Do█ █████ Memorial Library
Ge████ ████ College
P █████ █████████
B█ ████ ████████

D0056096

A World of Secrets

A WORLD OF SECRETS

THE USES AND LIMITS OF INTELLIGENCE

WALTER LAQUEUR

A TWENTIETH CENTURY FUND BOOK

BASIC BOOKS, INC., PUBLISHERS   NEW YORK

JF
1525
.I6
L37
1985

The Twentieth Century Fund is an independent research foundation which undertakes policy studies of economic, political, and social institutions and issues. The Fund was founded in 1919 and endowed by Edward A. Filene.

BOARD OF TRUSTEES OF THE TWENTIETH CENTURY FUND

Morris B. Abram
H. Brandt Ayers
Peter A. A. Berle, *Chairman*
Jonathan B. Bingham, Emeritus
José A. Cabranes
Alexander M. Capron
Edward E. David, Jr.
Brewster C. Denny
Charles V. Hamilton
August Heckscher, Emeritus
Matina S. Horner
James A. Leach

Georges-Henri Martin
Lawrence K. Miller, Emeritus
P. Michael Pitfield
Don K. Price, Emeritus
Richard Ravitch
Arthur M. Schlesinger, Jr.
Albert Shanker
Harvey I. Sloane, M.D.
Theodore C. Sorensen
James Tobin
David B. Truman, Emeritus
Shirley Williams

M. J. Rossant, *Director*

Copyright © 1985 by The Twentieth Century Fund
Library of Congress Catalog Card Number: 85–47567
ISBN: 0–465–09237–3
Printed in the United States of America
Designed by Vincent Torre
85 86 87 88 HC 9 8 7 6 5 4 3 2 1

CONTENTS

PART III

INTELLIGENCE ABROAD

PART IV

THEORIES OF INTELLIGENCE

PART V

CONCLUSION

FOREWORD

Political intelligence is critical to the making of U.S. foreign policy. Despite technological advances in data gathering, the assessments provided our policy makers are frequently wrongheaded, either because abundant data is analyzed incorrectly or because sound intelligence is ignored. Due to miscalculations on the part of the intelligence community, or its failure to anticipate the course of political and military developments, all too often policy makers have been taken by surprise, unprepared to cope with untoward events.

As part of the Twentieth Century Fund's continuing commitment to informed analysis of U.S. policy in the international area, we turned to Walter Laqueur, an accomplished author and analyst, to assess the role of intelligence in American foreign policy making. He has provided a critical appraisal that should serve to improve our performance in this critical area.

Laqueur points out that American intelligence agencies are probably unsurpassed in their ability to collect intelligence by such advanced technical means as satellite surveillance and the interception of electronic communications. It is in the evaluation of that intelligence that the system sometimes falls down. The art of intelligence assessment, he contends, is far from what it should be.

The need for reliable political intelligence in the years ahead cannot be overstated. It is essential that accurate information on the domestic and external affairs of foreign countries—their military strength, and their political, economic and social trends—be made available. Much of this information is contained in books, newspapers, radio and television broadcasts, and diplomatic reports. The flow of such information is greater now than ever before. But the quantity and the quality of intelligence are two different matters.

In part, the dissatisfaction with foreign political intelligence can be explained by exaggerated hopes that intelligence can be made "scientific."

The truth is that it can not. Scientific methods cannot solve the problems of coping with an explosion of knowledge, of reducing bias in assessment, of dealing with deception and surprise.

The fact of the matter is that intelligence assessment is really an art, not a science. Laqueur makes clear that whatever improvements are made in so-called scientific information gathering, the real secret of more informed and accurate appraisals lies in better human intelligence, the artistry of men and women who use their knowledge to make considered judgments. In the final analysis, it is human intelligence that is more likely to be illuminating than the accumulation of vast amounts of new data.

M. J. ROSSANT, *Director*
The Twentieth Century Fund
July 1985

PREFACE

Knowledge, if it does not determine action, is dead to us. The validity of Plotinus's saying can be endlessly discussed; with regard to intelligence, the proposition is probably correct. The main question to which this study addresses itself is: How important is intelligence? In the course of this investigation I had, of course, to deal with the collection, analysis, and transmission of intelligence, but there are many more competent men and women who have commented on these topics. My main concern was with intelligence as a guide to action—its impact on policy making. I have been preoccupied mainly with political, not military, intelligence. Sometimes the dividing line is obvious; often, it is obscure. The military potential of a country is a very important factor in the political intelligence equation. Conversely, the political intentions of the rulers of a country are very important for the military analyst. The absence of a clear dividing line makes for untidiness, but untidiness is inherent in the real world. I shall, then, frequently refer to problems of military intelligence; these have, after all, been among the main bones of contention within the intelligence community. But decisive issues in the recent past have been political rather than military (in the narrow sense) in character, and this is unlikely to change in the near future. It is easier to monitor Soviet ship building or to count missile launchers than to trace changing and often intangible political trends. But the success or failure of the U.S. intelligence effort in the years to come will be measured, to a large extent, by its performance in the political, economic, and scientific fields.

In the research for this book, I have been helped by former intelligence officials in this country and abroad. Without their published and unpublished work, this book could not have been written. Some officials also gave me to understand, very politely of course, that in their view, something of value on intelligence could come only from a person who, unlike this writer, had spent a lifetime in the profession, preferably at a high level.

As the Spanish proverb says: It is not the same to talk of bulls as to be in the bull ring.

I was not shocked. As a contemporary historian, I am familiar with the argument that firsthand experience counts. The academic student of the subject may have scanned tons of documents, but unless the student has personal recollections of the world before 1914, unless this person was a Communist, or lived in Nazi Germany, or fought in the wartime underground (to mention but a few arguments that I have encountered), he or she could not possibly have that deep understanding of time and place that documents cannot convey. Of course, all this goes *a fortiori* for intelligence, in which records frequently either do not exist, have not been declassified, or, if declassified, may be misleading. Many typewriter ribbons have been worn out dealing with all kinds of intelligence institutions and committees with impressive-sounding titles. But most of these organizations were of less importance than another institution about which, to the best of my knowledge, no monograph exists now or is likely to be written in the future—namely, the executive dining room of CIA headquarters in Langley, Virginia. The reasons for its importance—and its neglect in literature—need hardly be spelled out.

It is true that the ideal book on intelligence could be written only by an insider, for only an insider could combine all the qualities needed for understanding the subject. Yet I do not expect such a book to appear. Illuminating and valuable personal accounts have been produced, but while insiders are in a unique position to describe *wie es eigentlich gewesen,* * they are also subject to constraints from which the outside observer is, or should be, free. They are not permitted to relate the whole story; even if they were, their knowledge is usually restricted to parts of the whole picture. This is not surprising, because intelligence is now such a huge enterprise, impinging on so many topics, that no single individual is in a position to know all, however hard working and inquisitive, however long and varied their career in intelligence. Anyone who has worked any length of time as an intelligence agent is bound to have become involved in the internal and external struggles that went on much of the time, which is bound to impair one's judgment somewhat. In this respect an outsider with no axe to grind, with no personal ambitions in the field, is perhaps in a

---

*Even the most knowledgeable and reliable insiders have their lapses of memory. Allen Dulles, giving evidence (as "Mr. B.") before a congressional committee in 1947, claimed that during World War II he was in touch with Admiral Canaris, head of the German military intelligence unit, *Abwehr,* and especially with General Oster, his chief of staff. Dulles went on to say that in one way or another, about 10 percent of the *Abwehr* (that is, several hundred officials and agents) had been involved in such cooperation. The best that can be said about this account of cooperation between the OSS and the heads of the *Abwehr* is that it is greatly exaggerated. (House Committee on Expenditure in Government Departments, 27 June 1947, declassified December 1982.)

more favorable position. Many senior intelligence officials were shabbily treated in the convulsions of the 1970s, and the subsequent bitterness shown by some of them is only natural. But bitterness and the assumption that no outsider can possibly imagine what the situation was like, or the pressures and constraints under which intelligence had to act, are not sound bases for balanced judgment. Furthermore, while insiders undoubtedly know better than anyone else what happened within their organization, they are not necessarily in the best position to judge the importance of their operations.

All of which is to say that the noninvolvement of the outsider, with all its drawbacks, may have certain compensations. Insiders have often complained—not without justification—about the sensationalism, the fixation on personalities, the distortions, and the one-sided polemics typical of the literature on intelligence in the 1970s. I have tried to avoid these pitfalls. This is not a book of revelations, nor a book primarily on the CIA, but a study of the decisive questions facing intelligence. In the course of my work I encountered all kinds of fascinating events and aspects that I thought had been inadequately covered so far. The danger of getting lost in these many intriguing byways of intelligence had to be resisted.

Sometimes I had to deal in a paragraph or in a footnote with events or problems that could be adequately discussed only in a chapter or perhaps even a book. Though this is a work of synthesis, experts may find from time to time assertions insufficiently substantiated or new material for which they would want more detailed sources. I assure them that the reasons were almost always lack of space; the desire to provide even more detailed references collided with the need to respect practical boundaries.

In the course of my work, I had the opportunity to discuss certain problems with all recent directors of the Central Intelligence Agency but one, and with the present incumbent, as well as other senior intelligence officials and their main customers: former secretaries of state, secretaries of defense, and national security advisers. I am grateful to all those who have given of their time and advice.

Apart from these conversations, I received no help from the CIA or other intelligence agencies. I have studied recently declassified material, but most of it was disappointing and of little use for the purposes of this work, though some of the recently released OSS documents dating back to 1943–45 were of considerable interest to me as a student of World War II.

All along, Mark Lowenthal has helped me with this study. The chapters on intelligence performance are based on the indefatigable work of David Thomas; the sections on Allen Dulles as director of central intelligence, on technical intelligence, on economic intelligence, and on the KGB are based on special papers that were written by Victoria Price, Carl Duckett, Herbert Block, and John Dziak. Among those who read sections of the book and offered detailed and most helpful criticism were Paul Henze, Cord Meyer, Roger Hilsman, Roberta Wohlstetter, M. R. D. Foot, Richard Betts, George Carver, Robert Hunter, Penelope Thunberg, Raymond Rocca, and Daniel Silver. I had advice from some eminent men and women in the field of clinical diagnosis, but I feel it would be wrong to mention their names, for the invocation of these authorities might be wrongly interpreted. David Kahn and the late Ronald Lewin helped me with advice on SIGINT, Leon Furth on "producers and consumers," Professor Yehoshafat Harkabi on the history of Israeli intelligence, and Professor Robin Winks on the spy story. I have talked to or corresponded with more than two hundred people in half a dozen countries while working on this book. Some I cannot mention; others, I suspect, will not agree with what I write. To all of them, I would like to extend a collective, if anonymous, note of thanks. Last but not least, my gratitude to those who helped me in my research: Seth Carus, Jay La Monica, Desmond Dinan, Michael Warner, Sophia Miskiewicz, Marshall Salter, Eva Bellin, Debbi Wilson, Maja Latinski, Laura Blum, Jon Metropoulos, and Bernard Krikler, who helped me (not for the first time) with editing.

I would like to note my debt to the Earhart Foundation of Ann Arbor, Michigan, which greatly helped the completion of this study with two generous grants. This study was sponsored and financially underwritten by the Twentieth Century Fund.

A World of Secrets

Introduction

EVER SINCE humans first began to collect information about the powers and intentions of neighboring clans and tribes, there have been intelligence agents and a craft—or science—of intelligence. And from the beginning of intelligence gathering and analysis, there has been criticism of its usefulness and effectiveness. The critics have usually had their own ideas about how to improve the performance of intelligence. In the post-World War II period in the United States, there has been a remarkable swing from the view that the intelligence community is virtually omnipresent and omnipotent to equally immoderate criticisms of its spectacular failures.

For example, *The Invisible Government,* a widely read 1964 journalistic exposé of the intelligence establishment, opened with the ominous claim that "There are two governments in the United States. One is visible. The other is invisible."[1] At the heart of the darkness, the authors claimed, was the Central Intelligence Agency (CIA). Dozens of books and hundreds of articles, both in this country and abroad, have pointed to intelligence as the hidden hand, the prime mover and shaker behind important events all over the world. Of course, "The Company" itself was partly responsible for the inflated importance conferred on it—Allen Dulles, its director in the 1950s, had claimed that the National Security Act of 1947 gave intelligence a more influential position in the American government than it enjoyed in any other country. But after much research and discussion with the leading consumers of intelligence, I have concluded that, far from being an invisible government, far even from wielding great influence in the councils of state, intelligence has frequently been disregarded or ignored by decision makers. No one claims that intelligence has been of major importance in the conduct of affairs of state, which, while it may be unfair or inaccurate, certainly shows that intelligence is not held in very high esteem by those in high places. On the contrary, intelligence in some ways has been the Cinderella of contemporary politics: long hours, unpleasant work, humiliation, lack of recognition, and no Prince Charming in sight.*

In this book, I will examine intelligence analysis, not covert action, counterintelligence, propaganda, disinformation, or other such topics. Although most intelligence agencies have also engaged in covert action and counterintelligence, there is an obvious functional difference between the collection of information about the capabilities and intentions of other participants on the world stage, and operations undertaken to affect directly the course of events in other countries, either by secretly supporting or destabilizing a foreign government, or by conducting black propaganda or terrorist campaigns.[2]

Contrary to popular belief, what the Soviets call "active measures" is not necessarily a synonym for violent operations; most are, in fact, nonviolent. To give but one example: American diplomatic representatives cannot establish and maintain contact with opposition elements in dictatorships. It would be illegal, and it might well be mortally dangerous for those concerned. Yet contact with the opposition is vital, even if it should violate the laws of the land. It is in this context, in the "gray zones" between official diplomacy and direct military force, that active measures, overt and covert, acquire considerable importance.

The same holds true in terms of counterintelligence. As far as it is concerned with the detection and the frustration of the activities of foreign agents, counterintelligence has little bearing on the problems discussed in this book. But counterintelligence must also address itself to foreign interference in our intelligence process and—increasingly—in our politics. There are many ways that intelligence can be skewed by provision of wrong, doctored, or misleading information, or in which an intelligence agency can be lured into unproductive efforts.

I also devote little attention to the vast area of disinformation, the frequently successful effort to affect processes of judgment between countries and statesmen and to distort public opinion through disguised means. Much publicity has been given to invented or distorted letters, diaries, and

---

*It could be argued that, almost by definition, intelligence is always bound to fail. If it correctly predicts the political or military initiative of another country, and if as a result, countermeasures are taken and the initiative does not take place, it will be blamed for making false predictions.

memoranda. Additionally, there exist far more subtle and insidious forms of disinformation. There is nothing new in these forms of deception and political warfare; they have a long history. What is different today is their scope and perseverance. The influence exerted by a well-placed influence agent may well be as great as that of a spy.

I have devoted considerable space to the basic assumptions underlying intelligence work because these seem to me to be of critical importance. These assumptions are sometimes of a philosophical (or at least method-ological) character and to understand them, to follow them to their roots, calls for moving beyond the confines of intelligence in its narrow defini-tion. And to understand the influence of intelligence in the decision-making process, it is essential to cast an occasional glance at the informa-tion available from the open sources that intelligence must compete with.

It also is important to check our perception of intelligence work against the images that have been created through fictional accounts of the work of the services and agents in literature and in film. After all, the impres-sions we receive from the world around us color our perceptions of reality. Moreover, the problems faced by the intelligence services today are evi-dent in the changes in the portraits of both the services and agents in fiction, which might reflect the truth or influence it.

There has been a metamorphosis in popular novels and movies of the spy-story hero into a sleazy, cynical, and frequently materialistic antihero. Of course, fictional portrayals deal almost entirely with Human Intelli-gence, or HUMINT, an inelegant term for a profession not lacking aspects of elegance. The reasons for selecting HUMINT and counterintelligence themes are obvious. Neither the "national technical means of verification," involving satellites, sensors, and computers—PHOTINT and SIGINT in the current nomenclature—nor the desk-bound work of intelligence ana-lysts offers much intrigue, romance, or human drama.[3]

Quite apart from its entertainment value, spy literature is of considera-ble sociological interest. It tells us not only about the public image of the "spook" but also, as Robin Winks puts it, about changing values, about what people take pride in, about trust—and about how one might become world-weary even without betrayal.[4] On the other hand, the older kind of adventure-intrigue-espionage story in the John Buchan tradition has also prospered. Whereas the sympathies of Eric Ambler, Graham Greene, and Le Carré were clearly on the left—or at least anti-American—other authors have moved in the opposite direction. The genre is now so broad that almost everyone can find something to his or her taste. In addition, the demand for "documentary" accounts is perhaps stronger than ever; biographies and autobiographies of individual traitors and double agents abound. Not only have major spies such as Kim Philby and Gordon Lonsdale written their memoirs, but lesser figures in the espionage world have done the same.

In film, espionage has proved even more popular than in literature. A decade ago, James Parrish and Michael Pitts counted some 450 spy films produced since the early days of the industry.[5] Some of these films took their inspiration from the activities of real spies, including Mata Hari (played by Greta Garbo) and Edith Cavell for World War I and Moyzisch, the Nazi who was Cicero's case officer in Ankara, during World War II. Igor Gouzenko, the Soviet spy who defected in Canada in 1945, was the subject of a movie as well as a radio series. Both the filmmaker and the novelist need for their protagonists men of action, not administrators, and least of all intelligence analysts.

The spy movie has followed intellectual fashions just as the private-eye movie did. The attractive, patriotic, uncomplicated spy of the early period became a modern Hamlet, torn by competing loyalties, or a disagreeable "professional" engaged in ruthless, immoral actions of doubtful necessity. In the pre-World War II period (and with a vengeance during the war) there was no doubt about who were the heroes and who the villains. Enemy agents were foreigners in leather coats, speaking with a marked accent, walking alone in dark streets, behaving in a blatantly suspicious way. Nor was there any doubt that espionage against Nazi Germany was vitally necessary: it was a heroic enterprise. This often simplistic patriotism of the war years continued to prevail, more or less uncontested, for another two decades in film. It was replaced by the slick, glamorous-thug genre typified by the James Bond series. Such films were not only commercially successful, they echoed what had been said—with a slightly higher level of sophistication—in the pseudo-realistic school of spy novels, beginning with LeCarré's *The Spy Who Came in from the Cold* (1966).

Like its protagonists, the subject matter of the spy novel or film is enveloped in a shroud of secrecy inappropriate to other genres. In a realistic novel or film we can easily detect a false characterization, as we have some personal knowledge of how ordinary people behave, whether they be carpenters or physicians. With intelligence and espionage it is different.

John Buchan was quite frank in calling his *The 39 Steps* a "dime novel," while Graham Greene has described his spy novels as "entertainments." Few of their counterparts today display such modesty. Critics have attempted to transform the spy story from its legitimate function as a vehicle of entertainment into a cultural critique, nothing less than a metaphor for the moral burden of our times.

Some readers and filmgoers turn to the espionage genre as entertainment, a modern equivalent of the adventure story. Others read or watch because they believe that by doing so they will learn about the hidden hands that determine the really important events in world affairs. And there are those who, as Jacques Barzun noted, want their weekly dose of anxiety to keep in step with the current intellectual fashion of being at least vaguely disturbed or outraged at the prevailing state of affairs. What should be borne in mind is that media treatments are generally far removed from the real motives of spies and the real enterprise of intelligence and rarely deal with the tedious, painstaking work involved in political intelligence gathering and analysis. The media's focus and their alternately tawdry, sloppy, and/or demonic portrayals of intelligence operations in recent years help to explain the public's mood surrounding the investigations of the intelligence community that occurred in the 1970s.

Returning, then, to the real world, one does not need an exceptional memory to recall that success as a director of intelligence has been as elusive as success in "fine-tuning" the economy has been in recent decades. Allen Dulles, John McCone, William F. Raborn, Jr., and Richard Helms were forced to resign. George Bush was not reappointed, and both William E. Colby and Stansfield Turner were under bitter criticism as they ended their terms in office. Similarly, the careers of many senior U.S. intelligence officials have ended on an unhappy note.[6]

It is ironic that whereas no reasonable person expects the Department of Health to stamp out disease altogether, or the Department of Agriculture to provide for good harvests every year, that the various organs of intelligence are expected to be right every time. Whenever intelligence is inadequately informed, fails to warn of impending disasters well before they happen, or presents incorrect assessments of current developments, angry voices are heard in the corridors of power, committees of inquiry are set up, and bureaucratic reorganization becomes the order of the day.

The American intelligence community has been exposed to scrutiny by permanent supervisory boards and by special committees of investigation almost from its inception. Among the better known of the committees are the Dulles-Jackson-Correa commission (1949) and the two committees headed by Herbert Hoover (1950 and 1955). General Mark Clark, who was chief-of-staff of the Hoover committee, conducted an investigation that was a spinoff of Hoover's second committee, while General Doolittle looked into problems involving covert action. In 1960 the Kirkpatrick report concentrated on organizational and managerial aspects of intelligence. Ten years later Dr. James Schlesinger's report focused on the costs and benefits of intelligence,[7] and in the 1970s the Church committee investigated the whole field of intelligence while the Pike committee concentrated its fire on the CIA.

A military metaphor is appropriate here, for such investigating committees (there were a good many more) were mainly interested in examining covert action operations, the degree to which secrecy was compatible with free institutions, and the CIA's role as (in Senator Frank Church's phrase) "a rogue elephant." During these investigations, occasional lip service was paid to improving the quality of intelligence, especially the end-product, or intelligence analysis, "for which we spend so much money." (In fact, only one percent of the intelligence budget was spent on analysis.) But cost was, for all the committees, a side issue—they were more interested in exposing than in improving performance.

An indisputable authority assures us that intelligence about foreign affairs is a simple and self-evident thing, and this is certainly true on the level of abstraction; all attempts to develop ambitious theories of intelligence have failed. But in practice in the real world this simplicity is deceptive, and intelligence remains a vexing and complicated affair, enough so to have taxed the best of minds and the most blue-ribbon of panels.

This book is concerned with the main issues involved in this continuing controversy: the impact of intelligence on policy, the causes of intelligence failures, and the prospects for improvement in intelligence gathering and analysis. In part, intelligence in the United States remains a vexing and complicated affair simply because it is not altogether clear whether the American people and their political elite have decided that they really need and want a secret intelligence service. Certainly accurate and detailed information is desired about the state of the world in general and intentions of potential antagonists in particular. But there is often reluctance to provide the conditions in which a service of this kind can function effectively. This refers above all to the issue of secrecy: official secrecy runs against the American grain and is believed to be a threat to the American way of life, particularly as embodied in the Bill of Rights.

While some of the restrictions imposed on intelligence in the mid-1970s have now been removed, this has not brought about a dramatic recovery in either the status or the license given to intelligence activity. Many laws, regulations, and controls still hamper intelligence operations. Strict rules and supervision may be necessary, but at some point too much control conflicts with essential requirements—such as secrecy—without which intelligence cannot carry out its mandate. This is not to argue in favor of unlimited and uncontrolled secrecy.[8] But it would be unrealistic to expect intelligence to function along the same lines as, say, the Department of Transportation. Unless a measure of secrecy is accepted and safeguarded, it is pointless to maintain a costly, and in some respects risky, intelligence service. This is a real dilemma, but there has been notable reluctance to face up to it.

Criticism of intelligence has been partially based on exaggerated notions of what it can, and can not, accomplish. On the one hand, there is the popular image of the master spy, to whom no doors are closed, who knows all the secrets, and whose feats decisively influence world history. In fact, there have been no such spies in recent history; as for their exploits in earlier periods, closer scrutiny reveals a good measure of exaggeration. In spite of some spectacular coups, it is doubtful that these legendary heroes and heroines truly changed the course of history.

On the other hand, there have been excessive hopes attached to the technological revolution in intelligence that began in the 1950s. An immense amount of hitherto inaccessible data have become available making it appear for a while as if the dreams of generations of master spies had materialized. But while these new technologies are of great value in establishing the presence, or absence, of certain weapons systems, they are of no help with many other problems. This is particularly true of political, as distinct from military, intelligence. Thus human intelligence, which had never been quite as important as commonly believed, further declined in perceived importance, and the fields wherein technical intelligence could achieve results were strictly limited. Because there are wide areas in which technological breakthroughs have not taken place and are unlikely to occur in the foreseeable future, intelligence has to rely on more time-honored approaches: diligent research and human intelligence. Political intelligence, furthermore, can never give its customers the near certainties that technical intelligence provides. Secret data on the performance of various devices, or a purloined code book, can be assessed for accuracy with relative ease, but this is not so with a report about a debate in the Soviet Politburo.

The crisis of intelligence is, in part, the disappointment that results from unrealistic hopes. But there is also, in part, a real crisis that manifests itself in various ways. Intelligence has become more important than ever before; it is, to give but one obvious example, an essential precondition for arms control. Intelligence has to cover much more ground than ever before— many more countries and many more problems. It employs more people and machinery and suffers from the problems besetting all big bureaucracies. Its practitioners justify their existence by producing memoranda, reports, and surveys. Information of real importance may get lost in the process. The stream of paper never subsides, but as the distance between the source and the consumer has grown, so has the danger that important information may be lost.

It has always been difficult to obtain intelligence of political importance from totalitarian countries. High-grade codes can be unbreakable; intelligence has had a hard time attracting recruits as talented as in World War II and the first postwar decade. Veterans of the Office of Special Services (OSS) held most of the critical positions in U.S. intelligence during the 1950s and 1960s. Not every one of them was a brilliant intellect, a dynamic operative, or an organizer of genius. But the general intellectual level was higher and the motivation deeper than in later years, when the public climate became hostile and the attraction of intelligence as a career declined. A similar process took place in other countries, but this does not provide much comfort to the United States. Successive committees of inquiry noted these weaknesses and made various proposals to improve the state of affairs. Roughly, these proposals can be divided into two groups: those coming from inside government are usually organizational in character. Those made by certain political scientists suggest that if intelligence were made more scientific it could be mastered not only by highly gifted people, but by men and women of average talent.

Organizational reforms involve the establishment, transfer, or elimination of some departments and working groups and the weakening of others, the reorganization of the intelligence production system, the abolition of various oversight boards, and the creation of new ones. The many suggestions for a scientific theory (or theories) to guide intelligence were based on concepts and techniques borrowed from other disciplines.

Neither approach has helped. Organizational problems are important; poor organization creates unnecessary complications or even harm. Good organization can contribute to a clearer division of labor and generally make the most of existing resources, but it cannot of itself produce more reliable intelligence. Most jobs in intelligence demand no superior talents; solid competence and common sense suffice. In top positions, however, outstanding qualities of leadership, political judgment, and technical genius are needed. These cannot be provided by a set of programmed formulas based on quasi-scientific assumptions. Indefatigable "reorganizers" and "theorists" will continue their labors, but the enthusiasm has gone out of their efforts, and the hopes for either organizational or conceptual breakthroughs to solve the crisis of intelligence have grown dim.

Accident sometimes plays a role, ineffective collectors may have a streak of luck, and ignorant analysts could end up with the right conclusion for the wrong reason. Yet it would be imprudent to build on such accidents. Broadly speaking, able people will produce good intelligence, while those lacking flair, knowledge, and general competence will not. The qualities essential for producing superior intelligence are still needed in the age of the computer and the satellite because, quite apart from the all-important question of the interpretation of intelligence, for various reasons systems of collection may occasionally dry up and have to be replaced by new ones. Innovation is critical: U.S. intelligence would have been in poor shape in the late 1950s if not for the pioneering efforts of Richard Bissell and others in promoting the U-2. And were it not for the satellites, there would have been a crisis a few years later, when the U-2 had to be grounded. But because work on the satellites had started well before the U-2, they became operational soon after the U-2 crisis.

But are innovators welcome in conservative bureaucracies? As a rule, big governmental institutions do not put a premium on the qualities that make a good intelligence officer. Or, to be more precise, they may appreciate some of these qualities but not others. It may be possible to accommodate mild eccentrics who do not adhere to certain basic rules, provided they have powerful protectors. Yet there are limits beyond which such organizations cannot go, and, as a result, intelligence will lose in peacetime some people it needs, whom it could get in war.

In what has been said so far, it has been taken for granted that intelligence fulfills a vital function. It does not follow that intelligence is always important. Even when it is timely, accurate, and important it is not always usable. Hence consumers have been ambivalent throughout history about intelligence.

Statesmen and leaders in a state of ignorance about the intentions of rivals or enemies during war have been compared to blind men. Napoleon reportedly said that a well-placed spy was as important as several divisions, yet in his campaigns he paid little attention to intelligence.[9] The ancient Romans did not think highly of espionage, though they had their *speculatores* and *frumentarii*. They were too proud and arrogant, sure that they would defeat their enemies in any case. Frederick the Great once wrote, "If one knew the enemy's intentions beforehand one could always defeat him even with an inferior army." Like Napoleon, his own record does not bear this out. For there is much that can go wrong, even if one knows enemy intentions. In fact, the possession of superior intelligence may induce leaders to take decisions that in retrospect will appear counterproductive.

Intelligence is never an end in itself, almost always a price must be paid for it. Both intelligence success and failure may have unforeseen consequences. It is difficult to think of a more complete intelligence failure than Pearl Harbor. But if not for this stunning defeat, it is doubtful whether the American people would have been galvanized into action.[10]

Sun Tzu the sixth-century B.C. author of *The Art of War,* claimed that he who knows his adversary can win a hundred battles. But Sun Tzu's statement ought to be prefaced by "other things being equal, or nearly equal." The czarist regime is no longer in power in Russia, even though it had the most effective espionage organization of its time. If Sun Tzu had been right, the French would not have been close to defeat in World War I and would not have been defeated in World War II, for the *Deuxième Bureau* was then second to none, and the Allies should have won World War II by 1943 with their enormous superiority in intelligence. So unless a country has a more or less effective foreign policy, the quality of intelligence at its disposal is of little or no importance. There is a definite temptation to overrate the importance of intelligence in the world of power politics, but it is as wrong to exaggerate the importance of intelligence as it is to underrate it.

The term "intelligence" has thus far been used without clearly defining it, and not without purpose. Like "history," it has more than one meaning. On one hand, it refers to an organization collecting information and on the other to the information that has been gathered. Those in favor of more detailed and more rigorous definitions will find them in the textbooks, which also deal with the differences between strategic and tactical intelligence. In the present context, all that needs be said is that "intelligence" is by no means the only collector and producer of intelligence. Information reaches the policy maker from a great many other sources, and intelligence agencies draw their information largely from open sources. Thus the intelligence agencies have no monopoly, perhaps not even an oligopoly, in the product they bring to market. Unfortunately the missing information in open sources may be of decisive importance. However many Japanese newspapers American analysts had read in 1941, they would not have come across the plan for an attack of Pearl Harbor, nor does *Pravda* supply numbers and other specifications for Soviet missiles.

The "crisis of intelligence," then, involves the frequent failure of intelligence agencies to predict and give timely warnings of major events and to assess ongoing developments correctly. It remains to be investigated whether failures are always bound to happen, irrespective of the excellence of intelligence agencies. No one doubts that there is always room for improvement, but it is also true that change and reform normally exact a price. Changes should certainly not be made unless and until the causes of faults and failures are known. Have they occurred in the field of collection or in the assessment of intelligence? Or are the consumers to be blamed for not stating their requirements clearly or not paying attention to the information submitted to them? Are intelligence services in democratic societies perhaps bound to fail simply because they operate in an unfriendly environment, because their activities cannot be kept secret, and because their resources are inadequate?

PART I

THE ANATOMY
OF INTELLIGENCE

CHAPTER 1

The Production of Intelligence

WHO GETS what information, where does it originate, how is it collected, in what way is it transmitted—and what may go wrong in the process? Intelligence successes and failures can be discussed in the abstract, but the value of such exercises is dubious. Mention must be made of the specific components of intelligence to provide a framework for understanding its functions, scope, and limits under our political system.

Just as a tour of a factory should take the early stages of production and not the finished product as its starting point, a discussion of the production of intelligence has to begin at the beginning. The quality of the product, the price paid for it, possible improvements that can be made to it, the competition it faces, how it is packaged, the problems of marketing it—these and other important questions can be discussed only following a preliminary sketch of the way the American intelligence establishment has been built and the capacities (and deficiencies) of its resources in the branches of human intelligence (HUMINT), photo intelligence (PHOTINT), and signal intelligence (SIGINT).

In our time the technical means of collection have attained extreme importance, but it is dangerous to expect more from these intelligence branches than they can provide. As experience has shown, the product of signal and photo intelligence can be interpreted in different ways. Furthermore, such means of surveillance are not immune to deception. It is also important to note recent changes in the assignment of intelligence, above all the growing importance of economic and scientific-technological intelligence.

Once these parameters have been explored, we can proceed to a discussion of the relationship between the producers and the consumers, both in open and closed societies. Despite the myths created and disseminated by popular fiction and spy movies, intelligence production, quality, and consumer demand varies enormously according to the political regime under which these take place.

The current organization of U.S. intelligence began in July 1941 when President Roosevelt created the Office of Coordinator of Information (OCI) under William J. Donovan. In June 1942, it became the Office of Strategic Services (OSS) and control was shifted from the White House to the Joint Chiefs of Staff. The early OCI was very small; about half of its staff of 1,600 was employed in propaganda rather than intelligence work.

The OSS developed rapidly and played a role of note in the invasion of North Africa, the Sicilian landing and, to a lesser degree, in the preparation of D-Day, and in Southeast Asia and other special operations. The nation's most highly decorated soldier in World War I ("the last hero," in Eisenhower's words) and an excellent diplomat, Donovan needed all his energy, persistence, and shrewdness to hold his own in Washington's bureaucratic infighting. However tense and antagonistic they were with one another, military intelligence, the FBI, and the State Department all denied that yet another agency was necessary.

While the war lasted, Donovan managed to do more than hold his own. But his proposals for a peacetime worldwide intelligence agency responsible to the president ran into opposition. One month after the capitulation of Japan, the OSS was dissolved by order of President Truman.[1]

While the OSS was very much in the public eye, there was another intelligence-gathering organization that was less glamorous but perhaps even more important for the conduct of the war. This was the MAGIC group of cryptologists operating under the supervision of Army G2, the intelligence branch. It broke its first complete Japanese message in August 1940. Pearl Harbor was certainly one of the greatest intelligence failures in history, but that was not the fault of the intelligence collectors. The MAGIC group played a decisive role in the battles for the Pacific in 1942–43. American victories depended to a large extent on information obtained from this source.

The interregnum after the dissolution of the OSS did not last long. Facing growing turbulence in Europe and the Middle East, President Truman issued a directive in January 1946, establishing a National Intelligence Authority (NIA) consisting of the Secretaries of State, War, Navy, and the president's personal representative. Under NIA a Central Intelligence Group (CIG) came into being; it was headed by Rear Admiral Sidney W. Souers, a personal friend of the president. While in theory the CIG was responsible for the coordination, planning, evaluation, and overt collection and dissemination of all intelligence, it was not independent—its funds and staff were provided by other departments.

When General Hoyt S. Vandenberg succeeded Souers, the CIG expanded in size and scope, prepared its first national intelligence estimate, and above all, began to engage in an independent collection of both clandestine and overt information. As a result, the role of the CIG changed from coordinator to producer of intelligence, but as yet it had neither legislative status nor, even more important, budget authority.

The breakthrough came with the National Security Act of 1947 when the CIG became the Central Intelligence Agency (CIA), which was made responsible to the newly founded National Security Council (NSC). According to the act, the CIA was to advise the NSC on intelligence activities; make recommendations for coordinating intelligence activities; and correlate, evaluate, and disseminate intelligence. It was to act as a central evaluator, not as a separate collector or producer. But the act was vague (probably deliberately) in this respect, for there were also references to certain unspecified intelligence functions that could best be performed centrally. Thus, perhaps inevitably, the CIA did not assume the role of central coordinator of estimates but instead became another independent producer of intelligence—in part because all organizations tend to expand and in part because there then existed a genuine vacuum in the field.

The wartime OSS provided both the structure and much of the manpower for the cold war CIA. It also adopted the CIA's practice of housing analysis and operations under the same roof. In addition, it began producing the National Intelligence Estimate (NIE), which could legitimately be regarded as the offspring of the OSS Board of Analysts set up by Donovan during his OSS tenure.

From the beginning, the CIA was criticized for not performing its original duties and for operating without overall policy guidance. Admiral Roscoe Hillenkoetter replaced Vandenberg as Director of Central Intelligence and during his term of office the Korean War broke out, highlighting all the weaknesses of the CIA. In October 1950, General Walter Bedell Smith took over. A forceful administrator, he had been Eisenhower's chief of staff, and it was under his leadership that the CIA, hitherto an almost negligible entity, became a factor of some importance. Smith created the Office of National Estimates (ONE) whose sole task was to produce coordinated National Intelligence Estimates. The other important development that took place under Bedell Smith was the growth, much too rapid, of covert action—from 300 employees in 1949 to more than 5,000 in 1952, including those under "overseas contract."*

Bedell Smith was replaced in 1953 by Allen Dulles, who had played a notable role in the OSS, and had later served as Deputy Director for Plans, a euphemism for "operations." During his eight years in office, the CIA reached the pinnacle of its influence. Dulles showed little interest in intelligence coordination, but due to his close contact with President Eisenhower and with his brother, Secretary of State John Foster Dulles, he had a great deal of political influence.

Dulles's last years in office were marred by two controversies, one analytic, the other operational. The missile gap controversy arose from an overly pessimistic intelligence projection with regard to the growth of Soviet heavy bomber and ICBM capabilities. It had a lasting effect on CIA psychology and the intelligence community, having cried wolf once too often, learned its lesson only too well. For years thereafter there was an inclination to tone down arms estimates so as not to be charged with alarmism. The operational failure was the Bay of Pigs disaster; it damaged the CIA's standing even more and eventually brought about Dulles's downfall.

In Autumn 1961, the CIA moved from downtown Washington to its present headquarters in Langley, Virginia. In some ways the move was symbolic: no longer a makeshift organization with temporary and unsatisfactory quarters, the agency now enjoyed universal recognition. Although its organizational structure was more or less firmly set, the move had negative effects: during the early days, intelligence philosophers had argued that it was dangerous to be too close to the politicians; now they were to learn that it was equally dangerous to be too far from the policy makers they served.[2]

The changing fortunes of the CIA in the 1960s and 1970s have been related many times, so suffice it to say that the technical developments of that time were of great consequence. In 1961, a new military intelligence agency was established, the Defense Intelligence Agency (DIA), that took over many of the responsibilities of the three armed services intelligence groups. In principle, its assignments were narrowly circumscribed, but just as the CIA had come to disregard its statutes, so did the DIA. In theory, there should have been a clear division of labor between the DIA and CIA; in practice, there was rivalry. The competition extended to the Air Force as new technological capabilities in intelligence collection were developed, first by U-2 aerial reconnaissance, and later through satellite systems run

---

*The National Security Agency (NSA) was set up in 1952 by a presidential directive to unify cryptological activities. It was the most secret of all major U.S. intelligence agencies; the text of the order has not been published to this day.

by the air force. Part of the rivalry was due to priorities—the air force was most interested in tactical intelligence, while the CIA was eager to obtain long-range strategic information.

The late 1960s and the 1970s were, moreover, difficult years for the intelligence community. Neither Johnson, Nixon, nor Carter thought very highly of it. At the same time, the CIA was blamed for various misdeeds committed, or allegedly committed, in the past. The Pike and Church committees investigated CIA activities with the goal of strengthening control rather than that of improving the quality of intelligence. The Hughes-Ryan Amendment restricted CIA freedom of action. The CIA found itself under heavy media attack for having exceeded its mandate by engaging in unauthorized, allegedly criminal activities and then, under Carter, for the unsatisfactory quality of intelligence and for underestimating the Soviet threat—the Team-B episode. A great many leaks and the politicization of the CIA contributed to a deterioration of its morale. The reforms introduced in response to political criticism mainly affected oversights and the production of NIEs, their de facto importance limited. As a result of the "purges" of the 1970s, the counterintelligence and covert action capacities of the CIA were severely hit.

In recent years intelligence has received greater support from the Reagan administration, and there has been a favorable shift in public attitudes. Today the Director of Central Intelligence (DCI) has wider authority than in the early years of the CIA. According to a presidential order dated December 1981, the director is the primary adviser to the president and the NSC on national foreign intelligence. His duties include implementation of special activities (that is, covert action), the authority to "task" other intelligence organizations, and even to decide on conflicts in tasking. This is not to say that interagency disputes over budget tasking, resources, and the substance of intelligence have come to an end—a strong secretary of defense is still likely to prevail in disputes with a DCI.

The director of central intelligence has a dual role; he is not only in charge of the CIA but exercises control of the entire U.S. intelligence community. To help him to carry out these community-wide responsibilities, he has at his disposal a relatively small unit created in 1972, the Intelligence Community Staff (ICS). But he does not have authority over the budgets and the resource allocation of intelligence agencies other than the CIA's, which lessens his ability to fulfill his responsibility as the supreme controller of all intelligence.* Of course, it is unlikely that the

---

*A special monograph ought to be written about the attempts made by successive DCIs "to provide effective guidance and coordination" to the entire intelligence community, to quote an internal directive issued by Kennedy to John McCone. Kennedy's initiative resulted in the creation of NIPE (National Intelligence Program Evaluation), which first established a mechanism for the DCI to supervise aerial reconnaissance and for the CIA participation in

armed forces will ever surrender such control to a civilian authority. For this reason proposed reforms, such as separating the DCI from the CIA, are unlikely to bring about real change in the distribution of power. As for the DCI's role as the president's chief intelligence adviser, much depends on circumstances and personalities. A strong national security adviser will almost certainly arrogate this function to himself. Because his access to the president is much closer, an adviser is likely to prevail in a conflict with the CIA, as the experience of two decades has shown.

The CIA in public parlance has become a synonym for U.S. intelligence, even though it represents only a relatively small part—perhaps 15 percent —of the manpower and the total budget of the intelligence community. A larger share goes to the National Security Agency, which engages only in the collection of information, and to the secretary of defense's DIA. In addition, there is the Bureau of Intelligence and Research (INR) in the Department of State, staffed partly by foreign service officers, partly by civil service analysts. There are army, navy, marine, and air force intelligence groups, the latter including the important National Reconnaissance Office (NRC) in charge of satellite operations. The FBI engages in counterintelligence, and government departments such as the Treasury and the Department of Energy also have small intelligence units. But as far as foreign political intelligence is concerned and its analysis and transmission to policy makers, the CIA is the most important agency. And popular belief in its importance is not altogether wrong.

The Intelligence Cycle

According to the textbooks, the first stage in the intelligence cycle is an indication by its consumers of the kind of information needed. These needs are conveyed to senior intelligence officials, who in turn inform the collectors. The collectors obtain information, then the "raw" intelligence

---

the design, development, and operation of systems devoted to this end. It also investigated the utility and costs of various kinds of information acquisition. NIPE was replaced by the National Intelligence Resource Board (NIRB) in the late 1960s, which tried for the first time to review the independent budgets of the various intelligence agencies to determine which kinds of intelligence were to get highest priority and the largest allocation. Following the Schlesinger report (1971), NIRB was succeeded by yet another committee. Today most of the attempts to coordinate the intelligence efforts are done through the Intelligence Community Staff. The U.S. Intelligence budget consists of two elements. The director of Central Intelligence is responsible for the National Foreign Intelligence Program (NFIP), whereas the secretary of defense supervises TIARA (Tactical Intelligence and Related Activities) which refers to various complicated reconnaissance, surveillance, and acquisition programs.

is turned into finished intelligence which is eventually supplied to the consumers.[3]

In reality, theory and practice frequently diverge. In the first place, consumers may not know exactly what they want. A former secretary of state reportedly said: "I don't know what kind of intelligence I need, but I know when I get it."[4] The policy maker cannot possibly be aware of all the problems and challenges likely to confront him, so it is precisely one of the tasks of intelligence to alert him to the dangers and opportunities that he may face. But even if the policy maker does know what he wants, it is by no means certain that he will receive it. The difficulties may be insurmountable, the resources of intelligence are limited, and established priorities must be respected. But it has frequently been found that these systems of priorities work poorly, and sometimes they do not function at all.

Vice Admiral Rufus Taylor noted in a comment on the Cunningham report: "After a year's working on intelligence requirements, we have come to realize that they are not the driving force behind the flow of information. Rather, the real push comes from the collectors themselves—particularly the operations of large, indiscriminating technical collection systems —who use national intelligence requirements to justify what they want to undertake for other reasons, e.g. military readiness, redundancy, technical continuity and the like." The Cunningham report had criticized the existing Priority National Intelligence Objectives (PNIO) as "lamentably defective documents," and "ritual justification of every kind of activity anybody believes to be desirable." Six years earlier, there had been similar criticism, and five years after Cunningham, a future DCI (Schlesinger) called the formal requirements "aggregated wish lists," which could mean all things to all people.[5]

The attempts to establish priorities frequently result in bureaucratic nightmares. At one time the DIA listed 200 intelligence issues with regard to foreign countries, assigning a numerical priority for country and topic from one to eight. The CIA had at one time 83 intelligence topics concerning 120 countries, with assigned numerical priorities from one to seven. Furthermore, the DCI distributed a list of "Objectives" (for the next year) and "Perspectives" (for the next five years). Under Colby, the CIA system of key intelligence questions (KIQs) was introduced, but this did not solve the problem either. In the early 1980s NITC (National Intelligence Tasking Center) was created to direct collection efforts in the field of espionage, photos, and electronic intercepts. But its authority was contested from the first day and after a few years it was abolished. Obviously, once a war or other emergency had broken out, the area automatically became a priority intelligence target. But the decisive test for an intelligence agency is to warn the policy maker of the trouble before it occurs.

There have been widespread and probably exaggerated feelings that the inadequacy of guidance is one of the most striking deficiencies of intelligence, and that the reforms intended to remedy the situation have been of no avail. Some observers believe the system worked better, on the whole, as it was constituted prior to 1960. National Security Council meetings began with intelligence briefings, followed by short presentations in which the policy makers expressed their chief concerns. Thus, the DCI received immediate and systematic guidance that he transmitted to the intelligence agencies. The major drawback was that this system led to the suppression of differences, to manipulated consensus, and "an emphasis on the lowest common denominator."[6] President Kennedy's abolition of the NSC procedure sometimes led to the total absence of guidance and sometimes to an overload of the system with questionnaires so comprehensive as to be virtually meaningless.

The role of the president should be emphasized in this context because his requests for information will not normally be taken lightly even by the most obstreperous bureaucracy. The authority of even a strong secretary of state or defense or national security adviser may not always be sufficient to make intelligence comply with his wishes. But presidents are usually too busy to impose ordered priorities. As a result, no satisfactory procedure has emerged. But not too much should be made of this failure—to a considerable extent "tasking" will always depend on collectors. Reasonably competent intelligence officials will know more often than not what to look for without being told in so many words.

"Collection" is the second stage in the intelligence cycle. Until this century, human intelligence (HUMINT) was by far the most important means of collection. It includes the readily accessible intelligence found in books, periodicals, newspapers, radio broadcasts, or reports from diplomatic sources or travelers. More notoriously, it also encompasses clandestine collection—that is, espionage.

Overt information is of paramount importance as far as background knowledge is concerned, but it can also contribute significantly to the understanding of current events. Overt information means different things under different political regimes. Facts and figures considered state secrets of the highest order in a dictatorship are freely published in democratic societies. Such material embraces not only political information but, with even greater force, scientific and technological data. It has often been noted that subscription to a good clipping service covering the Western press produces an enormous amount of significant military, political, and industrial material. Clearinghouses in Virginia and New Jersey are under contract with the Soviet government to supply nearly the total of the U.S. media. All, or almost all, publicly available government documents are shipped to Moscow by the Government Printing Office (GPO) in Washington; and the National Technical Information Service, an agency of the U.S. government, provides the most extensive list available of all technical publications. To paraphrase Lord Acton, the chief problem facing the heads of Communist research and monitoring institutes is not drought, but drowning.

In open societies there is a gray zone of material which, while not readily available for sale, is not considered a state secret. A Swiss parliamentarian recently drew attention to the fact that Swiss local communities face an almost insatiable demand for detailed maps and blueprints of railway stations, bridges, tunnels, and similar installations from Hungarian and East German students who allegedly need them for seminar papers. These data usually detail installations of vital importance for the mobilization of the Swiss army and national defense in general.[7] In the same category in open societies belong in-house bulletins of industrial enterprises, publications by think tanks, and internal news letters of professional groups.

Western analysts will extract much less from Soviet-bloc publications; their effective system of censorship covers just about every aspect of daily life, not just political-military information. Yet precisely because clandestine collection is so difficult in these countries, the use of overt sources is of great importance. Total denial of information, while perhaps the censor's dream, is virtually impossible even in the most efficient dictatorship.

There is no direct or obvious correlation between the effort invested in receiving certain information, the excitement surrounding the circumstances of doing so, and the intrinsic importance of the information obtained. The *vita activa* of John Buchan's spy heroes—and their successors —is infinitely more interesting than the nine-to-five *vita contemplativa* of the professional newspaper reader or radio monitor. But the two are equidistant to the god of intelligence—the discovery of the secret.

What overt intelligence very often cannot give are specifics about the intentions and plans of adversaries or potential adversaries. At this point other forms of intelligence take over, among them clandestine collection. So much has been said and written about the subject that even a mere summary may seem unnecessary. In view of the enormous success of the modern spy story, there cannot be many people who do not know what a "safe house" is, or a "sleeper," a "dead drop," or a "burst transmitter," and few literate people have not heard about "residents" and "case officers." Nevertheless, the human spy in intelligence has declined in importance in recent decades; many of the tasks that were traditionally carried out by spies have been taken over by photography, radio intercepts, and other, more esoteric, means. The spies of ancient Sparta, however assiduously they tried, could not discover whether the island of Chios had a navy.[8] In our age the question could rapidly be answered by the so-called national means of technical verification—in the unlikely case that the Chios newspapers had not disclosed the information in the first place.

Perhaps the importance of the spy has always been exaggerated; the experience of both world wars has demonstrated that human intelligence has been of limited overall significance. The general trend in the United States since about 1960 has been to allocate fewer resources to HUMINT.* This greater reliance on technology was due in part to the traditional American fondness for gadgets, but it was also traceable to the belief that human agents are essentially unreliable.

The American trend has not been unduly influential in the secret services of other nations. They believe that however much may be found out through photography, intercepts, and other technical means, decisive confirmation of a hunch or a suspicion frequently can come only from the agent on the ground. Even within the American intelligence community, there has been growing criticism in recent years of the de-emphasis on human intelligence and the mistaken belief that space satellites can take care of almost all intelligence collection.

Advocates of HUMINT point to the fact that the decisive confirmation of the impending Egyptian attack in the Yom Kippur War came from a human agent; the fact that it was disbelieved until the very last moment is not relevant in this context. Similarly, the decisive advance warning of General Jaruzelski's coup in Poland in 1981 came from a human source. Human agents can acquire information on political intentions that cannot possibly be provided by photographs, laser beams, and sensors. They can supply economic intelligence, and, perhaps of the greatest importance, occasionally they may provide scientific-technological information that has been successfully hidden from surveillance.

The satellites and other technical means (to mention but one obvious example) could not possibly have given any warning about the weakened position of the Shah, and unless U.S. human intelligence in Iran has dramatically improved since, it must be assumed that U.S. policy makers are no better informed about the situation in Iran now than they were six or seven years ago. More dangerous yet, there is reason to believe that the intelligence intake by way of technical means has declined over the years, and this process may well continue: The size of the intelligence window has not shrunk but, according to some who ought to know, what can be seen through that window is less than in the past. Hence, the danger of overreliance on the so-called new technical systems.

*In 1975 about 87 percent of the collection budget was spent on machinery and only 13 percent for both overt and clandestine HUMINT. The ratio did not basically change in the following fiscal years.

What are a spy's motives? It is doubtful whether anything of general validity can be said about the psychology of espionage. Money has frequently played a role, though it has seldom been the only motive. Sex and blackmail have sometimes been decisive factors in the recruitment of spies, but most frequently such inducements are of no consequence at all.

On the Soviet side, ideological motivation is now much less important than in the past. Soviet intelligence in the 1930s and 1940s could count on a reservoir of goodwill and ideological fervor that accounts for Kim Philby, Guy Burgess, Klaus Fuchs, Anthony Blunt, and others, as well as for some American atomic spies who funneled information to Moscow. Alexander Orlov, the highest ranking Soviet intelligence official ever to defect to the West, told a senate committee that in his time (the 1930s) about 60 percent of the most efficient Soviet spies were Communists "and the Communists were supposed to work for their spiritual fatherland, for Russia, not for money."[9] For the "typical" Soviet spy in the 1960s and 1970s, that is, the post-Philby generation, mercenary motives or weakness of character seem to have been far more important.

The difficulties facing American and other Western intelligence services operating inside "denied areas," that is, effective dictatorships, have been touched on. In 1940 Britain found itself without a single agent inside Germany, a situation that did not substantially change up to the very end of the war. Even when there are spies, the transmission of information frequently presents great difficulties despite all the technological innovations intended to counteract police surveillance.

Western intelligence has never had many spies in "denied areas." What spies it has had have been mainly "walk-in agents," such as Fritz Kolbe, the German foreign ministry official who appeared one day in 1943 in Allen Dulles's office with documents of considerable importance and continued to deliver similar material to Bern fairly regularly. Lieutenant Colonel Pyotr Popov and Lieutenant Colonel Oleg Penkovsky, America's two main spies in the 1950s and 1960s, were likewise not recruited but made contact on their own initiative. Cicero (of World War II fame) and Christopher Boyce and Daulton Lee (the "Falcon" and the "Snowman") were also walk-ins, and the same applies to several American spies who offered their services to the Russians. Much critical information has come from KGB defectors and other former East European state security service officials.

There is a long-standing belief in the critical importance of highly placed agents and a corresponding inclination to underrate the significance of the "small" spy. This is particularly true with regard to agents in positions of significance inside an enemy intelligence service. The defection of Philby or the betrayal of Felfe (the West German official who was in charge of operations inside the DDR) can virtually nullify the efforts of a whole organization. He can provide invaluable information, but this information is often more limited in scope than commonly realized. Even the most highly placed mole of this sort is not omniscient. He may, in fact, know relatively little about the political and military decisions about to be taken by his own masters or about new weapons systems. Compartmentalization in modern bureaucracy is such that most secrets are usually not within his own province, nor are political leaders in the habit of telling their secret service chiefs more than they need to know about their intentions.

Paradoxically, a chauffeur, a cipher clerk, a junior employee in a laboratory or factory, or a night watchman may be almost equally well placed as far as access to secrets is concerned, and he (or she) will be much less conspicuous than a Philby. In recent decades there have been hundreds of cases in Western countries that show the danger that an apparently insignificant spy can create. Cicero was valet to the British ambassador; David Greenglass, the atomic spy, was a draftsman; Houghton and Vassel, the British spies, were lowly administrative workers; Sergeant Jack Dunlap was the chauffeur of the NSA's chief of staff; and Geoffrey Prim, who betrayed many Western SIGINT operations from his base in Britain for ten years, was a translator. East German security services have specialized in sexually seducing spinsters among the secretaries in Bonn and at NATO headquarters in Brussels, sometimes with spectacular results. Top secret documents, after all, have to be typed, copied, and filed, and the secretary is bound to know almost as much as the boss. No one normally pays much attention to secretaries, chauffeurs, draftsmen, and night watchmen, whereas the more highly placed, the more the spy will be under scrutiny —and the greater the danger of discovery.

In addition, there is a fairly sizable number of people who do not need security clearances because they do not have access to top secret materials; nevertheless, they are very much in the know due to their proximity to national leaders. Guenther Guillaume, Willy Brandt's assistant, was in that category. In its post mortem on the Guillaume case, an investigation committee found that for an intelligence service everyone is of interest who has anything to do with important political, economic, or military affairs, even if the person does not have direct access to official secrets.

Nor do all spies face equal risks. For East European citizens found guilty of spying against their own countries, there is the high probability of a death sentence. Spies in the West, whatever their nationality, face at worst a lengthy prison term, and there is always the hope of being exchanged for a Western agent caught in the Soviet Union. Nazi Germany serves as a good illustration of the difficulties facing intelligence services trying to infiltrate totalitarian societies. This was true even during the last two years of World War II, when police control had been severely weakened as the result of mass bombings, evacuations, the presence of hundreds of thousands of foreigners performing forced labor, and general dislocation. A few U.S. agents were parachuted into Germany during the last year of the war; some survived, but only because they remained inactive. British intelligence infiltrated very few agents during the war. Of the several dozen Soviet agents parachuted into Germany, only one was not apprehended. An ethnic Pole, he hid in his native Upper Silesia and later in Czechoslovakia, thus managing to survive.[10] The only allied spies inside Germany who were not caught were those operating outside the network, without the benefit of radio communication, couriers, and so forth. But, with a few exceptions, their role was of only limited importance.

Lastly, there is the problem of the double (or treble) agent, which has not only provided interesting material for novelists and film makers, but also a great deal of anxiety for counterintelligence services throughout the world. In our context the issue is not of central importance. The main assignment of the double agent is to spread disinformation rather than information. However, in order to establish credibility, the double agent has to reveal at least some secrets—to gain a bishop, a few pawns must be sacrificed.

Technical Means of Reconnaissance

Of the various means used in technical reconnaissance, photo intelligence is the youngest, though not by much.[11] Most studies on the subject make mention of the balloon view of Boston's downtown area taken by James Wallace Bleck in October 1860; even earlier, aerial pictures had been taken in Europe. In 1890 the first of many textbooks on the subject was published, and in 1909 the first motion pictures were taken from an airplane (piloted by Wilbur Wright). From that date on, the airplane replaced kites and balloons as the main platform for aerial photography. The two world wars, especially the second, gave a great boost to the new art. Comparative coverage (repeated checks to discover changes) had already been developed in World War I, night photography was developed in the 1930s, and infrared film came into use during World War II to detect camouflaged targets. Stereoscopic vision and other basic tools of the trade were introduced, and it was quickly recognized that the shape of objects observed was of great importance, as were tone and texture, configurations, shadows, and halation.[12]

According to a prediction, probably apocryphal, by the German General

Fritsch, the side with the best photo reconnaissance would win the war. According to General Chennault, 80 percent of all vital U.S. wartime intelligence came from aerial photos. This may have been true in the Far Eastern theater of war, but elsewhere it was not. By and large, World War II was a SIGINT, not a PHOTINT war.

Following some abortive attempts at aerial reconnaissance, the major intelligence breakthrough in the postwar period came with the appearance of the U-2, which made its first flights over the Soviet Union in 1956. This plane, a CIA-sponsored project, had a range of 3,000 miles and could fly at an altitude of over 70,000 feet. At one time the plane produced some 90 percent of the hard data on Soviet military developments. Each over-flight of the Soviet Union had to be authorized by the president. The era of the U-2 came to an end when Gary Powers's plane was shot down (or exploded) over Sverdlovsk in May 1959. The U-2 was succeeded some five years later by the SR-71 (Blackbird), another plane developed by Lockheed, flying at Mach 3 and at a height of nearly fifteen miles. It was equipped with optical and infrared sensors, radar and television cameras, and transmitted data back to earth instantaneously. But the SR-71 has not been used for flying over the USSR except for some peripheral flights along Soviet borders. Its main task has been reconnaissance in other parts of the world.

Today the term "remote sensing"—exploration by means of electro-magnetic sensors, mainly from airborne and spaceborne platforms—is frequently used to cover the whole range of activities of which aerial photography is just a part. Other tools include aerial thermography, which measures the radiant temperature of earth surface features through thermal and multispectral scanners. Another technique, spectral pattern recognition, is largely an automatic process based on a numerical key that identifies and classifies the physical features of the target through pattern recognition. A third method is microwave sensing, better known as radar, which can see through clouds and other obstacles that were otherwise impenetrable during World War II. Side-looking airborne radar (SLAR) was a major innovation of the 1950s; in contrast to most previous radar, it produced images. The part of radar in remote sensing has further expanded with the utilization of lower wavelengths on the one hand and the application of space exploration to intelligence on the other.[13]

Not all remote sensing is carried out from space. Aircraft, ships, and ground bases are involved, and in at least one case, a large helium balloon carrying sensitive antennae. In 1978, fifty-four Soviet fishery research ships were identified as electronic platforms of various types; some of them came close to Cape Canaveral, Vandenberg Air Force Base, and the Charleston, South Carolina naval base.

American ground intelligence operations of this kind are mainly run by the National Security Agency and usually serve more than one purpose. Electronic listening posts equipped with over-the-horizon radar designed to intercept radio transmissions can monitor Soviet missile tests. Some of these posts in Pakistan, Iran, and Ethiopia were lost in the 1970s, but others continue to operate.[14]

Several basic considerations should be borne in mind about remote sensing. Techniques are steadily advancing, military application is probably ten to fifteen years ahead of usage in the civilian sector, and information on the precise resolution of photographs is classified. For the fourth generation of satellites, which came into use in the 1970s, it was claimed that they could identify various makes of automobiles, read car license plates, and even distinguish between Guernseys and Herefords on the range.[15] Specific claims have been questioned, and some even ridiculed, but it is certain that there is steady progress in this field.*

Since the early 1960s, the burden of intelligence collection in highly denied areas has passed to space-borne sensors. The first recovery of a film canister from a satellite *(Discoverer 13)* was accomplished just a few months after the U-2 had gone down over Sverdlovsk. The first Soviet surveillance satellite is thought to have been launched two years later. Since then both nations have launched hundreds of satellites designed to intercept signals from various points along the electromagnetic spectrum.

The most important surveillance satellites have been those for early warning using infrared telescopes to detect quickly the hot emissions of missile boosters. The multipurpose use of satellites—early warning and verification of arms control, "close look" cameras carrying multispectral scanners, and "search and find" techniques covering a wider area to locate unidentified targets—became possible with the fourth generation of satellites, the "Big Bird" since 1971 and the "Key Hole," or KH-11 system first orbited in 1977.

Other new techniques in reconnaissance include thermal imaging, using infrared scanners that measure temperature differences between the earth's surface and its targets. Thermal imaging can detect emissions from tank engines, and even evidence of underground construction. Other recent

---

*The size of objects that can be identified as "resolved" is obviously a factor of paramount importance. Further improvement in this direction is hampered for the time being by the grain size of photographic film emulsion or by the atmospheric scattering of light. This may be corrected by further development of the new technique in adaptive optics that eliminates "image wander" as the atmosphere changes. The traditional kind of film is gradually being replaced by light-sensitive silicon with integrated circuits embedded in it.

innovations include long-wave infrared technology for the detection of radiation, and digital-image processing systems using sonar and satellite data for the detection of submarines and the analysis of aerial reconnaissance information.[16]

After the outbreak of the 1973 war between Egypt and Israel, the Soviet Union was able to launch five additional surveillance satellites within two weeks to supplement its coverage of the Middle East, which had previously been handled by a single satellite. By contrast, shortly after the start of the Iran-Iraq conflict in the late 1980s, one of two U.S. reconnaissance satellites over the region failed. As no backup was immediately available for launch and collection, capabilities were halved for some time.

Seen in historical perspective, the dividing line between photo intelligence, or remote sensing, and signals intelligence has become less rigid with the development of modern technologies. In the popular mind, SIGINT until recently was the breaking of codes, a preoccupation going back at least a few thousand years. In its modern form it came into being with the use of electronic communications. While cable lines were tapped and telegrams purloined in the nineteenth century, systematic military monitoring began only on the eve of World War I, when monitoring and decoding became established practice. The achievement of the British Admiralty's "Room 40," where up to 2,000 signals were daily intercepted are well known, especially because of the political uses to which intercepts such as the Zimmerman Telegram were put. Signals intelligence (ULTRA, MAGIC) played an even more important role in World War II. The British military historian Ronald Lewin wrote that every large war has its salient characteristics, and if the unprecedented use of masses of artillery was the most striking feature of World War I, SIGINT was the dominant feature of World War II.[17] Since then enormous technical progress has been made in SIGINT technology, with its main components of COMINT (radio communications intelligence), ELINT (the interception of electronic signals), and RADINT (radar intelligence).[18]

Specially designed satellites are an important source of SIGINT. Since the early 1970s, electronic surveillance, or "ferret," satellites have been orbited, deploying huge antennae capable of eavesdropping on broadcast transmissions along the electromagnetic spectrum. Some SIGINT satellites are launched into geosynchronous stationary orbit 22,300 miles above the earth, providing uninterrupted, full-time coverage of the targeted area. Other electronic intercept satellites are in lower orbit to detect signals such as radar emissions and local radio broadcasts. The satellite network can also pick up and broadcast back to earth telemetry data from satellites and missile tests.

These miracles of modern technology are impressive. But paradoxically, the overall importance of SIGINT seems to have declined since World War II, and the cost effectiveness of the NSA has been repeatedly questioned. There has been outspoken criticism of "collection for collection's sake." While SIGINT may know the precise location of any battalions and the first names of pilots and supply 80 percent of all raw intelligence collected, it is said to have produced less and less *important* and useful information. At a time of real crisis, such as on the eves of the Soviet invasion of Czechoslovakia in 1968 or of the Polish coup in 1981, the battalions and the pilots tended to get lost. The advances in computer science have given an advantage to the cryptologists; virtually unbreakable cipher systems are now in use. The codes are breakable in theory, but only a stolen codebook or a lucky accident will result in decrypts of exceptional interest.[19] The NSA and its Soviet counterparts can presumably continue to read the W/T (Wireless-Telegraphy) traffic of many other nations, intercept interesting commercial information, and engage in important military traffic analysis. Yet they are unlikely to learn what is most essential for them to know. Quantity, even of unimportant information, has its uses, but seldom does quantity in contemporary intelligence transform itself into quality.

Which of the various intelligence methods mentioned so far—in a needless to say incomplete listing—is the most important? In this categorical form the question is, of course, unanswerable. The methods of HUMINT, as well as PHOTINT and SIGINT, produce wholly credible information. Remote sensing, however, inspires most people with greater confidence than SIGINT, probably because they trust their eyes more than their ears. In turn SIGINT will frequently be trusted more than reports by human agents.[20] To put it differently, it is widely believed that deception or error is most difficult in photo intelligence, and easiest and most frequent in HUMINT.[21] It is known from World War II that military installations can be successfully hidden just as phantom tanks, planes, airports, even whole phantom armies, can be established—at least for a while. It is said that technological progress has made deception more difficult, but as a distinguished photo interpreter once quipped, "We have never found anything the Soviets have successfully hidden."[22]

The experience of the last two decades has shown the limits of both photo intelligence and SIGINT. Neither has been of great help collecting information about international terrorism and drug traffic, two issues that have increasingly preoccupied U.S. intelligence in recent years. There was much information available, mainly through technical intelligence, on topics such as the Soviet ICBM buildup in the late 1960s and SLBM construction in the 1970s, on the appearance of mobile ICBMs, on ballistic missile defense capacity, and on new types of bombers. But there were always widely diverging estimates, provoking heated debates. Official assessments were frequently wrong, sometimes by a wide margin, and it took years after the event for a realistic consensus to emerge. Considering that these disputes were not about intangible issues such as intentions, but about objects that could be observed and counted, it appears that the quantity of intelligence available frequently fails to reduce uncertainty. With all this, it is perfectly true that but for the existence of photo intelligence and SIGINT the possibilities of error would be infinitely larger.

In the final analysis, one does not know whether to marvel more at the achievements of modern technology, which have made much of yesterday's science fiction anachronistic, or be dismayed that despite all these achievements there still remains an enormous margin of ignorance and doubt, above all with regard to political intelligence.

Intelligence Production

Say the information asked for by the policy maker has arrived. It has come from a variety of sources, and according to intelligence doctrine, the CIA's Directorate of Intelligence (DDI) should now take over and turn this intelligence into finished products to be forwarded to the consumers. In practice, one intermediate stage—information processing—will usually be needed. Foreign language documents have to be translated; photo intelligence has to be interpreted. Furthermore, the enormous mass of materials has to be sifted, indexed, and prepared for storage and retrieval.

But the information may be taken out of the hands of the DDI even before assessment. Some top consumers are more interested in raw intelligence than in evaluations; this is particularly so at a time of crisis, when there is great pressure to obtain the most recent information. This is a fact of life with which the DDI has to live. Most of its effort goes into long term, in-depth studies, yet most of its influence is exerted through the supply of current intelligence and as an early-warning, round-the-clock "Watch Center."

The Schlesinger report noted in 1971 that although the provision of analysis to policy makers was the major purpose of intelligence, the production of intelligence was referred to as the "stepchild of the community." It has been traditionally overshadowed (in the words of the Church report) by the glamor of clandestine activities and the love of exotic collection systems.[23] Even in 1985 Admiral Turner referred to it as the Achilles heel of intelligence. It is the CIA directorate which has the smallest budget, yet its scope is global, with an interest in political and military as well as economic affairs all over the world. Scientific reporting is largely left to the Directorate of Science and Technology.

Military reporting has been a source of conflict ever since the birth of the CIA. Originally it was the responsibility of the Department of Defense, but since the 1950s the CIA has been increasingly drawn into strategic intelligence which has become one of its main preoccupations. A division of labor had to be established for the collection of military intelligence, but with regard to its interpretation, the dividing line has been less clear and a matter of contention. A strong argument has been made in favor of intellectual diversity and alternative hypotheses about the matters at hand. Members of the various branches of the intelligence community have (more or less) access to the same data, but their outlook is rooted in different bureaucratic perspectives and traditions. Seen in this light, a case can be made not just for tolerating overlap and analytical competition, but for extending it even further. Another issue which agitated the intelligence community was the nature of organization within the production units— the choice between regional or country desks and functional organization. Both have their merits and drawbacks; both offer different types of expertise. Reorganization in recent years has put the emphasis on regional rather than functional lines. It seems likely that these structural problems matter less than commonly believed as long as the subdivisions of a big organization are at least on speaking terms.

For many years, the national intelligence estimates were the most substantial products of the CIA. Some have estimated that 70 to 80 percent of the time of those concerned with the production of intelligence has gone into the preparation of these documents, but this is no longer true today. The NIEs had their origin in World War II when one of the main problems facing American intelligence was the coordination of reports received from many sources, both open and covert. Colonel Donovan's Research and Analysis Branch assembled all the information available and prepared reports for the president; these were in the nature of academic studies— descriptive, not analytical or estimative in character.[24]

These reports were not coordinated with the armed services and the Department of State. The first directors of the CIA did not think that "crystal gazing" was one of its tasks. Moreover, the armed services refused to cooperate with the CIA (or CIG, as it was called then) in preparing the intelligence estimates. They took a long time: the first study, commissioned in early 1947 to produce the "highest possible quality of intelligence on the USSR in the shortest possible time," actually appeared in March 1948, a delay of twelve months.

The CIA acted as editor of various independent estimates and no attempt was made to integrate them. The Dulles Committee of 1949 blamed the CIA for its failure to coordinate information as envisaged in the National Security Act of 1947. The situation changed in October 1950, after General Walter Bedell Smith became DCI and asserted his authority. The Office of National Estimates was established, and the finished NIEs were submitted for final consideration to the United States Intelligence Board (USIB). The power of decision was with the DCI, under whose signature the NIE eventually went to the president.

Certain NIEs became an annual fixture, such as those dealing with Soviet military capabilities.[25] In later years Special NIEs (SNIEs) were prepared on short notice—sometimes within twenty-four hours or less—in response to specific and urgent requests. The NIEs were CIA reports; if other intelligence agencies wished to register their dissent they were free to do so in footnotes, or sometimes in appendices, which they did freely. The practice of footnoting was mentioned in a directive as early as 1948, and a 1953 directive stated that any agency was free to express dissent about any feature of an estimate.[26] Minority views from within the CIA, on the other hand, would not be footnoted.[27] The monopolistic position of the CIA with regard to strategic NIEs was weakened in the 1970s; both the State Department and the Pentagon published their own studies on political and economic problems, even if these overlapped with the CIA. Whereas in 1978–79 the CIA had predicted rapidly declining Soviet oil production, the DIA published a report in 1981 arguing the contrary.

For many years the makeup of the NIE remained the same. First the problem would be stated, for instance: "To review significant developments affecting the USSR's internal political situation, relations with Bloc states, economic situation, military programs and foreign policy, and to estimate probable Soviet courses of action through 1962."[28] This would be followed by a summary estimate of several pages, many pages of text and when called for, figures, charts, graphs, and maps. While the average strategic NIEs in the 1950s seldom exceeded 40 to 50 pages, 250 pages in two or more volumes were not uncommon in later years. Strategic predictions usually covered a period of three to five years.

From the policy maker's point of view, perhaps the main weakness of the NIEs was that they seldom offered certainties. Adjectives like "possibly," "probably" or "likely" abounded. Sherman Kent, who headed the ONE for sixteen years, warned his colleagues against such "weasel" words. Yet even Kent would not do without them because they reflected the uncertainty inherent in most situations. As a veteran NIE drafter noted:

> The wise drafter will stop and point in both directions. He will give a scrupulously complete list of arguments why the enemy might do what we want him

to do. Then he will give an exhaustive set of reasons why the enemy might do just the opposite. . . . It gets the policy maker to think about all the factors, the unpleasant as well as the pleasant ones. And it insures that he cannot dismiss the conclusion which follows on the ground that the intelligence people forgot something important. . . . A competent drafter will marshal his facts and his ideas and construct an argument which leads to a single or a few major conclusions. If he does not, there is no use writing the estimate. If he does, and if he constructs well, then his betters may tug and pull at his paragraphs, alter his adjectives and qualify his estimative passages, but his message still comes through.[29]

So much for estimates with a clear message. But what is a policy maker to do with intelligence estimates that either present sharply divergent views, with detailed majority and minority arguments resembling a Supreme Court decision, or try to accommodate conflicting views in favor of the lowest common denominator? Kissinger reportedly rejected NIE: 11-8-68, which concerned the state of Soviet military preparedness, calling it inconclusive and bland, and noted that the few certainties it contained were modified, refuted, or taken back in the footnotes.[30] This was neither the first nor the last time that an NIE was sent back by senior policy makers.

For many years the NIEs were prepared by the ONE staff. In 1973, after the ONE had come under heavy criticism, it was decided to change the system of production. The ONE had been attacked both for being too academic and for lacking intellectual rigor.[31] Its defenders maintained that the existing system had provided a guarantee against pressure from policy makers to tailor assessments in accordance with their wishes.

The question of outside pressure is a constant problem for intelligence. Many CIA analysts have argued that military intelligence is always suspect, simply because in a military hierarchy independent views will not be tolerated—if they do develop, they will be rapidly suppressed. Senior military officers, however, have claimed that they were never in any way coerced to slant intelligence to fit policy.[32] There is no reason to disbelieve the claims of the generals and the colonels. But pressure can be generated from within as well as from above, and self-censorship may be far more frequent and effective than censorship from above. Such self-censorship may occur equally frequently in civilian intelligence services.

Sherman Kent has described the dilemma of the analyst who, "looking before the leap" from the realm of fact to the realm of judgment, realizes that his conclusions may be bad news to at least some of his consumers. He may undercut long-held positions, indicate the unsoundness of a plan or the misallocation of money. In such circumstances, temptation will be great not to take the leap, or perhaps simply not to complete the estimate and just "let the facts speak for themselves," which they seldom do.

Alternatively, with a small amount of tinkering—by giving greater stress to some facts and less emphasis to others—conclusions less dangerous to job security or more appropriate to the requirements of policy preconceptions may be reached.[33] This explanation assumes deliberate manipulation on the part of the analyst. Yet unconscious, or partly conscious, motivation is probably much more frequent. Military analysts have a prime obligation to defense—and hence to "worst-case analysis." In the CIA and INR, on the other hand, there may be an anti-military reflex at work, the feeling that DIA "exaggerations" have to be resisted.

Years ago a writer on the intelligence establishment observed that the NIEs were, potentially at least, the single most influential document in national security policy making.[34] But this promise has never really been fulfilled, if only because the NIEs had competitors.

The Murphy Committee noted in 1975 that NIEs "appear to have little impact on policy makers," in large part because the main consumers preferred to base their own estimates of future developments on competing sources of information and analysis. A Senate Select Committee in the late 1970s stated that the failure of the NIEs to serve their fundamental purpose for senior officials was indicative of the overall failure of intelligence to influence policy. It was suggested that all but the major military (Soviet) NIEs be discontinued. Even some of the leading CIA insiders occupied with the preparation of the NIEs stated in 1980 that the NIEs had not been published in a timely manner over several years.[35]

The daily bulk of material produced in intelligence is staggering, impossible even for the most diligent expert to digest in toto. Great advances have been made in storage and retrieval of information, but this is no substitute for evaluating and assimilating it. The decisive test of intelligence is quality, not quantity. If human beings had infinite resources of memory, mental energy, and time, there could be no such thing as too much intelligence data. In reality, overproduction of intelligence can be a serious problem. The fact that the tocsin was sounded concerning ominous developments in an in-house bulletin read by a few specialists will be of historical significance in a post mortem on intelligence performance. It will be evident that someone, somewhere, was on the alert, but it will be of no political significance. The more intelligence there is, the more difficult it will be to establish priorities, and the greater the danger that truly important developments and events will be lost in a tidal wave of information ranging from the mildly interesting to the irrelevant.[36]

The question of how much intelligence is enough is one of many confronted by the intelligence manager daily. He or she also faces the dilemma of current intelligence vs. estimates in depth. Preoccupation with current intelligence, however great the immediate rewards, will almost invariably block the view with regard to long-term developments.

Problems that loomed large thirty-five years ago—such as the question of whether analysts should cooperate closely with policy makers or whether they should keep their distance—were not of critical importance in the long run. The relative merits of organization by area or by function have been argued endlessly and without great benefit.* What matters in the final analysis is that an intelligence agency has people of competence and integrity available in an emergency for every topic of importance. Periodic reorganization will complicate or even block channels of communication; it will misdirect resources and waste valuable time with unnecessary meetings and consultations. Sometimes reorganization may bring about improvements, but it cannot replace individual excellence.

---

*Jeffrey Richelson, *The U.S. Intelligence Community* (Cambridge, Mass.: Ballinger Publishing Company, 1985), provides many facts on the structure of the various U.S. intelligence agencies, military and civilian. Admiral Stansfield Turner, a former DCI (1977–1981), offers similar data as well as suggestions for reform such as the separation of the role of the DCI from that of head of the CIA and the merger of the espionage and analytical branches of CIA. *Secrecy and Democracy: The CIA in Transition* (Boston: Houghton Mifflin Company, 1985).

CHAPTER 2

Economic and Scientific Intelligence

I N the public mind intelligence has usually been a synonym for military and political intelligence; a spy was someone eager to find out such state secrets as the enemy's order of battle or his rulers' intentions. But this image has never been the whole picture and is now less complete than ever. The minicomputer and Minox camera should be the professional emblem of the modern spy, not the cloak and dagger.

Economic and scientific-technological intelligence have always played roles in intelligence, and sometimes very important ones. The instructions Moses gave to his spies about Canaan predominantly concerned economic information, such as the quality of the land. The travelers who went to China in the Middle Ages to study the silk industry's secrets were engaging in technology transfer. British intelligence in the 1930s, whatever its weaknesses, fully understood that the production lines of the German aircraft industry were a matter of the highest priority.[1]

Germany neglected economic intelligence in World War I; its intelligence directors were the first to admit this failure in later years. They did not commit the same mistake twice, however. With the help of the major industrial corporations, German economic and scientific-technological intelligence was heavily developed in the 1930s. It assisted the German commanders in deciding whether to commit submarines to the Atlantic or the Mediterranean, in selecting targets for air raids, and in other important

command decisions. On the whole, German economic intelligence functioned well during the war, but not their scientific intelligence. The main
problem was that Hitler had no interest in the subject.

Paradoxically, wartime scientific-technological intelligence was neglected in America. The reason was primarily overconfidence, the feeling
that the U.S. economic outlook was so great, its technical know-how so
superior, that there was little, if anything, to be learned from potential
antagonists. During World War II the OSS had a research and development
section, but it was not very important; its main task was the production
of exotic weapons for OSS use. There was also a Special Projects Office
which dealt from time to time with scientific intelligence. One such project
was Operation Simmons, set up toward the end of the war to find out
details about German secret weapons, but this was not ever remotely on
the level of the British effort in the same direction.

Economic intelligence, on the other hand, played a growing role during
the war. Agents of the OSS and analysts were asked to find out not only
about enemy military dispositions but also about tungsten and diamond
smuggling, about the production of ball bearings, Swedish iron ore supplies to Germany, and other such topics. It was recognized that these were
strategic issues of great consequence for the conduct of war. Economic
analysis and research, and science and technology (S&T) have been part
of the American intelligence effort, and that of other nations, ever since.
Following the technological breakthroughs of the late 1950s, S&T was
elevated to the rank of a directorate, one of four inside the CIA. Economic
research, on the other hand, had lower priority; it was a mere "area."
Today it is an "office," part of the intelligence directorate.[2]

The problems facing these agencies today are practical in character, such
as how to concentrate on the most important topics and how to attract (and
keep) highly qualified specialists who could find more rewarding jobs in
private enterprise. There are certain basic differences between the techniques of collection of economic research and S&T. There is nothing mysterious about the methods used by the economists: a considerable part of
their knowledge comes from overt sources, photo intelligence is often of
great help in some respects, and further information is supplied through
diplomats, agents, defectors, and visitors. The S&T collection methods are
far more complicated, and they are also among the better kept secrets of
U.S. intelligence. Usually incomprehensible to the layman, they have frequently escaped the attention of the media.

Economic research and S&T maintain many more open lines to outside
experts than other branches of intelligence. If intelligence in general has
no monopoly on intelligence, this is even more true of economic and
scientific research. Exchanges and contacts are not just desirable, but vital

for success. Such contacts no doubt exist in other countries as well, including the Soviet Union. But in other respects there is little similarity; virtually every economic indicator of importance is freely available in the West, no particular intelligence effort is needed to obtain it. Few recent scientific and technological developments in the West are kept secret, but those few have been the target of intense interest on the part of Soviet bloc agencies. American S&T intelligence, though, cannot possibly obtain information about the Soviet equivalent of Silicon Valley. It can merely monitor Soviet weapons development, estimate the capacities of these weapons, and give more or less informed guesses about future trends.

Economic Intelligence

What is economic intelligence? To paraphrase Schumpeter, it is what economists do in and for intelligence agencies. This definition excludes the endeavors of private individuals and organizations to obtain confidential and privileged information about technology, business connections, prices, and financial plans of rivals or clients. Furthermore, it excludes assessments of the current or future economic scene by private individuals and firms or even government offices outside the intelligence community. The CIA may make use of reports prepared by the Federal Reserve Board or Citibank, but these do not constitute economic intelligence. What differentiates economic intelligence from these activities is its task, which is to support the nation's strategy and tactics by means of economic data collection and analysis.

Government agencies concerned with national security and foreign affairs need to know the intentions and strategies of international rivals, friends, and fence sitters, their capabilities and vulnerabilities. Aside from answering questions of this nature, intelligence has frequently had to tell its patrons what questions to ask or how to formulate them. The function of intelligence economists can be compared to that of the employees of a service station. They use the theoretical, historiographic, and statistical tools of their disciplines just as mechanics apply technology derived from scientific principles; their obligation is not to abstract scientific truth, but to provide services to their clients. Whether the drivers choose to follow their advice, whether they prefer Exxon or Mobil, whether they take their cues from the CIA, the DIA, or the INR, is another story.

In its effort to provide government decision makers with information and counsel, economic intelligence tries to uncover vital facts and documents that other players on the world scene wish to keep for themselves. Furthermore, using whatever information is available and applying historical insight, theoretical reasoning, and intuition, it makes judgments on economic decisions and developments abroad. If economic intelligence is successful in ferreting out the secrets of other players, its assessments have at least a chance to prevail over judgments without such ingredients.

Every individual needs a privileged sphere, so does a nation as represented by its government. There are candid individuals and open societies, though in dangerous times even they will be vigilant. There are also secretive individuals and secretive regimes. Open societies in the West, of course, also classify documents, though the secrets often find their way into the public domain. In the economic field, democratic governments may try to protect information on actions they are planning—a currency revaluation, for example, or purchases of strategic items. They also try to keep confidential their negotiating tactics, opinions of other governments, and the like. Such information ranges from truly vital matters to mere trifles classified only to satisfy their authors' vanity. Because foes and friends alike are curious about such secrets, they try to ferret them out with time-honored as well as newfangled methods of spying, yielding the intelligence collectors a considerable amount of information.

The bulk of information for all economies is available in print for analysis in the news media, in business or academic publications, or in intelligence reports. If intelligence reports are classified even when they rely entirely on open sources, the justification may be of two sorts. They could disclose the policy interest that led to their preparation at a specific time, or they could tell the foreign government what one's own observers know and, in particular, what they do not know.

Economic analysis poses different problems for different countries.[3] The advanced, open societies publish a wealth of information, fully annotated and usually quite reliable—or, when uncertain, with appropriate warnings. Less developed, non-Communist countries are more inclined to keep secret unwelcome data. The United Arab Emirates, for example, after conducting a census in 1980, chose not to disclose to what extent foreigners outnumber the native population. But while clandestine investigation may yield a few nuggets of information, badly collected or fabricated statistics can be made useful—if at all—only by patient analysis. Such analysis can be performed just as well outside as inside intelligence organizations.

All Western observers begin their analysis of Soviet economic topics with a perusal of official and other published materials from the U.S.S.R. This statistical universe, however, is full of black holes. The Soviet regime is inclined to conceal, or at least delay such data as would diminish their prestige—grain harvest figures are a good example. Other phenomena may be pushed into the foreground, but it is up to the Western observer to find out the truth behind the glitter. It would be useful—though not indispensably so—if the Soviets were to publish material making it possible for Western statistical offices to translate the Soviet "Net Material" to the more familiar Western concepts of GNP.[4] Far more troublesome is the inadequacy or even absence of Soviet explanations about the methodology used in calculating statistics and the irritating habit of changing definitions and areas of coverage without informing the reader. Such statistical bad manners have the same effect as outright disinformation. How else can one consider the fact, admitted in Soviet writings, that investment series reporting includes unknown quantities of military procurement?

Even worse, the official Soviet defense budget covers perhaps as little as one-fifth of the real security outlay. Since the late 1960s it has remained officially pegged at roughly 17 billion rubles, with actual expenditures ostensibly matching appropriations. This is irrespective of expanded Soviet preparedness measures, unexpected conflicts in various regions, and without adjustment for a mild but nevertheless real inflation. (For ideological reasons, Soviet inflation is as impossible to confront realistically as is unemployment; the regime itself may not have a full understanding of inflation's impact.)

Just as the Soviet regime has always tried to embellish its image, the directors of plants and enterprises as well as the administrators supervising them have always engaged in window dressing. The data they supply their superiors cover up failures to live up to plans; their motives may be to protect their jobs or to boost their bonuses. Illicit dealings in the "second economy," for example, may even be necessary to achieve unrealistic quotas, but such dealings are naturally concealed from view. Thus to some extent disinformation is built into the internal system of the U.S.S.R.

Soviet secretiveness, imitated to varying degrees by other Communist countries, must be acknowledged as an achievement of sorts in statistical and personnel administration. Over the decades the Kremlin has been able to prevent those in the know—and they must number in the thousands—from disclosing countless "secrets," whether on purpose or by blunder. The few exceptions confirm the rule. In all likelihood this pervasive secretiveness serves the Soviet economy and Soviet economics poorly, but by now it extends upwards as well as downwards.

Of course, the top Soviet leaders have all the available data at their disposal. Are they successful in discounting the warped accounts that have traveled up the line to their desks? Stalin was often misinformed because it would have been too dangerous to disabuse him. Khrushchev was not always willing to accept facts he disliked. For being less formidable, Brezhnev may have been better informed. Andropov's KGB background should have put him in a good position to recognize the difficulty, and we do not know yet how his successors fared in confronting the problem.

The problems facing economic intelligence can best be illustrated by reference to several historical cases. Given the tension between the superpowers and Soviet secretiveness, it is only natural that the examples relate chiefly to Western concepts of the U.S.S.R., but economic intelligence also played an important role in World War II. Several months before the Japanese struck at Pearl Harbor, on 2 April 1941, Winston Churchill wrote a letter to Foreign Minister Matsuoka enumerating some economic facts that Japan ought to ponder before choosing between Germany and the Allies. Point 8 read:

> It is true that the production of steel in the United States during 1941 will be 75,000,000 tons and in Great Britain about 12,500,000, making a total of nearly 90,000,000 tons. If Germany should happen to be defeated, as she was last time, would not the 7,000,000 tons steel production of Japan be inadequate for a single-handed war?
>
> From the answers to these questions may spring the avoidance in Japan of a serious catastrophe and a marked improvement in the relations between Japan and the two great sea powers of the West.[5]

It is unlikely that such important and openly available data were not provided by Japanese intelligence to its superiors. Yet the leaders chose to disregard them—either because they were gamblers, did not grasp the facts of economic life, or (to give them the benefit of the doubt) assumed that military and political successes would decide the struggle in their favor before American capabilities could be fully mobilized. They could not have counted much on contributions to the supply of armaments and other essential manufactures by their "co-prosperity sphere" because it was largely a producer of primary commodities.

During the war Germany was chronically short of motor oil; the Soviet oil fields remained a mirage. Refineries were vital for the Nazi war effort, and they were pinpointed as targets by Walter Levy, then a young analyst in the OSS and later a well-known petroleum expert. He calculated the exact location of refineries from the freight tariffs for petroleum products as published by the German railroads; once the refineries were located they became obvious targets for the Allied bombers. This was a perfect example of solid but imaginative intelligence work; a clever mind using overt materials and a minimum of tenuous assumptions swiftly led from conclusions to actions of major consequence.

As World War II drew to an end, Washington began to ponder the problems that might arise in the postwar era when the global power constellation would be dramatically different. Not everyone shared the illusions surrounding the creation of the United Nations. American-Soviet disagreements had surfaced even during the common fight against the Axis powers. In the economic area reconversion was bound to create dislocations everywhere; many economists feared a new Great Depression. The ravage of the war-torn regions appeared even greater than it was in reality,[6] with at least one important exception. The staggering losses the Soviets had suffered through casualties and low birth rates became known only when, three years after Stalin's death, the U.S.S.R. published its first statistical handbook since the 1930s. Demographers all over the world had to correct their calculations, a prime example of the effectiveness of the Iron Curtain in the Stalin era.

Whatever the nature of international relations after the war, the outlook for Soviet rehabilitation was vital. In 1944, it was examined by the U.S.S.R. Division of the OSS, a remarkable assembly of the best minds then involved in Soviet studies. Under the direction of Abram Bergson and Wassily Leontief, the division issued a report entitled "Russian Foreign Trade Developments," one of the major achievements of American intelligence analysis. Despite Soviet losses, the report stated:

> The Russians should be able to reconstruct their economy in about three years after the cessation of hostilities. If the war ends late in 1944, the Russian national income could reach the 1940 level in 1948. . . . Russian involvement in the Japanese war is unlikely to retard markedly the rate of reconstruction of the Soviet economy. . . . The tempo of total reconstruction might have to be slowed down if, in view of the international political situation, Russia feels constrained to maintain a high level of military preparedness. In such case, consumption will be below that attainable under more favorable international political conditions . . . the success of Russian reconstruction will depend only to a very limited extent upon foreign loans. . . .[7]

Researched and written one year before the end of the war, this was a perfectly correct appraisal of things to come.

The U.S.S.R. did indeed feel "constrained to maintain a high level of military preparedness." Restraint and postwar fatigue prevented the tensions that arose between the former allies from causing more than a Cold War. It is not known how Soviet intelligence viewed the East-West power ratio. American intelligence may possibly have overestimated Soviet military strength, as Zbigniew Brezezinski implied in 1972.[8] Economically the U.S.S.R. was underrated in many quarters, particularly by military men, some arguing at the time of the Berlin blockade that once the resulting American trade embargoes took effect, the Soviet economy would "stand still like an unwound clock." The U.S.S.R. division, transferred to the Department of State and now including the entire Soviet empire (CIA research in the area had yet to come into its own), examined the vulnerabilities of the adversary and the likely results of available measures. It came to the correct but not always popular conclusion that, while the embargoes could hardly be avoided as a minimal response to hostile Soviet policies, they would be no more than a great nuisance for the Soviets, more effective in the short run than over a longer time. And so it turned out, even though the productive capacity of the Soviet realm in the late 1940s was only one-fourth as large as today, while American influence in the Western world was far stronger than it is today.

Reconstruction in the West did not, of course, usher in a repeat of the Great Depression. Between 1949 and 1955 the American gross national product increased on an annual average, including the first of several minor recessions, by close to 5 percent. Worldwide economic growth was even stronger. The Soviet clock did not stop either; in fact, the U.S.S.R.'s GNP expanded in the 1950s by almost 6 percent. Not only did living and working conditions improve somewhat over the miserable 1940s, but the Soviet Union manufactured atomic and hydrogen bombs, launched *Sputnik,* created a respectable military arsenal and started economic and military aid to Third World nations. The U.S.S.R. did all this in the face of NATO ("CoCom") controls, rebellions in Eastern Europe, and much grumbling, and even some rioting, at home. The average Soviet citizen would probably have been glad to trade the cosmonaut in the sky for goulash on a plate, and almost surely took a dim view of the Aswan Dam. It was exactly the pressure of public restlessness and the predicament of de-Stalinizing without either wrecking the system or provoking a conservative backlash that induced Khrushchev to promise a Communist society in the near future and challenge the United States to economic competition. Soviet growth accelerated for a few years through heavy investments, while American growth was slowed by recessions.[9] This lent a degree of credence to Khrushchev's boast to "bury" the United States. As a result, numerous series were calculated in the West showing, on the authority of compound interest tables, how in years to come the U.S.S.R. would overtake this country in industrial production and other measures of economic performance.

Although the U.S. intelligence community dismissed Khrushchev's aspirations to be funeral director for Western economies, it differed within itself as to the prospects for Soviet growth. Allen Dulles stated in 1958 that, "The Soviet economy has been growing, and is expected to continue to grow through 1962 at a rate roughly twice that of the United States. Annual overall growth has been running between 6 and 7 percent, annual growth in industry between 10 and 12 percent." Stanley H. Cohn presented average annual GNP growth rates of 6–6.5 percent for the U.S.S.R.

and 4–4.5 percent for the U.S. This would have meant a change of the Soviet-U.S. GNP ratio from 47:100 to 57:100 between 1960 and 1970.[10] At hearings on this issue the same year, Roger Hilsman, Director of the INR Department of State, discussed "the present and future ratio of Soviet versus American national product and its more or less mechanical projection into the future. This ratio is now roughly 45 to 100 and whether, by 1970, it will be 48 or 50 really does not matter greatly; the change in the ratio is likely to be minor."[11]

Although twenty years ago intelligence and academic experts discussed all these rates and ratios with considerable passion, even those forecasts that gave the Soviets the benefit of the doubt erred only by a small percentage.[12] More meaningful were three facts emphasized by Roger Hilsman:

> Since Stalin's . . . burial, i.e., in the last 10 years, the U.S.S.R.'s national product has grown by about six percent in the annual average. . . . What is interesting about this figure is not that it is so high, but that it is so low. Considering the enormous efforts and sacrifices forced upon the Soviet population, one should have expected a faster rate of progress.

Hilsman underlined the Soviet system's paradoxical nature:

> You have a planned economy, but it is irrational—[it] is planned on two levels, and the two levels are out of balance. You have a great economy and yet a great poverty.

Finally, he pointed out that:

> Much more important [than mechanical projections into the future] is the impact that America . . . has and will have on the U.S.S.R. and its policies . . . and our actions . . . will, whether Moscow likes it or not, have a decisive influence on future Soviet allocations. . . .[13]

This last point remains valid today: at all times there is an inevitable "interdependence" between the two rival superpowers. Khrushchev had strengthened the American will to assert its economic and military power. Wishing to match the American military efforts elicited by its own aspirations and actions, the Soviet regime decided to forge ahead with its long-term military preparations while also improving the living standard of the general population, insofar as the system's resources permitted. The victim was capital investment, though this downgrading in priority was clouded by illusions of compensatory gains in productivity—illusions that were disabused time and again. As a result, capital stock shrank and the growth in GNP followed suit.

As in other fields, one should be careful not to overestimate capacity for foresight in economics. Although Soviet-style economics are "centrally planned," its directors have frequently misjudged their prospects—not only because the natural or political climate proved unpredictable. Western economic developments have continually confounded their observers, Marxists as well as analysts sympathetic to capitalism. Economists have become gourmets when it comes to eating crow. Those who speculate about the end of "stagflation" or the size of future federal deficits might read with fear and pity what Wharton Economic Forecasting Associates of the University of Pennsylvania predicted for the past decade. We do not know yet whether U.S. intelligence was more successful in judging the momentous events in Western markets during the past fifteen years, but there is no reason to believe U.S. intelligence to have been either more or less accurate as a forecaster.

In the quarter century since U.S. intelligence and academic observers first scrutinized prospective Soviet growth, economic forecasting has greatly expanded, profiting from econometric refinements and the electronic revolution. Almost every economist now embraces a model that, while costly, brings prestige and greatly varying results. The advantages that models can furnish are indisputable, but their users must keep in mind that the results, for all their elegance, can only be as solid as their underlying theories and assumptions. And the latter tend to resemble each other at any specific place and time, as programmers have a way of influencing each other.

Around 1960, Sovietologists inside and outside intelligence correctly predicted rapid economic growth fueled by heavy investment, though due to an underestimation of military outlays and the effects of errors in planning the anticipated rates were on the high side. The experts accurately foresaw capital inputs leveling off in the 1970s and labor inputs declining shortly before 1980. But they tended to overstate the expected rates. After actual Soviet GNP growth in 1971–75 had declined to 3.6 percent in the annual average, forecasts made soon after reckoned with a better performance for 1976–80, with an annual GNP growth of 4 percent or more. Models offering a base-line case seemed "reasonable" as well, as alternate scenarios had little difference in their variations. In reality, the average GNP growth continued at 3.6 percent during 1976–78 then slumped to 1.1 percent in 1979 and 1980.

This renewed Soviet decline of recent years was neither predicted, nor has it even now been sufficiently diagnosed by Western observers. It may be a temporary aberration; administrative and managerial failures may have caused an inefficient economy to fall below its usual level. But the system's malfunctioning may actually have deepened. Of course there is also the deflection of resources from civilian sectors to the national security apparatus to be reckoned with. One cannot be certain that the experts in the Kremlin themselves have sorted out the causes of the decline.

As the U.S.S.R.'s military posture is of central concern for Western intelligence, its evaluation is far more complicated than, say, stock, value, and costs of Soviet gold or other valuable resources. But the categories needed to assess these apply also to military might; estimates must be made of the arms and the men available at a given time or added over the course of a year, and this must be done in physical terms or in dollar or ruble costs. The physical picture is constantly being surveyed by a variety of methods, both traditional and ultramodern; it is incomplete if only because what is stored in silos or going on under the roofs of Soviet R&D buildings escapes satellite observation. Justified or imaginary, suspicions are easily aroused about missile gaps, or chemical, biological, or laser weapons, because secrecy has an unsettling effect on the other side. Nevertheless, the West's picture of the Soviet physical inventory appears reasonably complete.

The value in dollars of all these disparate components and their increase over the years permits a comparison of overall military capabilities in the East and the West, and an estimate of the costs (in rubles) permits analysts to form an opinion of the military burden carried by the Soviet population. For such estimates the few official Soviet announcements of "defense" and "science" budgets and the official ruble-dollar exchange rate are practically useless. It is therefore necessary to assign a dollar or ruble value to each of the physical components. The analysts assume that the list of physical data (weapons and installations, men in service, products consumed in operations) is sufficiently accurate in quantity and quality, including items eluding observation. They further assume that the costs and prices they apply to each class of items—the so-called building blocks of the procedure—are reasonable. On the dollar side of the calculation many prices are easy to arrive at (for example, prices for petroleum products used by the military). But there are many products used by the Soviets that are not manufactured in the U.S.: Soviet novelties, at one end of the range, or goods of low value, but not necessarily unserviceable, at the other. For such unknowns American "shadow prices" must be obtained. Pay and maintenance costs for the Soviet armed forces equal the dollar outlays for their U.S. counterparts even though it cannot be assumed that Americans and Soviets would be equally destructive in action. A whole array of U.S. price indices is available to deflate the dollar costs to some base-year price level but, as American budget discussions demonstrate, opinions differ as to what index to select even for our own defense outlays.[14]

Ruble prices are difficult to ascertain; the Soviets are reluctant to reveal costs for civilian goods, not to mention military items. Prices for civilian products, if known, are used as substitutes for military goods (for example, trucks); otherwise dollar prices must be hazardously translated into rubles, using purchasing power equivalents. Ruble inflation has to be taken into account, but so does cost reduction when prototypes move into serial output. Moreover, prices and costs (plus profit) for civilian and military goods are by no means identical; some products used by the military are taxed, and many are subsidized. These problems are mentioned because they go far to explain the rationale behind the CIA's sudden change of its 1974–75 estimates of Soviet military spending. This increase was largely limited to the ruble costs; estimates in physical terms and their dollar equivalent remained more or less unchanged.

What prompted the drastic revision of the CIA's estimates was a rare happening—the appearance in 1974 of an intelligence source with specific data for the year 1970. Someone had been allowed to see classified Soviet documents and then remembered a significant series of figures. Because these were roughly double those of Western calculations at the time, the new evidence was not readily accepted. But after lengthy examination it was decided that the source was not a Soviet plant to spread disinformation, that his memory could by and large be trusted, that the secret document he had seen some time earlier and only for a short while was probably bona fide, and that the value data were probably in current rubles.

The information obtained in 1974 had many implications: an official Soviet defense budget absurdly small compared with the actual outlay: a military burden twice as heavy as previously assumed, absorbing perhaps the highest share of GNP for any nation in peacetime; an armament industry technically competent but, in contrast to previous beliefs, economically not much superior, if at all, to a generally inefficient civilian industry; and civilian investment somewhat smaller but apparently slightly more productive than previously supposed.

Information of this type is in the nature of a revelation. A skeptic cannot check the records hidden in the Kremlin. Once he or she accepts the revelations as true, all that remains is exegesis, which may be sophisticated or sophistical. The CIA adopted the figures disclosed (with minor adaptations) feeling justified, especially in light of more recent information on Soviet prices. Its price investigations for the preceding years had not been up-to-date, but it is worth remembering that price research of this type is time-consuming and expensive. Using prices set by administrative fiat rather than prices reflecting scarcities is, moreover, a problem in itself. Before 1974 the CIA's ruble figures had been criticized for being on the low side both from within the intelligence community and from the outside, but none of the critics' alternate estimates were close to the magnitudes disclosed in that year.[15]

The economics of the U.S.S.R.'s military posture can hardly be successfully tackled without some penetration of Soviet silence or misinformation. Because national security activities appear to absorb roughly one-seventh of the U.S.S.R.'s GNP, even the analysis and extrapolation of national aggregates can be marred by uncertainty about an important component.

ECONOMIC INTELLIGENCE AND THE OIL ISSUE

In the course of history, the political importance of various commodities has changed. Long ago, the supply of salt was vital enough to lead nations to war; oil has been a comparable modern factor. Ancient oracles were probably no more accurate with regard to the price of salt than modern economic model builders concerning oil prices. Intelligence errors in this field are paralleled by numerous misjudgments on the part of internationally well-known oil experts. In 1977, when President Carter had called adjustment to the oil crunch the moral equivalent of war, the CIA issued a paper that created quite a stir.[16] The report concluded that by 1985 the OPEC group would have to provide the rest of the world with 48 million barrels per day (b/d), an amount they would be neither able nor willing to produce. This would result in an energy deficit—a lack of crude oil—of roughly 21 million b/d, including even a considerable shortfall within the Communist world.

This last aspect of the forecast rested on the belief that Soviet crude oil output was bound to decline in the 1980s because important oil fields would approach exhaustion at that time. From a 1975 production of slightly less than 10 million b/d the U.S.S.R. would move to a peak of, at most, 12 million b/d around 1980, then fall to 10 or 8 million b/d by 1985. Such an output would not be enough to supply the U.S.S.R. and its client states. Thus, "We estimate that the Soviet Union and Eastern Europe will require a minimum of 3.5 million b/d of imported oil by 1985. At worst, slumping production could lead to import requirements as large as 4.5 million b/d."[17] Expressed differently, the Soviet bloc would be dependent on outside oil to the extent of one-third to one-half of the U.S.S.R.'s total output. Instead of a large hard currency gain from oil exports (at that time $3–4 billion), the Soviet Union would have to put out $20 billion a year or, at higher prices, perhaps twice as much.

The CIA was aware that the U.S.S.R. could neither earn nor borrow that much money. How would the Kremlin behave after becoming dependent on foreign technology, foreign grain, and—soon—foreign oil? Would it try to appease the West, or would it try to extend its empire to a country in the Middle East with an oil surplus large enough to cover Soviet bloc requirements? Would the worldwide energy scarcity slow economic growth everywhere (except in oil- and gas-exporting countries) with the result that resources would be idled, protectionism would increase, and the masses would become more and more restive? This scenario was certainly suited to stimulate American efforts regarding the oil crunch. However, when the classified version became known to the intelligence community and the "sanitized" version was shortly thereafter made public, many found the picture overdrawn. Because even within the CIA opinions were divided, the agency published a second report in the same month that reaffirmed its initial conclusions while admitting the need for further research.[18]

Viewed five years later, the perspective was that the alarm was shrill indeed. Soviet energy production in all its forms had most certainly been laboring under difficulties for many years before.[19] Nevertheless, in 1980 the Soviet Union earned $12 billion in hard currencies by oil exports. Since the oil shortages of 1973 and 1979, the whole world has increased domestic energy output while economizing on its use. The CIA had indicated that by 1985 OPEC would have to export 48 million b/d, but in 1981 the figure was only 20–21 million b/d. Today, the oil crunch has given way to an oil glut. This is in part the result of a recession which, in turn, induces OPEC to attempt a reduction in its own output so as to keep prices high. As far as the market mechanism is concerned, the oil cartel has spent its force for the time being. As we have seen, however, oil is a thoroughly politicized commodity and future surprises of a political nature cannot be ruled out.

How to evaluate the 1977 CIA report's mistakes? The exaggeration of the U.S.S.R.'s difficulties was apparently the work of technological specialists. They had convinced their bosses, after some argument, of the approaching exhaustion of the Soviet oil fields. Herbert Block, an economist with many years service in government, tried to explain in 1978:

> Western technologists are sometimes inclined to disparage ways of doing things that are not as sophisticated as procedures in their countries. . . . The U.S.S.R. does face acute difficulties and an agonizing reappraisal of its options for the 1980s, but all economies are flexible and the Soviet people have become accustomed to rough conditions. . . . The authors of the two CIA reports are experienced analysts. I do not doubt their expertise, responsibility and veracity. To vary Oscar Wilde's report from the Wild West: "Please do not shoot the analyst. He is doing his best."[20]

What should an organization do in a case like this? Should it conceal the findings, only to be told perhaps at a later time that it had again missed the boat? The CIA directors decided to make what looked like a sensational discovery widely known. The oil issue was of great topical interest, and the document supported the administration's energy policy. Was the support effective? Exaggerations rarely help, and they were not needed at a time abounding in warnings that appropriate remedies had to be applied soon.[21] Did the CIA report stir the Kremlin to action? We do not know. If it did, then in all likelihood it strengthened the Soviet leadership's determination to take measures, perhaps even stronger measures than had been considered, to improve their position as a supplier and consumer of energy.

About the CIA paper of April 1977, the intelligence community agreed to disagree. The directors of the Defense Intelligence Agency told the Joint Economic Committee in 1981 that:

> The outlook for Soviet energy, from the perspective of the U.S.S.R.'s leadership, is highly favorable. Prospects for the full satisfaction of domestic needs, planned energy exports to Eastern European Communist countries, and negotiated quantities for customers in Western Europe appear to meet Soviet expectations through the 1980s and beyond. . . . Soviet planners clearly understand the politics and economics of oil. . . . The Soviet petroleum industry is well organized, tightly structured and closely monitored. . . . [22]

This account, in turn, may be too optimistic. Nowhere in the DIA document is the CIA report mentioned, but the silence calls attention to itself. In regard to energy estimates, U.S. intelligence is certainly a pluralistic community.

The preceding comments on a few interesting cases among many over the course of four decades are not post mortems. Official post mortems are usually carried out only after assessments go wrong. The evil that men write lives after them, the good is oft interred in their files. An inquest into the failure of an intelligence report has more than once led those concerned into making the same mistake in reverse. Comment on the performance of economic intelligence ought to differentiate between the research for secrets and the analysis of more or less open materials and the analysis produced for confidential policy deliberation or for the public domain.

The main target of Western economic intelligence is the Communist (in particular the Soviet) realm because of its all-pervasive secretiveness. Soviet economic intelligence in regard to the West has a plethora of unclassified materials at its disposal, not to mention security leaks; its efforts in the economic field, aside from the obvious strategic issues, seem concentrated on what Western firms regard as company secrets of a technological, organizational, or negotiating nature.

Soviet economic secrets can be uncovered by Western agencies in several ways: through observation by intelligent and discriminating observers with a good memory (considered "spying" in the Soviet Union); through careful analysis and interpretation of selected Soviet statements and literature, and the systematic perusal of Soviet broadcasts and publications; and through gleanings obtained by surveillance satellites and similar devices. The information from these various sources is enormous. Because there is always the danger that interesting items will be lost, the operation requires a large organization with up-to-date, expensive equipment. The limit on costs and manpower determines priorities in the search for evidence; "hard" knowledge of Soviet military component availability is obviously more important than data on currency aggregates. Whether classified or not, facts require analysis and adjustment to the special (and frequently confidential) interests of the decision makers. How good the results are, and some of the reports previously mentioned were outstanding, depends not only on the expertise of the analyst, which is indispensable, but must be combined with I.Q.—and good luck.

Those who undertake intelligence analysis, economic or otherwise, must understand, as Goethe said, "that everything factual is already theory." Each fact derives its significance from its place in the context of a consciously or unconsciously adopted economic or political theory. Because the elements that constitute the historical universe are numerous and there is no equivalent of the Periodic Table to give them their specific weights, and because even the theories connecting them are in flux, the same facts can be interpreted in different ways. Some people seem to possess an insight that cuts through the maze of history-making facts and factors to bare those that exert an overwhelming force. They select valid assumptions that lead to valid conclusions. When Churchill wrote that he had suggested a few questions which deserved the attention of the Imperial Japanese Government and the people, he exhibited that type of intuition and intelligence. Unfortunately, Japanese intuition was not as acute.

Analysis grows more uncertain as it approaches the margins of its capacity. Unfortunately, the marginal magnitudes—and not just in economics—are usually the real points at issue. We can be reasonably certain that both the United States and the Soviet Union will still have enormous GNPs in the years to come. But beyond this obvious truth we wish to know whether their growth will be 2 percent or 4 percent or perhaps a negative percentage.

Even if one disregards what Marxists call "false consciousness," the influence of national, religious, and cultural traditions on our thinking, it is still true that analyses and forecasts share in the world view prevalent at the time of their gestation. The mood of the period may be upbeat or despondent, aggressive or peaceable, reckless or fainthearted. In its effort to sustain the nation's policy makers, diplomats, negotiators, and military chiefs, moreover, economic intelligence is an eminently political task. Political pressures exist at all times, though stronger at some times than at others; and there are agencies that are more exposed than others. In economic intelligence, the pressure is often not so much explicit as it is part of the atmosphere emanating from the powers that be—from Congress and the White House to the particular government organization. But U.S. intelligence has always been able to count on those who would voice opinions that might not be popular; it has frequently had the courage to reverse its stand when confronted by convincing evidence to the contrary. Intelligence has usually remained sufficiently public to provoke and meet criticism from government agencies outside the intelligence community and from academia. In economic intelligence, such pluralism is aided by free movement between the academic world and government. There are no grounds to support the notion that intelligence competition is more expensive than an intelligence monopoly; even if this were the case, it would be worth the cost.

Scientific Intelligence

Of the four main directorates of the CIA, that for Science and Technology was the last to come into being (August 1963), and the number of people it employs today is relatively small. But the origins of scientific intelligence go back far beyond 1963, and the importance of the subject cannot be measured by a headcount of employees. Most scientific and technological research is not concentrated in the hands of one agency but dispersed over a wide range of government bodies and private corporations. There can be no doubt concerning the crucial role of scientific intelligence. The great majority of Soviet agents apprehended since World War II, from the "atomic spies" to those most recently identified, were engaged in technical intelligence.[23] Their assignment is not that of the classical spy,[24] that is, to report the views, intentions, and moods of foreign potentates and cabinets. Their interest is in such esoteric matters as advanced computers, space technology, fiber optics, directed-energy weaponry, and antisubmarine warfare. If they can harvest this field, the rewards will be rich indeed. Arrayed against them is a formidable combination of counterespionage brains and technology.

Scientific intelligence has come a long way since the OSS days, when a special section devoted itself almost exclusively to support for covert action with the construction of small weapons, miniature radio transmitters and receivers, forgery of passports and other documents, and so forth.[25] The CIA in principle was dealing with scientific questions from the very beginning (there was an Office of Scientific Intelligence as early as 1948) and notable work was done in the field of photographic intelligence (by NPIC, the National Photographic Interpretation Center, founded in 1953). Nevertheless, most of the research and development efforts in the 1950s took place in the Department of Defense as well as under contract to such corporations as Mitre, Sandia, and Rand. Direction was provided by two major study panels: the Technological Capabilities Panel headed by James R. Killian and the Security Resources Panel directed by H. Rowan Gaither, Jr. In October 1957 the shock caused by the launching of *Sputnik* provided fresh impetus to military research and development. One result was the establishment, or rather the elevation and reconstruction, of the President's Science Committee (PSAC) and the appointment of the President's Special Assistant for Science and Technology.

Most of these scientific developments deal with the construction of guided missiles and other major weapons systems, and are discussed later. Indirectly, they also had a considerable influence on the development of scientific intelligence. The Gaither Panel had a great deal to say about the subject in its "conclusions"; the panel was directly involved in the development of the U-2 plane and the plans for building reconnaissance satellites.[26] On the other hand, the PSAC—headed at the time by Killian and George Kistiakowski, a chemist who had been with the OSS in World War II—had to review every major high-technology project concerning national defense, including those sponsored by the CIA. Edwin H. Land of Polaroid served first as chairman of Subpanel Three (intelligence) of the Gaither Panel and later as a member of the President's Foreign Intelligence Advisory Board (PFIAB) where, with others, he helped pioneer the application of advanced satellite sensors for intelligence collection.

With the establishment of the CIA's Directorate of Science and Technology under Albert Wheelon, most of the components created during the previous decade were brought under one roof: the old office of Scientific Intelligence, ELINT, Richard Bissell's Development Projects Division, the Data Processing staff, the Foreign Missile and Space Analysis Center, and others. A great many vested interests had to be overcome to carry out this merger but John McCone, who was DCI at the time and an engineer by training, was firmly resolved to strengthen scientific intelligence—a subject in which Allen Dulles had been less interested. The Kirkpatrick report on intelligence, which had been published shortly before, strengthened McCone's hand with its emphasis on the need for integration of the scientific-technical efforts.[27]

Only one section was left out, the Technical Services Division which continued to execute all technical research and development concerning CIA clandestine activities.[28] From the point of view of the new directorate, this turned out to have been a blessing. It meant that in the 1970s, when the CIA came under fire, TSD was left virtually alone, with the exception of some searching questions about CIA ventures into the field of pharmacology.

The position of the science directorate was different from that of the other main CIA sectors. To a far larger extent than the other directorates, it made use of outside expertise and developed its new technical systems through outside contracting. While this made it vulnerable as far as the maintenance of secrecy was concerned, in fact it was responsible for fewer leaks than most other divisions. For this reason it is difficult to list even the major achievements of science and technology over the past two decades with any assurance that one has covered the field. Apart from the U-2 and SR-71 reconnaissance aircraft and satellites such as the KH-11, the directorate developed and improved ELINT systems (synthetic aperture radar and the "senior Ruby") providing for the simultaneous collection and transmission of COMINT and ELINT. Other important innovations included a major sensor camera that uses heat sensitivity to photograph images "in the past,"[29] the safe-X satellite identification system, digital-image processing systems, miniature generators, new all-source SIGINT systems, communication receivers-demodulators, "Cross-Ears" and "Cross Jade" for the integration of intelligence collections, and special devices making covert hearing possible by way of laser beams, directional microphones, and so on. In many of these fields U.S. technical intelligence has been considerably in advance of other countries. These remarkable achievements were entirely autochthonous. The main focus of U.S. intelligence over the past thirty years, however, has been the number, deployment, and accuracy of Soviet strategic weapons.

In its simplest form, scientific and technical intelligence activity involves research and development of technical devices used in the intelligence process as well as the operation of technical systems used in collecting and processing information. Perhaps even more important, it also covers the *analysis* of information as to what is happening in the scientific and technical arena in foreign countries.* Seen in this light, virtually every field in the physical sciences and many in the life sciences ought to be covered by scientific intelligence. Its interests range from questions concerning the accuracy of a Soviet ICBM guidance system to the state of health of various world leaders.[30]

Scientific intelligence is done by small groups of specialists in myriad technical disciplines. Each group tends to feel that its subject matter is of the highest importance. Cryptographers argue that their efforts produce more useful intelligence than any other group of specialists, while photo interpreters make a similar claim. But a new era in scientific intelligence dawned with the coming of the space age and with it many new technical problems and new sets of tools for the collection and processing of information.

Sputnik raised immediate questions as to what the Soviets intended to do in space, and with that came a more immediate concern as to other applications for their newly demonstrated ability to orbit a small payload. It was obvious from the outset that a rocket powerful enough to put a satellite into space could hurl a highly destructive nuclear payload across intercontinental ranges. Just in case U.S. and other world leaders missed this connection, Mr. Khrushchev was quick to point it out to them.

In October 1957, the month that *Sputnik* was launched, the first group of outside expert advisers was brought together in Washington to study U-2 photos of key Soviet guided missile and space test ranges at Kapustin Yar and Tyuratam. The conclusions of their study, published in November 1957, were that the Soviets had a very large and diverse effort in missile and space technology either already underway or planned for the near future.

Technical analysts were soon flooded with questions as to the types of missiles under development, their ranges, the sizes and types of warheads they would carry, the accuracy of their guidance systems, and so on. Political analysts were required to join in estimating how soon these missiles might be deployed, particularly those capable of threatening the United States. An additional urgent question was how many missiles might be deployed, and at what pace this deployment might proceed.

Information on these issues, both technical and political, was very limited; analysts' views varied widely and heated disagreements were frequent. Estimates were regularly issued, but as an old-timer in the national intelligence estimate business often pointed out, "You estimate when you

---

*The most detailed and most fascinating account in the open literature on scientific intelligence at work is chapter 40 ("The V Weapons in 1943") in the third volume of *British Intelligence in the Second World War,* ed. F.H. Hinsley et al. (London: Her Majesty's Stationary Office, 1983), pp. 357–401.

don't know." Answers to vital questions certainly were not known in 1960, but due to the foresight of intelligence leaders like Richard Bissell it was in the same year that the United States *began* to get some of the answers.[31] With the first film recovered from a U.S. satellite reconnaissance system, the "open skies" policy became a reality. True, these early photos tended to raise more questions than they answered. Many things were seen that were not understood, but given the large size of the facilities required for early Soviet ICBMs, questions as to the numbers of deployed missiles were soon authoritatively answered. Policy makers were relieved when the issue was settled in favor of those who had argued that few, if any, ICBMs had already been deployed.

Soon, however, another threat appeared: the emplacement of Soviet missiles in Cuba. These were not ICBMs, but their medium and intermediate ranges could bring much of the United States under fire from Cuban soil. The 1962 missile crisis resulted in the reorganization of missile intelligence efforts. Higher priority was given to both the collection and analysis of data on this vital subject. During the same period, U.S. concerns broadened from a preoccupation with offensive ballistic missiles to other strategic weapons programs.

Some limited information about Soviet interest in antiballistic missiles (ABMs) had been provided by German guided-missile engineers who had worked in the Soviet Union during the 1950s. Now photography confirmed that testing of such systems was underway. As a result, many new questions confronted the technical intelligence analyst. Details were required as to what type of radar—at what distance, and with what accuracy—could track a U.S. missile. To determine the vulnerability of U.S. systems then being deployed or planned for the future, it was necessary to know with what speed and accuracy the intercepting missile could engage a target.

These new requirements spawned a new family of electronic intercept systems located in space or around the periphery of the U.S.S.R. Electronic intelligence also included the interception of telemetry signals from all types of Soviet weapons as they were tested (telemetry is the information radioed from a missile in flight to stations along its flight path, providing development engineers with detailed performance information). Analysts in the U.S. gradually learned to interpret performance data and convert it into the technical characteristics needed to describe the capability of these systems.

Digital computers had been widely used among cryptographers for many years, but the increased importance of processing large quantities of electronic intelligence required new computer systems. A good example of the ambiguity in the early processing and analysis of some of the electronic information is the debate over the size of the SS-8, a second generation Soviet ICBM. Even after the missile had been tested many times, there was a vast difference of opinion on the subject and thus on the payload or warhead it could carry. Although the term was not to become popular until the SALT I talks, the SS-8 inaugurated the "throw-weight" dispute. Some analysts held that the SS-8 had a 3,000-pound payload, while others were equally convinced that it was in the 30,000-pound range. The importance of the argument was highlighted by the fact that those who held to the 30,000-pound figure also believed that this vehicle would allow delivery of the 100-megaton bomb which Khrushchev had bragged about. It was obvious that this type of technical disagreement greatly undermined the credibility of the entire technical intelligence effort. Analysts realized the need to improve their skills and techniques. Eventually, it was agreed that the SS-8 throw-weight was in the lower range. Those who had been wrong learned why, and this type of mistake was not repeated.

The 1960s saw an aggressive Soviet effort in space. Their long list of "firsts" included the first man in space, the first woman in space, the first multimanned spacecraft, and the first photos taken on the lunar surface. American intelligence was expected not only to identify each successive Soviet space project, but to determine details about each system, its objective, and degree of success. Once President Kennedy declared that putting a man on the moon during the decade of the 1960s was a top national priority, the dominant question was whether or not the Soviets were competing with the United States for this objective, and if so, what their progress toward that goal had been. By the mid-1960s, technical intelligence analysts were convinced that the Soviets were not trying to compete with the Apollo schedule. Nevertheless, when asked by the policy makers "whether the Soviets could beat us to the moon," they phrased their reply carefully: the Soviets had no chance to beat the Apollo *schedule*. To have gone further would have violated the ground rules of conveying intelligence to consumers. It would have forced intelligence to make judgments as to the probability that the Apollo schedule would be met. An intelligence analyst trying to second-guess U.S. programs in such a manner would have invited challenge from the program managers and their credibility would have been questioned.[32]

If the Soviets were not competing with the Apollo schedule, what were the objectives of their lunar program? The answers were not immediately apparent. As Soviet tests continued over the next few years, it became clear that they were countering Apollo with a dual approach. They planned to fly a manned spacecraft around the moon and back to earth. They also planned to land an unmanned vehicle on the moon, pick up a very small sample of lunar soil, and return it to earth. Despite repeated failures in both programs, the Soviets were persistent—in fact, a sample-return vehicle was in orbit around the moon when the successful *Apollo II* mission was launched. Up to the last day, the Soviets were trying for another "first." Had they succeeded in one or both of their missions before the first U.S. manned lunar landing, they would probably have claimed that they had sent the first man to the moon, had brought back the first sample of lunar soil, or both, even though the technological achievements of Apollo were of a higher order of magnitude.

Soviet plans may also have banked on an Apollo failure or at least a significant delay in the Apollo schedule. In addition to the manned circum-lunar and sample-return projects, they also developed a giant space booster (with about twice the lift-off thrust of the *Saturn V,* Apollo's first stage). This was the major building block for their own manned lunar landing try. After three successive failures, the program was terminated. Though some Soviet space systems continued to work well, their overall record in the late 1960s and early 1970s was disastrous. Because the two superpowers were in a declared space race, it was important for U.S. policy makers to be fully informed on the competition's progress or lack thereof. Technical intelligence met this need in exemplary fashion.

During this period of lunar competition, one Soviet achievement proved of particular interest to the officials responsible for Apollo. Soviet *Lunar 9* landed on the surface of the moon and took a series of facsimile photos of the surface. At that time there was still debate among U.S. scientists as to the most likely composition of the lunar surface, some fearing that the surface might not support the weight of the Apollo vehicle. Careful study of the *Lunar 9* pictures put that fear to rest. Soviet data, analyzed by U.S. technical intelligence specialists, had provided NASA with clear evidence that the Apollo spacecraft could land safely on the moon.

The question of outer space was of the greatest importance for the monitoring of SALT and other strategic arms agreements. Without the existence of satellite reconnaissance systems there would have been no SALT agreement, even though the very term "satellite reconnaissance" is not used in any SALT documents. (Neither country was eager to highlight that term during negotiations and the phrase agreed on was "national technical means of verification.") Recognition of the great importance of verification to both the Soviet Union and the United States led to a provision in the various agreements that neither party would interfere with the "national technical means of verification" of the other side.

After the SALT I and SALT II negotiations, the U.S. government made public the existence of satellite reconnaissance without providing details on the quality of satellite cameras and other collection systems. Studying the provisions of the agreements, experts will draw their own conclusions as to the monitoring inputs needed for verification. But secrecy as to the details is still fully justified, for uncertainty as to monitoring capability is a significant deterrent to cheating.

Strategic arms negotiations and monitoring of the resultant agreements has been one of the major challenges to scientific and technical intelligence for more than a decade and is likely to remain so as long as interest in arms limitations or reductions persists. SALT I was based heavily on the ability to count large, highly visible weapons systems. As negotiations move further into qualitative aspects of weapons systems monitoring and verification, the task becomes increasingly difficult. Improvements are needed in existing collection systems and new types of collection devices are required. Counting the number of ICBM silos or ballistic missile-launching submarines is relatively simple compared to establishing the range or payload capability of a small, air-launched cruise missile.

Additional challenges are ahead as new types of strategic weapons are considered. Some believe that high-powered lasers in space with an anti-satellite capability, or even antiballistic missile capability, are soon to come. Other experts doubt the feasibility of such systems, at least for the next decade or two. Technical intelligence cannot afford to be part of that debate, however. Its role is to carefully follow developments, advise decision makers as to the rate of progress, and reevaluate estimates based on new observations.

There is a tendency toward worst-case analysis in scientific intelligence, just as there is an inclination to believe that if *we* have not been able to do it, others cannot do it either. History has shown that there is no consistent pattern by which Soviet success or failure can be forecast. The Soviet space program in the decade of the 1960s went from an impressive string of successes to a rash of dismal failures. There have been similar examples in a variety of other Soviet weapons programs. If U.S. policy makers had attempted to counter every new Soviet system on the assumption that each one would be a success, the results would have been ruinous. It is useful to know and describe worst-case fears, but the policy maker has to act on the basis of a "best" estimate, and must have confidence in those who make it.

Emphasis on the missile and space aspects of technical intelligence may create the mistaken impression that it is the only, or at least the primary, thrust of scientific and technological intelligence.[33] But its scope is far broader; furthermore, it changes over time. The study of "technology transfer" has attracted great attention during the last decade. Technology transfer is not a new term; researchers have always considered the free exchange of ideas vital to scientific discovery. Academies of science and other professional groups around the world have long advocated and sponsored exchange programs.

But of late the term "technology transfer" has taken on a different connotation. As the recognized leader in many areas of science and technology, the United States has relied heavily on its technological edge in its military programs as well as in its economic sector. Gradually it has become clear that other nations have been buying (sometimes illegally) or stealing technological secrets from the United States. Secret ideas, techniques, and actual hardware "transferred" in these ways have included those classified for national defense purposes as well as those for civilian use.

Efforts to curb the flow of U.S. technology to other nations have required much close scrutiny by the technical intelligence community. Intelligence specialists must identify the areas of technology most sought by foreign governments and determine the use being made of acquired information. Detailed specifications or actual hardware from a U.S. missile guidance system might save the Soviets years of effort. Proprietary information on U.S. computers might give a foreign interest an advantage over its U.S. competitor. Those in technical intelligence are not responsible for enforcing U.S. regulations or laws, but they play a key role in providing enforcement agencies with leads as to where violations are occurring. Here again, coverage includes a wide range of technical disciplines and expertise.[34]

Impressive as the new machines and instruments are, the judgment of qualified people is the most essential factor in technical as in other fields of intelligence. While virtually every physical and life science discipline must be in the purview of modern-day scientific intelligence, the CIA and other intelligence agencies cannot possibly have a world expert in each discipline on a full-time basis. Priorities for highly trained technical personnel must be continually reevaluated. Today a laser expert is far more important than a decade ago. As in most other technical organizations, an effort is made to bring young engineers and scientists directly from university campuses, but it is also necessary to attract individuals with many years of experience. The national importance of the work and the technical challenge have been sufficient to attract first-class people in both categories.

All the same, outside help is still required. Despite investigations, revelations, and criticisms of intelligence operations during the 1970s, most universities, research laboratories, and industrial organizations continue to provide individual specialists and organizational support. Whenever a challenging new scientific problem faces the intelligence community, it has been traditional policy to bring the problem to the attention of the best brains in the United States. This has to be done quietly, and often without remuneration or public recognition, but the objective is frequently met. When the policy maker reads or hears the results of a new study on nuclear weapons, he is more often than not getting more than the opinion of a few full-time analysts. A Nobel Prize winner—or perhaps even two or three— may well have assisted in the study, or at least critiqued it, before it was finished.[35]

There is a growing consensus that the capabilities of the National Technical Means (NTM)—for example, the photo reconnaissance satellite systems and the telemetry-collection satellites—have been oversold. These systems are frequently the only means to find out anything at all about denied areas and a potential enemy's order of battle. But it is by no means certain that the United States will always be able to intercept and interpret telemetry, just as there are endless possibilities of *maskirovka* (masking) against U.S. sensors and cameras, especially if the other side is familiar with the specifics of the U.S. NTMs.

The controversies as to what can and what cannot be discovered through technical means have continued for a long time and no end is in sight. It is unlikely that Hitler's buildup against Russia in 1941, or the Japanese naval concentration directed against Pearl Harbor would have escaped the national technical means of verification. But the experience of the Yom Kippur War shows that there may be situations in which technical intelligence is not of much use. The technology of war is no longer that of 1941, and if there is no guarantee of sufficient early warning in modern conditions, the NTM will tell us even less about a potential enemy's long-range intentions. They are of little help with regard to the various species of low-level violence, which in our age are the most likely to occur or the strategy of penetration, coups d'état, civil wars, and warfare by proxy, destabilization, and so on.[36] If the NTM could not provide over many years conclusive answers about the one subject they were uniquely prepared to observe, namely the number of Soviet strategic weapons, their size, and other specifics, it would be unrealistic to expect information on subjects they are not designed to address.

Admiral Bobby R. Inman, former head of the NSA and deputy director of the CIA, noted after his resignation in 1982 that there had been a major reduction in manpower to pay for technical collection systems; there was plenty of communication intelligence but too few analysts to cope with it. The data on the Soviet Combat Brigade in Cuba (just one example) had been available for years, but had not been processed because of lack of manpower.

Technology has caused a revolution without parallel in the annals of intelligence. Without it we would have few hard facts and the margin for speculation would be immense. Yet the technologies have developed identities of their own, and in America, more than in any other country, intelligence has become the captive of technology on the road from intuition to computation. Again the similarity with modern medicine is striking. It is a mistaken belief that modern technologies can produce all, or almost all, the answers; that they are free of distortion and therefore more valuable than brainpower, experience, and analysis. But technology *cannot* provide all the answers and is *not* entirely free from distortion even in a field like verification. This applies with added force to other, nonquantitative aspects of intelligence.

Nor is it likely that salvation will come as the result of the revolution that has taken place in the modern office. True, offices are now very different from what they were twenty years ago, and as the information revolution gathers speed, it will again look different ten years hence. Data processing and office automation are increasingly affecting not just clerical activities but also the conduct of management. Answers to communications can be expected immediately, teleconferences, data and voice communication, and facsimile are all undergoing dramatic changes, and all-comprehensive data banks are just a pushbutton away.[37] Looking further ahead into the future—as the superconductor replaces the semiconductor—there seems to be no limit to the expansion of information technology. American intelligence promises computers not only able to smell and to detect emotions in people but that will be able to distinguish human faces from each other. Machines are envisaged that will educate themselves, turn into geniuses, and then reach out far into the unknown.

Quite apart from the long-term dangers of artificial intelligence, there are problems and pitfalls that have arisen already. All who do research are familiar with "Xerox syndrome," the mistaken belief that once an article, or a few pages from a book, has been copied, it has also been mentally digested. The syndrome has many facets, and one of the most serious and at the same time one of the most transparently naive is the idea that something published in the "open literature," ranging from newspapers to scholarly journals, need not be taken into account when making intelligence assessments that have to be based on secret information. This has often meant that important information and significant judgments were ignored.[38]

The new technology has also resulted in a colossal paper explosion. More and more is turned out faster and faster, much of it quite needlessly. It has been estimated that 72 billion documents are produced annually in U.S. offices and 300 billion are on file; therefore the chances of misfiling important material increase proportionally. There are compensating filters to ensure that important messages will "travel over a privileged network in a curt, staccato shorthand, like the one which evolved in the Department of Defense's ARPA [action and research projects] computer network." The critical signs will be delivered verbally, and the rationale behind the decisions will be lost in the noise.[39] Thus we are back to the old signals/noise problem. Who will decide what is "more important," what the "critical signs" are, and generally speaking, what information should be stored and how?

The problem is not made easier as the flow of information increases and the centralization of knowledge causes the magnification of error to become even more likely. Data banks and efficient information retrieval systems have enormous uses in military intelligence, as well as in other fields. They can provide, for instance, constantly updated tables on arms systems in position. Yet there still remains the crucial question of who will turn information into knowledge. There is much evidence that the skills and the knowledge of the new encyclopedists and censors who handle the data banks are declining. Much of the information that has been poured into electronic databanks is of mediocre or poor quality. In the early years after the invention of printing anything printed had semi-sacred status and was considered reliable simply because it was in print. Today there is a tendency to glorify databank information simply because it came out of a computer. The frequent experience of ordinary citizens with computer errors in bank statements and billings should act as a corrective.

The uses of the new technology are real but limited.[40] An abundance of information and greater speed of transmission will not be enough to compensate if the tendency is to store everything more or less indiscriminately. The decision maker who has asked for relevant information will receive it, but will also get a great deal more that is irrelevant. Then the process of sifting will have to start all over again.

Under these circumstances, it may become more difficult to detect the planting of false information and create a greater vulnerability to espionage. The concentration of information makes its retrieval easier for potential enemies as well as for those entitled to know. In the private sector, computer-related crime has reached a staggering level and only an estimated 15 percent of the crimes involved are detected and reported.[41] There are countless ways to cheat, or induce a computer to perform an unauthorized act, both from the inside and the outside. The advice given to the private sector to "instill a high level of ethics" or to "keep employees happy and fairly treated" will hardly deter a determined enemy agent.

The CIA was a pioneer in introducing computerization and claims that it has pioneered security precautions so secret that they are not discussed in the public literature.[42] The agency sensibly starts from the assumption that there is always the potential for "compromise," and that such attempts will be made. No system, no matter how physically secure, can be truly secure unless the personnel who work it can be fully trusted. Low-level CIA personnel are subjected to periodic reinvestigation. Both computer and information have to be protected against hostile penetration and destruction. Physical security means "protective rings and barriers," that is, vaulted areas, controlled access, alarms and other security procedures including certain forms of self-protection on the part of the computer (which may not always be possible), and ways to encrypt, or scramble, data during transmission (data communication has become largely dependent upon encryption for security).

Yet with all this, there remains an area of vulnerability affecting national security and highly competent computer spies may not find it impossible to get access to a mainframe's operating system. Codes hitherto believed unbreakable are broken and the danger of breaking into a computer increases with the number of computer terminals and the centralization of data.[43] It is generally agreed that it is now more difficult to steal $2,500 from a bank than millions from a computer.[44] The spy, needless to say, will not go for $2,500 but for the greater sum, figuratively speaking. If the CIA and the Department of Defense use far more sophisticated measures of security than the average company, the enemy agent works on a higher level, too. There can be no watertight security; there is always the danger that the positive vetting of those employed will be insufficient. But whereas yesterday's spy got away with one, or a few secrets, today's spy will have at his disposal a veritable Aladdin's cave full of secrets.[45]

So far mention has been made solely of scientific requirements and operations of U.S. national security. Among other countries only the Soviet Union has a technical intelligence capacity comparable to the United States, at least as far as military technology is concerned. Much of the effort of Soviet intelligence has been directed toward obtaining advanced U.S. technology, and much of that technology, as it becomes computer based, has become more vulnerable. As Major General Doyle E. Larson, director of the Joint Electronic Warfare Center, has put it, with only slight exaggeration—for almost twenty years the West has been developing weapons systems for two separate defense programs, its own and on a steadily increasing basis, the Soviet Union's.[46]

Much of today's technology transfer is done quite legally because certain technologies (for instance in the computer field) are mainly of civilian use and have been commercially acquired. Yet the same advanced technology is also of use for the development of new missiles, tanks, and spy satellites, so the dividing line between legal and illegal is sometimes difficult or even impossible to draw. Other technology was illegally acquired, stolen at trade shows (some of the technology for the Soviet SS-18 was said to be stolen from Hewlett-Packard in 1972), or obtained through unlicensed exports to the Soviet Union.[47] Sometimes deliberate fraud is committed with the help of Western businessmen; on other occasions technology is obtained through graduate students' exchanges. While American students in the Soviet Union are directed to the study of Russian music and literature, preferably in the eighteenth century, Soviet graduate students in the United States, older and more experienced, work on topics such as "automatic control as applied to spaceships," or "interaction of ions and plasmas with solid surfaces."[48]

Over the last fifteen years, certain points about the main effort of Soviet technical intelligence collections have emerged clearly. The emphasis is on U.S. guidance technology, rocket propulsion, aircraft technology, missile defense, antisubmarine warfare, "smart" bombs, and computer equipment in general. The Soviet Union has also been keeping a close watch on other new technologies which may be of high military value at some future date. These include recent advances in the computer industry, advanced large-scale integrated circuit design, magnetic bubble memory technology, genetic engineering, fracture mechanics, and superplasticity. According to a 1982 CIA study, Soviet intelligence now employs several thousand collection officers in the United States, Japan, West Germany, and other countries "under various covers ranging from diplomats to journalists to trade officials."[49] This concentration on technical intelligence involves the employment of highly skilled operators; according to German sources, the majority of Eastern bloc agents arrested or identified in West Germany in the early 1980s were university graduates. Time-honored espionage practices, such as bribing Western experts and establishing "dummy companies" for technology export, have been supplemented by pioneering new techniques. In computer penetration, for example, linkups with some of the world's most advanced computers in Britain and the United States come from a base in Austria.[50]

As far as can be ascertained, these Soviet intelligence efforts have been quite successful; the great progress in Soviet arms technology—in radar, smart weapons, various guidance systems, communications, and so on— can to a large extent be traced back to U.S. technology, both legally and illegally acquired.[51]

This problem, one of the most serious facing U.S. national security, is of direct concern to counterintelligence rather than to intelligence; it has been mentioned here mainly in order to point to the fact that the priorities of the secret services of the two superpowers are different in character. While one of the main issues facing U.S. intelligence has been the question of verification and strategic deception—whether compliance with any arms limitation treaty can be effectively monitored—Soviet intelligence has been preoccupied with the acquisition of high technology.

Is this likely to change in the future? The United States still has the edge in most aspects of military technology but its lead has been shrinking. For this reason a change in the function of Western technical intelligence can be expected. The Soviet research and development effort, both in the civilian and in the military field, has been considerably greater than the American one for a long time and this is now showing its results.[52] In 1981 the Soviets placed 125 payloads in space, of those about 100 were military in character; the United States orbited eighteen payloads, of which five were military. Quantitatively, U.S. intelligence is facing a growing challenge; qualitative assignments are far more difficult than in the past, when Soviet technologies were relatively primitive. Scientific intelligence, together with other agencies, will monitor nuclear proliferation in various parts of the world, and it will pay attention to new fields of science and technology. Much of its success will depend on the general state of the American R&D effort. American preeminence can no longer be taken for granted and scientific intelligence depends very much on the general health of U.S. science research and technological development.

Economic intelligence and science and technology intelligence have committed mistakes over the years. It is not difficult to find instances of bad judgment, misplaced priorities, or important developments that were not recognized in time. The economic analysts of the CIA, for instance, have devoted an inordinate amount of time and effort to various ruble/dollar conversion estimates that are of limited practical value. Their projections of oil production and consumption have frequently been off target. The Directorate of Science and Technology has been criticized for both developing and running its own collection techniques and for evaluating the results, thus making objective assessments more difficult. By and large, however, these branches of intelligence have performed as well as could be expected and it is pointless to engage in abstract prescriptions for change and reform. Changes will become necessary as the result of new economic trends and new scientific and technological developments—some of these can be anticipated, others cannot.

Success in intelligence is more often than not the result of patient and painstaking work. But on many occasions the element of creativity is also of crucial importance. So far, psychologists have been able to tell us little about the act of creation, except that intelligence (with a small *i*) is needed, along with hard work and imagination, as in Pasteur's "Opportunity coming to the prepared mind." And lastly, luck is needed, for as Thomas Fuller, distinguished eighteenth-century British doctor said: "He who is not lucky, let him not go a-fishing." There is, unfortunately, no prescription, scientific or otherwise, for making fortune quicken her steps in our direction.

PART II

A HISTORY
OF INTELLIGENCE
PERFORMANCE

CHAPTER 3

Intelligence and Its Customers

IT IS a truism that intelligence does not exist in a vacuum, even if its practitioners sometimes tend to forget this. Even excellent intelligence is of little consequence unless its most senior consumers, the president and secretaries of state and defense, take cognizance of it and believe in its accuracy. The relationship between them and the Director of Central Intelligence (DCI) is of paramount importance and this, of course, also goes for their closest advisers.

This relationship ought to be based on trust, if not a perfect personal chemistry, on the understanding on the part of policy makers about the way in which intelligence can help them, on what it cannot accomplish, and on the ability of intelligence to get important information across. The policy maker-intelligence relationship is in many ways an obstacle race. Many things can go wrong and frequently do. Because intelligence is the "silent service," it has usually had to accept responsibility even if the blame was not its own. To shed some light on the problematical character of this relationship it would help to review the presidential attitudes and changing fortunes of directors of central intelligence in recent administrations.

President Truman's attitude toward intelligence was ambivalent. He writes in his memoirs that he considered it very important to the United States to have a sound, well-organized system, both in the present and in the future. Properly developed, such a service would require new concepts as well as better trained and more competent personnel. But Truman also noted that while it was imperative to make plans, it was also imperative to refrain from rushing into something that would produce harmful and unnecessary rivalries among various intelligence agencies, and he added in his memoirs, not once but twice, that "this country wanted no Gestapo under any guise for any reason."[1]

Truman's conviction about the importance of intelligence was not shared by everyone in the administration and Congress. Opposition came mainly from conservative elements in Congress and the Department of State. Some opposed the very idea of a professional intelligence, some had no comprehension as to what purposes intelligence was to serve, and others, while not denying the importance of intelligence in principle, argued that the OSS men who were to constitute the core of central intelligence were "collectivists" and "do-gooders," their ideology "far to the left of the views held by the President and his Secretary of State."[2] If Secretary of State Byrnes had no use for intelligence, General George Marshall, his successor, did understand its functions, and so after almost endless distractions, the CIA was set up in July 1947. But it was established as a compromise; the agency's assignment and authority were not clearly defined. Dean Acheson warned Truman that as the CIA was organized, neither he nor the National Security Council would be able to control it.

· To note that the CIA under its first three directors was of no great importance is an understatement. Rear Admiral Sidney W. Souers carried no weight on the Washington scene; Lt. Gen. Hoyt S. Vandenberg was well connected but intelligence for him was a stepping stone in his military career. And while Roscoe Hillenkoetter had been Head of Naval Intelligence, he had no particular experience in political intelligence, nor was he influential by Washington standards. He was a "sea captain in mind and heart," according to one source; and he returned to a command at sea after his resignation from the CIA.[3]

It was perhaps indicative of the standing of the CIA that, as former CIA deputy director Ray Cline has noted, when the National Security Council was convened by President Truman for its first meeting about the Korean crisis, Hillenkoetter was not even invited. The CIA was then a very minor cog in the wheel with a small staff and a minute budget. True, the president had asked for more money, but Congress had cut the allocation, and Truman had not fought very hard for the new agency, whose performance (to the extent that he was aware of it) he did not consider too impressive.[4]

President Truman's views on intelligence became a subject of some controversy among historians. In a speech to a CIA orientation course on 21 November 1952, Truman said that he was appreciative of the service he had received as the chief executive: "You are the organization, you are the intelligence arm that keeps the Executive informed so that he can make decisions that always will be in the public interest for his own country. . . ." Twelve years later, he wrote the following inscription on a photograph he presented to the CIA: "To the Central Intelligence Agency, a necessity to the President of the United States, from one who knows." In December 1963, however, an article signed by Truman was distributed by the North American Newspaper Alliance that said he was disturbed by the way the CIA had diverted from its original assignment. He had never thought when the CIA was set up that it would become part of peacetime cloak-and-dagger operations, and he wanted to see the CIA restored to its original task as the intelligence arm of the president. Allen Dulles (by that time in retirement) and others reminded Truman that he had been the first to ask the CIA to undertake covert action assignments in Italy, Greece, and Turkey and that Truman had asked the National Security Council to authorize the creation of a new office within the CIA to carry out covert operations against secret Communist subversion—the Office of Policy Coordination. It later emerged that the article had been written by David Noyes, a former White House assistant, but Truman did not dissociate himself from its general tenor.

Among the five general tasks allotted to the CIA under the National Security Act of 1947, the stress was on the coordination of existing intelligence. (The act said nothing about national estimates; the DCI's estimative role developed only under General Walter Bedell Smith.) Yet it did not fulfill this basic function, as noted in the Dulles-Jackson-Correa Survey commissioned by the NSC in 1948. The report said that instead of coordinating intelligence, the CIA had become just another intelligence agency in competition with the established agencies. Its director was not in intimate contact with day-to-day operations, he provided no policy guidance, and he was surrounded by administrative staff.[5]

Such criticism was unfair, for if the CIA was not doing its duty the reason was that military intelligence, with far greater resources in manpower and money, provided little raw intelligence to the new agency. The assumption that a bureaucratic agency would share its information voluntarily with another was against all the rules of bureaucratic politics, and the idea that a military agency would do so with a civilian body was even more far-fetched. Nor was military intelligence willing to cooperate in the preparation of basic documents for the CIA. During the first years of its existence, the CIA was almost entirely dependent on current intelligence received from the State Department.

The heads of the CIA were not of a stature likely to impress the likes of General Marshall, Dean Acheson, or Secretary of Defense Louis Johnson. General MacArthur wanted to remove the CIA altogether from the Far East, just as he had tried to keep out the OSS during the war. MacArthur disliked civilian intruders he had no control over. Nor did the higher echelons of the State Department take much notice. The preparation of NSC-68, the most important policy document of the period, was the work of the newly founded Policy Planning Staff under Paul Nitze and George Kennan. If intelligence made an input, it must have been modest.

Thus, Truman's fears of creating an all-powerful "Gestapo" seem in retrospect more than a little exaggerated. With the outbreak of the Korean War, it became patently obvious that the CIA was not too strong but much too weak. It was this realization that prompted the appointment as DCI of General Walter Bedell Smith in October 1950. He had been Eisenhower's chief of staff during the war and subsequently ambassador to the Soviet Union. It was said about him that he was the most even-tempered man in the world—he was always angry.

> Beetle, as his friends called him, was a man with no more than a high school education, who had enlisted in World War I and worked his way up through the ranks in the Regular Army. He had an intimidating personality and was a perfectionist. Largely self-educated, he had a photographic memory, encyclopaedic knowledge and shrewd judgment about people and ideas.[6]

Ironically, the Dulles-Jackson-Correa report had just recommended prior to Bedell's appointment that the DCI should be a civilian, because for a military man the position would be more than a short tour of duty. It is doubtful in retrospect, however, whether anyone but a senior military man like "Beetle," Eisenhower's brilliant workhorse, respected by all and feared by most, would have been able to assert himself and put the agency on the map at that stage of CIA history.

Bedell Smith was the equal of, or outranked, the military men with whom he was dealing; the politicians took him very seriously, and under his leadership CIA manpower and budget greatly expanded. The budget grew from $4.7 million in 1950 to $82 million in 1953. There were seven CIA foreign stations at the beginning of the Korean War and forty-seven overseas offices when it ended. Smith took an active role in most CIA activities, such as the preparation of the NIEs, and while in favor of competitive discussion, he overruled military intelligence if he thought Pentagon arguments were poorly reasoned. He took care that these were presented to Truman clearly and unambiguously and that the "assessments" were not just a summary of ill-digested and frequently contrary briefings of the various agencies.

It had been Truman's basic complaint that the CIA was a "bulletin board" rather than an intelligence agency; in other words, it offered something for everyone, to be picked up according to personal preferences. As DCI, Hillenkoetter had always argued that he had no crystal ball with which to foresee the future and assess enemy intentions. Only under Bedell Smith did the CIA assume the responsibilities of assessing and predicting. Smith and other members of the agency worked closely with the National Security Council, but they also showed initiative in producing intelligence reports on subjects for which no specific requests had been made. Senior members of the agency said in later years that this was a period when they felt that their work was used by the upper levels in government.

The Dulles Years

President Eisenhower once said: "I would rather have Allen Dulles as my chief intelligence adviser than anyone else I know." Eisenhower's trust did not stem from personal whim. It was based on respect and a certain amount of healthy distancing, by which each man acted according to a traditional unspoken code of behavior. "Arms length and proper," as Gordon Gray, Eisenhower's last national security adviser, described it.[7]

Both Eisenhower and Dulles believed in the importance of unbiased intelligence and its neutral role in policy making. It was Allen Dulles's dream to improve the intelligence gathering and analytic capacity of the CIA to create, within government, a separate and strong civilian intelligence arm. Hence his legendary reluctance during the NSC and other presidential meetings to overstep his intelligence role. "This is a policy matter," he was apt to say, "and not my job."[8] It will be shown here that in actual fact such Olympian detachment could not be maintained for long.

President Eisenhower, for his part, wanted the facts and, like most presidents, wanted these to be unrefined facts. General Andrew Goodpaster, Eisenhower's assistant and later chief of staff, recalls one of the occasions when Eisenhower compelled the DCI to surrender raw intelligence. This occurred when Dulles was reluctant to pass on a radar report of unidentified aircraft near U.S. shores until it was analyzed, suspecting it was mere electronic noise. Eisenhower insisted, three times in conversation, that it was appropriate to send raw, unevaluated intelligence to the president. Eisenhower, needless to say, prevailed.[9]

Allen Dulles's role as chief fact finder was enhanced by Eisenhower's natural suspicion of Pentagon reporting, a fear not unconnected with budgetary considerations. Eisenhower had thus been determined at the outset that a civilian be director of the CIA. On average, Dulles saw the president twice a week, including every Thursday morning at NSC meetings. Eisenhower was briefed each morning by Goodpaster on the CIA's written daily intelligence summary, and about once every two weeks, the president would request more information on a specific subject.

Eisenhower's NSC staff (then under Gordon Gray) was a smoothly functioning mechanism for briefing the president and its members and discussing policy options. It was not a decision-making body. Allen Dulles's role in the weekly NSC meetings was to ensure that the intelligence he delivered in the first twenty minutes was lucid, concise, and relevant to the policies under consideration (an agenda having been set in advance). Dulles opened each meeting with a summary of the latest news on the world scene and introduced new national intelligence estimates. Observers report that Allen Dulles's intelligence briefings were some of the best ever delivered to the NSC.[10] They included verbatim agent reports, biographies, country sketches, maps, and, if asked, Dulles's own analysis of the personality or intentions of a foreign dignitary with whom he was acquainted.

The picture that emerges is not one of intimacy between the president and Allen Dulles; the popular image of Dulles strolling into the Oval Office to chat daily with the president is unfounded. The two did not engage in open-ended musings about world affairs; their relationship was formal and stable. Almost no appointee saw the president alone, with the exception of John Foster Dulles.[11]

Relations between Allen Dulles and his brother, the secretary of state, were close, and it is difficult to determine where their reciprocal influence started and stopped. On intelligence matters, Allen and John Foster Dulles communicated almost daily, posing questions and problems. These conversations were a critical element in Allen Dulles's access to the president. As one official observed, if Allen Dulles had something to relay or say in a hurry, he told Foster.[12] The secretary of state became an early, and natural, conduit for intelligence to the White House.

Evidence now available reveals the significance of the brothers' simultaneous appointments to office.[13] When in town, they typically talked on the telephone several times a week. Foster Dulles continuously queried Allen about new intelligence, his estimate of its implications, and made requests for new work. During a typical week in the spring of 1954, he telephoned Allen to inquire about the latest in French defenses at Dien Bien Phu, how the Chinese Communists might view U.S. intervention there, and what the situation was in Guatemala. He also asked Allen to prepare a memo about the history of conflict on the offshore islands and to think about Soviet reactions to a U.S. nuclear test ban treaty proposal. As Robert Amory, Allen Dulles's deputy director of intelligence, relates, one of his main responsibilities was to ensure that Allen was always aware when Foster called.[14]

During crises, the Dulles brothers' conversations were even more numerous. They talked several times a day during the Guatemala crisis of May–June 1954 and during the Suez Canal and Hungarian crises of October and November 1956. If the CIA was planning or conducting covert operations, such as aid to the forces seeking to overthrow the Arbenz regime in Guatemala, this was acknowledged by Allen and reported on to Foster.

The offices of the two brothers were a short block away from each other and they visited two to three times a week. These meetings went unrecorded, as no secretary was present. There were, of course, many social calls, meetings, family gatherings, and dinners as well. Rare was the time that Foster left the country without a final briefing from his brother. When Allen left town, a CIA official was designated as liaison to Foster Dulles.

The day before an NSC meeting, Foster Dulles might call to ask whether Allen planned to discuss a certain topic, such as Soviet arms to Red China or instability in Syria. Was the intelligence sufficiently crystallized or so significant that it was appropriate to inform the president? At other times, Allen called to see whether the secretary advised his attending an ad hoc meeting. Foster might suggest that the president would be interested in a subject and "it might be a good idea to be there."[15] If Allen Dulles was too busy to attend, he sent a deputy or provided a memo.

Sometimes Foster Dulles passed on Allen's opinion directly to the president. Memoranda of telephone conversations between the secretary of state and the president, or a close aide such as Sherman Adams or James Hagerty, indicate that Foster Dulles often said, "Allen thinks that . . . ," or "I have checked with Allen and he feels . . . ," or "Allen is handling that and will let you know." After the East Berlin uprising in June 1953, the secretary relayed his brother's predictions and preference for a U.S. propaganda response. As everyone knew about their close relationship, the result was that more importance was attributed to the CIA's intelligence and Allen Dulles's opinion than would otherwise have been the case.

Allen Dulles had many personal acquaintances in the State Department and in the White House with whom he kept constantly in touch. They included: James Hagerty, press secretary; the three successive National Security Advisers—Robert Cutler, Dillon Anderson, and Gordon Gray; C. D. Jackson, the first head of the Psychological Strategy Board; Nelson Rockefeller; Gabriel Hauge, economic adviser; Undersecretaries of State Bedell Smith, Herbert Hoover, Jr., and Christian Herter; Robert Murphy, the State Department's undersecretary for political affairs; Admiral Lewis Straus, Atomic Energy Commission chairman; and many others. Allen Dulles's World War II experience and New York political contacts meant that he was also well-acquainted with many U.S. ambassadors, such as Clare Boothe Luce and John Hay Whitney.

Whatever Allen Dulles's hesitancy to offer policy advice to the president may have been, there was no reticence when it came to private conversations with his brother, the secretary of state. Allen and John Foster Dulles had discussed foreign policy as youngsters around the dinner table, as law partners in New York, in attendance at the same international conferences, and as collaborators in political campaigns. They spoke the same language. They conversed in a cryptic fashion, darting from subject to subject, interjecting ideas out of context, each intuiting what the other was thinking.

Memoranda of telephone conversations between the brothers reveal that, on 19 April 1954, Allen Dulles asked with some disfavor "if the Secretary was going to get hooked on U.S. ground troops in Vietnam."[16] In July 1958, Allen opposed the landing of American marines in Lebanon and the evocation of the Eisenhower Doctrine in this matter. In this case, he asserted his views strongly to the secretary and then stood back. Kermit Roosevelt and NSC members observed that on more than one occasion Allen Dulles stood firmly with the secretary when the latter displayed an inclination to regard President Nasser of Egypt as the primary threat to Middle East stability.[17]

Allen Dulles generally adopted a wait-and-see attitude in foreign policy. He proposed that economic aid to Poland in mid-1956 not be linked to a Soviet commitment to show restraint in the use of force and that assistance to Egypt in 1954 be granted with no strings attached. He believed that internal change within the Soviet system was possible, but it would be gradual. He was opposed to reversing the U.S. propaganda line in Eastern Europe following Stalin's death and delayed releasing Krushchev's 1956 secret speech condemning Stalin, preferring to save it to use at a later, more opportune time.

Intelligence policy lines in the Eisenhower era were blurred because, more than in recent years, the CIA was an instrument of foreign policy. The president had a spectrum of specific policy responses from which to choose, including the CIA's covert programs. Often CIA programs such as psychological warfare or covert aid existed side-by-side with army missions, economic aid, or diplomatic initiatives.

Not only did the Dulles brothers collaborate on presidential speeches, messages, and U.N. addresses, they also consulted on setting policy guidelines for Radio Free Europe and Radio Liberty. Likewise, they cooperated in establishing special aid programs, such as in Berlin. Allen Dulles influenced the president and the secretary of state through facts, hunches, and educated guesses. He also influenced them by advocating a certain course of action. The administration's moderate policy vis-à-vis President Nasser is a case in point. Allen Dulles believed that an aggressive stance toward Egypt—toppling President Nasser, refusing him aid, or arming his opponents—would destabilize the whole region. Wait-and-see and selective Middle Eastern country intervention became the chosen courses.

In the Eisenhower era many conditions for effective intelligence-policy cooperation were met. Eisenhower did not accept all CIA intelligence, such as its "missile gap" estimates from 1957 to 1961. Nonetheless, he believed that on the whole he received good intelligence, a balance of raw facts and coordinated predictions. Of course, because Allen Dulles was fully informed by his brother what the president's mood was on an issue, what the president personally intended to accomplish on a meeting abroad, the latest in State Department forecasting, Pentagon positions, Allied and other ambassadorial communications, and Soviet messages, he was greatly helped in making the CIA more effective. Even the CIA's long-term estimative work, which does not revolve around U.S. options, assumed more relevance. The DCI's judgments were not made in a vacuum; they were influenced by his knowledge of the available policy alternatives.

The dire warnings about the perils of close cooperation between intelligence chiefs and policy makers were not borne out by the record for the Eisenhower years. Intelligence certainly did not function worse than either before or after, and in some respects it functioned better. In many ways, it was a different era—of strong personalities and of more human-oriented and less technological intelligence. Government was smaller; people knew one another; keeping informed was easier. It was a unique period in which two brothers held high office simultaneously. It demonstrated the benefits of early, close, and noncompetitive communication between intelligence and policy makers.

But after the Bay of Pigs disaster Kennedy decided that Allen Dulles would have to go. Following a long search for a suitable candidate, his choice fell in September 1961 on John McCone, a wealthy California Republican and an engineer by training, who had the reputation among liberals of a "rigid cold warrior."[18] He had been undersecretary of the air force under Truman and head of the Atomic Energy Commission during the Eisenhower administration. The intentions behind the choice of McCone were threefold. Kennedy wanted a competent administrator at the helm of the agency—as for interpretation of intelligence, he thought that the White House staff would be able to cope. He also wanted to keep the DCI and the agency free from any taint of appearing politically partisan, thus his choice of a Republican. At the same time, he wanted Congressional support against attacks from the right, feeling that the "experts"—meaning the chiefs of staff and the CIA—had let him down; therefore he planned to cut the budget of the agency for 1962–63.

McCone, however, was not the man to preside over a CIA reduced in size and power; he had the reputation of an "alley fighter." A man of great self-confidence, he had stated quite openly at the outset that he wanted to become a power in the administration. In this he succeeded within a very short time, partly as a result of the Cuban missile crisis, which convinced a lot of doubters that a strong intelligence agency was needed after all. His position was also strengthened because of an internal realignment of forces in Washington. Opposition to the CIA had come not only from the Pentagon but also from the State Department, which had rejected a prominent CIA role in the conduct of foreign affairs. In 1961 the Defense Intelligence Agency had been established at the Pentagon and within a short time it developed into a substantial bureaucratic apparatus, with the Defense Department controlling 80 to 90 percent of the money for "big ticket" technology collection. Thus the State Department was forced into an uneasy coalition with the CIA on the assumption that a balance of power within the intelligence community was in its own best interest. The real battle was McCone asserting himself as DCI.

McCone made himself known within a relatively short time in the agency. Most of the CIA's senior officials had been admirers of Allen Dulles and were decidedly skeptical about the newcomer without previous intelligence background or experience; they reserved their judgment, some of them quite pointedly. But McCone soon impressed the higher echelons of the CIA with sensible appointments and administrative changes and by staunchly defending CIA interests against those of its rivals. McCone identified himself with the agency, inspired loyalty, and showed good sense in most of his decisions. Allen Dulles, the "Great White Case Officer" as his subordinates called him, with all his sterling qualities and great personal influence, had had no taste for bureaucratic infighting, even if it were necessary from the CIA point of view. McCone was tougher in this respect. For instance, he succeeded in obtaining from the Pentagon top secret data on U.S. strategic capabilities and force dispositions; in the past, the absence of such knowledge had severely hampered CIA strategic research. To provide an authoritative assessment of an intelligence situation one needed to know not only essentials about enemy capabilities, but also the strength of one's own side.

McCone also showed more interest than Dulles in scientific-technological developments that were of enormous importance for the CIA's collection capabilities; under him the new Directorate of Science and Technology was set up. McCone's reputation was finally established when he, going against expert advice, claimed in September 1962 that the Russians were about to introduce offensive nuclear weapons into Cuba. The story has been told many times—how a national intelligence estimate in September had observed that it would be incompatible with Soviet policy to introduce strategic missiles in Cuba and that the Soviets "would not do anything so uncharacteristic, provocative and unrewarding."

McCone was not a Soviet expert, but he followed the useful rule that when in doubt one should suspect Soviet intentions. He felt instinctively uneasy and, before leaving for a honeymoon in Europe, told President Kennedy that "something new and different was going on."[19] The famous U-2 flight on 14 October proved that McCone's hunches had been right. Once Soviet intentions had been established, the CIA follow-up was excellent, which was fully appreciated by Kennedy and his advisers. Throughout the crisis, McCone was involved in all major deliberations between the White House and the CIA on the interpretation of intelligence. He met several times weekly with McGeorge Bundy, the president's national security adviser, and there was a sharing of diplomatic correspondence of top priority (Kennedy to Khrushchev). Ray Cline wrote later: "I cannot imagine a more intimate linking of intelligence in all functional categories with the highest level policy decisionmaking."[20] It is only fair to add that there had been similar intimacy between Allen Dulles and Eisenhower and John Foster Dulles, but this had not affected the cooperation of the lower echelons to the same extent. McCone's standing and that of the agency as counsels to government was now high, even though some of the leading White House staff became a little tired of being continually reminded that he had been right on Cuba where they had been wrong.

McCone came out against the version of the bomber gap propagated by the military in the early 1960s. He thought the air force estimates of Soviet ICBMs in 1963 (of 700 to 800) was too high. It later emerged that these estimates had been, broadly speaking, correct and that the lower estimates had underrated the extent of the Soviet strategic buildup. On Vietnam McCone was a hawk, but at the same time he was quite critical of the policies pursued by Kennedy, Johnson, and their chief advisers. He warned from an early date against a long, drawn-out jungle war that America could not win. He felt McNamara's policy was too little and too late. The only sensible course of action was to force a quick decision in Vietnam, and this could be done only by using overwhelming force in the air and on land.[21] The influence of the CIA in Washington declined as the Vietnam War spread, simply because so much of the intelligence needed was tactical in nature. Furthermore, President Johnson's work style was different from Kennedy's in many respects; the fact that he wanted his daily bulletin late in the day rather than in the morning was among the less important differences. He read the information he was given, but unless it concerned Vietnam or domestic affairs, he was not very interested. Work with McCone did not proceed harmoniously. Johnson did not take him into his confidence as Kennedy had done. Partly it was a matter of personality, but it is also true that as the war spread, the CIA became more and more a harbinger of bad tidings, whereas the president and his advisers wanted a little optimism. Some important decisions were made by a small group at the NSC in which the CIA was not represented and frequently not even discussed. At the same time CIA influence in the Pentagon, which had never been great, declined even further. Inasmuch as military intelligence was concerned, the armed services preferred to rely on their own agencies.

In April 1965, McCone decided to resign when he realized that Johnson no longer paid attention to him and that he was frequently excluded from the regular weekly meetings of the senior advisers. Johnson chose Admiral William F. Raborn as McCone's successor, an officer without experience in the field and also without political knowledge. It was an unfortunate choice, for it exposed a gallant sailor unnecessarily to ridicule. After only a few months it appeared that he was unsuitable for the job and while it was impossible to ask for his resignation immediately, he was effectively isolated and much of the agency work was done by the senior staff. The episode certainly showed something about President Johnson's attitude toward intelligence: he could not have known much about Raborn's suitability, but if he had thought of the position of the DCI as an important one in government, he would have chosen a man of proven ability who was well known and trusted by Congress and the public.

Richard Helms became Director of Central Intelligence in June 1966; not counting Allen Dulles, it was the first appointment made from inside the intelligence community. Helms had been with the OSS and joined the CIA in its earliest days. Under Dulles and McCone, he had served in key positions for many years, notably as deputy director for plans, that is, in charge of all operations. He remained DCI for more than six years, during the unhappy period in American history overshadowed by Vietnam and, of course, Watergate. Like virtually everyone in high public office at the time, Helms suffered as a result and quite frequently became the scapegoat for the mistakes—and worse—of others. The personal tragedy was all the greater because Helms was a very able director, loyal and self-effacing, a genuine public servant.

Helms established fairly good relations with President Johnson, but his position under Nixon became exceedingly difficult. There was no personal rancor on Nixon's part; on the contrary, the Republican president had inherited Helms from a Democratic administration and it would have been only natural had he picked a man of his own to replace Helms. The problem stemmed in part from Nixon's general indifference toward the CIA and, during his later years in office, his attempts to involve the agency in the Watergate cover-up.

Nixon was one of the few presidents in recent history who was interested in and well informed on foreign affairs. But there was never a feeling of trust between him and the members of his cabinet and other key advisers, except for leading personal advisers, such as Haldeman and Ehrlichmann. Nixon saw plots and conspiracies even when they did not exist, and seen in this light, the CIA was an obvious target for him. It was no secret that most senior CIA officials had liked and admired the Kennedys; socially and culturally—East Coast, upper middle class—they were close to them. It was only natural that Nixon should attribute his narrow defeat in the election of 1960 at least in part to the Central Intelligence Agency, which he thought was responsible for the "missile gap" that became an issue in the election campaign and was blamed on the Republicans.

Yet it is also true that Nixon was genuinely unimpressed by the kind of intelligence he received from the CIA. He found it bland and of little use; he frequently criticized the agency at NSC meetings and on other occasions. Eventually he asked his national security adviser, Henry Kissinger, to deal with all intelligence affairs as chairman of a special NSC subcommittee. Whatever Kissinger's disagreements with the president, he shared his penchant for secrecy and would not dream of informing Helms of Nixon's meetings with foreign statesmen, let alone his plans. This was the beginning of the era of the big security leaks, and Kissinger's behavior appears in retrospect not altogether unreasonable. Thus the CIA was less well informed in the Nixon years about policy making than ever before. And because the CIA did not know what the policy makers were up to, it was handicapped in its search for relevant information—a vicious circle.

Helms tried to make the best of an increasingly difficult situation. Discreet and unobtrusive, he was trusted by the members of Congress with whom he had dealings and also by most other top officials.[22] Relations with the Pentagon, however, were not good; tensions with the military had existed from the earliest days of the CIA and had been aggravated by recurrent disputes on Soviet strength. In these confrontations the CIA had, almost as a reflex, taken a position antagonistic to the DIA, questioning the accuracy of their figures. Military intelligence had tended to be alarmist in the 1950s, but in the late 1960s it was closer to the mark than the CIA's assessments, as was later seen.

Helms's critics said that he was overcautious and indecisive; for quite a few years, there was no NIE on Vietnam. Helms, they said, had only limited interest in certain aspects of the intelligence business. There was a grain of truth in this criticism, but given the prevailing conditions, there was not much room anyway for new initiatives and innovations. Trying to shield the CIA from outside attack, Helms spent most of his time resisting executive pressure to involve the agency in domestic politics, defending it against attacks from various quarters, and minimizing damage caused by various revelations and leaks. Frequently circumstances compelled Helms to deal with events that happened years ago—to explain, to defend, and sometimes to cover up—not an ideal situation to ponder the future and prepare for upcoming contingencies. At the same time, Nixon and those around him were fighting for their political survival and had little interest in any but issues directly connected with this struggle. They were more interested in the intentions of their enemies at home than those abroad.

It was an extreme situation, and precisely for this reason it teaches us little about normal working relations between producers and consumers in intelligence. Nor did conditions become more stable after Helms was sacked by Nixon. On the contrary, the CIA was still very much on the defensive; it had to devote much of its energy and time to defending itself against the many accusations concerning past misdeeds, real and alleged. It took almost a decade to recover, at least in part, from the shocks of the 1970s—the scandals, the leaks, and the self-inflicted wounds. It was a period in which most of the "barons," the old-timers who had risen to positions of power in the agency, left, and, while such a generational change would have been inevitable in any case, the manner in which many of them were dismissed, or forced to resign, caused much bad blood and prevented a smooth transition. Their successors were not always people of equal stature, and frequent organizational changes caused further confusion. It was said in the late 1970s that there was as much intelligence know-how and knowledge outside the CIA as inside. The collectors and their various technical systems continued to function and the analysts turned out their reports and studies, but it was not a happy period for intelligence, and its influence on policy making reached a nadir.[23]

The CIA has had six directors since 1973. Two of them served for very short periods: James Schlesinger from February to July 1973 and George Bush from January 1976 to January 1977. Schlesinger was followed by William Colby (1973–76), another CIA old-timer, who was succeeded by Bush who was followed by Admiral Stansfield Turner, Carter's chief of intelligence. He was succeeded by President Reagan's appointee, William Casey. Everyone of them had, for better or worse, considerable influence on the CIA's internal affairs, but none played a role comparable to that of Bedell Smith, Allen Dulles, and John McCone. Colby and Turner came in for much criticism, the former because of what were thought harmful and unnecessary revelations in front of Congressional committees and also because of internal reforms that were deemed misplaced. In Turner's case, the dismissal of many of the more experienced intelligence officials was not forgiven, and his style of work and general attitude toward intelligence generated hostility. Outside pressure continued, and successive DCIs still had to devote much of their time to defending their work before Congressional committees and, of course, lobbying for money and political support in all kinds of quarters. Morale in the agency was low, and the position of intelligence began to improve slowly only in the late seventies. This was part of the general process of disillusion with détente among the public: as the Soviet Union continued to intervene in various parts of the globe and as the United States became involved in various crises, there was a growing feeling that intelligence had been run down so much as to endanger national security.

But old enmities disappeared slowly. The American "left" would not forgive the CIA for engaging, however amateurishly and ineffectively, in covert action against Castro and other revolutionary movements. In fact, it opposed the very existence of intelligence. On the other hand, the CIA was upbraided by the "right" for having systematically underrated the extent of the Soviet military buildup. There was a feeling in the U.S. and abroad that U.S. intelligence was not remotely as good as it should be, which, given the blows that had rained down on the CIA, should not have come as a surprise to anyone. There is always criticism of the extent and the quality of intelligence, but there probably never was as much as during this period. From time to time semi-public expression was given to the dissatisfaction of the policy makers, such as in President Carter's famous note of 1978 in which higher quality intelligence was requested.*

President Ford was less active than Nixon in the foreign political field; authority under him was delegated to a greater extent. If under Nixon the general trend was toward concentration, the pendulum was now swinging again in the direction of decentralization. Executive order 11905 abolished the 40 Committee which had been in charge of covert action (and "sensitive collection"). It was replaced by a five-person Operations Advisory Group (OAG). The DCI became chairman of a three-person Committee on Foreign Intelligence (CFI) which was supposed to enhance his stature in the White House. The President's Foreign Intelligence Advisory Board (PFIAB) was succeeded by a three-person Intelligence Oversight Board (IOB).[24] Mondale and Aaron, whose enthusiasm for intelligence was lim-

---

*This refers to a handwritten note from President Carter dated November 11, 1978 to "Cy, Zbig, Stan," in which Carter stated he was dissatisfied "with the quality of our political intelligence." While this memorandum was ostensibly also addressed to the secretary of state and the national security adviser, it was obvious that the criticism was mainly directed against Stansfield Turner, who was DCI at the time. The occasion was the lack of reliable intelligence on Iran.

ited, felt that regardless of what precautions were taken, the board was inherently inclined to become a defender of the CIA. Stansfield Turner, on the other hand, did not look on the board as a potential ally but as an intruder. In practice, however, the real importance of the DCI still depended largely on his personality, not the chairmanship of a committee. Nor was it altogether clear how three part-time overseers, however distinguished, could effectively review a huge bureaucracy whose operations extended in so many directions. Most insiders continued to regard this and similar boards as little more than window dressing, albeit useful window dressing, considering the intricacies and pitfalls of Washington politics.

The appointment of George Bush as DCI was not universally welcomed in view of his deep political involvement, but after some initial doubts and resistance from inside the intelligence community, Bush acquired a reputation as an effective and trusted director who helped to restore confidence and morale in the CIA.

The fortunes of intelligence varied under President Carter. Admiral Turner, his new DCI, had fairly free access to the president in the beginning, but this changed in later years, and the overall impact of central intelligence on the conduct of foreign policy and defense was small. The reason was partly that President Carter (like Nixon before him) was more ambivalent about the CIA and its personnel than he was of intelligence as such, of which he was an avid reader. He discovered early on that he liked intelligence, and even when it did not produce a justification for some courses of action he felt committed to, he read it (and forgot it) but did not disparage it. When surprises and misfortunes befell him, he asked for more intelligence. But like Nixon, though for different reasons, he did not have much affinity for or trust CIA professionals, nor did he like to see them often. President Carter, most of the White House staff, and the State Department were deeply committed to a policy of détente; early in his presidency, Carter had warned against the unhealthy preoccupation with the "Soviet danger." Yet, the tide was running against détente, and in these circumstances, the CIA was back to its old role of the bearer of unwelcome news for the president.

The story of Carter's education in world affairs is known. He was kept informed in detail on all developments that preceded the Soviet invasion of Afghanistan. Intelligence on this topic was both excellent in quality and extensive in quantity and there was no delay in its receipt. But its importance simply did not register until much later. At the end of his presidency Carter was a sadder and wiser man, but there was no vote of gratitude to intelligence.

New turmoil occurred in the CIA when Admiral Turner brought in some of his naval staff to run the agency, sacked hundreds more of senior staff, and abolished an even larger number of jobs. Many hundreds of employees who had other job opportunities opted for an early retirement.[25] Manpower and budget declined in the CIA during the first years of Turner's incumbency but rose again toward its end. Among the many criticisms voiced of Turner was that he lacked tact in dealing with his staff and that he put too much emphasis on technical means of collection despite the known, limited range of this kind of intelligence.

To be fair to Admiral Turner, it should be recalled that during the first three years of the Carter administration the White House stress was still on putting restrictions on intelligence rather than improving it. Intelligence was not considered important, but a source of potential trouble; it was considered to have an inherent tendency to do evil, to go wrong, and to cause a president embarrassment.[26] One could not do away with it, but one could at least hedge it in with restrictions. One could also ensure that its wrongdoings would be exposed and that the administration would get credit for exposing them. There was initially a strong feeling in the administration that the investigation the Church Committee had begun into the state of intelligence had never really been finished and that a great deal more wrongdoing should be ferreted out.

By late 1978, Zbigniew Brzezinski and some other Carter advisers came to understand the need for more and better intelligence, realizing that the real problem was providing the simple capacity to perform. But by that time disillusionment and frustration about intelligence had reached a new climax. The PFIAB might have played a useful role in this situation; its prime reason for existence was concern about the adequacy of intelligence. But the PFIAB no longer existed and the Carter administration remained adamant about the supervision of intelligence until the end.

With all the extenuating circumstances, the Turner period was again not a happy one in the history of U.S. intelligence. He had his admirers in the CIA, but they were not many; in addition, he lacked influence in the White House and Congress. Senator Moynihan, a member of he Senate Intelligence Committee, was quoted in 1979 to the effect that "there is no intelligence agency of any kind in the United States today." This was, no doubt, an exaggeration, but it reflected the growing uneasiness with the state of intelligence and those responsible for its collection, assessment, and dissemination.

Under President Reagan higher priority was given to intelligence. Allocations rose appreciably "to enable the intelligence community to adjust from a prolonged period of cuts and freezes in the wake of the Vietnam War and to meet expanding requirements."[27] These requirements included intelligence on topics such as grain and oil production, state-sponsored international terrorism, human rights violation, and new buildings for the

CIA in Langley and for the DIA at Boling Air Force Base. William Casey, the new head of the CIA, had better access to the president than any of his predecessors of the last two decades, had more manpower at his disposal, and carried out some sensible reforms, such as the reorganization of the directorate of intelligence responsible for analysis and evaluation, which had come under increasing criticism in the late 1970s. It is only fair to add that some of these changes predated the Reagan presidency and that some of the boost to intelligence came owing to the initiative of the bipartisan House and Senate oversight committees, (HPSCI and SSCI). It is too early to give a conclusive answer to the question to what extent the quality of intelligence improved as a result of the new, more favorable climate, with greater resources at its disposal.

Seen in retrospect, it still seems that, as former senior government official Chester Cooper wrote in 1972, the salad days of the CIA were during the Eisenhower administration when it directly participated in the policy process through the National Security Council. In the Kennedy administration, the NSC lost at least some of its erstwhile importance, and the impact of the CIA was limited on the whole to current intelligence. Kennedy, like Carter, was an avid reader of intelligence and would sometimes get involved in the discussion of minor points in estimates (in Carter's case, it was problems of punctuation). But, to quote Cooper again, estimates, think pieces, and in-depth analyses were far from best-sellers in the 1960s.[28]

President Johnson was preoccupied with the problem of how to get out of Vietnam without making it appear that America had lost a war. He had little use for other information or estimates. But even on Vietnam, intelligence was not listened to, and Johnson's memoirs contain no reference to intelligence analysis as being among the factors that influenced his thinking about Vietnam.[29] Nor was Nixon greatly influenced by intelligence. His references were either cryptic ("CIA was closed like a safe and we could find no one to give us the combination to open it") or derogatory, noting that as recently as the day before the outbreak of the Yom Kippur war, the CIA had reported that war in the Middle East was unlikely.[30]

The late 1960s were years of stress and upheaval, "untypical" years for the study of the normal relationship between intelligence and the policy makers. But it is precisely at a time of crisis that this relationship is tested, and if it fails, the question of responsibility inevitably arises. Again, it could be argued that even if intelligence did not have a major impact at the top, the flow of information would continue at midlevel and that this was all the intelligence community could realistically hope for. This leads to the basic question concerning the purpose of foreign political intelligence: Whom does it serve? And, in the light of past experience, how can intelligence keep its customers reasonably happy? Or do the intelligence officials have to anticipate that their tasks will be like that of Sisyphus— not only thankless, but forever renewed and ultimately futile.

For a long time, the central issue in the minds of those concerned with the relationship between intelligence and foreign policy was where to draw the boundary line between the two. In the CIA's early days, the prevailing view was that intelligence was called on simply to provide facts, and that their interpretation as far as possible should be left to those responsible for policy. But "facts" are by their nature virtually unlimited. A preliminary selection must always be made in order not to swamp the consumer with information, important and unimportant, correct and false. Furthermore, there must be some kind of interpretation at an early stage because selection, needless to say, implies certain assumptions about the reliability of source and content.

Others believed in a more ambitious role for intelligence, including an active part in the policy-making process. But for many years the consensus was that intelligence needed administrative and substantive integrity, and that this could only be safeguarded by keeping it independent of its consumers. If intelligence were brought too close to the customer, it was feared that it would be diverted into doing less intelligence work, by its use for current intelligence only, and by lack of engagement in long-term projects. But the greatest danger according to this school of thought, was that the substantive integrity of intelligence would be compromised. As Sherman Kent asked: If under the best of conditions intelligence found itself guilty of hasty and unsound conclusions, how much more likely were such conclusions if it were subjected to the administrative control of its customers?[31] Human nature being what it is, how could intelligence escape from falling in line behind the policy of the employing unit and "prostituting itself in the production of what the Nazis used to call *Kämpfende Wissenschaft* [fighting science]?"

The only institutional safeguard for impartial analysis was, in Walter Lippmann's opinion, to separate as absolutely as possible the staff that executed from the staff that investigated. The two should be recruited differently, paid from separate funds, be responsible to different heads, and even "intrinsically uninterested in each other's personal success."[32]

For a considerable time after its foundation it was the official line of the CIA "not to take sides." Roscoe Hillenkoetter, former head of Naval Intelligence, thought that it was not the task of an intelligence agency to evaluate reports or make predictions; that it should not advocate, oppose, or make policy; but that it should fit together the pieces of a giant jigsaw puzzle.[33] Experience, in his case, was no guide to an adequate theory.

General Vandenberg, like the OSS's Donovan before him, stressed that an intelligence organization should never presume to suggest decisions, a tradition continued by Allen Dulles and Richard Helms. Dulles reportedly said that his job was to provide the facts; he refused to discuss policy implications at NSC meetings. Richard Helms resisted Kissinger's pressure for more predictive CIA statements about SALT verification.[34] Under Colby and Turner, the CIA was too weak, or its prestige too low, to take an important part in policy making.

Thus it would appear that both according to doctrine and in practice, intelligence has always played the role of neutral observer. The impression is misleading, for even if there were no explicit advice, the course of action bound to follow from the intelligence estimate or memo submitted to the policy maker was frequently obvious. Furthermore, most of the DCIs mentioned presided over covert actions, some part of the initiative for which must have emanated from them.

The debate about integration versus separation of intelligence now seems to be over. The fears expressed by Sherman Kent, William Langer, and their contemporaries were by no means groundless. But the experience of several decades has shown that the danger of loss of objectives in the intelligence process would have existed even if the CIA had been a totally autonomous organization. In the last resort, more depends on the integrity, the self-confidence, and the strength of character of the analysts than on their bureaucratic affiliation. Conversely, it appears that to be helpful intelligence has to draw closer to the core of the policy-making process; without doing so, intelligence cannot focus its collection effort. Unless there is traffic in both directions on the intelligence road, it cannot properly fulfill its function—this is true whether intelligence is under the direct control of the consumer or not.

The problem of finding the right balance between isolation and domination continues to exist, but it is not of such decisive importance as the founders of modern U.S. intelligence believed.[35] The distance from producer to consumer in the best of circumstances can still be long; the path is full of obstacles and pitfalls; and communication, from one end to the other, is often inefficient.

Among the most frequently cited causes for inadequate collaboration between policy makers and intelligence officials are (1) the cumbersome nature of bureaucratic organization; (2) demoralization and confusion caused by constant changes in administrative structure; (3) compartmentalization of knowledge due to the need for secrecy; (4) data overload, which makes it impossible for analysts and decision makers alike to distinguish between important "signals" and mere "noise"; (5) the impatience of decision makers with long-range, as opposed to crisis-generated, intelligence perspectives; (6) decision makers' tendencies in such situations to seize upon raw data, preempting the role of analyst for themselves; and (7) pressures, both externally and internally generated, to shape intelligence reports to confirm and support policies already decided upon.

Before examining these obstacles, a basic question remains to be asked: How important is the flow of intelligence? It has been said that information from worldwide public sources constitutes some 90 percent of what policy makers need to know, what is going on, and what will happen next, but that the missing 10 percent is critical: "Taken by itself, the vast mass of open source information is as useless as an uncompleted bridge that takes us not quite across a river when it comes to some of the things we need know most."[36]

Two CIA investigators who studied the subject during the Carter presidency have reached the general conclusion that policy makers will remember intelligence as less useful than it actually was, while intelligence producers will think their inputs were more helpful than was the case.[37] Unfortunately, it is impossible to say which side is "right"—or at least, more nearly right. As the authors of the CIA study note, it is impossible, except perhaps in a few isolated cases, to recreate the atmosphere in which decisions were taken and then to "audit" the impact of intelligence information and the way it influenced policy makers. Thus, they have focused not on intelligence in general, but on the impact of intelligence on PRM (policy review memoranda) and the products of the Special Coordinating Committee (SCC).[38] Having established a time-and-action sequence and interviewed most of the participants, the investigators realized that they would have to concentrate on the *perceptions* of the policy makers about the utility of intelligence, rather than try to establish objective criteria for the value of intelligence.[39]

The belief that intelligence operators tend to overrate the importance of intelligence may apply more to low-level analysts than to their senior colleagues, let alone DCIs and their deputies. My impression is that intelligence officials who are (or were) in constant touch with high-level policy makers have few illusions about the role of intelligence in policy making; on the contrary, almost all show more than a little frustration—or resignation at best. Policy makers on the highest level maintain that, on the whole, intelligence has usually been of limited importance and almost never decisive. When they say this, they have political intelligence in mind. On second thought, they usually add that intelligence has sometimes been useful in important negotiations with foreign statesmen or on other occasions. Nor do they deny the importance of strategic-military intelligence, which has become even more vital than in the past as America's margin of safety has shrunk. To give one obvious example, without intelligence, unilateral SALT verifications would be impossible. Senior policy makers are likely to conclude that in some cases intelligence constituted far more than the "crucial 10 percent," whereas in other cases intelligence was not critical at all. It is worth mentioning that politicians are most willing to grant special importance to scientific, economic, or strategic intelligence, which they themselves are incapable of evaluating. Where political intelligence is concerned, though, almost everyone will feel entitled to his or her own opinion: it is usually more difficult to collect, it is frequently ambiguous, and policy makers will feel that their own judgment and experience may be equal, if not superior, to the judgment of the analysts.

Bureaucratic Distortion and Administrative Discontinuity

One of the basic complaints of intelligence producers concerns the lack of continuity in American intelligence. It will soon require a Homeric memory to recall the successive CIA directors—Souers, Vandenberg, Hillenkoetter, Smith, Dulles, McCone, Raborn, Helms, Schlesinger, Colby, Bush, Turner, and Casey—let alone their deputies, who have been appointed since the agency's founding in 1947. It does not require special expertise in personnel or business management to conclude that an average tenure of less than three years is too short for optimal performance.[40] Between the time Andropov became head of the KGB in 1967 and the summer of 1982 when he moved on to higher office the CIA had six directors, in addition to one acting director. Each administration, and almost every new DCI, has introduced new directions in intelligence work. Intelligence has had to adjust to radical shifts in emphasis, to changes in the regions of the world considered most important, and to changes in styles of operation. The effects of these innovations have been felt not only in the daily workload, but also over the longer term. Intelligence capabilities built up with the agenda of one administration in mind often reach full development when it is time for the next one, which may or may not welcome the legacy. It has become a tradition for new administrators to tinker with the intelligence and policy systems they inherit in the hope that reorganization will improve their performance: what was centralized is decentralized and vice versa; specialists and generalists take turns drafting estimates; boards and committees of coordination and oversight are established and again disestablished; various oeprative sections are united and separated; and new publications appear, only to be discontinued.

Many such shifts in the structure of intelligence involve no more than the recycling of ideas that were previously tried and discarded. Karl Mannheim, the well-known sociologist, noted many years ago that it was the fundamental tendency of bureaucratic thought to turn all problems of politics into problems of administration. The problem of intelligence is predominantly political in character; administrative solutions promoted by enthusiasts have missed this essential point. Worse, they have quite frequently disrupted practices and mechanisms that, while not functioning ideally, have worked better than those that succeeded them.

The advent of new administrations results in particular strains on the intelligence policy-making relationship because new public officials frequently have an "instinctive distrust of bureaucracy."[41] Trust and confidence must be established, and even in the best of cases this does not happen overnight. The early years of the Nixon administration are an example of such a strained relationship, but it is difficult to think of any transition that was entirely smooth.

Two fundamental complaints of intelligence vis-à-vis policy makers concern the procedure for setting priorities and the failure of superiors to communicate these priorities adequately to those who are to attend to them. As the Church committee observed, consumers rarely take the time to define their intelligence needs, and even if they do, there is no effective and systematic mechanism for translating them into intelligence requirements. Successive commissions of inquiry have noted that consumers have treated intelligence products as free goods: "Instead of articulating priorities, they demand information about everything, and the demand exceeds the supply."[42] As consumer demands are constantly growing, as is the amount of data collected, analysts are overloaded. They, in turn, react by swamping customers with a great volume of memoranda. Modern systems of storage and retrieval make it easy to increase the flood of paper on short notice. But the customers want knowledge, not just large amounts of paper, and will therefore complain about lack of quality and discrimination.

Traditionally, intelligence consumers have stated what they wanted to know and have posed specific questions, or "requirements." This process was formalized in the 1950s with the Related Mission Directive (RMD), rechristened and refined in the late 1960s as the Operational Directive (OD), in which various tasks were listed in order of importance.[43] There has always been an inherent tendency toward extreme bureaucratization in this kind of process, since virtually everything gets listed.[44] Station chiefs in the field found in these lists everything they could reasonably be expected to do, as well as a great many things they could not; having something listed as second or third priority was tantamount to authorizing its being ignored. Thus, the wish lists became a grab bag that officers in the field realized was not taken too seriously, even in Washington. They were supposed to be reviewed yearly, but in fact they often were not, and the whole system became moribund. Under Colby, the agency adopted the "Management by Objectives" doctrine—everything was numbered and eventually the whole system was computerized. Elaborate quarterly, semiannual, and annual operational reports had to be submitted, which consumed an enormous amount of manpower. Such formalistic micromanagement led to further bureaucratization and had a debilitating effect on morale.

Under Turner, a National Intelligence Topics List (NIT) was established. This was a set of fifty-nine questions concerning the fifty-nine topics of highest priority to national decision makers. A special group chaired by the DCI met periodically to rank the fifty-nine NITs in order of priority. Broken down into current and long-range issues, this list was to guide the collectors and producers of intelligence. Yet a 1980 in-house inquiry found that the new system had not worked better than the previous one. It was too static and bureaucratized; above all, it did not really present the concerns of the policy makers but "rather an interpretation of those concerns as drawn up by the Intelligence Community."[45] Another observer noted that the system broke down when it came to translating the wide range of collected information into papers and studies that intelligently responded to the consumers' requirements.[46]

This leads to a related complaint on the part of intelligence—that they are insufficiently briefed by the policy makers about their intentions; intelligence producers are then bound to write their reports in a void, knowing more about the policies and weapons systems of the other side than about their own. An example of this is the case of a memorandum prepared in April 1970 by the Office of National Estimates on the situation in Indochina. Richard Helms, the DCI, had been told about the impending invasion of Cambodia but had been strictly forbidden by his superiors to inform anyone else. Not surprisingly, he decided *not* to forward a document to the White House that had been written by someone in ignorance of an already decided upon U.S. policy step.

The need to improve feedback on the part of policy makers to intelligence is recognized, but there is at present no mechanism, except an incomplete one at the top level, to provide policy information to analysts. Exaggerated secrecy and excessive compartmentalization of intelligence aside, there are objective difficulties to consider: on some occasions it may be impossible to take the analysts into confidence. To a certain extent intelligence will always have to operate by *guessing* rather than by *knowing* the intentions of its own government. This is true for all countries, and in some, such as the Soviet Union, analysts are much less well informed. Furthermore, priorities tend to change quickly as the world situation changes, when there are no remedies for the problem except the obvious ones: keeping requirements as simple as possible, reviewing and updating them as frequently as necessary, and, whenever possible, making sure there is close interaction between policy makers and intelligence officials —and not only at the most senior level. The absence of such interaction may be due to lack of curiosity by the policy makers, or, equally, the reason may be technical, such as the absence of secure telephone systems for on-the-spot discussions.

Policy makers are frequently criticized by their opposite numbers in intelligence for asking the wrong questions and for having unrealistic views on what intelligence can, and cannot, do. A litany follows: policy makers are too busy (or too lazy) to read information supplied to them; they prefer raw or current intelligence, however ephemeral, to long-term strategic intelligence; they want to hear their views confirmed; and they are intolerant of information contrary to their own opinions.

Consumers constantly demand that intelligence go beyond what the facts will bear; they pressure intelligence to move outside prudent "best estimates." Yet they also tend to believe that they can do better as analysts than intelligence personnel; they abuse their access to raw intelligence data, avoiding the views of competent intermediaries. They are resistant to bad news; messengers bringing such news are no longer physically killed, as in ancient times, but the damage to their careers may be severe, if not fatal. Consumers are quick to criticize the intelligence services in general terms, while doing little to provide adequate guidance or detailed, constructive criticism.

Compartmentalization of Knowledge

Quite often policy makers are insufficiently informed about the various intelligence agencies and their resources.[47] It is easy to understand, there-fore, that policy makers are sometimes bound to ask the wrong questions. But the intelligence community—even during its most liberal phase—has not, and perhaps could not, fully educate its customers as much as desired. It is well known that the free flow of information is the best stimulus for new knowledge and the elimination of error. But in the real world of government bureaucracy, sensitive intelligence information is compart-mentalized; in other words, it is denied to as many persons as possible. The assumption is that the more delicate the information, the smaller the circle of those who may be exposed to it: if something is really very secret, no one hears about it.

Compartmentalizing knowledge exacts a price. Although it reduces the chances that error will be detected in proportion to a diminishing number of "cleared" persons, a problem occurs when information tightly compartmentalized for security reasons happens to have important practical implications. It may mean that at the base of the intelligence and policy-making system, where staff is trying to break new ground, information critical to their endeavor is withheld. It is not certain that the damage may be undone by subsequently briefing a handful of top officials who may, or may not, be in a position to use this knowledge.

Compartmentalization affects both intelligence producers and policy makers, but the latter may be at a greater disadvantage. They are usually excluded from understanding what sources and methods were used to collect intelligence data in the first place. The existence of such barriers puts a heavy premium on the judgment and discretion of those who do have the means to appraise the strengths and weaknesses of intelligence assets. Their desire to protect these assets collides with their responsibility for getting information to those who need it.[48]

The proliferation of government agencies charged with collection or analysis of foreign intelligence represents a special—and evidently insoluble—problem of compartmentalization. Although the DCI is mandated by law to be the coordinator of intelligence from all of the agencies in question,* he is undeniably "the boss" only in his own organization, the CIA. Armed services rivalries make it virtually certain that a good deal of information will be withheld by military agencies from the civilian who is titular head of the intelligence community, as we have already noted. The former CIA deputy director, Admiral Rufus Taylor, hit upon an accurate if critical term when he compared the intelligence community to a "tribal federation."

Data Overload

The absorptive capacity of consumers clearly has its limits. There has always been more intelligence on some subjects collected than can be used, even though some 90 percent of intelligence never leaves CIA offices.

*CIA, NSA, DIA, Army Intelligence, Naval Intelligence, Air Force Intelligence (including the very secretive National Reconnaissance Office), State Department (Bureau of Intelligence and Research), FBI (Internal Security Division), Departments of Commerce, Treasury, Energy, Agriculture, Drug Enforcement, and so on.

Customers have complained about oversupply and excessively wide dissemination: "Some customers get too much material but at times will miss the one item they need."[49] But some degree of redundancy is usually desirable in the intelligence business and negative information also has to be collected. Furthermore, intelligence, once started, continues to grow in massive quantity. Systems for collection have a dynamism of their own; once devised, set in motion, and operated successfully, no one wishes to take the responsibility for turning them off. Technical operations are particularly susceptible to this syndrome and Americans are especially prone to favor technical operations.

Yet while intelligence operations are extraordinary in their comprehensiveness, timeliness, and scope, they are incapable of producing much of the information needed to form political judgment about what is going on in the world and how to relate to it. Overemphasis on technical collection leads to the illusion that there is more real (hard) intelligence than actually exists. This makes the lack of political intelligence even more glaring. A senior government official once noted in discussion: "The product is so full of judgment and so unclear about what the evidence is."[50] He thought that in the final analysis, analysts had little more to go on than someone who studied only open sources.

Attempts to improve the quality of political intelligence have been undertaken from time to time—most recently in the late 1970s—with mixed results. Political reporting from the field improved—to some extent from embassies, to a greater extent from CIA field stations. But there was still little real improvement in analysis.

Developments in Iran in the late 1970s highlighted a fundamental aspect of this problem. Consumers could have clearly absorbed much more information on Iran in 1978, but nobody got much reporting on political developments in that country. The first Carter administration debate about Iran dealt with the sale of AWACS to Iran, the assumption being that the Shah's government was as stable as it needed to be. During most of its history, the CIA's Teheran station had been oriented toward maintaining friendly relations with SAVAK, the Iranian secret police, and the Shah in order to ensure favorable conditions for U.S. technical collection sites targeted at Soviet missile testing, the highest priority intelligence operation in the country. This was an interesting example of an operation that though designed to protect valuable operations actually undermined them, or at least contributed to their loss. In Iran, the United States neglected to see the necessity of providing itself with the information necessary to judge the viability of the single most important factor on which the continued performance of these highly sophisticated sites depended: the Shah himself.[51]

In the Iranian debacle, producers and consumers seem equally at fault. Questions were not asked, so no attempt to answer them was made—at least until things had begun to fall apart and it was too late. A similar pattern can be found in the case of most "intelligence failures": "No warnings were given . . ." and "No questions were asked. . . ."

Excessive reporting needs to be brought under control periodically. Once-high priorities often outlive their usefulness, resulting in a vast flow of detailed information that no one any longer wants. Such an overgrowth of intelligence has to be cut back. Yet pruning operations have to be carried out with good judgment, not indiscriminately. Two illustrations come to mind. There was no high priority demand from any consumer for Caribbean operations in the 1960s. Yet contacts were still made and basic data assembled, because those in charge sensed that the area might eventually become more important from the viewpoint of American interests, as it eventually did.

Another example concerns the visit of the Pope to Poland in 1979. A seven-page DIA report on the subject was singled out for criticism as an example of duplication and overreporting; INR, after all, had devoted only a few paragraphs to the topic. Yet, as it subsequently appeared, the visit of the Pope was an event of historical importance, contributing to the rise of "Solidarity" and the ferment in Poland in 1980–81.

Short-Term Perspectives: "Butchers" vs. "Bakers"

The amount and kind of intelligence supplied must be a judicious balance between intelligence requested and intelligence volunteered. Many of the problems of U.S. intelligence stem from the fact that it has been too crisis-oriented and too little directed toward studying situations in depth and identifying trends that could eventually lead to serious problems or, conversely, that may not turn out to be so serious after all. Intelligence has been infected—in large part no doubt as the result of consumers' pressure —with the disease that is the bane of American journalism: news is only what is news today, tomorrow doesn't matter, and yesterday's headlines are yesterday's. Once a crisis breaks, the reader is exposed to a relentless flood of information—unfamiliar names, an abundance of isolated facts that are frequently irrelevant, and conflicting viewpoints of all kinds of experts, real and spurious. But the moment the shooting is over (literally or figuratively), the country in question again disappears from the headlines and often from the columns altogether.

It has been argued that this excessive preoccupation with current intelligence is not mainly the fault of the intelligence agencies. For it is known that while in theory the greatest prestige in the intelligence world is attached to formal long-range estimates, which supposedly serve to shape opinion and illuminate important policy issues, in the real world the only intelligence that most policy makers read from cover to cover on a daily basis is current intelligence.[52]

Thomas Hughes, a former head of INR, noted that daily competition to reach the policy makers is usually won by the "butchers" (the current intelligence man) with the hot item, whereas the "bakers," the authors of the substantial estimates, are much less successful.[53] The demands on key figures in the world of politics are so severe that the U.S. foreign affairs bureaucracy usually spends two-thirds of its time in meetings and on the telephone. Although ten- to twelve-hour days (more at high levels) are the norm for such officials, they can devote little time to reading, even if they like to read and read fast. If the subject of a substantial study is one they are keenly interested in, their frustration will be all the greater, for they know they will not find time to read it. Ponderous estimates wind up on the bottom of in-boxes or are relegated to subordinates, who may be too busy to get much beyond a well-written executive summary. Richard Helms related that he could be certain to have the undivided attention of President Johnson for about 90 seconds; the daily bulletin of intelligence information submitted to President Reagan has been brief. Even under Kennedy, the president's daily check list was kept short, despite Kennedy's known interest in the subject.

What, then, are the ideal vehicles for communicating information to the most senior policy makers? Obviously, their desires must be taken into account; some still prefer oral briefings to written documents, though this practice seems to be on the decline. Senior intelligence officials agree that on some occasions the best way to convey information about a large and important subject is a good oral briefing with slides, viewgraphs, charts, and perhaps videotapes.[54] It is impractical, however, to make this a standard practice, for few high-level officials can afford the time for many such briefings. On other occasions a plausible case can be made for submitting bulky studies replete with statistics, graphs, and appendices to the White House and other high officials in order to emphasize the complexity and importance of a certain issue. But it would seem that what is easiest to read is most likely to be read—a document that provides the basic facts and a brief interpretation, avoiding bureaucratic ponderousness. Yet at a time of crisis, high officials may also ask for executive summaries of long studies otherwise neglected; they may wish to see even esoteric material from unusual sources if they feel that it might be relevant. The real difficulties arise when the attempt is made to get high-level attention either for an unpopular viewpoint, for a subject that no one wishes to grapple with, or for a critical situation not yet perceived as such. Routine presentations or formats will only reinforce the disinclination to pay attention. Chances of success are greater if a dramatic vehicle is used for presenting information.

While composition and format are important for the more comprehensive studies, form and representation seem to be relatively unimportant as far as daily intelligence is concerned. According to some intelligence consumers, the daily morning summary issued by INR—which was the messiest in format—tended to be the most influential.[55] It was popular because it had a freshness and readability lacking in the more polished DIA and CIA daily intelligence briefs, even though it was no more accurate. Other material with a relatively broad readership includes biographical summaries of individuals whom the reader would soon be meeting, with whom consultations of some sort are being conducted, or who are simply getting new attention in the world.[56]

Further down the line, almost all intermediate-level officials like to receive cable traffic directly from the field. This refers to embassy cables as well as to CIA field reporting. Most NSC staff members read field reporting and embassy cables in preference to other material and would not be content with receiving summaries of such material, both because the originals are more rapidly available and because they seem more authoritative. Military reports are less often read in the original, partly because of their complicated nature, and partly because they are less interesting.

The traditional rivalry between the CIA and the State Department should be mentioned in passing.[57] A great deal depends, of course, on the individual temperaments and abilities of those involved. It is also true that the disparagement or at least studied ignorance of intelligence thirty, or even fifteen, years ago is now much less common in the State Department. It is still true, however, that the preeminence of the State Department in foreign policy usually means a certain downgrading of intelligence.[58] More reliance is placed on short-term diplomatic and procedural considerations at the expense of longer-term, more basic national security requirements. Comprehensive political reporting is rare, and Mr. Kennan's famous cables from Moscow in 1946 were the exception rather than the rule.

The decline in the standards of diplomatic reporting since World War II is obvious to students of diplomatic history. News is transmitted infinitely faster, but it does not contain more insight and judgment. In embassies, there is a disinclination, partly caused by lack of time, to think about discontinuities and disruptive developments, about the impact of economics on politics, and about developments in sections of society that do not seem immediately relevant to the political process. An experienced ambassador knows well that he or she will not be judged too harshly for lack of analytical reporting if the home desk is kept fully informed on what the embassy is doing on a day-to-day basis—persuading the host government to vote with the United States in the United Nations, arranging for a visiting congressional delegation, and so forth. Ambassadors know that trend reporting may turn out to be wrong, and that it can be dangerous to become overly concerned with threatening phenomena that do not materialize. It may be safer not to report these circumstances at all than to report what might later be questioned. Absence of serious political reporting is not a chargeable offense, whereas wrong predictions may provide ammunition for one's critics in Washington. With these conditions, the CIA has a political advantage over the diplomats. Whether its people in the field seize that advantage is a different question.

It cannot be repeated too often that intelligence summaries and cables have to compete each morning with the newspapers for the attention of the leading policy makers, who may well have seen the morning press papers before they read the intelligence reports. The DCI or his deputies will be submitted to annoying queries as to why they were scooped by the national press or the news agencies. In any case, certain items carried by the press are likely to attract more attention for the simple reason that a report in the *New York Times* will be widely read and may provoke calls from Congress and from other newspapers; press officers will also want to know what to say in response to inquiries.

Because the highest-level consumers are usually too busy to deal with even very important intelligence, it is essential to have the middle-level well informed so that their superiors understand the overall significance of what is provided to them. The president and the secretaries of state and defense, for example, will insist that their immediate subordinates and staff officers receive the same material as they do in order to summarize it and offer comments.

In effect, then, much—perhaps even most—of the detailed output of the intelligence community is produced primarily for the middle levels of the foreign affairs and defense bureaucracy, for these officials are likely to be the only ones who systematically follow developments in a particular country or area over a long period of time. The upper levels expect the middle-level officers to brief them from time to time and to provide expertise for a trip or a meeting with a foreign official as required. A field officer gathering information on developments in a political party in Portugal will have no illusions that his reports are read by the president or the secretary of state, but he will expect them to be read by the analyst following Portugal in the INR, by the desk officer for Iberian affairs in the political department of the Pentagon (DOD/ISA), and so on.

The middle levels are important in yet another way. They provide the only permanent constituency for intelligence analysts and field reporters. They are the intelligence equivalents to colleagues in the academic field who follow articles in scholarly journals and criticize papers at professional meetings. Isolation is a chronic problem for intelligence officers. Their work needs to be exposed to other knowledgeable people so that they can receive advice, correction, collaboration, or praise, as the case may be. This feedback can come only from the middle echelons of the bureaucracy.

External and Internal Pressure for Conformity

Of all the obstacles in the way of communication, political pressure exerted by the consumer is often thought to be the most important and the most dangerous. Such pressure did not prevent the CIA from sticking to its often unwelcome positions during the Vietnam War. A former DCI told me that intelligence may have an almost glacial effect on the unwilling customer: even unwelcome intelligence, if well documented and reasoned, will usually have its effect if repeated often enough and without softening the essential points.[59]

Intelligence must provide information and assessments for cabinet officers who often have vested interests in specific policies. There are well known, almost institutionalized differences of view between the Departments of State and Defense. Instances are known of intelligence memoranda being modified as the result of intervention on the part of the White House and the Pentagon. There is a natural tension between intelligence and policy or, in the words of a former DCI, "There is no way to isolate the DCI from unpopularity at the hands of presidents or policy makers if he is making assessments which run counter to administration policy."[60] The effect of these pressures should not be exaggerated, however, if only because they hardly ever come from one side. Kissinger was blamed on at least one occasion for trying to make the CIA provide a "hawkish" assessment, according to which the Soviets had produced an SS-9 with a MIRV capacity in 1969. "Dovish" pressure was probably even stronger: Richard Helms relates that when Fulbright was chairman of the Senate Foreign Relations Committee, a DCI who attempted to demonstrate that the Soviets were bent on achieving superiority would have been laughed out of court. Granted this was not direct interference with intelligence, but since intelligence officers are only human, the prospect of public ridicule can be an effective form of pressure.

In 1968, the top policy makers in the Johnson administration were so committed to the planning then underway for arms control negotiations that they discounted any possibility that the Soviet Union might intervene with troops in Czechoslovakia, at least so long as Dubcek did not threaten to remove his country from the Warsaw Pact. When Richard Helms tried to raise a warning flag at a White House meeting just before the actual invasion, he was dismissed as an alarmist. He later called this incident a classic example of important intelligence that was disregarded because it ran contrary to a major policy objective previously decided upon.[61] But the CIA also contributed—without evident outside pressure—to the "anti-alarmist" mood. The NIEs published in the 1960s and, indeed, up to the late 1970s manifested a clear reluctance to accept mounting evidence that the Soviet Union had no intention of stopping at the point of missile parity.

During the early years of the Carter administration there was reluctance to accept intelligence indicating that the Soviet Union was engaged in a massive military buildup and that as a result the SALT process could be in danger. The problem in that instance and others is not simply that consumers want confirmation of views they already hold, but that on really important issues they want to be spared the consequences of changing comfortable assumptions. This is especially true when the problem involves difficult moral issues; its most extreme form is the "terrible secret" syndrome—the reluctance on the part of many to accept the information about the mass murder of European Jewry in World War II.[62] In a milder form the phenomenon appears quite frequently, for most people are reluctant to confront evidence of immorality or inhuman behavior. Statesmen, high government officials, and intellectuals are perhaps more prone to such reluctance than others simply because they are expected to set standards and call for action. Ordinary citizens may be morally indignant, but they find it easier to offer political impotence as their reason for inaction.

It has been argued that largely because of the lack of high-level commitment, intelligence for a number of years did not actively pursue such issues as "yellow rain," poison gas, germ warfare, and international terrorism. In these areas, policy makers tended to treat the symptoms while ignoring the disease. As for terrorism, the inclination was usually to look for sociological explanations or to blame specific incidents on an isolated, demented fanatic. Quite apart from the psychological reasons given in the previous paragraph for failure to explore this problem adequately, this area is not only dangerous, but exceptionally complex. Chances for quick success are never good when the terrain is so largely unexplored. Western intelligence services subjected to economizing do not have the funds or manpower to deal with the enormous infrastructure, encompassing hundreds of channels, through which money, people, and weapons are transferred. The quest for legal proof in suspected cases of terrorism is very difficult, for the whole purpose of the complicated arrangements of terrorism is to ensure that no traces are left for further investigation.[63] Intelligence performance in this specific field has been deficient, but there is reason to assume that this has been the responsibility of consumers to a large degree.

Intelligence operators have understandable misgivings about the inclination on the part of some policy makers to reject evaluations, believing in their own superior ability to assess situations. The case of Churchill is well known. As one experienced witness puts it, few leading officials of the U.S. government would have gained their positions of influence without considerable self-confidence, hence their tendency to regard themselves as their own best intelligence officers on at least some issues.[64] This is particularly true with regard to "soft" appraisals of general trends. Furthermore, such intelligence seems much less significant than the policy makers' own high-level exchanges or conversations with foreign leaders.[65]

In a wider perspective, however, the "just-give-me-the-facts" attitude no longer seems to be a major problem in relations between producers and consumers. It appears most frequently in political reporting, as military, economic, and technical reporting require the study of formidable bodies of statistical data, as well as specialized training that individual consumers usually lack. Political intelligence is on the whole more subjective. Some of it involves masses of data on elections, political trends, polls, and public opinion. But most political intelligence has to do with less readily quantifiable matters: what leaders think and what they aspire to do, how societies work, and how they react to stimuli and changes. A consumer with a keen feel for such factors, perhaps through personal experience of foreign societies, is likely to be highly skilled in the interpretation of raw data. The consumer may well be more competent in such matters than an analyst who is meticulous in the systematic weighing of the evidence, but has less feel for the country in question. In such circumstances, the consumer is justified in wanting the facts and in drawing his or her own conclusions; it would even be irresponsible not to do so. Direct political interference is rarer than indirect influence, no less real for being less than overt:

If an administration bent on a specific policy course has made decisions leading it in a certain direction, then any information to the contrary may not be viewed with favor. However, there are no pronouncements related back to the intelligence community that contrary information will not be accepted. Rarely if ever by direction, but usually by inference, analysts sense pressure, know how options and alternatives that might not suit policy preferences are likely to be viewed, and hence are swayed to skew their analyses towards the easy way out

—analyses that if not in agreement with a proposed policy are framed so as not to be flatly opposed to it.[66]

Far more frequent than direct interference and outright censorship by higher authority is a degree of self-censorship, the psychological adjustment someone termed "a subtle cultural thing"—the conformity to a certain mold of political preference deriving from similar background and academic perspectives. In the long run, this is probably more important than working-level officers' fear of dissent from the views held by their superiors.[67] Thus, as a reaction against popular identification of the CIA with conservative, right-wing, or reactionary views, CIA officials may attempt to demonstrate their nonconformity and independence of mind by overcompensating in the other direction—by opposing, for instance, "alarmist" assessments made by the DIA.

There is almost always room for disagreement among intelligence services; differences of view are normally legitimate and signs of healthy competition. But given such disagreement, what is the best way to get at the truth? Some have advocated an adversary procedure comparable to our legal system. For example, under Colby and Turner at the CIA, unorthodox interpretations were encouraged and experiments were sanctioned with against-the-stream analyses, especially if these took the form of challenges by younger officers. The State Department maintains an institutional channel for dissent. These approaches, as well as devil's advocate evaluations, have been useful on occasion. But on the whole they have not greatly appealed to intelligence experts who argue that most dissent initiatives center on special pleadings and narrow interpretations of developments.

Experimentation with these approaches to dissent was, no doubt, a reflection of the preoccupation in American society with challenging authority and a manifestation of the tendency to find government at fault. The CIA never went as far as the State Department in establishing a formal "dissent channel," but there were similar schemes. They all emphasized the values of challenge and of youth—frequently, it seemed, as values in their own right. Not to mince words, there was a great deal of self-righteous posturing. The result was that those with strong emotional biases got more hearing than they deserved, while more reserved men and women (some of whom were more competent) received less than their share. The net result was deleterious to intelligence.

It is not undesirable if a chief of station or an ambassador sends reports that include alternative interpretations and scenarios, provided some perspective is also supplied. But it is another question whether analysts in Washington should systematically prepare devil's advocate analyses. This can be a useful way of testing for weak points in a seemingly plausible interpretation and occasionally a stimulating exercise in its own right. To some degree this procedure takes place in the normal course of preparation of all major intelligence studies or estimates. Carried too far and formalized too rigidly, it becomes a time-wasting exercise as it did during the Nixon administration.[68]

In actual fact, high-level consumers do not want an infinite range of speculative interpretations and implications. They want a trenchant explanation of developments reflecting the judgment of informed intelligence analysts and a range of likely future developments based on the best information currently available. It is important to reexamine evaluations and estimates periodically, to see whether they have stood the test of time and whether new information substantiates earlier conclusions.[69] It is much less important—even counterproductive—to construct elaborate systems for feeding contrasting interpretations into the intelligence process.

Some of the attitudes of policy makers toward intelligence have changed over the years, others have remained constant. It is instructive to compare the results of a mid-1950s investigation by former INR chief Roger Hilsman with the conclusions of a CIA study carried out almost a quarter of a century later. Hilsman found a strong reliance on "experience" on the part of diplomats and policy makers; many were suspicious of the warning and estimating functions of intelligence because intelligence usually lacked such field experience.[70] In this connection, a fairly strong anti-intellectual bias could frequently be detected. The analyst, as the policy maker saw it, was a bookish dreamer, an egghead unaware of the difficulties of getting things done in a world of competing groups and conflicting desires. Research was of limited usefulness when it came to taking actions: "Accordingly the researcher's contribution, if at all, must be checked carefully by someone who is accustomed to doing rather than theorizing."[71] As those whom Hilsman surveyed saw it, the Foreign Service produced professionals and provided experience and proper training, whereas the intelligence people were by and large amateurs on leave from academe. As one man put it, if he had a choice between a man who knew everything about history and another who was a professional with operational experience, he would take the operator.[72] Like an experienced policeman walking his beat, the operator might not *see* anything suspicious, but he would be able to *sense* trouble in the offing.

Such criticism referred to central intelligence as it existed at the time. There is no denying that the creators of the ONE had a tendency to organize their business too much along academic lines. Intelligence was usually on a high level of sophistication, but it was so detached that policy makers were frequently not interested in what it had to tell them. The early analysts were not starry-eyed utopians and their view of the world was as informed and as realistic as that of the policy makers. But by keeping aloof from the practical concerns of American foreign policy and defense, they limited the impact of intelligence on the conduct of policy.

Twenty-five years later, analysts are seldom criticized for "excessive intellectualism." Today there is little difference between CIA and State Department personnel as far as background and training are concerned. Nevertheless, intelligence is still frequently criticized for its irrelevance to immediate policy considerations. Such complaints indicate a failure of communication rather than some sort of innate inability to produce relevant intelligence. Policy makers still claim from time to time that the intelligence material told them nothing that they did not already know, told them things they knew were incorrect, or showed them that they knew more about the situation than the analyst. Occasionally this impression may be correct—a junior analyst in the Soviet field reporting to a policy maker with many years experience in the Soviet Union will not be able to report much that is new unless the junior analyst is uncommonly talented. But this kind of dilemma is likely to arise in any organization.

Another complaint frequently heard is that intelligence analysis had been "overcoordinated," presenting only a vague, meaningless level of consensus that conceals many of the most important arguments. If such overcoordinated intelligence contains a warning, it is so well hidden that it fails to warn until it is too late. Complaints about aimless or arbitrary dissemination have already been mentioned—certain materials are distributed too widely, whereas others never reach the individuals most interested in them.[73] Some of these difficulties are mechanical in character and can be overcome without much difficulty; others lie at the core of the intelligence process and involve problems that may never be solved to everyone's satisfaction. Close contact on all levels between intelligence and policy makers is necessary for psychological as well as other reasons. There is frequent resistance against anonymous writings even if they are well reasoned and adequately supported by data. Quite often analysts are not in a position to name the sources behind the analysis or state the assumptions on which it is based. In these circumstances, intelligence officers have to establish their credentials with the policy makers, which they cannot expect to do with formal, impersonal publications. Policy makers are most willing to listen to intelligence analysts they know and trust. Their observations can be of decisive importance from the DCIs downward. The larger the bureaucracy, the greater the danger of anonymity and the risk of the message being lost on its way to the consumer.

From what has been said so far, it would appear that the relationship between intelligence and foreign policy is so full of pitfalls, difficulties of communications, and intrinsic tensions that breakdowns must happen all the time. Yet in actual fact, intelligence usually functions as well as can be expected; it has, in any case, become an essential part of the process in making national security decisions. The relationship between intelligence producers and consumers is more reciprocal than most critics claim. But it must be emphasized that of the two, policy carries the heavier responsibility when things go wrong. Intelligence helps to define what kinds of policy approaches may be workable, while policy exercises not only a daily influence on the intelligence agenda but a long-term influence on overall intelligence capabilities.

Furthermore, intelligence is not always the initial source of information setting the policy process in motion. Many other sources may provide that stimulus—diplomatic exchanges, the media, and even scholarship. But once the policy process is under way, intelligence becomes essential to the government's pool of information, reaching levels of data otherwise inaccessible.

Compared with the state of affairs thirty years ago, there is now closer contact between intelligence officers in the field and analysts in Washington and their policymaking consumers. Thirty years ago HUMINT, which still accounts for a significant part of the more exciting foreign intelligence, was much less well regarded because it was of much poorer quality and less timely. Since then standards have been set, methods of communication have improved, and field stations are given a better idea of what sort of reporting is expected from them. The various kinds of intelligence are now more effectively integrated. The distinction between what can be obtained by human sources and what by technical means is better understood. As a result, no serious foreign policy official would want to be without intelligence reporting today.

Intelligence has come to be recognized as a profession. It is no longer regarded as an avocation to be practiced by gentlemen for brief periods when their country needs their services. Consequently, other professional services in the U.S. government—the soldiers and the diplomats—have come to accept intelligence professionals as legitimate, important members of the country's team abroad and of the government establishment in Washington. This change in attitude was easiest for the professional military services to make; for a long time conventional Foreign Service officers looked upon intelligence as a distasteful but temporary burden, which would disappear once the world returned to sanity.[74]

Thus, the picture is by no means one of unrelieved gloom. For all the ups and downs, the unsolved problems, and the recurring breakdowns in communication, there has been overall progress in the relationship between intelligence collectors, producers, and consumers. There is no room for self-congratulation or for despair, but only for continued efforts aiming at further improvement, mindful of the fact that total and uninterrupted success is beyond human ability.

CHAPTER 4

Early Experiences and Later-Day Trials

I MMEDIATELY after World War II intelligence played a very minor role in U.S. foreign policy. The OSS had been dissolved in September 1945 and for the next two years there was no central intelligence organization. The summary President Truman received every day at noon "was not an evaluated job at all," but simply a synopsis of army, navy, and State Department dispatches.[1] Only with the outbreak of the Korean War in 1950 did central intelligence come into its own. Top U.S. officials decided on foreign policy up to this time according to their own views of the world and on the basis of reports received from American embassies around the world.

Investigating the quality of intelligence reporting before 1950 is therefore largely an academic exercise. The reports were primarily "think pieces," and it is open to doubt whether they were widely read in the higher echelons of the bureaucracy, let alone by the president. Most "sensitive" information was received from refugees, returned prisoners of war, and occasional defectors.[2] At that time there was no aerial reconnaissance and decryptions, if any, produced little of interest about the all-important subject of the Soviet Union's intentions.

Assessments of the immediate postwar period are nevertheless of a certain interest. To a large extent postwar intelligence came from the same people who had written the OSS reports during World War II, and who were again in key positions during the 1950s and 1960s. The OSS had no "party line," and there were considerable differences between various departments. Some were to the right of center, but the majority was liberal, extending to sympathies for democratic socialism. There was even a sprinkling of the far left within the community. Reports on the Soviet Union during the war and immediately after were strictly matter-of-fact. The clampdown on Soviet intellectuals was duly noted,[3] but most reports dealt with such recondite topics as the Soviet silk industry. No systematic anti-Soviet bias can be detected in these analyses; on the contrary, there was a tendency to underrate the extent of Soviet ambitions in Eastern Europe and the Balkans. Many U.S. diplomats on the spot, however, took a dimmer view of the situation.

In 1947, the CIA began to publish its *Review of the World Situation as It Relates to the Security of the United States.*[4] It continued to appear for a number of years —referred to as the *Review*—and presents a fairly accurate picture of political thought at its headquarters. The analysis in the very first issue of this monthly journal deserves to be quoted, for it laid out guidelines that long remained in force:

1 Among foreign powers, only the USSR is capable of threatening the security of the United States.
2 The USSR is presently incapable of military aggression outside of Europe and Asia, but is capable of overrunning most of continental Europe, the Near East, Northern China, and Korea.
3 The USSR is unlikely to resort to open military aggression in present circumstances. Its policy is to avoid war, to build up its war potential, and to extend its influence and control by political, economic, and psychological methods. In this it is deliberately conducting political, economic, and psychological warfare against the United States.
4 The greatest danger to the security of the U.S. is the possibility of economic collapse in Western Europe and the consequent accession of power to Communist elements.
5 Stabilization and recovery in Europe and Asia would tend to redress the balance of power and thereby to restrain the USSR.
6 From the point of view of containing the USSR and eventually redressing the balance of power the order of priority among the major regions of Europe and Asia is:
   a   Western Europe;
   b   the Near and Middle East . . . ; and
   c   the Far East.[5]

Looking back, this analysis seems to have been a fairly realistic estimate, although "Asia Firsters" would dispute the "one-sided orientation of the Europhiles," and those who think Communist advances should have gone unopposed would argue that Soviet interests and ambitions should have been met with greater sympathy. Subsequent CIA assessments were less sanguine—the Communists had launched a concerted campaign of disorders, strikes, and sabotage in France and Italy. The overriding objective of Soviet policy was to defeat the European recovery program without the risk of war. The trend in Europe was generally favorable, but the immediate prospect was grim.[6]

One month later the *Review* took a more optimistic attitude. The European Communist parties, with Soviet approval, were falling back upon the electoral process. There was a chance that the Kremlin was revising its policy and seeking an accommodation with the West—without giving up its ultimate objectives.[7] This particular assessment contained a major misreading of the situation, for it predicted that the Soviet Union was retreating from violent action because it wanted the Communists to do well in the upcoming Czechoslovakian election. Any astute observer should have known that the Communists did not trust the outcome of free elections after their electoral failures in Hungary and Poland. Five days after publication of the CIA assessment, the non-Communist ministers in Prague were forced to resign, and the Communists carried out their coup in Prague, a watershed in the postwar history of Europe and of the cold war.

The following CIA assessment, not surprisingly, was markedly more pessimistic. Communists had made progress in Europe and Asia; Europe's resistance had stiffened, but the situation in Italy and France remained precarious; and the existence of Chaing Kai-shek's government was threatened.[8] The CIA seems to have been oblivious to the quarrel between Tito and Stalin that led to the expulsion of Yugoslavia from the Cominform in 1948, even though Belgrade and Moscow feuded openly for several months before the final break.[9] Once the split had taken place, however, there was a tendency to exaggerate its importance. The CIA predicted correctly that it would probably cause a disruptive purge of Communist ranks, but the announcement that it would "complete the elimination of communism as a formidable political movement in Western Europe" proved to be premature, to say the least.[10] Yugoslavia's chances of survival were rated high. There would be a very hostile (and ultimately ineffective) propaganda campaign, but no direct Soviet military aggression.[11]

Estimates on the situation in Asia also showed political astuteness. An evaluation in early 1950 predicted that most of the crises during 1950 would arise in Asia, the new Chinese government would be recognized by most nations, and there was danger that India and Pakistan would go to war.[12] Even before this, the *Review* had stated that within the next two years the French would fail to hold Indochina.[13] In June 1950 a theme appeared that was to play an important role in U.S.-European relations in later years, that of neutralist stirrings in Western Europe and European fears that the United States might use the North Atlantic Treaty to prepare for war. Hence, Europeans were discussing the idea of a "third force," or, at the very least, expressing the desire to have an independent European component in the Atlantic Community.[14]

A slightly manic-depressive tendency was evident in these forecasts, or at least an inclination to exaggerate, whether the tidings were good or bad. Whenever an immediate crisis had passed, a mild case of misplaced euphoria ensued. For example, the Berlin blockade had never been appraised in an alarmist manner. It was seen as consistent with the Soviet goal of compelling the Western powers to reopen four-power negotiations with respect to Germany as a whole.[15]

When the Berlin blockade ended in early May 1949, there were visions of détente. The U.S.S.R. had two basic alternatives: to enter negotiations in an attempt to delay and confuse Western policy, or to attempt reaching an agreement that would remove Germany as a cause of friction, thus making détente possible. The CIA analysts favored the second choice,[16] but Stalin did not. One year later, following the outbreak of the Korean War, which took intelligence by surprise, there was again deep CIA pessimism.[17] The Soviet Union was likely to create a whole series of incidents comparable to Korea, while Western military reserves were inadequate to cope with such contingencies. A general war, in which all Western Europe and most of Asia could probably be quickly overrun, seemed to be a real possibility.[18]

Coverage of East European affairs was generally accurate, but again the intelligence evaluators were inclined to be a little too optimistic. They assumed, for instance, that the socialist and other democratic parties in Poland would be permitted a measure of independence for a long time to come.[19] Less than a year later, in December 1948, the forced merger of Socialist and Communist parties took place. Yet their optimism was justified for Finland and Greece. They did not think a direct Soviet takeover in Finland was imminent because the U.S.S.R. was too preoccupied with other parts of the world. In Greece they saw the main danger in an attack from outside, but this seemed unlikely because it would lead to a general war, which the Soviet Union did not want.[20]

Intelligence analysts, like many others, were long fascinated by General Charles de Gaulle, subjecting his actions and ideas to detailed scrutiny. His prewar outlook was said to have been rightist, "with semifascist tendencies"; during the war he entered into an alliance with the leftist-dominated resistance movement, but only because he was "forced by circumstances." This approach did not betray very deep knowledge of Gaullism. The CIA predictions of October 1948 were not much better. It appeared inevitable that de Gaulle would return to power soon—if not upon the fall of the current government, then certainly after the next one.[21]

Analysis and prediction were more accurate for West Germany and Britain. The results of the first all-German elections were meticulously analyzed and their political consequences convincingly outlined by a CIA writer, or group of writers, who obviously possessed intimate knowledge of Germany and who had social democratic sympathies.[22] Of almost equal excellence were the reports and forecasts on Britain. It was realized that Britain would have to choose soon between Europe and the Commonwealth. In view of its reduced power position and the continuing struggle for economic recovery, Britain was no longer a wholly free agent and could not undertake a major defense effort unless sacrifices of wartime dimensions were imposed or additional outside assistance provided.[23]

In August 1949, a special study on "Europe's will to resist," offered an optimistic picture. Britain was showing the greatest determination to resist, and lacking a Communist threat from within, was more capable of self-defense than the other countries studied. But in France and Italy also, the will to resist aggression had increased by comparison with earlier periods and Organization of European Economic Communities (OEEC) participation had boosted morale. There, as elsewhere, the continuation of U.S. economic aid was of great importance. The comments on the Netherlands are of considerable interest for their perspicacity:

> The will of the Netherlands to resist aggression is not surpassed by that of any other North Atlantic power. The deep religious convictions of the Dutch and their emphasis on the maintenance of the basic human freedoms make them irrevocably opposed to Communism. Moreover, the extension of Soviet influence over the small countries of Eastern Europe and Czechoslovakia brought home to the Dutch the menace of the USSR and was a principal factor in impelling them to abandon the U.N. as their principal bastion of security in favor of regional arrangements.[24]

Some general observations emerge from reading the intelligence reports of the period from 1945–50. The assessments were based almost entirely on open sources and diplomatic reports. If information was received from covert sources, it was of no discernable consequence. The reports from East European embassies, and above all George Kennan's famous memorandum (telegram number 511) from Moscow had infinitely greater impact. At first these warnings were dismissed rather easily in Washington. As Robert Falson, then a young U.S. diplomat in Budapest, later wrote, "For months

I know we were regarded by those in the State Department as Russo-phobes if not warmongers and that our reporting was discounted."[25] Eventually the facts created by the Russians in Eastern Europe and the Balkans began to register. In this process of political reorientation, the CIA played no significant role, except perhaps by providing occasional information on Soviet military capabilities that said the Russians did not intend to launch a general war.[26]

The heavy emphasis on Europe in intelligence coverage is not surprising, as Europe and China were the main political battlefields of the immediate postwar period. While there was nothing the United States could do about the outcome of the struggle in mainland China, its capacity to act was much greater in Europe. If reporting was biased, this appeared most clearly in the tendency to underrate Soviet ambitions and the tenacity with which these were pursued. The CIA was certainly not prepared for the ruthlessness with which the non-Communist forces in Eastern Europe were eliminated or for the internal purges and show trials that followed.

United States intelligence had not believed the danger of war very great until the Korean War provided a new catalyst to its thinking. Suddenly the estimates changed:

> On the basis that the longterm object of the Soviet rulers is immutable and dynamic [*sic*], and that the Western powers are not prepared to succumb to Soviet domination without a fight, there is, and will continue to be, grave danger of war between the Soviet Union and its satellites on one hand, and the Western powers and their allies on the other.[27]

This assessment estimated that the risk would exist for the next four years, by which time the NATO forces in Europe would be built up to minimum strength; the year of maximum danger would be 1952. Such predictions may seem alarmist in retrospect, yet one should not forget that in 1950 the Soviet Union and China were allies, continental Europe was a military vacuum, and American rearmament did not begin until after the Korean War broke out.

It should be said in fairness that the late Stalin period was not an easy one for predictions of any kind. There should have been few illusions about Soviet intentions, but Soviet capacity to pursue them was another matter; moreover, the Kremlin's policies were by no means consistent. All the same, it appeared that the CIA and other intelligence groups had little expertise in Soviet affairs. The main thrust of U.S. intelligence during the war had been in different directions, so a great deal of effort had to be devoted to retraining and to the acquisition of new expertise.

Overall, the quality of intelligence was as good as could be expected from a relatively small, recently established service with little authentic information from inside the Communist countries. In these circumstances, intelligence could not provide warnings against unpleasant surprises, nor was it aware of welcome developments, such as Tito's defection or, later on, the Sino-Soviet split. But its comments were sensible, and its general evaluation was more often right than wrong. It is a moot point whether its record was superior to that of well-informed and experienced newspapermen or of seasoned students of international affairs. The Dulles-Jackson-Correa report noted in 1950 that State Department intelligence produced "Ph.D. intelligence, scholastically admirable but of somewhat limited use in the day-to-day formulation of policy." The policy planning staff and the regional offices of the State Department were the principal recipients.[28] It would no doubt have been more valuable and certainly more exciting to have spies in the Kremlin as well as in the other capitals of the world. But in the absence of such highly placed sources "Ph.D. intelligence"—namely, detailed and reliable background information—was preferable to no information at all. Policy makers, however wise and experienced, unless they happened to be experts in the field, no doubt benefited.

During the 1950s, Soviet military capabilities and intentions remained the most important topic for American intelligence. Before examining the CIA record in this respect, assessments on three related topics ought to be mentioned: the question of Stalin's succession, the turbulence in Eastern Europe, and the arrival of the Sino-Soviet conflict.

The issue of Stalin's succession first came up, as far as can be ascertained, in an ORE memorandum in January 1948. At the time, Molotov appeared to be the most likely candidate, and several reasons were given to explain why the Soviet Union was more likely to be governed by a single heir than by a committee. According to that estimate, the succession was likely to be orderly, with only insignificant political effects expected. The estimate did not, however, rule out a struggle for power within the elite if the U.S.S.R. were confronted by a series of domestic or foreign adversities. Such a struggle would result in the "rapid disintegration of the Soviet Union," which was an astonishingly sweeping prediction on the part of otherwise cautious people. State Department intelligence went on record with two important (and prophetic) reservations to this estimate: the concentration of power in the hands of one man after Stalin's death would probably not occur at once, and because the distribution of power in the Politburo was not stable, there might well be several "palace revolutions" before the real successor to Stalin could consolidate his position. That is, of course, exactly what happened.[29]

In a special estimate on the probable consequences of Stalin's death

(5 March 1953), the CIA provided an estimate of remarkable fairness and accuracy. It noted that while Stalin had been a ruthless autocrat determined to spread Soviet power, he did not allow his ambition to lead him into a reckless course of action. His status in the Soviet Union had been that of a demigod, so his death was bound to be a psychological shock for many Russians. By and large, however, the regime was stable; even if a struggle between his successors should break out, the Communist hold on power was not likely to be shaken quickly. The CIA expected Stalin's successors to continue his policy in both domestic and foreign affairs. Yet the new leaders would lack Stalin's prestige; they would be unsure of themselves in the face of difficult decisions, and while the immediate transfer of power had been smooth, a struggle for supremacy might break out at any time. As Mao's stature as a leader was bound to increase, the Moscow leadership would probably deal cautiously with him to avoid the development of serious strains in Sino-Soviet relations.[30] This assessment did not foresee the gradual and partial de-Stalinization under Khrushchev; that phenomenon still lay three years in the future. Given the fact that the assessment was produced within a few days after Stalin's death, it is an impressive piece of work.

Intelligence was less perspicacious with regard to the unrest among the Soviet satellites, which broke out soon after Stalin's death. The uprisings in East Berlin in 1953 and Poznan in 1956 came as a surprise, even though the steady stream of refugees testified that there was ferment in East Germany. There was no inkling that 1956 would be the year of major revolts in Hungary and Poland.[31] A subsequent NIE explained that Moscow apparently had not recognized or seriously attempted to cope with discontent in the satellites. Generally speaking, Moscow had underestimated the strength of forces seeking reform and change.[32] The intelligence community had shared this mistake. The most likely explanation for which would seem to be that although information on unrest was available in the form of reports forwarded by Radio Free Europe and other sources, it did not receive sufficient attention.

Nor was the intelligence community successful in its analysis of the growing tensions within the Sino-Soviet alliance. During the 1950s divergencies in the ideological field became apparent, the two regimes had followed different economic policies and China had reacted bitterly to Khrushchev's de-Stalinization campaign. Nevertheless, the intelligence estimates seemed to rule out any serious conflict. It was conceded that Russia and China had separate and potentially conflicting national objectives, but "they will certainly maintain a relationship of close alliance throughout the period of this estimate." China depended on the Soviet Union for support of its economic and military programs, and even if some minor points of friction arose in the next few years, there were basic points of agreement: ideological bonds, common hostility to the United States, and the belief that their concerted political and economic activities were mutually beneficial. Intelligence concluded that the advantages of this interdependence were fully appreciated in both Moscow and Peking.[33]

This was clearly a serious misreading of developments. Intelligence should have taken into account that the Sino-Soviet relationship was shaky from the very beginning; the precedent of Yugoslavia should have been given more weight, especially because, as with Yugoslavia, communism had not been imposed on China from outside and the Soviet hold was correspondingly weak. Finally, "common ideology" was naively overrated as a cohesive factor. Misperceptions about Chinese politics continued to bedevil U.S. intelligence for many years to come.[34]

The possibility of Soviet military attack overshadowed all other issues facing U.S. intelligence for many years after the war. Perhaps the first to sound the tocsin (in 1948) was General Lucius Clay, commander in chief in Germany. The CIA, in one of its very first estimates, thought a Soviet attack unlikely during the next two months, but would not go any further. After the Korean War began, the appraisals became very pessimistic: the Soviets had a crushing superiority; although the West was now making efforts to counter the threat, [they] would not be effective for years to come. Would the Russians wait that long, or would they launch a preventive war? A special estimate published in October 1951 noted a

> constant and serious threat to the security of the NATO powers. Politically, economically, and militarily the Soviet Bloc is capable of undertaking a major war. Its overall strength and war potential should increase considerably by mid-1954. . . . In view of the high state of war-readiness of the Soviet economy and armed forces, the USSR is at present capable of initiating hostilities against the NATO powers with little or no warning.[35]

This estimate—and there were many of its kind over the coming years —was based on the following assumptions:

1.   The internal position of the Soviet government was now more secure than at any time since 1971 and it was also in effective control of the Soviet bloc and most Communist parties.

2.   Its ultimate objective was to achieve a Communist world order dominated by the U.S.S.R. It operated on the premise of a permanent conflict with the West.

3.   The immediate Soviet aim in Europe was to obstruct the further growth of Western strength and unity, to divide the Western powers, and to frustrate their rearmament plans.

4.   In contrast to the West, the Soviet leadership could act quickly,

secretly, and decisively, unencumbered by public opinion and parliamentary restraints. It could use Communist ideology as a magnet for attracting local and foreign support.

It is difficult to quarrel with these propositions. Any reader of *Pravda* and of Stalin's speeches was bound to reach similar conclusions. The argument frequently voiced in later years—that the Soviet leaders did not really mean what they were saying—does not deserve to be taken seriously. The CIA did not assert that Soviet military attacks were inevitable, either on the local or global level. Assessments took a "temporary relaxation of international tensions" into account but regarded it as a tactical shift, a "different method of political and psychological warfare, to lull the West into a false sense of security and undermine growing NATO strength."[36] As central intelligence saw it, there was a basic threat in the aggressive nature of the Soviet regime on the one hand, and Soviet military superiority and war preparedness on the other.

The assessment was correct as far as it went, but it was incomplete. It was based on Soviet proclamations and the intentions behind them. But it certainly overrated Soviet *capabilities.* In a way it was a purely defensive estimate, focusing almost entirely on ultimate Soviet aims. The fact that a great deal could be done by non-Communist powers to thwart these designs was hardly mentioned. While some argue that an intelligence agency has no business discussing the policies of its own government, it is also true that these policies have a direct bearing on evaluation of the other side. Reviewing Soviet intentions in a vacuum, as it were, was to undertake the task with a one-sided perspective.

Furthermore, the military argument was inconsistent. It claimed that the main danger would be around 1952, but said that the Soviet war potential would substantially increase by mid-1954. A 1952 estimate seems to have recognized this inconsistency, announcing that while the Soviet Union was now much better prepared to support a major war effort than it had been in 1940, and while it had a significant quantitative superiority over the Western powers, "the Kremlin almost certainly estimates that in some respects the position of the West is stronger than it was in the early postwar years."[37] Thus, even at the height of tension, the CIA did not argue that war was the most likely possibility. The Soviet Union would continue political warfare, trying to isolate the United States and supporting various armed rebellions in the Third World. But a Communist armed revolt in the West had no prospect of success, nor were conditions ripe for bringing additional areas into the bloc through armed aggression without the serious risk of global war.[38] This was a basically correct appraisal. It was made in Stalin's last year of life, when the world situation was more difficult than ever to interpret. According to Khrushchev and other Soviet sources, Stalin had by that time convinced himself that a third world war was inevitable, but this was not the same as saying that he was actively preparing an all-out attack.

The CIA almost certainly overestimated Soviet conventional strength. It is quite likely that the Communist bloc, including China, had some nine million soldiers under arms at the time. But it is most unlikely that Stalin would have been able (as one estimate argued) to launch simultaneous attacks (each with sufficient air support) against Western Europe (including Italy) with seventy to ninety line divisions; against the Near and Middle East with twenty-five line divisions; against the Far East with twenty-five divisions; and with an aerial bombardment against Britain, Canada, and the United States.[39]

Even the help of Chinese divisions would not have been sufficient for so ambitious a design. The estimate was not just an exercise in worst-case analysis, it verged on paranoia. The Soviet Union had suffered tremendous losses in World War II; its economy could not continue indefinitely on a wartime footing and had already been converted to reconstruction in substantial part. The Soviets did have a great many divisions, but they were usually understrength; in any case, America's nuclear weapons made any Soviet attack infinitely more risky. In short, the assessments overrated Soviet strength and underrated Soviet prudence and caution. Stalin wanted to expand his sphere of domination, but unlike Hitler, he felt no pressure to do so within a given number of months or years.

By late 1957, Washington had taken account of the changes in Soviet foreign policy since Stalin's death. There had been "change and innovation, flexibility, and pragmatism." The conflict was still thought to be irreconcilable, but the confidence shown by the new Soviet leaders augured a change in tactics. Their growing nuclear capabilities gave them greater freedom of action in local situations, and the use of threats would remain a basic element in Soviet policy. There would be warfare by proxy, perhaps even Soviet "volunteers" fighting in foreign parts. Thus the risk of general war as a result of miscalculation could actually increase. But in general the Soviet leaders preferred to achieve their objectives by nonmilitary means. The concept of "peaceful coexistence" was to promote divisions within the Western world while Soviet influence increased in the key underdeveloped areas of the world.[40]

The 1958 *Important Points in the Estimate of the World Situation* likewise made a number of long-range predictions that were borne out by subsequent events. The United States and the U.S.S.R. would soon achieve a state of mutual deterrence under which each would try to avoid a general nuclear conflict. There was no indication of deterioration or disintegration as far as Soviet power, policy, or determination to achieve its aims was concerned. But there were evolutionary changes going on in Soviet society that might ultimately turn Russia into a nation with which the Free World could live more peacefully. But the estimate also warned that the near future was likely to witness a dangerous jockeying for position between the United States and the U.S.S.R., "involving the most difficult calculations of risk of actions or inactions in particular situations." Above all, the *Estimate* foresaw a gradual erosion of the Western Alliance:

> Under these circumstances, (a) some friendly nations fear that the U.S. will no longer be willing to threaten nuclear retaliation in order to deter Soviet actions in matters of vital concern to them; (b) the Soviets will take more bold actions in the field of economic penetration and subversion, perhaps in the area of limited war; and (c) there will be a weakening in the Free World Alliance, less confidence in U.S. leadership and military power, increased respect for Russian achievements in science, technology, rocketry, and nuclear weapons, more susceptibility to Russian propaganda for East West negotiations, all in the hope of escape from tension.[41]

There remained one crucial problem which plagued the intelligence community for many years: Soviet nuclear strength. It has been mentioned that American intelligence underestimated the speed with which the U.S.S.R. was able to develop an offensive nuclear capacity. In October 1949, a special group consisting of members of the various intelligence services began a long series of meetings to consider what this unpleasant surprise meant for the security of the United States. Their tentative report (published in April 1950) stated that the Soviets would probably have a stockpile of one hundred atomic bombs by 1953, perhaps twice as many sometime between mid-1954 and the end of 1955, and that it had produced or could easily produce enough TU-4s (comparable to B-29s) to attempt the delivery of all bombs in its possession against key U.S. targets.[42]

But *would* the Soviet leaders engage in such a course of action? The CIA admitted there was no factual information permitting an authoritative answer, but their belief was that they would probably *not* do so unless they gained military superiority and at the same time lost confidence in the inevitable collapse of capitalism. The Soviets would launch a nuclear attack only if they had no reason to fear retaliation or, more frighteningly, as the result of miscalculation.

Having underrated Soviet capacity to produce an atomic bomb, one might have expected U.S. intelligence to be more cautious in its future scientific-technological forecasts, but it was not. An NIE of November 1952 was unduly skeptical about the other side's ability to produce a thermonuclear device; some nine months later the Russians detonated their first hydrogen bomb.[43] An intelligence estimate prepared for the

National Security Council in 1956 went even further astray in its prognosis that the Soviet Union would not have an intercontinental ballistic missile for another five years—it had one within a year.⁴⁴ Most U.S. nuclear scientists had shared the "conservative" views of the CIA. In fact it seems likely that the underestimation of Soviet scientific and technical ability was due not to any independent sources—which did not exist at the time —but on the mistaken expectations of American physicists themselves.

By way of overcompensation for recent surprises, Washington showed a tendency to overrate the Soviet nuclear potential for a while. The estimate that Russia would have 200 atomic bombs by 1953 was probably exaggerated, and the TU-4 could reach the United States only on a one-way, Kamikaze-type mission. The first true Soviet intercontinental bomber (the TU-95) appeared only in 1955; by 1960 only 135 seemed to have been in operation. Yet the CIA had argued in July 1954 that the U.S.S.R. could already launch 850 long-range aircraft against the United States and that by 1957 this number could be increased to 1,000.⁴⁵

The year 1956 was not only that of the abortive Hungarian Revolution, but also of the surprise Anglo-French invasion of Egypt. President Eisenhower subsequently made it known through his press secretary, James Hagerty, that he got his information through the press: "The attack had come as a complete surprise to us." Allen Dulles was furious: in a deliberate leak (and in articles published in later years) he charged that the president would have known what was going to happen if he had only read the CIA reports.⁴⁶ Even today we cannot say whether Eisenhower or his chief of intelligence was right, partly because the daily flow of intelligence in 1956 is not accessible, but mainly because it raises the important question of what constitutes a "warning."

The U.S. government received information from many quarters that the use of force against Nasser was a likely option; British Prime Minister Anthony Eden had said so himself in his communications with American leaders. The military buildup itself was not kept secret. Yet there was always an element of doubt. Perhaps the British and French were engaged in a war of nerves against Nasser to reinforce their diplomatic demands. Or perhaps they were trying to destabilize his regime by means short of a full-scale military mission. A SNIE dated 19 September 1956 concluded that the temptation for the British and the French to use force would be great over the next few weeks. On balance, however, the CIA believed that military action would come only in the event of some new provocation, such as violence to British and French nationals or property in Egypt. In such a case the two powers might use force even without U.S. support. Lastly, it was thought possible, but unlikely, that the Arab-Israeli conflict would resume in such a way as to furnish an occasion for British-French military intervention against Nasser.[47] By the time this estimate was published, two dates that had been set by the British for an invasion had already passed. Nothing certain could have been known to the CIA about "collusion" with Israel; a high-level delegation left for Paris only ten days *after* the estimate was issued. But the possibility of such cooperation should certainly have been taken into account, in spite of Anthony Eden's well-known hostility to Israel. American intelligence clearly underrated how hurt and humiliated the governments of Britain and France had been by Nasser's unilateral action in nationalizing the Suez Canal Company.

During the weeks preceding the Israeli and Anglo-French invasions, Washington received contradictory intelligence reports. Some sources were certain that an invasion was impending, others discounted its likelihood.[48] So both the president and his director of intelligence were correct: one in claiming that he had not been told in advance of the Suez expedition —certainly not explicitly—the other in insisting that there had been frequent warnings. Like all realistic assessments, these had been couched in careful language and riddled with all kinds of stipulations and provisos.

In closed session Allen Dulles was hard pressed by several senators as to whether events in Poland, Hungary, and the Middle East had taken his agency by surprise. Dulles answered:

> Senator Mansfield, it is something like spontaneous combustion. You know that a mass is likely to erupt and burst and go into flames. It is extremely difficult to predict the exact day and hour when that would happen. These movements are touched off by labor unrest here and there, by labor conditions that become intolerable, by political pressures and by a great variety of events. We were not caught by surprise as to the general condition or the general reactions, except in Hungary it went beyond what we expected.[49]

Dulles insisted that no one could possibly predict the exact day when such "spontaneous combustion" would happen; all the same, he had anticipated that Hungary would move first. As for the Middle East, his feeling was that the performance of the intelligence community had been satisfactory. American intelligence had been quite well informed about the events leading up to the Israeli attack, and when the British and French forces moved in no surprise was involved.

Unfortunately, the intelligence records themselves do not quite bear out this assessment. There were reports about growing tension in Poland and Hungary; indeed, one could have learned that much from the radio. But there was no clear indication that there would be some kind of major upheaval. In other words it was not—as Dulles would have had it—just a question of when it would happen, for the CIA did not seriously consider the possibility of an open uprising. As for events in the Middle East, the records reveal no assessment specifically pointing out the high probability of an Israeli attack and of Anglo-French intervention.

Allen Dulles counts the 1958 coup in Iraq, which toppled the monarchy in favor of General Kassem's radical republican regime, as one of the CIA failures that occurred under his leadership. He told an executive session of the Senate Foreign Relations Committee in 1958 that the CIA had failed in Iraq. He said that rumors of plots and assassinations were extremely common in the Middle East, that hardly a day passed without such reports, and that it was consequently very hard to isolate the small amount of valuable information: "I do not state this as an alibi, but the government itself, which was one of the few governments in the Middle East that had a reasonably good security service, was caught entirely napping."[50]

The CIA failure in Iraq continued to bother Dulles in later years, and he returned to the subject in his book on "the craft of intelligence." But the true failure was not that the CIA (and the Iraqi police) had been unaware of the conspiracy against Nuri Said and the Hashemites, but the basic assumption that the Iraqi regime was stable and that there was not much reason for apprehension.[51]

A State Department intelligence report predicted in early 1959 that a "drift into a Communist takeover of power" was already perilously close in Iraq. Largely by default, the Communist party was winning a major victory.[52] Yet Kassem lasted another four years, his honeymoon with the Communists was of short duration, and in the next coup many Communists were massacred. It is perfectly true that when this report was composed, the Communists were making headway, but the analysts failed to realize that their influence was not deeply rooted, and, above all, that the key positions in the army and police force were not in their hands.[53] Within a few months Kassem had turned against the Communists and little remained of their erstwhile influence.

Intelligence from Middle Eastern capitals was generally of mixed quality, despite the fact that it was possible to operate much more freely there than in the Communist countries. For example, OIR reported in April 1957 that recent events in Jordan had been building toward a showdown between King Hussein and the extreme nationalists. Army support for the king could not be regarded as assured, nor could the ability of the king to act decisively at the right time be taken for granted.[54] This prediction was right about the showdown, but its fears proved unfounded. The crisis occurred within eight days after publication of the report; the king prevailed with relative ease.

On the other hand, an assessment of the situation in Egypt managed to misread the situation in almost every essential respect. Egypt and Syria were united as the United Arab Republic at the time, and while the report foresaw "serious internal and external difficulties for an extended period of time," it also said that it was "unlikely that the union will break apart, at least during the next year or two." Break apart it did, and with quite a noise, within eighteen months. The same report also noted that "a return to the 1955–57 honeymoon period in Soviet-UAR relations was unlikely" —again a mistaken asumption. Looking a little further ahead it said: "Nasser's death from natural causes, however, would be much less likely to disturb the relationship between Cairo and the [Soviet] bloc, since the value of cooperation would probably be equally apparent to his successors."[55]

Nasser did die of natural causes, but the value of cooperation was not appreciated by his successor, and the Russians were duly expelled from Egypt. In the case of Egypt, Washington analysts had overrated the importance and duration of Middle Eastern alliances and mergers. Perhaps they watched events in the Arab World through Western glasses, in which case they could hardly avoid the tendency to regard an alliance (let alone a merger between two countries) as a solemn and lasting affair. They were mistaken in assuming that Nasser's ambitions in the Middle East, Asia, and Africa were bound to lead him into a collision with the Soviets, ruling out a division of labor. They also failed to realize that Nasser's weak power base set narrow limits to what he could achieve, and that his ambitions would eventually drive him into greater dependence on Moscow.

In the context of two decades, an evaluation of the perceived role of Saudi Arabia as a "disruptive force in Western-Arab relations" makes interesting reading. The kingdom was seen as a "problem state even in a problem area of the world"; it encouraged neutralist and anti-Western groups in all the Arab countries. In view of the contradictions inherent in its character and the perspectives of its regime, no significant improvement in relations between Saudi Arabia and the United States was likely so long as that regime remained in power. "The Saudi policy is such that far from tending to work toward a solution of the basic problems of the area, it tends to complicate the problems and to harden existing attitudes toward them." As far as survival of the regime was concerned:

> Saud's failure to make a constructive approach to the Saudi internal situation had led to the development of dissidence on all levels of Saudi society. Eventually, these, now-fragmented, may find common cause and engage in assassination or terrorism as a prelude to complete overthrow of the regime.[56]

Washington saw the shortcomings of the regime clearly, but it overestimated the power of the opposition. The government was weak, but its opponents were even weaker. The very conservatism of King Saud, who lasted for another six years, was his strength. Given the character of the Saudi regime, any other policy would probably have brought about the downfall of the dynasty. Faisal, Saud's successor, was wise not to pursue a radically different course himself. Saudi Arabia was soon driven into a much closer relationship with Washington by the hostility of Nasser and his allies. The subsequent story of the U.S.-Saudi entente is well known.

The difficulties of political forecasting emerge clearly from a post mortem of two intelligence memoranda by the directorate of current intelligence. One, which appeared in 1965, dealt with instability in Latin America; the other, published the next year, discussed the likelihood of coups in various parts of Africa.[57] The memorandum on Latin America correctly noted that instability there was endemic, and that the factors responsible —economic difficulties, ineffective government, distaste for the old order, and so on—varied from country to country. The situation was considered most critical in the Dominican Republic, Bolivia, Haiti, Panama, Guatemala, Ecuador, Honduras, Uruguay, Colombia, Venezuela, Argentina, and British Guiana. These countries were ranked in order of "criticality" and intelligence concluded that a coup in any one of them was likely to happen quickly, with little or no prior warning. Yet no coup took place for five years afterward in the Dominican Republic, Haiti, Guatemala, Honduras, Uruguay, Venezuela, or British Guiana. In Ecuador there was that rare thing, a civilian democratic coup in 1966, and in Argentina the Ilia government was overthrown the same year. But in Colombia there was a peaceful change, and even in Bolivia, a country of innumerable coups, this period was one of relative calm (General Ortuno, who had come to power in Bolivia in 1965, perished in an aircraft crash, not of human violence). This is not to deny that the situation in all of the countries mentioned was critical. The assessment of the analysts was perfectly sensible. In Uruguay, for instance, the government came under heavy pressure from the Montoneros; eventually the Congress gave President Areco dictatorial power to cope with the situation. On the other hand, violent change occurred during 1968 in Peru, which had been considered relatively stable. Nor did the memorandum anticipate Allende's rise in Chile, the massive riots of 1970 in Trinidad, or the emergence in 1968 of a full-fledged military dictatorship in Brazil. In such a volatile situation as Latin America virtually anything can happen. In such circumstances, long-term specific forecasts are risky, to say the least.

The analysts seemed to score better with their predictions on Africa. The memorandum noted that at the time of writing (1966), only a few countries there seemed immune to coups. Change could come at almost any time, and these countries appeared to be the best candidates for "quick and perhaps violent change": Burundi/Rwanda, Dahomey, Ethiopia, Nigeria,

Uganda, and Sudan. Within four months after the publication of the memorandum, Prince Charles had deposed his father in Burundi; within the same period General Ironsi had been overthrown in Nigeria. Coups took place in Dahomey in 1967 and 1969. There were riots in Addis Ababa in 1966, but Emperor Haile Selassie stayed in power for almost another decade. General Idi Amin took over in Uganda, but five years later. The expected coup in Sudan (led by Numeiri) eventually took place, but also with a delay of four years. Thus, governments were overthrown in all the countries on the list of critical countries, at first sight an impressive record of forecasting. Yet there were also coups in most of the other African countries, for instance, Togo in 1967, Mali, Sierra Leone, Chad, and the Congo in 1968. In 1969, there was even a coup in Somalia, which the authors of the memorandum had singled out as "stable enough to be in no danger now." All of which showed again how very risky specific forecasts about coups are, even where they are the rule rather than the exception.[58]

In contrast to the CIA, the State Department's intelligence section relied upon reports from its diplomats in the field (a very important source) and some of the memoranda supplied by other sections of the intelligence community. Even though it lacked the full collection resources of the CIA, some of the INR's "Intelligence Reports" were influential; quite a few of them were prepared for, or became part of, the National Intelligence Estimates.[59] Two topics especially preoccupied the INR in the 1950s and 1960s: the Soviet Union and Eastern Europe, and Western Europe (particularly France). The general impression is that INR intelligence was usually good, and sometimes excellent.

Analysts for the INR correctly assessed the reasons for and circumstances leading to Beria's downfall and were quick to identify Nikita Khrushchev as the central figure in the Soviet "collective leadership." They predicted the emergence of a dissident movement in the post-Stalin era, but they thought that it would be limited to the intelligentsia, thus underrating the role of the subjugated nationalities. In 1960, they noted that the Soviet Union was preparing itself for a showdown with China "even at a risk of causing an open break." But they were mistaken in assuming that it was "more likely that a partial accommodation or truce would be reached," and erred even more profoundly when they claimed that only "irrationality" would cause a break, for "both powers acting rationally must realize that they will benefit more by remaining closely allied."[60] This argument was based on misconceptions about rationality in politics in general, and it clearly underrated the importance of the national component in both Soviet and Chinese foreign policy.

The INR provided sensible analyses of Soviet attitudes toward negotiations with the West, and its interpretations of Soviet attitudes toward peaceful coexistence, limited détente, and disarmament were cogent. The INR analysts also noted fairly early that the Third World would be the most important area of struggle between the two blocs.[61] But some assessments on Eastern Europe had shared a myopia widespread in the intelligence community. Before the Hungarian uprising in 1956, the general tendency had been to overrate the strength of the Soviet hold on the satellites (although the Polish ferment had been duly taken into account). A detailed analysis of the Hungarian events, written many months afterward, concluded that the Hungarians had demonstrated that "a nation can throw off its Communist system, Soviet occupation, and satellite role, changing by force the regime's personalities, policies, and programs," and that it could "abolish a system which had been fully in force for nearly a decade." Yet three years later the INR concluded that the Kadar regime had not been able to live down its past, it had not become respectable, and it was implied that it would not be able to do so in the future, either.[62]

What had gone wrong in both assessments was that prior to 1956, Soviet rule in Eastern Europe seemed unassailable, a monolithic bloc—even though the events of 1953 in East Berlin and Poland should have served as warning signs that Soviet domination was not as secure as it seemed. Once a spontaneous rebellion had occurred, taking the West by surprise, the tendency was to overrate the revolutionary potential in Eastern Europe. But the lesson of 1956 was definitely not that a nation can "throw off its Communist system." The opposite was the case. The Soviets had shown their determination and their ability to retain control of the countries they had occupied in World War II. Intelligence analysts were clearly misled by their sympathy for the Hungarian cause. The same was true with regard to their negative appraisal of Kadar's chances of making his regime respectable, in which intelligence was again guilty of wishful thinking. The idea that the traitor who had helped the Russians to suppress his country should prosper seemed clearly unacceptable; the analysts seemed to have forgotten that virtue is not always rewarded, nor crime punished, in world history.

On non-Communist Europe, the INR had a great many sources at its disposal and most of its reports show an excellent grasp of the situation. In 1957, before the Italian economic *miracolo* really began, the INR predicted that even prolonged prosperity would not eradicate the appeal of Italian Communism. A well-informed review of the British Labor party in 1956 noted its tendency to underestimate the role of communism, which at the time was no more than a tiny cloud on the political horizon. Twenty years later the far left, including sundry Communists, Ex-Communists, and Trotskyites, had become a major force in both the unions and the Labor party.[63]

Even more important was the question of how France was going to deal with the problem of Algeria. At first, the INR underrated de Gaulle. To be precise, it believed that the new consensus of the Fifth Republic was "specious and lacking in depth." For this reason de Gaulle's government would succumb to the same erosions that had eventually destroyed the old. It is quite true that many things might have gone wrong, but not all of them did; consequently, de Gaulle was able to solve the Algerian problem abroad and defeat the extreme Right at home.[64] Not until 1961 did the INR analysts grudgingly agree that only de Gaulle could have led France out of the Algerian quagmire.

Most intelligence reports were well informed and closely reasoned, even those which were proved wrong by subsequent events. Often their learning was not carried easily—it is difficult to imagine Dulles, Herter, or Rusk reading a paper of forty-six single-spaced pages about the extreme Right in France, especially as there were many more of the same awaiting their attention. Granted, the reports were of a high standard, but the fact remains that they contained little, if anything, that was not known and published by observers outside of government. Even if the intelligence reports contained an occasional nugget of additional information or if they enjoyed greater credibility because of their official status, they were hesitant to take clear positions, to accept risks, and to entertain unorthodox ideas. To say this is not to denigrate State Department intelligence because while not startling, the information policy makers received was by and large correct—which was all they could reasonably expect.

The detailed report provided by Allen Dulles to the Senate Foreign Relations Committee in January 1959 is a good example of the strengths and weaknesses of U.S. intelligence. Khrushchev, as Dulles saw it, was firmly in control; the man most likely to succeed him was Frol Kozlov. (This was a good guess, for Kozlov became second secretary of the party in 1961, though he died a few years later.) The CIA estimate up to 1963 was that because the Soviets knew they could not be certain to win a general war they would rely mainly on political struggle. According to CIA figures, the Soviet economic growth rate was very high—two to three times that of the United States—and was expected to continue growing. Soviet GNP was 45 percent that of the United States; in 1965 the figure would be 55 percent. The CIA was mistaken in its projection—by 1982 the Soviet GNP was probably not yet quite 55 percent of the American. On the other hand, the CIA apparently underestimated Soviet defense spending at 16 percent of the total Soviet budget (or 22–23 percent, if indirect expenditure was included). "I would like to tell you that the Soviet Union is a hotbed of unrest and dissatisfaction," Dulles said, but this just wasn't so—all in all, the situation in the Soviet Union was stable. There was some dissent among students, and Dulles dealt at some length with the dissent caused by the publication of *Dr. Zhivago,* but neither of these was a major political factor.[65]

The CIA appraisal of the Soviet Union was, then, realistic, even as seen with the benefit of hindsight. Dulles was also correct when he noted that Eastern Europe was much less stable; the satellites "would revolt tomorrow if they had any chance of getting free."[66] He thought that Poland and Hungary were the most dissatisfied countries, followed by East Germany and probably even Rumania. Only Bulgaria and Czechoslovakia would be slow to join in a revolt. This may have seemed a fairly realistic assessment of the situation at the time, for Hungary was still traumatized and bitter over the events of 1956, and the exodus from East Germany showed no sign of diminishing. Yet as subsequent events were to show, Hungary quieted down, and so did East Germany after the Berlin Wall was built. Rumania, by contrast, began in 1960–61 to detach itself cautiously from Soviet tutelage, and toward the mid-1960s Czechoslovakia became the main focus of dissent in Eastern Europe.

Even the best-informed observer could not have predicted these latter events with any great confidence, though the possibilities probably should have been mentioned. Speaking in January 1959, Allen Dulles must certainly have been aware of the incipient rift between the Soviet Union and China. There was already more or less open dissent between the two major Communist powers on a number of issues, such as Chinese agricultural policy, the "great leap forward," "peaceful coexistence," attitudes toward Yugoslavia, and the Soviet claim as leader of the Communist camp. But the CIA, wedded to the belief that open conflict between Russia and China was most unlikely, belittled the importance of information to the contrary. True, said Dulles "there is some friction," and "Khrushchev and Mao regard each other with misgivings," but the CIA nevertheless expected that "the cohesive factors in the Sino-Soviet alliance will remain stronger than the divisive factors for some years to come."[67]

Finally, Dulles turned to a discussion of Cuba. Castro had just come to power, and Dulles said that this was "a tough one" for the CIA, even though intelligence had not done badly—it had predicted Batista's fall weeks before it happened and had even urged him to depart through "extradiplomatic means." On the whole Dulles took a sanguine view of the situation. "We do not think that Castro himself has any Communist leanings," Dulles said, though he had certain suspicions about Che Guevara. Castro, Dulles said, had shown great courage. If so many people were now executed in Cuba, well, the same had happened in the French Revolution. There had been cruelty and oppression before Castro's victory and "when you have a revolution you kill your enemies. It will probably go much too far but they have to go through this." But the present cabinet in Cuba was not a bad cabinet. American intervention had had disastrous effects in the hemisphere in the past, and it would be counterproductive now.[68] Dulles's optimism was shared at the time by most observers of the Cuban scene. It is probably unfair to blame Dulles and the CIA for failing to predict that soon after his victory Castro would openly turn to communism. But should there not have been greater wariness about such a possibility? In December 1961, Castro explained during a famous television appearance that he had been a Leninist since his student days, but had hidden his true beliefs in order not to jeopardize his chances for gaining power. If Castro was telling the truth, then U.S. intelligence had certainly been misled, but many believe that this was no more than a half-truth. Nevertheless, the fact that some of Castro's closest advisers were Communists should have caused more concern than it evidently did.

The main issues facing U.S. intelligence in the 1960s were military-strategic in character, even though the question of political intentions always figured prominently. These issues will be reviewed in the following chapters. The underestimate of the Soviet ICBMs, like the "missile gap" in the decade before, became a major political issue in the 1960s. It also generated a great deal of heat inside the intelligence community; understandably, no one wanted to accept blame for the mistakes that had been made. It could always be argued that even if the Russians had deployed more ICBMs, it was really of no great consequence, for it did not give the Russians a decisive strategic advantage. After all, the Soviet leaders always believed in quantity, irrespective of whether such concentration on numbers was rational from a political, economic, or military point of view. Those who had erred could also fall back upon the traditional Russian fear of the "Yellow Peril" and of "encirclement."

These issues have been discussed for a long time and the debate still lingers on, though the number of those explaining the Soviet buildup in purely defensive or "reactive" terms has dwindled. It had been the issue that most sharply divided the CIA and DIA for a number of years. But there was a related debate which began in the early 1960s, and continues in one form or another to the present day. It concerned the economic implications of the Soviet arms buildup and the question of what percentage of the Soviet GNP was spent on armaments.

Unlike the missiles debate, it was fought out among a handful of people, professional economists (both intelligence officials and scholars) with a special interest in the Soviet arms industries. The implications were not as far reaching as the strategic debates, for it could be argued that regardless of how much the Soviets spent on arms, what mattered was how much they produced. Even if it emerged that the Soviet leadership spent much more on arms than had been believed in the past, it could be argued that this effort was bound to place the Soviet economy under a heavy strain, and in view of that economy's general weaknesses, the military effort could not expand much further. This view was excessively sanguine, for it implied that Soviet priorities were only a matter of abstract interest. Could the American government afford to ignore the extent of Soviet military spending or should it have a direct bearing on its own allocations?

Throughout the 1960s and the early 1970s some observers had maintained that CIA estimates of Soviet military spending were much too low —2 to 4.5 percent growth per annum for weapons production. Their views were rejected as hawkish and alarmist. But in 1975 covert means provided new information, as a result of which the CIA estimate of Soviet military outlays was doubled almost overnight. According to the official version, an individual had had the opportunity, so to speak, to inspect the books of the Soviet Ministry of Defense. What really happened was anyone's guess. But the evidence was so strong that it induced the CIA to revise its estimates of Soviet procurement for 1970 (and consequently for the years after) from 5.5 to 18.5 billion rubles and its estimate of total defense spending from 25 to 50 billion rubles. If the CIA had underrated Soviet procurement growth by a factor of three over two decades, this put its methodology in doubt, to say the least. But it also raised some important political questions, undermining the arguments of those who had claimed the Richardson-Cournot-Stackelberg hypothesis—that the Russians had merely *reacted* to the U.S. lead in the arms race. The new information made it clear that the Soviet aim was not parity, but superiority. Their commitment to arms control and restraint could no longer be taken for granted. Thus the issues at stake were no longer academic quarrels about the computation and evaluation of Soviet procurement in dollars and rubles.

The issue is highly complex and the answers are uncertain. To give but two examples, the estimates of the Soviet gross national product vary considerably, so the percentage of military spending cannot accurately be established, and we do not have any exact figures about hidden inflation inside the Soviet Union. But when allowances for uncertainty are made, it is still true that the CIA had underrated the extent of Soviet procurement. The only question was, by how much? Those like economic analysts William Lee and Steven Rosefielde who had argued all along that the CIA figures had been too low felt vindicated by the 1976 revisions. Others were a little shaken, but they tended to downplay the new findings. The official CIA line was that, while the revised estimate of the ruble costs of Soviet defense had a major effect on some intelligence judgments, it did not affect its appraisal on the size or capabilities of Soviet military forces.[69]

But this left open the question whether the overall impact of the upward revision was of importance or not. It is likely that unknown ruble price inflation played a role in underestimating Soviet spending and perhaps the inefficiency of the Soviet machine-building sector, as it does make a difference whether estimates are made in dollars or rubles. But these factors were known, after all, even before 1975 and cannot explain the very considerable discrepancy between the CIA figures before and after that year. It is one thing if the Soviet Union spends 8 percent of its GNP on its military buildup, but the assessment of Soviet priorities is clearly affected if it appears that the Soviet defense burden is 16 percent or even 20 percent. It has been argued that "alien influences" (that is, disinformation) might have affected the CIA evaluation of Soviet arms buildup.[70] But this cannot be proven, and it seems far more likely that what error there was, was home grown, as had been the case with the miscounting of the ICBMs. In both instances the estimates were based on some general assumptions regarding Soviet political behavior. Once wedded to certain theories, analysts were reluctant to change their position.*

It is too early to investigate in detail the more recent record of U.S. intelligence performance. A general picture has emerged of a recurrent pattern that in virtually every case of surprise, warning signs had been received but were not given sufficient weight for one reason or another. Yet, the exact timing of a surprise attack, coup, or popular uprising is hardly ever known early enough beforehand to make the information of practical value. The rise and fall of "socialism with a human face" in Czechoslovakia gives this truism a special poignancy.

Before the August 1968 invasion of Czechoslovakia by Soviet forces, the Russians' intentions had been discussed at great length in Washington. But the first news of the event was received from Prague radio. American technical intelligence had learned of the invasion several hours earlier, but

---

*In late 1983, CIA (and NATO) assessments of Soviet military expenditure was revised downward. If the Soviet annual growth rate had been 4–5 percent in 1971–1975, it was thought to have declined to 2 percent in 1977–1982.

A West German study of CIA methodology in assessing Soviet expenditure published in 1985 reached, broadly speaking, the following three conclusions: (1) that there is a high degree of uncertainty involved in these estimates; (2) that the revisions of 1976 and 1983 were not motivated by political considerations; and (3) that methodologically the CIA approach was probably sounder than the approaches used by the critics who thought that its estimates were too high or too low. Franz Walter, *The Reassessment of the Trend in Soviet Defense Expenditures —How Reliable and Meaningful Are the Estimates?* BIOst Report 1/1985 (Cologne: January 1985.)

The DIA did not accept the CIA estimates, however, and maintained in 1984 that during the previous year the Soviet Union spent 5–8 percent more (in rubles) on defense production than it had during 1982. Eventually (in early 1985) the two intelligence agencies concluded an armistice agreeing to concentrate in their future estimates on "outputs," meaning the hardware rolling off Soviet production lines, rather than on "inputs," meaning the costs involved in producing these arms. *Defense Week,* 4 March 1985.

this information did not reach Washington until after the official radio broadcast. President Johnson got the information from Ambassador Dobrynin, who delivered the news in person. In his report to the PFIAB in October 1968, Richard Helms wrote that he was distressed by the failure of intelligence to detect the attack earlier. An internal memorandum issued by the Directorate of Intelligence the day after the Soviet invasion provided an explanation which may or may not have been correct, but provided no comfort as to the CIA's ability to avoid similar surprises in the future. The memorandum explained that the Soviet Politburo had been "divided in mind" even three weeks before, when it had met the Czech leadership at Bratislava. Thus, "the decision to execute the plan of intervention came at a fairly late stage."[71]

It is quite likely that the Soviet leadership was indeed divided as to the most effective approach to the Czech reform movement. What the CIA apparently failed to make clear to the policy makers, however, was that the Soviet leadership could not, and would not, accept the Czech liberalization process. At the very least, the CIA should have stressed that the Soviet leaders had not only the capability to invade, but that they were likely to do so. Intelligence performance during the Czech crisis was worrisome for yet another reason: whatever the political intentions of the Soviet leaders, which could not easily be divined, it had been assumed that the U.S. government would always be reasonably well informed about Soviet troop movements. Yet in early August, U.S. intelligence suddenly "lost" a major Soviet combat group that had moved into Poland. Such phenomena should give pause to even the most enthusiastic advocates of the "electronic battlefield."*

Detailed information was received in Washington about an impending Middle Eastern war during summer and autumn of 1973. A NIE which appeared in May 1973 took the possibility of an Arab-Israeli war "within a few weeks" quite seriously. An INR memorandum of 31 May 1973, stated that the resumption of hostilities "will become a better-than-even bet." But by September, U.S. intelligence was persuaded that war was not likely. On 23 September, the CIA and DIA had information that Syrian armed forces had moved toward the border; the next day intelligence learned that maneuvers in Egypt were being conducted for the first time on a divisional scale, that live ammunition was stockpiled at the Suez Canal, that leave was cancelled, and that a huge communication complex had been installed. Taken in isolation, none of these items was very signifi-

---

*One famous earlier indicator of the consequences of overreliance on electronic intelligence was the Battle of the Bulge. Since ULTRA had not specifically forecast a major German counterattack, U.S. thinking was that there could not be one. See Omar N. Bradley and Clay Blair, *A General's Life,* (New York: Simon & Schuster, 1984), pp. 351–55.

cant, but taken together they should have set off all kinds of alarms. The Israelis were duly informed, but they did not seem very concerned, so the CIA drew the conclusion that if *Aman*—Israeli military intelligence, which had an excellent reputation, was not worried, there was no reason why America should be.[72]

In 1974 several events of international importance occurred, and in none had intelligence given adequate forewarning. The government of Archbishop Makarios was overthrown in July by General Ionnides of Greece, leading to the Turkish invasion of the island five days later. In April a group of junior officers ousted the Caetano regime in Portugal, and India exploded a nuclear device in May. Post mortems revealed that neither the events in Portugal nor the Indian nuclear development had been as closely monitored as their importance merited. On Cyprus the reasons for the failure were more complex. Contradictory reports were on hand, one of them an urgent memorandum with 20 July as a likely invasion date. But this memo was not disseminated to the intelligence community. There had been much, perhaps too much, SIGINT material, mostly of a highly technical nature. In the words of the post mortem there had been "too little analysis of the facts." The analysis that had been performed attributed too much rationality to the antagonists. None of the well-known theoretical models fitted cases in which passion was involved.

When the Soviets invaded Afghanistan, the U.S. was not taken entirely by surprise; there had been at least two warnings by intelligence prior to December 1979. Amin's ouster—the crucial event—was not anticipated, however. The Soviet military buildup could have been deduced from collected PHOTINT and RADINT imagery and intercepted signals, but the connection between the buildup and the invasion that followed seems to have escaped the analysts. A basic assumption was partly at fault: whereas it had been assumed in 1973 that the Egyptians and Syrians would not attack Israel because they were not ready and could not win, the assumption in 1979 was that direct Soviet military intervention was out of style and that the Russians would always act through proxies in the Third World.

While intelligence analysts had always attributed excessive importance to the new phenomenon of Eurocommunism, in Cuba they seemed to believe that the status quo would continue indefinitely. In the late 1970s they were reluctant to believe that the Soviets were willing to station offensive weapons on the island. The presence of MIG-23 and MIG-27 fighter bombers, the construction of submarine pens, and the presence of a Soviet combat brigade roused few from this dogmatic slumber. Of course these forces were insufficient for engaging in operations against the United States. But at issue was whether the Soviets had adhered to the 1962 agreement ending the Cuban missile crisis. In the words of the Senate Intelligence Committee:

> Until the summer of 1979, however, it was not widely believed that the Soviets maintained an organized, independent ground forces unit in Cuba. By August, an analysis of all available intelligence information resulted in the conclusion that the Soviets did have such a unit, termed a "brigade," in Cuba, that it had been there for a number of years, and that it consisted of between 2,000 and 3,000 men.[73]

The real problem, to repeat, was not the presence of several thousand Soviet soldiers in a combat unit in Cuba, but the fact that the U.S. government had not known it—perhaps because U.S. intelligence had not wanted to know it.

When the Polish coup occurred in December 1981, senior government officials complained that they had received no warning. That the Soviets would intervene in Warsaw seemed probable, perhaps even certain. But whether this would be done through the local forces, satellite assistance, direct Soviet invasion, or perhaps some mixture of various approaches, was not known. There were, as always, mitigating circumstances. If the Israelis were surprised in 1973, so was Solidarity in 1981. Later on, two salient facts emerged. First, several months prior to the coup, U.S. SIGINT had "lost" the Russian and Polish traffic because a new communications system had been installed. Not much seems to have been made of this, though it certainly merited alarm. Second, U.S. intelligence had an impeccable source in the Polish General Staff to keep abreast of developments inside Poland. But information from this source was kept so secret that only a few people in the U.S. government knew about the preparation of the coup, nor was Solidarity informed, as it was riddled with Polish secret police and Soviet agents. In brief, no operational use was made of this information.

The intelligence failure in Iran has come in for closer scrutiny than any other such event in recent times. As late as August 1978, a twenty-three-page CIA Intelligence Assessment stated that "Iran is not in a revolutionary or even a pre-revolutionary situation." On 28 September 1978, the DIA said that "the Shah is expected to remain actively in power over the next ten years." The INR did not even have a full-time Iranian analyst, therefore it produced no reports on the subject during 1978. During most of 1978, intelligence community analysts struggled in vain to produce an NIE on Iran.[74] Harold Saunders, John D. Stempel, and others in government with some expertise on Iran claimed that the problem was much broader. That Iran was vulnerable, the experts agreed but in 1977 none, whether inside or outside the government, predicted the events that would bring about the downfall of the Shah. According to the same sources, the embassy did have contacts with the opposition, though there were no direct encounters with the radical clergy prior to March 1978. In July 1977, a ten-page analysis of the opposition had identified the major actors; other U.S. studies had pointed to growing economic unrest, rampant corruption, SAVAK brutality, religious discontent, and so on. Some of the reports from Teheran anticipated the coming events and the others were quite wrong. The policy makers were unable to make the right choice between conflicting estimates. Nevertheless, it seems clear that insufficient attention was paid to political Islam in the Iranian context. It was not realized early enough that the opposition, evidently disunited and weak, might cooperate at least temporarily, becoming the formidable force that it did. Policy makers and intelligence officials alike believed (somewhat unrealistically) that the monarch, having survived so many challenges before, would also survive this one, and that the new middle class—like the bazaar—was an effective counterweight against the "revolutionary" movement.

In 1982 a congressional committee took note of the weaknesses in U.S. intelligence performance in Central America. The overall performance was judged competent, and in some instances worthy of high praise. But there were charges of "occasional oversimplification," and the suggestion of greater certainty than seemed warranted by the evidence. The committee suggested that these "minor faults" were perhaps symptomatic of a more important problem, namely the desire to produce intelligence welcome to the (Reagan) administration, although nothing so crude as deliberate suppression or distortion of evidence was suggested.[75] The specific question at issue was to what extent the Central American revolutions were driven by indigenous factors as opposed to outside instigation, guidance, or direct assistance. The committee report was by no means unanimous, however, as it represented only the views of the majority, the Democrats. A nonpartisan source, Admiral Bobby Inman, who had shortly before resigned as CIA deputy director, charged that the report was far from objective. The majority report made it clear that though the amount of aid and degree of influence was difficult to assess, intelligence had established the involvement of Communist countries in the El Salvador insurgency beyond reasonable doubt. Furthermore, the CIA had predicted Somoza's downfall in mid-1978, but it had depended too much on Salvadoran government sources for coverage of developments in that country. The CIA's intelligence on El Salvador and Nicaragua was criticized for pretending to greater certainty than was warranted. The report was critical not only of the Reagan administration but also of President Carter's. The earlier administration had kept the CIA from publishing evidence about Cuban, Nicaraguan, and even Soviet support to the Salvadoran insurgents; at one stage there was even a presidential order not to brief the committee staff on this subject. The CIA had concluded that there was a "very high likelihood" of such support activities, whereas President Carter's administration—wishing to avoid cancellation of aid to Nicaragua—stated that the evidence was substantial but not conclusive. "What mattered in terms of intelligence performance," the committee concluded, was "that the intelligence process had retained its independence and had not been undermined by this policy."

What emerged from the controversy was, firstly, that intelligence on Central America had been on the whole satisfactory. Secondly, Democratic and Republican administrations to a certain extent had interpreted the information submitted to them according to their preconceived notions—not exactly a unique phenomenon in the history of intelligence producer-consumer relations. Lastly, it appeared that it was unrealistic to expect totally conclusive intelligence on such inherently difficult subjects as international terrorism, insurgency, and civil war. Policy makers have to draw their conclusions based on evidence that would never satisfy a criminal court.

CHAPTER 5

The Missile Gap Controversy and the Cuban Missile Crisis

MOST PEOPLE, LaRochefoucauld observed, judge men only by their success or their good fortune. This is doubly true for intelligence performance. In most fields of human endeavor allowances are made for difficulties and obstacles, failure may be counted as a step on the way to success, and even the unsuccessful effort may hope for recognition.[1] Intelligence cannot count on this kind of sympathy; it is thought that to fail in intelligence is to fail utterly. To compound the problem, intelligence successes frequently remain unknown for a long time, whereas failures usually become known soon after they are recognized.

Intelligence professionals deplore this fixation on success and failure. They know how often success depends on accident; they have seen people reach the right answer on the basis of false assumptions. They admit that sometimes it is absolutely crucial to have the correct information in time to take action. But in many situations success and failure are relative, not absolute, categories. Indeed, a rough idea of the intentions and capabilities of the other side is more useful than a detailed and accurate statement that leads to wrong policy decisions which will be stubbornly adhered to. The simple fact is that last minute, unforeseen changes on the part of the enemy can never be ruled out.

In this chapter, certain important problems that preoccupied U.S. intelligence will be examined and an attempt will be made to establish how well informed intelligence was, whether it interpreted information correctly, and how well it predicted coming events. Such a picture cannot possibly be complete as evidence is more fully available for earlier periods than for recent years. The evidence consists largely of substantial estimates and only to a smaller extent of intelligence notes provided on short notice. Moreover, it is by no means certain that the impact of the NIEs and SNIEs on policy makers was always proportionate to their length. There was also hardly ever a consensus on any topic in the intelligence community. Sometimes its member components confronted each other with radically different views, but there were differences of opinion even on issues which did not fully engage the prestige and emotional commitment of the rival services. There was almost always someone (occasionally a sizable minority) who disagreed; strictly speaking, therefore, it is incorrect to refer to a CIA or intelligence community "view."[2] All the same, certain opinions and attitudes did prevail in the intelligence community at a given time. A full record may never be established, but the researcher can piece together a general picture of achievement and failure. The purpose of such an exercise is not to distribute marks of excellence or negligence, but to try to understand why the record was mixed, what made for correct appraisals, and in what circumstances major errors were committed.

During the early years of postwar American intelligence—roughly the first decade of the CIA's existence—it suffered from a dual handicap. First, it was without adequate staffing and financial resources to cope with the many new problems posed by the worldwide cold war. Second, until the aerial reconnaissance provided by the U-2 began in 1956, the traditional HUMINT approach of the intelligence community was unable to provide reliable data on military capabilities in "denied areas." As a consequence, many of the early NIEs and other assessments compiled by the CIA relied almost exclusively on diplomatic reports and open sources. If they attained no more than the level of sophisticated journalism written for a discriminating readership, one had no right to expect more from them at the time.

In addition to the staffing, financial, and technical limitations of American intelligence between 1945–56, its performance was often flawed by an "academic" tone that policy makers took to be tantamount to equivocation, and a tendency to oscillate between optimistic and deeply pessimistic analyses—the Pollyanna and Cassandra syndromes, which we shall discuss in chapter 9.

In defense of the "academic" approach, it should be said that it would be irresponsible for intelligence analysts to pretend to scientific accuracy in their forecasts about political and other developments. The unexpected death of a leader—at the hands of enemies or of natural causes—may unbalance the equation so laboriously worked out to deal with reality. Since there are so many imponderables of this sort, even the best intelligence must hedge its forecasts and talk in terms of probabilities. Seen from the decision maker's perspective, however, this caution may seem to be merely a manifestation of the bureaucratic impulse to avoid responsibility —a twentieth-century variant of the peasant soothsayer's prediction that "If the cock crows at exactly twelve, it will rain, or it will not rain." Hence, in the controversy between Eisenhower and Allen Dulles over the "intelligence failure" regarding the Suez War of 1956, both men were right. Dulles was correct in saying that CIA-prepared reports had warned of the *possibility* that Britain and France would use their military buildup not just to put pressure on Nasser, but actually to invade Egyptian territory. Likewise, Eisenhower was at least subjectively truthful when he claimed to have known nothing of the invasion except what he read in the papers. Presumably he had looked in vain for the kind of straightforward prediction which, in the nature of things, intelligence can seldom provide.

At least equally serious, but more specific to early years than later, was the periodic retreat from a mildly euphoric outlook to one of deepest gloom in intelligence. The most notorious example of this was the persistent underestimation of Soviet scientific and technical advances, first with the atomic bomb, then with the hydrogen bomb, and finally with the launching of *Sputnik*. Analysts could be relied upon for a long time thereafter to provide worst-case scenarios with regard to Soviet military technology.[3]

In this chapter we take up the story of U.S. intelligence performance just as it began to get its stride by clearing up the exaggerations and hysteria of the "missile gap" controversy to which it had earlier contributed. Our case histories here and in chapter 6—the "Missile gap" debate, the Cuban missile crisis, America's role in Vietnam, and the nature and intent of the Soviet ICBM buildup during the late 1960s and early 1970s—lead to further reflection on the causes of intelligence failure, discussed in chapter 9. If one conclusion stands out more clearly than any other, it is that the single greatest defect in U.S. intelligence performance is the tendency toward "mirror-imaging," the assumption that an adversary will behave in a rational manner calculated to secure national security *as we understand those terms.* This was clearly at the bottom of the CIA's initial reluctance to believe that Khruschev would attempt such a risky venture as the placement of ballistic missiles in Cuba, for example. Unfortunately, even when the CIA has done an exemplary job of intelligence gathering and analysis, its input has sometimes been neglected in favor of assessments more congenial to policy decisions that have already been made—this was surely what happened in Vietnam. But let us proceed to our in-depth consideration of the missile gap controversy. It offers an interesting combination of a provincial approach to potential HUMINT assets, a predilection for worst-case analysis, and—at least for air force intelligence—more than a hint of outside pressures to provide answers congenial to special interests.

And Then There Was None: The Missile Gap

The missile gap controversy of 1956–61 concerns the United States intelligence community's performance in assessing the general development of the Soviet missile program.[4] A journalist was the first to use the expression "missile gap,"[5] but the controversy—debated first within the intelligence community, then in Congress, and then among the public—arose from contradictory and inaccurate estimates of a future strategic environment. These estimates were presented in both public and classified official testimony; some were "leaked" to selected politicians and journalists. Briefly stated, the prediction which caused the uproar was that the Soviet Union would soon be able to deploy reliable intercontinental ballistic missiles in larger numbers than the United States.[6]

As far as the intelligence community's performance—especially that of the CIA—is concerned, the main reasons for the inaccurate forecast seem to have been the unavailability of reliable strategic intelligence on the Soviet missile program and inaccurate estimates of the production and deployment rates of enemy ICBMs.[7] The tendency to overestimate Soviet capabilities was influenced to some extent by the U.S.S.R.'s previous (1955–57) success in convincing the United States that a bomber gap was imminent, by elements in the armed services and the Congress who hoped to profit from predictions of future strategic inferiority, and by Soviet success in launching its first successful ICBM.[8] Yet the inaccuracy of the estimates was not due to extraneous political pressure. Thus the missile gap controversy, which was concerned with inadequate performance by U.S. intelligence in assessing the Soviet missile program, should be differentiated from the public missile gap debate. The latter began late in 1957 following the first Soviet ICBM test firing, the launch of *Sputnik,* and the leakage of conclusions from the Gaither Committee report.

Three explanations for the intelligence failure have been emphasized in subsequent analysis. The first is the scanty and ambiguous nature of the intelligence available to the intelligence community about the Soviet ICBM program. The second relates to the atmosphere of uncertainty in which responsible analysts purportedly worked. The third concerns political support between 1957 and 1961 for the alarmist projections of the air force by congressional Democrats who had a partisan interest in discrediting the defense policies of the Eisenhower administration.

THE SOVIET MISSILE PROGRAM: THE STATE OF U.S. INTELLIGENCE TO 1955

For the first decade after World War II, U.S. intelligence is said to have possessed only "scant knowledge" of Soviet missile development.[9] Open intelligence sources available for this period are limited and give few details on the extent of American knowledge in this area.[10] For this reason it is impossible to provide a definitive picture either of the range of intelligence sources, or of the quality of the information procured. On the evidence available, assessment of Soviet missile progress to the end of 1954 was based on four sources.

The first was a Soviet defector, Lieutenant Colonel G. A. Tokaty-Tokaev, a military engineer who was involved in the initial development of the Soviet rocket program. Before he defected to British intelligence in 1948, he was employed at a level that apparently included contact with Stalin.[11] Tokaty-Tokaev is credited with providing Western intelligence with information about the establishment of a major Soviet rocket development program in 1947.[12] This program utilized captured German rocket scientists and technicians, German technological data, and V-2 rocket prototypes seized by Soviet army intelligence in 1945 at Peenemunde and other research facilities in the Soviet occupation zone in Germany.[13]

The second intelligence source came from the interrogation of German scientists and technicians who had worked on the missile program in the Soviet Union until their repatriation in 1951.[14] Because they were used independently of the main rocket program and were kept ignorant of the full extent of the Soviet effort, they could apparently furnish only limited information about actual missile prototypes, testing results, and arrangements for missile production.[15]

A third source was the military intelligence obtained by the CIA beginning in 1953 from a GRU (Soviet military intelligence) officer in Vienna, identified variously as "Major B" or as Colonel Pyotr Semyonovich Popov. Popov functioned as a "defector in place," and is said to have furnished descriptions of Soviet tactical missile systems.[16]

The fourth source, beginning in the late 1940s, consisted of electronic and signal intelligence collected by airborne electronic eavesdropping along the frontiers of the Soviet Union and by systematic monitoring of Soviet domestic civilian and military telecommunications and internal transmissions. This source provided evidence about the development of rocket boosters and large rockets and was responsible for the discovery of a missile testing site at Kaputsin Yar.[17]

ESTIMATES OF SOVIET ICBM DEVELOPMENT—1955–61

The thrust of intelligence estimates drawn up on the basis of these sources is not clear.[18] In the late 1940s there was a tendency in the West to dismiss ICBMs as delivery vehicles, either under the assumption that bombers were more accurate and cost-effective, or because the fledgling United States missile program had not yet progressed very far.[19] The intelligence community, and in particular the air force, seems to have assumed that the Soviet Union would reach a similar conclusion.[20] In the early 1950s it was agreed that the Russians conceivably could hit the United States using the ICBM, but not until the end of the decade.[21] However, no clear evidence shows a pronounced official concern over the danger of a major Soviet buildup of ICBMs, nor did the intelligence community consider the possibility that the Soviet Union would appraise the strategic military potential of the ICBM differently and alter its doctrine accordingly. Official intelligence estimates seem to have become more cautious only in 1954, after the discovery of Kaputsin Yar and evidence about Soviet development of large booster rockets.

Between 1954 and 1956 the quantity and quality of intelligence concerning Soviet missile development improved substantially. A line-of-sight radar installation was built at Samsun in Turkey; it became operational in the summer of 1955. Thereafter, radar surveillance of Kaputsin Yar permitted accurate monitoring of Soviet rocket testing that included the number of tests, their success or failure, the general configuration of the missile prototypes under test, and their speed and thrust power.[22] The construction of a network of additional radar and electronic eavesdropping facilities in Turkey in the Elburz Mountains, in Iran at Meshed, and in Pakistan at Peshwar permitted the expanded monitoring of Soviet test ranges and installations for missile development near the Aral Sea.

The U-2 high altitude reconnaissance plane had been developed under a crash program to meet the need for reliable strategic intelligence about the Soviet bomber force and the Soviet rocket program.[23] The first U-2 overflight of the Soviet Union took place in mid-June 1956. From this date to the shooting down of the plane piloted by Francis Gary Powers in May 1960, there were an estimated two hundred U-2 flights across the Soviet

Union. It is, however, uncertain how many of these overflights involved strategic reconnaissance connected with the Soviet ICBM program.

Although the U-2 was limited both as to the frequency and the areas of its overflights, it became the most important technical means of monitoring Soviet missile development.[24] The U-2 furnished high-resolution photographs of test facilities and suspected production centers. These photographs served as the most reliable evidence of the construction or existence of ICBM launching pads on a certain date in a given area of the Soviet Union. In addition, the U-2 provided a reliable check on other sources of intelligence related to the detection of Soviet military activities.

Foremost among these supplementary sources were tourists who carried out simple assignments such as visual observation—from trains, planes, and roads—of intelligence targets in metropolitan areas and along major transportation routes. After the launching of the first *Sputnik,* many of these travelers were guided by detailed instructions to focus on specific missile installations. Photographs of missile installations taken from a civil aircraft are reported as having been of the greatest value in pinpointing a missile assembly plant and a storage area.[25] According to a former CIA officer, the coverage of observable targets by legal travelers contributed directly to the settlement of the missile gap debate. Between 1958 and 1960, Russian-speaking American tourists visited the Soviet Union on prearranged itineraries and reported in depth on key installations identified by U-2 flights. These travelers are reported to have furnished photographs of the facilities for ICBM production and of the actual deployment sites for ICBMs.[26]

The first consequence of U-2 reconnaissance photography was the lowering of previous estimates of Soviet bomber production.[27] But if photographic intelligence provided by U-2 flights proved that the bomber gap was a fiction, the downgrading of bomber production estimates had no direct results on the assessment of Soviet defense production capabilities. To the contrary, air force intelligence interpreted the palpable slackening in Soviet long-range bomber production as evidence of a Soviet decision to concentrate industrial resources on an ICBM program. The reduction in estimates of bomber production was accepted as an indication of a Soviet "leap-frog" into ICBM production.[28]

This interpretation was buttressed by the classified report by the Gaither Panel to President Eisenhower on 7 November 1957.[29] The Gaither Report was one of the most comprehensive studies of overall U.S. strategic defense posture and requirements ever undertaken by an ad hoc civilian group. Unlike a normal NSC document, its views embodied neither a compromise among a number of government departments and agencies, nor an amalgam of considerations. The members of the committee were not bound by previous government policy decisions, nor by any consensus as to the meaning of the intelligence information upon which they based their report. It emphasized the vulnerability of American strategic forces as a result of the Soviet Union's calculated risk in shifting a large part of its effort from manned bombers to long-range missiles.[30] One of the conclusions of the Gaither Report was indeed disturbing: by late 1959 the Soviet Union could possibly launch an attack against the United States with one hundred ICBMs carrying megaton warheads.[31]

Because only the Gaither Report itself has been declassified, it is impossible to establish what intelligence data or finished intelligence estimates were used by the committee as the basis for this conclusion. Moreover, it cannot be known what use, if any, the component agencies of the intelligence community made of the report, particularly its conclusion, in their own evaluations of the Soviet missile program.

In late 1956, radar surveillance detected some forty to fifty Soviet missile test-firings. In this same period, radar revealed the existence of an ICBM test center at Tyuratam, near the Aral Sea. Early in the summer of 1957, U-2 surveillance of this site provided the first photograph of an actual Soviet ICBM on its launcher.[32] On the basis of this hard intelligence, the CIA notified the Eisenhower administration of the imminence of long-range ICBM tests in the U.S.S.R. On the available evidence, the testing program began in the spring of 1957 with four to six firings and concluded in August with two launches; the estimated range was approximately 3,500 nautical miles.[33]

The Soviet ICBM tests of August 1957 served as decisive evidence of a genuine technological breakthrough, then unmatched by the United States. From this time on, the intelligence community was deeply concerned about the effect of this development on U.S. security. The reports of these tests, however, did not have any immediate impact on the administration. Real concern among both government and the public dates from the autumn of 1957. At this time, two events combined to conjure up not only the danger of a missile gap, but also to arouse fears of an approaching period of maximum peril in which the Russians' ability to deploy the missiles they had tested would allow them to destroy American strategic bombers on their airfields before the United States had developed and deployed its own ICBMs.

The first event was the successful launching of *Sputnik,* the first artificial satellite, on 4 October 1957. The second was the leakage of the conclusions of the Gaither Committee Report of 7 November. The public debate over the existence of a missile gap started from the premise that the United

States had been surprised by the rapid development of the Soviet missile program and that this surprise amounted to an intelligence failure.

The fact was that the possibility of a Soviet satellite launch had been predicted for three years by the CIA.[34] Moreover, as noted previously, there was no question of surprise in the case of the ICBM tests, for the CIA had anticipated them as well. Thus, in the fall of 1957, the CIA did not change its estimates of Soviet ICBM capabilities, and spokesmen for the Eisenhower administration could honestly deny the existence of any technological lag or surprise. The available intelligence confirmed that there were irregular intervals between ICBM tests, established the different types of tests conducted, and documented the occasional failures—all of which indicated, but did not prove, that the Soviet ICBM was still in its development phase.[35] Accordingly, the estimate of Soviet initial operational capability that seeped into the published literature was partly based on the assumption in the 1957 NIE that the development of ICBMs would be pushed at all possible speed, and that all technical problems could soon be mastered.[36] In fact, the evidence from tests monitored down to the end of 1957 was inconclusive and remained that way throughout the period of testing monitored up to April 1958.

As of that date, between ten and fifteen test firings had been carried out; no launch had exceeded 3,700 nautical miles in range. The assumption of the intelligence community was apparently that the Russians could not effectively monitor a longer test firing, which would require a seaborne tracking capability down-range in the Pacific Ocean. Accordingly, the short range in this group of tests was attributed to the geographical limitations of the Soviet Union proper, not to any technical problems with the ICBM prototype. Therefore, the suspension of Soviet test firings after April 1958 caused immediate disagreement as to its significance. This dispute led to a divergence in subsequent intelligence estimates of the probable rate of Soviet ICBM development.

Allen Dulles was obliged to testify on the subject of Soviet ICBM development before the Preparedness Investigating Subcommittee of the Senate Armed Services Committee, which included among its members two critics of the Eisenhower administration's defense program. Dulles's testimony was not released even after being censored. However, at the time of his testimony Dulles was quoted to the effect that the Soviet satellite and recent ballistic missile tests had not altered the overall appraisals of Soviet capabilities and intentions reached a year or more previously.

The overall estimate of Soviet ICBM development and missile capabilities as of autumn 1957 are still not accessible. Thus it is difficult to evaluate the response of Senator Symington to Dulles's testimony, which the former described as a "sad, shocking story." Nor can one confidently judge the accuracy of Senator Styles Bridges's reference to "very unpleasant information," which would shock any complacency out of various officials and the American public.[37] Secondhand accounts of the November 1957 NIE indicate that the CIA assumed the Russians might have ten operational ICBMs by early 1959, provided that the development was pursued with all possible speed and that the technical problems were resolved.[38]

The CIA interpreted the hiatus in testing as due to technical performance difficulties; it seems to have extended its estimates by approximately six months, thus assuming that the Soviet Union's ICBMs would not be operational until late 1959. Air force intelligence drew the opposite conclusion from the interruption in testing. It interpreted the halt as signifying the resolution of all technical problems and the initiation of mass production of the previously tested ICBM prototype. It predicted that the first operational Soviet ICBMs might appear by the end of 1958.[39]

In January 1959, Secretary of Defense Neil McElroy testified before the Senate Preparedness Subcommittee at which time he submitted estimates of Soviet missile capabilities for the next few years and explained the Eisenhower administration's position regarding estimates of Soviet ICBM capability and U.S. ballistic missile programs.[40] The secretary's testimony is informative in assessing the intelligence community's knowledge about Soviet missile development at this date; it also helps to clarify the assumptions upon which the NIEs were based.

> SECRETARY McELROY: It is not our intention or policy to try to match missile for missile in the ICBM category of the Russian capability in the next couple of years. Our position, Mr. Symington, is that our diversified capability to deliver the big weapon is what we are going to count on as our ability to deter general war.

> SENATOR SYMINGTON: What you are in effect saying is that we are planning in this fashion in spite of our intelligence estimates that the Russians are going to produce a great many more missiles, ICBMs, than we are, is that correct?

> SECRETARY McELROY: We are planning based on an assumption that they have the capability and if they use that capability—and we are also assuming that they will from the standpoint of our counterforce—then they will have a year from now, two years from now, a larger number of this particular element in the retaliatory force than the United States will have.[41]

The National Intelligence Estimates assumed, then, that the Soviet Union would realize its full ICBM potential as to numbers and production schedule, as surmised from various intelligence sources. The secretary's testimony presumed an ICBM ratio of three to one in favor of the Soviet Union; Senator Symington believed that a ratio of four to one was a more realistic estimate.[42]

Soviet ICBM testing resumed in March 1959 at the rate of four test firings per month; the intelligence community regarded this as an indication that the testing program was in its terminal stages. As of September 1959, however, U-2 flights had found no launching sites apart from the testing centers at Kaputsin Yar and Tyuratam. Nonetheless, the November 1959 NIE posited the existence of a small number of operational ICBMs. Intelligence obtained in the winter of 1959–60 from radar surveillance of the tests and U-2 photographs of the first ICBM prototype—NATO designation SS-6—converged to show that this ICBM was large and unwieldy, requiring transportation and servicing by rail. Intensified U-2 reconnaissance of the Soviet railway system and, in particular, of newly constructed trunk lines and sidings, apparently failed to uncover any new ICBMs or launch complexes. In February 1960, Chief of Naval Operations Admiral Burke testified that no missile sites other than the Soviet test missile sites had been securely identified.[43]

Within the intelligence community, the number of failures and the weaknesses manifested by the SS-6 tests raised the question of whether the Soviet Union in fact intended to deploy this missile in large numbers, assuming that it could do so.[44] The intelligence community presupposed a relationship between testing and deployment criteria. The series of tests monitored by radar was thus the harbinger of actual deployment. Analogy with the U.S. ICBM testing program, however, indicated that the exact relationship between testing and deployment was not easily determined. For instance, in February 1960 the United States had carried out some thirty-seven Atlas missile flight tests but it had only three operational ICBMs.[45] In contrast, at the end of 1959 the Soviet Union had conducted roughly forty firings, yet it had no known ICBMs in place except at the two test sites. Moreover, by further analogy with the American ICBM program, the Soviet ICBM program was subject to a constraint that had to be taken into account, which was the time needed to design and construct a launching pad at a specific location. It was also necessary to estimate when the construction program for operational deployment would commence. An Atlas launching pad at a given site required five to six months for design and fifteen to seventeen months for construction, with an overlapping period of as long as nine months to install and prepare the missile.[46] Even assuming a faster rate of construction and installation for the Soviets, in theory at least one year would be needed to complete the deployment of the first Soviet ICBMs. This phase would therefore provide a year's notice or more before deployment. Yet the November 1959

NIE credited the Soviet Union with a small number of operational ICBMs in spite of testing failures and no known launch sites except Kaputsin Yar and Tyuratam.

This was perhaps the beginning of a change in the way estimates were made. During the winter of 1959–60, some members of the intelligence community, particularly within the army and navy, began to doubt that the Soviet Union intended to deploy the SS-6. They maintained that the Soviet ICBM program was more restricted than previously estimated. But this analysis, as far as it can be reconstructed, depended upon the failure to locate launching sites other than Kaputsin Yar and Tyuratam; technical constraint was not part of the equation. To be sure, the CIA agreed that the Soviet program was more restricted than had been thought. But it hesitated to conclude that SS-6 deployment had been, or would be, minimal. The limited coverage of the Soviet land mass and rail system by the U-2 was responsible for this uncertainty.[47]

In the absence of pertinent U-2 photographs, there was considerable debate as to the ground configuration of an operational ICBM launch site. It was assumed by the CIA that such sites would resemble the test installations at Kaputsin Yar and Tyuratam. Air force intelligence is recorded as arguing that no set configuration for Soviet ICBM launching sites could be assumed; consequently, the air force identified all unusual construction sites and structures photographed by the U-2 as missiles and launching sites until they were proved to be something else.

The dispute went unresolved until the first ICBM site was positively located. In the meantime, during the winter of 1959–60, signal and communication intelligence was used to supplement the gaps in U-2 photography. A number of spurious missile sites were located. These "discoveries" may have influenced the intelligence estimates of operational or nearly operational sites. If so, the Soviet Union was credited with a larger ICBM capability than it in fact possessed.

Communications intelligence and agents' reports finally combined in the spring of 1960 to provide convincing preliminary evidence of an ICBM base under construction at Plesetsk. On 1 May 1960, the U-2 mission arranged to photograph this site ended in failure when the aircraft, piloted by Francis Gary Powers, was shot down near Sverdlovsk. Further U-2 overflights of Soviet territory were canceled by President Eisenhower; as a result the intelligence community was left with no reliable means of confirming the true nature of the Plesetsk site or expanding the aerial reconnaissance search for other Soviet ICBM bases.

The nascent satellite reconnaissance program offered the only certain alternative source of photographic intelligence. The first launching of a Samos satellite, however, did not take place until October 1960. Of the five

Samos craft launched, only two were successfully placed in orbit—*Samos II* on 21 January, and *Samos V* on 22 December 1961.[48] No information about the quantity or quality of photographs provided by these has been declassified; it is therefore impossible to say whether or not these satellites were able to compensate for what the U-2 had done to provide intelligence on Soviet ICBM base construction.

By contrast, the so-called Discoverer Biosatellite Program appears to have been quite fruitful. *Discoverer 14,* launched on 19 August 1960, photographed the suspected ICBM base at Plesetsk. The photographs revealed railway lines absent from World War II German maps, thereby adding to the evidence that Plesetsk was an ICBM site.[49] But the photographs were of poor quality, and after two additional sets of photographs before the end of the year, Discoverer satellites furnished no further intelligence for six months.

It is clear, therefore, that the last NIE of the Eisenhower administration (November 1960) and the first NIE of the Kennedy administration (June 1961) could not have used extensive photographic intelligence for their estimations of Soviet missile development and the construction of ICBM sites. Apart from radar surveillance and communications and signals intelligence, the only other likely source of hard intelligence on the Soviet ICBM program was the defector in place, GRU Colonel Oleg Penkovsky. From April 1961, Penkovsky is said to have supplied Western intelligence with "the most valuable strategic military information produced by an agent since World War II," including detailed reports on Soviet strategic capabilities relevant to American intelligence estimates of Soviet ICBM strength.[50]

By mid-1961, army and navy intelligence harbored serious doubts as to further Soviet ICBM deployment. The CIA and air force intelligence appear to have adhered to the early premise that the pattern of Soviet ICBM testing implied the commencement of operational deployment. While the official working estimates of the number of Soviet ICBMs are not known, open sources mention between 50 and 150 missiles.[51]

The decisive intelligence for assessment of Soviet ICBM deployment was furnished by Discoverer satellite photographs between June and September 1961. These photographs revealed an actual ICBM launching site, showing the SS-6 deployed on launching pads, whose arrangement replicated precisely the known site-plan of Tyuratam. Owing to this evidence, and by virtue of the expanded geographical coverage of the U.S.S.R. afforded by Discoverer satellites, many sites that the air force had previously insisted on counting in the interim as ICBM bases were eliminated from consideration. Thus, in this matter the CIA's skepticism was proven well founded.

Satellite reconnaissance may fairly be credited with resolving the debate within the intelligence community over Soviet ICBM deployment. By September 1961, the intelligence community appears to have reduced its estimate of Soviet ICBM deployment to a new figure of about ten SS-6 missiles. The first instance in which the full panoply of technical collection systems was employed to furnish strategic military intelligence was the effort to analyze the Soviet ICBM program.

THE ESTIMATION OF SOVIET ICBM PRODUCTION RATES

The existence of a Soviet testing program justified the assumption that ICBM deployment would occur; the first question, therefore, was when operational deployment would begin. The second question was how rapidly deployment would occur.

In both cases, the answers depended upon the rate of production of Soviet ICBMs. But the intelligence needed to determine the rate of Soviet ICBM production was even more difficult to collect and evaluate than information on the initial testing and deployment arrangements had been. The need to estimate the production rate of Soviet ICBMs confronted the intelligence community with a limitation that has bedeviled the entire U.S. espionage effort against the Soviet Union and frustrated the most sophisticated attempts to assess its military power. The limitation is the paucity of consistent, high-grade human intelligence from within the Soviet Union, its armed forces, defense industries, and intelligence services.

But intelligence from any source about the Soviet defense industry was limited. For the first decade after World War II, what hard intelligence there was at hand was assembled by components of German military intelligence, Foreign Armies/East, and the War Economy and Armaments Department of the *Wehrmacht.* This was supplemented after 1945 by the Gehlen organization—the forerunner of the West German intelligence service—largely through the systematic interrogation of repatriated German prisoners of war, returned German rocket scientists, and other civilian refugees from Eastern Europe.[52] Before the advent of the U-2 in 1956, additional information was procured by the CIA using agents, tourists (directed travelers), and through the analysis of Soviet scientific and technical literature. Presumably the NSA and its predecessor, the Armed Forces Security Agency, contributed to this effort by means of signal and communications intelligence. As in the case of the Soviet atomic bomb program, however, so it was with Soviet military technology and defense industrial production capabilities—there was a serious lack of hard information.

Before U-2 photography became available, the only aerial photographs of Soviet industrial areas were those taken by the German Air Force in World War II (which covered only European Russia west of the Urals) and from CIA-sponsored travelers flying in civilian aircraft. Photographs taken by the U-2 of Soviet factories, combined with analysis of the particle content in the air in overflown areas, permitted a determination of the type of manufacturing activity within them; given these data, estimates of monthly production rates could be calculated from the area of the factories. The number of shifts in a given factory could be estimated in accordance with the amount of ancillary civilian housing, and an estimate of productivity per shift could be contrived on the basis of comparable Western or American production norms. Additional evidence about the production rate of a particular factory might be gleaned from the analysis of railway traffic from a site and from the number and size of observable packing containers.

Without agent reports, however, there could be only very limited success in identifying those factories specifically engaged in ICBM production.[53] For example, an assembly facility for ICBMs was identified at Tyuratam, but the factories that provided the components could not be located. Thus aerial reconnaissance or communications intelligence, supplemented with comparable estimates of American productivity per shift, yielded little more than educated guesses. Nevertheless, it seemed certain that the Soviets were able to build a large number of missiles.

Portions of the competing estimates appear to have been leaked at different times, but little confidence can be placed in these open figures, which are set forth in Table 5-1.

Debate within the intelligence community as to the speed of the anticipated Soviet ICBM buildup dates to October 1957 and became more strident with the launching of *Sputnik.* As we have seen, the air force circulated the information that the Eisenhower administration deliberately underestimated the Soviet ICBM threat and the Gaither Report concluded that this threat had not been adequately appreciated, warning that a major ICBM attack was possible by 1959.[54] The air force contribution to the November 1957 NIE credited the Soviet Union with a substantial ICBM capability by the end of 1959, with an estimated deployment of 500 missiles by the middle of 1960 and 1,100 by the middle of 1961, implying a production rate of 500 missiles per year. The CIA estimates seem to have been less alarmist with 100 ICBMs by early 1960, and perhaps 500 by early 1961.[55]

Despite the downward revision in the estimate of ICBM operational deployment in the November 1959 NIE, the air force did not think it necessary to reduce its estimates of ICBM production rates. Instead, the anticipated start of the buildup was moved back by six months. The rate

TABLE 5-1

Summary Estimates of Soviet ICBM Strength[1]

	Source	1959	1960	1961	1962	1963
Actual Figures[2]	U.S.S.R.	0	30	50	100	150
	U.S.A.	0	0	75	250	400
Date						
Nov 1957	NIE (newspapers)	10	100	500	——	——
Jul 1958	Alsop[3]	100	500	1,000	1,500	2,000
Jan 1959	NIE (newspapers)	——	100	300	500	1,000–1,500
Mar 1959	Symington[4]	——	——	——	3,000	——
May 1959	Alsop[5]	——	300	1,000	——	——
Jan 1960	NIE (newspapers)	——	——	100–150	——	400–500
Mar 1961	Air Force	——	——	200	——	——
Mar 1961	NIE (newspapers)	——	——	50	——	——

SOURCES: 1. Based on R. Licklider, "The Missile Gap Controversy," *Political Science Quarterly* 85 (1970): 615. 2. Lincoln P. Bloomfield, Walter C. Clamens Jr., Franklyn Griffiths, *Khrushchev and the Arms Race: Soviet Interests in Arms Control and Disarmament, 1954–1964* (Cambridge: M.I.T. Press, 1966), p. 95. 3. See T. R. Phillips, "The Growing Missile Gap," *Reporter* 20 (8 January 1959). 4. Senate Committee on Armed Services and Committee on Aeronautical and Space Sciences, Senate Preparedness Investigating Subcommittee, *Missile and Space Activities,* 86th Cong., 1st sess., 1959, p. 220; *New York Times,* 16 March 1959, p. 2. 5. *New York Times,* 6 December 1959, p. 1; Joseph Alsop, "Our Gamble with Destiny," *Saturday Evening Post,* 16 May 1959, 117.

of production to support this buildup, however, continued to be calculated at about 500 missiles per annum.

In the absence of full documentation it is impossible to know either how the CIA and the other members of the intelligence community arrived at the figure of 500 missiles per year or what assumptions and data underpinned the two dissenting estimates in the same NIE. The first of these estimates appears to have posited an orderly program with an initial production rate of 3 missiles per month increasing to 15 a month and thereby yielding a projected total of 36 operational ICBMs by the end of 1960 and as many as 400 by 1963. The second assumed the operation of a crash program with an initial production of 15 missiles per month, giving the Soviet Union 140–200 ICBMs on station by mid-1961 and 500 by 1963.[56]

From the testimony of new Secretary of Defense Thomas Gates in January 1960, it seems clear that the CIA at least endorsed the assumption of an orderly program, not a crash effort. Gates's testimony offers some insight into the method of evaluating Soviet missile production and operational ICBM strength, a method that may plausibly be attributed to the CIA in the case of the November 1959 NIE.

In his January 1960 testimony, Secretary of Defense Gates fixed the year of maximum Soviet ICBM superiority as 1962.[57] This testimony provoked the public debate over a missile gap for the remainder of 1960. Within the intelligence community, the CIA estimate of an orderly program acquired additional credibility, presumably owing to data furnished by U-2 flights, radar surveillance, and CIA-sponsored tourists and directed travelers to the Soviet Union. As of the November 1960 NIE the intelligence community is reported to have abandoned belief in a major Soviet SS-6 production and deployment program. Within a year, the new satellites furnished additional evidence of the failure of the Soviet first-generation ICBM program. The lack of launch sites for the SS-6 indicated to intelligence officials that no large-scale production or deployment would occur. Tests of a new 6,500-mile-range missile were good evidence that the SS-6 program was to be abandoned in favor of developing a second-generation ICBM to counter the coming deployment of America's Atlas and Titan missiles. Early in February 1961, new Secretary of Defense Robert McNamara tacitly acknowledged the nonexistence of a missile gap, presumably reflecting the consensus within the intelligence community.[58]

In retrospect, there can be no doubt that Soviet missile development and production was overestimated and that projections for the future were inaccurate. The reasons for this poor performance remain to be determined. Was the intelligence upon which the assessment of the Soviet missile program was founded so meager or ambiguous that contradictory estimates were unavoidable? Or did these deficiencies in the available data combine with earlier experiences of underestimation—for instance, Soviet bomber strength—resulting in a resolution of uncertainty by deliberate adherence to worst-case analysis?

The categories of intelligence information that would have permitted accurate and confident assessments of the Soviet missile program were either late in acquisition and equivocal or could not be procured because of Soviet secrecy and counterespionage. There had been few signs that a new missile program was being initiated. As Allen Dulles commented, "drawing boards are silent."[59] Plans, specifications, test records of components, data on materials, information about Soviet industrial technologies, and the organization of the Soviet defense industry are technical data that could not be adequately procured in the Soviet Union through traditional human espionage, although these data could be collected in the United States by Soviet intelligence.

The true extent of Soviet ICBM development was not adequately comprehended until several years after the missile gap controversy, when it was uncovered, so to speak, at the start of the testing program. Having previously identified a missile testing site at Kaputsin Yar by technical means (communications intelligence), radar installations were constructed to monitor the testing. Thereafter radar surveillance, communications monitoring, and, soon, overhead reconnaissance combined to furnish the minimum intelligence sufficient to follow the progress of Soviet ICBM tests. If open sources are an accurate guide, the building of radar sites in Turkey, Iran, and Pakistan and the crash development of the U-2 were undertaken in response to, not in anticipation of, the Soviet test program.

On the logical assumption that testing presaged deployment, the collection of photographic intelligence was initiated. It alone could provide the one incontrovertible kind of physical evidence for actual operational deployment, the construction of launching pads and the existence of missile sites. Even in this instance ambiguity arose, as it was impossible to conduct comprehensive overhead reconnaissance of the entire Soviet Union. Even sophisticated cameras could be deceived by systematic camouflage of missile bases, whether under construction or completed. The intelligence community nonetheless handled this area of ambiguity adequately. Uncertainty did occur over the meaning of the 1958–59 hiatus in testing, at least for air force intelligence. But the CIA and the army and navy correctly interpreted the pause; in any case, neither radar surveillance nor overhead reconnaissance could have provided definitive evidence as to the reason for the halt. When testing was resumed in May 1959, the assessment that deployment would shortly follow was in accord with the available physical evidence.

Only at this stage can failure in estimation be fairly attributed to ambiguity in the intelligence data. Here, the progression from technical and observable evidence to an accurate conclusion broke down. From 1958 to 1960, the estimates of Soviet ICBM deployment capabilities were founded on an extremely narrow and uncertain base—namely, the estimation of production capacity. No technical means could furnish definitive intelligence for a reliable judgment about Soviet technological progress and defense industrial organization; therefore, the true rate of ICBM production, planned or achieved, could not be reliably known. Only two sources of evidence could furnish such intelligence: (1) industrial espionage within the Soviet Union, including inside information on the allocation of economic resources by GOSPLAN (Soviet state economic plan), Soviet economic constraints, technical difficulties prior to testing, production schedules, and so forth; and (2) American analogies, with the concomitant assumption that the Soviet defense industry would face similar difficulties in solving problems in missile development and fabrication.

The CIA penetrated the Soviet defense establishment or defense industry in only one case—that of Penkovsky—as far as our evidence indicates any success at all in this endeavor. Even if there were more penetration, the information obtained could not have been very reliable to judge by the wildly inaccurate estimates of the Soviet ICBM production rate served up in the published versions of the 1959 and 1960 NIEs. With regard to the use of American analogues, the projected initial rate of ICBM production was 50 missiles per year, increasing to 100 per year after two years. This estimate is hard to reconcile with the production rate of up to 500 missiles per year attributed to the Soviet Union. The explanation offered by Secretary of Defense McElroy in 1959 stated in effect that the gap in prediction arose because the number of missiles the United States *planned* for production was compared with the numbers that the Russians *could produce.* A more unconvincing excuse would be hard to find.

It is a reasonable conjecture that the worst-case estimate, which required a belief in Soviet ability to produce ICBMs between two and five times as fast as the United States, was either a deliberate exaggeration intended to justify increased production of American strategic weapons without reference to the true state of the arms race or the result of ambiguous and scanty intelligence. I believe the latter explanation is closest to the truth, although significant sources of information were culpably overlooked.

It seems clear that the judgments of the intelligence community, and in particular of the CIA (which had the decisive coordinating role in the national estimation process), were founded on an excessively restricted set of data obtained from technical collection systems and observation: missile testing, missile prototypes on test stands and launchers, missile-site configurations, and missile launching pads. When faced with the necessity of estimating an aspect of the Soviet missile program which could not be so monitored or observed, intelligence turned to other kinds of evidence, but without success.

The intentions of the Soviet Union might have been illuminated by other forms of evidence, forms that were apparently excluded from the estimative process until 1960. This evidence included, for example, Soviet strategic military doctrine, economic constraints, political-bureaucratic demands, and propaganda and deception.[60] Little attention seems to have been paid to unclassified Soviet material concerning Soviet military and political doctrine and Soviet strategy.[61] As a result, the connection between Soviet strategic concepts and Soviet weapons systems was not adequately understood. In the case of Soviet missiles, both ICBMs and IRBMs (intermediate range ballistic missiles), openly proclaimed doctrine and strategy available in Soviet publications pointed to the future course of weapon-system development. The intelligence community apparently did not accept such indications of policy as true indicators of Soviet long-range goals.

There was no realization of the importance of Eurasia to Soviet political and military leaders or of their perception that the strategic threat to the Soviet Union came from Europe and regions in Asia where the United States had bomber bases. Consequently, intelligence did not anticipate the Soviet decision to build 700 M/IRBMs instead of several hundred SS-6 ICBMs in the late 1950s. Having failed to understand the Soviet strategic concepts behind the missile program, America misjudged priorities as to IRBM versus ICBM development.

What was the role of Soviet propaganda and deception in the mistaken assessment of the Soviet ICBM program? Soviet claims made during 1957–61 by Premier Khrushchev and others were designed to heighten Western uncertainties regarding the strategic balance and to conceal the Soviets' own uncertainties and weaknesses. Soviet claims of strategic superiority also concealed from Western intelligence the Soviets' decision *not* to begin deployment of a first-generation ICBM by making it appear that the Soviet Union had in fact the capability to do precisely this. Moreover, these claims, enunciated repeatedly in Soviet propaganda, attempted to deter the United States from launching an attack when the Soviet Union was strategically vulnerable.[62]

Yet in no account of the missile gap controversy is there any indication that this aspect of Soviet behavior influenced the evaluation of the Soviet ICBM program in the National Intelligence Estimates. The NIEs were based primarily upon observable actions of the Soviets, not on an appreciation of their intentions or strategic thinking, even though evidence on these matters was available in Soviet military and doctrinal writings, overt propaganda, and Politburo rhetoric. Secretary of Defense Gates said in his testimony that "there is obviously no intelligence whatsoever on U.S.S.R. intentions as to specific military or political policies or action. Of course, it is impossible to have such intelligence. What we have is a refined and better set of facts pertaining to the probable or what the Soviet ICBM may be [sic]."[63]

In sum, the intelligence available regarding the Soviet missile program was always incomplete. The amount of high-grade human intelligence from traditional espionage was small, at least before Colonel Penkovsky appeared. Technical intelligence—aerial reconnaissance, signal and communications intelligence, and radar surveillance—was comparatively ample after 1956, but remained ambiguous. Open sources of potential information and insight that might have yielded clues to the purpose of Soviet missile development were not quarried, an oversight that was not the least of the factors that led to the erratic performance of American intelligence in the notorious missile gap controversy.

The Cuban Missile Crisis

Intelligence had a far greater arsenal of resources at its disposal in the 1960s than in earlier years. It soon became clear, despite all the technological breakthroughs, that more facts did not necessarily make for less ambiguous intelligence. The major intelligence issues of the 1960s and early 1970s provide vivid illustrations. Deliberate deception never played a decisive role. If so, what were the main obstacles to a realistic understanding of events? The experience of U.S. intelligence in the Cuban missile crisis, in Vietnam, and in the debate about Soviet missile strength in the 1970s shed some light on this question.

Why concentrate on conflicts that were mainly military in character rather than discuss the U.S. record in foreign political intelligence? For one thing, the dividing line between "political" and "military" is seldom clear-cut in the real world—all the crises discussed in the following pages were both military and political confrontations. More important yet, the U.S. intelligence effort was preoccupied with "military" affairs from the very beginning. It concerned itself to a much lesser extent with political, social, and economic trends—fields in which it was in any case less adept. Most of its resources were, and are, devoted to "bean counting." It has accomplished this sort of task with considerable success on the level of collection, if not always on that of analysis.

Overemphasis on military affairs to the neglect of other aspects of world affairs is one of the basic weaknesses of American intelligence. The Kirkpatrick report drew attention to this weakness in 1961, but nothing much seems to have changed in this respect. While the outside observer may disagree with this order of priorities, he or she cannot ignore its dominant role in U.S. intelligence during the period under review. Finally, there is a practical consideration involved in that a good deal of documentation is available on the Cuban missile crisis, on intelligence in Vietnam, and on the internal intelligence community debates about Soviet military strength. Political developments and crises in the past few decades are *terra incognita* by comparison.

The Cuban missile crisis provides a unique opportunity to study the record of U.S. intelligence before it becomes "ancient history," because the data used for analysis are largely in the public domain.[64] The crisis period involved several stages: (1) the initial military buildup in Cuba in the summer and fall of 1962; (2) discovery of the Soviet strategic missiles there in October 1962; (3) identification of these missile systems and their capabilities; (4) monitoring the missiles' dismantlement and removal from

Cuba; and (5) post-mortem analysis of Soviet objectives. This treatment focuses upon the discovery of the missiles, for it was there that the performance of the intelligence community was questioned, whereas its accomplishments in the other phases were outstanding.[65]

The introduction of medium- and intermediate-range ballistic missiles into Cuba was not anticipated. If the installation of the missiles came as a surprise, was this the result of an intelligence failure? Did the CIA or other components of the intelligence community later succeed in explaining the Soviet Union's objectives in deploying the missiles? Neither question can be answered with total assurance; the official CIA and DIA post mortem evaluations are as yet inaccessible. On the available evidence, however, it appears that U.S. intelligence was unable to reach a definite judgment about the ultimate goal of the Soviet Union.[66] The only available assessment of intelligence community performance, the "Interim Report of the Senate Preparedness Investigating Subcommittee," attributes the failure in anticipation to a misconception about Soviet policy.[67] If this was the case before the crisis, and if this faulty view influenced the estimation process, it is not hard to understand why no satisfactory explanation of Soviet actions was provided after resolution of the crisis.

Before proceeding to a discussion of performance, a brief comment on sources. The Cuban missile crisis has become the classic study for the role of the intelligence community in crisis management; many epistemological questions about intelligence turn on this case.[68] Recent assessments have tended to address only the general criticisms and conclusions set forth in the Senate Interim Report.[69] These evaluations have been shaped by the available dossier of intelligence records, NSC documents, Kennedy's presidential records, and congressional testimony supplemented by the memoirs of contemporary official participants.[70] As a result, the discussion will not move beyond the restricted framework of this evidence. No official post-mortem evaluations of performance are at hand and the first-person accounts of officials involved in the crisis are of limited utility, for they do not discuss any intelligence except that available in open sources. The "hard evidence"—in the form of intelligence records—is limited to four Special National Intelligence Estimates, CIA memoranda relating to the military buildup, some supplemental reports,[71] and an analysis of variant views of the Kremlin's intentions.[72] The documents do not provide sufficient information with which to assess either the full range of intelligence data collected in the summer and fall of 1962, or the analytical process whereby the raw intelligence was fashioned into analyses and estimates. Furthermore, no intelligence record of the DIA pertaining to the crisis is presently available[73] though the DIA appears to have been the first intelligence organization to tentatively identify San Cristobal as a Soviet ballistic missile site.[74]

THE MILITARY BUILDUP

Intelligence discovered strategic ballistic missiles in Cuba while conducting a comprehensive collection and analysis intended to detect the types of military weapons and the numbers of Soviet personnel brought to Cuba in the summer and fall of 1962.[75] As was the case with the Soviet ICBM program, incontrovertible proof of the installation of missiles in Cuba was first provided by high-altitude photography. But the U-2 reconnaissance flight that discovered the MRBM (medium-range ballistic missile) site at San Cristobal was not the culmination of prescient deductive analysis about Soviet strategy and policy but resulted from a chain of evidence assembled in a pragmatic, inductive manner.

Three questions are important for this phase of the crisis. First, what sources of intelligence were available and what clues did these provide? As in the case of the "missile gap," we need to know whether the intelligence community possessed adequate sources of intelligence and whether these sources could provide the necessary information on time. Second, there is the question of timing. On 4 October 1962, a DIA hypothesis led to a U-2 flight over western Cuba, with particular emphasis on the area of San Cristobal. The genesis of this hypothesis began after 21 September, when an agent reported that ballistic missiles were perhaps being installed there.[76] In the aftermath of the crisis, it was established that no ballistic missiles were shipped to Cuba before 8 September, and that initial construction of the missile sites began between 15 and 20 September. Reconnaissance over western Cuba on 5 September had detected no missile activity in the San Cristobal area and no military activity at Remedios and Sangua La Grande, the two locations at which IRBM sites were discovered in October. But no additional U-2 flights were carried out over western Cuba between 5 September and 7 October.[77] Did other sources of intelligence provide any evidence of missile activity before early October or before 14 October?[78]

Third, how accurate were the intelligence analyses and estimates? The SNIE of 19 September said nothing about Russian plans to install strategic missiles.[79] The estimate recognized the possible advantages, but it discounted the likelihood of such action by the U.S.S.R.[80] Did the available evidence support this judgment? Was the evidence overriden by preconceptions about the Soviet Union and its behavior? Or did the evidence admit of no other conclusion?

In the spring of 1962 the Soviet Union furnished Cuba with large quantities of conventional military armaments, including MIG aircraft and motor torpedo boats. In July and early August this buildup was accelerated. An unusually large number of Soviet ships delivered military cargos to Cuba under conditions of extraordinary secrecy during this period. In addition, recently arrived Soviet personnel began construction activity at several locations, from Oriente Province in the east to Pinar del Rio Province in the west. By mid-August, refugee and agent reports suggested that the Soviet Union was introducing surface-to-air missiles (SAMs) and building ancillary radar and communications facilities as part of a comprehensive air defense system. Special collection efforts were directed at known locations of military activity and construction. The next U-2 reconnaissance mission, on 29 August, provided positive identification of SAM sites at two of the suspected locations and at six other places in western Cuba.

Throughout July and August, high-altitude reconnaissance missions were the primary source of hard intelligence about the progress and extent of the military buildup in Cuba. Until the positive identification of the SAM sites, these missions were carried out according to a regular schedule. The areas photographed were pre-Castro military sites still in use after Batista's overthrow. Aircraft deliveries, airfield improvements, construction of military bases, and the delivery of naval craft were closely monitored. High-altitude reconnaissance missions between 5 September and 5 October discovered new SAM sites and missile installations, although they did not uncover any evidence of offensive missile capability.

THE DISCOVERY OF THE STRATEGIC MISSILES

Intelligence about the missiles was developed in three stages. From April until late September, reports and rumors from agents, refugees, and exile organizations were received and collated with intelligence from other sources. No individual report sufficed to prove that there were strategic missiles in Cuba.[81] Before 14 October, the interpretation of high-altitude photographs of the areas in question either disproved the presence of missiles or connected the suspected activity with SAM or cruise missile deployment.[82]

The second stage, in late September, took place when a recently arrived agent provided the first credible description of military equipment corresponding to a medium-range ballistic missile. Only with this item of human intelligence did it become acceptable to argue that strategic ballistic missiles were stationed in Cuba.

In the third and final stage, the missiles' presence was proved by the correlation of this agent's report with other intelligence. The deployment of SAM sites in the region of San Cristobal was suspicious. This was the same area in which the agent had observed the movement of military equipment, but where there were no identified military installations. Analysis of this report resulted in the designation of a specific location as a suspected medium-range ballistic missile site.[83] Soon afterward, a U-2 flew over San Cristobal. It returned with incontrovertible photographic evidence of the MRBM complex under installation there.

High-altitude reconnaissance subsequently obtained aerial photography of the entire island. This project was designed to ascertain the precise nature of missile deployment and the exact configuration of missile sites. It also provided information about location, number of missiles, and their degree of operational readiness. Locations detected by high-altitude photography were later photographed by low-flying aircraft. The result was the discovery of two additional MRBM sites near Sangua La Grande and three fixed IRBM sites under construction at Guanajay and Remedios.[84]

SOURCES OF INTELLIGENCE

The intelligence community was intensely interested in the military buildup in Cuba that began in the summer of 1962. Yet the best efforts of intelligence were in vain, as offensive missiles were being introduced into Cuba and there was no avoiding detection of them by shipping intelligence, agent and refugee reports, high-altitude photography, and SIGINT.[85]

High-altitude photography furnished proof of the presence of offensive missiles in Cuba, but the first MRBM site at San Cristobal was detected at an installation stage that no longer required concealment.[86] What other sources of intelligence were utilized before 14 October?

The first source to alert the intelligence community to the military buildup in Cuba in 1962 was shipping intelligence. This included the tabulation of the volume of Soviet merchant ship traffic to Cuban ports, photography of individual ships to determine deck cargos, regular aerial reconnaissance over port areas, and monitoring of naval communications. The cargos of the ships, however, remained unknown unless they were carried above deck.[87] Nothing in the available shipping intelligence provided any indication of the Soviet plan to introduce offensive missiles. The ships that brought the ballistic missiles, the *Omsk* and the *Poltava,* were duly observed; at the time, however, intelligence analysts did not perceive the significance of their large hatches or of the fact that they rode high in the water—an indication of space-consuming cargo of low weight and high volume.[88] Because there was no climate of expectation, the only clue that shipping intelligence could have provided was missed. There seemed no need to relate these specific pieces of evidence to any wider context or to speculate as to their possible implications.

Survey work for the MRBM and IRBM sites must have been carried out by July or August 1962. The decision to deploy the missiles must have been taken not later than the spring of that year.[89] Colonel Oleg Penkovsky was still providing information in the spring of 1962, but there is no indication that the CIA received forewarning from Penkovsky or other human sources.[90] Penkovsky did provide detailed information on Soviet medium-range missile systems that later permitted CIA agents to estimate the construction stages and timetables of the missiles in Cuba. The September SNIE reflects deductive analysis based on diplomatic sources, Soviet and Cuban statements,[91] and private exchanges between the Kennedy administration and the Kremlin.

HUMINT. Did the CIA have agents in Cuba able to provide warning or confirmation, either before or after the event?[92] There is no evidence that the Havana station had succeeded in establishing a long-term, stay-behind network of agents in the Cuban armed forces, intelligence service, or government before the United States broke diplomatic relations with Cuba. The CIA possessed indigenous agents in Cuba, but their number and effectiveness were surely reduced by the massive internal security operation mounted after the failure of the Bay of Pigs invasion. The CIA also had access to intelligence from the other Western intelligence services in Cuba and collected many reports from interviews with refugees and from exile organizations.[93] But all told, the quality of human intelligence received from Cuba was poor. Most of the intelligence by agents and refugees seems to have been obtained through local visual observation.[94] The difficulty of communicating with agents in Cuba precluded sending agents to suspected or identified military installations and construction sites to observe, sketch, or photograph the different weapons systems being deployed. As Cuban and Soviet internal security measures were highly effective, had the intelligence community been compelled to rely entirely upon human sources no accurate picture could have been formed.

Nonetheless, intelligence from human sources between April and September 1962 provided useful information on the ports receiving military equipment, the secrecy under which it was unloaded and transported to the interior, the locations of Soviet personnel, and the construction sites connected with the military buildup.[95] The report of an agent who had observed and estimated the length of a missile transporter near San Cristobal prompted analysts at the CIA to correlate the evidence of long-trailer convoys heading west with the photographic evidence of SAM construction sites in western Cuba.[96] There is no evidence, however, of a link between this report and the decision on 3 October to overfly the San Cristobal area. Although the inland region of western Cuba had not been photographed since 5 September, the decisive factor that led to examining the SAM sites appears to have been due to two suspicious facts that had only recently been revealed: the installation of a SAM complex in an area not known to contain any military installation and the trapezoidal pattern of the identified SAM site, which replicated the usual configuration in SAM complexes protecting ICBM bases in the Soviet Union.[97] The DIA analyst who recognized this congruity of pattern for the respective SAM complexes also realized that the center of the pattern was near San Cristobal. This correlation was almost certainly the stimulus that convinced the CIA, the military, and CIA director John McCone that the Soviet Union was installing strategic missiles in western Cuba.

SIGINT.[98] Signal intelligence is not acknowledged in congressional testimony, CIA estimates and reports, or in secondary treatments of the Cuban missile crisis. The National Security Agency's contribution is never mentioned.[99] Yet SIGINT in some form must have supplied intelligence about the military buildup in Cuba; it may have helped to discover it, in fact. With SIGINT, the "argument from silence" carries no weight; unfortunately, there is no converse example—SIGINT provided important intelligence that could not be revealed without betraying American techniques of breaching Soviet security. In the Cuban missile crisis, it had to appear that human intelligence and aerial photography provided the decisive intelligence information.

Soviet intelligence services and military units in Cuba maintained rigorous communications security before and during the military buildup. The NSA was presumably unable to break into the strategic cryptosystems used for communication between the Soviet Union and Cuba to obtain a forewarning either of the military buildup or of the plan to install the ballistic missiles.[100] Cuban communications were supervised by the KGB, so it is improbable that coded traffic related to Soviet plans and Soviet units was carried by the Cuban military communications network.

Apart from the KGB communications center in Havana, which would have handled all diplomatic traffic, it is certain that the Soviets established a major communications network in Cuba in the summer of 1962 to parallel their military buildup. Elements of the Soviet armed forces trained and advised the Cuban army, air force, and navy; they also supervised the installation and operation of the various weapons systems under Soviet control in Cuba. Each military site, and each civilian location where Soviet intelligence, security, and military personnel were stationed, had a direct link to the Central Soviet command center near Havana. Each separate element of the Soviet armed forces in Cuba, moreover, was equipped with its own tactical communications network, including land lines, which allowed them to dispense with the existing American-built telephone and microwave systems.

There were at least seven separate tactical networks in Cuba in the summer and fall of 1962:

Network	Responsibility of Organization
1. KGB and GRU	Security, communications, arms shipment
2. Strategic Rocket Forces	MRBM and IRBM site operation
3. Air Force	MIG and IL-28s, training, maintenance
4. Air Defense Command	SAM systems
5. Army ground units	SAM bivouacs, training, missions, logistics
6. Army engineers	Site preparation and construction
7. Navy	missile boats, training, bases

As soon as a network came into use, direction-finding (D/F), the taking of bearings on a Soviet radio transmitter from two or more intercept stations, could pinpoint its location or confirm its movement. Theoretically, a combination of D/F, network analysis, and call-signal identification could have determined the entire communications grid of each Soviet military element. On the other hand, the Soviets sought to ensure the greatest secrecy in respect to the location of the SAM sites and ballistic missile complexes by using land lines for coded messages and voice communication.[101]

The congressional testimony of Secretary of Defense McNamara implies that SIGINT helped to provide hard intelligence about missile sites and Soviet military units' locations:

> That information [the agent report of 31 September] over a period of days, extending beyond the 4- or 5-day period you refer to, up into early October, was correlated with other information which was not received and not included in such reports, and which, following the correlation, led one or two individuals to the hypothesis that there might possibly be missile activity in a particular area of Cuba.[102]

Because the last U-2 flight over western Cuba was made on 5 September, where could this "other information" have come from, if not from SIGINT? According to the secretary's testimony, the agent report of a long-trailer convoy heading west plus the identification of a trapezoidal SAM site at San Cristobal, where there was no known military installation for it to defend, led to the identification of San Cristobal as a possible ballistic missile site. But it is also possible that SIGINT D/F or traffic analysis had drawn attention to unusual military activity near San Cristobal within the area of the trapezoidal SAM deployment pattern.[103]

The discovery of two additional MRBM sites at Sangua La Grande and of the IRBM sites under construction at Remedios and Guanajay contributes further circumstantial evidence of the importance of SIGINT. These sites were identified by search reconnaissance ordered after the discovery of the MRBM complex at San Cristobal.[104] The official explanation implies that discovery of the launch positions at Remedios and Guanajay was an isolated event resulting from chance observation by the U-2 aircraft.[105] Since Remedios and the other sites had been overflown in September, something must have drawn attention to them as possible locations of military activity. Otherwise they would not have been included in the flight plans, first in August and September, and then on 17 October. It is my conjecture that a Soviet presence in the area had been established tentatively by SIGINT.[106]

THE DISCOVERY OF THE MISSILES

The available intelligence sources were apparently unable to reveal either Soviet intentions or the types of weapons systems that would be installed in Cuba. These sources did permit the intelligence community to monitor the buildup as it proceeded and to estimate the capability of each weapons system introduced into Cuba. At this point, the analysts had to relate *capability* to *intention* in order to assess the military and strategic implications of the buildup and the possible future developments arising from it. The first Special National Intelligence Estimate of 19 September on Soviet military activities in Cuba derived in part from the insistence of John McCone that the deployment of SAMs foreshadowed the Soviet Union's intention to install offensive ballistic missiles in Cuba.[107] This first attempt to estimate Soviet intentions in Cuba also appears to have been motivated by concern about the connection in Soviet policy between Berlin and Cuba, by the instinctive suspicions of the intelligence collectors of the CIA, and by the conviction of intelligence analysts in both the CIA and DIA that something strange was afoot in Cuba.

The September SNIE was a failure inasmuch as it did not predict that the Soviet Union would install strategic missiles in Cuba that fall. The document's descriptive analysis focused on the assessment of military capability rather than on Soviet intentions.[108] On the other hand, at the time the document was drafted there was no basis for an unequivocal prediction that the Soviet Union would deploy offensive missiles in Cuba, though the estimate did admit that this was a possibility. Was this kind of move one that would be incompatible with Soviet policy?

Analysts concluded that the SAM deployment fitted the more conservative explanation. The buildup in general was defensive in nature, designed
to ensure the survival of the Castro regime,[109] and did not reflect a radically
new Soviet policy toward Cuba. The pattern of Soviet military aid was
intended to strengthen the defenses of the island, thereby raising the price
the United States would have to pay to eliminate it by invasion.[110] Albeit
indirectly, the SNIE explained the emplacement of the SAMs in areas
presumed to lack military installations as a function of an area air defense
system. It ignored the question of why particular SAM sites were located
in certain areas.

On the empirical level—where the estimators appear to have operated
—could one infer from any aspect of their overall military capability that
the Soviets intended to deploy offensive missiles? The answer must be yes.
For John McCone, the emplacement of SAMs at sites apparently unrelated
to the defense of specific military installations was sufficient evidence of
Soviet intentions to install offensive missiles. Given his background in
business and engineering, McCone could not believe that such an expensive weapons system would be installed unless it was intended to defend
very important military targets. He rejected the CIA analysts' explanation
that the SAM deployment was designed to provide an air defense system
against possible American invasion. The Soviets could not possibly assume
that anti-aircraft missiles and MIG aircraft would seriously hinder the
United States if it chose to invade Cuba.[111] Instead, McCone concluded
that the SAM network was intended to prevent American reconnaissance
aircraft from penetrating Cuban airspace, so that they would not discover
the next stage of the military buildup—the installation of offensive missiles. McCone was predisposed to believe that the Soviet Union sought to
augment its strategic nuclear capability by deploying ballistic missiles in
Cuba and made the leap from capability to intention. He acknowledged
that he had no evidence, only his intuition, to support his belief. In a word,
he had the *imagination* indispensable to superior intelligence work.

In fact, the construction of the MRBM and IRBM sites was begun before
the entire SAM network was fully operational. But this does not vitiate
McCone's hypothesis. A U-2 aircraft was downed by a SAM over Cuba
—proof that the system, though not completed before the ballistic missile
sites were operational, was indeed intended to preclude U.S. overhead
reconnaissance.

If McCone was able to make the leap from capability to intention, what
prevented the CIA estimators from doing likewise? Analysts in the CIA
were aware that offensive missiles might be placed in Cuba. But the
19 September SNIE still claimed that the military buildup was defensive

in nature and that the establishment on Cuban soil of nuclear strategic forces would be incompatible with Soviet policy. The estimators could have reached McCone's conclusion only if they had shared his somewhat primitive views about the objectives of Soviet military strategy and the psychology of the Soviet leadership. But the estimators in the ONE were more sophisticated in their approach; furthermore, there may have been a disposition to avoid the type of overstatement that had occurred in the missile gap controversy.[112] The primary reason seems to be that the estimators were inclined to foist American constructs about nuclear strategy on Soviet policy and to attribute American conceptions of rationality in policy making to the Soviet leadership.

Soviet behavior and strategy in Cuba were interpreted according to an American perspective. The official statements of Soviet Foreign Minister Gromyko and Ambassador Dobrynin to the Kennedy administration in August and September seemed to take full account of President Kennedy's warning that America would not allow Cuba to become an offensive military base for the Soviet Union. It is clear that these statements were designed to reinforce the American assumption that the Soviet Union would act according to American canons of rationality.[113] This argumentation seems to have been shared by those responsible for the SNIE,[114] who underestimated the risks that the Soviet Union was prepared to take in Cuba.[115] They failed to consider the possibility that the Soviet leadership was operating under a set of premises different from their own. The impression left by the reasoning in the SNIE is that the estimators could not accept the worst-case analysis[116] so congenial to John McCone, whose view of Soviet strategy and behavior was permeated by a visceral distrust.

To this day, there is no firm consensus as to why the Soviet Union decided to introduce strategic missiles into Cuba.[117] The supposed inconsistencies in the way individual elements of the Soviet intelligence services and armed forces carried out the deployment puzzled intelligence analysts at the time; those who believed there were such inconsistencies have still not explained them satisfactorily. It is possible that the Soviet aim was to maneuver the Kennedy administration into a formal commitment not to invade Cuba in exchange for the removal of the missiles.[118] The Soviet Union almost certainly did not bring the nuclear warheads for the MRBMs and IRBMs to Cuba. The warhead storage bunkers were under construction, so it is possible that these components were being carried to Cuba on the Soviet ships, which turned back after imposition of the quarantine.[119] The central point is that without warheads the missiles were strategically useless. Whether the Soviets ever intended to arm the missiles in Cuba remains a subject of conjecture. Since they made little or no effort to camouflage or conceal the preparation of the missile sites, it is possible that discovery was anticipated before the missiles could be armed—for which reason there was no need to bring the warheads to Cuba in the first place.[120] Soviet behavior in Cuba has been explained in a number of different ways,[121] but in the present context all that matters is that the process of analysis and estimation manifested both a rigid empiricism and a lack of imagination. Intelligence was handicapped by its inability to entertain the hypothesis that Soviet leaders were acting on assumptions quite different from what Americans assumed them to be.

CHAPTER 6

Vietnam and the Case of the Missing Missiles

Vietnam

T HE Vietnam War, 1961–75, is a frustrating, albeit fascinating, topic for the student of U.S. intelligence performance.[1] Intelligence—whether strategic or operational—was not a decisive factor. The records available suggest that intelligence *facts* were seldom in dispute.[2] Yet the most important American decisions in the conflict were reached without adequate study of intelligence information and without a thorough consultation with intelligence officials. Strategic intelligence was generally accurate, but often ignored in the formulation of military policy. Operational intelligence, which is of more importance in the actual conduct of war, was frequently inadequate, but was not a prime factor in determining how the war was waged.

Unlike World War II, in which strategic intelligence was of decisive value in devising military and political strategy, during the Vietnam War strategic intelligence was commonly ignored unless it supported the views of high-level civilian and military decision makers.[3] The often pessimistic strategic intelligence assessments and estimates produced by the main civilian analytical branches, the Offices of Current Intelligence and National Estimates at the CIA, and the Bureau of Intelligence and Research at the State Department (INR), were used very selectively or discounted as the judgments of habitual pessimists. Scrutiny of the decision-making process in the period shows that leading officials in the Kennedy, Johnson, and Nixon administrations often applied traditional maxims of American military strategy and academic precepts of "policy analysis" and "crisis management" to a situation in which they were quite irrelevant.[4] From time to time, the civilian intelligence agencies furnished analyses that differed from the prevailing perception of reality in Southeast Asia and questioned the assumption of U.S. military strategy there. Some officials have admitted that their own beliefs may have been wrong. But it would be hard to prove that National Intelligence Estimates restrained many of them from making decisions as though their perceptions of the war were true.

On the operational level, a great number of human and technical intelligence resources were mobilized in 1965 when U.S. ground combat forces landed in South Vietnam and the air campaign against North Vietnam began.[5] The combined capabilities of the CIA, DIA, NSA, INR, and the military services, however, often failed to provide the categories of tactical combat and police security intelligence necessary to deprive the Communists of the strategic initiative and tactical surprise and uproot their clandestine apparatus.

For example, the Tet Offensive—at least the scope of the attack and its initial targets—was such a surprise largely because there had been no effective penetration of the North Vietnamese hierarchy. For most of the war, the best source of intelligence about the enemy's short-term intentions and tactical combat behavior was tactical COMINT and airborne direction-finding. When these technical systems failed, U.S. commanders found themselves dangerously ignorant about the intentions of the other side.

Difficulty in establishing contacts with the enemy's personnel and the efficiency of the Viet Cong counterintelligence apparatus partly explain the CIA's poor performance in human espionage before 1968, but at least three other reasons should be noted: (1) Until the middle of 1966, when the CIA established a Viet Cong branch and began to operate unilaterally against the Viet Cong, U.S. intelligence relied on South Vietnamese intelligence and police services for information about the enemy supplied by agents. These services were penetrated by the Viet Cong. Accordingly, they were an inadequate, sometimes dangerous, source of human intelligence. (2) Only a small number of CIA case officers could speak Vietnamese, and many CIA officials and senior U.S. army intelligence officers had only an imperfect knowledge of the country and the enemy.[6] (3) The average one-year tour of duty was usually too short to permit a case officer or an analyst either to understand the Vietnamese mentality or to develop the necessary intuitive grasp of the enemy's military and political behavior.

The most important requirement of operational intelligence in the ground war was to locate the enemy in order that they be brought to battle on the ground or attacked from the air. The intelligence available to U.S. and South Vietnamese forces was usually unable to satisfy this requirement. For the Americans, as for the French before them, the major question of operational intelligence was to predict where the Communists were or where they were going to strike. But the Viet Cong, like the Viet Minh, were sheltered by the almost impenetrable secrecy of the Communist world and by the obscurity of the jungle. American intelligence never had much success in penetrating this secrecy through human espionage,[7] and even the array of electronic ground sensors and technical collection systems was often to no avail. In spite of the mass of intelligence information stored in American computers in Saigon, U.S. intelligence in the Vietnam War knew everything in general about the enemy, but nothing in particular.[8]

Operational intelligence did establish, however, the basic facts about the nature of the war as waged by the Viet Cong and the North Vietnamese,[9] while the large quantity of operational intelligence about the enemy's strategy, combat methods, and organization eluded appreciation and application by the American high command in South Vietnam. Rarely was this information applied to the design of forces, tactics, and operations corresponding to the nature of the war. The U.S. army in particular persisted in the attempt to fit the Viet Cong organization and the Communist form of "revolutionary warfare" into its own "strategic concept" of the war. Both in the ground war and in the air offensive against North Vietnam— and later Cambodia and Laos—each of the military services remained committed to its own style of warfare, which was often irrelevant to the actual hostilities under way.[10] This stubborn attitude persisted despite the abundance of intelligence proving its futility. Orthodox military strategy and tactics adapted from World War II and the Korean War, or even the "counterinsurgency warfare" which so beguiled the Kennedy administration was unable to defeat the kind of revolutionary warfare waged first by the Viet Minh, and later by the Viet Cong and the North Vietnamese army. By 1964, the stamp of conventional U.S. army tactical doctrine had been imposed on the South Vietnamese forces.[11] In 1965, the American field commander began to deploy U.S. combat units according to a strategy of firepower and attrition that ignored both the conception of "revolutionary warfare" and military development in North Vietnam since the French Indochina War.[12]

A brief assessment of intelligence performance in Vietnam can deal only briefly with the most important reasons for conceptual errors in analyzing traditionalist, non-Western societies.[13] Therefore, focus should be selective on some of the major phases of the war, emphasizing the best-documented period, 1961 to 1968.

THE KENNEDY COMMITMENTS, 1961–63

The Kennedy administration bound the United States to preserving South Vietnam from Communist domination. Between 1961 and 1963, a confluence of events and decisions enmeshed the United States in progressively larger commitments in support of this objective.[14] Strategic intelligence provided a background to the decision-making process at this time. A number of NIEs alerted high-level policy makers to the general nature of the Communist insurgency and delineated the increasingly adverse political-military trends in South Vietnam.[15] But as the administration conducted no extended debate or study about the appropriate courses of action, strategic intelligence played little role in shaping policy recommendations.[16] No intelligence estimate before 1964 questioned the assumption that the United States had no choice but to prevent the fall of South Vietnam, nor was there a thorough examination of the assumption that the Communist insurgency posed an unavoidable challenge to American credibility and security regionally or around the world.[17]

During this preliminary phase of the war, most of the available National Intelligence Estimates confined themselves to descriptive analyses of the situation in South Vietnam.[18] Although reassuring data was provided at times, the tenor of these estimates was consistently pessimistic. These documents show that neither the CIA nor the INR was under any illusions about the essentially political nature of the insurgency or about the character of the enemy. There were many warnings about Communist shrewdness and tenacity that proved more accurate as the conflict continued. The question of numerical accuracy was more difficult—neither the CIA station in Saigon nor the U.S. Military Assistance Command Vietnam (MACV) was able to provide a detailed account of the Communist insurgent organization before 1963.[19] Estimates by the CIA in 1961 and 1962 miscalculated the numerical and political strength of the Viet Cong.[20] Yet the CIA and INR recognized that the transition of the Communist effort from a clandestine political movement to an overt military organization—which greatly expanded the scope of the insurgency—inaugurated the opening phase of the "people's war" described in the writings of General Vo Nguyen Giap. All in all, these agencies arrived at a useful understanding of Communist military strategy and long-term objectives in Indochina and Vietnam, but whether this assessment was more accurate than the contemporary writings of Bernard Fall and other French and American "Indochina hands" is debatable.[21]

Inadequate and uninformed intelligence reporting has been blamed for the unfounded optimism of U.S. policy in 1962 and 1963. Certainly, American civilian and military intelligence lacked a systematic approach to Vietnamese culture and society, which made accurate perceptions of Vietnamese attitudes and behavior with respect to the war almost impossible. The available record discloses how the CIA, MACV, and the U.S. Mission in South Vietnam misjudged the extent of rural disaffection with the Diem regime, misunderstood the internal political weakness of the government, and misrepresented the morale and military ability of the South Vietnamese army. The difficulty in assessing the situation in South Vietnam was compounded by the dependence of U.S. intelligence in Saigon on the Diem government for raw information about Viet Cong activity, the "strategic hamlet" program, the pacification effort, and so forth.[22] Much of the optimistic reporting about the progress of the war and the performance of the army can be traced to the U.S. Military Assistance Advisory Group (MAAG), to its successor (MACV), and to the bureaucratic structure of the reporting system in Saigon and Washington. General Paul D. Harkins, the MACV commander in 1962 and 1963, was not the last senior American military officer who preferred his own wisdom—or hunches—to less optimistic intelligence reports. During Harkins's tour, finished intelligence assessments for Washington produced by the CIA station and the U.S. mission were coordinated with MACV before dispatch. In the process, they were edited to reflect the optimism of the MACV commander lest any acknowledgment that the war was not being won, or that U.S. military programs were not succeeding, might serve as an admission of failure.[23] General Harkins's tenure began the fateful closing of the intelligence evaluation circle; its vested institutional self-interest and self-deception afflicted U.S. intelligence for the remainder of the war.

True, the distortion of reporting was recognized in this specific case. An independent evaluation of the situation by a special CIA survey team commissioned by Secretary McNamara redressed the optimism reported earlier and revealed the serious deterioration of the counterinsurgency program. It pointed out the failure of the "strategic hamlet" program, the decline in rural security, the increase in Viet Cong activity, and the military ineptitude of the South Vietnamese army.[24] Although this evaluation did not weaken the U.S. military's adherence to its own version of reality, it did force a more pessimistic view on Washington, one that undermined the belief that South Vietnam was capable of defeating the Communist insurgency alone.

The intelligence community's formal forecasts from 1961 to 1963 expressed skepticism about the long-range prospects for the survival of a non-Communist South Vietnam; they did not highly rate the policies recommended to President Kennedy as far as chances of success were concerned.[25] In general, these estimates furnished an accurate assessment of the Communist insurgency. However, the CIA, whose Office of National Estimates was mostly responsible for the tone of the NIEs, hardly ever placed its judgments about the enemy and the consequences of American policies in historical context. An invaluable perspective was thus lacking: the French experience in the so-called First Indochina War of 1946–54. Whatever lessons the CIA drew from the record of French failure, and whatever wisdom it distilled from French official and academic assessments of the war and the enemy, was seldom apparent in the National Intelligence Estimates. This in turn made it difficult for the officials who used these documents to place American involvement in Vietnam in the proper perspective. For none of President Kennedy's chief advisers read the French literature on Indochina themselves or knew much about recent Vietnamese history. The failure to learn from the French is of fundamental importance in assessing the decisions of senior American policy makers.[26]

One of the important instances in which the neglect of French precedent weakened the influence of an intelligence estimate bearing on a major policy decision was the mission of General Maxwell Taylor to Saigon in the fall of 1961. The Taylor mission, or "Taylor-Rostow" mission, recommended the dispatch of 6,000 to 8,000 U.S. troops to Vietnam and emphasized the probable need for a program of "graduated measures" against North Vietnam which would include conventional bombing attacks.[27] Neither the final report of the mission nor the memorandum of Secretary McNamara endorsing its recommendations envisaged large-scale infiltration patterned upon previous Viet Minh tactics against the French. Experience would have shown that such infiltration was impossible to interdict with air power. As General Taylor stated in a secret message to the president:

NVN [North Vietnam] is extremely vulnerable to conventional bombing, a weakness which should be exploited diplomatically in convincing Hanoi to lay off SVN [South Vietnam]. Both the DRV [North Vietnam] and the Chimcos [Chinese Communist forces] would face severe logistical problems in trying to maintain strong forces in the field in SEA [Southeast Asia]. . . . There is no case for fearing a mass onslaught of Communist manpower into SVN and its neighboring states, particularly if our airpower is allowed a free hand against logistical targets.[28]

The Special National Intelligence Estimate commissioned to analyze Taylor's proposed courses of action raised three objections: North Vietnam would increase its infiltration of men and supplies in response to the commitment of U.S. troops; the bombing of the North would not cause Hanoi to stop its support for the Viet Cong; and the infiltration could not be prevented by American airpower. This was a prophetic estimate indeed; any reader of Bernard Fall knew that combat air power had proved ineffective in the First Indochina War.[29] That war showed (as had the Korean War) that air superiority and interdiction bombing were of limited military utility in underdeveloped areas. In spite of total French mastery of the air, the Viet Minh had built a logistic system able to switch from truck convoys to human carriers. But this historical parallel was not pointed out. Had it been, the CIA might have convinced President Kennedy's chief advisers (and perhaps also the military) that conventional bombing in Vietnam would be ineffective. Instead, the belief in the efficacy of strategic air power and interdiction bombing continued without challenge among many high-level decision makers in the Johnson administration.

THE AIR CAMPAIGN AGAINST NORTH VIETNAM, 1965–68

The failure to appreciate the weakness of strategic air power was a fateful mistake, made in spite of contradictory intelligence estimates. The decision to launch Operation Rolling Thunder, the bombing campaign against North Vietnam, produced exactly the opposite result from what was expected—the bombing did not weaken Hanoi's will to resist or compel North Vietnam to negotiate on American terms.[30] Instead of persuading North Vietnam to end its support of the Viet Cong, the air attacks induced Hanoi to introduce its regular forces into South Vietnam on a large scale, thereby creating a military stalemate on the ground. This North Vietnamese response resulted in the decision to send more U.S. ground forces to Vietnam. Concerning this, I will confine discussion here to some general observations on the role of intelligence in the course of these events.

The intelligence community was consulted during the 1964 policy debate that preceded implementation of "graduated escalation"—beginning with the bombing of North Vietnam—as advocated in General Taylor's report. As early as May 1964, a SNIE commissioned to analyze this policy concluded that North Vietnam would resist U.S. military pressure because it believed that U.S. troops in Vietnam could be defeated like the French in 1954. A year later, in April 1965, President Johnson approved National Security Action Memorandum 328 which included the significant decision that U.S. Marine ground units already in South Vietnam should go over from a static defense to active combat operations against the Viet Cong.[31] In a memorandum submitted shortly after the president's decision, CIA Director McCone issued a prophetic warning against sending more troops to South Vietnam:

> I think what we are doing . . . involves ground force operations which, in all probability, will have limited effectiveness against guerrillas, although admittedly will restrain some VC advances. . . . We can expect requirements for an ever-increasing commitment of U.S. personnel without materially improving the chances of victory. . . . I envision that the reaction of the North Vietnamese and Chinese Communists will be to deliberately, carefully, and probably gradually, build up the Viet Cong capabilities by covert infiltration . . . and thus bring an ever-increasing pressure on our forces. In effect, we will find ourselves mired down . . . in a military effort that we cannot win, and from which we will have extreme difficulty in extracting ourselves.[32]

This warning embodied as much sagacity as could possibly be wished of an intelligence estimate or expected from an intelligence service; it had no effect on the president or his closest advisers. In the same month, another pessimistic assessment was submitted to President Johnson by the Board of National Estimates: If the United States deepened its involvement by expanding the combat role of U.S. ground forces and intensified the bombing campaign, the Viet Cong and the North Vietnamese would try to offset this by stepping up the insurgency. Moreover, the deployment of U.S. troops on a large scale might cause North Vietnam to send its own regular forces to the South.[33]

The NIEs produced during this period supplied a number of correct evaluations as to the consequences of the actions carried out or proposed under this strategy.[34] In general, however, these assessments were ignored. The most influential assessment in the debate was produced in late 1964 by the intelligence committee of the National Security Council Working Group on Vietnam. The NSC Working Group conducted the policy review culminating in the recommendation of a two-phase expansion of the war, including an escalating air campaign against North Vietnam. The intelligence assessment of the NSC Working Group was based on judgments about the effectiveness of a bombing campaign contained in previous NIEs.[35] But the final NSC document was a mixture of the skeptical evaluations of the CIA and INR with the more favorable assessments of DIA (which shared the views of the Joint Chiefs of Staff, or JCS), so the net result was an equivocal, composite estimate, implicitly endorsing a modified program of interdiction bombing. It was presumably this NSC intelligence assessment (and the NSC recommendation that went with it) that persuaded National Security Adviser McGeorge Bundy, and subsequently President Johnson, to adopt the bombing policy in February 1965.

Once the air campaign was begun, the civilian agencies in the intelligence community quickly recognized the ineffectiveness of Rolling Thunder. The several assessments of the bombing issued by CIA during 1965 and 1966 are among the most astute intelligence estimates of the Vietnam War.[36] The official resistance to the unwelcome conclusions of these documents is renewed proof of the insignificant role played in this period by objective intelligence analysis in the decision-making process. In April 1965, Director McCone advised President Johnson that "the strikes to date have not caused a change in the North Vietnamese policy of directing the Viet Cong insurgency." A Special National Intelligence Estimate of 28 April provided this analysis of the enemy's expected reaction to Rolling Thunder: "It appears that the DRV, with strong Chinese encouragement, is determined to ride out the U.S. bombardment."[37] In July, another SNIE estimated that the limitation of the bombing to military targets in the Hanoi-Haiphong area was unlikely to impair significantly the Viet Cong's perseverance or to persuade North Vietnam that the price being paid was unacceptably high. Notwithstanding these evaluations, Secretary McNamara, reviewing the bombing in a memorandum for President Johnson, came out in July with a broadly optimistic assessment: "There is no doubt that the bombing program has become an important counter in the current tacit and explicit bargaining process. . . ."[38]

When Rolling Thunder was resumed in February 1966, after the deliberate pause during December 1965, the intelligence community debate bifurcated along civilian and military lines. With the exception of a CIA study issued in March 1966, which argued that Rolling Thunder had been ineffective because of restrictive ground rules (thus supporting the JCS proposal for the expansion of the bombing), the CIA and INR consistently questioned JCS arguments that the bombing was having the desired results. On the other hand, DIA, NSA, and army, navy, and air force intelligence tended to agree with the JCS assessments of the air campaign.[39]

In any event, the bombing of enemy petroleum, oil, and lubricant facilities was approved. As the CIA had predicted, North Vietnam was able to switch to a less vulnerable storage and distribution system. But neither the failure of the intensified air campaign nor a CIA-DIA joint assessment of Rolling Thunder in September 1966[40] induced the JCS or President Johnson's chief civilian advisers to abandon their strategy. The decisive impetus for reconsideration of Rolling Thunder was provided by a series of reports prepared by the Institute for Defense Analysis (IDA), which had been commissioned by Secretary McNamara to obtain a neutral assessment of the air campaign.

The conclusions of the IDA provide a useful comparison with earlier assessments of the bombing by the CIA and the rest of the intelligence community. The IDA emphasized the inability of the bombing to achieve the psychological objective of bending the enemy's will: "The great variety of physical and social countermeasures that North Vietnam has taken in response to the bombing is now well documented in current intelligence reports, but the potential effectiveness of these countermeasures was not stressed in the early planning or intelligence studies."[41]

The IDA study also pointed out the tendency in current intelligence assessments to regard the bombing of North Vietnam as one set of operations and the war in the South as another, evaluating each separately. It also emphasized the proclivity to tabulate and describe data on the military, economic, and physical effects of the bombing without addressing the relationship between such effects and other data relevant to the North Vietnamese ability and will to continue supporting the Viet Cong.

Neither the IDA study nor a CIA estimate of Rolling Thunder in early 1967 prompted serious reexamination of the bombing strategy in the first part of the year. At the end of 1967 two additional studies of the bombing, the second IDA study and the Joint Staff-IDA assessment, confirmed the pessimism of previous CIA estimates. The second IDA study concluded, again, that the bombing of North Vietnam had had no measurable effect on Hanoi's ability to mount and support military operations in the South. In addition, it knew of no alternative bombing strategy that might be effective.[42]

But the fifteen-month debate among President Johnson's principal advisers did not end because the controversy within the intelligence community about the air campaign was resolved in favor of a halt. The bombing was stopped in 1968 as the result of a *political* decision, not because of the second IDA study or the contributions of the intelligence agencies. The entire process of evaluating the bombing strategy was repeated at the beginning of the Nixon administration. National Security Study Memorandum Number 1 merely reaffirmed the assessment of the CIA that the bombing was of little military value.[43] This advice was ignored, and Laos, Cambodia, and North Vietnam were again subjected to strategic saturation bombing.

THE DEPLOYMENT OF U.S. GROUND FORCES, 1965–68

President Johnson's decision in July 1965 to approve large-scale deployment of U.S. combat troops to South Vietnam was made more quickly, and with less consultation with the intelligence community, than any other important decision in the Vietnam conflict.[44] Yet intelligence was used in the formulation of basic U.S. ground strategy, the establishment of appropriate U.S. troop requirements, and the assessment of the enemy's capabilities and intentions.[45] Pessimistic intelligence estimates about the situation in South Vietnam buttressed the argument advanced by MACV and the JCS for an offensive U.S. ground strategy.[46] But the intelligence community—in particular, the main civilian and analytical offices, the Board of National Estimates, and the Office of Current Intelligence at the CIA—was not asked for a broad assessment of the fundamental strategic issues that were arising. Intelligence was not asked for views on such matters as the strategic logic of direct American involvement in the ground war, the chances of achieving the main U.S. objectives in South Vietnam, the level of military commitment that would be needed to win the war, the reaction of North Vietnam to direct combat participation by U.S. troops, and how much effort in terms of men and material the North Vietnamese were willing to devote to the struggle. Neither in 1964 nor in 1965 did a NIE address the most important question of all: whether even a large-scale commitment of U.S. forces would be able to defeat its Communist adversaries, and thus succeed where the French had failed.

From time to time the intelligence community attempted to question the prevailing military wisdom and assess strategic problems in an indirect manner in its National Intelligence Estimates. In addition, over the period of 1963–64 John McCone repeatedly warned the president and his inner circle of the risks involved in changing U.S. strategy by committing American ground troops. But little notice was taken either of analytical doubts set forth in intelligence estimates or in the formal or informal warnings by intelligence officials. By the spring of 1965 the U.S. military, the president, and his chief advisers seem to have become convinced that a long, drawn-out war in Vietnam involving U.S. ground forces was inevitable.[47]

Strategic intelligence estimates seem to have led military and political decision makers to conclude that everything had been tried and nothing had worked—the "strategic hamlet" program, "counterinsurgency warfare," covert military action, and perhaps even the bombing campaign. Direct participation in the war on the ground by American forces seemed to be the only remaining option.[48] The intelligence community's reservations were insufficient, or at least formulated in a manner inadequate, to weaken the conviction of the military and the president that U.S. military power was equal to any challenge. Nothing intelligence did or said could overturn the belief at high levels that the Sino-Soviet bloc must be contained at its periphery in Southeast Asia.

Once American ground combat forces were committed, operational intelligence became more important in the conduct of the war; strategic intelligence exercised almost no influence in the determination of force deployments from 1965 to 1968. At least two "official" versions of reality about this war came into being in this period. The first version was that of the main civilian intelligence agency, the CIA, which was increasingly skeptical and fundamentally pessimistic about the long-term prospects for American victory. The second version was that of Commander U.S. Forces Vietnam (COMUSMACV) and the JCS. This variant held that the war in Vietnam was winnable, that it was not a stalemate, and that it was steadily being won.[49] Until 1968 the Johnson administration was committed to a military victory in South Vietnam, but it did not really know what was needed to achieve such a victory. The result was a tendency to accept the field commander's estimate of what was required and of what was happening in the war. The intelligence estimates of COMUSMAVC showed that progress apparently continued with the steadily increased commitment of American forces, but 1968's Tet Offensive revealed that this progress had been illusory. The military and civilian intelligence agencies were forced by this shock therapy to accept the earlier version of reality: unconditional American military victory was impossible.[50]

Only a few National Intelligence Estimates are available for the period 1965–68. They concern subjects such as Communist military capabilities, "pacification," the situation in South Vietnam, Soviet Union and Communist China reactions to particular U.S. courses of action, and Communist strategy and intentions.[51] In general, these estimates were both accurate and skeptical. They tended to descriptive analysis, eschewing prediction concerning the outcome of the war and the chances of achieving announced U.S. policy objectives. But these estimates never came to grips with the question set by MACV in 1965: how much effort were the North Vietnamese prepared to expend? The estimates failed to assess how effective the South Vietnamese armed forces and police service would be in establishing security in the countryside. Finally, neither MACV intelligence nor any NIE seems to have accurately assessed the relationship between the U.S. force structure and the nature of the war. The lessons of the past went unheeded.

WITHDRAWAL, "VIETNAMIZATION," AND THE FALL OF SOUTH VIETNAM, 1968–75

In the final phase of the war, the performance of strategic intelligence improved, even though strategic intelligence per se became ever less relevant to the conduct of the fighting or to the outcome of the conflict.[52] After the Tet Offensive, a CIA estimate of North Vietnamese intentions presented the evidence of military stalemate in the ground war to the Johnson administration. Given this stalemate, and the decision to refuse the U.S. field commander's request for an increase in the number of troops in South Vietnam, anyone with knowledge of the First Indochina War should have been able to foresee North Vietnam's strategy.[53] Thus, it was no unique revelation of genius when the intelligence community advised the Johnson administration (in 1968) and the Nixon administration (in 1970) that North Vietnam would probably adopt a "prolonged warfare strategy" to wear out U.S. resolve and encourage the eventual withdrawal of U.S. forces from the South.[54] Several intelligence estimates between 1968 and 1972 correctly assessed the conviction of the Viet Cong and the North Vietnamese that their basic strengths and advantages would prove decisive once South Vietnam was deprived of U.S. support.[55] In the context of "Vietnamization" and the withdrawal of all U.S. troops, this assessment was no more than an expression of common sense and elementary logic. The pessimism of intelligence estimates was no longer unfashionable; no one in the Nixon administration could, or did, entertain any serious doubt about the ultimate fate of South Vietnam. By now the only question seriously debated in strategic intelligence was the North Vietnamese operational timetable for the invasion and occupation of the South.

During the last five years of the Vietnam War, the accuracy of intelligence estimates improved as the result of the CIA's penetration of the Communist high command.[56] Assessments by the CIA of North Vietnamese intentions, the factors affecting North Vietnam's war policy, as well as the implications of Prince Sihanouk's removal in Cambodia[57] demonstrate a subtlety and a capacity to analyze the situation from the enemy's perspective not found in earlier estimates. But these assessments no longer mattered against the background of inevitable collapse.

The final Vietnam NIE in 1974 did not foresee a countrywide military campaign in the South before 1976.[58] When the so-called "improvisatory offensive" of North Vietnam began in early 1975, agent reports and captured documents were at first misinterpreted. The series of individual attacks in particular regions of South Vietnam coalesced into the final offensive of the war before the CIA and the rest of the intelligence community recognized the last shift in North Vietnamese strategy.[59] The First Indochina War ended with the intelligence failure of Dien Bien Phu. The American Vietnam War may have concluded with the realization that intelligence had been irrelevant to those who made policy.

INTELLIGENCE LESSONS OF VIETNAM

The Vietnam War testifies to the frequently observed fact that the leaders whose decisions shape fateful events often have a more sanguine outlook than is merited by the facts. True, career officers and politicians may have a vested interest in "cooking raw intelligence to make their master's favorite dishes."[60] But in the case of Vietnam, the decision-making record shows that the bad decisions, and much of what went wrong with the conduct of the war from 1961 onwards, owed far more to the decision makers' misinterpretations and their dismissal of certain important but inconvenient facts than to any sort of deception or falsification by the intelligence community.

It is easy enough to document the unwillingness of high civilian and military officials to believe or to act on intelligence information with awkward political implications or that ran counter to conventional wisdom. Given the shared belief in the doctrine of containment, American military intervention in Vietnam seemed more or less inevitable. American warfare in Indochina emerges in broad perspective as essentially a bureaucratic phenomenon, only distantly responsive to the realities of the conflict as anticipated, reported, and assessed by intelligence. The official record depicts an almost unbroken series of seemingly unavoidable decisions all based on the assumption that unless such and such a step was taken, there was no alternative to a Communist victory in Vietnam. These decisions were all conceived with the best intentions, either in a mood of official pessimism or with cognizance of the pessimism contained in intelligence estimates and the warnings of intelligence officials.

But this notion of unavoidable decisions can also be applied in the case of the First Indochina War. The fact that "the system worked," making it possible to decide among alternative courses of action, does not of course retroactively validate all of its decisions—which did, after all, lead to failure. But it would be difficult or impossible to prove that nothing American leaders might have done could have changed the result or that nothing left undone could have altered the outcome.

Other decisions and courses of action could clearly have been chosen. No specific decision in the Vietnam War was logically unavoidable, whatever the premises for assuming that such an action was necessary. In this sense, the Vietnam War was no more inevitable or unavoidable than the Athenians' Sicilian Expedition. Human psychology, not the momentum of bureaucracy, must be held responsible for bad choices and perseverance in the face of cautionary intelligence. Historical decisions seem unavoidable to us only because we know what for the persons who made them was unknowable—the future. Warnings about the difficulty of resisting, for a second time, Communist revolutionary warfare in Indochina were discounted. Intelligence estimates consistently depicted or predicted deterioration and stalemate, in contrast to many of the formal evaluations served up by the State Department and the U.S. military. Interestingly, the most important decisions to increase American involvement and enlarge the scope of the war were made in periods of pessimism. Once these decisions had been made, reservations and analytical pessimism were regarded as counterproductive for the actual management of the war and received little attention at the government's top levels. Only dramatic events—for example, the Pleiku attack in 1964 or the Tet Offensive in 1968—could induce high-level officials and presidential advisers to recognize that official optimism was illusory or that the tide of the war was changing.

As a result, expert knowledge about Indochina within the intelligence community was an essentially underdeveloped resource. Neither the U.S. military nor the chief advisers of three presidents seem to have been familiar with the special circumstances in Indochina. The many "policy studies," presidential memoranda, recommendations, and programs devised by these officials betray a fundamental ignorance about Indochina and Vietnam.[61] The French experience was either unknown to most high-level decision makers or considered to be basically irrelevant to U.S. policy.[62] American's leaders had long ago made up their minds about the importance of defending Vietnam and the manner in which the war should be waged and declined to be confused by the facts available from history and their own intelligence services.

That unwelcome intelligence was dismissed or ignored cannot be denied. The question then arises whether the vagaries of human psychology and the dynamic factors of bureaucracy, taken together, can explain this phenomenon. A partial answer is that the *form* of intelligence reports and estimates did indeed contribute to their neglect. Posterity has ratified the accuracy and perspicacity of many of the judgments presented in intelligence documents such as the NIEs, but in some cases the greatest accuracy was achieved not in prediction but in analytical description.[63] In certain instances prediction amounted to nothing more than common-sense deduction presented as the revelation of intelligence. To cite only one example, a 1965 CIA memorandum on Communist military capabilities predicted that the Viet Cong military campaign for 1965 "would certainly be carefully tailored to exploit and increase South Vietnam's political and morale problems."[64] Furthermore, the apparent prescience of certain judgments sometimes seems to derive as much from their oracular language as from genuine foresight.[65] The use of Delphic language and cautious formulation—beyond what was required for candid recognition of the range of uncertainty—combined to diminish the credibility and practical usefulness of some intelligence estimates.[66]

In addition to their proclivity for Delphic formulae, intelligence reports did not always avoid the predilection for quantification and statistical indices of progress and effectiveness typical of much analysis during the war.[67] No statistical index or quantitative variable could properly be attached to the essential attributes of the enemy: surprise, deception, cunning, and agility. Many quantitative evaluations of certain aspects of the enemy's behavior, which appeared to be numerically precise, were thus in fact numbers games that added up to precisely nothing.

Some facts of the war were quantifiable, however, and these were often subjected to statistical analysis to produce indices of progress—for example, measurements of trends in the "strategic hamlet" program and the pacification effort, assessment of bomb damage in North Vietnam, infiltration statistics, evaluation of enemy casualties, and so forth. But in general, the capabilities of U.S. intelligence to measure particular facets of the war dictated its performance—the measurable was measured, but the relevance of the evidence so quantified was not always analyzed. For example, precisely what did statistics about the percentage of enemy base camps destroyed mean? If x percent of camps were "neutralized" at any given time, could not the enemy rebuild them or construct new ones at any time? Similarly, if "activity" of friendly forces in a sector was to be gauged by the number of operations per week, there would arise a natural tendency to improve the score by sending out as many patrols as possible, even if they did not engage the enemy. Or, if "structure" destructions were adopted as a criterion, a structure, whether a Viet Cong concrete bunker, a tunnel complex, or a rice-thatched hut, became a performance statistic. In the aggregate, these indices did not add up to a measurement of progress.

The Case of the Missing Missiles, 1962–69

The Defense Department's annual classified posture statement of March 1970 acknowledged that previous NIEs had underestimated the deployment of Soviet ICBMs. An unofficial analysis of U.S. intelligence forecasts of Soviet strategic offensive forces later provided additional evidence.[68] American intelligence in general, and the CIA in particular, had underestimated Soviet ICBM deployment from 1962 onward. The underestimation grew progressively worse at the end of the decade, just when the different technical collection systems began to yield more raw data than had ever been available before.

The reasons for the Soviet ICBM underestimation are, as in previously discussed intelligence failures, multifaceted and complex. One is at a special disadvantage in examining this case, however, because it belongs to the recent past. In the absence of the pertinent national intelligence estimates and their supporting technical analyses we must sometimes rely on informed guesswork. But it will not surprise the reader to find here that American miscalculations owed a great deal to their (dangerous) propensity to view their opponent in terms of their own canons of political rationality and national self-interest. Whatever other factors were involved, the by now familiar *deformation professionnelle* we call "mirror imaging" was surely one of them. A naive methodology of strategic analysis, largely oblivious of the larger political picture and excessively reliant on the technology of "bean counting," was also to blame. Because the CIA played the central role in the estimation process, both drafting the first versions of the NIEs and coordinating the main annual forecasts of Soviet strategic forces, this discussion will focus mainly on its performance.[69]

In 1962 the small number of "soft" operational Soviet ICBM launchers, the low ICBM strength (75–100 missiles as of July), and the slow pace of deployment for the SS-7 and SS-8 systems suggested that the Soviet Union was not interested in attaining numerical ICBM parity with the United States. The actual deployment rate of Soviet ICBMs between 1961 and mid-1965 seemed to offer the requisite corroboration: the projections for mid-1963 Soviet ICBM strength made in 1959, 1960, and 1961 (350–640, 200–700, and 100–500 respectively) had proved excessive. From an actual estimated total of 100 operational launchers in mid-1963, the Soviet force grew to approximately 200 ICBMs in 1964–65. By 1965 it had become rather conventional wisdom that the Soviets were not seeking to develop an ICBM force as large as that of the United States, but were prepared to settle for a level of capability in vogue with American theorists of "minimum deterrence." As Secretary of Defense Robert McNamara put it, the Soviet Union had no intention of catching up; the arms race was effectively at an end.[70]

As the NIE for 1965 is not available, we do not know whether the CIA and the rest of the intelligence community endorsed this belief. In a 1967 CIA analysis of Soviet military policy, U.S. analysts were uncertain about how the Soviets would react to the announced intention of the United States to level off its strategic missile deployment in 1968. The 1967 classified posture statement contains a judgment that seems to reflect the thinking of the intelligence community at the time about the future magnitude and pace of Soviet ICBM deployment: "While it is possible that the Soviet ICBM force could grow in the later years of this decade at a higher rate than we now estimate, present deployment trends and economic, strategic, and technical considerations do not appear to support a higher estimate."[71]

In any event, the Soviet ICBM force expanded to 570 operational launchers as of mid-1967. The 1967 classified posture statement acknowledged the faster-than-anticipated rate of hardened silo construction starts, but did not interpret this increase as presaging a major ICBM buildup.[72] The January 1968 posture statement reported a one-year increase (October to October) in the number of ICBM launchers from approximately 340 to 720, but maintained that the rate of deployment would slow down.[73] The statement reported only an incremental change in Soviet strategic offensive forces and betrayed no anticipation of a continuing ICBM buildup exceeding U.S. projections. It was believed that deployment of large numbers of SS-11s and SS-9s would be accompanied by the phasing out of older and less accurate SS-6, SS-7, and SS-8 ICBMs deployed at "soft" launching sites.

The posture statement of 1969 provided an estimate of 896 operational ICBM launchers as of 1 September 1968, noting the threefold increase in the number of operational ICBMs in a period of two-and-a-half years.[74] But this increase was attributed to the deployment of the new SS-9s and SS-11s. For the period after mid-1969, the statement predicted that the Soviet ICBM force would continue to grow, but at a considerably slower rate to a total of 1,020–1,251 operational launchers by mid-1972. The assumption that numerical parity with the United States was the final objective of the Soviet buildup thus persisted. American intelligence estimated Soviet defense expenditures at essentially the same levels as those given in the published Soviet budget. The growth rate, the scale, and the scope of Soviet defense spending for strategic weapons procurement in the 1960s were substantially understated, for the main Soviet national priorities were not well understood.[75] But there is no good evidence that CIA estimates of Soviet defense expenditure ignored altogether the increases in defense outlays or discounted the financial capacity of the Soviets to build a large ICBM delivery system. Admittedly, the estimates of Soviet defense spending in the 1960s were on the low side, but it is unlikely that they were mainly to blame for the underestimates of Soviet ICBM deployments.

There were other reasons nearer at hand to explain why the estimates went astray. Setting aside the numerical totals and the issue of percentages of error in long-range prediction, it is clear that the underestimates were largely due to the methods and preconceptions by which the intelligence data was analyzed—or not analyzed;[76] the material was superior to the workmanship. Soviet deployments were not placed in a coherent strategic context and the dynamism of their ICBM buildup was neither anticipated nor apprehended, for Soviet objectives escaped explanation.

Methodology. After the resolution of the "Missile Gap," there was no substantive change in the methods used to prepare the annual NIE of

Soviet strategic offensive forces. The section of the assessment that dealt with Soviet missiles continued to be a numerical estimate of Soviet capabilities. The tabulation of extant and predicted Soviet operational ICBM strength was not correlated with an analysis of Soviet military doctrine and decision making. The estimative process consisted merely of counting physically and technically observable manifestations of Soviet strategic weapons systems: operational missile launchers, missile silos under construction, ancillary ground installations, missiles under storage at launching sites, technical performance capabilities and traits. The emphasis was on inference from the collected data, which itself was mainly of a technical character—photographs, telemetry signals, ELINT, RADINT, and signals and communication intelligence. Presentation of the data was largely confined to descriptive analysis; seldom were questions asked about why, or how, a particular type of Soviet weapons system was being developed or deployed. For this reason there was inadequate analytical effort devoted to the possibility that the growth pattern of Soviet missile forces reflected a coherent strategy at the political level, or that there might be a direct relationship between Soviet capabilities and intentions.

During the time of the "missile gap," neither the U-2 nor the first photographic reconnaissance satellites could provide continuous, comprehensive surveillance of the entire Soviet landmass sufficient to reveal all the details of identified or suspected missile sites. The capabilities of U.S. satellites improved rapidly over the years, however, to the point where technical intelligence could furnish photographic and technical data of such high quality that the "counting problems" previously hindering U.S. intelligence were virtually eliminated.

Consequently, the short-range predictions of operational ICBM numbers were generally accurate from 1965 on. But they did not anticipate the ultimate magnitude of the Soviet ICBM program, so long-range estimates of operational ICBMs did not begin to catch up with the true Soviet levels until 1970. True, by 1966 yearly deployment rates for both soft and hard launching sites had been established; in theory this should have helped to predict 1970 as the terminal date for the new ICBM program that came on line in 1964 and 1965. By assuming that the extensive launching site construction required for this program was part of a 1966–70 Soviet Five Year Plan, a reasonably accurate prediction of the aggregate ICBM deployment levels for 1970 should have been possible.[77] But the estimators did not aggregate the figures for different ICBM types, nor did they plot yearly missile-silo construction starts.

Although the aggregate of construction starts should have been the primary indicator for estimates of the eventual size of the Soviet ICBM force, no one seems to have plotted this indicator during the 1960s. Otherwise, the trend line of construction starts would have been manifested, and the underestimates would probably not have occurred. The so-called "construction-start" method of estimating ICBM deployments was known at the time, but the "operational accounting method" was preferred in its place. This procedure ignored the date when silo construction began, using the date when a missile was inserted in the completed silo as its basis for calculation. In other words, only the completion of actually operational launches was used to date, estimate, and count ICBM deployments, thus gauging Soviet deployment rates by single, observable events. As a result, the annual U.S. estimates of Soviet ICBM strength tended to project past trends, because they lacked specific, concrete data about new ICBM deployments at a given time in the future.[78]

The trend lines for Soviet operational activation plotted in a recent unofficial evaluation of U.S. intelligence estimates show that in the 1960s the approximate construction period for ICBM launchers was one-and-a-half to two years. If the projections of Soviet ICBM deployments in the classified posture statements are compared with the actual construction starts and operational activations, it is clear that operational activations followed silo construction starts by not more than two years, and that after 1966 the NIEs underestimated the pace of Soviet deployment every year until 1970.

It has been argued elsewhere that 1964 marked the beginning of a previously determined plan: the constant "construction-pace line" throughout the rest of the decade reflected the implementation of strategic decisions made in 1963 in connection with the 1966–70 Five Year Plan. The "activation-trend line" certainly makes this appear to have been the case. The silos begun in 1964 and 1965 were to be activated in 1966 and 1967 in accordance with the revised 1959–65 Seven Year Plan, and so on. However, the NIEs apparently took no account of these known Soviet plans. On the face of it, U.S. estimates assumed that all the ICBM silos under construction each year would be completed, but that no new silos would be started. Consequently, each year's NIE estimated that Soviet ICBM strength would peak when all the silos being built at the time were completed. The construction-start line is constant from 1964 to 1970, arguing quite a different conclusion. But because they relied on the operational accounting method, the estimators appear not to have taken serious notice of the continuity and consistency in Soviet ICBM deployments from 1966 on. The result was that U.S. estimates lagged behind actual deployments until the cumulative, systematic repetition of error no longer admitted of rational denial.

Mirror imaging. The second cause of the Soviet ICBM underestimation was the pervasive but perhaps least obvious error of "mirror imaging," the implicit, subconscious assumption that Soviet military and political objectives were similar to those of their American counterparts. The failure to understand Soviet strategic concepts and priorities—responsible for the "missile gap" fiasco of the 1950s—had not been redressed in the 1960s. Specific Soviet requirements were generally neglected in long-term forecasts of Soviet strategic force development; in fact, U.S. intelligence assessments left out of account those Soviet capabilities without direct counterpart in American strategic doctrine. Analysis of the Soviet ICBM force assumed a more or less common technological culture, and overall Soviet norms of military behavior derived from a common system of calculating strategy, strategic weapons deployment, and their respective "cost-benefit" characteristics. No one in authority seems to have seriously contemplated the possibility that the calculations that determined Soviet military policies were the product of an environment, a view of the world, an experience with war, and a decision-making process—none of which had an American analogue.[79]

The fallacy of mirror imaging can be discerned in various CIA analyses from the late 1950s and the 1960s. A 1959 memorandum of CIA Director Allen Dulles asserted that Khrushchev recognized the concept of "mutual deterrence."[80] In 1962 a SNIE on the military buildup in Cuba attributed to the Soviet leadership an essentially American conception of strategic military power and the calculus of risk. For some time after the Cuban missile crisis, CIA analyses ascribed to the Soviets an American conception of the balance of power, deterrence, and a degree of disillusionment about the efficacy of military force somewhat like that exhibited by American strategic theorists and Defense Department systems analysts.[81] For example, an assessment prepared for the Office of National Estimates asserted that the advent of hardened ICBM silos and mobile missile launchers made it impossible both to destroy an enemy's military and industrial capabilities and simultaneously protect one's own country from unacceptable damage. Hence, the only "valid and rational" concept of nuclear strategy was "mutual deterrence."[82]

A CIA analysis of Soviet military policy in 1967 shows how the debate initiated by Secretary of Defense McNamara about U.S. nuclear strategy and the interaction of Soviet and American strategic forces had influenced the assessment of Soviet military doctrine, political-military decision making, nuclear strategy, and weapons development. This study claimed that a marked change in the Soviet Union's strategic situation had occurred because of the continuing growth of Soviet offensive strategic forces. This growth had bolstered "Soviet assured destruction capabilities" and had cut into the margin of U.S. superiority, which had clear implications for military policy: the Soviet Union was "approaching maturity in the nuclear missile age." The point was approaching at which the Soviet Union must ask, as the United States had done under Secretary McNamara, "not merely how much and what kinds of additional military power it needs," but rather, how it can improve "the efficiency of its management of military power." The Soviet Union was improving its "nuclear deterrent posture" relative to the United States, and it had undertaken strategic offensive programs of sufficient scope to affect the existing military relationship with the United States, thus inviting the risk that the United States might take compensatory actions. The analysis concluded, however, that the issues of military policy in the Soviet Union and the United States had never been more delicately interrelated. This would provide the Soviet Union with strong incentives to curb at least some of its current programs.[83]

The shifts in American nuclear strategy from deterrence to assured destruction and finally to mutual assured destruction, which presupposed the bilateral desirability of stable deterrence, were projected upon the Soviet leadership and read into Soviet military doctrine; Soviet strategists and leaders were taken for granted as educable. It was implicitly assumed, in a somewhat patronizing manner, that the "backwardness" of Soviet strategic doctrine and the Kremlin's "misunderstanding" of American objectives in the ICBM buildup of the early 1960s would be ameliorated by greater Soviet maturity arising from the improvement of its strategic situation.[84]

This projection of American strategic concepts and defense policies upon those of the Soviet Union naturally affected the assessment of Soviet ICBM development. Published Soviet military doctrine received no substantial analytical attention for most of the decade. The inconvenient tenets of Soviet military doctrine were dismissed as ideological rhetoric. Fundamental asymmetries in American and Soviet strategic concepts and doctrine certainly were recognized by U.S. analysts. These asymmetries included the U.S. concept of "mutual assured destruction" compared with Soviet strategic thought. The aims of Soviet military policy, stated in the available Soviet military literature, did not recognize the status quo or aspire to erect a platform of "stable deterrence"; these aims were quite simply to change the "correlation of forces" in favor of the U.S.S.R. by achieving maximum military advantage. Contemporary Soviet writings on nuclear strategy even used a technical vocabulary different from that to be found in U.S. documents. Terms such as "strategic sufficiency," "realistic deterrence," "assured destruction," and "flexible response" were initially avoided, and the concepts expressed by them were rejected.[85]

Because these incompatibilities were either ignored or dismissed as mere rhetoric, the actual number of Soviet ICBMs, deployed according to Soviet strategic goals, came as an unpleasant surprise. The neglect of Soviet military doctrine had impaired assessment of the Soviet ICBM program in two important ways. It tended to restrict attention to the counting and technical evaluation of a narrow range of tangible military capabilities and consequently, U.S. analysts in the early 1960s did not realize that the establishment and growth of the Soviet ICBM force involved the structured interaction of political-military theory with centralized and interlocking institutions.[86] The ICBM systems finally deployed were the result of a consistent effort to achieve the objectives laid down by Soviet doctrine and strategy. Yet this interconnection was missed.

In this context, the response of U.S. analysts to Soviet Chief of General Staff Marshal Sokolovskiy's *Military Strategy* is of considerable interest. The book contained the first thorough Soviet analysis of nuclear war strategy.[87] When it appeared in 1962, U.S. analysts refused to believe that the document outlined the Soviet leadership's requirements for building a strategic nuclear force whose size would exceed that of the United States in a decade. This disbelief was due in part to the memory of the Cuban missile crisis and the mirror-image assessment of Soviet military policy in the aftermath. United States analysts found it difficult to relate Soviet doctrinal writing—especially the precepts set forth in *Military Strategy*—to current events and the observable Soviet strategic forces between 1962 and 1967, when the United States enjoyed an absolute numerical and technological superiority in long-range bombers, ICBMs, and SLBMs (submarine-launched ballistic missiles).[88] Instead, there was a tendency to concentrate on nuances in Soviet writings, searching for evidence of power struggles and doctrinal controversies that might somehow explain the uncompromising thrust of *Military Strategy.*

A common American interpretation held that the first edition of *Military Strategy* represented a debate between opposing Soviet military groups—"modernists" and "traditionalists." This interpretation is a classic example of American mirror-imaging that projects the disagreement between civilian defense analysts and the U.S. military in the 1960s over U.S. nuclear war strategy into a Soviet context. Between 1964 and 1966 the most influential version of this supposed Soviet debate asserted that the new Soviet leaders, the "modernists," would give less attention to Soviet nuclear weaponry because they had accepted the concept of mutual assured destruction. In actual fact, there was no important change in Soviet military concepts. Decisions about the development of particular ICBM prototypes and silo basing made no later than 1963 by Khrushchev were reaffirmed and executed in full under Brezhnev under the 1966–70 Five Year Plan. All of this was in perfect conformity with the strategic and doctrinal requirements revealed in *Military Strategy* and other Soviet military writing.

The analytical climate in which estimates of Soviet offensive strategic forces were prepared in the 1960s was influenced by the prevailing wisdom about deterrence and nuclear strategy. The classified posture statements after 1965 expressed no doubt that the Soviet Union could build a large ICBM force, if it chose to do so. But the intelligence community was the captive of a preconception that the Soviets would hold themselves at, or under, American ICBM deployment levels. This assumption was based on speeches by Soviet leaders intended for foreign consumption and on the belief that the concepts of stable deterrence and mutual assured destruction were congenial to the Soviets. Because the Soviet Union had needed to acquire an "assured destruction capability" in the early 1960s, the first increase in its ICBM force—up to two hundred missiles between 1962–65 —was easily explicable. But given the continued numerical and technological superiority of American strategic forces in 1965, "mutual assured destruction" was impossible unless the Soviets further enlarged their ICBM force to what American strategic theorists called the "properly equilibrated" force structure needed for stable deterrence. The Soviet expansion from 1965–66 was therefore actually thought to be desirable by some defense officials, including Secretary of Defense McNamara.[89]

When the Russian ICBM force continued to grow beyond the requirements of parity, it was assumed that the Soviets had somehow misunderstood the technical implications of "mutual assured destruction.[90] This being the case, it is not surprising that the intelligence community was initially not alarmed at the increase in the number of ICBM deployments and continued to anticipate that the Soviet Union would stop adding "unnecessary" ICBMs to its inventory. American analysts wanted to avoid worst-case assumptions and therefore underestimated the scale and pace of the Soviet ICBM buildup.

Deception. In the final analysis, the underestimation of Soviet ICBM deployments between 1962 and 1969 did not result from a lack of intelligence —plenty was available from technical sources or from information in the Soviet military press. The Soviet Union did not deceive U.S. intelligence as to its doctrine—the broad strategic military intentions underlying the development and deployment of Soviet forces in the 1960s. Neither the long-term miscalculation of Soviet defense expenditures nor errors in methodology explain the inaccuracy of U.S. estimates of the Soviet ICBM force. The failure to recognize the Soviet commitment to a massive ICBM buildup in its Seven Year Defense Plan for 1963–70 and the misinterpretation or dismissal of evidence that did not fit American preconceptions about the enemy are best explained by the stubborn persistence of mirror imaging.[91]

Analysts were confident in the 1960s that Soviet ICBMs were neither accurate nor reliable enough to threaten the hardened silos in which the Minuteman and Titan II forces were deployed. Analysts recognized as early as 1960 that Soviet improvements in missile accuracy would constitute the most destabilizing of developments.[92] But the intelligence community of the 1960s accepted hard intelligence data obtained from the different technical means of collection as evidence of serious failures in Soviet missile guidance systems and instrumentation. This evidence provided the basis for technical intelligence predictions about the performance characteristics of the new generation of Soviet ICBMs, especially regarding accuracy and multiple independent targeting reentry vehicle (MIRV) capability. These predictions seemed to indicate that the Soviets would not soon be able to mass-produce ICBMs sufficiently accurate or reliable to destroy U.S. underground missile command centers and land-based ICBMs in hardened silos.[93] The possibility of Soviet counterforce strategy was discounted also on economic grounds. The apparent technological weaknesses already noted led analysts to conclude that the Soviet Union would have little reason to continue the heavy rate of investment in its ICBM program and the large-scale deployment of ICBMs.

The extent to which U.S. intelligence failed to understand the performance characteristics of Soviet ICBMs before the SALT I negotiations is a matter of dispute. It is certain, however, that some performance characteristics were incorrectly evaluated. The question is whether this failure resulted from inadequate technical intelligence collection and imperfect measurement pertaining to Soviet missile systems or whether it was caused by Soviet strategic deception.

Predeployment and postdeployment estimates of technical characteristics are unreliable; these features can be measured only imperfectly, even for U.S. missile systems.[94] Thus random, accidental, or systematic errors in the measurement of Soviet ICBM performance could have resulted from imperfections in the technical means of collection, inaccurate measurements (such as acceleration or CEP—Circular Error Probable), or flaws in geophysical and geodetic data. But U.S. intelligence underestimated Soviet ICBM performance for so long that such explanations appear unlikely.

There remains the possibility of deception. It may be recalled that between 1954 and 1962 the Soviet Union attempted to deceive U.S. intelligence about Soviet long-range bomber production, the size of the Soviet ICBM force, and about Soviet military intentions in Cuba. In view of the habitual Soviet obsession with secrecy, the Soviet leadership would naturally try to conceal as much as possible of its ICBM program as well. Having adopted a counterforce strategy, the Soviets had every incentive to misrepresent the accuracy of the new ICBMs in order to conceal those technical performance characteristics that could confirm the feasibility of such a threatening strategy. If the accuracy of Soviet ICBMs could be misrepresented, their probable mission might be misunderstood, resulting in the neglect or delay of appropriate U.S. countermeasures.

Soviet officials could establish—in large measure from the public record —the preconceptions of the U.S. Defense Department and U.S. strategic theorists about Russian nuclear and strategic goals. Defectors and spies from the National Security Agency, a high-ranking U.S. Army officer attached to the staff of the Joint Chiefs of Staff, and a Soviet agent in the communications center of U.S. Air Force Headquarters surely furnished the KGB and GRU with valuable knowledge of the U.S. technical collection systems.[95] This knowledge constituted a powerful resource for Soviet planning staffs. They knew, at least in part, what U.S. analysts and Defense Department officials wanted to believe. Furthermore, the Soviets knew how much confidence U.S. intelligence had in its technical collection systems and possessed some insight into the estimative process and the role of technical indicators in analysis. Circumstantial evidence points to Soviet recognition of the possibility that they could distort the measurement and interpretation of that technical intelligence upon which the Americans placed the greatest reliance. By intentionally incorporating systematic error into the precision guidance systems of Soviet ICBMs during flight tests it would be possible to compensate for the systematic error in Soviet measurement and at the same time buttress American belief that Soviet ICBMs were inaccurate and unreliable.[96]

There were two technical performance indicators critical to intelligence estimates about the Soviet ICBM force: the parameters of instrumentation error in Soviet guidance systems and median system delivery error (CEP). Poor performance by both of these indicators led U.S. analysts to underestimate not only Soviet technological capabilities but also the numbers and deployment rate that the Soviets adopted. For instance, technical biasing of instrumentation data would explain why the SS-7 and SS-9 systems were originally evaluated as too inaccurate to threaten U.S. ICBM silos and why the SS-9 was initially rejected as a possible counterforce weapon. Technical deception also might account for the fact that American intelligence judged the SS-11 and SS-13 to be less accurate than they were, as it believed that these missiles used the same guidance components as the earlier systems. If, as it would seem, U.S. interpretation of Soviet targeting performance affected intelligence estimates of future ICBM deployments, the errors in the projections of ICBM deployments in the classified posture statements are explicable. The expectation that the pace of Soviet ICBM deployments would slow down seems to have been premised partly on the assumption that the SS-7 and SS-11 lacked the accuracy to be "silo killers." Belief in the insufficient accuracy of Soviet ICBMs also led to the conclusion that the SS-13 was essentially a retaliatory weapon for use against cities.[97] The conviction that Soviet ICBMs were, in varying degrees, inaccurate thus reinforced the conventional wisdom that the Minuteman and Titan II systems in their hardened silos were invulnerable to a Soviet first strike. This belief in turn diminished incentives to upgrade U.S. silos and undertake the analysis of other nuclear war strategies.

What advantages would have accrued to the Soviet Union from technical deception? Mainly, a delayed American recognition of the vulnerability of U.S. land-based ICBM forces. Khrushchev had attempted in the late 1950s to deceive the United States about the size of the Soviet ICBM program. This intention was, in part, to gain time until the next generation of ICBMs moved from development to operational deployment. His subterfuge might have succeeded, except for the rapid development of U.S. overhead reconnaissance capability. With regard to Soviet ICBM programs in the 1960s, U.S. intelligence was for some time uncertain about the performance characteristics of Soviet ICBMs. Initially, the CEP of the SS-9 and SS-11 was inaccurately determined.[98] By the end of the decade, as the United States and the Soviet Union joined in the SALT negotiations, U.S. intelligence had only begun to accept the Soviet buildup as fact. In the early 1970s the earlier underestimation of Soviet progress in missile accuracy was compounded by an overestimation of the rate of deployment and an inadequate anticipation of improvements in the technical performance of the newer Soviet ICBMs.

In 1839 the Marquis de Custine, the author of the classic work on the subject, complained in effect that Russia's policy of working in the shadow concealed all that was thought and done there, leaving the observer as ignorant as if he were blind, thus permitting Russians the strengths of secrecy. But the errors of U.S. intelligence in estimating the numbers of Soviet ICBMs cannot only be ascribed to the strength of Soviet secrecy or to deception. As we have seen, U.S. intelligence failed in the period under review not because of Russian deception nor from lack of evidence, but from American refusal or inability to confront alien ways of political and strategic thought.

The record of U.S. intelligence has by no means been entirely negative: after some initial hesitations it performed well in the Cuban missile crisis, and it was more often right than wrong in Vietnam. Yet even when it was right, it has seldom had a decisive influence on the conduct of U.S. foreign policy. A conclusion of this kind may sound defeatist, but the same could be said with regard to other instruments of foreign policy. In recent decades the formal conduct of diplomacy has not made a tremendous difference in U.S. relations with the outside world, for example. The truly crucial issues in the history of nations are not usually decided by intelligence successes or failures. Intelligence can do no more than serve as a useful guide, a compass in a complicated world. A compass indicates the general direction, but it cannot warn of all the obstacles one may encounter.

PART III

INTELLIGENCE
ABROAD

CHAPTER 7

Secret Services in Open Societies

THE QUESTION of how secret services function in free societies, and how well they *can* function, given the constraints of their own political and social frameworks, is interesting in itself. In addition, American intelligence has in some cases been hindered by the peculiarities of bureaucratic organization, political pressure for results attuned to policy, the compartmentalization of knowledge, duplication of effort, and so on. The purpose of this chapter is to survey the manner in which other democracies—Great Britain, Germany, and Israel—have dealt with the contradiction of secret services in open societies, and to evaluate their success in overcoming the problems that vex the relationship between intelligence producers and consumers. In undertaking a sketch of the global context, some attention must also be devoted to the financial costs of intelligence operations. Due to the technological revolution in data collection and analysis, today's expenses are not only greater than ever, but there is an ill-defined point at which an increased quantity of resources produces a qualitative change in results. Once that threshold is crossed, the United States and the U.S.S.R., as we shall see, are literally in a league of their own. Only when we have assimilated the comparative perspectives will we be in a position to evaluate the purposes and functioning of the KGB in chapter 8.

The aims of intelligence are the same all over the world, but the way these services function varies from country to country according to objective requirements, historical traditions, and, above all, the political context in which they operate. American intelligence constantly encounters other intelligence services as allies, rivals, or foes. It can learn from them as well as from historical experience. True, the political circumstances, scope of interest, structure, and means of collection of intelligence services, have changed enormously, especially in this century. But human emotions and behavior have not changed since the first intelligence operations began, and they, not technology, are the source of the problems as well as the achievements of the craft.

American intelligence—systematically and continuously conducted—is a relative newcomer on the international scene. It is well known that the OSS learned from the British in its early days, though the extent of this should not be exaggerated; the tricks of the trade were not all that many, nor were they exceptionally difficult to master. Today there are three main differences between American intelligence operations and those of other democratic societies. First, America is a global power with interests extending much further than that of other countries. Second, America has means of collection far surpassing what other countries can muster. Each of these differences affect the whole of intelligence management, both as to style and as to substance. The third difference is that U.S. intelligence functions today in an adverse political climate, more adverse than that faced by intelligence among its allies. True, the political climate is subject to changes —under direct threat American public opinion will tolerate even covert action. But during the last two decades, U.S. practices that cause hardly a murmur when performed by other countries have often provoked a major outcry from the world. American expectations of openness in politics are such that even when the CIA was least under attack, far more was known about it than about any other secret service. Without such openness, a study like the present would have been impossible. Whether a secret service can function effectively in such conditions is less clear.[1]

In the global context, there has been no real consensus on the standing of spies and their masters in international law. Spying is surely one of the oldest professions,[2] but it was not until the anarchic period of religious and dynastic wars in seventeenth- and eighteenth-century Europe that systematic philosophical attention was paid to the problem. Grotius, citing the biblical precedent of Moses, found espionage to have a basis in the law of nations. At the other extreme was Kant, who argued in his essay *On Eternal Peace* that even in wartime, espionage was in itself a diabolical act which undermined the last remnants of international trust.

On a practical level, it seemed appropriate to threaten the spy and his or her accomplices (even unknowing ones) with quartering—as in Polish military law around 1690—or with similarly draconic measures. Yet the spy's employer was not regarded as a necessarily dishonorable person for all of that. Perhaps this attitude was merely a reflection of the power relationships of the day, as it was easier to trap a spy than a spymaster. Guy Fawkes was subjected to condign punishment—an occasion for an annual holiday in Britain—while Francis Walsingham, who ran countless operations employing much less savory characters for Elizabeth I, is a national hero. Insofar as consensus exists on the matter, it seems to be that a belligerent acts lawfully in employing spies, but the other belligerent acts with equal justice in punishing them.[3]

While espionage may still be punishable—even in the West—by death, reality has usually mitigated the rigors of theory. As virtually all countries engage in espionage, if truly severe punishment were always meted out to spies, they would be a sparse if not vanishing species. In fact, frequent exchange of convicted spies is the rule, not the exception, among sovereign states.

The *definition* of espionage, not its punishment, is one of the most accurate indicators of whether a society is free or totalitarian. In the latter, it is almost true that whatever is not expressly allowed is forbidden—perhaps as good a definition of a "closed society" as one might hope for. But this chapter attempts to evaluate the problems of intelligence/espionage in "open societies" basically similar to the United States. It is therefore logical to begin with Great Britain, if only to see how widely attitudes, organization, and degree of success diverge.

Great Britain

The striking difference in attitudes toward intelligence in Great Britain and the United States is well illustrated by the case of Sir Robert Baden-Powell, the founder of the Boy Scout movement who had no hesitation about spying for his country in peacetime.[4] While there have been fluctuations in its prestige, intelligence has usually been regarded as a legitimate and indeed essential instrument of policy throughout English history; Sir Francis Walsingham in the sixteenth century, and Cromwell's John Thurloe in the seventeenth stand out among the leading practitioners of early modern spying and counterspying.

Military intelligence first came into being under Wellington, but fell into disrepute soon after the close of the Napoleonic era. Not even the many setbacks in colonial wars and the Crimean War brought change until the end of the nineteenth century. In 1887, the post of director of military and naval intelligence was created. Only in 1909 did a Secret Service Bureau come into being; it dealt with both foreign and domestic affairs, thus anticipating the future MI 5 and MI 6. Even on a purely tactical level, early British intelligence had a lamentable record, as the Boer War showed. In later years, there were outstanding achievements, such as the activities of Room 39 (naval intelligence) in World War I and ULTRA in World War II. But there were also outstanding cases of failure. About Burma, General (subsequently Field Marshall) Slim wrote in 1942 that "our intelligence was extremely bad, we were like a blind boxer trying to spy an unseen opponent."[5] The Venlo incident in 1939, when two leading British agents were seized at the Dutch border, left few Special Intelligence Service—SIS (MI 6)—secrets unknown to the enemy. While the British succeeded in smashing all German spy rings in their country early in the war, inside Germany they did not have any espionage success themselves. The main achievements in both world wars came from technical rather than human intelligence.*

The high reputation of British intelligence in the 1920s and 1930s was on the whole undeserved. Apart from some isolated breakthroughs, such as breaking the Soviet diplomatic code in the 1920s and the Comintern code in the 1930s, it could not point to many achievements. This was partly due, no doubt, to its minute budget (less than £100,000 after 1919). Political intelligence hardly existed; naval intelligence, which had been quite effective in World War I, became a backwater staffed by officers who had not particularly distinguished themselves and were about to retire. The collection of information was woefully insufficient and whatever intelligence did come in was largely ignored by the planners. As a result, the commanders of the British fleet were wrong about the German navy in the 1930s and ignored the Japanese naval buildup altogether. They did not anticipate new German tactics in the use of submarines or the use of air power at sea. Only after 1936 did some of those in positions of influence begin to realize that something was seriously amiss in the field of intelligence, and then it took several years to build up an effective organization.[6]

But the failure was not due merely to limited resources. In the SIS (MI 6), nonchalance prevailed until well into World War II. Those in charge of the secret services were, with rare exceptions, well-connected clubmen or former army, navy, or Indian police officers who did not always have the necessary political understanding to cope with the new perils facing Britain. Their patriotism was not in doubt, but their judgment was.

---

*To a considerable extent, human intelligence from Nazi-occupied Europe reached London from Polish and Czech sources. Thus far insufficient credit has been given to these sources in official and unofficial accounts of wartime intelligence.

They lacked imagination, knowledge, and, on the whole, professionalism
—which in this context meant the ability to operate under conditions very
different from those prevailing at home. Thus, when World War II broke
out, Britain lacked a secret service adequate to its needs.

This failure was surprising. England had been the home of the spy and
of the detective story. Millions of readers had read with fascination the
adventures of Sir Percy Blakeney *(The Scarlet Pimpernel)*, and those of Richard
Hannay and Sandy Arbuthnot, two of John Buchan's best-known heroes.
Noted authors like Somerset Maugham, A. F. W. Mason, and Sir Compton
Mackenzie drew on their own experience on active duty when writing
their intelligence novels. It is difficult to think of a similar preoccupation
with intelligence in any other country at the time. Yet the Richard Han-
nays were gentlemen spies, brilliant amateurs serving their country in an
hour of peril. Once the danger had passed, they retired to their farms or
clubs; it was never clear who would replace them. The tremendous interest
in intelligence and the reservoir of ingenuity and daring were never really
tapped in a systematic manner. Even in World War I it was clear that the
age of the great individual spy had drawn to a close. As Captain Roskill,
a leading historian of the British navy, put it, the major exploits of an
intelligence organization no longer depended on rifling the safe of a foreign
diplomat or the seduction of officers by beautiful women, but on the
systematic collection of small pieces of information from scores of different
sources.[7]

When World War II began, a new crop of men and women appeared in
Whitehall, ready to serve in intelligence. Among them were young lectur-
ers from universities, scientists, classicists, philologists, journalists who
had lived abroad—all brilliant young people on the whole, many of them
eccentrics. The management of the services themselves did not change very
much; the old-timers received the new crop of recruits without enthusiasm
but with recognition of the fact that they were needed, even if not all of
them had been to the right public schools. But Britain's wartime intelligence success was to be generated by these new recruits.

The director of the SIS (commonly called "C") during the war was
General Stewart Menzies, a product of Eton and the Guards. Menzies's two
predecessors had been naval officers, whereas Kell, the head of counterintelligence (MI 5), was a military man like all his predecessors. The director
of naval intelligence during World War I had been Admiral Reginald Hall,
who virtually ignored the Foreign Office and conducted his own foreign
policy; the publication of the Zimmermann telegram was his most noted
feat.[8] In World War I, Admiral Hall had been directly in control of "Room
40," the source of most intelligence. By contrast, in World War II Menzies
was only nominally in charge of Bletchley, where the Ultra traffic was

decrypted. His influence was therefore much smaller, compared to his predecessor.

During the period between wars British intelligence lacked adequate functional coordination and unified leadership. The SIS was engaged only in the collection of information; the other functions of intelligence—evaluation and dissemination—remained outside its scope. Far from fighting for the control of intelligence (as the United States had after World War I), no one really wanted it in Britain. The Foreign Office provided a small budget and (reluctantly) some cover: operators for the SIS appeared abroad as employees of the passport control division. The Foreign Office did not think highly of the SIS; most diplomats were convinced that the information gathered through their own channels was infinitely superior, despite the fact that the Foreign Office did not even have a proper research section at the time. Ambassadors and their aides served not only as collectors of information and evaluators, but also as providers of background information for the foreign secretary. The Government Code and Cipher School (GC and CS), which was to play a central role after 1939, had been founded after World War I. Headed by a retired naval officer, it was "an adopted child of the Foreign Office with no family rights, and the poor relation of SIS, whose peacetime activities left little cash to spare."[9] At the same time, intelligence organizations of sorts continued to exist in the armed services. Aerial reconnaissance, which was to play an important part in World War II, was inaugurated by the RAF in the mid-1930s, but almost in a fit of absentmindedness. As there was no mechanism for properly developing the new techniques, such reconnaissance was "farmed out" for a while to a private firm which acted as subcontractor.

A fresh impetus to coordinate the various intelligence activities came in 1937, on the eve of the war. This impulse arose from the realizations that economic considerations were likely to be of paramount importance in a coming conflict, that modern war would involve all the resources of a nation, and that the zone of operations had been vastly extended by the progress of aviation.[10] Yet it took two years before the Joint Intelligence Committee (JIC) began to function under the chairmanship of a representative of the Foreign Office. Up to that date, military and political intelligence had been kept apart. The Foreign Office did not trust the military assessments and supplied little information to the armed services. Systematic evaluation hardly existed before the outbreak of the war, except in the form of annual estimates prepared by the armed services. Raw intelligence was received and passed on, in a more or less haphazard way, to various consumers. From 1939 on, a Situation Report Center published daily reports and a weekly commentary on the international situation.

During the war years intelligence greatly expanded, though there were few major organizational innovations. The JIC recruited its own staff (JIS) to coordinate, assess, and disseminate incoming intelligence. This made it possible for the JIC to concentrate on its basic function, which was to provide guidance to intelligence. The other major departure was the establishment of Special Operations Executive (SOE). The official assignment of SOE was not to collect intelligence, but to engage in covert action and sabotage—"to set Europe ablaze." But in fact, SOE became a source of important information from several European countries, including Denmark, Poland, and France.

There was continuous friction between SIS and SOE; organizationally, the latter was part of the Ministry for Economic Warfare. The SIS regarded the rival enterprise as amateurish and misguided; furthermore, there was intense competition for the limited financial and logistic resources, probably the most important cause of conflict. On occasion, the two organizations got into each other's way in neutral or enemy countries because they hardly ever exchanged information. The existence of rival organizations made it somewhat more complicated for the Germans to penetrate British intelligence networks. In the final analysis, however, it would seem that duplication did more harm than good.

British wartime intelligence achievements and failures have been widely discussed. By and large, success came relatively early in the battle against the German air force; by contrast, naval intelligence's repeated failures bordered on disaster—the turning point toward success was not reached until the late spring of 1943. British intelligence on the German army, beginning with the North African campaigns, was at its most effective by the summer of 1942, when it was needed most. Detailed political intelligence existed from as early as 1940–41; thus British leaders knew about Hitler's preparations to invade the Soviet Union, though the JIC, for a variety of reasons, did not fully believe the evidence until about two weeks before the event.

The achievements of British HUMINT were rather modest. By and large, neither the British, Americans, nor Russians succeeded in penetrating Germany. Networks of agents did not survive long, infiltration proved nearly impossible, and what information that did emanate from these sources was in no way comparable to the systematic flow received through SIGINT. Most of the reliable information came from "technical means," especially SIGINT, and to a lesser degree from photographic intelligence. If World War I's distinguishing characteristic was the duel between artillery batteries, World War II was a SIGINT war. Never before or after in the history of warfare did each side know so much about the other's preparations and sometimes about its intentions. From 1942 on, the Allies certainly knew much more about the Germans than vice versa. At the same time, there were whole areas of intelligence that SIGINT could not cover; even under ideal conditions, when information was detailed and reliable, there was still room for doubt about enemy intentions.

If the finest hour of British intelligence had been during World War II, it was followed by years of disaster. Successive spy scandals shook Britain's reputation—Soviet penetration appeared to have been complete. Although uncertainty prevails to this day in some cases of alleged espionage, the proven instances of treason were many and disquieting. It could be argued that British intelligence had become less important with Britain's decline in world affairs. But though Britain was no longer a world power, it was still a key member of NATO and as such remained an important target for Soviet espionage. Until about 1970 there were suspicions that some contemporaries of Kim Philby and Anthony Blunt were still operating undetected. After that date, it was assumed that they must have reached the end of their careers. But the cases of Blake, Vassall, Bettaney, and Price, spies who were recruited in the postwar period, proved that internal security was still deficient, causing new problems between Britain and her allies.

Counterintelligence (MI 5) had to bear the burden of the scandals. Its successive directors had to devote much of their time to appearances before investigation committees to answer for the sins of their predecessors. With a minimum of publicity some farreaching changes took place. The basis of recruitment for MI 5 and MI 6 (renamed DI 5—the Directorate of the Security Services—and DI 6*) was changed and the new directors were no longer military people but diplomats and civil servants or officials who had risen from the ranks of the secret services. In 1965 the Ministry of Defense established a Directorate General of Intelligence (DIS), which incorporated the intelligence sections of the armed services. The first director of this new body was Major General Kenneth Strong—Eisenhower's chief intelligence liaison officer during the war. Navy, air force, and army intelligence were still responsible for collection and internal security, but evaluation and dissemination was done by a combined unit, the Joint Intelligence Bureau (JIB). This body deals not only with military intelligence but also with political and economic affairs that impinge directly on overall strategy. Directorate General of Intelligence has five main branches: Service Intelligence; Scientific and Technical Intelligence; Economic Intelligence; Management and Support of Intelligence; and Administration. The organization as a whole is subdivided into some fifty departments.[11]

Several more special features of British intelligence ought to be mentioned. The Foreign Office has a research department, similar in function

*For convenience, and since the older terms continue to be used, I refer here to MI 5 and MI 6, not to their new names.

to, though much smaller than, INR. The Joint Intelligence Committee established during World War II continues to function. Now called the Defense Intelligence Committee (DIC), it is headed, as previously, by a Foreign Office representative, usually a deputy undersecretary. It acts as a coordinating body for intelligence received from all agencies, both political and military. The Franks committee appointed after the Falklands war recommended that the JIC should be more independent from the government departments principally constituting it and that the chairman should in the future be appointed by the prime minister, be a member of the Cabinet Office, and operate on a full-time basis. Since 1970 there is also an official coordinator of intelligence and security in the Cabinet Office. The Official Committee of Security is an in-house body, not to be confused with the Security Commission, which is an outside supervisory group usually headed by a very senior judge and made up of former career undersecretaries and military officers. The coordinator is directly responsible to the prime minister, acting as a two-way conduit, providing the prime minister with current information from MI 5 and MI 6 and DIS and informing these agencies of the requirements of the prime minister. The British equivalent of the NSA is the Government Communication Headquarters (GCHQ) in Cheltenham, manned by officers and soldiers of two signal regiments as well as civilians; it employs more than six thousand people. The NSA itself has several bases in England and Scotland. Both GCHQ and MI 6 are under the control of the Foreign Office. This arrangement has been criticized by knowledgeable students of British intelligence, who believe that the special views and attitudes of the Foreign Office may have a negative impact on intelligence collection and assessment.

While hostile intelligence agencies knew—until recently at least—a great deal about the activities of the British secret services, the Official Secrets Act of 1911 has kept such knowledge from the public. As it cannot possibly have escaped the KGB's attention that the headquarters of MI 5 were in Curzon Street and MI 6 was in a building adjoining Lambeth North underground station, why bother to hide the facts? Nor is it readily obvious why, many years after the event, intelligence files should remain closed. Some suspect that this has less to do with the defense of the realm than with the wish to cover up past mistakes. By and large, successive British governments have accepted the advice given by Austin Chamberlain in the 1920s that it was "of the essence of a secret service that it must be secret, and if you once began disclosure it is perfectly obvious that there is no longer any secret service and that you must do without it."[12] After he resigned as prime minister, Harold Wilson wrote that he saw the heads of MI 5 and MI 6 so infrequently that he confused the names of their directors. Harold McMillan, a man of excellent memory, could not remember in later years, or did not care to say publicly, who had been head of MI 5 in his time. When Furnival Jones was head of MI 5, he noted that there had been "some erosion of what had been an extremely rigid position" (to keep secret the names of the security services' chiefs until they resigned) and he was clearly not happy about it: "I have no direct relations with the press. Where does one stop? If my name is published, why not my deputy's name? If my deputy's name is published, why not my director's? And before you know where you are, you are publishing the name of someone who is running agents, and his photograph appears in the press. . . ."[13]

This secretive approach has come under increasing attack from a variety of people—those who regard the secret services as pillars of a system they want to destroy, concerned citizens worried by successive spy scandals and the suspicion that there have been massive cover-ups, journalists who affirm the people's right to know. The official "D notices" to newspapers, which advised them not to publish information on certain "sensitive" issues, have been ignored on occasion. Several fringe periodicals even began to specialize in revelations about British intelligence. The authorities were in most cases reluctant to prosecute them, perhaps because they feared that in a trial even more such information would be divulged. Ironically, the Official Secrets Act had been promulgated precisely because the law otherwise made it impossible to get convictions in cases involving intelligence without revealing state secrets.

Because the British intelligence services exist in a kind of legal limbo— they are not established by statute nor are they recognized by common law —there is bound to be some ambiguity about the lines of command.[14] The MI 5 is not grounded in an act of Parliament, whereas MI 6 is sanctioned by the official Secret Service Vote. To whom are the agencies accountable? Clearly not to Parliament, which in a secret vote each year ratifies the MI 6 budget.[15] According to a 1952 order by the home secretary, the director general of the Security Service (MI 5) is personally responsible to him, even though the organization is not part of the Home Office. On appropriate occasions, the director general has the right of direct access to the prime minister. The directive of 1952 also said that MI 5 is part of the nation's defense forces; it is to remain absolutely free from any political bias; inquiries on behalf of any government department should be undertaken only if it involves the defense of the realm; and ministers are not to concern themselves with detailed information obtained by MI 5, but "are furnished with such information only as may be necessary for the determination of an issue on which guidance is sought."[16]

The "doctrine" of 1952 did little to clarify the position of MI 5. In 1945 senior government officials had agreed that appointment of the MI 5 director was a matter of the greatest responsibility, "calling for unusual experience and a rare combination of qualities."[17] But having appointed the right man, there was no alternative other than to give him the widest discretion in the means he used and the direction in which he applied them—provided he did not step outside the law. As MI 6 must not engage in any acts of violence and as MI 5 is forbidden to prevent anyone from leaving the United Kingdom, interrogate anyone without the person's consent, or even tap a telephone without the consent of the home secretary, the danger of illegal action should not be overrated.

Some postwar prime ministers have asserted greater control than others over the secret services. Prime Minister James Callaghan reported meetings with the secret service chiefs and even the subjects discussed; Mrs. Thatcher told the House of Commons that MI 5 had been ordered to report directly to the home secretary (and to her) if any minister, ex-minister, or senior civil servant might be or might have been a security risk.[18] Nevertheless, prime ministers are notoriously busy people; they cannot possibly devote much time and energy to secret service affairs. Consequently, whether control is exercised and guidance given depends very much on the personality and forcefulness of the prime minister's coordinator of intelligence. But as neither the coordinator nor the Defense Intelligence Committee commands a substantial staff, control and guidance may of necessity be limited to matters of vital importance. There is no supervision as far as the administration of the secret services are concerned. Once a director has been appointed, a great deal must be left to the director's discretion.[19]

The British secret services, with their weaknesses and strengths and inconsistencies, are very much a product of British culture and of the British political system. The record reveals brilliant efforts by individuals and groups, at times an imaginative approach unrivaled in any other country, admirable discretion, and in some respects great professionalism. The close relationship between national intelligence and the local constabulary, a peculiar but effective system, has been the envy of American intelligence. Yet, a kind of clannishness and a disinclination to "meddle" with colleagues' business have caused major internal security failures. For many years the system was based on the assumption that anyone who came from a good family and had been to a good school could not possibly be a traitor. (As Carruthers said in Erskine Childers' *The Riddle of the Sands*: "The Englishman acting for the enemy is the vilest creature on God's earth.")

But the Philbys, Burgesses, and Macleans no longer subscribed to this simple ethos; some of their friends argued that strictly speaking they were not even traitors, for how could one betray a cause if one did not believe in it to begin with? Negligence, a lack of elementary political understanding, and a public school ethos according to which informing on one's friend is the greatest sin led to a cover-up with disastrous consequences. Hence, the setbacks in recent years, which led to more soul-searching concerning internal security inside British intelligence. However, while the secret service is small, and while it does not have remotely as much influence as readers of espionage fiction have been led to believe, its professionalism is still highly regarded by other Western intelligence agencies.[20]

Germany

Contrary to widespread belief, German policy makers have not usually accorded much weight to intelligence. Bismarck had a private spymaster, a failed police official named Wilhelm Stieber, who brought him interesting personal information about his enemies and also, on occasion, some military intelligence, but he would not have dreamed of consulting Stieber on affairs of state. There was no political intelligence service in Germany on the eve of World War I, and on the military side, one general staff officer coordinated the activities of a dozen junior officers on the Russian and French borders. When Major Walther Nicolai was appointed chief coordinator of German intelligence in 1914, he noted with sadness that the Russians, the French, and the British had an enormous advantage, because they had realized the importance of intelligence in modern warfare so much earlier. Nicolai's work was not taken very seriously by his superiors —as a relatively junior officer he was not only in charge of intelligence throughout the war but also acted as chief censor and director of domestic propaganda.

Not surprisingly then, Germany's intelligence achievements in World War I were undistinguished. With some exceptions, mainly owing to telegraph intercepts, the German leadership did not know much about the state of affairs on the other side. Initially, the German leaders did not care, assuming that the war would be over within a few months. Once it emerged that it would be a protracted war, it was too late to build up a superior intelligence organization. German officers were even less interested in technology than British and French officers; tanks, for example, were a total surprise to the Germans. On the other hand, it would be difficult to point to any major victories scored by the Allies against Germany as the result of intelligence. Throughout the war the French had an exceedingly well-placed spy in German headquarters, just as the Germans had an important agent in the head office of censorship in London. Both remained undetected, but neither had any impact on the course of events, for there was no way the spies could keep their masters informed in time.

The second major phase in the history of modern German intelligence began in the early days of the Weimar republic and lasted to 1945. The small intelligence section of the Reichswehr concentrated on purely defensive activities, hence its name: *Abwehr,* or defense. Only when Hitler began to rearm was the *Abwehr* (now renamed *Ausland-Abwehr,* or Defense Against Foreign Powers) given wider scope and instructed to engage in both active espionage and counterespionage. The *Abwehr* also had a covert action section, but most sabotage and similar activities were entrusted to special units sponsored and controlled by the party through Section VI of the Security Head Office. For political and other reasons, Hitler decided to keep the two apart.

German wartime intelligence was as systematic and thorough as that of the Western Allies, but it did not show much imagination. Unlike Britain, Nazi Germany had no room for brilliant outsiders and eccentrics in intelligence. German postwar intelligence was initially based on General Reinhard Gehlen's *Fremde Heer Ost,* or Foreign Armies/East. In the beginning this was a semiprivate organization paid for by America; in 1956 it became the official German external intelligence service, the *Bundesnachrichtendienst* (BND) with Gehlen at its head.

During the first decade after the war, Gehlen's organization was generally well-informed about events in the Soviet Union and Eastern Europe, mainly as a result of the systematic interrogation of many thousands of German prisoners of war returning from the East (Operation Hermes). The border with East Germany was not yet sealed in those years and Gehlen's operators recruited agents in the East German party government; even the East German spy service was penetrated. After 1956, many of these sources of information began to dry up; there was now only a handful of returning prisoners of war, and East German counterintelligence made activities more and more difficult inside the German Democratic Republic (GDR). Furthermore, the BND's analytical and integrating capabilities were inferior to those of the CIA or the British intelligence services. Yet, the exodus from East Germany continued until the GDR built the Berlin Wall in 1961.

During the late 1950s, the character of the BND and its work began to change. Until 1956, the BND had concentrated on the Soviet Union and Eastern Europe, with an emphasis on military intelligence; now it began to cover certain other parts of the world as well. In addition, the BND's emphasis shifted from HUMINT to technical means of information gathering. It introduced modern monitoring services and was the first German institution to install a major computer.

The BND suffered a major eclipse in 1961 when it revealed that Heinz Felfe, one of Gehlen's close collaborators and a former SS officer, had been an East German agent. It soon appeared that Felfe had not been the only mole. As a result, most of the remaining agents of the BND in Eastern Europe were lost, and a major purge was carried out in Pullach—the headquarters of the BND in a Munich suburb. The damage to the reputation of the BND (and to Gehlen personally) seemed irreparable.

Gehlen had been running his service in a highly idiosyncratic manner. In some ways he was an accomplished intelligence officer of the old school, but books published after he retired reveal that he was lacking in political understanding and judgment. Legend had portrayed him as the master spy in dark glasses who never allowed himself to be photographed. He did wear tinted glasses, but that was about all the truth there was to the legend. A capable wartime intelligence officer, Gehlen was far less successful as the head of a modern intelligence service operating in peacetime. Many years later a senior CIA intelligence official familiar with German conditions wrote that the BND under Gehlen had a good record in the collection of military and economic intelligence, and that Gehlen's domestic activities were not nearly as sinister as his critics made them out to be. But the BND had been weak on political intelligence at a time when there was a growing demand for such information. Gehlen made little of his intelligence analysis department, and though not an operator himself, he loved operations for operations' sake and tended to measure the BND's performance by an operation's success or failure.[21]

In 1968 Lieutenant General Gerhard Wessel, a military intelligence officer during World War II, succeeded Gehlen. Wessel's style was unlike that of his predecessor; above all, it was far less personalized and splenetic. Wessel tried to restore confidence within the service and to improve relations with the government and the political party leaders. Yet he and the BND were at a disadvantage, partly because of domestic political pressures, and partly because of the continued Soviet/East German attempts to penetrate the service and to discredit it. It was also difficult for Wessel to provide the political intelligence Bonn demanded. Neither Gehlen nor Wessel was a member of a political party, but both were more or less identified with Christian Democratic Union (CDU) policies. Gehlen had the reputation of a die-hard "cold warrior," though he had maintained contact with Kurt Schumacher, postwar chairman of the Social Democratic party (SPD) and after his death with other SPD leaders. On one famous occasion—the Spiegel affair—Gehlen deeply antagonized Adenauer.[22]

As the West German leadership's deep suspicions of the Communist bloc gave way to great expectations during Willy Brandt's *Ostpolitik,* the BND came under attack as a reactionary anachronism harboring outdated fears of Communist danger. True, from time to time there were new revelations about Soviet and East German espionage in the *Bundesrepublik* (BRD), but policy makers considered these to be minor blemishes that should not be permitted to interfere with the spirit of détente. In 1969 the Social Democrats first shared power at the national level; subsequently, they became the senior partner in the Bonn coalition government. Not surprisingly, they wanted to establish control over the BND. Dieter Blotz, a Social Democratic politician, was appointed deputy director, and there were other changes in the higher echelons of the BND. When Wessel retired, Dr. Klaus Kinkel, a senior civil servant, was appointed president of the BND. This was not a political appointment per se, but the fact that Kinkel was known to sympathize with the Liberal party (the junior partner in the coalition) may have helped determine his selection. When the Christian Democrats replaced the government headed by Helmut Schmidt, they appointed Eberhard Blum head of the BND, a senior intelligence official and a sympathizer of the CDU.

The politicization of the service was blamed for information "leaks"; these caused the BND a great deal of aggravation and sidetracked some of its activities. More important, it was argued that as a result of outside pressure—or of the perception of pressure—intelligence reports lost some of their objectivity. If during the 1950s the BND had tended to take too somber and alarmist a view of Soviet capabilities and intentions, the inclination among policy makers in the 1970s was toward "good" news from the East, and they expected intelligence reports to bear out their predilection. According to some sources the distortion was even more palpably felt in the early 1970s than twenty years earlier because Gehlen had been more interested in military than political intelligence and had been much better at obtaining it, whereas in the era of *Ostpolitik* the emphasis was on political reporting. As the international situation again deteriorated toward the end of the 1970s, the high hopes among German policy makers gave way to a more realistic outlook. There was, generally speaking, greater readiness to acknowledge the importance of the intelligence function in the changed international climate. As a result, political pressures lessened or were less readily perceived.

All the same, political infighting and public controversies continued to bedevil the activities of the BND inside Germany. Constitutionally, the BND was defined as West Germany's foreign political intelligence organization. Its task was to collect and evaluate information on foreign policy and on economic, military, and military-technological developments. The BND was also expected to engage to a limited extent in counterintelligence inside Germany. (According to a 1958 regulation, it should deal with enemy penetration into its own ranks, but in reality an agent once uncovered may lead to others with different targets, so that an artificial division of labor may be incompatible with maximum effectiveness.)

Counterintelligence, in any case, was to be only a sideline for the BND. It was the main assignment of two other institutions: the *Bundesamt fur Verfassungsschutz* (BfV)—the state office for the defense of the constitution —which was also in charge of watching over the activities of domestic antidemocratic organizations; and the *Militärischer Abschirmdienst* (MAD), which was in charge of counterintelligence within the German armed forces.

This arrangement was bound to lead to duplication and internal disputes, for there was no division of labor that could cover all eventualities. For example, information about East European agents operating in West Germany frequently originated with the BND; such information should then have been passed on for action to the BfV, whose head was the government's senior advisor for internal security affairs. But for one reason or another the BND might not want to pass on such information at an early stage, which naturally led to distrust and friction between the two organizations. Quite apart from problems of an organizational nature, political differences also impeded the smooth functioning of intelligence. The BfV's former chief, Günther Nollau, claimed that Gehlen tried to operate the BND in a big way inside West Germany, and that, contrary to established norms, Gehlen had agents in the Social Democratic party, to which Nollau belonged. Gehlen's aim, according to Nollau, was to attain a "position of domination" in the country.[23] Gehlen's successors improved relations with the political parties and other intelligence organizations and political accusations against the BND came to an end, except, of course, from left- and right-wing fringe groups. The compromise provided that German citizens were not to be kept under observation by the BND, unless it was established that they were in contact with foreign agents. In such cases, warnings about those involved would be passed on to the BfV more or less automatically.

The structure of the BND has changed considerably over the years; it has been modeled fairly closely after the CIA. In the post-Gehlen era the BND was subdivided into four major departments: Collection; Technical Questions; Evaluation and Assessment; and Central Assignments. Collection has many area subsections; it is based mainly on HUMINT and receives its material from more than a hundred branches abroad, as well as from liaison officers with other German and allied institutions. The Technical Questions department is in charge of W/T interception; it also researches and prepares technical means for conspiratorial data collection. Evaluation and Assessment, like Collection, has many regional subsections. Within all major subsections there are separate desks dealing with political, economic, military, and technical issues that prepare daily, weekly, and monthly bulletins as well as special memoranda on current intelligence. Central Assignments deals with administration, personnel, finances, and general support for the other departments; it is also responsible for internal security. In 1981 a brief official survey mentioned the following topics as the main fields of BND inquiry: military policy and armaments in the Eastern bloc countries, the Afghanistan conflict, the war between Iran and Iraq, Chad's civil war, developments in Poland, energy problems, and the development of new technologies.

The head of the BND is appointed by the chancellor. This is a political appointment in a sense, but it is unlikely to go to someone strongly identified with one party, as the head of the BND has to enjoy the broadest confidence possible. The BND head reports directly to the head of the Chancellor's Office, traditionally a state secretary or a minister of state who has been designated as chief intelligence coordinator.[24] The head of the Chancellor's Office exercises a degree of control over BND activities, but there are also more than half a dozen institutions charged with a certain measure of supervision. These include the BND's two main customers, the Foreign Ministry and the Defense Ministry, and to a lesser degree, the Ministry of Economics. Parliamentary control is exercised through a commission consisting of the heads of the three main parties and a few other deputies. The G-10 Committee, made up of five parliamentary deputies, is responsible for making sure that the BND acts in accordance with Article 10 of the German Constitution *(Grundgesetz).* Three members of the G-10 Committee have to decide, on a case-by-case basis, whether circumstances involving state security make exemption from the Constitution necessary. There is a three-person financial subcommittee of the German parliament designated to ratify the budget of the BND. Finally, the Federal Budget Court *(Bundeshaushaltshof),* the main financial control institution, has the right to ask for explanations and to issue warnings.

With this multiplicity of interested parties the question arises whether there can, in fact, be effective control. The answer is yes, as far as finances are concerned. As for the rest, a considerable bureaucratic staff would be needed to monitor the performance of the BND on a permanent basis. Such a staff does not exist, and if it did, it might well prevent the effective functioning of a secret service. A former president of the BND told me that close control is virtually impossible, that government and parliament have to trust the integrity and competence of the director and his closest collaborators, and that organizational reforms will not change this state of affairs.

The Foreign Ministry and the Defense Ministry also have research and intelligence offices of their own. In the Foreign Ministry, there is a small but highly qualified policy planning staff, which functions somewhat differently from its namesake in the State Department. It does not engage in collection itself, but coordinates and evalutes all incoming information from in-house and other sources. Many German diplomats believe that political information received from their own representatives abroad is superior to that passed on from the BND, simply because diplomats have better access to information than intelligence agents, especially on a high level. In addition to MAD, its counterintelligence service, the German Defense Ministry has its own intelligence branch, *Führungsstab II* (Fus II), which engages in naval and aerial reconnaissance as well as electronic monitoring and receives information from other sources, such as military attachés in foreign capitals.

Attempts to achieve full coordination between the various intelligence agencies—for instance, within the framework of a German National Security Council—have so far not succeeded. While the BND reports to the chancellor, military intelligence is responsible to the minister of defense, and the BfV is the minister of the interior's special agency. Separate parliamentary committees deal with the operations of the three services. There is overlapping and duplication, but probably less of it than in the other major Western countries.[25]

The BND is better informed about East Germany than are other Western intelligence services; there is occasionally information via East Germany on other East European countries. Between 1950 and 1961, some 300 employees of the East German Ministry of State Security defected to the West. Over the last twenty years the number of defectors has been only about 55, but it has nevertheless been sufficient to gain a fairly accurate picture of the structure of East German intelligence and some of its activities. Among agents who were active for the BND in East Germany were the secretary of Prime Minister Otto Grotewohl, Assistant Prime Minister Hermann Kastner, the chief translator of the Soviet Embassy in East Berlin, and Lieutenant Colonel Dombrowski of the East German security service. More recent successes are naturally kept secret for the most part, but one of the few cases that did become known was Operation Schiller, in which an East German state security officer who worked for the BND was "exfiltrated" in 1979, bringing with him material leading to arrests in West Germany and other West European countries.

Today as in the past there are undoubtedly many more East German agents active in the *Bundesrepublik* than vice versa. Given the openness of a democratic society this is inevitable. On the other hand, even the strict controls exercised by a totalitarian regime have not been sufficient to prevent defections and the loss of East German state secrets. The BND also seems to have met with some success in Third World countries because

West Germany is an economic giant, but not a great military power. Consequently, it has faced fewer suspicions than either the United States or the Soviet Union.

Among the successes of the BND over the past two decades, the following are usually singled out: knowledge about Soviet policy vis-à-vis Germany in general and Berlin in particular; foreknowledge of the decision to invade Czechoslovakia in 1968; and advance warning of Israel's Six Day War in June 1967.[26] As far as can be ascertained, there were only non-specific indications in 1961 that some kind of stringent measures (that is, the Wall) would be taken by the East German leader Walter Ulbricht to stem the flow of refugees from East to West Germany.

The strengths of German intelligence lie in its systematic, orderly approach, its collection and sifting of great quantities of material, and in Germany's special relationship with some East European and Third World countries. Although Germany's direct interests in the Third World are mostly economic, intelligence in this field is worth a good deal in the exchange of information among Western secret services. The weakness of the BND lies in its bureaucratic, rigid character—perhaps inevitable in the given framework—which narrowly confines fresh initiatives. Some of the qualities that make for success in intelligence—unorthodox approach, willingness to take risks, imagination—are incompatible with a civil service routine which hems in the activity of government employees with hundreds of bureaucratic regulations. While intelligence is not neglected in West Germany, it is not very influential. The heads of the various services do not participate in the deliberations of the inner councils of the *Bundesrepublik;* they do not even have access to the chancellor except on rare occasions. This remoteness from decision making means that they cannot be sure which, if any, of their reports reaches the key political figures. Remoteness also means that the head of the BND is not always sufficiently informed about the policy and the needs of his own government. As a result, the BND routinely collects information it thinks the government *may* need; in these circumstances, current intelligence is most likely to suffer.

In a study not intended for publication, a highly placed U.S. intelligence official noted some ten years ago that the BND, with a broader charter than that of any other Western service, was not then a first-class intelligence organization. It was, however, "in a position to become one." In the decade since that was written, the BND has largely overcome the burden of suspicion and politicization that plagued it in the 1950s and 1960s. Other secret services in the West respect it and find the BND systematic and reliable. Whether it will someday merit the term "first-class" depends upon whether it can find a way to accommodate unorthodox approaches, while at the same time drawing nearer to those who must decide what national policies and priorities shall be.

Israel

Israeli intelligence is of interest as an example of the specific opportunities and problems facing a small nation which are necessarily different from those confronting the superpowers and former imperial nations such as Great Britain and France. While substantial in size, Israeli intelligence is by no means the largest of the secret services of the smaller countries (the Cuban DGI, for one, is substantially larger). Its three main components are: (1) the *Mossad*, which employs 1,500–2,000 men and women, of whom 500 are officers, and which engages in the collection of foreign intelligence; (2) the *Shin Bet* (counterintelligence) with about 1,000 employees; (3) *Aman*, or military intelligence, with 7,000 people, of whom only about 500 are officers. For the sake of completeness, the Foreign Ministry's relatively small research department should also be included.[27]

Of the *Mossad*'s eight sections, the Collection Department, the Operational Planning and Coordination Department, and Political Action and Liaison are the most important. The desks are organized on both regional and functional bases, and are highly specialized. The *Mossad* has a virtual monopoly on the collection of intelligence outside the state of Israel, with the exception of certain military targets (usually not far from Israel's borders), which are the concern of military intelligence. The *Mossad* is basically a HUMINT organization; the technical means of collection belong to military intelligence, as do most of the documentation and, more surprisingly, most of the production of intelligence.

Whether this division of labor is the most effective and rational is a moot point. It came into being as a result of Israel's unique international position. Except for Egypt, the state of war with Arab neighbors has never officially ended; therefore, the kind of information most urgently needed is military in character. Thus the preparation of the annual "risk of war" estimates, with their heavy emphasis on military facts and figures, was given to military intelligence—*Aman*—rather than to the *Mossad*.

The successes of Israeli intelligence have frequently been explained with reference to "Jewish solidarity," that is, the fact that Israel can count on the goodwill or active help of Jews in many parts of the world. But this is a mistaken assumption. Israel is vitally interested in the Middle East and in some Third World regions—places where there either are no Jews or where Jews live but are in no position to offer assistance.

Professionalism and achievement did not come to Israeli intelligence all at once or without great effort; its first decade was one of troubles, infighting, and interservice rivalry. Lacking tradition and experience, Israeli intelligence became involved in domestic rivalries and engaged in some disastrous ventures. True, even in those early days it had some spectacular exploits to its credit—such as obtaining the text of Khrushchev's "secret" speech in 1956—so in some important respects the foundations for later successes were built then. Early Israeli intelligence had an abundance of initiative, daring, innovation, and, above all, the ability to improvise. But seen in retrospect, the output was uneven: only toward the late 1950s did Israeli intelligence achieve a steady level of performance. Its achievements in the period since then can be explained largely by the fact that it was able to attract recruits of high caliber, that it used superior training methods, and that while applying the most up-to-date technological means of reconnaissance and surveillance within its financial reach, it never neglected the traditional approaches of HUMINT.

Relations between the various branches of intelligence were occasionally troubled, but smoother on the whole than in most countries. Perhaps the most important reason for this is that Israel was, and remains, an embattled country. The high priority given to intelligence is literally a matter of survival; hence it is prestigious. While Israeli intelligence has been bitterly criticized for its failures, it has never come under attack for political reasons. There have been no sensational revelations, scandals, or press campaigns against it. As far as we know, it has never been penetrated by enemy agents. It can count on a large reservoir of goodwill and cooperation from the population, of the kind found only in small countries at a time of emergency.[28] In view of these conditions, it is no surprise that there has also been less tension between Israel's foreign service and intelligence than in other countries, an intelligence background has never been an obstacle for a subsequent diplomatic career. In 1982 both the foreign minister and the director general of the Israeli Foreign Ministry were formerly senior officials of the *Mossad* and former heads of military intelligence had leading positions in the academic world and in economic life—two subsequently became cabinet ministers.

The greatest Israeli intelligence feat was the preparatory work done for the Six Day War in 1967. Other successes included the 1963 "acquisition" from Iraq of a MIG-21, a major coup because of the aircraft's secret technology. The failure of Israeli intelligence was the surprise attack achieved by the Egyptians in the 1973 Yom Kippur War. Over the years, this has become a textbook case of successful deception, discussed in dozens of articles all over the world. Knowledge of the essential facts can therefore be taken for granted, even though the full text of the inquiry (the Agranat Report) has not been released to this day.[29] Much less well-known is another Israeli failure—the inability to assess the "threat of peace," as a director of military intelligence subsequently put it. True, in its annual assessment (September 1976) Israeli intelligence asked itself whether the Arabs—or at least some of them—wanted peace, but it gave no clear answer. One year later the intelligence assessment was more decisive: Egyptian policy had reached a dead end, and more likely than not Sadat would turn to war.[30] Two months later, Sadat was addressing the Knesset in Jerusalem. If the underlying cause of the 1973 failure was overconfidence—the conviction that in view of Israeli military superiority an Arab attack simply would not make sense—the 1976–77 intelligence assessment drew the wrong lesson from the shock of 1973. Having once been caught napping in the face of military attack, the inclination was toward worst-case analysis.

Reforms carried out in the wake of the Yom Kippur War have not produced significant changes in the structure of Israeli intelligence. A special intelligence adviser to the prime minister was appointed, but the position was later abolished. The Foreign Ministry research department was strengthened, but not enough to make it a major factor in the intelligence community. Intelligence production remained as before in the hands of military intelligence—more than a third of army intelligence personnel deals with such production, including documentation. The devil's advocate approach was tried, but without conspicuous success.

The Israeli experience shows that the personality of individual service heads is of great importance, both for morale and for the quality of intelligence. This is even more the case with the senior aides who are the backbone of the service. While not one of the directors of the *Mossad* was an intelligence genius, all were extremely hard workers and none was a failure. Differences in stature were more pronounced among the various directors of military intelligence. Two of the last four directors of military intelligence proved excellent choices, while the other two were of lesser caliber. Except in 1982, the directorship of the *Mossad* has not gone to an insider.

Every secret service has its specific traditions and peculiar features. For instance, there have been relatively few major intelligence leaks in Israel. This may seem surprising in view of the fact that secrets are more difficult to keep in a small, intimate community than in a big country. If intelligence has been relatively "leakproof," the reason is not so much press censorship as the widespread feeling that survival depends on a strong defense. Activities detrimental to national security are seen as a luxury that a small, embattled country can ill afford. The "need to know" principle is strictly observed, and dissemination of intelligence is kept to a minimum.

The *Mossad* has had to engage in activities that are not customary among other Secret Services, again in view of Israel's unique international position. The Political Action and Liaison Department of the *Mossad* has functioned for many years as something like a second foreign ministry, maintaining relations with many African and Asian countries that broke off relations after 1967, or with which official relations have never existed. Another example is Israel's role as an arms producer and exporter of some significance; intelligence has often established contacts and paved the way for arms deals. There has also been more violent action than in other Western intelligence services.

Relations between intelligence producer and consumer have varied in Israel, as in other countries, according to the interests of the main consumers—the prime minister, the minister of defense, and, to a lesser degree, the minister of foreign affairs. While there has been much praise for the quality of *Mossad* political intelligence, military intelligence (including raw intelligence) has on the whole attracted greater interest. David Ben-Gurion was an avid consumer of intelligence, though he frequently preferred his own judgment to the assessments he received.[31] Moshe Dayan and Itzhak Rabin, in view of their military and political experience, also tended to trust their own hunches more than the combined wisdom of the intelligence community. By contrast, "civilians" such as Levi Eshkol, Golda Meir, and Shimon Peres were on the whole more open to intelligence reports. Menachem Begin was fascinated with the details of military intelligence; from the menu of political intelligence he is said to have picked and chosen what was most to his liking. He once told the director of military intelligence that he was not interested in the assessment of *Aman* but in the "facts." Such an attitude on the part of the senior intelligence consumer has a negative effect on morale in the intelligence community.

The directors of the *Mossad* and *Aman* address members of the Foreign Affairs and National Security Committees of the Knesset regularly, but these briefings are by necessity of a general character. The main impact of Israeli intelligence has been not so much on state policy as on the operational level, both in the political and in the military field (enemy order of battle, equipment, identification of personalities, and so forth). It has also served as an early warning system. Yet for all the recognition it has received, Israeli intelligence has not been free of frustration. Sometimes it has served as a scapegoat for the sins of political or military leaders, sometimes its warnings were not heeded, sometimes its information was wrong and misleading. The record of Israeli intelligence is a good yardstick for what a highly professional and deeply motivated service, aided by public support, can achieve. But it also points to the limits of intelligence: even a capable service, operating in nearly ideal conditions, may suffer failure when it can least afford it.

The Cost of Intelligence

Intelligence expenditures vary from country to country, much as the functions of intelligence do. Legislators and members of the executive branch, as well as the media and the average citizen, have often asked whether intelligence is worth all the money spent on it. Similar questions arise in other free societies. In recent years some have suggested that consumers should have to pay for information requested and supplied. Psychologically, the effect might be beneficial—goods supplied free of charge are seldom fully appreciated. But attaching a price tag to individual pieces of intelligence involves too many difficulties to be a practical proposition.

Even in the most open societies there are no accurate figures about what governments spend on intelligence. Before World War I, spymasters had special funds at their disposal; receipts and bookkeeping were not encouraged. Allocations for military intelligence were part of general defense budgets that had to be passed by parliaments, but these figures are not reliable—it was always possible to hide part of the intelligence allocations in other parts of the budget. The German military intelligence budget on the eve of World War I was 450,000 marks, a little more than $100,000. By far the richest intelligence services before World War I were the Czarist secret police, the *Okhrana,* the Russian military intelligence: together, they disposed of millions of rubles. The Russians paid one spy alone (Colonel Alfred Redl, head of Austrian counterespionage) a sum close to half-a-million dollars over a ten-year period.[32]

American intelligence expenditure in the last year of World War I was $2.5 million exclusive of salaries, but this was drastically cut once the war ended; during the 1920s and 1930s the military intelligence budget never exceeded $300,000. The OSS budget was about $35 million in 1943; it increased in the two years that followed, and was cut to $24 million in 1946, the year before it was dissolved. Great Britain, France, and most other countries made similar cuts. The budget of the British intelligence service (SIS) was about $1 million at the end of World War I, apparently exclusive of salaries, most of which were paid by the pass section of the Foreign Office. After the war SIS's budget was cut to $400,000; apparently it remained at this level throughout the 1920s.

Even after World War II, American intelligence expenditure was relatively low; it did not employ many people and the means of collection were, on the whole, inexpensive. A big change came with the appearance of the modern and costly technologies in the late 1950s. According to reliable estimates, the United States spent some $3 billion annually in the early 1960s, of which $500 million went to the CIA. By 1968, the number of those employed by all intelligence-gathering agencies had risen to 160,000; this increase was a result of the Vietnam War—most new personnel were in military intelligence. Many claimed that intelligence was spending too much. The foremost task of James Schlesinger's study of U.S. intelligence in 1971, and the main purpose of his subsequent appointment as DCI in 1973 was to halve the intelligence budget, which had risen to $6 billion in 1973. In April 1973, certain figures about the numerical strength and the budgets of the various intelligence community components were read into the *Congressional Record* by Senator Proxmire:[33]

	Budget (in millions)	Employees
DIA	$ 105	5,016
Air Force	2,800	60,000
Army	770	38,500
Navy	775	10,000
State Department	8	335
NSA	1,000	20,000
CIA	750	15,000
TOTAL	$ 6,208	148,851 (approximate)

According to one of the Pike reports in the 1970s, intelligence spent as much as $11 billion annually, but the report also said that it could not be sure of the amount. The only certainty was that intelligence spent more than it told Congress. The air force budget included the space program, whereas the NSA budget covered most of signal intelligence. Within the CIA more than half of those employed—55 percent—and considerably more than half of the budget went to operations; research and analysis received only a small part.

There was a further rise in the intelligence budget in 1974 and 1975, but during the Carter years the intelligence budget declined and the number of those serving in intelligence decreased. According to a 1978 estimate in a professional journal, CIA personnel had fallen to 16,500 (from more than 20,000); air force intelligence had been reduced to 56,000; army intelligence had remained more or less steady, but naval intelligence had gone up to 17,000.[34] Despite attempts to economize, the air force intelligence budget had more than doubled between 1973 and 1978 (from $2.8 billion to $6.5 billion) and NSA expenses had more then tripled (from $1 billion to $3.3 billion). It should be taken into account that equipment became more expensive every year and though these figures suggest an enormous expansion of the intelligence apparatus, it is likely that the U.S. government actually received less intelligence of importance in 1978 than five years earlier. One trend that emerges clearly from the available figures for the postwar period is the small (and declining) part of HUMINT in intelligence spending.

According to Marchetti and Marks, the CIA budget in 1973 was about $740 million, of which the Clandestine Services received $440 million; Science and Technology, $120 million; Management and Services, $110 million; and the Directorate of Intelligence, $70 million.[35] During the first year of the Reagan administration, CIA budget and manpower reportedly increased by about 20 percent; it is said that the 1983 defense budget allocated $12 billion for national foreign intelligence, including tactical intelligence programs. The defense budget allocation figure is for "intelligence and communication." Similar data have been published fairly regularly in the *Aerospace Daily* and other professional journals.

Considering the internal structure of the intelligence budget, which has not changed much over the past fifteen years, it can be assumed that the total intelligence community budget is now in the magnitude of $15–20 billion (this includes military communications systems that have little to do with intelligence as it is commonly understood). If this figure is correct, intelligence accounts for less than 10 percent of the general defense budget; in the perspective of two decades the percentage of defense spending for intelligence has remained fairly stable. America probably spends somewhat more on foreign intelligence than the Soviet Union because unlike the Soviet Union it confronts closed societies. On the other hand, the Soviet Union employs many more people in intelligence, and possibly gets more for its money. The budgets of all other intelligence services, including the British, French, West German, Cuban, and East European, are measured in hundreds of millions of dollars. There is a qualitative difference between big league and minor league intelligence collection.

While the budgets of the intelligence services have been going up and up, spies have not been doing all that well. Mention has been made of the great sums paid to Colonel Redl by the Russians; Mata Hari received 30,000 marks, 15,000 pesetas, and probably several more major remittances; Cicero in Ankara got $50,000 the first time he handed over British documents to his German case officer. Altogether Cicero received some

$700,000 (but then, he was paid in counterfeit money). Since World War II the sums that have changed hands have been small by comparison. Major Popov of the GRU—the most important spy the CIA had at the time —had a monthly salary of $400 from Washington. Alfred Franzel, the German Social Democrat member of parliament was paid $7,000 by the Russians over a period of four years (1956–60); Harry Houghton, the "bagman" of the Soviet spy group at the British naval station in Portland, received a little more, but over a longer period.[36] The American Kampiles sold the Russians the KH-16 spy satellite's manual for $3,000, probably the bargain of the century, with the possible exception of the $700 paid in 1944 to Allan Nunn May, the British nuclear physicist, for two samples of plutonium (but May was a Communist, and the Russians had their own plutonium). There have been spies who were paid more handsomely but their number is small. Higher sums were probably paid to influence agents, covert action operators, defectors, and so on, but this does not strictly belong to the realm of intelligence.

Comparing Intelligence Performance

Comparisons between American intelligence and the secret services of other nations point up some obvious similarities. The dominant form of intelligence up to World War I was human intelligence. A few weeks before the outbreak of World War I a writer discussing the "most colossal spy game in history" in the *New York Times* did so exclusively in terms of what would now be called HUMINT.[37] Since then intelligence obtained through technical means has become more and more important, a fact only belatedly recognized by the public. The basic difference between American and other Western intelligence services now is that only the United States owns and uses the most sophisticated and expensive means of reconnaissance.

Before World War I, French intelligence was arguably the best in the world; even up to World War II the *Deuxième Bureau* was considered a major factor in world espionage. Today French intelligence is no longer at the top; the *Service de Documentation Exterieur et Contre-Espionage* (SDECE) is a relatively small organization employing some 2,000 people with a commensurate budget.[38] It is affiliated with the Ministry of Defense but has access to the prime minister's office. Its present activities are mainly restricted to West Africa and the Middle East, both with regard to intelligence gathering and covert action. The SDECE became interested in economic intelligence only recently, and its electronic monitoring capacities are relatively small. French intelligence still plays a part of some importance on occasion, but its tasks are different in kind as well as in magnitude from those confronting the United States.

Many of the problems that Western intelligence faces at home and abroad do not trouble Soviet bloc intelligence. It is far easier to spy in an open society than in an effective dictatorship, and the risks are much smaller. True, in every dictatorship there are dissatisfied people who for personal, ideological, or even patriotic reasons may be willing to cooperate with an "enemy" secret service. But even once such a connection has been established, the difficulties of transmitting information are enormous for someone living under a modern dictatorship. By contrast, Soviet agents in the West more often than not accidentally stumble into being discovered, or are discovered because their case officers defect.[39]

For other reasons too, the task of the Western services has become more difficult since World War II. Secret services used to be small; senior officials were under no bureaucratic supervision, they were not hampered by regulations, nor did they have to render account; secrets were between the chief spymaster and the agent, and there was no paperwork, or only a minimum of it. The equipment of the spy and the means of communication were infinitely more primitive. But because a spy of some experience and shrewdness frequently operated alone, there was every chance that he would last for a long time unless he met with some unlucky accident.[40]

In some Western intelligence communities intelligence, counterintelligence, and covert action are concentrated in the same organization; in others they are kept separate. Whatever the arguments for either form of organization, covert action and intelligence—despite their essentially different functions—are combined in most countries, whereas intelligence and counterintelligence are kept apart.[41] Two important exceptions are the United States and the Soviet Union; the KGB and the CIA have their own counterintelligence units. But the difference may be more apparent than actual: the "distance" between two departments in the same huge bureaucratic machine, whether in Moscow or in Washington, may be so great that for practical purposes they could well be separate organizations.

The technical potential of a big (and wealthy) service is enormous, but a small organization may still be qualitatively better at fulfilling its specific function.[42] Large bureaucratic machines tend to be clumsy, slow moving, and hostile to innovation; they may also be easier for enemy agents to infiltrate. Due to a chain of command that is too long or complex, the achievements of the collectors may be lost in a surfeit of information or never reach those who could use them.

The French historian Marc Bloch once compared the difficulties facing the historian presenting his evidence with those of a detachment of soldiers moving along a road at night. As the enemy may be near, loud conversation is strictly forbidden, so the officers' commands are whispered from soldier to soldier along the line. There is a real danger that in the process of conveying the message from the front to the rear of the column, it will get garbled. In intelligence, the content of the message is unlikely to be affected in transmission because it will usually be in writing. But the greater the distance from source to consumer, the less the recipient will know about the message's general context, the atmosphere in which it originated, and how seriously to take it. In the intelligence service of a small country, this distance, and the consequent loss of vital information, is likely to be small.

Problems of transmission quite apart, a small service will concentrate on a few well-defined tasks of immediate concern. The intelligence service of a power with global interests may have to engage in the "scatteration" of its sources to the detriment of overall quality. Differences in function between the services of global powers and those of other countries are reflected in the composition of their budgets, making comparisons problematical.

Experience has shown that relations between foreign service diplomats and secret service operators have seldom been smooth. Diplomats traditionally view the activities of intelligence with some disdain, not only because they fear the complications that may arise, but also because they trust their own knowledge and experience more than those of the secret service. This has changed to a certain extent in the age of technical intelligence, but it is still possible to differ over the interpretation of photographs and decoded cables. In some countries civil and military intelligence have worked together more or less harmoniously on the basis of an agreed division of labor; in others there have been constant quarrels.

In the relations between secret services and their masters there is always the danger of politicization. An intelligence service serves the government of the day. Politicians may try to exploit intelligence for their own partisan purposes; ambitious secret service chiefs may wish to enhance their status (and that of their organization) by their willingness to serve such special interests. There have been political pressures on intelligence in virtually every country at one time or another: President Nixon never trusted the CIA, Harold Wilson firmly believed that MI 5 was out to discredit and overthrow him; and certain British intelligence officers were convinced that there were security risks in Wilson's entourage.[43]

Generally speaking, there is always a measure of distrust toward politicians and parliamentarians among those in intelligence. Secrecy is so essential to intelligence that its practitioners are reluctant to share their information even with the most highly placed politicians. There is always reason to fear that the secrets will be communicated by the recipient to friends, family, or assistants. The suspicions may usually be wrong, even ludicrous, but a single slip could be disastrous. As there have been a good number of such slips, by politicians, the fears of intelligence should not be dismissed as mere paranoia.

In most democratic countries the secret services are not permitted to investigate members of parliament (let alone ministers) except by permission of the president or the prime minister.[44] Nor are they allowed to enlist them for operational purposes, though such cases have happened in most countries at one time or another.

If there is a tendency in intelligence services to regard some of their masters as security risks, or at the very least, as potential leaks, the secret service tends to be unpopular among many politicians. In democratic societies, intelligence is the chief enemy of all those who want to overthrow the system. But even those who do not belong to extremist groups frequently suspect intelligence of various misdeeds or are at least perturbed by the thought that there exists an organization capable of such action. Because the service is secret it seems sinister; because there can be no full control over it, it is always a source of disquiet.

The reputations of American, Soviet, British, and German intelligence may be more or less deserved, and correspond with their actual performance. But this is a risky area for generalizations; if many of the failures of U.S. intelligence have been revealed, some of the successes have not.[45] American intelligence has a well-deserved reputation for collection by technical means; few cognoscenti doubt that in this respect it leads the rest, but it does not score high marks for political evaluation, judgment, and prediction.

Directors of intelligence in most countries are expected to shun the limelight, to be self-effacing. They do not meet the press except in special circumstances. (Most intelligence agencies have a "no contact with journalists" rule in their standing orders, except, of course, contact for operational reasons.) Not all directors have lived up to these expectations. Percy Sillitoe, head of MI 6 in the immediate postwar period, was an extrovert for whom such anonymity was impossible. Gehlen did not wish to be in the public eye, but he went out of his way to meet politicians. America has always been more open than other countries in this respect, but there too, successive DCIs have had greatly varying perceptions of their own role. The tendency in Britain since about 1950 was not to appoint any more military men to the top position, whereas in Israeli intelligence (in contrast to counterintelligence) the top jobs were for two decades the domain of retired major generals.

Access to the prime minister or president varies from country to country and from president to president. Until recently access was infrequent in Britain. Some German chancellors saw the heads of their secret services every Tuesday at meetings in which the general situation was discussed. In Israel too, the directors of civil and military intelligence regularly briefed the prime ministers, and on occasion the government and parliamentary foreign affairs and defense committees. Some presidents and prime ministers have put greater emphasis than others on being regularly briefed, but even the more avid consumers of intelligence have not attributed paramount importance to intelligence, except in times of acute crisis.

This leads to a more general question, that of recognition and appreciation. Praise is the sweetest of all sounds, as Xenophon wrote, but because the work of intelligence has always proceeded at least somewhat in the shadows, open recognition is seldom heard. During a visit to CIA headquarters in 1961, John F. Kennedy said: "Your successes are unheralded, your failures are trumpeted." A few years earlier Eisenhower had put it even more explicitly:

> By its very nature the work of the agency demands of its members the highest order of dedication, ability, trustworthiness, and selflessness, to say nothing of the finest type of courage whenever needed. Success cannot be advertised, failure cannot be explained. In the work of intelligence, heroes are undecorated and unsung, often even among their own fraternity. Their inspiration is rooted in patriotism, their rewards can be little, except the conviction that they are performing a unique and indispensable service for their country, and the knowledge that America needs and appreciates their efforts. I assure you that this is indeed true.[46]

Yet, there has been little encouragement and many public attacks for U.S. intelligence. This has had a negative effect on motivation and morale; at the very least it has led to excessive caution and inaction.

Other intelligence services have been more fortunate in this respect. Senior British intelligence officials are knighted at the end of their career; in Israel employees of the *Mossad* receive some special privileges and fringe benefits, and they face only seldom attacks in the newspapers. U.S. intelligence agencies are inclined to regard the attacks against them as part of a deliberate, worldwide disinformation campaign. There is no doubt that such campaigns are conducted by forces hostile to them. But in the final analysis, other factors have been equally important, such as the sensationalism of some of the media.

There has been fairly close cooperation since World War II among the intelligence services of the West.[47] Much information was and is exchanged, and it is noteworthy that the collaboration among services has been on the whole far more stable and enduring than the relations between governments—sometimes to the alarm of the politicians. By and large, the secret services have been little affected by transient political crises with friendly nations. There has been tacit or explicit understanding for the past decade or two that they will not engage in clandestine operations on each other's territories. Their intelligence representatives in other Western capitals act mainly as liaison officers.[48]

Intelligence is part of the general policy process; to regard it as an autonomous activity is misleading. It is one of the sources of information on which policy makers depend in their decisions, but it is by no means always the most important source. The functions of intelligence agencies in democratic systems vary from country to country in the light of traditional approaches toward intelligence and the specific perils, problems, and ambitions of each country. Nevertheless, they are all much more like each other than like intelligence agencies in totalitarian regimes, the prime exemplar of which is the KGB.

CHAPTER 8

The Antagonists: KGB and GRU

THE KGB and, to a lesser extent, the GRU (Soviet military intelligence) have been for many years the chief opponents of U.S. intelligence. Since World War II, most of the operations of American intelligence on almost every level have been connected with the Soviet bloc and its activities. Indeed, the CIA came into being only as the result of Soviet policies in postwar Europe; it would not have developed from a minuscule Washington working group into a major central agency but for the invasion of South Korea. A critical review of the CIA has to take notice of its main antagonist, even though the KGB's tradition is much older, its functions partly different, and its role in Soviet politics infinitely more important than the CIA's place in the U.S. context.

For one thing, the KGB operates on a very different scale. It employs at least twenty, possibly thirty, times as many people as the CIA, and its other resources are also much larger. But its assignments are also far wider, especially as a security force. The KGB is a main pillar of the system it serves; no one would claim that about the CIA.[1]

The Evolution of Soviet Intelligence

The Soviet security and intelligence system is rooted in a tradition both Russian and Bolshevik. Its creation coincided with that of the Soviet state, but its pedigree dates back as far as Ivan the Terrible's private army, the

233

oprichnina. It is subject to few legal restraints, notwithstanding Khrushchev's efforts to restore "Socialist legality." From the very beginning, the secret police was the guarantor of the party's monopoly of power. It soon became the central base for Soviet operations, both with regard to "active measures" (political action) and intelligence collection. Its organization and activities are among the most closely guarded of state secrets.

The Committee for State Security (KGB) and its predecessors are first and foremost security services. A little over a month after the Bolshevik coup of 7 November 1917, the All-Russian Extraordinary Commission, or Cheka, was established to combat counterrevolution and sabotage; it was intended as a temporary organ, but one whose operations would be unfettered by the existing legal system. On a number of occasions, both before and after the founding of the Cheka, Lenin categorically asserted that the new society had no need of state instruments of coercion: "Soviet power is a new type of state without a bureaucracy, without police, without a regular army. . . . "[2] He soon realized that the regime would be overthrown without the temporary expedient of the Cheka.

Beginning in 1921, the "temporary" Cheka passed through several organizational mutations (GPU, OGPU, NKVD) as a permanent organ directly responsible to the Politburo. The other two props of Soviet power, a standing army and a party bureaucracy, were similarly well established by the early 1920s—a development that, one gathers, left Lenin somewhat puzzled at his own creation.

If Lenin established the institutional basis, the tradition and operational style of Soviet security and intelligence were created by Feliks Dzershinsky, the first head of the Cheka. This work was in turn developed and expanded under Stalin's lieutenants. As the historian of the Cheka observes:

> Dzershinsky was admirably fitted for Chekist work; not for nothing had he spent 20 years as an operational revolutionary, mostly in the underground, engaged in a battle of wits with the pursuing Okhrana, living under false identities, organizing a clandestine party, spending many years in prison and Siberian exile and perpetually escaping in order to resume his struggle against Tsarist authority. He emerged a hardened, battle scarred revolutionary veteran; this practical education, this accumulated experience, had prepared him for leadership of the [Cheka].[3]

The ascetic "knight of the revolution," the founding father of the security service, shared these experiences with other old Bolsheviks. A conspiratorial mentality, acquired in the underground along with the corresponding operational tradecraft, secrecy, and compartmentalization, characterized the upper and middle echelons of both the party and the secret police as the Bolsheviks consolidated their rule. The ease with which so many party cadres moved into Cheka work, and the ferocity with which they executed their duties (and "enemies"), may be attributed in no small measure to their previous experiences. From the start the party and the security policy were an intertwined network of cadres with a common outlook, a common mission, and a common interest in protecting the exclusive power wielded by a small group of leaders. The clandestine mentality was also typical of the organs charged with foreign activities: the Comintern; the Foreign Department (*Inostranny Otdel* or INO) of the Cheka formed in 1920; and Military Intelligence (*Razvedyvatelnye Upravlenya*), probably created in 1921.[4] The operational style of these services paralleled that of the internal security organs, since all three were active in hostile environments. The information gathered by internal and by external intelligence was funneled through a highly centralized party-security service superstructure.

The centralization of internal security and external intelligence began even before the death of Lenin when Stalin was accumulating the instruments of party and state authority that enhanced his power at the expense of other Old Bolsheviks. It was probably Stalin's influence that raised Dzershinsky to the Defense Council in July 1923 (before Lenin's death), then made him chairman of the Supreme Council of the National Economy in February 1924 and a candidate member of the Politburo in June 1924.[5] This was the beginning of a broader effort on Stalin's part to transform the secret police into an instrument of personal rule at the party's expense. It eventually gave him control over all sources of information, domestic and foreign.

One of the most important moves toward central control of information and its use in decision making was the creation of the Secret Department *(Sekretny Otdel)* of the Central Committee (CC). The first record of the Secret Department dates back to April 1922.[6] Prior to that, there had been a CC General Department, also known as the CC Chancery. Still later it was known as the Special Sector *(Osoby Sektor)*; the literature also refers to it as "secret cabinet," "personal secretariat," "secret chancery," and "personal chancery."

The Secret Department/Special Sector soon formed the core of a larger chancery of sorts that wielded enormous power and included the heads of the secret police, Stalin's personal secretaries, the chiefs of the principal party and state control agencies, as well as selected Central Committee Secretariat personalities and officers. This organizational arrangement made it possible for Stalin to control the growing party-state amalgam by his monopoly of the most important information. The Secret Department/Special Sector was the controlling authority, both for the flow of information to Stalin and for personal access to him; it was probably identical with Stalin's personal secretariat. According to Boris Bajanov, an early defector who had been a personal secretary to Stalin in the 1920s, the department registered and checked "all incoming and outgoing secret documents" and was one of the "two most important departments in the CC" (the other was the Organization-Assignment Department, or Org-buro). While the Secret Department/Special Sector and the somewhat larger "chancery" concerned themselves primarily with internal matters, they were also central to Soviet foreign intelligence.[7]

In many respects the secret police supplanted the party apparatus to which it was theoretically subordinate. In Stalin's purges of the 1930s they drastically thinned the higher ranks of the party. But the secret police did not escape similar punishment when Stalin subjected it to a purge. The rapid change of personnel had little effect on the structure of power itself; Stalin retained his "chancery" and its Special Sector as the central mechanism of information control.

By the late 1930s, when the international situation was steadily deteriorating, Stalin had at his disposal a personalized mechanism of rule, which also determined the staffing for all types of intelligence, domestic and foreign. It was a viciously circular system because the users of the information determined the nature of the "take." Stalin had eliminated any tendencies toward the development of a more independent intelligence process. Although there were several separate foreign intelligence vehicles pumping information into the "chancery"—NKVD, Military Intelligence, Foreign Commissariat, the Comintern—all had been coordinated to say what Stalin wished to hear.

A number of examples illustrate the consequences. When Stalin deceived himself about the nature of his relationship with Hitler, there was no one to contradict him. The lies of Poskrebyshev, the head of Stalin's secretariat, Golikov, Beria, and Merkulov in Moscow, or Ambassador Dekanozov and B. Z. Kobulov (the NKVD resident) in Berlin, only reinforced the leader's predilections—despite contrary evidence from the field.[8] Undesirable information was attributed to Western provocations. Sources too solid to ignore were used selectively, as was Richard Sorge's network in Japan. "Skvor," the contact in Czechoslovakia's Skoda Works who reported the German buildup in April 1941 and the imminence of war was ordered punished.

In spite of the intelligence failures contributing to military disaster in 1941–42, the basic attitudes did not change either during the war or thereafter. The Special Sector, with Poskrebyshev still its head, remained in operation. In some respects it became even more difficult than before to penetrate this screen. Lavrenti P. Beria stood behind an expanded security service empire, having received a marshal's star and control over the acquisition of nuclear technology.

The passing of Stalin ushered in a period of ferment that interrupted the joint operations of the "chancery" and the security service. With the arrest and execution of Beria, a period of readjustment followed in which Khrushchev sought to restrict the power of the secret police and to make it serve the party as it had done in early years under Lenin and Dzershinsky. (He was not above using the secret police, however, against the "antiparty" group.) This period, which began with the breakup of Beria's empire and the renaming of the security service as the Committee for State Security, or KGB, culminated in 1959 with the appointment of a non-security service bureaucrat, Alexander Shelepin, as KGB chief. Shelepin's ascendancy ushered in a new phase of foreign intelligence operations.

While Stalin's "personal chancery" disappeared, the Special Sector resurfaced as the General Department *(Obshchy Otdel)* shortly after Stalin's death. V. N. Malin, a senior party official with earlier links to the security service, served as its head from 1954 to 1965, when he was replaced by Brezhnev's protegé, the late K. A. Chernenko.

The sweep of the General Department's responsibilities places it in a very powerful position with regard to information and the security and intelligence services. The following functions are evidently performed by the General Department, or Secretariat to the Politburo: oversight of party membership through issuance or withdrawal of party cards; maintenance of Central Committee records and party archives at all levels; receipt and investigation of complaints from within the party; supervision of the party's internal security (closely associated with party membership responsibilities); and control over use of all classified party material, according to guidelines established by the KGB.[9] As the Politburo's Secretariat, the General Department occupies a key position for filtering information into the senior party echelons. But its use as a private secretariat with authority over the rest of the party has not been revived; it is the Politburo's Secretariat, not that of one man.

While the domestic activities of the security service were restricted—though not very effectively—during de-Stalinization, its foreign activities were widened. Khrushchev had used the KGB chief, General Serov, to purge the Beria holdovers and to assist the new party boss in his struggles with the antiparty group. However, when it came to the task of improving the KGB's foreign operations, Khrushchev transferred Serov to the General Staff's GRU, replacing him, as already noted, with Alexander Shelepin.[10] His assignment was twofold: to return the secret police to the hallowed traditions of Dzershinsky, and to raise the level of its foreign operations to fit Khrushchev's "peaceful coexistence" policies.

One of the more interesting new ventures of the KGB was the establishment of the Disinformation Department in 1959. Its first chief was Ivan I. Agayants. From about 1947 to 1951, he operated under cover in Paris, where he may have played a central role in the fabricated memoirs published by an early Soviet defector who is believed to have been "turned" back to Soviet service. When Agayants died in 1968 he was a general, and his department had been elevated within the KGB to become part of the First Chief Directorate (Foreign Operations). In Soviet intelligence such upward movement comes only as a consequence of operational success.

The reorientation of the KGB in 1959 also affected the more traditional field of intelligence collection. The quality of KGB officers for duty overseas was improved, and the collection of scientific and technical intelligence was especially emphasized. Oleg Penkovsky, a senior military officer, shed light on this effort in his detailed discussions of the State Committee for Coordination of Scientific Research Work, heavily staffed with KGB and GRU officers. Known today as the State Committee for Science and Technology (GKNT), this organization is intimately involved in the coordination of basic scientific research under Central Committee authority and helps determine which scientific needs can best be met through intelligence collection. It has also been a central coordinating base for technology transfer from the West.

The general thrust of KGB operations initiated by Khrushchev remained essentially the same throughout the Brezhnev period. The appointment of Yuri Andropov as KGB chief in 1967 and his subsequent rise to full Politburo membership and the supreme leadership seems, if anything, to have enhanced still further the KGB's role in foreign operations.[11] Invocations of "socialist legality" and concern for proper procedures have been supplanted by new definitions of the unique position of the security organs in Soviet politics.

The report of the Central Committee to the Twenty-fifth Party Congress stated that

> The basic aim and direction of the state security organs are: the timely unmasking and denunciation of the aggressive plans and subversive actions being prepared by imperialism and constituting a threat for the security of the USSR and other socialist countries.[12]

Such documents clarify the idea that the security organs are expected to frustrate the enemy's designs. But the words "unmasking and denunciation of the aggressive plans of imperialism" refer not just to counterintelligence; they constitute an endorsement of intelligence and "active measures." The security organs, accordingly, are among the principal sources of foreign intelligence utilized by the political leadership in its decision making.

There has been no essential change in the approach of the Soviet system toward intelligence. It has been consistently careful to control access to important information, that is, state secrets, through such clearinghouse mechanisms as the General Department. The watchdog function has always been the prerogative of the intelligence and security organs. This is not to deny the importance of organizations such as Arbatov's Institute for the Study of the United States and Canada, but their main role is that of influencing agents rather than collectors and political analysts. As influence operations are now a central KGB activity in the West, these institutions play an important role. They are also employed in collecting and sifting information from open sources, but their access to sensitive information and political leaders is severely limited, and, like other state bodies, they are still objects of KGB penetration and cooperation. The keepers of the intelligence keys are still the KGB and the GRU.

Brezhnev pursued the initiatives begun under Khrushchev, fusing the Lenin-Dzershinsky tradition of KGB as faithful party servant with the institutional structure from Stalin's years. The stature of the security organs has since been enhanced legally and operationally. The top echelons of all three intelligence and security services—KGB, GRU, and the Ministry of Internal Affairs, or MVD—were staffed with men from Brezhnev's entourage. This renaissance of the security organs culminated in 1978, when the KGB ceased to be legally subordinate to the Council of Ministers and became the "KGB of the U.S.S.R." Although in reality the KGB had never been more than nominally answerable to the Council of Ministers, even that fiction was relegated to Trotsky's "dustbin of history" in 1978. Not since the days of Beria did the premier Soviet intelligence and security service enjoy such prestige.

Today's Soviet Intelligence Establishment

The two principal collectors of Soviet intelligence are the KGB and the Armed Forces General Staff's GRU, or military intelligence. They have shared this responsibility since the early 1920s in a rivalry that, at one point, turned bloody when Berzin's GRU was purged by Yezhov's KGB.[13] Despite the clearly preeminent position of the KGB and the fact that it alone has responsibility for military counterintelligence (the GRU, like the rest of the military, is penetrated by the KGB's Third Directorate for counterintelligence), the GRU is not a creature of the KGB. As a major directorate of the powerful and prestigious General Staff, it is a bona fide intelligence organization in its own right; it can display the laurels for numerous espionage successes that figure prominently in Soviet intelligence history (the Sorge, Rado, and Trepper networks of World War II, for instance). Although the KGB is the principal executor for party political action, "active measures," and "wet affairs" (assassination, sabotage, and so forth), the GRU also has a mandate for *spetsnaz,* or "special designation" missions ranging from commando-type special operations (sabotage, reconnaissance, assassination) to the training of foreign "diversionists," that is, saboteurs, insurgents, or terrorists. But the GRU's paramount responsibility is the collection and dissemination of a broad range of strategic intelligence to the military and political leadership of the country.

The KGB and the GRU run their foreign intelligence collection operations through geographic area directorates. Within the KGB, the First Chief Directorate is the operational focal point for all intelligence activities, including the use of "illegals" (spies with no diplomatic status), "active measures," and "wet affairs." Although the GRU similarly runs its foreign collection operations through a directorate subdivided into area desks, its *spetsnaz* and "diversionist" activities are organizationally separated.[14]

A key question concerns the way these services process and analyze the intelligence they collect. It is often assumed that because analysis is so important in the U.S. intelligence process, it must play a similar role in the Soviet system. Yet this is not the case. The KGB and GRU possess an Information Service and an Information Directorate, respectively, but neither is an independent body of professional analysts who attempt to distill the underlying meaning and import from intelligence. Although it has been reported that both the KGB and the GRU have augmented these processing elements in the course of the past decade's intelligence expansion, nothing remotely resembling the U.S. analytical structure has emerged. The Soviet intelligence tradition, unlike that of the United States, is one that puts a great premium on raw, unvarnished secret information. This is not to say that Soviet leaders spend hours interpreting raw telemetry relevant to American ICBMs. The General Staff, as an intelligence user, serves as a processor and repository of intelligence data on scientific and technical matters. (The SALT process bears witness to this.) But on broader subjects, the leadership still seems to prefer information untinged by bureaucratic analysis and manipulation.[15]

The KGB and GRU provide the overwhelming bulk of intelligence data to the Politburo and Central Committee, but other party and state bodies also contribute to the intelligence flow. The State Committee for Science and Technology (GKNT) is both a "tasker," or gatherer, of intelligence and a recipient of collected information, which it then funnels to various users in the political leadership and in defense industries. The Central Committee is a collector of intelligence through those departments that have extensive foreign contacts.[16] These are the following:

The International Department (ID). The true locus of Soviet foreign policy, the ID has extensive foreign access through its links with the Communist parties of capitalist and developing countries and with a number of national liberation movements. Such linkages provide ready intelligence conduits. In addition, the ID representatives are known to serve in select Soviet embassies abroad, where they possess plenipotentiary authority over the rest of the Soviet presence, including KGB and GRU *residents.* Their potential as direct intelligence links to the Central Committee is obvious. The ID dates from the dissolution of the Comintern in 1943 and may be viewed as its lineal successor. Its chief, Boris Ponomarev, was a member of the Comintern's Executive Committee. He currently holds a seat in the Politburo as a candidate member and is a secretary in the party's Secretariat.

Department for Liaison with Communist and Workers' Parties of Socialist States. This department split off from the ID in 1957 and has exclusive responsibility for the Communist Party of the Soviet Union (CPSU), and links to ruling Communist Parties (CPs). Following a tour as ambassador to Hungary, Yuri Andropov headed this department in the late 1950s. The nature of the Liaison Department's responsibilities makes it a specialized intelligence channel to the Central Committee.

Two other Central Committee departments—the Cadres Abroad and the International Information Department—are part of the Soviet foreign policy mechanism, but it is not clear whether they serve foreign intelligence functions.[17] They certainly are users of the intelligence generated by other Central Committee elements and the intelligence services, which is also the case with the International and Liaison Departments.

Other state agencies involved in the collection of foreign intelligence include the Foreign Ministry and the sundry trade, maritime, and other ministries engaged in foreign enterprises. Their activities provide access to information of interest and value to the state. The ready foreign entrée they enjoy make them valuable cover agencies for KGB and GRU operatives. The KGB and GRU frequently and routinely enlist individuals from these organizations for intelligence (and sometimes for security or counterintelligence) purposes.

Various research institutes, including those affiliated with the Academy of Sciences, provide expertise that occasionally or even regularly becomes part of the intelligence flow reaching the policy makers. They are not collectors of intelligence in the narrow sense, except when institute members traveling abroad are enlisted for intelligence purposes. The more technically oriented institutes engage in research relevant to intelligence and requiring access to intelligence data—that is, to state secrets, which are the domain of the security and intelligence services. By contrast, foreign policy-oriented institutes such as the Institute of World Economy and International Relations (IMEMO) can do their work, by and large, on the basis of published Western material. Given the Soviet leadership's penchant for compartmentalization on the one hand, and its fascination (or obsession) with secret data on the other, it appears that the scientific-technological institutes with access to secret data have a greater impact on the policy makers than the foreign policy institutes that lack these sources of information.[18] Even the Foreign Ministry—if the SALT experience is a reliable guide—is not a bureaucratic equal to the KGB and the military when it comes to information/intelligence access.

Whether such centralization and apparent lack (at least by Western standards) of analytical screening should be viewed as a drawback is a moot point. It has been claimed that Soviet intelligence reporting has been "adjusted" to fit the predisposition of the information users.[19] This was charged specifically with reference to Czechoslovakia in the middle and late 1960s and, more recently, with regard to Afghanistan in December 1979. Both examples bring to mind Stalin's self-deception about Hitler in 1941, which was reinforced by Ambassador Dekanozov in Berlin, Beria's secret police, and General Golikov's GRU.

The 1941 Stalin analogy may, however, be misleading. Whereas Stalin was more or less aware of his largely self-inflicted weaknesses during 1939 and 1941 and appeased Hitler in the hope of deflecting hostilities, Soviet leaders in the Czech and Afghan crises correctly judged that their moves would not trigger a major political reaction, much less Western military responses. Thus, even if the KGB and others were reporting incorrectly at the *tactical* level, Soviet leadership seems to have made the correct *strategic* evaluations of the broader implications of their decisions. A plausible case may be made for the Soviet style of intelligence use: data from the collectors, but estimates and "net assessments" from the leadership itself.

While it cannot be determined in detail how the Soviet leaders make specific strategic decisions, the structure that they have inherited from their predecessors leaves few doubts that the process itself is intimate and highly centralized. Access to state secrets, whether domestic or foreign, has changed little from the days of Dzershinsky. Indeed, the movement "back to Dzershinsky," a characteristic of the Brezhnev era, did little more than legitimize Stalin's centralizing practices without invoking Stalin's name. Even the nomenclature of earlier days has reasserted itself:

general secretary in place of first secretary, "Chekist" as an honorable title for anyone in security and intelligence, the 1968 reappearance of the Ministry of the Interior (MVD) in the guise of the innocuous-sounding Ministry for the Maintenance of Public Order (MOOP). When Andropov became one of the Party's general secretaries he was replaced as KGB chief by Vitali Fedorchuk, a veteran who had joined the organization in 1939.[20] In a similar way centralization has continued on the level of strategic leadership. This is borne out by the growing emphasis on the role of the Defense Council, with its membership drawn from a small elite of party, security/intelligence, military commanders, and industrial managers.

A structure of this kind is not at all similar to the U.S. National Security Council, which depends upon a fractious bureaucracy for its intelligence needs. The Communist party leadership and its intelligence/security apparatus are fused in a manner in keeping with a style and tradition that recognizes the intimate link between intelligence and the perpetuation of power. If the Soviet leaders had found this arrangement wanting they would no doubt have changed it. The fact that they have not done so seems to show satisfaction with the present system.

It will come as no surprise to the student of Russian history that the overall record of Soviet intelligence achievements has been excellent. The kind of political rule to which the Russian people have been subjected for centuries has engendered qualities such as dissimulation, suspicion, and skepticism on the part of rulers and ruled alike. These attitudes find an almost perfect embodiment in those parts of the legal code in the Soviet Union (and, by extension, in its satellites) that concern espionage. The interpretation of the term is sweeping; legislation against violations of the act is draconian. A section of the Soviet criminal code implies that the exercise of one's constitutional right to know may still be punishable, even if the information collected is not in the nature of a state secret. The sole criterion of guilt is that such collection is adjudged detrimental to the national interest. Even political, economic, and cultural information are state secrets unless their publication serves the national interest. Warsaw Pact countries follow the Soviet example—according to paragraphs 97 and 98 of the East German Penal Code, the collection and dissemination even of nonsecret information is punishable by prison terms of between two and twelve years if it is likely to aid the activities of organizations hostile to East Germany and other peace-loving (that is, Soviet bloc) peoples.

East German courts have argued in their verdicts that the dissemination of nonsecret information may lead to the discovery of state secrets. Seen in this light, the passing on of seemingly innocent information about the mood of the population, or even of an individual, is potentially the revelation of a state secret. People apprehended prior to their intended escape from East Germany have been charged with espionage on the grounds that, had their flight succeeded, they would have been interrogated by West German (or other) authorities—in which case they might have given away state secrets.

In other cases espionage has merely been a synonym for dissent, as for instance in trials against Jehovah's Witnesses in the U.S.S.R. From a Communist point of view, the systematic study of *Pravda* by critics of the Soviet regime might be construed as an act of espionage if undertaken with the intent to extract information not meant to be revealed. On other occasions Communist sources have referred to spies as "engaging in anti-Soviet propaganda." To Westerners this would seem to be a contradiction in terms, for espionage involves secrecy, and a spy cannot simultaneously engage in open propaganda and in clandestine espionage. But Communists reject such hairsplitting; as they use the term, espionage is a catchall term for activities inimical to their interests.

For the senior officials of Soviet intelligence, Czarist tyranny had been the mortal enemy, yet they were heirs to the same political culture and were soon to display similar mental attitudes. The Cheka and its successors had notable success in their foreign operations almost from the beginning. They penetrated virtually all emigré groups from the Trotskyites to the extreme Right and established espionage networks in all major countries. In the earlier years, the attraction of communism as an idea was an important ingredient of success abroad. The Soviet Union was, after all, the only power that could count on the support of a party (with branches all over the world) whose members regarded Moscow not only as the font of political wisdom, but also as the undisputed capital of a global movement that claimed their loyalty.

Soviet intelligence was less successful in its operations in an efficient dictatorship such as Nazi Germany. The intelligence provided by the "Red Orchestra" was not on the whole very important, the network operating mainly from France and Belgium did not last long, and attempts to infiltrate agents into Germany during the war failed without exception. Richard Sorge in Japan provided excellent information, but it was not believed. And the case of the "Lucy" ring in Switzerland during World War II is not clear to this day.[21]

In retrospect, it would seem that while the role of the Cheka and its successors *inside* the Soviet Union was absolutely critical, and that without it the regime might not have survived, its operations (and those of military intelligence) abroad were not of equal importance. Even if Trotsky had not been murdered, even if some of the monarchist generals had not disappeared without trace, their followers would not have been able to cause significant damage to the Soviet regime. The same is true for the role of Soviet intelligence during World War II; it was of some importance but seldom, if ever, a decisive factor.

Mention has been made of the fact that both the NKVD and military intelligence were purged during the late 1930s; most of their senior officials were executed. A few—such as Orlov, Krivitsky, Lyushkov, Barmine, and Reiss—defected to the West, but their accounts were dismissed there as exaggerated, even hysterical, at the time. Consequently, the harm done to the operation of Soviet networks in England and America, in Canada, Australia, and other parts of the world was less than might have been expected. The wartime alliance created a climate of trust vis-à-vis the Russians as far as the Western powers were concerned; this changed only in 1946, when conditions began to be more adverse for Soviet intelligence. Because many agents were flushed out as the result of defection or detection—even those who had long been in place—it became necessary to look for new ones, usually of a new type, that is, not ideologically motivated.

While the first generations of Soviet intelligence chiefs had been ardent believers in Communist theory and practice, this began to change—certainly with regard to those engaged in foreign intelligence—in the post-Stalin era. They were, and are, of course, Soviet patriots, and the fact that they belong to a very powerful elite enhances their self-confidence. Yet at the same time, the general erosion of belief in Marxism-Leninism, and the fact that they, more than other Soviet citizens, are exposed to "alien influences" was bound to breed cynicism. Western ways, however alien, frequently exercise a fascination over them, so, of course, do foreign standards of living. As far as can be ascertained, the likelihood of being stationed abroad for long periods is one of the strongest motives of those choosing KGB foreign operations as their career.

All this does not affect the overall efficiency and competence of Soviet foreign intelligence operations, which became increasingly sophisticated during the 1960s and were pursued on a broader scale than ever before. Soviet intelligence operators going abroad are more thoroughly trained (between two and three years) than their opposite numbers in the West. Unlike Western military intelligence, there is little moving into and out of the GRU—Soviet military intelligence is a lifetime career. Operations are planned on a very different time scale than in the West; moles are planted and illegals are placed with the intention of keeping them—according to the tradition—inactive for five to ten years or even longer. As far as technical intelligence is concerned, the KGB and GRU are as accomplished (or almost as accomplished) as the CIA. Yet they remain essentially HUMINT organizations, perhaps because operating conditions in the West are so much easier than for Westerners in Communist countries.

The internal structure of the KGB (and of the GRU) has not changed greatly over the years. The KGB's First Chief Directorate is the main collector of human intelligence outside the Soviet Union.[22] This is subdivided into many geographical and functional departments. Thus, the first department of the First Directorate deals with the United States and Canada; the second with Central and Latin America; the third with the United Kingdom and Scandinavia, and also Australia and New Zealand; the fourth with West Germany, Austria, and Switzerland, and so on. The Second Chief Directorate is in charge of counterintelligence. There is a Scientific and Technical Directorate, which has been given high marks for competence by Western intelligence officials. There are semi-independent departments such as *A* (formerly *D*), which covers deception and some covert action; *I* (formerly the Thirteenth Department), which carries out the more violent forms of covert action such as assassinations, terrorism, or assisting with guerrilla warfare. And finally there is the Intelligence Liaison Department, which coordinates activities with East European and other Communist secret services.

At the most, we can make informed guesses about the size and the budget of the KGB and other Soviet secret services. The KGB employs no fewer than 500,000 men and women, and the total number of people employed by Soviet intelligence cannot be too short of one million. Lest these numbers give rise to undue panic, it is important to point out that the KGB figure includes at least 200,000 border troops and about 120,000 men in other, special military units such as Kremlin guards, special signal troops, personal security staff for the Soviet leadership, and so forth. Another 60,000 are employees in the KGB Moscow head office and local offices throughout the USSR, more than half of whom deal with internal security. The one million figure does not, however, include the hundreds of thousands of part- and full-time informants—the *seksots,* the *sekretni sotrudniki.* Nor does it include some 250,000 MVD security troops, which can be put at the disposal of the KGB as something akin to a U.S. rapid (internal) deployment force. Estimates of Soviet agents operating abroad vary between 5,000 and 20,000. In NATO and other "enemy" countries, about half of the diplomatic personnel is thought to work part- or full-time for the KGB; elsewhere the percentage is probably less. Lastly there are the KGB cultural and communication "proprietaries," such as the radio station "Peace and Progress," the news agency "Novosti," a publishing house, and so on.

The GRU is much smaller; it probably counts no more than 50,000 staffers at home and abroad, including 30,000 men in *spetsnaz* units. But there are several hundreds of thousands more in Soviet arms, naval, and air force intelligence, and in the special departments collecting photographic and communications intelligence—the Soviet equivalent of NASA and NOR.

The "official" budget of the KGB is about $3 billion. A simple calculation shows that this figure makes sense only if one assumes that the KGB armed units are paid for by the Ministry of Defense, that its agents abroad are on the payroll of the Foreign Ministry, and that the rest do their duties on a voluntary basis. The real KGB budget may well be $20 billion or larger and that of the other Soviet intelligence organizations about the same. It is true that the KGB has to spend much less (or nothing) for obtaining information of the sort that Western intelligence receives at great cost, or not at all. But on the other hand its "control" function on the home front, its many other security duties, and the sheer number of people it employs make it an expensive apparatus.

In contrast to the relative continuity in organizational structure, the priorities of Soviet intelligence have changed substantially over the past three decades. While the KGB retains its interest in political, economic, and military intelligence, there has been a marked shift toward "active measures" in the United States, Western Europe, and in other parts of the world. The change involves the spread of disinformation, from the most primitive level (dissemination of forged documents) to sophisticated comments and speculation. This nuanced approach does not deny the deficiencies of Soviet society; on the contrary, Soviet weaknesses will even be magnified occasionally so as to make the country appear militarily weaker than it really is. The Soviet military buildup will be acknowledged and an aggressive foreign policy noted with regret. These will be explained as a reaction to Western animosity by a leadership that has not overcome the trauma of World War II, and which faces enemies both in the West and the East. At the same time, all possible support will be extended to neutralist, pacifist, and similar trends in the West.

A detailed analysis of these practices goes well beyond the purview of this study, but it should be pointed out that politically these operations may be as important as espionage. While Western societies are more or less equipped to cope with spies, they have found it more difficult to deal with disinformation and influence agents.

The other task of Soviet intelligence, which is even more important, especially in the most developed industrial countries, is the acquisition of technology—above all, in the military field. The Soviet Union has, of course, always been interested in this field; the activities of the "atomic spies" in Britain, the United States, and Canada were given high priority at the time. But in the 1970s these targets became crucial for the Soviet Union, partly in view of the fact that while general political intelligence is easy to come by in democratic societies, more effort has to be invested to obtain scientific-technological information. An article in *Aviation Week,* however interesting, usually will not contain all the specific details needed to make it of immediate practical use. Hence, the concentration on such issues as missile guidance, computer technology in general, radar defense, rocket propulsion, smart bombs, antisubmarine warfare, and so on, which has been reported from Silicon Valley, the Far East, and the centers of West European industry.[23]

Some Weaknesses of Soviet Intelligence

With all its undoubted achievements, Soviet intelligence is vulnerable to a number of professional deformations. One such weakness is common to all big bureaucracies that have to justify their continued existence—overlapping and the desire to expand. There is also the traditional Russian tendency toward excessive suspicion; Stalin was an extreme case, but the syndrome is deeply ingrained in the Russian national character. It may lead to the rejection of correct information. Where enemies do not exist they are invented, or their importance is exaggerated so as to show that the Soviet fatherland would be in great peril but for the vigilance and the excellence of Soviet intelligence. Equally there is the time-honored tendency toward caution and reinsurance *(perestrakhovka);* intelligence officials who want to be promoted do not wish to be unpopular with their bosses.

Soviet intelligence has difficulties in attracting recruits of more than average caliber; to be sure, some will be attracted by a KGB career because it offers the prospect of a life of greater freedom and privilege than most other positions in Soviet society, but the more intelligent young men and women—those of character and integrity—will look for a career outside the KGB, and usually as far away from politics as humanly possible. This may not be of great consequence as far as the medium echelons are concerned, for their activities usually do not involve superhuman feats of intellect and imagination. But unless there is superior intelligence and creativity in the higher ranks of Soviet intelligence, operations will become routine and there will be little innovation. Intelligence could become ossified, like most other institutions in Soviet society. This seems to have been the case, to a certain degree, over the past two decades. While the secret service has certainly become more professional, the quality of the intelligence agents and their masters has not been impressive; language proficiency and a certain shrewdness cannot compensate for lack of deeper political understanding.

Lastly, one should consider the question of ideology and its impact on the political judgment of Soviet intelligence. There is a danger of overrating the negative impact of Marxism-Leninism in the formation of a realistic political assessment. Soviet intelligence agents may frequently be primitive; for they may have an imperfect understanding of how foreign political systems work—though on the whole they have improved since the 1950s—but they are rarely "ideological fanatics." They may express themselves in the political language they were taught since childhood, but this is frequently no more than ritual incantation. Furthermore, a good case could probably be made proving that Marxism is at least as helpful for an understanding of the realities of political power as many of the theories taught in Western political science departments. A young Soviet citizen will certainly be less naive in passing judgment than many of his or her Western contemporaries.

If Soviet intelligence has been mistaken this has not been due to the presence of ideological blinkers, but rather to the absence of sufficient knowledge of the outside world, inadequate understanding of how foreign political systems work, a lack of general education, and a belief in stereotypes of various kinds. Sometimes these may be national prejudices (as manifested in the way the Soviets underrated the Israelis in the Six Day War), and sometimes simply the inability to understand that seemingly chaotic political movements and systems in the West may be stronger and more resilient than they appear at first sight.

Auxiliary Services: The Satellites

Most discussions of Soviet intelligence ignore the secret services of other Communist countries. Yet these services are active in most parts of the world and aid the Soviet Union in many ways. The satellite secret services are fairly substantial in size: the East German Ministry for State Security *(Stasi)* employs many more people than the West German BND (although, like the KGB, most of the *Stasi* officials devote themselves to internal security), and the Cuban DGI is probably larger than British and French intelligence together. While the Cubans have concentrated on Latin America, they have also been quite active in Africa and Western Europe. When 107 Soviet diplomats were expelled from the United Kingdom in 1971 because of espionage activities, the Cubans stood in for the Russians until new KGB agents were brought in.[24] Czech covert action in Italy, and Bulgarian covert action in Turkey, Italy, and other European countries were given wide publicity in the early 1980s. The Bulgarians seem to have been involved in the 1981 plot to assassinate the pope.

The very presence of satellite intelligence agents is of great assistance to the Soviets, especially in smaller countries where local counterintelligence may be hard pressed to keep a hundred Soviet agents under control; the presence of yet another hundred from other Communist countries may make real control impossible. The satellite secret services are totally controlled by KGB and GRU, whose representatives have access to all their information. Their operations are not just closely coordinated with Moscow; they are directed from there.

In the Third World, satellite intelligence has psychological advantages. While an Asian or African country may be reluctant to cooperate with a superpower, there is likely to be no such hesitation in collaborating with a small state like East Germany or an independent "bloc free" country such as Cuba. It is not by accident that the political policy and the secret services of Third World countries "of socialist orientation" are built up mainly under the direction of the East Germans; to a lesser extent, the Cubans also play this role.

Satellite secret services can be of help to the Soviet Union in recruiting sources among ethnic minorities in the West, such as Poles and Czechs, and also in West Germany. On the other hand, satellite secret services always remain a little suspect for the Russians—the ratio of defection among them has been relatively high, and the KGB faces the delicate task of making maximum use of the satellites' services without sharing too many secrets with them.[25]

The KGB's Western Competitors and Soviet Masters

Even a cursory discussion of Soviet intelligence shows profound differences with Western secret services. Soviet intelligence is much larger than its Western counterparts and operates more freely at home and abroad. While Western intelligence agencies may exchange information, they will rarely cooperate in collection or any other such activity. In the Soviet camp, cooperation is total. Soviet intelligence is above all aggressive in character; it does not just wait for things to happen, but creates opportunities. In contrast, U.S. intelligence (and intelligence in the other and smaller Western nations) more often than not merely reacts to events. The difference between Soviet and Western intelligence resembles the difference between the offensive and the defensive in war, or, to choose a less drastic example, in a football game.

The political importance of the KGB in the Soviet system is infinitely greater than that of the secret services in Western societies; together with the party and the army they constitute the three pillars of the political system. True, the predominance of the party has always been stressed. For two decades after Stalin's death the KGB was kept on a short leash, and even now there is a great deal of interpenetration between party and the "state organs." But under Andropov the KGB regained much of its self-confidence and power. And while it remains subordinate to the party, it cannot be ruled out that at a time of internal crisis it might become an independent factor in the power game.

PART IV

THEORIES OF INTELLIGENCE

CHAPTER 9

The Causes of Failure

THE TASK of intelligence is to obtain information and to assess it correctly. Because intelligence is not a science it is bound to have mistakes from time to time, which may be caused by factors like insufficient knowledge, general incompetence, deception, self-deception, or bias. A major mistake leads to surprise and thus an intelligence failure; the main function of an intelligence service, therefore, is to shield those it serves against surprise.

In recent times practitioners and students of intelligence have been extraordinarily preoccupied by the issue of surprise. Not to say that it is a new problem—surprise antedates regular warfare as well as modern diplomacy. The use of intelligence to achieve and to prevent surprise has been reported from virtually all parts of the globe, from the tribes of the Tetons and Comanches to the African kingdom of Dahomey and the Papuan Kiwais.[1] During the past decade—particularly since the Yom Kippur War—theories of surprise have been developed, debated, and rejected, and various integrated crisis warning systems have been proposed.[2] These debates, almost without exception, were about full-scale military attacks, of which there have not been too many in modern times; Pearl Harbor and Hitler's invasion of Russia ("Barbarossa") are the classic cases. This investigation will refer to strategic, and on occasion, even tactical surprise, but in the main it will address political rather than military surprise. We will attend not so much to Clausewitz's "fog of war," but to the fog of prewar situations on the one hand, and to developments that result in important political change, on the other: revolution, civil war, coups d'état, and sometimes even nonviolent action. The difference between these two kinds of surprise is obvious: it could be argued that almost all intelligence after the outbreak of a war is tactical, inasmuch as the question is no longer whether the other side will take military action but when, where, with what forces, and with what intentions. Changes resulting from political developments—everything short of full-scale war—have been much more frequent in recent decades, for a variety of reasons, yet they have been much less frequently studied.

Strategic Military Surprise

As Clausewitz notes, history has few totally unexpected wars to report, "unless, of course, we confuse them with instances of states being ill-prepared for war because of sheer inactivity and lack of energy."[3] "Ill-prepared" in this connection also means that psychological preparation was lacking. In recent decades the outbreak of the Korean War (1950) and of the Yom Kippur War (1973) come to mind. An analysis of these cases and a few others usually mentioned in this connection shows that there was a surprise effect and an inadequate response because the political assumptions of those attacked were erroneous.

There was always information about an impending attack, but as it was neither complete or irrefutable it was not given much credence. To paraphrase Roberta Wohlstetter with regard to Pearl Harbor: for every signal that came into the information net in 1941 there were usually several alternative explanations. A signal in this connection was any piece of information about a certain danger of intention of the enemy, regardless of its origin. Conversely, "noise" is everything that distracts from correctly reading the signals. It can be deception on the part of the enemy, but more often it is self-generated, or simply misjudgment. While hindsight makes it easy to differentiate between signals and noise, it was not so, of course, at the time.

Stalin's case is instructive because under him the Soviet Union was in a permanent state of siege—an attack from without had been predicted ever since the revolution. Stalin was also the most distrustful political leader of modern times. He saw plots and conspiracies everywhere and had virtually all the old Bolsheviks shot, as well as a great many people who were not potential plotters. Because Stalin saw dangers on every side, it must have been difficult for him to establish priorities and to take special precautions. It is also possible that, having become accustomed to imaginary dangers, he did not believe in real ones. Or perhaps he preferred to discover conspiracies himself, and resented being informed by those whom his psychological makeup made it impossible to trust.

Pearl Harbor was a case not of oversuspicion, but of overconfidence. The idea that a small and industrially backward country like Japan would dare to attack mighty America seemed so strange and outlandish that the president and the military leadership were disinclined to attribute much importance to information about an impending attack.[4] In this respect Pearl Harbor resembles the Yom Kippur War, another clear case of overconfidence. The consensus in Israel was that no Arab state would be in a position to attack Israel for at least another decade. The Korean War, however, does not conform to either of these patterns. There was information about an impending attack, but it was vague and coupled with similar information about possible attacks in other parts of the globe. Furthermore, General MacArthur had made up his mind that the North Koreans would not attack; later, he was sure that the Chinese would not intervene.[5]

There are always mitigating circumstances, but these do not count in the court of history. In the case of Pearl Harbor, there was no certainty about the direction of the main attack. No Japanese battleship had been sighted near Hawaii, which was thought to be an unlikely target in any case. As the result of intraservice and interservice rivalry—and also through incompetence—those on the spot were not informed in time about the general deterioration of the situation.[6] On the eve of the Yom Kippur War, it was not easy to provide correct estimates of Egyptian intentions, as the bulk of the attacking force had been concentrated in the Suez Canal for a long time. An unnecessary alert had been called only a few months earlier. There were also disquieting pieces of information available. In the end, there were irrefutable signals that overcame the existing consensus about the implausibility of the war. But these came too late to be useful.

A review of surprise attack shows that it can hardly ever be ruled out altogether. It may be possible to reduce the danger of attack by improving the means of observation, by devoting greater resources to this task, and by ensuring that all relevant information is carefully analyzed and transmitted to the policy makers. But while fuller information from a great variety of sources is always desirable, greater quantity does not necessarily make for greater certainty. The military power of the other side may be greater than assumed, or a military attack may be launched without clear warning signs. It may be launched in spite of rational calculations against its success—that is, from a position of inferiority, or intended as a calculated risk. Most major surprise attacks in recent times ended, after initial successes, in defeat or in stalemate. This was true for Hitler's invasion of

Russia, for Pearl Harbor, for the invasion of South Korea, and for the Yom Kippur War. Surprise, more often than not, is the weapon of the weaker side, the only weapon that holds any promise of success.

Of course, even minor tactical surprise may in theory have the most farreaching consequences for it may lead to the loss of a battle, which in turn may result in general defeat. Yet the relative infrequency of true surprise noted by Clausewitz has, on the whole, been borne out in the hundred and fifty years since his book was published.[7] Even when such surprise occurred it was seldom the decisive factor in historical change. Israel was certainly surprised in the Yom Kippur War and as a consequence its position vis-à-vis the Arab states deteriorated. But this would have happened in any case as a result of the growing political and economic power of the Arab oil producers. A decisive impact from surprise is likely only if there is a rough equilibrium of forces. Normally, surprise will not be able to compensate for substantial inferiority, unless of course it is coupled with far more than average incompetence on the part of the victim. The extent and speed of the Soviet missile buildup is seen by some as a case of major strategic surprise. But the essential facts and figures were known all along and were, in fact, the subject of seemingly unending controversy among the cognoscenti. At most, it was a genuine surprise to some but not to others.[8]

Military surprise may be sometimes inevitable, but political surprise should occur only very rarely. The statement that appears in an old U.S. Calvary manual applies to foreign policy: "A commander may be excused for being defeated but never for being surprised."[9]

Failure in foreign policy analysis means that there has been a mistake not just about the likelihood of a specific event (military attack) but in the general political orientation, the designs, behavior, ambitions, and strength of a certain country. For a great number of good reasons, analysts may fail to foresee a single event, but the foreign policy of a country should never be a riddle for any length of time. Yet, there have been such misreadings on more than one occasion. The four cases of strategic surprise mentioned —Barbarossa, Pearl Harbor, the North Korean attack, and the Yom Kippur War—were, at least in part, also political intelligence failures.

Political Surprise

It is possible to believe that in each of these instances of surprise attack, the military evidence (army, aircraft, and naval concentrations) was inconclusive. But military information must always be reviewed in the political context in which it arises. As Hitler's foreign political ambitions were not exactly a state secret in June 1941, Stalin's failure to read the signs correctly is difficult to understand, even given his unusual personal character.

In the case of Pearl Harbor and North Korea's invasion, there were few illusions about the peaceful intentions of the other side. But the potential enemies' willingness to take risks was clearly underrated, and their perceptions of America were insufficiently taken into account. American policy makers thought of their country as invincible, almost omnipotent, and apparently it was assumed that this belief was shared by the Japanese and the North Koreans. To a large degree, the same was true with regard to the Israelis on the eve of the Yom Kippur War. Reluctance to anticipate a possible Egyptian attack was reinforced by the Israelis' preconceived mental pattern of Egyptian behavior.

Foreign political surprise is more difficult to achieve than military surprise, if only because secrecy has to be maintained for a longer period of time. Nevertheless, it does succeed from time to time as a result of political misjudgment. Yet while an enormous amount of attention has been devoted by students of intelligence to the causes of military surprise, the reasons for political surprise have been consistently neglected.

Political surprise was, for obvious reasons, much easier to achieve in ancient times. Arminius, chief of the Cherusci east of the Rhine, pretended to be a great friend of Rome (he was, in fact, a Roman citizen), yet he inflicted on it one of the greatest military defeats it ever suffered. There was still some room for surprise in the age of secret diplomacy, but the realignments were usually not that sudden. Christian consciences were perhaps shocked by the treaty in 1536 between Francis I and the Turkish sultan Suleiman the Lawgiver, but were they surprised? Secret visits and missions and exchanges of correspondence did not as a rule go unnoticed.[10]

In the twentieth century, public opinion has to be consulted with regard to any major reorientation, and it is no longer possible to maintain secrecy about nonmilitary issues. This is true even with regard to relations between a democracy and a nondemocratic regime. Some secrecy was maintained in the Nixon-Kissinger era, and some successes achieved as a result. But these concerned negotiations for the liquidation of a war from which America wanted to extricate itself in any case and the establishment of closer relations with China—again a development that had long been in the process of development.

Thus, the results of the talks with the Chinese leaders were no surprise; if nevertheless many were astonished, it was more because of the secret manner in which the negotiations had been conducted, and the dramatic way in which they were announced, than because of the substance of the agreements. Genuine political surprise is theoretically possible in relations between two modern dictatorships, with their complete control of the means of communication. Yet even in these seemingly ideal conditions, there are always certain warning signs. The German-Soviet pact, the case that comes closest to real surprise, was preceded by the dismissal of Litvinov, the Soviet foreign minister, a very substantial scaling down of anti-Soviet attacks in Germany and anti-Nazi attacks in the Soviet Union, exchange visits by economic and diplomatic missions, and the breakdown of talks between the Soviet Union, Great Britain, and France. True, there were many rumors, but there were also more than a few hard items of information about a realignment of alliances. It was widely known that something important was in the wind, and a minority of observers in Moscow and Berlin were even positive that a realignment would take place —which they reported to their governments. If at some future date, for one reason or another, Albania or Yugoslavia were to rejoin the Soviet bloc, or if there were to be a rapproachement between China and the Soviet Union, it seems certain that this would not come about suddenly, but only after many prior indications.

Surprises in the foreign political field arise, in reality, from difficulties of comprehension. These may be formidable whenever one is dealing with authoritarian leaders subject to sudden impulses and liable to inconsistency. Sadat's policies were an obvious example, but even in that case, it was more the dramatic gesture than the substance of his policy which came as a surprise. Although the expulsion of Soviet advisers from Egypt could not be predicted far in advance, Sadat's general views about the Soviet Union were no secret; the only question was how these would manifest themselves. There was also his sudden decision to go to Jerusalem and to address the Knesset. But again, his desire to normalize relations with Israel had been known for a long time, and preparatory talks had already taken place in Morocco and elsewhere.

The greatest difficulties in political analysis usually concern the intentions of new regimes which have emerged as the result of radical internal change. These regimes raise the general question whether, and to what extent, predictions can be made about impending internal change by violent means. Such change has been far more frequent in the recent past than surprise attacks, and—in the absence of nuclear war—will be the central issue facing the West in the near future. It will be necessary, therefore, to deal with this issue in some detail here and to draw on the past for illumination and instruction of a complicated subject.

Opinion polls may indicate public dissatisfaction, but they cannot predict whether violent change will take place in a country or not. In a revolutionary period it becomes virtually impossible to foretell what will happen next. What makes a situation revolutionary, what signs provide warnings of danger? There are usually some indications, and coming events cast their shadows before them. But the shadows are seldom distinct; sometimes, to change metaphors, there is smoke without fire and sometimes fire without smoke.

In the case of the American Revolution there was little room for surprise. After the fall of Quebec in 1759, many observers foretold that the British conquest of Canada would be followed by the loss of the American colonies.[11] While the French had a foothold in North America, their presence had been the cement of the colonies' union with Britain. The moment that foothold disappeared, so did the objective need for the union. Even before the fall of Quebec, Montesquieu and others had predicted that American colonists would not indefinitely accept the burden of fiscal restraints. Unyielding British policies may have hastened independence, but it is safe to say that it would have happened anyway. In a similar way, no great powers of prediction were needed to forecast the disintegration of the colonial empires in the twentieth century—the two world wars only hastened the process.

Contrary to popular belief, the coming of the French Revolution was far harder to predict, based on the evidence at hand. On the one hand, there were countless French observers and foreign travelers reporting the lack of authority of the Bourbons at home and abroad. It was said that "there was no cheaper way to become popular than to defy the crown." Arthur Young, the great British traveler, predicted in 1788 that some great revolution would occur, as would a civil war and the total overthrow of government. He saw financial disarray leading to bankruptcy as the underlying cause for these calamities.

But similar arguments could have been used at the same time about other European states. The general assumption among informed European observers around 1770 was that England, not France, was decadent, and would be ruined and lose its liberty twenty years hence.[12] Albert Mathiez, the left-wing historian of the French Revolution, notes that despite passing financial problems the revolution broke out in a flourishing land, on a "rising tide of progress." There had been financial difficulties of similar or greater magnitude before, in France as well as in other countries, without their leading to revolution.

The storming of the Bastille thus surprised everyone, including the very knowledgable Paris police. According to a CIA guide, "Warnings of Revolution," published in 1980 by the Center for the Study of Intelligence, a "discerning analyst would have recognized the warnings of the revolution at least a year prior to the fall of the Bastille." Perhaps so, but the analyst would also have detected revolutionary situations in many other countries where revolutions did not occur. This guide makes various correct observations about the circumstances in which revolutions are likely to occur. It fails, however, to differentiate between a coup d'état, a rebellion, or a revolt leading to the overthrow of a government and a genuine revolution. It also states that "a revolution is almost invariably triggered off by the oppressive, harsh, unjust and arbitrary actions of a tyrannical regime but this is usually the final stage of the revolutionary process. There are earlier indications that powerful destabilizing forces are beginning to move. . . . It is the cumulative effect of outrageous events which sets the stage for revolution." This kind of definition is clearly pre-Toqueville; even Mallet du Pan (1749–1800), the Swiss-born, royalist writer, gave a sounder description in 1793: "A revolution is essentially a displacement of power, which is effected by necessity every time that the old power no longer has the strength to protect the commonwealth or the courage to protect itself. . . . Once the power has escaped from the king's hands, the feeling set in that it belonged to whomever would succeed in seizing it for himself. . . ." But Mallet du Pan did not try to provide an answer to the crucial question of why the old power should lose its strength in the first place.

The French security forces were convinced that the Paris crowds were far more civilized than the London mob. "They were, in fact, so confident that they kept the repressive forces in Paris down to a minimum."[13] True, in late June 1789, the police chiefs became uneasy; orders were given to concentrate more units in Paris. By 16 July (two days *after* the storming of the Bastille) about a quarter of the French army would have been concentrated in the capital.

The lack of a sense of alarm on the part of the authorities was intelligible in the light of the past. They failed to recognize that they faced a situation which, in important aspects, was essentially novel. The police paid attention to the so-called criminal classes, but they more or less ignored the fact that a new crowd had emerged of newly arrived provincials without roots and deference, the *meneurs* (agitators) who were hanging around aimlessly in the street. "A drink or a free meal might recruit them to any cause," writes Richard Cobb, and:

> There is no greater threat to established order than the nameless man who lives alone in a garret, receives no mail, has no friend and no occupation, no fixed hours, and no reason to be in one place rather than another. The events of July 1789 were exactly what such people had been waiting for for years.[14]

This new kind of crowd played a leading role in the nineteenth-century revolutions in Europe, as it did in Middle East capitals from the 1930s. The "new crowd" was at least as numerous in London as in Paris—but there was no revolution in England. Was the situation in London less revolutionary than in Paris? Or was it that the new crowd, volatile and highly excitable, was seldom capable of undertaking a sustained effort and therefore remained unpredictable?

There was much public dissatisfaction in both places, but revolution was likely to prevail only if the rulers lost their heads and their nerve and if the security forces—the army or the police—ceased to obey them. This was the case in Paris but not in London. Throughout history small units have dispersed great crowds without any apparent difficulty. Thus, the cardinal question is whether authority still functions more or less smoothly in times of unrest. Up to a certain point there seems to be hardly any danger, but beyond it collapse can occur suddenly, without further warning signs.

To choose another example, people had written and talked about the Russian Revolution for at least two generations before it. Some of the predictions were remarkably accurate. Pyotr Struve predicted in 1906 that in an extreme situation the army would join the revolutionaries and this would be the end of the Czarist regime. In 1915 Paleologue, the French ambassador, was told by Putilov, Russia's leading industrialist, that a catastrophe was inevitable. A great many people seemed to agree that the situation was hopeless.

Yet, as World War I continued, neither revolutionary spirit nor defeatism made any apparent headway in Russia. The German chancellor wrote in late December 1916 that there was no hope of a Russian collapse and Ludendorff admitted with regret that "our propaganda had failed." Buchanan, the British ambassador, reported to Balfour on 17 March 1917 (after the uprising had actually started) that it was "nothing serious"—a revolt at most, not a revolution.

Lenin had never given up hope for a revolutionary uprising during the years of despair after the defeat of 1905. Yet even Lenin, in a famous speech in early 1917 commemorating the revolution of 1905, said that while his faith in the coming victory remained unshaken, his generation would probably not live to see the great day. Less than two months later the revolution broke out.

Lenin had always stressed the essential importance of three factors—a "revolutionary situation," a strong revolutionary party, and weaknesses and irresolution among the ruling class. Of these three factors, the third seems to have been more often decisive than the other two. "Revolutionary situations" always exist to some extent and, seen in another light— never exist. It is not difficult to think of instances in which a relatively small group of militants seized power even though there was no acute political and/or economic crisis—Castro's rise is an obvious case. Equally, revolutionary movements, as in Russia in February 1917, have succeeded despite the fact that they were weak simply because the government collapsed with hardly a shot.

In some instances the personality of the leader of the revolutionary movement is of decisive importance, but not in others. There was no one central figure in the French Revolution, and the Chinese Communists might have prevailed after 1935 without Mao. But without Lenin, the Bolsheviks would not have made their bid for power in October 1917, and the opportunity might not have come again. Likewise, it is impossible to imagine Castroism without Castro. The central role of the leader in Fascist movements is well known—without Mussolini's and Hitler's relentless ambition and drive, their movements would probably not have come to power. Without Khomeini, the Shah's regime might still have been overthrown, but in the absence of a supreme authority it might have turned immediately into a free-for-all between the mullahs.

In a revolutionary period, political forecasts must pay attention to the factors making for an "objectively" revolutionary situation. This is not an impossibly difficult task—after all, happy, contented people do not mount the barricades. But analysts must also face the infinitely more difficult problem of deciding whether the government in question can still handle a serious challenge, whether it is still considered "legitimate," and whether, having once suffered an eclipse, it is likely to recover.* The forecasts have to take into account the possible dependence of a revolutionary moment on the presence of a single leader who might suddenly disappear. In short, it is a question not only of the interaction between incumbents and pretenders, but also of accidents.[15]

The difficulty of correctly assessing violent internal change abroad is compounded if the pretenders are the vanguard of some movement about which little is known. The rise of Bolshevism and Fascism are illustrations; Nasserism and Khomeinism are more modern examples. Even among experts in the West, few had heard about Lenin and Trotsky before 1917, let alone the lesser Bolshevik leaders. Russian experts in the West were familiar with the old Russia; they knew no more than anyone else about the new rulers who had seized power in 1917 and were determined to transform Russian society.

*CIA methodologists have long been preoccupied with the question of how and why coups happen, and this has led them to adopt an "indicators approach." A CIA paper submitted to a conference on this subject (March 1985) made various sensible points: that existing approaches are anchored in the social science trends of the day; that they usually contradict each other; and that they seek to explain rather than to predict. The CIA analysts rightly stress that coups are not random events, and that the dynamics of past coups might be of help in assessing the likelihood of future military takeovers. Unfortunately, the "indicators" are usually not clear cut. Can one really argue (as the CIA document does) that if a regime steps up repression of its civilian opponents, this ought to be regarded as one of the most important indicators of potential coup plotting? Halfhearted and incompetent repression may well trigger a coup but ruthless and effective repression will have the opposite effect.

The Russian case shows that at a time of violent change, expertise may be a deceptive guide. The specialist finds himself in a political landscape from which once-familiar landmarks have been removed. Though he still thinks that he knows his way about, in fact he is lost, and is likely to err more grievously than some of those with no claim to expertise. Bertrand Russell had no previous knowledge of Russia and did not speak the language, but unlike the established experts he was familiar with left-wing politics. The political philosopher had a far shrewder idea than the "experts" of what kind of society Lenin and Trotsky wanted to build and what kind of political regime was likely to emerge, as the book he wrote on Russia soon after the revolution demonstrated.

The emergence of fascism again confronted outside observers with countless riddles; it was a phenomenon that simply did not fit established categories. The experts could not make up their minds whether it was of left or right-wing inspiration, whether it was "a good thing" or "a bad thing," as someone put it. They only agreed that fascism was very different in character from previous dictatorships. The Communists (who should have known better) were equally puzzled. They thought of Hitler and Mussolini as traditional reactionaries, comparing them with the "white generals" of the Russian civil war. The essential new factor in fascism escaped them—that it was not a reactionary party in the traditional nineteenth-century mold, but a genuine mass movement.[16]

To turn to more contemporary illustrations, in 1976 and for quite some time afterward, it was fashionable in the media—but also in the State Department and the CIA—to point to the momentous and irreversible changes that had taken place in West European communism. The reference was to the phenomenon of Eurocommunism: its rift with the Soviet Union and the gradual development toward liberalism and democracy in all the more important Communist parties of Western Europe. It was virtually a matter of bad taste to doubt the genuineness of the West Europeans' conversion. According to a minority view, changes had indeed taken place in certain Communist parties; all of them had ceased to be revolutionary in the old-fashioned sense for a long time. But while conditions varied from country to country, it was difficult to imagine that parties which were strictly authoritarian in their own internal structure could become guardians of liberty in the sphere of national politics.[17] When such skepticism proved right and the confidence of the optimists was not borne out, there was, at first, reluctance to accept the facts and then surprise. What had gone wrong with the predictions? No doubt it was partly a case of insufficient information, but a more important factor was wishful thinking. The desire to move on to new ideas from the "tired old concepts of the cold war" was rooted in a misjudgment of basic issues, such as the internal structure of Communist parties, the nature of their ties with the Soviet Union, and other obstacles to such a farreaching transformation.

In the late summer and fall of 1978, Iran was nearing a crisis. Yet the DIA concluded on 29 September 1978, that the Shah would remain in power for the next ten years. In a twenty-three page intelligence assessment of August 1978, the CIA asserted that Iran was not in a revolutionary or even a prerevolutionary situation. The INR did not publish a full-scale intelligence report on Iran at all throughout 1978.[18] The situation in Iran was also of little concern to the U.S. media.

A more sober, careful reading of the situation should have shown in 1978 that the Shah's regime was unlikely to last. It was trying to liberalize itself under circumstances which made that virtually impossible. Iran was too advanced to continue under the rule of an autocratic monarch or to be taken over by an openly pro-Soviet clique. It should also have been clear that the next Iranian government would rule the country more harshly than the Shah, and that after his overthrow, the extreme left would have to submit to the demands of the ayatollahs, whose rule was likely to end in chaos, probably bringing some kind of military junta to power.

An assessment of this kind could have been reached by reading newspapers and listening to radio reports, supplemented by a working knowledge of Middle Eastern affairs. Such a prognosis would have taken seriously Tocqueville's dictum about the vulnerability of dictatorships at a time of reform; it would have scrutinized the balance of power inside Iran, concluding that the anti-Shah coalition was virtually certain to fall apart soon after victory. Those who thought that the Shah would weather the storm, as he had weathered many before, underestimated the vulnerability of his regime. The optimism of the Iranian oppositionists, who predicted not only the downfall of the Pahlevis but also the dawning of a new era of peace and goodwill, was based on a defective understanding of revolutions in general, and of the specific course one was likely to take in a country like Iran.

Iran showed once again that the human mind is ill-attuned to a very fast pace of events. Psychologists have referred to "cognitive dissonance," and theoreticians of "scientific international relations" have admitted that it is exceedingly difficult to come to terms with "novel conditions" that make forecasting impossible. Some have comforted themselves with the thought that radical change in the international system occurs infrequently. Even if this were true, it is of little help to the analyst—like a doctor, the analyst is needed when the patient is sick, not when the patient is healthy. Policy makers will have neither time nor respect for the analyst who argues that because systemic changes are taking place in a certain country (or worse, in the international system) there is no opportunity to provide a reliable estimate.

By about the mid-1930s, when many outside observers had more or less understood what the Russian Revolution had been about, the Soviet Union had again changed in significant ways. By the time a more or less realistic perception of Stalin prevailed in the West, Stalin was dead. Similar observations apply to many countries besides the Soviet Union.

The suggestion that radical change occurs but seldom in international affairs may well be true as a philosophical proposition; indeed, one could go further and propound that given the limitations of the human condition, truly extreme change itself is impossible. But there is constant change, even if it is never absolute. And the analyst of international affairs is concerned with the here and now, not eternal laws, and customers of analysis expect practical guidance, not philosophical observations.

Economic and Scientific-Technological Surprise

An intelligence service cannot, of course, be expected to predict the fluctuations of the stock market or the price of gold any more accurately than the great investment banks (which maintain intelligence and research units of their own). But intelligence should be able to identify dangers in the national and world economy, such as an overload of the banking system by potentially bad loans, or possible shortages of vital raw materials. It cannot predict the date or the extent of the next depression, but it ought to be aware of general trends, such as the availability or scarcity of strategic resources. The intelligence community should have been able to foresee the emergence of OPEC as a major power and the oil shock of 1973, but neither the CIA nor the intelligence service of any other country did so.

The reason was perhaps the fact that the oil shock came about as a result of economic and political factors. Economic analysts were analyzing models of oil prices in a political vacuum; given a reasonably stable political environment, it is quite possible that the increase would have come gradually over a number of years, rather than suddenly. Students of politics, on the other hand, were not even aware of the existence of the economic problem, except perhaps in a very general way. In such cases, multidisciplinary groups are usually suggested as a means of dealing more effectively with issues of this kind. The idea sounds impressive to the uninitiated, but it is frequently less than helpful in practice. In certain aspects of economics, surprises are inevitable; in others, they should never happen.

In today's scientific-technological field major surprises are improbable, given the relatively long lead between the emergence of a new concept and its application. But they are not impossible. It took the British a long time in World War II to make up their minds what the Germans were producing in Peenemuende; there were bitter quarrels on this issue. As scientist R. V. Jones, who worked in British intelligence during the war, later wrote, "What one could see in a photograph was often a matter of subjective interpretation"; this is still true today.[19] In our time the protracted controversy about Charged Particle Beam Technology (the "death ray") in the intelligence community provides another example, with the air force coming out in favor of one interpretation, and the CIA for another.

According to widespread popular belief, scientific intelligence can speak with scientific accuracy. But scientists (in contrast to political scientists) have been far less sanguine in this respect. A symposium on "Verification and Salt," seemingly a wholly technical and "objective" topic, opens with the statement that "this volume takes as its starting point the assumption that verification involves as much art (and politics) as science."[20]

One of the main sources of error in scientific intelligence has been a negative form of mirror-imaging which R. V. Jones called "postulates of impotence"; in the U.S. intelligence community it was once known as the NIH (Not Invented Here) factor.[21] To give a recent illustration, a Polish engineer who had defected described a Soviet jet with a huge diameter. Calculations showed that such a diameter would provide a thrust much greater than any U.S. jet had at the time; therefore the report was disbelieved.

Historical evidence concerning scientific surprises is ambiguous. In World War II the Allies knew about the German nuclear project only in general terms, and the same is true about the Germans and the Manhattan Project. The explosion of the first Soviet nuclear device in 1949 and the launching of *Sputnik* was, in principle, no surprise for American scientists, though they had expected it several years later.[22] The first Chinese nuclear explosion was known well in advance through intelligence (probably satellites) and was even announced beforehand by Secretary of State Dean Rusk. American intelligence was taken unawares when India exploded a nuclear device in May 1974, but only because there had not been much interest in the matter. The DIA had stated since 1971 that India might already have an A-bomb. In a special estimate the CIA had stated that the chances were even that India would conduct a nuclear test "some time in the next several years."[23]

Theories of Surprise

The debates about surprise—predominantly strategic-military surprise —have produced a great amount of literature, many post mortems, a number of explanations for past failure, but no predictive theory. Some have seen the fault in "naive realism," the assumption that it is not the task of intelligence to assess intentions but only capabilities, that the more information one amasses, the clearer the picture will be that emerges in the end. Once all the pieces of the jigsaw puzzle have been put together, there will be room for only one interpretation. This explanation is itself naive, for it presents an oversimplified picture of how political intelligence works. While there are many "realists" in the field, few are sufficiently naive to believe that information on a question, if sufficiently copious, speaks for itself, leaving no room for legitimate differences of interpretation. Many military leaders (and some statesmen) have discouraged assessment and interpretation on the erroneous assumption that their interpretative faculties are as good, if not better, than those of their subordinates. More recently, even in military intelligence, the evaluation of intentions has come into its own, and, thus, the reproach of "naive realism" is now seldom heard.[24]

Contemporary interpretations of the cause of surprise point to the perceptions (or rather, the misperceptions) of the analyst; the clumsy bureaucratic structures of the intelligence services and their problematic relations with the decision makers; the bias of decision makers themselves; or a combination of all these. Even among the "perceptionalists" there are different kinds of explanation. Some stress the inevitable ambiguity created by noise, that is, misleading or irrelevant signals. Others concentrate on the fact that observers and makers of foreign policy are strongly influenced by their images of the opponent, which may reflect national stereotypes or personal hopes and fears. They point out the dangers of a closed mind and the unwillingness to alter hypotheses in the light of new information. More generally, they emphasize the limitations of the human intellect when called upon to choose the right course of action amid conditions of uncertainty and in the face of new, unfamiliar phenomena.

A detailed enumeration of all the suggested causes of surprise and failures in intelligence will not be attempted here, partly because there are too many of them, and partly because some of the explanations are of little merit. By and large, the arguments can be summarized as follows: analysts cannot interpret information without hypotheses or a belief system. But this system may be wrong in the first place—for instance, it may err through wishful thinking (the Pollyanna syndrome) or, on the contrary, through excessive fear (the Cassandra syndrome). It may be affected by the stereotyped images one society has of another. There is frequently great reluctance to give up a hypothesis once it has been adopted, especially if much time and energy have already been invested in it. Intelligence may fail because it is too close to policy makers, thus subjecting it to the same influences and misperceptions characteristic of the political leaders. Or, on the contrary, it may be too remote from, and thus not attuned to, the needs of the political leadership. This in turn makes it more difficult to assess the intentions of the potential enemy, which will be influenced by the actions of one's own side.

Intelligence has to be guided by the experience of the past, yet invocation of the "lessons of history" can be a dangerous game because they refer to specific conditions which no longer exist. One of the most frequent sources of error is mirror imaging, which also includes the assumption that what the enemy knows about its own side is more or less identical with what the observer knows. Given the imperfections of human cognitive processes, given the additional stress of having to make a decision under pressure of time, uncertainty, and crisis, there is always the danger that intelligence will come up with wrong conclusions.

Next there is a group of explanations that puts most of the blame not so much on individual failings but on ineffective and overcomplicated organizational relationships. Intelligence services are unwieldy and hierarchical organizations; there is the danger that warning signals may be lost or filtered out in the bureaucratic channels. Overcentralization and overspecialization are dangerous, but so are their opposites. Correct information may be held back through self-censorship, in an effort to avoid being typecast as either Cassandra or Pollyanna. Interpretation may be distorted by "group thinking"—the pressures to reach a consensus—or by "boss thinking"—the fear of contradicting the basic political and strategic tenets of the decision makers. Bureaucratic politics do indeed hamper effective intelligence. The politics in question are not really interested in abstract "truth," but oriented toward action (or inaction); special interests, special rules of the game, even personal rivalries play an important role here.[25]

Some of these explanations point to real difficulties, others call for considerable skepticism. Those who have ridiculed the naive realism of the mosaic theory (the-more-information-the-better school of thought) have recommended instead "deductive testable knowledge," that is, scientific intelligence. Such knowledge itself rests on hypotheses, such as the assumption that decision makers tend to see other states as more hostile than they are, and that it is difficult for one side to believe that the other sees it as a menace. Assumptions of this kind may or may not apply to liberal democracies. There is no evidence that they are correct with regard to autocratic regimes; the hypothesis is, in fact, a good illustration of mirror imaging. Others have argued that occasional crises are bad, that urgency weakens the structural basis of good analysis and that, generally speaking, people under stress make bad decisions. But if there is no evidence that more information will always result in a clearer picture, there is no certainty that more time and less stress will necessarily do so. In fact, pressure may have a wonderfully concentrating effect, as Dr. Johnson observed apropos a scheduled hanging. Some of the symptoms described as typical for "group thinking"—namely, a shared illusion of invulnerability causing excessive optimism, unquestioned belief in the group's inherent morality, and a tendency to ignore ethical or moral questions—seem to appear in a few cases but not in others. On the contrary, group thinking may have the opposite effect: it may produce collective agonizing and magnify doubts, resulting in inactivity.

The hypotheses about surprise and intelligence failures have certain common features: most tend to play down accident, or good or bad luck; accidents are unrewarding material for theory building. There is consequently a frequent inclination to assume rationality, design, consistency, coordination, even a master plan or an overall blueprint on the opponents' part.

Some hypotheses express awareness of inherent difficulties, but still express confidence that shortcuts can be taken by way of mastering the "operational code" of the other side. There may be such a code, but it is not a set of formulas that can be mastered without a deep understanding of the political and social systems and the national traditions and culture in which the code is rooted.

Another shortcoming of the hypotheses on surprise and intelligence failure is a critical one: the focus on approach and method. However important knowledge of cognitive processes and of the subconscious mind may be, a substantive mastery of the topic at hand is even more important, be it the international oil market, the dynamics of communism in the Middle East, or indeed, any other subject.

Few will deny that there is a psychological dimension to the conduct of foreign policy. But it is wrong to overrate it, just as it is a sign of provincialism to ignore it. In America, and only there, the importance of the issue of perceptions and misconceptions has been exaggerated during the past two decades, partly as a result of Vietnam.[26]

Mirror Imaging and Questions of Rationality

With the advantage of hindsight, a report on the Cyprus Crisis of 1974 concluded that

> As was the case in the period before the Arabs' attack on Israel in October 1973, this inability to foresee critical events—in the face of mounting evidence to the contrary—seems to rest in part on an old and familiar analytical bias: The perhaps subconscious conviction (and hope) that, ultimately, reason will prevail, that apparently irrational moves (the Arab attack, the Greek-sponsored coup) will not be made by essentially rational men.[27]

The comment highlights two major related pitfalls facing the intelligence analyst: the problem of mirror imaging and the rational-actor hypothesis.

Foreign policy, by definition, deals with foreign countries—with political systems, cultural traditions, and mental attitudes quite different from one's own. This creates difficulties of a special kind, as it is difficult enough for a political observer to understand and interpret his or her own country, despite the fact that the observer has been steeped in its culture and traditions and shares, by and large, its mental makeup. How much more difficult, then, to understand distant people and their different ways. The problem has not become easier with the passing of time and blessings of modern transport. It was far easier for an eighteenth- or nineteenth-century traveler or diplomat to understand and even feel at home in a foreign capital than it is today. The number of sovereign countries was much smaller, the ruling class was cosmopolitan in background and outlook, and (quite literally) spoke the same language. Today this is no longer true. If Europe has become more complicated for an American despite a common political, cultural, and religious heritage, this is all the more true with regard to non-European peoples and countries. A hundred, or even fifty, years ago, a high proportion of Americans were immigrants from overseas who necessarily had a better understanding of their countries of origin. Before World War I it was customary to leave diplomats at their posts abroad for far longer than today; thus, there was a better chance that they would acquire a sound understanding of the countries to which they had been posted.

Today these links have become much weaker, or have ceased to exist altogether. Furthermore, America suffers from the "parochialism of bigness"; precisely because it is a big country, it is quite possible to get along without ever mastering a foreign language, traveling abroad, or displaying much interest in the world beyond the oceans. Even the leading American newspapers, and especially the other mass media, do not normally devote much coverage to foreign affairs, except in the case of some particularly sensational (but not necessarily important) happening. Even those with an interest in the subject cannot possibly form any deep understanding of world affairs solely on the basis of press, radio, and television reporting. Every country has parochial tendencies, but smaller, less powerful countries are more likely to be aware that they cannot ignore events outside their borders, which tends to offset their parochialism.[28]

It is against this background that American failures to interpret events correctly in foreign lands must be viewed. Americans have probably been worse than others in tending to project their own standards and values onto the world outside, from the quality of plumbing to that of political institutions. The proverbial innocents abroad include many from whom greater sophistication would normally have been expected.

Americans also frequently find it difficult to understand how dictatorships function; this is a problem of great topical relevance, because a majority of the countries in the world are dictatorships of one kind or another. Americans may be aware of the problems on an intellectual level, but that alone does not take them very far. As citizens of a free society, they have lived in a country which was never under foreign occupation, and in which the rule of law has prevailed. As a consequence, they have certain—largely unquestioned—basic tenets of belief and behavior. Reading about life in a less free political system may serve as a partial corrective, as will spending some time in such a country. But the American observer will still not understand certain elementary truths that are self-evident to a member of a society of this kind, and the behavior of the political leaders of such a regime will remain at least partly enigmatic. An extraordinary effort, not just of the intellect but of the imagination, is needed. Unless this effort is made, the tendency toward mirror imaging will always prevail. Information received from or about a dictatorship or a Third World country will be processed in familiar terms. The confusion starts with the use of language. The uninitiated will assume that "democracy" means something like the American political system, or at least development toward such a system; that a "political party" means something like the Democrats or Republicans; that "law" entails due process; and that "politics" means that disagreements will be handled in an atmosphere of reasoned argument.

For the United States, this is a major problem, and it has been the cause of many intelligence failures since World War II. American failure in Vietnam stemmed not from the incorrect reading of the Tet offensive, but from basically mistaken notions of Vietnam concerning the breakdown of traditional society, the public spirit of the upper class, the village populations, and the role of religions. Any misreading of the Iranian situation in

1978–79 resulted at least in part from underrating the intensity of religious passions in their specific populist Iranian form. Yet there are no ready-made lessons to be drawn from the Iranian example, such as a standing order henceforth to attribute high importance to religious opposition movements. In other countries, even in the Islamic world, these sects have a lesser political impact.

To overcome such difficulties and to gain a better understanding of the opponents' perspectives, various remedies have been suggested. More often than not governments act rationally in pursuance of their national interests. This is a useful rule of thumb; the chances of survival for a government which consistently acts irrationally and against its own best interest are not good. It has been said that prolonged study of a foreign country in many situations—especially at a time of crisis—will lead to a body of knowledge and a set of expectations that should form a solid basis for intelligence. Something like an operational code is learned or intuited by the observer, which may serve as a guide to understanding by foreign leaders. Once it is known what foreign leaders believe (and how strongly they believe it) it should be considerably easier to calculate how they are likely to react in a given situation and what considerations will influence their choices of strategy and tactics. It has been argued that the analyst needs explicit models to understand how foreign political systems work. Lacking such models, there is nothing solid to criticize, to correct, or to improve; it is just one person's opinion against another's, based on assumptions that are never made quite clear. Various games have been proposed to expedite this learning process; for example, what would you do if you were a Soviet leader (or Khadafi, or Castro)?[29]

These are eminently sensible suggestions; they address in slightly different form the problem already outlined: How can one gain a better understanding of one's opponents? Gaming is an educational aid that forces the analyst to try to understand the opponent's viewpoint and likely course of action, especially in crisis situations. As such it is of a certain value, but profound insights from this approach are unlikely to emerge, for no matter how hard Mr. Smith attempts to empathize with Soviet leaders, he will still be Mr. Smith. He will still find it exceedingly difficult to simulate the behavior of people so remote from him in so many respects.[30]

It is useful to be reminded from time to time that one should be explicit about one's expectations of foreign countries—there is no such thing as a value-free approach in international affairs. It is not possible to confront a government or a problem without at least some preconceived notions. An analyst who believes that there is a split in the Soviet Politburo between "hawks" and "doves," and who interprets Soviet foreign policy in the light of this split, real or imaginary, ought to state his hypothesis explicitly for his own benefit, as well as for the benefit of those for whom he works; the same goes, of course, for those who disagree with him.

But all this concerns methodology, not matters of substance. It would be most welcome if there were a simple, elegant model (an operational code, perhaps) that could be superimposed on reality and provide the answer to all uncertainties—serving, at the very least, as a guide to the perplexed. Unfortunately, simple models have the disadvantage of being simple; they are of little help in understanding a world which is both complex and in a constant state of change. Dynamic models, on the other hand, have other drawbacks; with them, the few certainties the simple model provides tend to disappear.* Such difficulties may not be major problems on the theoretical level, but in the world of intelligence these are decisive handicaps.

Thus we are left with the basic assumptions initially mentioned—the rules of thumb. But alas, even they are no panacea: it has been noted that even a fairly shrewd idea of the other side's intentions (a "reasonably good model of the opponent's behavioral style," to use more scientific language) does not guarantee a correct interpretation of how the opponent will act in any given situation. Information may be deficient, a calculation mistaken, there may be more than one equally attractive course of action open. In other words, chances remain good that things will not turn out as expected.[31] There is always the danger that the analyst, desperately in need of certainties, will be sorely tempted to underestimate the elements of doubt and uncertainty, of faulty and incomplete information on the other side. The analyst will be likely to underrate irrational and immeasurable factors and attribute too much more rational calculation and planning to the opponent. In brief, the inclination will be to bring artificial order into an essentially disorderly situation.

There are other difficulties. National interest is certainly a compass of sorts and no mystery surrounds the national interests of countries like

---

*The textbooks of the various intelligence agencies offer many choices of analytic method to the student, ranging from the obvious ("brainstorming," "breakthroughs," and "historical analogy") to the complicated and esoteric (such as "critical event filters" [CEF], "cross-impact analysis," "multi-attribute utility" [MAU], not to mention "projected alternative major national causes of action" [PAMNACs], and [DENs]). See, for instance, ORD/ACS, *Problem Solving Techniques for Intelligence Analysis,* 1981, and J. K. Clauser and S. M. Weir, *Intelligence Research Methodology* (Washington, D. C.: Defense Intelligence School, 1975). Most of these authors seem to be aware of the limitations of these approaches; in the words of one such textbook: "all analysis should be tempered by good judgement. . . ." The more interesting CIA contributions to intelligence theory and doctrine appeared in the late 1960s. See, for instance, Keith Clark, "Notes on Estimating;" Willard Matthias, "How Three Estimates Went Wrong;" Jack Zlotnick, "Theorem for Prediction;" and John Whitman, "On Estimating Reaction;" all published in *Studies in Intelligence,* 1966–68.

Sweden, France, or Venezuela. But national interest is interpreted differently in different periods; it meant one thing to the leaders of the Weimar Republic and the *Bundesrepublik,* but something quite different to Hitler. Nasser and Sadat viewed their national interest in different lights, so did King Idris and Colonel Khadafi. The yardstick of national interest will not be much use in understanding Stalin's purges or the Cultural Revolution in China. Nor is the key to the understanding of such phenomena to be found in the writings of Marx or Lenin, which do nothing to explain the Pol Pot regime in Cambodia or that of Idi Amin in Uganda. These, it will be argued, are extreme examples—but it is in dealing with regimes of this kind that intelligence is the most vital.

It is true, as some argue, that many American observers and policy makers did not know much about Asia in general and Vietnam in particular, that they did not understand the Vietnamese mind, culture, traditions, customs, and religion. It is quite another and misleading proposition, however, to argue that our habits of perception should be our principal concern, and that because we construct the reality in which we operate, the study of our perceptions about reality can be a substitute for the study of reality itself.

If it could be shown that most of the world's major conflicts during the past fifty years were caused by wrong inferences drawn from ambiguous evidence, in short, by misperceptions, the study of the subject would be of decisive importance. Misperceptions have been important, but it is nonsense to argue that Mussolini misunderstood the Ethiopians, or vice versa, or that the two sides in the Spanish Civil War misinterpreted each other's intentions, or that Hitler's decision to dominate Europe stemmed from cognitive failures. Even the outbreak of World War I, the favorite example of the "perceptualists," had to do only in part with perceptions of hostility and threat. At least as important were the internal political situation in Austria, the belief of the German Emperor and his generals that they could win quickly, and the conviction of the Russian leaders that war was inevitable. Israelis and Palestinians, another example, want the same territory—it is a genuine conflict, not a cognitive problem.

A student of world affairs may become steeped in the theory of cognitive dissonance and know all about selective inattention and the perceptual lag. The student may be freed from all cognitive and emotional biases and may then proceed to a thorough study of bureaucratic politics, crowning it all by immersion in Thomas Kuhn's *The Structure of Scientific Revolutions* and the critical literature that it inspired. Our student will have acquired a valuable education along the way, but will his judgment on world affairs have markedly improved?

Because the theories of surprise and intelligence failures have not provided the hoped-for answers, more attention should have been given to intelligence successes in the search for the causes of success and failure. As President Kennedy noted, intelligence successes are much less widely heralded than failures; sometimes they remain unknown for a long time. Yet, some are by now common knowledge, like ULTRA in World War II, R. V. Jones's exploits in scientific-technological intelligence, or political scientist Alexander George's story of American experts who, by analyzing German radio propaganda, correctly predicted enemy actions.[32] There was no major methodological breakthrough in these intelligence successes; there was, of course, a theory underlying the assumptions of the analysts, as there always is. But in the final analysis, the successes are to be attributed to the fact that both countries were able to mobilize a substantial number of gifted individuals (many of them somewhat eccentric) who had considerable knowledge of the subject at hand or superior reasoning powers—or both; that these people were much less encumbered by bureaucracy than today's intelligence personnel; and that as a result wartime intelligence was on the whole of high quality indeed.

Bias

The question of bias is fundamental in political understanding, as it is in history, psychology, and other fields. On a philosophical level the problem is insoluble, and there has been a tendency in the intelligence community to make heavy weather of the issue and to regard bias as the most dangerous source of error. A stream of articles on cognitive biases and their allegedly horrible consequences has poured forth in intelligence literature. At least in part, this anxiety is due to a misunderstanding of the problem. Insufficient knowledge of a country or a problem is an example not of bias but of ignorance. The wish to please one's master is not a result of bias but of deficient intellectual integrity. Lack of imagination is not bias but a serious weakness in an individual's thought processes. Denial of reality is not a bias, although it may require psychiatric care. Bias, as the great English historian Trevelyan said in a famous lecture on the subject, is a thing not necessarily good or bad; in any case it is inevitable. The true question is which *kind* of bias—conscious and/or unconscious—is permissible and which may lead to serious error.[33]

The ideal preached by nineteenth-century historians such as Leopold von Ranke and Fustel de Coulanges—that the historian should "extinguish the self" so as to attain total impartiality—is elusive for historians and altogether impossible for those dealing with current affairs. Even those who preached the idea never practiced it. The idea that the psychoanalyst undergoes analysis in order to "purify the self" is mistaken because the primary aim is not to resolve unconscious conflicts, but to acquaint the trainee with the techniques of analysis, to remove blind spots, and to make conflicts controllable.[34]

Even if it were possible to remove bias, there are a number of reasons why this would be undesirable. Saint Augustine once noted that nothing can be known except by sympathy—a statement only half true, for hate can also sharpen the senses.[35]

Edmund Burke's *Reflections on the Revolution in France* provides a good example. The *Reflections* were written in 1790 when there was still a monarchy in France. Hardly anyone had heard of Danton and Robespierre, and men of goodwill all over Europe welcomed the new freedom that had come to France, announcing what bliss it was to be alive. Reasonable, balanced analysts, free of bias, could have made an overwhelming case in favor of the proposition that now that the last vestiges of absolutism had been removed, France would become a constitutional monarchy more or less like England, that there would be no violent convulsions, and that the period of turbulence was more or less over. Burke, on the other hand, instinctively knew that this was not true. He foresaw that the revolution was only at a beginning, that it would gather impetus and ferocity, that it would lead to despotism, that the movement would not remain limited to France, and that it would end in a military dictatorship. No known method of warning system and crisis research, no associative forecasting capability, no quantitative or semantic analysis, no man or computer simulation could have possibly helped Burke to understand the repercussions of the storming of the Bastille and the resolutions of the Constituent Assembly. It was by inductive reasoning on a deeper level of political understanding that he realized that something in the social and political order had been broken, that the restraints mitigating despotism had been removed, that the revolution was only beginning, and that it would have to run its course.

Freedom from bias was not a good guide to the understanding of Soviet politics under Stalin or of China's development in the last years of Mao. Describing the state of Soviet studies in America during the Stalin period, historian Adam Ulam referred in retrospect to two fictitious characters, X and Y:

In his attempt to learn as much as possible about the Soviet Union, X . . . read nothing but the works of reputable, non-communist authors. He grounded himself on the writings of the Webbs and Sir John Maynard. Turning to the American academicians, he followed the studies of the Soviet government law and various aspects of Soviet society which might have come from the pen of a professor at Chicago, Harvard, Columbia or Williams. This serious intellectual fare would be supplemented by the reading of the most objective non-academic experts on Russia, and finally of those few journalists who had no axe to grind, especially the ones who had spent a long time in the Soviet Union.

His friend, Y, had an equal ambition to learn but his taste ran to the non-scholarly and melodramatic. Indifferent to objectivity, he would seek the key to Soviet politics in the writings of the avowed enemies of the regime, like the ex-Mensheviks; he would delight in the fictional accounts à la Koestler or Victor Serge. Sinking lower, Y would pursue trashy stories of the "I was a prisoner of the Red Terror" variety. He would infuriate X by insisting that there were aspects of Soviet politics which are more easily understood by studying the struggle between Al Capone and Dan Torrio than the one between Lenin and Martov, or the dispute about "socialism in one country."

Which of our fictitious characters would have been in a better position to understand the nature of Soviet politics under Stalin?[36]

A real-life equivalent of Y in China was Father LaDany, a Jesuit priest, who edited a Hong Kong newsletter, *China News Analysis,* based on Chinese news media as well as refugee reports. Among objective experts of the time it was considered distinctly bad form to quote this source because of its obvious bias and its refusal to pay respect to China's political and economic achievements, its military power, and so on. Yet in the late 1970s, when official Chinese spokesmen more or less freely discussed the various misfortunes that had befallen them during the preceding two decades, it appeared that Father LaDany's skepticism had been vindicated, while his unbiased critics proved to have been poor guides to Chinese reality.

It is one thing to acknowledge that bias is unavoidable and that it may even play a positive role. But it does not follow that one may in good conscience suppress evidence, or that since the ideal of impartiality is unattainable, one person's bias is as good as another's. Trevelyan, one of the most persuasive defendants of bias, always stressed that it must never invade the sphere of investigation or interfere with the collection and collation of facts. This, of course, is easier said than done, for there is often an unlimited number of facts and no one approaches them without some preconceived idea about which of these facts may be important, true, or relevant. A process of selection is inevitable. In this connection, awareness of one's bias is indeed of paramount importance. In the absence of such control, bias may indeed become a major danger.

Denial of reality is a phenomenon well known to psychologists, similar to repression but not identical with it. Denial is usually a defense against an outside danger.[37] Extreme cases of denial of reality manifest themselves in psychoses, and it is well known that the syndrome occurs more often in small children than in adults. Neurologists have coined the term *ano-*

sognosia for a condition in which people who are obviously very ill, suffer from pain, or recently underwent an operation, deny any of these things.

The analyst of international affairs is hardly ever likely to face problems of similar emotional intensity. But there are countless cases in which denial of reality in a milder or more severe form has manifested itself because people were wedded to concepts and ideas they found painful to give up even in the face of overwhelming counterevidence. They will rationalize their wish not to admit error, just as a neurotic will ignore the id and think of various explanations, sometimes ingenious, not to have to change his or her views and admit defeat.

Leaving "cultural bias" aside—which is not a true bias but parochialism, a deficiency of knowledge and imagination—one is still left with several frequent manifestations of negative and potentially dangerous bias. There is the danger of hypercredulity on one hand and excessive skepticism on the other. Primitive man tends toward credulity, reflected in beliefs in myth and magic. In modern times exaggerated skepticism is the more likely tendency. Modern man, while craving faith, tends to disbelieve; this is particularly true in a profession like intelligence, with its innate inclination to doubt. Intelligence analysts have been trained to regard the world as a place in which things seldom are what they seem to be but have to be subjected to rigorous investigation before they are accepted. Yet excessive skepticism does not necessarily lead to the truth, but may instead produce a very complicated, wholly incorrect interpretation.

Probably the most frequent forms of bias in the field of intelligence are the Cassandra and the Pollyanna syndromes. The term "Cassandra" refers to someone engaging in worst-case analysis. For example, toward the end of World War II, most economic analysts predicted a major crisis; there had been such a crisis after the first war, and there were sound reasons to assume that the transition from war to peace would cause grave shocks. This false prediction did not cause much harm, if any. A plausible cause can be made that the wise intelligence manager will err on the side of excessive caution, just as a doctor or a lawyer ought to warn a patient or client against all possible dangers, however remote. The doctor or lawyer will be blamed less for a disaster that does not occur than for one that takes place without forewarning.

But the price for a Cassandra approach may also be unacceptably high. Worst-case analysis may lead to excessive defense spending, to frequent alerts against possible attacks, or to the rejection of peace feelers by a putative enemy. Repeated false alerts will undermine the credibility of intelligence, and accurate forecasting will be the victim.

Pollyanna, Cassandra's opposite number, was the little orphan girl who was always glad; her father had once told her she *must* be glad and she obeyed him.[38] The Pollyannas of intelligence believe that worry is dangerous. The syndrome is seldom found in pure form, but its milder states—like smugness and overconfidence—are frequent. Certainly, the failure of Israeli intelligence on the eve of the Yom Kippur War derived largely from overconfidence. Israeli superiority was overrated, and Arab military strength, Egyptian ability to learn from previous military setbacks, and their capacity for deception were all drastically underrated.

Ignorance

Good intelligence can be produced with a minimum of theory; it is unlikely to come forth on the basis of a minimum of knowledge. The most obvious reason for intelligence failure is lack of knowledge. If bricks cannot be made without straw, even the most gifted analyst cannot provide an assessment without a minimum of information. This may take the form of absence of elementary information about a certain country or a certain problem from lack of interest, or for other reasons. Vital information may not be forthcoming because of wrong priorities. A nation preoccupied with internal problems may not be curious about foreign affairs and might regard them as unwelcomed intrusions on its main concerns. Between the two world wars, America lacked an intelligence service; its policy makers derived their knowledge about the outside world from the dispatches of ambassadors and, of course, the daily press.

During the interwar years, most people in Britain and the United States were in search of a quiet life. National interests, it was thought, would be reconciled by compromise. Propaganda and intelligence were regarded as distasteful wartime expedients that were no longer necessary. Sir Hughe Knatchbull-Hugessen, a distinguished diplomat, explained that while it was unfortunately true that the object of diplomacy of some countries was still to gain something for themselves at the expense of others, enlightened countries had long since realized the futility of such enterprises.[39]

The main reason for these mistaken assumptions about the state of the world was probably the shock caused by the losses and general futility of World War I. It was also caused by overconfidence on the part of the victorious powers. In these circumstances it seemed quite unnecessary to keep constant watch on events in foreign countries. Furthermore, intelligence always involved some distasteful practices; as Secretary of War

Henry Stimson put it so memorably: "Gentlemen do not read each other's mail." Such ethical (or aesthetic) qualms were admittedly more pervasive in the United States than in other countries.

In these circumstances, information was not available because it was not deemed necessary. But intelligence may be missing despite hard work and despite the recognition that it is badly needed. This is particularly true with regard to information on totalitarian regimes, in which effective power and decision making are concentrated in the hands of a very few people. In a closed society, where everything that is not expressly permitted is forbidden and secret, and where the few resident foreigners are closely watched, it may be impossible to obtain firsthand information about the views and the intentions of the ruling few; intelligence in general will be sparse and unreliable.

However effective an intelligence service, and however extensive its coverage, it will always have to establish certain priorities simply because its resources are limited. It stands to reason that the Soviet Union will devote more attention to the United States than to Ecuador and that the United States will be more interested in the Soviet Union than in Portugal. Yet it is always conceivable that a seemingly unimportant country, or an economic or technological problem, may suddenly assume major proportions. The Portuguese case is an excellent illustration. American intelligence had not given Portugal high priority in 1973–74, which is understandable. But following the military coup in 1974, Portugal was suddenly of very great interest because of the danger of a Communist takeover. American intelligence had had no information about the preparation of the coup. This is not particularly surprising, for if the conspiracy had been known that widely, it would have been doomed in the first place. When the matter was looked into, it was found that while U.S. intelligence had reported serious difficulties encountered by the old regime in Portugal, there had been no national intelligence estimate and the information transmitted to Washington contained little, if anything, that had not appeared in the general press.[40] Portugal is mentioned here because it is by no means unique; almost any country, almost any problem, may suddenly acquire great importance. The Falklands War in 1982 is another example.[41]

Lastly, vital information may not be forthcoming because of incompetence—the caliber of those manning the higher echelons or the rank and file of an intelligence agency may not be sufficiently high. In time of war the secret services frequently attract some of the best minds of a nation. At other periods, intelligence has less to offer, either by way of glamour or of job satisfaction.

Conservatism, and the Lessons of History

A frequent reason for intelligence failure is routine thinking: the inclination to judge every new phenomenon in the light of past experience, to miss essentially novel elements in a situation, or the failure to reexamine established tenets in the light of new evidence. That the human mind tends to look for confirmation of already held beliefs has long been recognized, and even praised as an element of stability. After all, if people constantly changed their beliefs, utter confusion would result. The same is true for historical experience. To ignore it would be tantamount to facing each new situation as if the world were created anew every night. Historical experience, even if inadequate, is the most reliable guidance system in existence. It may have to be discarded on occasion, but it must never be disregarded. In this sense, then, conservatism is mandated by prudence.

But conservatism becomes a danger, if it leads to the rejection of new information, however reliable and important, because this information contradicts existing beliefs. Stalin's reaction to the information he received about an impending German attack was a classic case of willful disregard of new evidence in order to preserve an already existing belief. His basic assumption was that Hitler had more to gain by keeping the peace with Russia, squeezing all he could from the nonaggression pact; he thought Hitler's military buildup in the East was a giant feint before his attack on England.[42] The countless warnings from British, American, and other sources were seen as no more than clumsy (or clever, but not clever enough) attempts by the Western imperialists to embroil the Soviet Union in war. Information from reliable sources was submitted to Stalin by his intelligence chiefs, but they marked it "doubtful," for they knew that their boss had already made up his mind. They were as eager to please as they were afraid to annoy him. When local commanders, worried by all-too-obvious German concentrations facing them, suggested putting their troops on alert and bringing up reserves, they were sharply rebuked by their superiors. They were told that ordering mobilization and concentrating troops on the frontier was a dangerous game, as the experience of 1914 had shown.

An interesting conflict of generations emerged in the *Abwehr*, German military intelligence, in 1938–39. The older officers, who had fought the French in World War I, remembered how well the enemy had acquitted itself and were skeptical about the chances of defeating France in a Blitzkrieg. The junior officers, unencumbered by memories of the past, took a dimmer view of the French army as a fighting force. They happened to be right, as subsequent events demonstrated.

The German leadership in both world wars refused to accept overwhelming evidence about America's great military potential. In 1915–16 it was said in Berlin that in military terms, America was like Holland or Switzerland—not a single American soldier would pass muster.[43] Hitler's attitude in 1940–41 was equally dismissive; Americans, he had decided early on, were bad soldiers. It should have been remembered in 1914–1915 that the "unmilitary" Americans had fought a bloody war in the previous century which, in many respects, had been the first modern war in terms of organization, logistics, and weaponry. A few German staff officers did indeed refer to it, but they carried no weight. Even Colonel Nicolai, the head of German intelligence in World War I, and a man not given to admitting he had been wrong, conceded that underrating the Americans had been one of his three intelligence failures.[44] In 1941 Hitler should have remembered the lessons of 1918, but he had forgotten or repressed this knowledge. Hitler believed in surprise: "Half the success is in surprise. But for this reason one must not simply repeat an operation with which one has succeeded."[45] Yet he did not think highly of intelligence. He did not need it as long as success favored him, and as the war began to go against him he simply refused to listen to the increasingly depressing information from intelligence.

Conservatism is frequent in scientific and technological intelligence; the not-invented-here (NIH) syndrome refers to a kind of intelligence blindness to facts indicating the possibility that an antagonist has taken the lead in some field where one believed one's own nation was preeminent. For this reason, Soviet technological achievements have more or less consistently been underrated. The obvious fact that the general level of Soviet civilian technology was not very high made outsiders forget that Russia had first-rate scientists and technicians, and that a system that gave the highest priority to military spending was able to compete with any other country. Thus, in 1941 the Germans were greatly astonished to face a tank (the T-34) which they were not aware existed; this was by no means the only such surprise awaiting them. After World War II, Allied intelligence thought it would take the Russians a long time to produce a nuclear bomb. In a top secret 1948 memorandum, the CIA reported that it was remotely possible that the Soviets would have a nuclear bomb by mid-1950, but that mid-1953 was a more likely date. The Soviet atom bomb was in fact exploded in September 1949 and was followed by the explosion of a hydrogen bomb in August 1953.[46] Just six days before the Russians exploded their A-bomb, there was another top secret report that it would not be ready before mid-1951.[47] The Soviet Union actually produced a hydrogen device before the United States did, something which no one in authority had thought possible at the time.[48] Another enormous surprise ensued when *Sputnik* was launched.

The assumption that "history always repeats itself" is mistaken, to say the least, but the fact that it has been naively invoked does not discredit history. No one would claim that because physicians have frequently failed to cure their patients they should stop practicing altogether, or that because there has been so much bad poetry no more poems should be written. Historical experience is used by everyone; the bone of contention is which analogy with the past is relevant and which is not. The rationale for the disastrous Suez expedition was partially based on Prime Minister Anthony Eden's analogy in 1956 of Nasser to Mussolini. He was right in seeing Nasser as a troublemaking demagogue, wrong in thinking the forces he and his allies could assemble were comparable to what Britain and France could have done in the early 1930s.[49]

The mind and outlook of a political generation are dominated by events that have happened in its own time or shortly before. And as diplomatic observers and intelligence analysts are not located outside time and space, they too are subject to these influences—they, like all mortals, may draw wrong inferences from the past. The impact of the Holocaust on the Jewish people (and also on Israeli politics) may serve as an illustration. The slaughter of one-third of the Jewish people led some to see in every enemy a new Hitler, in every manifestation of anti-Semitism or threat to Israel a renewed danger of genocide. The psychological roots were obvious, yet for all this, it was a potentially dangerous distortion of reality. Extreme cases make for bad laws; they are a risky base for generalizations.

Because every political assessment is influenced not only by contemporary constellations but also by the events that preceded it, the more momentous the events, the larger the shadow they cast on posterity. Clausewitz was one of the many voices warning against the temptation to judge new events only with reference to what has happened in the past. One example of such blindness toward a new situation was the reluctance of some political observers and intelligence analysts to accept the Sino-Soviet split as genuine when it occurred. Because the Soviet Union and China had a common ideology and because they had certain common interests, it was taken for granted that the alliance would last forever.[50]

Some "lessons of history" are misleading; others may be intriguing for the philosopher but irrelevant for the practitioner of intelligence and the policy maker. Some have argued that lessons of the past are usually negative in character, teaching what not to do, so as not to repeat past mistakes. Even if these were their only functions, they would not be purely negative, for they help narrow down the choices and thus point the way to correct interpretation and action. In the end there is no escape from the "lessons of history" as a guide, however imperfect. They are not to be uncritically accepted and mechanically applied: wisdom consists of choosing the right ones—a difficult task, but not an impossible one.

Deception

Deception is an integral part of warfare, yet the peacetime manipulation of potential enemies, while frequently attempted, is successful only under certain conditions. In wartime it is possible to influence the other side's assessment by "plants," or by the systematic fabrication of false evidence. World War II offers countless examples; among the best known are the story of the "man who never was," the *Englandspiel* carried out by the German *Abwehr,* and the successful British attempt to "turn" (that is, convert into double agents) virtually all German spies operating in Britain. In our time, the question of whether the Soviet Union has lived up to its commitments under the SALT Treaty, and how great its military expenditure has been, have been issues of intense debate. The same refers to the unending disputes about whether certain defectors from the Soviet Union were genuine or double (or even triple) agents.

On the other hand, it is difficult to think of successful strategic deception in peacetime. In the 1920s Germany tried to conceal the fact that it was rebuilding its army in violation of the limits set by the Treaty of Versailles. Yet the news still came out—in many different ways—and if Britain and France failed to react, it was not for lack of information.[51] The alleged German manipulation of Stalin in the 1930s has frequently been invoked as a classic case of successful deception. German intelligence informed Stalin that Soviet military leaders had conspired with German generals against him, whereupon Stalin ordered the execution of most members of the Soviet general staff. The story is probably apocryphal, for Stalin was engaged in a large-scale purge of the entire party and state apparatus anyway and there is no sound reason to assume that he would have excepted the army, no matter what information he received from Germany. He may even have used this information as evidence without believing it.

Another famous case of deception often cited as the cause of a major intelligence failure was the Stalin-Hitler pact in August 1939. The head of the Northern Department in the British Foreign Office later claimed that he and his colleagues faced a problem very similar to the captain of the forty thieves in the story of Ali Baba. That is, the enemy had provided so many possible clues as to what was going on that rational choice among them was impossible.

The reference to the story of Ali Baba is an interesting example of special pleading, but the analogy does not hold up. Had Hitler made a violent anti-Soviet speech while negotiations with Russia were proceeding, or had Stalin attacked Nazi Germany just then, we would be dealing with a clear case of deception. But there were no such blatant attempts to mislead the outside world. The real reason for the intelligence failure was far more prosaic—Great Britain and France were not informed about the talks between Berlin and Moscow, let alone the fact that the negotiations were going well.[52] So ignorance, not deception, was to blame.

In the Second World War neither American, German, nor Soviet military leadership was willing to devote very much effort to strategic deception. This was partly due to the innate conservatism of military leaders, but also to the firm belief that the really decisive components of victory would be elements like massive firepower, the concentration of troops, and speed of maneuver—not rumors spread by diplomats, wooden tanks, or other decoys. Major operations had to be kept secret, of course, but military leaders saw no reason to go beyond the elementary rules of caution. The British leadership on the other hand, believed in deception and it invested a good deal of effort in such operations, two of them of some importance. Fortitude South induced the German command to make false dispositions in France at the time of the invasion, and to a lesser extent, Fortitude North persuaded the Germans to retain troops in Norway and Denmark that were thus unavailable for the defense of France.[53]

Deception is rarely a total success even in wartime—the Trojan horse (if the tale is true) is an exception. Usually the most to be hoped for is to spread doubt, rather than to make the antagonist accept a specific untruth. If through Fortitude North or Fortitude South, the Allies had induced the Germans to concentrate all of their forces in Norway or the south of France in 1944, the war would have been over sooner. But then, the Allied invasion would probably not have succeeded had the Germans known the exact time and place of the landing. In that event, Allied deception was partly successful. The Germans knew about the impending invasion, but they thought that it was more likely to occur in the Pas de Calais, 300 miles from the D-day landings. Yet they took other possibilities into account and therefore did not concentrate all their forces in the part of France nearest to the English coast.

Is it true that Soviet counterintelligence successfully deceived the CIA during the 1960s and much of the 1970s about the extent of Soviet defense spending and the number and accuracy of Soviet missiles? It is no longer seriously questioned that the CIA underrated the Soviet military effort. It is also true that the Soviets were hiding whatever could be hidden but whether systematic Soviet disinformation played a decisive role is doubtful. Western errors were not based on false figures, procurement costs, or dollar-ruble conversion tables smuggled in by Soviet influence agents. They were rooted in mistaken fundamental assumptions about the nature of Soviet aims and strategy. The belief that the Soviet aim was strategic parity amounted to Western mirror imaging, not to successful Soviet deception.

One of the great masters in the field, R. V. Jones, once noted that "In principle it should always be possible to unmask a deception." However, he added the important corollary that "it is surprising how effective deception can be in the stress and speed of operation."[54] As there is usually far less stress and urgency in peace than in war there should be correspondingly little successful deception when the guns are silent.

Then how does one explain the frequent intelligence failures in peacetime such as, for instance, the misjudgment on the part of British intelligence of the extent of German and Italian rearmament in the 1930s, or the fact that Hitler underrated Soviet military preparations? It is certainly true that Mussolini greatly exaggerated both numbers and performance of his air force and navy, but he deceived himself and his allies even more thoroughly than his enemies. Despite the Duce's impressive claims, British intelligence had doubts about the Italian war potential from the beginning. Hitler used deception with regard to German rearmament, especially in the early years (1936–38) when he was trying to appear strong when he was still weak. British intelligence was admittedly feeble at the time; the information received from a retired group captain, Malcolm Christie, was more reliable than the estimates of the officials in charge of intelligence production.[55]

Yet even in its weakened state, British intelligence was never far off regarding the order of battle of the German air force; that applies both to the early years (they knew Hitler was bluffing in 1935) and to the time of the Munich crisis.* British intelligence predicted in December 1938 that the Germans would have 3,700 planes by the end of 1939; when war broke out Germany had 3,647 planes. The British committed serious mistakes in their projections up to 1937, underrating the German effort and assuming that the British aircraft industry could keep step. They were also mistaken in their appraisal of German strategy for use of the air force. They were

---

*Most governments were by and large correctly informed both on the eve of World War I and II about their potential enemies' capabilities. They mainly erred with regard to their intentions. See Ernest R. May, ed., *Knowing One's Enemies: Intelligence Assessments Before the Two World Wars* (Princeton, N.J.: Princeton University Press, 1985).

mistaken, however, not because Hitler deceived them, but because they made no real effort to understand the Nazi phenomenon—a combination of British conservatism and mirror imaging.

The Soviet Union was more effective in keeping its military preparations secret. Hitler and the German staff seriously underestimated the number of Soviet divisions, as well as the quantity and quality of Soviet equipment.[56] They underrated the capacity of the Soviet armament industry. They belittled the fighting spirit of the Soviet soldier and exaggerated (like everyone else) the impact of the purges of the late 1930s on the senior officer corps of the Red Army. Yet Soviet secrecy also had its dangers— if the Soviet Union had played down its military strength, its supposed weakness might have invited attack. But if it had made known the full extent of its preparedness, even exaggerated it, this could have provoked Hitler to attack "before it was too late."[57] In any case, it was not deception that misled the rest of the world about the state of Soviet armed might, but secrecy. The Soviet Union was a closed society, the opportunities of outside intelligence to obtain reliable information were minimal. Given the difficulties of penetrating a society of this kind, even the most accomplished theory of deception or counterdeception would have been to no avail.

Attempts have been made to compose a theory of deception, drawing heavily on work done in experimental psychology, especially that concerned with judgment under uncertainty. This approach rests on a number of indisputable propositions: that the evidence facing the intelligence interpreter is frequently incomplete, ambiguous, and fuzzy; that perceptions once formed are resistant to change; that human beings have a preference for consistency and are willing to base their judgment on a narrow basis of facts, or continue to cling to discredited evidence just to avoid inconsistency; and that there is a bias in thought (particularly pronounced perhaps among intelligence analysts and policy makers) toward causal explanations, to see direction and planning where there is just accident.[58]

All this is true, but it is not sufficient to ensure successful deception in time of peace. Deception is usually costly, and to prepare it with sufficient thoroughness requires a considerable expenditure of time and effort—as the cost increases with the scale of the deception.[59] The U.S. intelligence community in the postwar period has been influenced more by Sun Tzu, the great believer in deception, than by Clausewitz. No doubt Mao's victory has something to do with this.[60] Allen Dulles extensively quoted Sun Tzu, and so did many other practitioners and writers. But this reverence derives, at least in part, from a misunderstanding. For deception is bound to play a considerably greater role in the kind of partisan warfare conducted by the Chinese Communists before 1945 than in other forms of military and political conflict.

It is more than likely that on various occasions the Soviet Union has fed U.S. intelligence false information through spurious defectors. But unless inordinate importance was attached to the information, this cannot have been of decisive importance. A country may hide a certain weapon system for a while from the outside world, or conceal a certain part of its military power, but strategic misinformation is more than this. According to the KGB manual it consists in misleading the enemy concerning basic questions of state policy, military-economic status, and the scientific-technical achievements of the Soviet Union.[61]

That the United States or any other open society cannot mislead its enemies with regard to "basic questions of state policy" goes without saying. It may inadvertently confuse them because it has no clear policy, or it may pursue inconsistent policies. The Soviet Union (and other non-democratic regimes) is in many ways in a more advantageous position. But on *basic* questions deception should not be possible unless it is facilitated by more than average incompetence on the part of the side trying to get the information.

For years, Uriah Heep deceived Mr. Wickfield, the aged solicitor, and he fooled, but not for long, David Copperfield. Individuals can simulate or dissimulate, but states cannot do so for any length of time—at best, they can gain time. It cannot be said that strategic deception in peacetime is always the result of gross incompetence—there are exceptions to every rule. But it can be said that successful deception should be rare in politics once there is a general knowledge about the enemy's basic strategy.

Those who stress the dangers of deception are mainly concerned with the damage caused to the efficiency and the morale of an intelligence service that has been successfully infiltrated by the other side. Certainly, there is the danger that the service is fed disinformation by one or more "moles," or even more important, that the service may be deflected from its main assignment of obtaining information about the capabilities and intentions of the other side. In extreme cases this may lead to a partial paralysis of the service.

But it still does not follow that successful infiltration has decisive political consequences. Among the most successful instances of infiltration and deception were the *Englandspiel* (the manipulation of the Dutch Department of Special Operations Executive [SOE] by the Germans in World War II) and the infiltration of British security by Soviet agents like Philby, Burgess, and Maclean. These successes by German and Soviet intelligence cost the lives of dozens of people and the failure of various ingenious operations in which much thought, effort, and money had been invested. It caused demoralization in London and a certain amount of distrust among the Western Allies. Yet the *Englandspiel* had no influence on the course of World War II. While Philby and his friends played a lamentable role, it would be difficult to show that, but for their treasonable activities, British postwar history would have taken a different course.[62] As Lord Dacre (Hugh Trevor Roper) wrote many years later, the idea that men like Philby could influence British policy was absurd; mechanically it was impossible. Usually they were not even in a position to suppress intelligence passing through their hands, and on the rare occasions that this might have been possible, it was not likely to be effective, for "a Foreign Office does not base policy on the narrow trickle of evidence which a single counterespionage officer can occasionally block."[63]

Why has so much recent attention been paid to deception?[64] Partly, no doubt, because a great deal of shrewdness and inventiveness has been invested in various schemes and ploys of this kind, giving it a certain intellectual fascination. Another reason is that Soviet intelligence has greatly increased its disinformation effort during the last twenty-five years. Some students of deception, not content with the study of classic cases, have come to include in their purview not only active deception (fraud) but also self-deception, general confusion, incompetence, and "passive deception" (secrecy). But a certain amount of secrecy is the normal climate in which foreign policy has been and is conducted. It seems no more fair to put secrecy and active deception in the same category than to equate, say, a Trappist monk and a pathological liar.

Deception is an interesting subject; its importance has to be measured, however, not by the ingenuity of its methods but by its ultimate political results. Seen in this light there are obvious limits to successful strategic deception in war, and there is even less scope for it in peace, provided that elementary rules of vigilance are adhered to.

In sum, in intelligence the opportunities for mistake are almost unlimited. They may arise from a lack of sufficient information or from the fact that the enemy acts irrationally; failures of intelligence are bound to occur in wartime because information is sparse, because collection and interpretation have to be done under stress and pressure of time, and because there is more room for deception at such a time.

The special difficulties of assessing foreign internal trends at a time of domestic crisis have been emphasized as well; in this respect too, failures may be inevitable. But if the assignment of intelligence is seen as assessing correctly the motives, general intentions, and capabilities of foreign governments, major mistakes should not often occur. If they do happen, the failures, more often than not, are attributed to "bias," or deception. But bias is not usually the most dangerous cause, unless it is interpreted in such a sweeping way as to cover ignorance, lack of imagination, and the denial of reality. True bias is as inevitable as differences of opinion on political, philosophical, or religious affairs. What does matter is *awareness* of the bias and openness to new facts, even if these are unwelcome.

Over the years a great deal of experience has been amassed on such matters, and this body of knowledge is occasionally referred to as the "doctrine" of intelligence. Central to such doctrine is the recognition that some facts must be selected as pertinent from the many at hand. Further, the selection of those facts that are indeed pertinent and important must rest upon certain assumptions about reality—assumptions we may choose to call a hypothesis.

Intelligence collectors and evaluators alike have to rely on the experience gained and on general competence. They need imagination and instinct, or *Fingerspitzengefuehl,* to quote the favorite term of a former DCI. They have to be able to listen with the "third ear," to borrow a term coined by a psychoanalyst, and to the still, "small voice" mentioned in the Bible. These observations may not be startling or original. But they do have a decisive advantage over all other prescriptions: they are the only known way to minimize the risk of failure.

CHAPTER 10

Craft or Science?

THE QUESTION whether intelligence is, or ought to be, a craft or a science has heavily preoccupied some political scientists for more than a decade, but the leading intelligence managers have not spent sleepless nights wrestling with this issue. As far as they are concerned, intelligence is a tool needed by policy makers for political, military, and economic decisions, a wholly pragmatic enterprise, in which results are the only criterion of success. It is certainly not the most important question confronting intelligence today; just as the interest of most physicians in the philosophy of medicine is strictly limited. But it is still a subject of considerable interest because it sheds some light on the direction intelligence has taken in the past and is likely to take in the future, it has direct implications on what one may reasonably expect from intelligence, and it should guide the trainers of those who want to make intelligence their career.

In the late 1950s, the belief began to gain ground—largely outside the intelligence community—that intelligence had to be put on a sounder theoretical basis. Those favoring the search for a scientific intelligence theory pointed out that since World War II, the methods of intelligence had become more and more sophisticated, as the Mata Haris were replaced by scholars, or at least by technicians and computers. A widening gulf had developed between the scientific methods of collecting information and the primitive, traditional ways in which information was interpreted. Those engaged in evaluation were dependent upon certain subjective assumptions and beliefs held to be self-evident. But were they really self-evident? No attempt had been made to clarify their reasoning, to make it more precise, let alone to verify it. Those who advocated an intelligence theory referred to the great strides made in the social sciences in recent decades. Ignoring these insights would inevitably lead to a deterioration in the quality of the intelligence product; the world was becoming more complex and traditional methods no longer sufficed to explain events, let alone predict them.

Against this, the pragmatists, reacting with instinctive antagonism, argued that a theory was bound to create unnecessary complications. Only those who did not know how to cook needed cookbooks; only those lacking experience needed how-to manuals. But whereas a manual might be of some limited use in providing practical advice, an intelligence theory would not even serve as a guide to action, and therefore was altogether useless. Yet others, while in principle welcoming any attempt at more rigorous thinking on intelligence, thought the proposed new methods largely inapplicable and the goals overambitious.*

The 1950s and the 1960s were a time of great optimism among political scientists and students of international relations in the United States; hopes prevailed that the borders of knowledge about human behavior could be greatly expanded. If modern science, with its quantitative capacities, could replace the old-fashioned "contemplation" approach, then policy makers and those who provided them with intelligence could not afford to ignore the new methods.

The innovators were impatient with the traditional view that international relations was only for well-trained and mature graduate students with an intensive grounding in the histories of many countries, a mastery of several languages, and, if possible, extended experience abroad. Such a combination of talents and experience demanded an almost unending apprenticeship and was consequently in scarce supply. Furthermore, there had been no palpable progress in the field, which had been dominated since its beginnings by historians on one side and legal philosophers on the other. There was no objective testing, no one could say with any certainty who was right and who was wrong, and all too often the view of one appeared to be as good as another's.

How to transform the study of international politics from folklore to science, to go from mere description to explanation and prediction? A strong and coherent theoretical framework was needed as well as operational indicators of political and diplomatic variables (that is, data: accurate, standardized, comparable, and measurable). The innovators borrowed

---

*Hans Morgenthau, the most prominent representative of the "realistic school," argued that the new theories did not deal with what was most important in international politics—the struggle for power—that they neglected psychology, and that they were couched in language and underpinned with data accessible only to small groups of initiated experts, thus presenting the unintelligible as profound and mysterious knowledge.

from social psychology (decision making), management (operations research), mathematics (game theory), communication theory and biology (general system theory), anthropology, and other fields. While some put the emphasis on simulation, the psychologists focused on the importance of perception and misperception in international relations.

The general inclination was to give the innovating frontiersmen a sympathetic hearing in the universities, in the major foundations, and, to a certain extent, in the government. Even if only part of the promise were true, it was bound to be of great practical use. If wisdom and experience were not the main criteria, large numbers of educated nonspecialists who had mastered the right method and had some knowledge of statistics and mathematics would be able to understand international relations. Government would save a great deal of time, effort, and money training its employees, and America's considerable lead in the new science would give it an inestimable advantage over its rivals.*

Some maintained that a better understanding of conflict and cooperation, integration, negotiation, communication, and other processes had already been achieved. A decade hence, the claim that one could not quantify diplomatic variables or international politics would sound absurd. Others were more cautious; one should not claim too much, they said, for an adequate diagnostic and prescriptive base was still decades away. Furthermore, because the social sciences were by their nature probabilistic, they could be predictive only in terms of odds. Those even more skeptical emphasized that probabilities were not laws; they could not explain individual events, and this ruled out scientific prediction in politics. But could it not be argued that even statistical laws (that is, probability hypotheses) would still be an advance over the "prescientific generalizations" used in the past?

It is difficult to quarrel with this last proposition as far as it goes. But how far does it take the analyst? Let us assume that it can be statistically demonstrated that economic crises frequently cause political radicalization. The great political revolutions of our time, however, have not occurred mainly as the result of economic crises. Nor is it possible to predict whether the extreme right or the extreme left will benefit from polariza-

---

*In some important respects, the consequences seemed even more farreaching. If, as some of the frontiersmen argued, war was considered as a combination of epidemics and car accidents, one could eventually prevent war and the odds on human survival would improve immensely. By understanding the dynamics of war, one would at the very least reduce the likelihood of unintended war.

The historical sources of the idea that intelligence could be made scientific can be traced back, of course, much further. They are found, for instance, in pre-Clausewitz European strategy that based itself on geometrical concepts. In the 1930s General Maurice Henri Gauché, head of the French Deuxième Bureau, was a leading believer in the essentially scientific character of intelligence assessment.

tion. In any case, long-term prophecies can be derived from scientific conditional prediction only if they apply to systems that are well isolated, stationary, and recurrent. "These systems," to quote British philosopher Karl Popper, "are very rare in nature and modern society is surely not one of them."

There is no denying that quantitative research in history has produced interesting results on subjects as varied as electoral analysis, occupational mobility, and the social system of slavery. Yet cliometricians, as practitioners of historical quantification are called, were usually the first to admit the inadequacies of their technique. While statistical investigations were in many respects helpful, they could not produce certainties; arithmetical findings are no more indisputable than other findings and cannot supply a complete explanation of the events they covered, let alone establish a general law (or laws) predicting that certain consequences would invariably ensue from certain conditions. "Such expectations are the stuff that dreams are made of and not to be seriously considered for a moment by those who have any considerable experience with this kind of research."[1]

Inside the intelligence community there was no lack of sympathy for the new approaches in social science. Historian Sherman Kent, author of the most authoritative early work on intelligence, compared the method of those social sciences used in strategic intelligence favorably with that of the physical sciences.[2] No behaviorist could have asked for more.

Willmore Kendall went even further. He noted that while Kent quite rightly looked primarily to the social sciences for the skills needed, his book was deficient in appreciating the importance of theory. Kendall, to be sure, expressed grave misgivings about "the ability of our sciences to supply the sort of knowledge which Mr. Kent and his clients needed."[3]

A decade later, Princeton professor Klaus Knorr took it for granted that modern intelligence was unthinkable without social science inputs: "The conceptual structures, the repertory of research techniques, the generalizations, the indicators and data produced by social scientists, all have obvious relevance." There was an important reservation: "How successful social scientists have been in discovering useful hypotheses and tested generalizations is a question that even they find difficult to answer."[4] E. Raymond Platig, at the time director of external research at the State Department, paid respect to the rapid growth of research in international relations and "the input by new practitioners equipped with mathematical techniques of data handling and analysis, applying probability models, searching for quantifiable indices of basic processes and factors, searching the storehouse of mathematical models for those that might fit arms races, negotiating behavior, etc."[5]

These, then, were the expectations. In the early days of a new scientific departure, certain mistakes are always committed and extravagant promises are likely to be made, so to focus on such errors and exaggerations would be unfair. The problems were more basic. The issue at stake was not whether some kind of quantification was possible. No one doubted that statistics, and probability theory in particular, provide a powerful tool for handling numerical data. They make it possible to reduce complicated experimental results to more manageable proportions. But how to quantify patriotism, ideology, human passions, and weaknesses, that is, most of the stuff of which politics is made?[6]

Models of conflict are usually based on the study of small groups. But small groups operate in the framework of the nation-state, with the state acting as an arbiter. There is no such arbiter in international relations. Games theory, on the other hand, is based on the assumption that decisions are based on rational strategies and that the rules of the game are known. It may be of help when analyzing the reasons for conflict between, say, Sweden and Uruguay, or even between Sweden and Norway. But in the most important conflict situations facing policy makers, stability and rationality cannot necessarily be taken for granted. It is understandable that political scientists with a "rational man model" will prefer 1914 to 1939 as an object of study. If Hitler engaged in an armament race and ultimately went to war, it was certainly not because he was afraid of the aggressive designs of France and Britain. Some have argued that 1939 was the "untypical" exception. Unfortunately, most present-day major conflicts likely to be of interest to foreign policy makers are also "untypical."*

Some social science methods are of great value in democratic societies but inapplicable in the rest of the world. This is true, for instance, for public opinion research interview techniques and survey research. Assuming that public opinion exists in dictatorships, assuming furthermore that this public opinion has a certain influence on the conduct of foreign policy, there is no reliable method of measuring it, much less the motives, thoughts, ambitions, and fears of the rulers.

There has been much interest in cognitive science among students of international affairs and intelligence. Cognitive science—the study of thought—does indeed deal with a great many questions that are of critical importance in the context of this study. It explores problems of judgment and bias, of hypotheses and problem solving, and the relatively new field of artificial intelligence (computer thought). But while there have been many experiments on perception and memory, not many scientific certain-

---

*This goes for Soviet-U.S., Soviet-Chinese, and Israeli-Arab relations, the behavior of Khadafi and Khomeini, sundry terrorist and extremist movements, Vietnam, Cambodia, and so on. The players do not operate according to Western rules; they are "extremists" and "ideological."

ties have emerged. Most psychologists will admit that information processing, the prevailing fashion during the past three decades, has been somewhat disappointing. Nor has much progress been made with regard to problem solving, let alone the psychology of creative thought. It is, of course, always possible that a breakthrough will occur one day in one of these fields or the other. But optimism is not as pronounced as it was two decades ago, and it is unlikely to happen in the near future.

The CIA and Behaviorism

Two small methodological units were established at the CIA in 1973 following the initiative of William Colby, then director of the agency. In 1976 these two units merged and became the Methods and Forecasting Division of the Office of Regional and Political Analysis (ORPA). It was headed first by Richards J. Heuer, Jr., a veteran of twenty-seven years with the agency, on whose report the following account is based.[7] While the CIA had been innovative in the application of new methodologies in other fields—such as economic modeling of Soviet defense expenditures, and information storage and retrieval—the "behavioral revolution in academic political science had been virtually ignored by the Agency and the intelligence community as a whole." The timing of the establishment of the new division is certainly of interest; the CIA began its experiments with the new methodology at a time when it was viewed with growing skepticism by many in academe.[8]

The Methods and Forecasting Division used various approaches such as Bayesian Statistics to estimate the likelihood of military conflicts (Arab-Israeli, Sino-Soviet) and Content Analysis (mainly with regard to the Soviet Union). There was also interest in cross-impact analysis (a forecasting technique developed for industry), which uses the subjective judgment of experts to identify and estimate the probability of events that would have an impact on a situation. Simulation was given various trials, and a data base was established for the systematic study of incidents of transnational terrorism. According to Heuer, the early effort of the division benefited greatly from the CIA directors' support: "The simple statement that the director liked our work opened many doors—and minds. The initial attitude analysts adopted towards our unconventional proposals typically ranged from skepticism to hostility. . . ." Some of the projects sponsored and undertaken by the division were subsequently published.

They seem to convey a representative picture of the quality of the enterprise and its ultimate use. Two studies dealt with psephology: United Nations voting behavior in 1975, and an analysis of the impact of economic conditions on left-wing voting in France over the past fifty years. Other studies dealt with the Middle East, Rhodesia's future, and the support for Brezhnev among sixteen Soviet leaders. The research project on the Middle East used Bayesian analysis, a method that deserves attention because it has been used on frequent occasions in central and military intelligence and is generally considered one of the most promising of all the new techniques.[9]

Thomas Bayes (1702–1761) was the author of two short mathematical articles, of which "An Essay Towards Solving a Problem in the Doctrine of Chances" is the more famous. Bayesian analysis provides a method for recalculating probabilities in the light of new information. Its principles are commonsensical and are frequently used to solve a problem. A description of Bayesian technique *avant la lettre* has been given by the creator of Sherlock Holmes, who almost certainly never heard of Bayes:

> In the absence of data we must abandon the analytic or scientific method of investigation and must approach it in the synthetic fashion. In a word, instead of taking known events and deducing from them what has occurred, we must build up a fanciful explanation, if it will only be consistent with known events. We can then test this explanation by any fresh fact which may arise. If they all fit into their places the probability increases in geometrical progression until the evidence becomes final and convincing.[10]

"Fanciful explanation" in contemporary parlance would be a hypothesis, and the idea that with each fact the probability increases in geometrical progression will not now be generally accepted by scientists. But the principle is, no doubt, similar.

Bayesian statistics, virtually ignored for almost two centuries, were rediscovered and put to practical application in the late 1950s. An example of Bayesian inference applied to the medical field may serve as an illustration of the method. In solving a clinical problem, a physician will have to consider first the incidence of disease in the population at large, then the incidence of a specific clue in a disease, and then the incidence of this clue in people who do not have the disease. (For example, 85 percent of tuberculosis victims have a cough, but of those people who cough, only a few have tuberculosis.) Thus an equation can be prepared as the basis for calculating further clues and also as a guide for diagnostic procedures. Both positive and negative tests will be of value, because with each additional piece of information the probability that the patient suffers from a certain disease and not from another becomes more precise. Computer-assisted diagnosis, usually based on Bayes's Theorem or one of its variations, is now occasionally used in clinical medicine.[11]

In intelligence, Bayesian techniques have been used after the event to estimate the probability of a major North Vietnamese offensive during the dry season of 1974, the prospects of Sino-Soviet hostilities since summer 1974, and the likelihood of Arab-Israeli hostilities from autumn 1974 to summer 1976. Individual CIA analysts have investigated the utility of the technique by applying it to an earlier "intelligence situation." Their impression was that Bayesian analysis "can allow us to squeeze a little more information from the data we do receive," that it pushes the analyst faster and farther from a starting point than traditional intuitive procedures for revising judgment, and that in confusing situations (for instance, the interpretation of aerial photography) Bayesian technique made it possible to cut through the "noise" of contradictory items.

This sounds encouraging, but preparation of the data and the assignment of probabilities to the various clues demand so much knowledge and judgment that those doing this difficult job may not need Bayesian statistics in the first place. The analyst in charge of the CIA exercise summarized its value as follows:

> The ability to portray the results of the analysis graphically was one of the strongest arguments for using a quantitative method like Bayes's, and the graphs in the publication have been well received. . . . It is just possible that much of the success of the reports is due more to this informative brevity than to the validity of the estimative technique.[12]

There is a strong predilection for simple graphs and diagrams in top management, including politics and the military. Curves and diagrams can be of the greatest use—they are excellent teaching aids—but a precise verbal statement is bound to be fuller, more reliable, and less given to oversimplification.

In a study that was undertaken in 1973, outside social scientists were shown 545 documents prepared by INR, the State Department research department. These documents were classified no higher than "secret"; the general intention was to find out whether social science could help the Department of State improve its performance.[13] The authors, trying to counter criticism by some of their colleagues, maintained that if quantitative tools had been accessible to (dovish) State Department intelligence to the same extent as to the (hawkish) Department of Defense, the State Department might have been able to reverse American foreign policy earlier. They concluded:

Analysis found in INR documents tend to be of the most demanding kind
. . . the kinds of relationship found in the great majority of INR analysis represent such complexity that no single quantitative work in the social sciences could even begin to test their validity.[14]

When the chief of the methodological division drew an interim balance in 1977, his conclusions were similar. Bayesian analysis apart, there had been no guidance for the division, nor was there any consensus about what approaches would be the most fruitful. Social scientists defined policy-relevant research far more broadly than foreign policy analysts in government did, and "there were not a great many relevant methods and proven models just waiting for our use."[15] Technical obstacles—academicians' difficulties adhering to government-set deadlines, intelligence customers' unfamiliarity with academic jargon—were minor problems. They could have been overcome if there had been solid results or, at the very least, some promising leads in new directions, or some new light on the questions vexing intelligence chiefs and policy makers.

But the innovators were not greatly interested in the problems confronting intelligence. As Heuer put it: "The quantitative-oriented scholar tended to limit his work to variables that could be operationalized (i.e., expressed quantitatively), whereas the intelligence analyst seldom enjoyed that luxury. The academician was interested in the correlates of political violence in general and wanted to test certain theoretical propositions. The intelligence analyst, on the other hand, had to be specific; he was expected, for instance, to offer explanations of the coup in Thailand in October 1974 and what it portended for the future of that country. It was in many ways the old story all over again of the historian focusing on individual events and the political scientist searching for patterns: "While these two perspectives are complementary in theory, they tend to be contradictory in practice and require different skills and methods."[16] Hence the conclusion that there were "severe and intractable limits" on the applicability of behavioral insights to the needs of government agencies concerned with foreign affairs, because "most of the variables of interest" in this field simply were not amenable to quantification.[17]

The initial enthusiasm about impending scientific breakthroughs has waned. Many students of intelligence methodology now believe that no general prescription should be offered to the intelligence analyst as to whether to adopt quantitative techniques, to attempt theory building, or to continue to rely on narrative explanation.[18] Intelligence agencies in the U.S. have been criticized for concentrating their efforts on monitoring military indicators and neglecting indicators that could shed some light on an impending economic or political crisis. There has been a growing disproportion between the collection and analysis efforts; a reallocation is overdue if only because military indicators often give only hours of warning, whereas political indicators may yield longer lead times before crises.[19] But political indicators based on multivariate statistical analysis, transaction analysis, hierarchical inference structuring, influence diagramming, Bayesian decision analysis, operations research, game theory, and other such quantitative methods have not worked miracles either. A knowledge of statistics and computer science is important but it cannot, of course, replace historical, political, or economic knowledge in intelligence analysis; the other skills needed; and the ability to express oneself clearly and without too much jargon. Social science certainly has a considerable role to play in accelerating and improving intelligence data gathering, forecasting, and analysis—secret and otherwise—but the more extravagant promises made by some in the past ought to be forgotten.

Intelligence and the Question of Clinical Judgment

Students of intelligence methodology were looking in vain to the exact sciences for guidance. Technology might have done better service as a model, as it fulfills specific purposes and does not aim at establishing general theories. Another field suggested for inspiration has been meteorology. But the most promising analogy for the student of intelligence seems to be the one between political and clinical judgment. The doctor and the analyst have to collect and evaluate evidence about phenomena frequently not amenable to direct observation. This is done on the basis of indications, signs, and symptoms. As early as the sixteenth century, the pathologist Jean Fernel wrote: "Diseases hidden in the innermost crevices of the body, that cannot be distinguished or perceived through the senses, are understood by signs. With these as evidence, the mind is led by sound reasoning to penetrate into what is hidden."[20] The same approach applies to intelligence.

Medicine has made enormous progress since the Renaissance, and diseases once hidden can now be observed owing to such marvels as Computed Axial Tomography (or CAT scanning). The intelligence chiefs and the military commanders use sensors in the same way as the medical expert invokes X-ray scanning, and both electronic systems share most of their functional principles. The similarities extend to both collection and analysis or, in the case of medicine, diagnosis. References to medicine have become frequent in intelligence literature.[21]

There is at least one important difference, however. The patient usually cooperates with the medical expert; there is no incentive to hide and to mislead. The assignment of the observation satellite on the other hand is more complicated. In this case, the "patient" will make every possible effort not to reveal what he does not want to become known. In the nineteenth century, Sir William Osler said medicine was a science of uncertainties and an art of probability. This is all the more true with regard to intelligence. The problem facing the doctor is that just as no two faces are the same, no two bodies are alike. But even though every patient is unique, it does not follow that all patients are incomparable.

The debate on the scientific character of medicine dates back to its very beginnings. Hippocrates made the excellent observation that if medicine were not an art all practitioners *(demiurgoi)* would be equally good or equally bad, a point that seems also to apply to political analysts.[22] From Hippocrates onward physicians agreed that there were no certainties in medicine, only probabilities and approximations. Experience was transmitted through human sensations. As far as a doctor was concerned everything depended on the gift of observation and instinct.[23] As the result of the stormy development of the natural sciences, medicine began to move more and more toward a purely scientific orientation during the nineteenth century.

Yet, as so often in the history of science, great progress would trigger off new questions. In a little study published during World War I, a leading physician (and philosopher of medicine) drew attention to the basic difference between pure science dealing with infinite questions and medicine preoccupied with the "here and now." Clinicians—unlike engineers and technologists—were dealing with a subject that was incalculable.[24] There was a scientific doctrine of politics and of war as there was of medicine: no one in a leading position in politics or in the armed services could afford to ignore the body of up-to-date scientific knowledge that had been assembled. But this did not mean that professors teaching at war academies would necessarily make the best military leaders, or that professors of economics would succeed as ministers of finance. "Scientific" competence, while an essential prerequisite, was not the only quality needed, perhaps not even the most important one. The physician, like the statesman, had to make frequent decisions with reference to mathematical formulas, but these actions also grew out of experience, possibilities, and probabilities.

Toward the end of a long and distinguished career as a clinician, the British physician Sir James Mackenzie pondered the curious fact that no blood count, no bacteriological examination, no instrumental method could tell him as much as a glance at the face and the feel of the pulse. What was this "curious knowledge" that enabled the experienced doctor to estimate a patient's state with such precision? "The real source of this knowledge is the familiarity, derived from experience, of the appearance of the patient when stricken with an insidious disease, a subtle alteration in the expression of the face or a slight wasting, or a faint contraction of some of the muscles of expression, a faint change in color, coupled, it may be, with an alteration in the patient's temper, ideas or voice."[25]

The role of judgment in diagnosis has in no way lessened, and the label of "art" is by no means scientifically shameful. Some observers have de-emphasized the importance of brilliant insight or creativity, pointing to the fact that most clinical problems can be routinely identified and resolved.[26] But it is also true that it is precisely in critical situations in which there are elements of ambiguity that the dramatic insight comes back into its own, and this applies to both clinical medicine and intelligence.

To the student of foreign affairs and intelligence, many of the frequent sources of error in medical diagnosis sound familiar: a tendency to choose an exotic explanation over a simple one, missing an overall pattern due to concentration on details, stubborn adherence to a hypothesis in spite of strong evidence against it, and even time constraints and weariness. Both the physician and the intelligence analyst face the question of how to deal with unique situations by means of mathematical approaches.[27] They may be helpful in some instances, but usually they are not sufficient. The more distinctly human the phenomenon, the more necessary a human observer. "Whatever can be distinguished only by human speech, sight, smell, touch, hearing, taste, movement and cerebration cannot be discerned by inanimate devices which lack perception and the ingenuity of the human brain."[28] The programming of computers and artificial intelligence will no doubt make great progress in the years to come. But, as often noted, computer-based decisions cannot be more reliable than the information that was provided in the first place.

Given limited resources, in medicine as in intelligence, there is also the danger of overdiagnosis, of a perfectionism that is not just unnecessary, but possibly dangerous. The problem at hand may not be solved in time, and the "wider questions" to which this perfectionism leads may never be answered. The physician engages in diagnosis for therapeutic purposes, not to find some objective truth; the intelligence analyst is expected to reply to some specific question, not to propound a theory of social change. Diagnosis, like much intelligence work, has to be timely and cost effective, it cannot go on forever, and frequently it is needed for action here and now.[29]

The clinician has to be prepared for the unexpected, the apparently inexplicable and incongruous. Habituation—routine—in this field, as in others, is the great danger. Like the intelligence analyst, the clinician faces the problem of detecting signals. The problem of the weak signal drowned in background noise is common to both fields. There is the syndrome of the loquacious patient—the doctor hardly hears the many irrelevancies and reminiscences and the doctor's suppressive mechanism turns a deaf ear to them and they are unconsciously dismissed.[30] But equally there is the danger of selective deafness and blindness, of suppressing some relevant information.

The comparison between medicine and intelligence, however instructive, must not be carried beyond a certain point; the doctor engages not only in diagnosis but also in curing the patient. At this juncture the analogy tends to become weak unless, of course, one establishes a parallel between medical treatment and "active measures." They do, however, face common dilemmas. Science alone will not solve their problem nor will subjective judgment and intuition; only a combination of the two will work.

The Perils of Prediction

Intelligence analysts, like doctors, are expected to predict. Their customers wish to know not only what has happened but what is likely to occur in the future.[31] In intelligence this refers primarily to short-term prediction, though it is not difficult to think of examples of long-term prediction that directly impinge on policy planning—the development of weapons systems in other countries, for instance, or the energy situation and its likely political repercussions. Machiavelli believed that all history showed that no great public misfortune had happened that had not been foretold by someone possessed of the power of prophecy. He was perhaps the first to make a plea for the scientific study of prophecy, suggesting that men acquainted with things both natural and supernatural should investigate the phenomenon.

Our age has witnessed an unparalleled upsurge in rational attempts at prediction, in contrast to the prescientific forecasts of bygone ages. Yet for every bona fide futurist there are even now several believers in the occult sciences.[32] For every scientific study on the future, there are others in parasensory topics, alien mind control, consciousness expansion, clairvoyance, PSI, or the I Ching.*

*C. G. Jung was probably right when he wrote in an essay on UFOs, "The heyday of astrology was not in the benighted Middle Ages but is in the middle of the twentieth century, when even the newspapers do not hesitate to publish the week's horoscope." Carl G. Jung, *Civilization in Transition,* vol. 10 of the *Collected Works,* 2nd Ed., Bollingen Series (Princeton, N. J.: Princeton University Press, 1964), p. 370.

In the 1960s, Erich Jaentsch distinguished roughly a hundred techniques of rational forecasting, and additional ones have been introduced since. Trend extrapolation is still the most widely used technique. The projection of various scenarios based on intuition (or invention), analogy, and elimination is also widely used. Delphi has already been mentioned, as has the use of cross-impact matrices. Some approaches—the more modest ones—are based on structural certainties such as the assumption that Luxembourg will not be a superpower by the 1990s or that China will not have ceased to exist. Others rely on the operational "code" or the system; that is, the implicit "rules of the game" in a society and its institutional sources of power, assuming that these will not change—at least, not much.

Experience so far has taught a number of basic lessons on the uses and limits of prevision.[33] That forecasting underlies most human activities goes without saying; without some planning even the most primitive societies (based on hunting or agriculture) would not function, let alone modern industrial societies. Yet, the history of forecasting also shows that knowledge of the past is by no means a sure key to the future.

The first obvious way to minimize risks in forecasting is to eschew forecasts that are too precise, but in this case they won't be very helpful. Reviewing certain predictions made around the turn of the century by H. G. Wells on the future of warfare, S. Lilley found that while in questions of detail Wells had almost invariably been wrong, he did get the general trend of development astonishingly right (his scenario was more correct for World War II than for World War I). If his forecasts had been of a more general nature—that means of flight would soon exist, that speed of maneuver on land would greatly increase, and so forth—he would have been even more acclaimed.

Forecasting, to the extent that it is of interest in the present context is more frequently used in demography, in economics, and in technological development. While the technique of demographic projection methodology has continually improved over the years, the uncertainties of social, economic, and political changes are such that the outlook for more accurate population forecasting is not promising.[34] Likewise a comparison of econometric forecasts shows that predictions have not much improved over the years. These studies have also shown that judgment-free economic models have consistently scored worse than those using human judgment.

All this is not to suggest that because there has been little progress, prediction is neither possible nor desirable. It is both feasible and necessary, even though it is no more a science now than it was fifty years ago. Basic assumptions matter more than the methodology. If the basic assumptions are correct, almost any approach will do; if they are wrong, even the most sophisticated method cannot repair the damage.

Political and sociopolitical forecasting is the most difficult kind. The case in favor of the feasibility of foolproof (surprise-sensitive) forecasting is based, broadly speaking, on the argument that forecasters are not concerned with unique or random events, with the highly individual impact of the great (or maniacal) statesman or prophet, but with patterns of change and development that exist independently.[35] As there are no independent patterns of change, however, such forecasts will result either in exceedingly vague (or false) statements, or, alternatively, in a variety of scenarios trying to cover all the various possibilities open at a time of rapid change. Such predictions are not helpful to the policy maker. Because prediction is impossible without at least some measure of extrapolation, and because extrapolation does not work without at least some continuity, prediction becomes most difficult when it is most needed—at a time of rapid or radical change.

Of the future, says Aeschylus, "you shall know when it has come; before then, forget it." Yet we can never forget the future for very long, even though it is unfathomable before it happens. Most forecasters are concerned with modest and limited assignments, such as assembling data for industrial or town planning and economic and social demand in general; few will question the need for such projections. While truly scientific prediction in economics seems impossible for the present, a great many people, more than ever before, are making a comfortable living doing just that. Some of them, at least, have a fairly good record. The same is true with regard to political prevision. The fact that it is not scientific does not mean that a wise man's view on the subject is no better than that of a fool or a charlatan, and that therefore specialized knowledge and practical wisdom of long experience should be dismissed as of no consequence. Studies have shown that in various fields amateurs have predicted as well as professionals. International politics, however, is not one of these fields.

If political prediction is not a science, it still needs adequate political theory; it does seem to have the attributes of a craft, and there is something akin to a track record among its practitioners. Because there is no reason to believe that success or failure is based on mere accident, we shall examine in some detail the qualities that provide for better forecasting, and whether these can be improved, in the concluding chapter.

Over the years, a body of experience has been amassed, and there are generalizations on which intelligence work is based, even if there is no normative theory that would make intelligence per se more scientific. The body of knowledge that constitutes "intelligence doctrine" is based on certain tenets, none of them mysterious. One must consider the basic factors and motives shaping the politics of nations and the relations between them. At the same time, one must have recourse to traditional maxims of prudence and wisdom. The attempt has been made to verify the truth of these hypotheses, and in the course of such investigations terms such as "heuristic," "epistemological," and "cognitive" are frequently used. Such investigations are perfectly legitimate; as the great statistician Karl Pearson said, popular beliefs should be tested statistically. As a result it will emerge that Rome was indeed not built in a day, that birds of a feather do indeed flock together, but that it is not always true that great minds think alike.

The popular wisdom of the past has something to offer for everyone, but there still remains the problem of choosing the right advice for a specific situation. At this point the decision will be left to judgment, and the judgment of a trained and experienced mind will be more likely to get things right than the judgment of a mind lacking these qualities.

If intelligence is a craft, it is not one that is easy to master. Apprenticeship in medicine today takes, at the very least, seven years, and not much less time in many other professions. A discipline such as intelligence involves competence not only in current affairs, in history and geography, in psychology and sociology, in economics, science, and technology, but it should include firsthand experience of at least some foreign countries and at least a working knowledge of a foreign language. Much thought has been given in recent decades to improving medical education, but very little to the acquisition of the skills and the knowledge needed in intelligence. Yet the quality of analysts will remain the decisive factor in intelligence in the future as it has been in the past.

PART V

CONCLUSION

CHAPTER 11

The Future
of Intelligence

THE Dulles report of 1949 was optimistic about America's ability to create "the best intelligence service in the world." It had the resources and the human material, people from many lands, and the needed technical and scientific skills. Above all, it could develop the individual initiative, skill, and ingenuity of a free people, whereas its adversaries had to rely on iron discipline. As Allen Dulles put it, "free men could be more efficient than the unfree"—in this respect as well as in most others. History has not so far born out such optimism. While America *may* have the necessary potential to achieve the goal Dulles set, there are great obstacles to overcome before that potential can be realized.

Organizational Reform

Dulles and his colleagues were prophetic about one thing, at least—organizational charts could never replace individual initiative and ability. Lyman Kirkpatrick, inspector general of the CIA at the time returned in his 1960 report to this question, complaining that his committee was fed on a constant diet of such organizational charts; he himself had gone through eighteen of them. Gradually the question of whether or not the Office of Estimates should be combined with the Office of Current Intelligence, and similar proposed reforms, struck him as less and less earthshaking.[1] Every reorganization, Kirkpatrick noted, took two years; James Schlesinger's committee of investigation subsequently observed that reforms could at best create conditions in which wise and imaginative leadership might flourish.[2]

The intelligence investigation committees of the 1970s dealt mainly with covert action, the compatibility of secrecy with the principles of democracy, and—from time to time—with improvement of the intelligence end product. Given the mood of the 1970s, the main concern of these committees was directed to instances of abuse, and the pressure they exerted for more and more revelations was successful. As Philip Agee put it, "Who would have dreamed, two years ago, that such a great volume of information on secret American intervention in foreign countries would ever be made public?"[3]

The revelations poured forth, but the improvement of intelligence performance did not ensue. It is, of course, naive to believe that intelligence can actually be perfected, but some improvement is usually possible. Various proposals suggested improvement through organizational reform; others put the main emphasis on technical innovation; and there were some who insisted that intelligence must first of all be established on sound theoretical foundations. These approaches were not mutually exclusive; in some cases all three have been advocated simultaneously. There is another school of thought—the correct one, in my opinion—which insists that there are no quick fixes to be had in this matter: intelligence will improve only if those engaged in it reach a higher level of competence.

Intelligence has been subject to a bewildering zeal for organizational reform:[4] NIPE became the I.C. staff; OCI and ORR were merged into OSR; IRAC and USIB came and went; ONE was dissolved and replaced by the NIO system; PBCFIA became PFIAB, which was liquidated under Carter, only to be resurrected under Reagan. It is a subject of limited interest; the "reforms" of the 1970s were more often than not restrictions, inhibiting experimentation and in some cases technological innovation. There was so much preoccupation with bureaucratically safe procedures that little energy remained for anything else. Creative people became discouraged by being caught up in what to them seemed irrational organizational change.

Reforms may become inevitable as the result of changing priorities, new political constellations, or technological innovations. But much of the organizational change affecting the CIA has been unnecessary, and in some cases it was positively harmful. It reflected the growing bureaucratization of modern intelligence and the unhealthy preoccupation with managerial problems—the tendency, to paraphrase Karl Mannheim, to turn substantive problems into problems of administration.

Every student of modern bureaucracy knows that it is subject to certain fundamental laws. As bureaucracy grows, so does specialization. Specialization, however, does not necessarily lead to greater effectiveness.[5] A century ago a foreign minister ran his department singlehanded and knew virtually everyone he employed and everything that went on. Today a minister or intelligence chief controls many thousands of subordinates, which is to say that he does not really control them. He has difficulties in getting his directions carried out; often he does not so much do what *he* wants, but what circumstances dictate. Once a policy has been established, it becomes very difficult to alter it. The larger a bureaucracy, the more *paperasserie*—the production and dissemination of paper. An inordinate amount of time and effort goes into bureaucratic empire building, hierarchy becomes a deadening influence on the use of one's own initiative, and leadership and direction become more and more difficult. Bureaucracies increase the natural disinclination toward change and instill an aversion to planning and clear delegation of authority. The watchword of bureaucracy is authority without responsibility and responsibility without authority.

To remedy such problems, committees are often established on the assumption—not always confirmed in practice—that several viewpoints are most likely to produce useful results. Committees have often been defined in malicious ways: as "the unfit, selected by the unwilling, to do the unnecessary"; or as "the place where the loneliness of thought is replaced by the togetherness of nothingness." Of course, these definitions are untrue as a general proposition, for committees can also fulfill vital functions by coordinating policies and sharing information. The drawbacks, however, are well known: committees consume a great deal of time, and sometimes money; they tend to compromise on the lowest common denominator; and they often prefer to avoid taking action. Thus, while committees can coordinate, they can seldom manage, engage in research, or, generally speaking, execute policy.

The "science" of management has developed more fully in America than perhaps anywhere else. Thinking about organization is a legitimate and useful activity, but the achievements have been modest so far. No one is likely to dispute the fact that large organizations have to be rationally managed, or that certain effective rules of thumb have evolved from that practice. Bureaucracies are good for certain types of work, but not for others, and the general tendency in America has been more toward overorganization than its opposite. This is as true with regard to intelligence as to government and to private enterprise. It has led to a "machine bureaucracy" with the emphasis on hierarchy, specialization, control, and abstract rationality. Decisions are likely to be guided not by wisdom, intuition, and common sense; their place may well be usurped by abstract rules and an overemphasis on quantitative results—those that can be measured by modern machinery.

These trends may not constitute a mortal danger to certain branches of modern administration, but their impact on intelligence can be debilitating. Perhaps more than any other activity, intelligence depends on qualities such as initiative and creativity that are difficult to accommodate into bureaucratic routine. A good example of this problem was the entrenchment of various "programming-planning-budgeting" procedures adopted in the 1970s in imitation of the business world, though they had little relevance to the more complex world of intelligence. A parallel instance was the so-called "Management by Objectives" procedures that permeated all aspects of CIA activities in the mid-1970s. These procedures diverted energy to compliance with bureaucratic rituals; they distorted the whole process of judgment as to who was successful and who was not. The officer who faithfully completed all the reports and computerized programs was almost certain to be ranked as more effective than one who did some really creative thinking, intelligence collection, or analysis.[6] In all fairness, in the end none of these techniques had much impact.

The basic ideas of the Pentagon reforms of the early 1960s were sound insofar as they stressed the necessity of policy planning and dispassionate judgment. The analytical techniques used—operations research and systems analysis—no doubt benefited some fields, but they did not prevent grievous mistakes. The performance of organizations which have been run according to the most scientific principles is not very impressive, and the new American interest in how others manage betrays considerable dissatisfaction with current practices. Organizations that have prospered did so because decisions at critical junctures were based on creativity, foresight, and common sense. Those which lacked these qualities are now lagging behind.

What can realistically be expected from organizational reform in intelligence? Above all, clear lines of communication and a reduction of unnecessary paper flow and of unproductive committee meetings. Would it be preferable to maintain a smaller, but highly competent and truly secret intelligence service? A small, truly secret secret service—William C. Donovan's legacy for the postwar world—may be impossible to maintain in today's American society. Nor is the small-is-beautiful doctrine necessarily applicable to intelligence which requires, after all, a great deal of detailed work. But if there are not enough competent and experienced people, if initiative, quick communication, and secrecy cannot be assured in a big organization, a good case can be made for employing fewer people. Lower standards may not mean just less intelligence. It could mean wrong intelligence.

The Limits of Technology

Ever greater expectations have been attached to modern technology and its effect on intelligence. That the most advanced means should be applied in the collection of intelligence, that one should always try to perfect them and to look for new departures is, of course, beyond dispute. In most respects American technology still leads the rest of the world; in some cases reality now exceeds what only yesterday was the fantasy of science fiction. But given the American fascination with gadgets, given that American intelligence has always been better at collecting facts than at putting them together to assess intentions, the advances in the means of collection have not been an unmixed blessing. In some respects, the means of technical collection have outstripped the capacity to exploit the information collected. More dangerously, the large amount of technically collected information has tended to downgrade sparser and more fragmentary information from other sources, which may be intrinsically more important.

Enormous technical changes have occurred in the field of information management. This information revolution will probably continue, even gather speed. But overfascination with the most recent gadgets, or preoccupation with package rather than substance is a very real danger. The intelligence community has now used computers and related techniques for almost three decades, but few will argue that there has been a striking improvement in foreign political intelligence during this period. It would be utterly wrong to blame the silicon chips or those using them, for the situation in other fields is similar. Forensic medicine, to give but one example, now uses machinery unheard of even a decade ago. Scanning electro-microscopes can produce evidence on shotwounds; GC/MS (gas-chromatograph-mass-spectrometer) produces evidence on even minute quantities of poison. Computers can now provide enormous help in matching handwriting and fingerprints. Yet these breakthroughs have not significantly increased the detection rate. For the truly vexing questions in intelligence, high technology is vitally needed, but very often has no answer.

The Future of Scientific Intelligence

What changes are likely to take place in technical intelligence in the years to come? It will continue to become more important, if only because technology is playing an ever-increasing role. The managers of scientific intelligence will need more people and resources, but such increases will not be easy to obtain—particularly if economic conditions are unfavorable. Managers will have to find more efficient methods and reevaluate their priorities.

Computers have revolutionized the ability to process, store, and manipulate information. The selection and training of personnel is becoming increasingly important, and the selection of scientific fields to be covered will be the key element in this process. Intelligence will never be able to assign full-time employees to all areas of technical intelligence, nor should it try to do so.

A more efficient way to cope with future requirements is to improve the exchanges of ideas and information between government specialists and those in the private sector and, of course, in the academic world. This has already been done on relatively narrow, well-defined projects. Such exchanges ought to be across a broader range of technical subjects and disciplines.

In the past, U.S. technical intelligence analysts have been able to analyze foreign development by comparing information on it to what American laboratories had done several years earlier. This will become increasingly difficult as the technological gap narrows. In addition, a greater degree of mutual trust between scientific intelligence officers and those engaged in private or academic research must be established. But such cooperation will depend upon recognition that assisting the government to understand foreign research is not morally reprehensible. Professional societies could provide an important two-way communication channel in this respect.

Greater involvement by nongovernment scientists and technologists seems the only sensible way to follow the numerous foreign technical advances in fields that are not on today's top priority lists. Genetic engineering may not be as high on the scale of importance as high energy lasers at the moment, but it may equal or surpass them after some years. If the subject is not covered in government now, it is vital to know that outside researchers are doing so, and that they will alert the intelligence community to important changes as they occur. To make this approach effective, informal understandings are necessary in addition to formal contractual arrangements.

316

The increased technical intelligence work load will prompt a reexamination of government organization for this effort. In addition to the CIA, the Defense Intelligence Agency and components of each of the military intelligence services are currently engaged in scientific and technical analysis. There is overlap and duplication, but this is not always undesirable. Some breakthroughs in scientific and technical intelligence came about only because there was duplication, and often an element of competition as well. Duplication forced more careful examination of the data, leading to more complete understanding and more informed conclusions. Duplication, however, is expensive, and constant review of the division of labor should be mandatory. As new scientific subjects and discoveries arise, it will have to be determined which organization is best qualified to deal with them. In other words, duplication—where it exists—should be the result of a conscious judgment, not of bureaucratic inertia.

Scientific intelligence may have to turn its attention to more countries. "Technology transfer" has already accelerated to major proportions among most developed nations, and though the future may see stricter controls, one must anticipate an increased flow of scientific and technical exchange among nations great and small. Increased attention is necessary because an important technological discovery in a small country may rapidly find application by a superpower.

No Dramatic Leap Forward

Some have claimed that modern computer technology can set up a global integrated warning system to detect every kind of crisis situation, thus developing the art of forecasting into a "hard" science;[7] these claims have come, admittedly, from outside enthusiasts rather than intelligence officials. If these claims ever turn out to be true, most of the assumptions about intelligence would have to be changed. Having for so long moved in a morass of doubts and uncertainties, we would at long last have our feet on terra firma.

But it has not happened yet, and it is unlikely to occur in the near future. If consumers complain about the low level of political intelligence analysis, if they claim that they find more interesting and accurate information in journals like the *Economist,* the fault lies partly with those who promised more than they could deliver. The call to place intelligence gathering (including measuring, monitoring, and evaluating) within a firm social science tradition is perfectly legitimate. Furthermore, it would be incorrect to suggest that the historical (or wisdom) and social science approaches are diametrically opposed. They have much in common and they certainly deal with many of the same issues: objective and subjective factors; the place of partnership in practice; and explanation and prediction in the social, as opposed to the natural, environment.

In any case, social research is not the initiator or executor of policy decisions, though some of its practitioners have been guilty of such a mandarin misperception of their roles. Prime responsibility for policies—whether successful or not—belongs to the bureaucracies that welcomed approaches that seemed to fit so well into their ways of thought and organizational frameworks.

A good grounding in social science tradition is an important asset in intelligence analysis. It cannot replace, but it usefully complements, area expertise, knowledge and experience of important personalities and national characteristics, and basic economic facts that can easily be quantified. In theory, students should acquire this kind of knowledge in colleges and universities. Recruits ought to join intelligence agencies with a basic area knowledge, foreign language skills, and a good grounding in history and geography, but seldom do. Geography, to give one example, is one of the most neglected disciplines in American education. As a consequence, even intelligence analysts have shown lamentable ignorance in this respect. Seen in this light, intelligence schools mirror a common American shortcoming—emphasis on procedure and method at the expense of substance. Remedial courses in English are taught in leading universities, so there is no good reason why intelligence schools should not provide remedial tuition in other fields. It is pointless to teach procedure and method if substance is lacking.

The record in the United States shows that neither frequent organizational reform nor technological advance—except in the field of collection —let alone an elusive scientific theory of intelligence has significantly improved the quality of foreign political intelligence. Intelligence performance depends on those who perform it, their ability, competence, and experience. The idea that the quality of intelligence can somehow be improved beyond the level of its producers is a dangerous delusion. There will always be an element of accident and luck involved, for which there can be no accounting. But in the long run, ignorant people will not be consistently lucky, nor will competent individuals be consistently wrong.

The Genius of Intelligence

The only promising way to improve intelligence performance is to select recruits who have at least some of the faculties needed, and then give them a good training. The faculties needed by a director of intelligence are easier to define than are those needed by those who serve under him. A director does not have to know too much about the business itself, but he must be open-minded. No single individual can be equally well informed on the political and economic state of the world, on military issues, and on technological developments. He cannot even know all that happens in the organization which he directs. But he must not be the prisoner of preconceived notions. He must have a mind of his own, yet be willing to change his views if there is convincing evidence to merit it. Above all, he must enjoy the respect and trust of his subordinates and able to get the best out of them.

Such qualities of leadership are not all that frequent, and they cannot automatically be expected of those in high authority. But judgment is essential for a leader—this refers above all to the choice of close advisers. There have been chiefs of intelligence who were poor organizers, and others without politically brilliant minds. But they are still regarded as successes owing to their good teamwork and ability to delegate authority. Lastly, the head of intelligence needs a relationship of trust with his main consumer, the president, and also with the secretaries of defense and state. Short of such relationships, even excellent intelligence will not reach its destination, or be paid sufficient attention.

In some important respects intelligence differs from other branches of government. Deeper motivation is needed; a merely perfunctory interest in one's job will not do. Senior officials in many government departments will not be effective if they restrict their activities to normal office hours. This refers with special force to intelligence, but by no means only at the very senior level.

The qualities needed by a good intelligence officer have long been known; they were described by writers on early modern diplomacy like Wicquefort, de Callières, and Jean Hotman.[8] Their writings can still serve as guidelines. The comparison with diplomacy is not fanciful—while Wicquefort called the ambassador a "messenger of peace," he also called him "an honorable spy." De Callières noted that spies were of critical importance in negotiations; more than any other agency they contributed to the success of great plans, for they alone could keep an ambassador informed of all that happened in the foreign country of service.

The early political messengers and reporters knew from Machiavelli not to be deceived by appearances, and that *fortuna* was fickle and mysterious —one might have to act quickly to seize her. Shakespeare impressed on them the art of dissimulation: "Why, I can smile and murder while I smile" *(Henry VI)*. August Vera stressed the importance of *sang froid*—to listen much and to talk little. Among other qualities stressed, one finds discretion, infinite patience, tact, vigilance, calmness, subtlety, firmness, force of mind, and prudence.

How was the intelligence gatherer of old to acquire background knowledge about the country to which he was accredited? An anonymous Spanish diplomat of the late seventeenth century provided detailed guidance, which still applies:

> He must spend his spare time in reading its histories or chronicles, must gain a knowledge of its laws, of the privileges of its provinces, the character of the natives, their temperament and inclination; and if he should desire to serve in his office with the goodwill of his own and of a foreign people, he must try and accommodate himself to the character of the natives, though at the cost of doing violence to his own, he must listen to them, talk to them and even flatter them. For flattery is the magnet which everywhere attracts goodwill. . . . Anyone who listens to many people and consorts with them, sometimes meets one who cannot keep a secret and even habitually makes a confidant of someone in order to show that he is a man of importance. . . . Should he lack friends and ability to discover the truth and to verify his suspicions, money can help him, for it is and always has been the master key to the most closely locked archives.[9]

Should he consort with members of the opposition? The issue was raised by de Callières, and it still preoccupies American diplomats today. Our eighteenth-century guide advised against it, except perhaps in England and Holland, as such contacts were least risky there. Whether representatives should be left abroad for a long time at the risk of their "going native" was much discussed. The tendency was to leave them for many years, even decades, at their post, though a British report of 1861 warned against the possibility of divided loyalties.

The early writers also reflected on what kind of people would be best fitted to serve abroad. De Callières believed that though diplomatic genius was born, not made, there were many qualities that could be developed with practice. He and Wicquefort agreed that the study of history was the best teacher, and that the knowledge of languages was absolutely essential. To this, needless to say, a knowledge of literature, science, mathematics, and art was added. Last, but not least, one needed the ability to express oneself clearly and objectively in reports.

Most of the problems vexing these early experts have not gone away. This also refers to recruitment and training; the present practice of selecting young recruits straight out of college is wasteful, if not pernicious.[10] They are unlikely to know their own minds sufficiently, nor is it easy to assess someone accurately before he has been exposed to the turbulence of "real life"; it is unlikely that his character has already been fully formed. The applicant may have an excellent record as a student of the theory of decision making, yet his most important decision to date may have been the choice of a course or a subject for a research paper.[11]

There are, of course, some profound differences between the diplomat and the intelligence agent—the assignments are different and in some respects even opposed. But both diplomats and intelligence agents have the same overall tasks—to observe sharply, to understand politics, and to convey their findings to their superiors in clear, objective, and succinct reports.

How can some of these qualities be taught to young recruits? The present state of affairs is unsatisfactory. The Church report noted that the post mortems of major U.S. intelligence failures "pointed in all cases to the shortage of talented personnel."[12] This should have been no surprise, for most of the effort had gone into training operators, rather than analysts. At the time of the Church report, the CIA's Office of Training (OTR) provided some in-house courses on management and executive development. Only one-quarter of those going to external training went for courses lasting longer than six weeks. The training department announced that it was also providing programs in "methodology and research techniques," and that "much of the substantive training for intelligence analysts takes place outside the agency, both in academic institutions and in other government departments."[13] There is no reason to return to the painful subject of methodology again. As for the "substantive training" in other academic institutions and government departments, of course, all efforts to broaden cultural horizons ought to be welcomed. There are excellent universities providing fine courses in history, literature, foreign policy, psychology, economics, and (rarely) national security. But there are no courses teaching political judgment or the specific skills the intelligence analyst needs.[14] Courses on political intelligence hardly existed ten years ago. Today, political science professors or senior former intelligence officials teach the subject in a few universities as part of general national security programs.[15] Perhaps the best way to study intelligence is to go over past experience, with famous cases in the history of the field reviewed and critiqued by former intelligence professionals.

But such reviews cannot replace systematic training, which should take place in a national defense university or special intelligence college. At present the scope of existing institutions is too narrow and the duration of the program too short to meet intelligence needs. What the U.S. offers today is not even remotely comparable in depth with the courses given at the Military-Diplomatic Academy in Moscow. An aspiring American intelligence officer may learn such useful arts as shaking off a tail in Washington's K Street, how to prepare a meeting with an agent, or when and how to use a dead drop; intelligence analysts will receive lectures about the fundamentals of intelligence production (two hours), document security (one hour), "Delphi" and "Group Think" (one-and-a-half hours). There are textbook-style politico-military exercises, and a great deal of time is devoted to statistics, including the minicomputer programs available for the Washington area.

It is unrealistic to take for granted that the recruit has a more or less rounded education, or knows languages, or is familiar with at least the rudiments of Marxism-Leninism and other political doctrines, or has read the essential literature in the field of international relations. Unless the recruit has traveled, he or she will be naively ignorant about foreign countries and will know very little about the philosophy and practice of communism, of social democracy; indeed, of any form of government that of their own country. However eager, intelligent, and adaptable the recruit may be, ignorance of the outside world would make it highly irresponsible to assign him or her to a position in intelligence at home, let alone abroad, without further training. This training should start from scratch, be highly intensive, and last for several years.[16]

But is it possible to teach political judgment? Up to the end of World War II, the leading Soviet agents abroad and the main Western spies were self-made men. In his autobiography, Leopold Trepper, the head of the *Rote Kapelle,* the main Soviet espionage network in Western Europe during World War II, ridiculed the authors who had credited him with long and intensive training in a military academy. Rudolf Abel pontificated in his retirement about the qualifications of a spy: he must be a hard and painstaking worker, have a broad outlook, erudition, knowledge of foreign languages, perseverance, stamina, willpower, and skill. To the extent that Abel possessed these qualifications, he had not acquired them in a special college but in the school of life. Trepper and Abel belonged to a bygone period in the history of intelligence, but as long as HUMINT is in demand, agents will need pretty much the same set of attitudes and skills.

Paraphrasing de Callières, it may well be that intelligence genius is born, not made. But it is also true that intelligence needs not only geniuses, and that political judgment and understanding can be taught—at least up to a point. The same applies to writing. Few will attain the standards of a Bertrand Russell or a George Orwell, but almost everyone can be taught to write clearly and simply, to avoid neologisms and bureaucratic gibberish.[17] A full-scale effort to improve the quality of intelligence recruitment and training is clearly called for if we hope even to approach optimal performance.

Intelligence in a Cold Climate

The CIA and other intelligence agencies have suffered from grave handicaps in their recruitment for many years. The revelations and the attacks of the late 1960s and 1970s deterred many potential recruits from even considering a career in intelligence and CIA recruiters were often banned from campuses. The leaks and sensational allegations created the impression that most if not all members of the intelligence community were involved in activities which, if not criminal, were at least morally reprehensible. Wrongdoings, even mere errors of judgment, were frequently exaggerated and described in the most lurid light, and the basest of motives were attributed to those responsible.

True, a former DCI (Admiral Stansfield Turner) has claimed that during his period of office during the late 1970s the CIA succeeded in casting its net much wider than earlier, when so many of its recruits had come from certain elite schools, especially the Ivy League colleges. This broader base may have been all to the good, but it remains true that the CIA seldom attracted young people equal in caliber to those who had joined in the late 1940s and 1950s. Frequently, the new personnel lacked the international background, intellectual stature, and motivation that had characterized its predecessors.

Toward 1980 the situation began to change. In the late Carter years there were the events in Afghanistan and Poland; at the same time, job prospects for new college graduates became dimmer. Such developments made recruitment easier, but some of the old problems were no nearer to solution. What could intelligence offer by way of career advancement? Intelligence, like other government branches, offers security but little else to help it compete with rival employers. The financial rewards are modest, particularly considering the hardships undergone by the employees and their families. The first three DCIs received a category *V* salary—four levels below cabinet rank. Although the rank is higher now, the earlier situation showed how little importance government attached to its "first line of national defense." Today the CIA has some supergrade positions (GS 17 and 18 in current jargon); this is more than most government agencies have, but virtually all of these positions go to people with managerial responsibilities. According to the Church report, only the small Office of

Political Research (which no longer exists) still retained some supergrade analysts. There had been more in the Office of National Estimates, but the ONE was abolished in 1973. The salary difference between a supergrade and the ranks below was admittedly small, often literally zero, but it was at least a symbolic reward.

The intelligence community enjoys few other compensations: the CIA staff officers posted abroad are almost invariably given a position in embassies and other organizations well below their real rank, which is reflected in such matters as accommodations and social status. While the CIA is exempted from certain civil service constraints, these exemptions are not very significant. A good technologist or a specialist in energy problems, for example, could easily find more remunerative employment outside the agency.[18] Even the Department of State has more to offer to its employees; their achievements are openly recognized and there are fewer restrictions on their social life.

When the absence of rewards coincides with constant accusation and defamation of the intelligence community, morale is bound to sink. This is, of course, what happened in the 1970s. Since then changes have taken place, but the process of rebuilding American intelligence is neither quick nor easy. What was destroyed in a decade may take longer to reconstruct. Nor is it merely a question of rebuilding confidence, for it is imperative to improve intelligence well beyond what it was.

Even under optimal conditions, there are limits to what can be done. It has to be understood that intelligence was never as important in the conduct of policy as is commonly believed, nor is it ever likely to be. Furthermore, American intelligence cannot aspire to be the world's best in peacetime; Allen Dulles's dream cannot be achieved within the restraints of a democratic society. This, at least, seems to be the prevailing view among intelligence consumers, who are in the best position to judge. It is characteristic for an open society such as America that even crucial secrets can frequently be kept no longer than a few years, perhaps a decade at the most. The history of the intelligence community during the last two decades is a history of leaks that continue to the present day.

Even the most ardent critics of intelligence usually do not oppose intelligence across the board, if only because it may have a useful role in arms control, and perhaps in the fight against terrorism. Some critics do not even rule out covert actions in principle, as long as they are undertaken infrequently and under strict supervision. Furthermore, there remains the question of the uses of intelligence: Is the intelligence effort worthwhile if the policy makers are either unable or unwilling to make use of it?

The training of new recruits should start almost from scratch, but the intelligence community is not prepared for an educational effort of this magnitude. This leads back to the argument made earlier, that a smaller intelligence operation might function better; there seems to be today too much intelligence in terms of quantity but very little that can be rated as being of consistently high quality. To function well, even a smaller intelligence establishment would have to be freer of bureaucratic restrictions than is the case today. An intelligence establishment ought to combine orderly procedure with a maximum of freedom for creative thought and action. It should offer its employees work and salary conditions comparable to those they can find elsewhere.

By way of contrast, consider the situation in the academic world. Universities have shown great flexibility in their endeavor to attract and keep not just superstars but whole disciplines such as clinical medicine, offering both better conditions of work and higher salaries. Intelligence should have similar freedom of action. But could this be achieved in a tight bureaucratic framework? Most jobs in intelligence (as in other disciplines) are routine; geniuses are seldom needed. It could also be said that the difference between the best people in a given field and those behind them may be relatively small—that it may not be worthwhile to cause a great commotion to get marginally better results. All this is true, and it is also correct that more money is not always the main attraction for the very best people. But in the last resort there *is* a difference between competence and excellence, and while financial rewards are not all important, neither are they negligible. By and large, customers will get what they are willing to pay for—at least in peacetime.

Let it be assumed for argument's sake that all these prerequisites can be met; that all obstacles have been removed; that excellent people have been recruited; that good training has been provided; and that intelligence will not be disrupted by frequent organizational reforms, misled by false technological dawns, or sidetracked by methodological searches. Even in these ideal conditions success cannot be guaranteed, partly in view of the inherent uncertainties of intelligence, but also because politicians are often unwilling to listen to intelligence or are incapable of acting on the basis of the information received.

In view of these reservations, the initial question arises once more. Is intelligence not a luxury—desirable enough, if one can afford it—but not of decisive importance, and certainly not worth a great investment in manpower, money, and other resources. No major country so far has been willing to accept the risk of conducting its policy without some form of intelligence or another, and it is unlikely that anyone ever will.

Secrecy and American Political Culture

It is tempting to blame the politicians' shortsightedness for their unwillingness or inability to act "upon information received." The real reasons go considerably deeper. American society's hostility to intelligence is a political fact of life. True, from time to time—after some particularly humiliating political or military defeat, or in the face of obvious danger—the call goes out to strengthen intelligence, to give it a freer hand, and to allocate more resources to it. But once the immediate crisis passes, the feeling again prevails that the public has a right to know everything (or almost everything), and that the denial of this right is bound to result in abuse and crime. Secrecy, it is said, erodes the system of checks and balances on which constitutional government rests.

These fears are not groundless; there *is* a contradiction between free societies and secret services, and there are no easy ways to resolve the problem. There is great reluctance to accept the fact that without secrecy there can be no diplomacy, much less intelligence. American attitudes toward intelligence arise from a high standard of morality, but there has also been some humbug involved. Justice Brandeis's dictum that "sunshine is the best of disinfectants" is sometimes cited by those who oppose secrecy. But, of course, those who quote it also know that as far as human beings are concerned, sunshine is wonderful only in moderation. Those most embittered about secrecy—and intelligence—argue that American administrations have been lying to the American people, lying about the Bay of Pigs and about Laos, about operations MONGOOSE and CHAOS and COINTELPRO, about Indonesia and Chile, about projects MKULTRA and CHATTER. There is no denying that the authorities have been lying; all governments do at one time or another—some, admittedly, far more often and outrageously than others. It is one thing to argue that a government that consistently misleads its people has effectively lost its legitimacy and should be replaced. But it is preposterous to demand that governments should *always* tell the whole truth, as if that single moral value everywhere and forever transcended all other values. An individual may legitimately decide to act this way, even at the cost of life, but governments are not free to choose this "ethic of ultimate ends." Their decisions are necessarily determined by a process of weighing alternate goods.[19]

The fact is that intelligence runs against the grain of American political culture. It is true that President Wilson, when he talked about diplomacy proceeding "frankly and in public view," did not really mean anything more than the *results* of secret negotiation. His rhetoric certainly did not prevent him from having secret sessions with Lloyd George and Clemenceau while U.S. marines with fixed bayonets stood at the door and patrolled the garden outside.[20] But intelligence is in an even worse position than diplomacy; it has to hide not only its operations but also the final product from the public. Hence the aversion to intelligence, which is seen as an unfortunate necessity in war, but certainly not a profession for decent people at any other time. With the appearance of fascism, nazism, and bolshevism, there was reluctant realization that the rules of the international game had changed. But there was equally the feeling that if the democracies used the same methods their enemies did, they might become like them. Bertrand Russell, for example, predicted in 1939 that if Britain and France went to war they would inevitably transform themselves into fascist states.

Few carried this argument to its logical extreme; during the cold war there was not much criticism of U.S. intelligence except on the radical fringe. The underlying assumption remained, however, that unless the CIA was kept on a short leash it would become uncontrollable, an attitude that became more pronounced with the advent of détente. As Nicholas Katzenbach, former undersecretary of state and attorney general suggested, the U.S. government "should abandon publicly all covert operations designed to influence political results in foreign countries."[21]

The Church Committee, in a serious attempt to investigate and confront the dilemmas facing the U.S. intelligence community in the 1970s, considered its main assignment to be to answer the following questions:

- What should be regarded as a national secret?
- Who determines what is to be kept secret?
- How can decisions made in secret, or programs secretly approved, be reviewed?

As the Church committee saw it, the main problem was that U.S. intelligence activities had infringed on the rights of U.S. citizens, and that Congress must have access to secret information to carry out its constitutional responsibilities of advice and consent. Hindsight showed that many secret operations had indeed been ill-advised and that secrecy had wrongly been demanded in the interests of national security, sometimes serving merely as a cloak for mistakes.

Congressional criticism was restrained in comparison with attacks against intelligence in the media. Not only did the role of intelligence in Vietnam come under scrutiny, but revelations of assassination plots well before that, Operation Mongoose, CIA activities in Chile, illegal NSA surveillance, CIA influence on student and other groups (exposed by

Ramparts magazine), the testing and use of chemical and biological agents by the intelligence community, and many other real and alleged misdeeds.

As a result of congressional investigations, constant adverse publicity, and extracted or volunteered revelations, the level of intelligence—which had not been too high in the first place—further declined. If there had not been many secrets about the CIA before these revelations, there were few left after. Most of the competent senior personnel were purged or left, budgets were cut, collection operations were stopped. Relations with foreign informants and other agencies were damaged because these assumed —not unreasonably—that any information conveyed to Washington would find its way, sooner rather than later, into the media. Covert action and counterespionage activities of the CIA were virtually dismantled. Other branches of intelligence were also affected, for those engaged in collection and assessment could well reason that given the prevailing climate, the more cautiously they moved and the less they did, the safer they would be. In short, the investigations of the 1970s aimed at a moral cleanup of intelligence; the quality of intelligence, let alone the question of what use should be made of it, was, at most, a marginal issue.

Both Congress and the White House prepared guidelines as additional checks on the activities of intelligence. Under Carter's Executive Order 12036, two National Security Council committees were to have direct supervision of all U.S. intelligence.[22] But the intelligence agencies were also to be subject to scrutiny by the Intelligence Oversight Board, which was concerned solely with questions of loyalty or impropriety. The Senate was to confirm the appointment of the key positions in the CIA and the NSA. Legislation proposed by Congress went even further: congressional committees were to be notified in advance about covert activity.* Intelligence was to operate much more publicly than in the past and covert actions were to be resorted to sparingly, if at all. Most of these proposals —such as advance notice of covert activity to congressional committees— are now of purely academic interest because the political climate changed soon afterward, and with it attitudes toward intelligence.[23]

The charges of the early 1970s rested on the argument that secrecy is always a potential danger to a democratic society, and that government officials may try to shield themselves from public scrutiny by keeping their actions unknown. In Britain, for example, the Official Secrets Act has been used to protect the government and the civil services from all kinds of

---

*The Hughes-Ryan act of 1974 stipulated that eight congressional committees would have to be notified in advance, which, while not ruling out covert action in principle, would have made such action in fact impossible. The Hughes-Ryan act was superseded in 1980 by the Intelligence Oversight Act, which amended it in certain important respects. Covert action is now commonly defined as operations in foreign countries other than activities intended solely for obtaining necessary intelligence.

inconvenient probes.[24] In the U.S., the labels "confidential," "secret," and "top secret" have been used on many occasions without any obvious need. At present some 20 million documents are classified each year (about 350,000 as "top secret"), two-thirds of them by the Department of Defense. While a presidential order explicitly forbids classifying information to conceal violations of law, inefficiency, and administrative error, the general tendency has always been to overclassify.

Intelligence in a Democratic Society

The intelligence control reforms proposed in the 1970s took a number of assumptions more or less for granted. These assumptions were that intelligence could function—and even function better—in a democratic society under the supervision of outside officials and in the limelight of the media; that while regrettable, the betrayal of secrets by leaking was part of an unofficial system of checks and balances; that the right to know usually took precedence over the need for secrecy; that there was no fundamental clash between secrecy and the right to know; and that it was almost always more important to protect the citizen against intelligence abuses than to shield intelligence against its adversaries.

These assumptions were themselves based on certain political beliefs— namely, that America, with its democratic values and free institutions, was in no immediate danger if it behaved prudently, and that those who pointed to external dangers were either grossly exaggerating or were engaged in special pleading. Some argued that even if there were certain dangers, it would be wrong to use questionable means in the defense of one's values. The big debate centered on what means were permissible in the conduct of foreign policy, and whether America could afford to play according to a set of rules much more stringent than those used by its adversaries.

Secrecy and the right to know are not absolutes that preclude each other; various democratic countries have developed arrangements that, while not ideal, work tolerably well most of the time. America is ill-suited for such experiments. Its position cannot be compared with that of Costa Rica, which has abolished its army and presumably has few state secrets. Nor can it afford a kind of modern-day "armed neutrality," like Sweden.[25] American interests are global, and the anonymity of its big cities provides many more opportunities for espionage and leakage than is the case for countries like Sweden and Costa Rica. The United States lacks that elementary national solidarity and responsibility which in some smaller democratic countries frequently prevents leakages damaging to the national interest. The U.S. investigative journalist sees it as his or her job to ferret out secrets and to publish them; protection of the national interest is up to government officials, who are paid for doing so. If the journalist happens to be one of radical persuasion, the claim may even be made that "the national interest" is merely the shibboleth of paranoid right-wingers. Of course, to blame journalists as a group for leaking would be grossly unfair; politicians and government officials, for whatever motives, have been worse offenders.[26] They are the wholesalers of what journalists later retail. In other democratic societies such behavior would be frowned upon and the perpetrators would be ostracized, if not punished. This is not the situation in the United States, where revealing state secrets is not punishable, provided it is done in the proper way, such as in a public speech, in an interview, a newspaper article, or a book.[27]

Leaking may have an honorable history, and it may provide the public with valuable information for judging its elected officials, but intelligence officials (who were not elected) cannot be expected to do a reasonable job in the full glare of publicity. Another common justification for such leaks is that without them abuses would never become known. But the leaks affect the legitimate uses of intelligence, not just its abuses. If details are published about the U.S. capacity to decrypt enemy codes or to observe a strategic buildup through satellites, this will enable the other side to hide its activities, and the operations of U.S. intelligence will become that much more difficult.

Even at present, the United States has an Espionage Act (18 U.S. Code, sections 793–798). This act deals with gathering, transmitting, and losing defense information, photographing or sketching defense installations, the disclosure of classified information, and other such subjects. While these statutes are not entirely ineffective, they do not provide national security protection comparable to that of other countries. The reasons for this are rooted in the Constitution and in the protection afforded by American criminal justice procedures.

The statutes are contradictory with regard to the definition of national security and state secrets. The government must prove that those accused of violating the Espionage Act intended to injure the United States or aid a foreign nation—the so-called "specific intent" requirement. The government has to persuade judge or jury that the information involved was classified, and if it was, that the classification was necessary and proper. Then all the secret details concerning the case have to be disclosed in court and made available to the defense.[28] Thus a spy, not to mention a leaker, may enjoy de facto immunity from persecution because the price of disclosure would be unacceptably high to the government. Lastly, the statutes do not provide sufficient protection against "subversive leaking"—if a spy, instead of selling secrets to a foreign power, decides to have them published by a group or press in the United States which supports that foreign power, the spy might not be prosecuted.

Two leading American legal experts, Edgar and Schmidt, have summarized the state of affairs as follows:

> The ideological spy can argue in good faith that his revelations are designed to advance the interests of the United States by bringing it under a different political system. Spies interested in pecuniary gain may plausibly claim that the information selected for transfer was harmless, or already known to the foreign government or some such.[29]

A former legislative counsel in charge of CIA relations with Congress put the situation even more drastically in focus. He noted that, whereas there are criminal laws in the United States likely to send a Department of Agriculture employee to prison for up to ten years if he revealed advance information on next year's soybean crop, defense secrets are not protected in a similar way.

Legislation against leaks and legislation to strengthen the espionage statutes is opposed by those who argue that the Constitution protects the right to receive and disseminate information and ideas, and that the First Amendment and the Bill of Rights are intended to protect citizens against the government, not the government against its citizens. Without the dissemination of information, they argue, there can be no informed public discussion.[30] Such views have, no doubt, been behind much of the resistance against attempts to introduce a state secrets act in the United States.[31] The desire for openness is so deeply rooted in the American tradition that it seems unlikely that more effective laws against espionage and leaking will be passed.[32] An Intelligence Identities Protection Act became law in 1982 after a three-year legal battle, but this addresses only a small part of the general problem.

Could intelligence function without secrecy? To some extent its role can be fulfilled by research institutes or think tanks that analyze newspaper clippings and radio broadcasts, diplomatic and travelers' reports, and perhaps some other occasional pieces of information. A great deal of intelligence can, in fact, be assembled on the basis of such material. Suggestions of this kind have frequently been made. They aim at disassembling the CIA and assigning its two principal functions to separate organizations. The central analytic and estimating responsibilities would be placed in a new agency, organized and staffed to perform only those functions, fully isolated from all clandestine activity.[33] An organization-ally separate agency would be responsible for any and all kinds of "active measures."

Active Measures/Covert Action

The maintenance of two (or even three) separate intelligence agencies is not unheard of; it has been tried before—in Great Britain during World War II, for example. Collection of intelligence aims at knowing about the state of affairs in a foreign country; covert action aims at doing something about it.[34] The analysts, to paraphrase Marx, are the philosophers who have interpreted the world in different ways; those in covert action have been commissioned to change it—a little bit, and from time to time. The National Security Act of 1947 was not altogether clear (perhaps on purpose) about the functions of the CIA in this respect, for it mentioned not only the coordination of intelligence, but the performance of "such other functions and duties related to intelligence . . . as the NSC may from time to time direct." This clearly meant covert action, but it is doubtful whether those who composed and passed the act envisaged that covert action would soon emerge as a very important component within the CIA.

The arguments for separation aim at removing the stigma attached to the CIA. Some expect that a new agency, under a different name, would gain more public support, attract better recruits, and perhaps even get greater financial allocations. George Carver, a former senior intelligence official, holds that the aim of the proposal is to "separate the virtuous analysts from the leprous operators." Carver's definition is extreme, but not far from the mark. He continues: "This is nonsense. The Intelligence process is seamless, both analysts and operators serve the same country. Neither have any monopoly on virtue, objectivity, or integrity."[35]

The issue is not one of principle but of utility. Those opposed to covert actions would not be any happier if clandestine activities were continued under different management, and under a different name. The practical difficulties involved in such an organizational scheme would be formidable. Members of the two agencies would run the risk of getting in each other's way. The cost would be great; two parallel worldwide networks would be required, as it cannot be known beforehand in which country covert action might be needed. The Foreign Assessment Center would still need HUMINT, otherwise it would have only the same sources at its disposal as other organizations, such as material supplied by the State

Department's INR. Because human intelligence involves secrecy and illegal activity, covert action might reenter through the back door.

Nevertheless, in certain circumstances, a new division of labor in the intelligence community might be viable. It is, to repeat, a practical question, not one of principle. But the issues involved in this debate lead in the end to a reconsideration of our fundamental question: Why intelligence?

It is not quite true that there is no point in producing intelligence of any sort if it cannot be used.[36] A case can be made for producing "pure intelligence" just as a case can be made for doing basic research in science. An institute bringing together some of the best brains in the country with an annual budget of a few hundred million dollars would provide basic intelligence which, for all one knows, might be superior to what is produced at present. But it could not provide the practical information politicians need most—whether or not Argentina will actually land on the Falkland Islands at a certain date, whether the Soviets are massing troops for an operation against an unruly satellite, and so on. Roberta Wohlstetter has provided an excellent illustration in her study on Pearl Harbor:

> Foreign correspondents for the *New York Times,* the *Herald Tribune* and the *Washington Post* were stationed in Tokyo and Shanghai and in Canberra. Their reporting as well as their predictions on the Japanese political scene were on a very high level. Frequently their access to news was more rapid and their judgment of its significance as reliable as that of our intelligence officers. For the last few weeks before the Pearl Harbor strike, however, the newspaper accounts were not very useful. It was necessary to have secret information in order to know what was happening.[37]

Intelligence is primarily action-oriented, frequently calling for immediate political action to cope with dangers abroad. The country in question might be of no vital importance to U.S. security, in which case no action would be necessary. But *if* vital U.S. security interests are involved, what should be done? If a covert action capacity exists, all kinds of possibilities are open. If not, the United States will either have to mount a full-scale military intervention, which is unlikely, or refrain from supporting its friends, which is undesirable.

In the conduct of foreign policy there is a "gray zone" between full-scale military intervention and doing nothing. This part of the political spectrum has grown a lot in recent years, and is now of great importance.[38] There is every reason to assume that most of the action touching on U.S. security in the 1980s and 1990s will be in the "noncommitted" countries of the Third World, where there is wide scope for active measures.

Covert action is only one of the tools of foreign policy, but it is not a negligible one—in certain conditions it may be decisive. It is not an option to be chosen lightly, but in the absence of such an option a global power may be doomed to impotence. Most people, albeit reluctantly, have reached the conclusion that a covert action capacity should exist as long as international politics remains what it pretty much always has been. But there is yet another argument against covert action. It runs as follows: that while the existence of a covert action capability may be in principle desirable, America frequently does not have the know-how, the trained individuals, the surrogates, or the experience to carry it off. If indeed these preconditions do not exist, if such action is hemmed in by too many restrictions, if it is impossible to keep preparations secret, success may not be possible—in which case it may in fact be preferable not to engage in an operation of the covert kind.[39]

It is also true that covert action was abused to carry out operations that were dangerous, morally questionable, stupid, or unnecessary. It is unlikely that without these misguided covert actions the general campaign against intelligence would have been as extensive and as damaging as it was. Given the circumstances in which it operated, U.S. intelligence might have been better advised to refrain from covert action of the violent kind in the 1960s and 1970s—the results were meager, and there was little public support for it. Some notable instances apart, U.S. covert action in its more violent forms has not been successful. Investigations showed that while the assassination of foreign leaders had been considered several times, in only one case was it really attempted, and no foreign leader is known to have been killed or actually even injured as the result of a CIA plot—surely an almost unheard of record in the history of secret services. There is something of a contradiction between covert action and violence, for violence cannot remain covert for long. What is frequently overlooked is the fact that most covert action has *not* been violent, and in this respect U.S. intelligence has been at times very successful. Yet, the greater part of these successes is still unknown to the general public.

A detailed discussion of this issue is well beyond the scope of this study.* Mention should be made, however briefly, of the dilemmas facing policy makers and heads of intelligence. The connection may not be seamless, but there is still much in common between active measures and the other branches of intelligence. The question of their relationship is a legitimate concern.

---

*For this reason, certain issues that have been of much concern to Congress, the media, and sections of the public are of no direct relevance in the framework of this study. This refers in particular to paramilitary operations in Nicaragua carried out by elements of the intelligence community, the Boland amendment, the "Tayacan" manual on "Psychological Operations in Guerrilla Warfare" (1983), and so forth.

Oversight

Assuming that intelligence will have a freer hand in the years to come than in the 1970s, assuming also that effective measures will be taken so that intelligence can engage in clandestine operations with improved hopes for success, how will effective control be established? Supervision should cover both the quality of intelligence and possible abuses. There are various official organs designed to attend to these duties, but none has proved very satisfactory in the past. The quality of intelligence will always be under some scrutiny, if only because the customers will evaluate its usefulness for their own work. But neither their satisfaction nor their complaints need be assumed accurate; only systematic monitoring can establish whether intelligence could have done better, and whether it has kept within its legitimate areas of activity.

Congress has conducted various hit-or-miss investigations of intelligence in the postwar period. Such inquiries have been mounted by the armed services and appropriations committees of both houses, by subcommittees of the House Permanent Select Committee on Intelligence, and others.[40] Some reports published by these committees were of interest; others did not serve any obvious purpose.[41] While congressional briefing by the most senior intelligence officials has benefited both Congress and the CIA, these committees are not really able to exercise a true oversight or evaluation function. Their members have only limited time to spare for this purpose, not all of them are adequately educated about intelligence, and membership of the committees changes—sometimes too frequently for the necessary continuity. Intelligence, for its part, has no wish to supply information beyond the call of duty. William Colby was a rare exception as DCI in this respect; senators and congressmen will usually be told the truth by those briefing them, but rarely the whole truth. Nor are the committees ordinarily equipped for systematic and detailed investigations.*

There is also always the danger that the committees' attitude toward intelligence, be it praise or criticism, will be dictated by party political considerations; a recent example of this phenomenon was the debate over Central American policy in 1982–83. There are aspects of intelligence that

---

*Standing Congressional intelligence committees exist only since 1976; their status was defined by the Intelligence Oversight Act of 1980. Today, the House Permanent Select Committee on Intelligence has three subcommittees dealing with legislation, oversight and evaluation, and program and budget. The Senate Oversight Committee has four subcommittees: collection and foreign operations, budget, legislation and the right of American citizens, and analysis and production. Furthermore, the CIA Directorate of Intelligence now has its own internal evaluation staff.

can and should be subject to congressional oversight, but it is difficult to envisage how committees of this kind can conduct systematic evaluation of intelligence performance. Commenting on "Soviet support for international terrorism and revolutionary violence," the chairman of the Congressional Subcommittee on Intelligence Oversight and Evaluation wrote to the deputy director of the CIA that "after an indisputably difficult production process, the result was a very high quality product."[42]

The chairman could, no doubt, comment intelligently on whether the SNIE was well written, whether it was well structured, with detailed evidence, or whether perhaps farfetched conclusions were drawn from a dubious factual basis. But he could not reasonably judge whether the SNIE in question was "a very high quality product." To make such an evaluation he would have had to know more about the subject than the intelligence community itself, which could not have been the case. A well written, well organized, seemingly objective intelligence estimate may still be fundamentally wrong. On some issues it is possible to know after a few weeks or months whether intelligence assessments were correct or not, in which case evaluation may be possible and indeed desirable. But for broader, long-term issues, years may have to pass before a definitive conclusion can be reached. It is beyond the capacity of congressional committees or subcommittees to engage in historical post mortems of this kind.

The president's Foreign Intelligence Advisory Board (PFIAB) played a role of importance under some presidents, such as Eisenhower, who created it, but not under others, such as Johnson. Members of the PFIAB have included distinguished scientists, corporation presidents, and retired senior naval and army officers. They have offered important technical and military advice, and on occasion important economic and political guidance.[43] The PFIAB met as a rule for two days every other month; it had a minute staff, which prevented leaks. But its post mortems on intelligence failures, or on the advisability of certain covert actions, apparently had limited impact.

When PFIAB was first established, it was meant to act as a quality control oversight group charged with seeing that intelligence performed effectively. Under the Carter administration the emphasis was placed on preventing abuses and punishing wrongdoing. Inquiries as to whether the administration was getting adequate intelligence on situations in Iran, Afghanistan, Cuba, Ethiopia, and so on, came only after some major setbacks to U.S. foreign policy had occurred; by this time the PFIAB had been abolished.[44] From the intelligence community's point of view, the fact that the PFIAB had only a small staff was no doubt a blessing, for the CIA and the other intelligence agencies knew from experience that if staffs operating in the name of prestigious senior bodies were large enough, they tended to become meddlesome, another bureaucratic impediment to their work.

The reconstituted (1982) PFIAB has shown much initiative, but it is too early to say whether it will enjoy much influence. In theory, PFIAB has direct access to the president.[45] But successive directors of intelligence have regarded the PFIAB as neither a formidable threat nor a strong ally; consequently, their cooperation with it has been less than wholehearted. The PFIAB has been regarded as a necessary evil, not to be antagonized unduly, but also not to be taken too much into confidence. This is probably a mistake; even for purely political reasons it is advisable for the intelligence community to work closely with the PFIAB in case things go wrong. Such cooperation would also help to secure greater backing in Congress.

Internal oversight bodies include the CIA general counsel and the inspector general. Both report directly to the DCI. The general counsel is technically responsible for ensuring that CIA operations are in compliance with the law, but he does not often initiate inquiries. While he has a sizable staff of lawyers, it is not certain that he is kept truly informed about the more sensitive intelligence operations. The inspector general has a similar function, but is also concerned with the level of CIA performance. In addition, his office acts as a forum for grievances by CIA personnel and engages in periodic inspections of CIA offices concerning both their effectiveness and their observation of regulations. Under certain conditions, the inspector general can be denied access, but this must be done by the DCI in person and in writing. It is likely that illegal activities and other intelligence shortcomings will occasionally escape the inspector general's attention.[46] Despite these shortcomings, and although the inspector general has never influenced "high policy," his office has played a positive role in the intelligence community.

True control over the CIA should by right have been exercised by the National Security Council—or, to be precise, by the various subcommittees it set up in the past (the 40 Committee, the Special Group, the 54/12 Group, and the 303 Committee), each of them slightly different in scope, outlook, and responsibility. The NSC was created in 1955, and is chaired by the president's national security adviser; other members are the chairmen of the Joint Chiefs of Staff. This group has been in charge of approving proposals for clandestine operations, and its importance in the decision-making process has been considerable. This is more than can be said for other groups, such as the NSC intelligence committee (SIG-1), various subcommittees (for example, on economic intelligence), the Resources Advisory Committee, and the Net Assessment Group, all of which hardly ever convened.[47]

A review of the oversight process shows that more can be done, both inside and outside government, to make the controls more effective. But, in the words of a former European secret service chief, "they [the elected authorities] have to trust in the final analysis the man whom they have appointed and his closest aides. It is difficult to control an intelligence service from within; it is impossible to do so from outside." This has been a permanent source of resentment for critics of intelligence. As they see it, directors of intelligence by definition cannot be trusted. Critics do not want to give a blank check to intelligence, yet there are many situations in which intelligence cannot succeed unless it has a free hand. Unfortunately, there seems to be no constitutional or practical remedy.

Some DCIs have tried to involve outside experts in the process of intelligence review, but such discussions of current problems and tactical issues have not always been fruitful. In the case of Allen Dulles's Princeton Group, periodic meetings with distinguished figures were successful in some areas, but failed in others. Similar attempts in Europe have not been more successful.[48] On the other hand, exchanges with outside experts on broad issues of political, scientific, or economic interest can be of considerable value to the intelligence community. Intelligence officers absorbed in day-to-day tactical work will frequently benefit from exchanges of views about long-term, strategic issues of which they may lose sight. While "ethical" control of intelligence from the outside is exceedingly difficult, the assessment of the quality of intelligence is entirely possible, given the openness of the American system. Such evaluations have been made with considerable competence by researchers from abroad without privileged access; it should be possible, therefore, to expect at least this much from others with at least some such access.[49]

Intelligence has many functions and aspects, and the problems confronting it are even more numerous. Very roughly, they can be summarized as follows:

1.   In contradiction to Sun Tzu and other Chinese and Western sages, the function of intelligence is more modest than is generally believed. It is a prerequisite for an effective policy or strategy, but it can never be a substitute for policy or strategy, for political wisdom or military power. In the absence of an effective foreign policy even the most accurate and reliable intelligence will be of no avail. True, those responsible for intelligence must act as if the fate of all mankind, or at least of their nation, depended on their success or failure. Seen in a wider perspective, there are periods and political constellations in which intelligence is more important than in others. Intelligence could have been of considerable importance in the immediate postwar period when the future of Europe and the Near East was in the balance. It is again of growing importance today in view of the

more or less equal strength of the two main power blocs. What the British historian David Dilks wrote about the eve of World War II applies with added force to the situation in the 1980s: "It is precisely when the resources are stretched and the tasks many, when the forces are evenly matched and the issue trembles in the balance, that good intelligence and sensitive interpretation matter most."[50] In a situation of this kind, even relatively minor factors may make a decisive difference. Intelligence must always be viewed within the wider framework of foreign policy. The crucial questions are: If what was not known had been known, would the outcome have been different? And conversely: If nothing had been known, would those in question have acted differently?

Seen in this light, many intelligence failures of recent decades mattered less than is commonly assumed. Even if U.S. policy makers had known about the weakening position of the Shah, or the anti-Amin coup in 1979, there is little they could have done about it. American leaders knew about the impending Polish military coup in November 1981, but this in no way changed their course of action. On the other hand, there have been instances in which available information would have been of great importance if decision makers had been willing to act upon it. Such willingness cannot be taken for granted. The British and French had fairly accurate facts and figures on German rearmament in the 1930s, but they were unwilling to act. The decisive factor, then, is always the capacity to make use of intelligence.

2. The performance of U.S. intelligence since World War II has been uneven. While it has pioneered technical means of collection, it has been weak on human intelligence. It has been excellent in ferreting out facts and figures, but it has been less accomplished in putting them into a coherent picture—analyzing trends, assessing situations, and warning of future contingencies. The objective difficulties facing HUMINT must not be underrated; the need for HUMINT has not decreased, but it has become fashionable to denigrate the importance of human assets because technical means are politically and intellectually more comfortable. On the other hand, the opportunities for hostile intelligence agents operating in democratic societies are incomparably greater than for their Western counterparts. Technical means of collection frequently do not result in unambiguous evidence. These seldom help in the assessment of intentions rather than capabilities, so that their uses for political intelligence are strictly limited. Yet precisely because U.S. intelligence has been so much better in technical intelligence than in HUMINT (including analysis), it has invested more and more in the former to the neglect of the latter.[51] Such overreliance on technical means of collection would be dangerous in any case. It is doubly dangerous at a time when intelligence faces additional requirements such

as state sponsored terrorism and the narcotics trade, for satellites are only of limited utility in coping with these new problems. And, the crucial importance of intelligence analysis quite apart, there is always the danger that the stream of information received through technical means may decrease, or even dry up.

3. The main reasons for intelligence failures have been discussed. To some extent such failures are inevitable, because indetermination prevails in international affairs. Yet certain events and trends are more predictable than others, and no one can fairly expect intelligence to do more than provide warnings based on probabilities. Bias is among the causes of intelligence failure most frequently adduced. It may take various forms, such as an unwillingness by analysts or consumers to accept evidence contradictory to their preconceived notions, or which is for some other reason inconvenient. Such bias has, on occasion, had fatal consequences. Yet bias has probably been of less overall importance than ignorance, lack of political sophistication and judgment, lack of training and experience, lack of imagination, the assumption that other people behave more or less as we do (mirror imaging), that their governments generally share our psychology, values, and political aims. The impacts of ideology and of nationalism, militant religions, and so forth, have always been difficult for deeply pragmatic and nonideological people to understand.

Other weaknesses have included the politicization of intelligence; bureaucratic reluctance to accept risks and to present unambiguous intelligence assessments; and reluctance on the part of consumers to pay attention to intelligence warnings. But these and other shortcomings are of minor importance in comparison with the basic weakness of inferior political knowledge and judgment. The inclination to exaggerate the role of bias and deception is as strong and constant as is the tendency to underrate incompetence and self-deception.

4. There have been periodic attempts to improve intelligence; most of them have had no positive effect. In the perspective of three decades, it has at least become clear which approaches do not work. This goes above all for attempts at organizational reform. Managerial principles that work in other fields are not necessarily applicable in intelligence—by and large, the less bureaucratization the better. While changes may become necessary in the light of new technical or other developments, frequent organizational change always has a detrimental, unsettling effect. The uselessness of most organizational changes should have been manifest a long time ago. Nevertheless, they seem to be forever with us, partly because of a feeling that "something ought to be done," and partly because such reforms are much easier to carry out than substantive changes that would improve the quality of intelligence. The overemphasis on organizational reform also

stemmed from the erroneous belief that America is particularly good at solving managerial problems.

Another misconception that has played a negative role is the belief that modern machinery (or gadgetry) will provide judgment superior to the human mind. The corollary of this error is the assumption that enough quantity automatically turns into a new quality; that is, if there is an unsolved question, more intelligence data will provide the answer. This may be so in some cases, but not in most instances. Technical means of collection already produce more information of certain kinds than can be analyzed, whereas other secrets cannot be penetrated at all. Lastly, there is the belief that if only intelligence were firmly grounded in certain "policy sciences" concepts, it could improve intelligence performance all along the line.

5. There is no panacea for providing better intelligence, no sensational breakthroughs or approaches which no one has thought of before. The only realistic prospect for genuine improvement depends upon prosaic measures. These include the recruitment of promising individuals, careful personnel evaluation, thorough assignment processes, extensive and systematic training in relevant subjects, a constant search for better means of collection, and the pursuit of efficiency with a minimum of bureaucratic procedure. To this one may add that analytical competition also has its uses and should be encouraged.

Intelligence agencies need employees in many fields; in some of them, technical proficiency may be an adequate criterion for recruitment. In others the requirements are broader, and while recruitment mistakes are unavoidable, there have to be mechanisms to remedy such errors. This refers not only to cases of incompetence or major deficiencies of character —intelligence can afford mediocrity only within limits. The record shows that relatively low priority has been given to the selection of recruits. The methods and requirements used ought to be reexamined.

Far greater emphasis ought to be given to training. The courses presently taught inside and outside the intelligence community constitute an advance in comparison with the state of affairs ten or fifteen years ago, but they are still quite insufficient. Intelligence needs either a high-quality central academy—or several such institutions—specializing in military, political, economic, and scientific-technological intelligence. Such an institution or institutions should engage in systematic, full-time training, employing the best talent available. There should be a heavy emphasis on subjects directly relevant to intelligence; in particular, subjects not systematically covered in university education should be stressed. Such study should be combined with practical work, at headquarters or in the field. In the course of a training period of several years, the specific abilities and weaknesses of the trainees would become obvious. Thus it would be easier to direct new members to the kind of work in which they are most likely to feel at home and achieve most.

Recruitment and training are critical for the future performance of intelligence. While lip service has always been paid to the need for superior recruitment and training, the attention actually devoted, the financial allocations made, and the quality of appointments tend to show that these tasks have never been given the priority they deserve.

6. Intelligence should never be satisfied with its performance. There will always be a great deal of reliable and detailed information on subjects not in demand, whereas information on the most urgent issues will often be sparse, unreliable, or even nonexistent. Unless intelligence tries constantly to improve its performance, it is bound to deteriorate. Intelligence is necessarily bureaucratic in structure and part of a wider bureaucratic network. Therefore it is always threatened by the negative features of bureaucracy, such as routine, innate conservatism, preoccupation with questions of procedure and organization rather than substance, and the stifling of creative thought and fresh initiatives. In the final analysis, intelligence will be judged by performance—not by the number of memoranda circulated or by adherence to rules established to promote the smooth functioning of a bureaucratic organization. In many respects intelligence is—or should be—the very antithesis of bureaucratic thought and practice. It can fulfill its functions only if it constantly resists the encroachment of bureaucratic routine. Eternal vigilance in this matter is the precondition of success.

7. The central effort of U.S. intelligence has been on strategic-military intelligence. The importance of knowledge about the Soviet strategic effort (and, to a lesser extent, that of other countries) or of the order of battle, need not be stressed. America's defense and that of its allies depend on the findings of intelligence in this field. But the decisive developments in world politics in the last decades have been political and economic in nature, a situation that is unlikely to change soon. These developments are taking place in Asia and Africa, in Europe and Latin America. It is much easier to monitor the deployment of missile launchers than the frequently intangible and inchoate political trends in faraway countries which cannot be quantified and are open to divergent interpretations. A reorientation of the intelligence effort in this direction is long overdue precisely because of these difficulties, and because certainties in the political field are so elusive. The shift of attention to the political scene raises the question whether intelligence should also serve as one of the tools of foreign policy— not only watching the course of events, but also trying to influence it.

8. There are various ways and means to exert influences abroad—

diplomacy, both public and secret; propaganda; aid and trade; friendly or hostile speeches; arms supplies; visits and conferences; the export of feature and propaganda films; and invitations to scholars. There are also active measures, carried out directly or through surrogates, which have come to play a central role in the Third World. Whether the United States is capable of undertaking an effort of this kind may be sometimes open to doubt; whether such operations should be executed by a separate organization may be debated at length. If ill-conceived or badly executed they will certainly do more harm than good. Active measures are not a game to be entered thoughtlessly or routinely. They constitute a weapon to be used in cases of dire necessity, but all the same, they are an integral part of the contemporary instrumentarium of foreign policy. Foregoing active measures may mean the paralysis and abdication of foreign policy. Intelligence without such a capacity is comparable to a warning system. But even a loud noise will not deter the burglar who knows that the neighbors are on vacation and that the police have instructions to look the other way.

9. Intelligence not only has to train new recruits but also to educate its customers. This is a formidable task because the latter, at a more advanced age, are very busy people, sure of their own judgment; some may be uneducable. They have to be convinced of what intelligence can, and what it cannot, achieve. They must learn that an overload of requests will result in diminishing returns; that intelligence should be taken into the confidence of policy makers if they wish to obtain relevant information. In short, there is everything to be said in favor of close cooperation. The old fears of intelligence being too close to the policy-making process, thus losing its independence, were misplaced. Much depends on the quality of the senior intelligence staff: if they are worthy of their responsible positions, they will not shield their superiors from inconvenient information. If, on the other hand, they lack sufficient backbone, or if the consumers are congenitally incapable of listening to unpleasant facts, it will not make any difference whether intelligence is organizationally close to, or remote from, the seats of power. It will be ignored anyway.

10. Intelligence needs both secrecy and supervision. A small think tank, working solely on the basis of open material, may provide as much —or more—valuable information and advice to a government than a big and bad secret service. But a research institute of this sort cannot possibly produce the kind of detailed military and political intelligence that governments need. Secret services can function only in secrecy; attempts to have them operate openly are futile.

The absence of real deterrents against leaking state secrets is not conducive to the effective working of intelligence. This is one of many unavoidable handicaps confronting intelligence services operating on behalf of democratic societies. Experience in other Western countries has shown that it is possible to maintain greater secrecy than the present prevailing level in the United States without surrendering reasonably effective control.

American intelligence ought to be subject to stringent supervision with regard to performance and possible abuse, from within the intelligence community, from within the White House, and from within Congress. Such control mechanisms have existed in the past, but they have not worked very well. They could be improved if greater authority were given to a small group of people of stature and energy exercising a full-time control function. While absolute control is impossible under the specific conditions in which a secret service operates, the very presence of such a body would deter abuses.

11. Intelligence is an essential service, but only a service. It is an important element in the decision-making process, but only one element; its usefulness depends entirely on how it is used and guided. It has been a factor of some importance in providing continuity, such as there was, to American foreign policy since World War II. It has contributed to the education of all levels of the U.S. foreign policy establishment. It can identify options and probabilities and illuminate the consequences of action or the failure to act. It has produced technological marvels without which U.S. strategic weapons policy would have been chaotic. Its performance can be improved. It has no access to revealed truths: the days of "Magic" are over in more sense than one.

NOTES

Introduction

1. David Wise and Thomas B. Ross, *The Invisible Government* (New York: Random House, 1964).

2. For information on such topics, see Roy Godson, ed., in vol. 3 of *Intelligence Requirements for the 1980s: Counterintelligence* (Washington, D.C.: National Strategy Information Center, 1981), and vol. 4: *Covert Action* (Washington, D.C.: National Strategy Information Center, 1981).

3. A partial exception must be made for *Three Days of the Condor,* in which Robert Redford plays an intelligence analyst. Some writers, such as Len Deighton and Ian Fleming, follow the lead of some early spy novels as William Le Queux's *Cipher Six* in their preoccupation with technical aspects such as cryptology, supplemented now by all kinds of electronic and computer wizardry.

4. Robin W. Winks, *Modus Operandi* (Boston: David R. Godine, 1982).

5. James R. Parrish and Michael R. Pitts, *The Great Spy Pictures* (Metuchen, N.J.: Scarecrow Press, 1974). Their list could be considerably augmented by the addition of French, German, Russian, and other foreign films. See also Leonard Rubenstein, *The Great Spy Films* (Secaucus, N.J.: Citadel Press, 1979).

6. The United States is not unique in this matter. Foreign secret services have gone through their own periods of trouble. The life expectancy of senior Soviet intelligence officials has improved since the time of Stalin, when few died a natural death. But even in the following years, from 1953 to 1967 (when Yuri Andropov took over), there was a rapid turnover at the KGB helm, and few of its directors escaped considerable trouble. For years the heads of Britain's MI 5 and MI 6 had to spend much of their time proving to various judges and committees that they and their staffs were neither incompetent nor enemy agents. Germany and France have had their own "intelligence crises" in the postwar period; luckily, those found wanting are no longer "terminated with extreme prejudice."

7. In the early 1960s Gordon Gray conducted an important survey of HUMINT and technical means of intelligence data collection. The resulting study has not been declassified to this day.

8. The critics are right to complain about the tendency of the intelligence bureaucracy to blanket almost everything with one of the "classified" labels available to them. In the 1950s a story made the rounds about how a copy of the "Communist Manifesto," transmitted to Washington from some exotic country in an equally exotic language, arrived stamped "Top Secret."

9. This is true, for instance, with regard to the battles of Jena, Wagram, and Preussisch Eylau, when Napoleon disregarded intelligence. Most of the time he was in ignorance of enemy movements and did not even know the fate of his own troops. He paid no attention to the warning of Caulaincourt, Segur, and others against the invasion of Russia.

10. Rear Admiral Claude Bloch, one of the participants, later wrote: "The Japanese only destroyed a lot of old hardware. In a sense they did us a favor." Gordon W. Prange, *At Dawn We Slept* (New York: Penguin Books, 1982), p. 737.

Chapter 1: The Production of Intelligence

1. The main sources on the foundation of the CIA are Thomas F. Troy, *Donovan and the CIA* (Frederick, Md.: Univ. Pubns. of America, Aletheia Books, 1981); Richard Dunlop, *Donovan: America's Master Spy* (Santa Monica, Calif.: Rand, 1982). Interesting material connected with the passing of the National Security Act of 1947 is contained in the *House Committee on Government Operations, For the Establishment of the Commission on Organization of the Executive branch of the Government,* 80th Cong., 1st sess., H.R. 2239, v. 6, 27 June 1947, declassified in 1982.

2. Anne Karalekas, *Supplemental Detailed Staff Reports on Foreign and Military Intelligence,* vol. 4: *History of the Central Intelligence Agency* (Laguna Hills, Calif: Aegean Park Press, 1977), p. 64.

3. Following the official CIA definition, the intelligence cycle "is the process by which information is acquired, converted into intelligence, and made available to policy makers." There are usually five steps that constitute the intelligence cycle: planning and direction, collection, processing, production and analysis, and dissemination. Yet the very concept of an "intelligence cycle" is unfortunate, for a cycle in accepted parlance is an orbit (as in astronomy) or, as in thermodynamics, a series of operations at the end of which the working substance is brought back to its original state. The whole goal of an intelligence operation is that at the end there should be more knowledge than at the beginning.

4. Quoted in R. Betts, "American Strategic Intelligence: Politics, Priorities and Direction," in R. L. Pfaltzgraff, U. Ra'anan, and W. Milberg, eds., *Intelligence, Policy and National Security* (Hamden, Conn.: Archon Books, 1981), p. 252. The saying is apocryphal, but Mr. Kissinger confirmed in conversation that if he did not say it, he easily might have done so.

5. Karalekas, *Supplemental Detailed Staff Reports.*

6. Murphy Report, House Commission on the Organization of the Government for the Conduct of Foreign Policy, June 1975, p. 35.

7. Dr. Rudolf Friedrich, *Neue Zürcher Zeitung,* 1 July 1981. From several West European countries the presence of East European trucks has been reported, measuring the width of the high roads and the strength of bridges. *L'Express,* 5 November 1982.

8. Frank Adcock and D. J. Mosley, *Diplomacy in Ancient Greece* (London: Thames & Hudson, 1975), p. 176.

9. Senate Committee on the Judiciary, Subcommittee to Investigate the Administration of the Internal Security Act and Other Internal Security Laws, *The Legacy of Alexander Orlov,* 93rd Cong., 1st sess., (Washington, D.C.: GPO, 1973), p. 83. Orlov's evidence was originally given in 1957 before the Senate Subcommittee on International Security.

10. The British files on penetration into Germany during the war are not accessible; the German files are for the time being our only source of information. On the time of the other Soviet parachutists, see Günther Nollau, *Gestapo ruft Moskau* (Munich: Blanvalet, 1979). There may have been one or two more agents who were not caught—Soviet sources have been reticent about the subject—but this is not certain.

11. Aerial reconnaissance by men in a balloon was apparently first used in the battle of Fleurus (July 1794), but photo intelligence was not applied systematically before World War I. The origins of modern SIGINT came a few years earlier when, in 1911, Austrian military intelligence (the *Evidenzbüro)* intercepted Italian signals exchanged during the war in North Africa. In 1914, during the first weeks of World War I, SIGINT was already widely used—by the Germans with farreaching consequences against the Russians in East Prussia, and by the French facing the German army advancing on Paris. According to some authorities, 90 percent or more of the usable intelligence in World War I was of SIGINT origin.

The real origins of SIGINT are to be found much further back, for the ancient Greeks and Romans (and many other peoples) used smoke signals at day and fire signals at night and these were, of course, also intercepted. There is a fine account in Aeschylus's *Agamemnon,* §281, of how the system worked; it is discussed in great detail in W. Riepl, *Das Nachrichtenwesen des Altertums* (Leipzig: B.G. Teubner, 1913).

12. Constance Babington-Smith, *Evidence in Camera* (London; Chatto & Windus, 1958); Roy M. Stanley II, *World War II Photo Intelligence* (New York: Scribner, 1981).

13. Remote sensing has many civilian applications, such as in the environmental sciences. Many textbooks on data acquisition and interpretation have been published during the past ten years, among them Thomas M. Lilles and Ralph W. Kiefer's *Remote Sensing and Image Interpretation* (New York: Wiley, 1979); *The Manual of Remote Sensing* Robert G. Reeves, ed., (Falls Church, Va.: American Society of Photogrammetry, 1975); Philip H. Swain and Shirley M. Davis, *Remote Sensing: The Quantitative Approach* (New York: McGraw-Hill, 1978); Eric C. Barrett

and Leonard F. Curtis, *Introduction to Environmental Remote Sensing,* 2d ed. (New York: Chapman & Hall, 1982); W. L. Smith, ed., *Remote-Sensing Applications for Mineral Exploration* (New York: Academic Press, 1977); Floyd F. Sabins Jr., *Remote Sensing: Principles and Interpretation* (San Francisco: W.H. Freeman, 1978) and others. On satellite launchings see, *Proceedings of the Institute of Electrical and Electronics Engineers,* Special Issue on Image Processing (May 1979).

14. The Iran posts were "line of sight" (LOS) and for this reason more reliable than the "over the horizon" (OTH) installation.

15. Cecil B. Jones, "Photographic Satellite Reconnaissance," *Proceedings of U.S. Naval Institute* (June 1980): 45. It has been calculated that a telelens with a focal length of 6 meters could be accommodated in the spacecraft and might result in a ground resolution of 15 cm. (six inches) from an altitude of 150 kilometers. Hans Arnbak, "Observations in Space, Past, Present, and Future," *NATO's Fifteen Nations* (April 1982). According to other sources, the resolution was even better than six inches, and the six-meter camera lenses were developed as early as 1959–60. On the part of Edwin Land and others in these initiatives, see James R. Killian, Jr., *Sputnik, Scientists and Eisenhower* (Cambridge, Mass.: MIT Press, 1977).

16. The part of the satellites in the detection of submarines remains modest for the time being. While submarines generate many disturbances it is not yet clear that they can be detected from space. James W. Lisanby and Reuven Leopold in *Sea Power* (April 1982): 140. Satellite communication, on the other hand, plays an important part in antisubmarine warfare. T. S. in *Scientific American* (February 1981).

17. Ronald Lewin, "A Signal Intelligence War," in *The Second World War,* ed. Walter Laqueur (London: Sage Publications, 1982), p. 184. For a divergent view in the same volume, see Ralph Bennett, "Ultra and Some Command Decisions," pp. 218ff.

18. The nomenclature has been the source of some confusion. The interception of emissions in radar frequency range has been known for the past decade as ESM—Electronic Support Measures. In practice, the various components of SIGINT are increasingly used in combination. On recent trends see *Defense Electronics* (April 1982): 13.

19. Far less has been written about SIGINT than about other branches of intelligence; satellite photos are widely circulated on occasion, whereas the list of recipients of SIGINT intercepts is very short indeed. The standard work on modern cryptology is David Kahn's *Codebreakers* (New York: Macmillan Co., 1967). For summaries of the state of the art, see the periodical *Cryptologia,* also edited by David Kahn. Cryptoanalysts have faced interesting problems in recent years, some of which were discussed in open meetings with academics. There is no such thing as an unbreakable cipher, at least in theory, quite apart from the fact that cryptographic secrets may be stolen by agents. It is assumed that the very complex keys used today for important messages are safe, but they are also costly and they may take too long to decrypt in situations in which speed is of the essence. And there is always the possibility, however remote, that even the most complex key may be broken as the result of some technical breakthrough, by a stroke of genius, by a mistake committed by an operator —or by means other than code breaking.

20. Only the United States and the Soviet Union operate photo intelligence satellites, but SIGINT is practiced by many nations. The United States cooperates in ocean surveillance with Great Britain, Canada, and Australia. This system is based on satellites code-named *Classic Wizard* and *White Cloud,* as well as on SIGINT direction findings—that is, location through radio transmission. Israel, and presumably other countries, practice a more primitive form of aerial photography by means of "drones"—small, unmanned aircraft that were also used for SIGINT purposes. Such photo intelligence methods can be quite effective for specific purposes.

21. A former director of the NSA (and deputy director of the CIA) has been quoted to the effect that SIGINT is not only infinitely more reliable than HUMINT but also beats photo intelligence "by a wave length." James Bamford, *The Puzzle Palace* (Boston: Houghton Mifflin, 1982), p. 378. According to this source, "SIGINT is the one that is immediate, right now" in contrast to HUMINT but also in contrast to photo intelligence, which can be misrepresented by the reader or intentionally made deceptive by those targeted. There is no denying the immediacy of SIGINT, but it is also true that it can be misused with equal ease. Radio frequencies and communication channels are changed and codes modified. It can be taken for granted that through Soviet agents such as Geoffrey Prime (arrested in Britain in 1982), misleading information was fed by means of SIGINT. The question whether deception by means of SIGINT is difficult or not remains a live issue among the experts. See the debate of the Consortium for the Study of Intelligence meeting in *Intelligence Requirements* vol. 5:

Clandestine Collection ed. Roy Godson, Godson (Washington, D.C.: National Strategy Information Center, 1982), pp. 118–25. The experts have not even been able to agree on whether SIGINT is the cheapest or the most expensive form of intelligence collection.

22. Amrom Katz, *Verification and SALT: The State of the Art and the Art of the State* (Washington, D.C.: Heritage Foundation, 1979).

23. Senate Select Committee to Study Governmental Operations with Respect to Intelligence Activities, Final Report, vol. 1: *Foreign and Military Intelligence,* 94th Cong., 2d sess., no. 94–755 (Washington: GPO, 1976). Analysts have never attained the highest positions in the agency.

24. This tradition was continued in the National Intelligence Studies (NIS) encyclopedic handbooks on various areas and problems.

25. See Victoria S. Price, *The DCI's Role in Producing Strategic Intelligence Estimates,* Naval War College, 1980.

26. DCID, "Production of National Intelligence Estimates," 9 January 1953.

27. Price, *The DCI's Role,* p. 39.

28. NIE: 11–4–57.

29. John Whitman, "On Estimating Reaction," *Studies in Intelligence* (n.d., internal CIA periodical).

30. Price, *The DCI's Role,* p. 55.

31. The ONE had been headed for many years by distinguished academicians, first by William Langer and subsequently (for sixteen years) by Sherman Kent. Kent was succeeded by Jack Abbott Smith, also a former university professor. John Huizinga was the last director of the ONE. Other prominent members of the ONE were the historian Raymond Sontag and the economist Calvin Hoover. Ray Cline mentions in his memoirs that the ONE never exceeded a hundred staff members, whereas the then DCI (Bedell Smith) had suggested an office of about a thousand people. Ray Cline, *The CIA under Reagan, Bush and Casey* (Washington, D.C.: Acropolis Books, 1981), p. 142. On the debate concerning the abolition of the ONE, see Murphy Report app. U, p. 37ff.

32. Lt. Gen. Daniel Graham, a former head of DIA, relates that in his whole career he witnessed only one such case, when General Curtis Le May (of SAC fame) exerted pressure at a time when he thought that air force intelligence was dangerously wrong. Daniel O. Graham, "The Intelligence Mythology of Washington," *Strategic Review 4,* (Summer 1976): 63.

33. Sherman Kent, "Estimates and Influence," *Foreign Service Journal* (April 1969): 18.

34. Harry Howe Ransom, *The Intelligence Establishment* (Cambridge: Harvard University Press, 1970), p. 147. There have been great fluctuations in the number of NIEs published annually. It fell to an all-time low of about a dozen annually in the late 1970s, but then rose to thirty-eight in 1981. Philip Taubman, "Casey and His CIA on the Rebound," *New York Times,* 16 January 1983.

35. The House Select Committee on Intelligence noted an improvement in the quality of the NIEs in the 1980s. Its 1985 report said that "The Committee is pleased that the current Director of Central Intelligence has continued and expanded the effort to improve the NIE process." Report on the Activities of the Permanent Select Committee (Washington, D.C.: GPO, 1985), p. 12. Other sources reported that the number of NIEs had grown from twelve in the last year of the Carter administration to about fifty in 1984. John Lelyveld, "The Director," *New York Times,* 20 January 1985; Robert M. Gates, "Is the CIA's Analysis Any Good?" *Washington Post,* 12 December 1984. Mr. Gates is at present CIA deputy director for intelligence, the final approving official for all daily production of current intelligence that goes to the president and senior government officials.

36. In view of universal bureaucratic practice it can safely be assumed that other intelligence agencies also publish too much. It has been the practice in some countries for many years to bring out long estimates, supplemented by a short (one or two pages) and a medium-sized (five to ten pages) version to assure that the message will get across.

Chapter 2: Economic and Scientific Intelligence

1. The "Oslo report" was one of the most important documents in World War II intelligence. This was a list of Germany's most important scientific and technological advances in the military field, sent anonymously to the British naval attaché in Oslo in November 1939.

It included essential technical details. The text of this amazing document appears as Appendix V in F. H. Hinsley, ed., *British Intelligence in the Second World War*, vol. 1, (London: Cambridge Univ. Press, 1979). See also volume 3 of *British Intelligence* (London: Cambridge Univ. Press, 1983) for the importance of economic intelligence in World War II.

2. Recently, there has been a general trend to upgrade economic intelligence. Australian intelligence experts (just one example) have suggested the establishment of a National Economic Intelligence Agency which would be responsible for all reports and assessments on international affairs.

3. For the first decade of its existence the CIA covered only Soviet bloc and Chinese economic activities. According to a formal agreement in March 1965 between the DCI and Secretary of State Dean Rusk, the CIA was permitted to engage in worldwide economic intelligence cover. Previously the Department of State had a monopoly on non-Communist economic intelligence. This ratified a practice started in 1956—following Soviet bloc activities in less developed countries (LDCs). Nevertheless, economic intelligence, unlike scientific intelligence, was not given a directorate of its own. Until 1967, it remained a subsection of the Office of Research and Reports which belonged to the Directorate of Intelligence. It then became the Office of Economic Research (OER), still within the same general framework. Following yet another report in the 1970s, one of the eleven national intelligence officers was given special responsibility for economic intelligence. Because foreign economic policy is conducted by several government departments and agencies, the circle of economic intelligence consumers is fairly wide, including the Department of State, the Treasury, and the Departments of Commerce and Agriculture.

4. In October 1978 the CIA published an excellent research paper, *USSR: Toward a Reconciliation of Marxist and Western Measures of National Income*, ER: 78–10505. It is one example of the useful research carried out by CIA analysts, that is indispensable for the more eye-catching overall surveys of Soviet performance.

5. Winston S. Churchill, *The Grand Alliance*, vol. 3 of the *The Second World War*, (London: Cassel, 1950), pp. 189–90.

6. See for example the gloomy picture drawn for Germany in Gustav Stolper's *German Realities* (New York: Reynal & Hitchcock, 1948).

7. "Russian Foreign Trade Developments," R & A, no. 2060, 9 September 1944, declassified in 1972.

8. Zbigniew Brzezinski, "How the Cold War Was Played," *Foreign Affairs* (October 1972): 188–209.

9. Average annual GNP growth in the U.S.S.R. from 1954–58 was 7.7 percent (versus 2.5 percent in the United States).

10. "The Gross National Product in the Soviet Union: Comparative Growth Rates," a contribution to the 1962 Joint Economic Committee's *Dimensions of Soviet Economic Power*, 87th Cong., 2d sess., pursuant to sec. 5(a) of public law 304, 79th Cong., (Washington, D.C.: GPO, 10 and 11 December 1962), 67–90.

11. Ibid., p. 42. The 1970 ratio, as recorded in Herbert Block's *Planetary Product in 1980* (Washington, D.C.: CSIS Georgetown University, 1981), Table 1, was 49:100.

12. The actual GNP rates for the U.S.S.R. and the United States were 5.2 versus 3.2 percent for 1962 over 1957 and 5.2 versus 3.9 percent for 1970 over 1960.

13. *Dimensions of Soviet Economic Power*, pp. 40–42.

14. See, for instance, a paper by Richard F. Kaufman on *The Defense Build-up and the Economy*, a staff study prepared for a subcommittee of the Joint Economic Committee of Congress (Washington, D.C.: GPO: 17 February 1982). In this timely and wide-ranging report, Kaufman deals with a "defense inflation gap" created by an insufficient deflation of estimated future defense outlays (the Department of Defense [DOD] deflator rises faster than the GNP deflator), and he complains of inadequate information about the defense sector.

15. The disputes over Soviet military spending will be briefly discussed. In March 1983 some CIA experts claimed that previous estimates of an annual increase of 3–4 percent may have been exaggerated and that the rate of growth may have been closer to 2 percent. This was based on the fact that less Soviet military material had been observed and counted than had been expected. Others—in the CIA, and above all in the DIA—argued that weapons systems had become costlier all over the world and that Soviet military spending could not therefore be deducted simply from the number of weapons counted. This was in addition to the fact that counts of this kind are always open to doubt and that it is most difficult to compare American and Soviet industrial efficiency.

16. Central Intelligence Agency, *The International Energy Situation: Outlook to 1985,* CIA-ER: 77–10240, (Washington, D.C.: GPO, April 1977).

17. Ibid., p. 13.

18. Central Intelligence Agency, *Prospects for Soviet Oil Production,* CIA-ER: 77–10270, (Washington, D.C.: GPO, April 1977).

19. See, for example, J. Richard Lee, "The Soviet Petroleum Industry," in Joint Economic Committee, *Soviet Economic Prospects for the Seventies,* 94th Cong., 2d sess., (Washington, D.C.: GPO, 27 June 1973), pp. 283–90; Emily E. Jack, J. Richard Lee, and Harold H. Lent, "Outlook for Soviet Energy," in Joint Economic Committee, *Soviet Economy in a New Perspective: A compendium of papers* 94th Cong., 2d sess., (Washington, D.C.: GPO, 14 October 1976), 460–78. See also Herbert Block, "Energy Syndrome, Soviet Version," Jack M. Hollander, ed., *Annual Review of Energy,* vol. 2 (Palo Alto, Calif.: Annual Reviews, 1977), pp. 455–97.

20. Herbert Block, "U.S.-Soviet Ratios and Relations," *Washington Review* #1, no. 1 (January 1978): 116–17 (since renamed *The Washington Quarterly*). Seen from the perspective of 1983, OPEC production and Western demand had also been greatly overrated; even in 1979 a CIA study erred by 40 percent. But many other experts made the same mistake, failing to realize that the price rises were bound to bring down consumption. Donald F. B. Jameson, "CIA Petroleum Prophecy," *Washington Post,* 29 March 1983.

21. For example, the widely read *Energy: Global Prospects 1985–2000, Report of the Workshop on Alternative Energy Strategies,* a project sponsored by the Massachusetts Institute of Technology (New York: McGraw-Hill, 1977).

22. Defense Intelligence Agency, "Allocation of Resources in the Soviet Union and China —1981," 8 July 1981, pp. 41, 42, 50.

23. Those engaged in "disinformation" and penetration of the Western secret services *may* number more, especially of late.

24. Technical intelligence concerning fortifications, naval bases, and new weapons was part of the standard fare of "classical espionage" even before World War I.

25. While British intelligence was quite unprepared for a major scientific technological effort in 1939, it rapidly made up for the delay; by 1942–43, it was well ahead of U.S. intelligence. The story is admirably told in Reginald Victor Jones, *Most Secret War* (London: Hamilton, 1978).

26. Thomas J. Kuehn and Alan L. Porter, *Science, Technology and National Policy* (Ithaca, N.Y.: Cornell University Press, 1981), p. 205.

27. Even after the foundation of the Science Directorate, a considerable part of the Science and Technology intelligence effort remained outside the CIA. Several committees were set up to coordinate these efforts and exchange information, such as the SIGINT Committee, the Scientific Intelligence Committee, the Guided Missile Astronautics Intelligence Committee, the Joint Atomic Energy Intelligence Committee, and so forth. The Science and Technology Directorate is today divided into seven subsections; their names are not always a clear indication of their activities (for example, "Office of Special Projects," "Office of Special Activities," and so on). The annual budget of TSD was thought to be about $120 million in the early 1970s and is, no doubt, considerably higher now. These figures are to some extent misleading, for the costs of the planning, construction, and maintenance of modern collection systems are very high and have to be covered by the air force or other outside agencies with larger budgets at their disposal.

28. Anna Karalekas, *Supplemental Detailed Staff Reports on Foreign and Military Intelligence,* vol. 4 of *History of the Central Intelligence Agency* (Laguna Hills, Calif: Aegean Park Press, 1977), p. 78.

29. Harry V. Martin, "Electronics Remains Keystone to U.S. Intelligence Mission," *Defense Electronics* 13 (December 1981): 71–72.

30. When it became known that the late Gamal Abdul Nasser suffered from diabetes, the results of his laboratory tests became a matter of priority for various intelligence services. The state of Mr. Brezhnev's health was a topic of enormous solicitude (and remote diagnosis) probably without parallel in the annals of medicine.

31. These leaders also developed the SR-71, successor to the U-2. Initial work on a reconnaissance satellite was carried out by the air force, but discontinued in 1956. The Developments Project Division (DPD) under Richard Bissell took over; the DPD later became part of the Directory of Plans headed by Bissell, whose stay in the CIA was relatively short (1953–62). The DPD operated quite independently from either the Technical Services Direction (also belonging to DPD), which provided technical operational support for covert action, and the Office of Strategic Intelligence (OSI), which was part of the Directorate of Intelligence

and conducted basic scientific research. The early administrative history of scientific intelligence is highly complicated; it was mainly due to Bissell's strong personality that a unified Science-Technology Directorate did not come into being prior to 1963, for such a body would, by necessity, have been outside his control.

32. See chapter 3, "Intelligence and Its Consumers."

33. There has been in the work of the Directorate of Science and Technology a traditional stress on technology rather than on other subjects. The same is true, incidentally, with regard to the work done by the president's scientific advisors. William T. Golden, ed., *Technology in Society* vol. 2, no. 1–2 (New York: Pergamon Press, 1980), p. 55. But the reasons were different, intelligence followed the "technological imperative," whereas the presidential advisers learned by trial and error that issues other than those connected with physical sciences (for instance, biomedical research) were politically far more contentious and likely to land them in trouble.

34. In the intelligence community, there is a special technical assessment agency, the name of which is kept secret, which monitors high technology developments throughout the world and the shipment of U.S. technology to foreign countries, with special emphasis on laser and electronics technology. Harry V. Martin, *Defense Electronics* 13 (December 1981): 62.

35. Paul Hoffman, "The Crypto Censors," *Science Digest* (July 1982) and many other publications in 1981–82. Other areas of contention were biotechnology and VHSIC (Very High Speed Integrated Circuits). See, for instance, *Military Electronics/Countermeasures* (January 1982): 60–66. There is, of course, a wider problem. In some sections of the academic community there has been reluctance (or unwillingness) to collaborate with intelligence. This has partly to do with the negative public image of intelligence, even though none of these agencies is involved in the design or production of means of mass destruction. (Ironically, they have concentrated on the technology of reconnaissance, without which there could be no arms control.) But there is also the belief that in science as in the arts, there should be no national boundaries, that new discoveries should be shared and that, generally speaking, "patriotism invading the realm of science is a dirty wretch who should be thrown out" (Arthur Schopenhauer, *Parerga und Paralipomena,* vol. 2 (Leipzig: P. Reclam, 1891), p. 523). These scientists recall the problematical role played by their predecessors in both camps in World War I. There were no such scruples preventing contributions to the war effort in World War II, but with the development of modern arms technology, hesitation to cooperate with governments has increased. Schopenhauer was probably right—the establishment of national frontiers in science is a major misfortune. Yet so was the emergence of totalitarian governments depriving whole nations of the freedom of movement and strictly censoring intellectual exchanges. Sharing of information under these conditions is a one-sided affair. Western nations practice it in any case, simply by being open societies. But some information will be kept secret as long as antagonistic political systems and national states exist, just as producers of certain foods and drinks will keep their special recipes secret as long as competition exists.

36. American intelligence has always tended to be preoccupied with the radical discontinuity and the cataclysmic at the expense of detecting the slow change, the trend, the subtle variations in mood, atmosphere, or firmness of resolve that may be more important. The most obvious examples are the preoccupation ever since the Korean War with indications of the outbreak of major hostilities and with coups d'état at the expense of efforts to understand the subtler dynamics of other governments, the pressure upon them, and the potential of groups contending for power.

37. Russell Jack Smith, a former DDI, has provided some insights into new techniques for assisting intelligence analysis that came into use in the early 1970s:

"One such [text processing] system would display incoming cables on the analyst's desk, machine sorted appropriately for his individual mission and coded by number. Scanning these cables on the video tube before him the analyst would select those items he would like to have delivered to his desk for more intensive study and comparison with other material. . . . Another system just coming into use which will be widely available . . . stores information in such a way that it is retrievable by key phrases punched on a console on an analyst's desk. It can provide the sentence in which the key phrase, or proper name, appears and can provide sentences both immediately preceding and succeeding. The context enables the analyst to decide whether he needs to see the full report or can reject it. This system has the greatest utility for handling information which is easily codified."

Russell Jack Smith, "Intelligence Support for Foreign Policy in the Future," App. U to Murphy Report: House Commission on the Organization of the Government for the Conduct of Foreign Policy, *Intelligence Functions Analyses,* (Washington, D.C.: GPO, June 1975), 85. Such innovation in intelligence support helps the analyst to scan the daily traffic—the flow of cables that reach their desks. It is a useful contraption to speed up this process, but not a qualitative breakthrough. It has not resulted in better intelligence.

38. A striking example was a series of important articles in the French newspaper *Le Monde* during the spring of 1978 on events in Iran. These were only taken into account by the intelligence community after an academic had called them to high-level White House attention in the fall of that year. British intelligence ignored the Argentinian press campaign immediately prior to the invasion of the Falkland islands. According to the Franks report (January 1983) this was one of the main reasons for the intelligence failure. A senior U.S. Government official noted in 1982 that overt sources were still inadequately exploited and inadequately appreciated, and that little enthusiasm could be found in the intelligence community for information derived from open sources. Roy Godson, ed., *Intelligence Requirements* vol. 5: *Clandestine Collection* (Washington, D.C.: National Strategy Information Center, 1982), pp 123–24.

39. Tom Forester, ed., *The Microelectronics Revolution* (Cambridge, MIT Press, 1981).

40. Ibid., p. 231.

41. *LEEA Newsletter,* December 1979; C. R. Swanson and Leonard Territo, "Computer Crime," *Journal of Police Science and Administration* 8, no. 1 (1980).

42. Senate Committee on Government Operations, *Staff Study of Computer Security in Federal Programs,* 95th Cong., 1st sess., February 1977, "The Central Intelligence Agency," p. 134ff.

43. "Data Communications Dependent upon Encryption from Security," *Defense Electronics* 13 (December 1981); "New Code is Broken," *Science,* (28 May 1982); Paul Hoffman, "The Crypto Censors," *Science Digest,* (July 1982).

44. Leslie D. Ball, "Computer Crime," *Technology Today* (April 1982).

45. A British Security Commission which published its findings in 1982 stated that the use of computers in public service for the storage and retrieval of classified information was the area of physical security that caused the greatest disquiet. "The amount of data that is capable of being stored upon a single disk or magnetic tape and the rapidity approaching instantaneity with which the data can be retrieved means that any vulnerability to access by hostile intelligence services of material stored in computers or word processors could be a major disaster to this country and in particular to the efficacy of those involved in intelligence work." *Statement on the Recommendations of the Security Commission,* Cmnd. 8540 (1982).

It is not fanciful to assume that the same worries apply to the United States. True, the British situation may be different in certain respects as there was even greater computer concentration in Britain than in the United States. But other observations made by the British committee apply equally to America. The system of codewords and personal keys for preventing unauthorized access may become or may now be no longer adequate as rapid changes take place in computer and microchip technology. This kind of computer penetration had gone on for years. Working from a base near Vienna, the Soviet Union has established computer links with an unclassified commercial data service and with British installations that enabled them to carry out complex nuclear design calculations for which their own computers were not suited. Above all, there is, and will continue to be, a great demand outside the public sector for those with the highest form of expertise in this field. There is a comparatively rapid turnover of computer staff after they have acquired the skill and experience that enables them to earn higher salaries elsewhere. Compared with other officials, computer staff have to be regarded from the security point of view as birds of passage. And this in turn means that in the case of classified information stored in computers there are likely to be persons outside the government with intimate knowledge of the programming and the hardware and software of the computers in which governmental information is stored.

46. Doyle E. Larson, *Journal of Electronic Defense,* (August 1982) 41–46.

47. A typical example was the case of a high-technology computer system for enhancing photographic images from satellites which was sold to Great Britain under a valid export license and was sent on from there to the Soviet Union in 1981. In addition, "front corporations" shipped fifty high-energy laser mirrors to the Soviet Union through consignees in West Germany and Switzerland. In yet another case, also in California, two individuals were convicted for exporting state-of-the-art computers and other equipment to West Germany to be forwarded to the Soviet Union.

48. The same refers to Soviet interest in other industrially developed countries. Of the forty-odd Soviet citizens expelled from France in early 1983 the majority had engaged in technological espionage. For a comprehensive list of major fields of technology of interest to Soviet intelligence see F. Kapper "Soviet Acquisition of Western Technology," *Signal,* January 1983; see also E. A. Burkhalter in *Signal,* March 1983.

49. CIA, *Soviet Acquisition of Western Technology,* April 1982.

50. Gerhard Mally, "Technology Transfer Controls," *Atlantic Community Quarterly* 20, no. 3 (Fall 1982): 233–38; Senate Committee on Government Operations, Permanent Subcommittee on Investigations, *Transfer of High U.S. Technology to the Soviet Union and Soviet Bloc Nations,* 97th Cong., 2d sess., May 1982.

51. In one recent spy case (Bell-Zacharski), information was acquired by Soviet intelligence (operating through Polish agents) on the "Stealth" bomber, on "look-down, shoot-down" radar, on a new rapid-firing, radar-controlled antiaircraft gun, and on a new antitank missile. On Soviet collection of Western scientific and technological intelligence see CIA, *Soviet Acquisition of Western Technology,* April 1982; and *Scientific Communication and National Security,* Washington, 1982, in particular the memorandum from the intelligence subpanel, pp. 91–96. See also Senate Subcommittee on Investigations, *Transfer of United States High Technology to the Soviet Union and Soviet Bloc Nations, Report of the Committee on Governmental Affairs,* 97th Cong., 2d sess., (Washington, D.C.: GPO, 15 November 1982).

52. It is widely known that many more scientists and engineers are trained in the Soviet Union than in the United States. The U.S. federal budget for basic applied research in constant dollars was the same in 1982 as in 1972. Center for the Study of Intelligence Strategy, *R & D for National Strength,* ed. David Williamson (Washington, D.C.: CSIS Georgetown University 1982).

Chapter 3: Intelligence and Its Customers

1. Harry S. Truman, *Year of Decision,* vol. 1 of *Memoirs by Harry Truman* (Garden City, N.Y.: Doubleday, 1956), pp. 98, 226.

2. Dean Acheson, *Present at the Creation* (New York: W.W. Norton, 1969), pp. 159–62.

3. Anne Karalekas, *Supplemental Detailed Staff Reports on Foreign and Military Intelligence,* vol. 4: *History of the Central Intelligence Agency* (Laguna Hills, Calif: Aegean Park Press, 1977).

4. *Presidents of the United States on Intelligence.* Central Intelligence Agency, November 1976, pp. 12–13. *Washington Post,* December 22, 1963. "What Did Truman Say About CIA?" in *Studies in Intelligence* (n.d., internal CIA periodical). Thomas Troy, "Truman and the CIA" in *Studies in Intelligence* (n.d.).

5. Allen Dulles et al, *The CIA and National Organization for Intelligence* (Washington, D.C.: GPO, 1949).

6. Ray S. Cline, *The CIA under Reagan, Bush and Casey* (Washington, D.C.: Acropolis Books, 1981).

7. Gordon Gray, interview with Victoria Price, 28 May 1980. For more on Eisenhower and intelligence, see Steven E. Ambrose and Richard H. Immerman, *Ike's Spies: Eisenhower and the Espionage Establishment* (New York: Doubleday, 1981).

8. Ray Cline, interviews with V. Price, 8 November 1978.

9. Andrew Goodpaster, interview with V. Price, 9 April 1980.

10. Bromley Smith, interview with V. Price, 12 September 1978; John Bross, interview with V. Price, 29 May 1979.

11. Sherman Adams, Papers of John Foster Dulles, Oral History Collection, Princeton University, Princeton, N.J.

12. Gordon Gray, interview with V. Price.

13. Released by the Eisenhower Library, the *Memoranda of Telephone Conversations of John Foster Dulles* are written summaries of most of the phone conversations of the secretary of state, including those with the president. They were usually prepared by Dulles's secretary, Phyllis Bernau (Macomber). A few remain classified.

14. Robert Amory, interview with V. Price, 6 March 1980.

15. *Memoranda of Telephone Conversations of John Foster Dulles,* telephone call to Allen Dulles, 21 May 1954, 5:15 P.M.

16. Ibid., 19 April 1954, 8:50 A.M.

17. Eleanor Lansing Dulles, interviews with V. Price, 2 May 1978 and Eleanor Lansing Dulles, Papers of John Foster Dulles, Princeton University Oral History Collection, pp. 93–94; Kermit Roosevelt, interviews with V. Price, 13 October 1978 and 1 April 1980; Gordon Gray, interview with V. Price.

18. Arthur M. Schlesinger, Jr., *A Thousand Days* (New York: Houghton Mifflin, 1965), p. 428; Roger Hilsman, *To Move a Nation* (Garden City, N.Y.: Doubleday, 1967), p. 46.

19. John Bross, interview with V. Price.

20. Cline, *The CIA Under Reagan,* p. 221.

21. This briefest of summaries does not, of course, do justice to McCone's position on Vietnam. He modified his position between 1961 and 1963, and again after the Diem coup in 1963.

22. As Congress became more active in foreign policy making in the late 1960s, CIA relations with Congress assumed considerable importance. According to John Maury, the DCI and his deputy averaged some thirty to thirty-five committee appearances annually, not counting a hundred individual briefings and an average of over a thousand written communications. Maury says that "all of our Directors have subscribed to the view that the Congress was entitled to know as much about the Agency and its activities as it thought necessary to carry out its responsibilities." But he also notes a few paragraphs later that "a week rarely passes that we don't have a couple of real lulus—perhaps a request from the Foreign Relations Committee for copies of certain National Estimates. . . ." John M. Maury, "CIA and the Congress," in *Studies in Intelligence,* (n.d., internal CIA periodical).

23. Central intelligence is barely mentioned in Nixon's and Kissinger's memoirs. The CIA is mentioned only three times in President Carter's *Keeping Faith* (New York: Bantam, 1982); Admiral Stansfield Turner also appears three times, but always as a participant among several others in some meeting or another. The same lack of coverage is true with regard to many other books written by public figures covering the late 1960s and the 1970s. The authors would not have endangered national security by disclosing secrets, but if intelligence would have had a decisive effect on policy making, there certainly would have been hints and allusions. Journalists and authors who work without such constraints have not written much on the impact of intelligence on policy either. Thomas Powers in his massive book on Richard Helms *(The Man Who Kept the Secrets,* New York: Alfred A. Knopf, 1979) altogether has two or three pages about Helms's relations with Johnson and Nixon and the function the CIA fulfilled in providing intelligence for policy making. Hundreds of books and countless articles have been published on Castro's poisoned cigars and other such topics, but with very few exceptions there has been nothing about intelligence proper. Such absence of comment may reflect the lack of overall impact intelligence has had on policy making.

24. The primary function of the IOB was not to supervise the intelligence community or the CIA but to be a "Super Inspectorate General," designed chiefly to guard against abuses. In actual fact, it was preoccupied with trivia.

25. Among the reasons given for the sackings was that the large cohort who had entered service in the early years of the Cold War outnumbered younger staff and blocked advancement. There is some truth in this, but the newcomers were not always of the same caliber. Another reason was that the operational side of the agency had been bloated as a result of Vietnam. This, too, was true but it had resulted in starving other CIA activities that had to be restored. In any case, the sackings caused much bad blood and demoralization, but the fact that individuals suffered was, though regrettable, less important in the long run than the decline in the quality of intelligence.

26. Paradoxically, Carter was the most voracious reader of intelligence since Kennedy. Nixon, Ford, and Regan reportedly sometimes did not even read the executive summaries of intelligence reports.

27. HPSCI, Report, 2 January 1985, p. 2.

28. Chester Cooper, "The CIA and Decision Making," *Foreign Affairs* 50 (January 1972): 227.

29. Lyndon Baines Johnson, *The Vantage Point* (New York: Rinehart & Winston, 1971).

30. Richard M. Nixon, *The Memoirs of Richard Nixon* (New York: Grosset & Dunlap, 1978), pp. 515, 920. Henry Kissinger, in *Years of Upheaval* (Boston: Little, Brown, 1982), pp. 459–64, mentions that the DCI had forwarded a report in May 1972 according to which the Egyptian general staff had been ordered to prepare a detailed plan for crossing the Canal. At the same time INR reported that "in our view the resumption of hostilities by autumn will become a better than even bet." But by late September the CIA appraisal was that Sadat

would not attack, and INR too had abandoned its prediction. Even after the war actually had broken out the intelligence agencies announced that they could not find hard evidence of a major coordinated Egyptian/Syrian offensive across the Canal and in the Golan Heights. According to the same sources, it was at most a raid or some other such small-scale action that had escalated into something bigger—"an action-reaction situation" (p. 458). It remains to be added that intelligence during the first week of fighting was equally bad. Answering the question, "Why were we surprised?" Kissinger responds that the breakdown was not administrative but intellectual. Following (at the very latest) the Soviet evacuation of their dependents from the Middle East on 5 October, it should have been clear that big events were impending, not just another state in the action-reaction cycle: "We uncritically accepted the Israel assessment . . . we had become too complacent about our own assumptions. We knew everything but understood too little" (p. 467). A CIA post mortem prepared in later years reached the same conclusion—the facts were known but they did not register.

31. Sherman Kent, *Strategic Intelligence for American World Policy* (Princeton: Princeton University Press, 1951), pp. 195–201. For many years this remained the basic text on the subject.

32. Walter Lippmann, *Public Opinion* (New York: Harcourt, Brace & Co, 1922), chap. 26. Sherman Kent did not go so far; of the two dangers—that intelligence might be too far from the users, or too close—he thought the greater danger was that of remoteness.

33. For contemporary sources, see Roger Hilsman, *Strategic Intelligence and National Decision* (Glencoe, Ill., Free Press, 1956), p. 89.

34. Victoria Price, p. 38. Dulles drew a fine line (perhaps often blurred or overstepped in practice) between discussing policy implications and making policy recommendations. Helms followed his example.

35. The problem of finding the right balance exercised minds with regard to the question as to whether intelligence should be organized "geographically" or "functionally." Obviously both kinds of structure are needed, according to conditions.

36. Cord Meyer, *Facing Reality* (New York: University Press of America, 1978), p. 361.

37. Arthur S. Hulnick and Deborah Brammer, *The Impact of Intelligence on the Policy Review and Decision-Making Process. Part One: Findings,* (Washington: Center for the Study of Intelligence, CIA, 1980), p. 7; R. J. R. Heuer, "Cognitive Biases," *Studies in Intelligence* 22, (n.d., internal CIA periodical): 21.

38. The studies ranged from "Conventional Arms Transfers" to "Economic Implications of a Middle East Peace" to "Assessments of the Situations in the Horn of Africa and in Nicaragua."

39. Focusing on perceptions makes it impossible to judge whether the intelligence was really more helpful or less helpful. The difficulty is partly of the investigator's own making, for as has been shown, it is easy to exaggerate the importance of cognitive biases: the distance between reality and perception is not necessarily always that great. Furthermore, the researchers linked their investigation to a certain type of intelligence product, long- and medium-range studies. Such studies are prestigious, but they usually have little impact on actual high-level policy making. An excellent major document may be totally ignored by policy makers, whereas an item of raw intelligence transmitted in a crisis situation may be of decisive importance.

40. If one excludes the unusually long terms of duty by Dulles (1953–61) and Helms (1966–73), the average comes out just short of two years per director.

41. William J. Barnds, in App. U to Murphy Report: House Commission on the Organization of the Government for the Conduct of Foreign Policy (Washington: GPO, June 1975), pp. 31–32.

42. Senate Select Committee to Study Governmental Operations with Respect to Intelligence Activities, Final Report, vol. 1, *Foreign and Military Intelligence,* 94th Cong., 2d sess., no. 94-755 (Washington, D.C.: GPO, 1976), 275.

43. There was a certain difference between an RMD and an OD inasmuch as the former was intended to define roles, missions, and patterns of command subordination in a wartime environment.

44. Even "concise lists" tend to be formidable, as witness the following illustration. On 17 March 1977, the national intelligence officer for the Near East and South Asia forwarded the following "limited, prioritized list" to the U.S. Embassy in Teheran:

Guidance: Iran

I. Political
   A. *Internal*
      1. Long-range objectives and policies of the Shah and his key advisers, both civilian and military.
      2. How and by whom major political, national security, and economic decisions are made.
      3. The role SAVAK plays in the government.
      4. The Government of Iran's involvement in human rights violations.
   B. *External*
      1. Sources of foreign military threat to Iran.
      2. The balance of forces in the region as it affects Iran.
      3. Relations with the Soviet Union and the Gulf countries, particularly Saudi Arabia and Iraq.
II. Economic
   A. Economic development programs, especially the National Iranian Oil Company strategy and sales policies.
   B. Plans being formulated for nuclear development.
III. Military capabilities of the Royal Iranian Armed Forces.

The head of the CIA Human Resources Division who transmitted the list to Ambassador Sullivan added that since the list was so concise no order of priorization was indicated. CIA Documents, vol. 8 (Teheran: CIA, 1981), p. 151.

45. Hulnick and Brammer, *Impact of Intelligence,* p. 14.

46. Richard Giza, in *Intelligence Requirements,* "The Problems of the Intelligence Consumer," vol. 2: *Analysis and Estimates,* ed. R. Godson (Washington, D.C.: National Strategy Information Center, 1980), p. 184.

47. Hulnick and Brammer, *Impact of Intelligence,* p. 13.

48. Delicate judgments have to be made in this context, and they can never be made to everyone's satisfaction. Without compartmentalization, particularly of the most sensitive information or information from the most sensitive sources (the two are not quite the same), the sources from which such information comes will soon disappear. This dilemma is occasionally referred to as the "Coventry conundrum," the widespread belief that the British military leadership knew about German preparations for a mass air raid against Coventry in 1940, but decided not to take any special measures to intercept the German bombers. This was in order to preserve the secret that the British had broken the German air force code. More recently it has become known that the British leadership had only vague knowledge of a major raid against a target in the Midlands, not about a specific raid against Coventry. But the dilemma is nevertheless a real one—in the 1941 battle for Crete the British generals did not make use of all the foreknowledge they had for reasons similar to those just discussed.

49. Giza, "The Problems of the Intelligence Consumer," p. 196.

50. R. Godson, p. 215.

51. A massive CIA study published in early 1976 provided a critical review of the quality of reporting during the preceding two decades. It noted certain major lacunae: "The religious community, even though a principal opponent of the Shah, is little known." There was little or no information about the influence of religious leaders, and on such areas of society as the bazaar and the intellectuals, the relations between small-town mullahs and officials, and so forth. These happened to be, as it later appeared, crucial sections of society. Ernest R. Oney, *Elites and the Distribution of Power in Iran,* Research Study (CIA Directorate of Intelligence, February 1976), pp. 82–83.

In a nondemocratic regime, diplomats and intelligence agents always face problems trying to maintain contacts with oppositionists, whether it be a friendly country or a hostile one. It is precisely in facing such difficulties that good intelligence proves itself.

52. This is not to denigrate the importance of current intelligence, a fine and demanding art. It requires that analysts spot policy-relevant data the instant they appear, under circumstances where the analyst is working almost entirely on his own initiative. The editing of current intelligence is quite often drafted as a spin-off rather than a primary product, and the contents of a day's work seem to be determined more by random factors than by policy insight.

53. Thomas L. Hughes, *The Fate of Facts in a World of Men—Foreign Policy and Intelligence-Making* (New York: Foreign Policy Assoc., 1976), p. 42.

54. Graphics such as photographs, charts, and diagrams are increasingly used to good effect in the intelligence community; they can sum up pages of written analysis. But they can also be misleading, because charts and diagrams invariably oversimplify, making issues seem more clear-cut and data more authoritative than they may actually be.

55. The INR morning summary was typed up hurriedly from overnight embassy cables and CIA intelligence reports, but also often included material from press agency wires, FBI monitoring, military traffic, and USIA cables.

56. Thus, reports containing photographs, information on educational background and family situation, along with anecdotes and illustrative information on how the individual thinks are likely to be more appreciated than more demanding analyses of complicated political issues.

57. Such rivalries seem to be fairly universal. Zarah Steiner, a leading student of foreign ministries, notes with regard to the state of affairs on the eve of World War I that there was more competition than cooperation between the diplomats and the military even in such countries as France and Russia, where cipher-breaking techniques were well advanced and could have been more effectively exploited if the military and the civilians had cooperated. Zara S. Steiner, *The Times Survey of Foreign Ministries of the World* (London: Times Books, 1982), p. 17.

58. The same applies, I am told, to other Western countries.

59. "Tactical" rather than "strategic" concessions may be necessary in the process. For instance, it may be unwise to choose a certain turn of phrase if it is well known that the president dislikes it. Carter disliked the term "regime" in the daily reports, and Nixon was irritated by excessive use of such phrases as "right-wing reactionary circles." The producer can take account of such idiosyncracies and still get his point across.

60. Senate Select Committee to Study Governmental Operations with Respect to Intelligence Activities, Final Report, vol. 1: *Foreign and Military Intelligence,* 94th Cong., 2d sess., no. 94–755 (Washington, D.C.: GPO, 1976), 75–82.

61. Helms likened his experience—retaining the expletive—to "peeing up a rope."

62. Walter Laqueur, *The Terrible Secret* (Boston: Little, Brown, 1980).

63. In terrorist support operations, the need-to-know principle, developed in the Soviet Union to a degree inconceivable in the West, is rigidly observed. There is strict compartmentalization, careful cut-out and camouflage arrangements, the use of a chain of countless subcontractors, and so forth. Even in the most obvious cases, such as the assassination of Trotsky, the murderer never admitted his links and it is doubtful whether even now, more than forty year later, his ties could be proved in a court of law.

64. Barnds, Murphy Report App. U, p. 31.

65. I have heard this complaint from intelligence officials in several countries.

66. R. Giza, "The problems of the Intelligence Consumer," in *Intelligence Requirements* vol. 2: *Analysis and Estimates,* ed. R. Godson, p. 204. In the interest of balance and completeness it must also be stated that, in the words of a former senior intelligence official, analysts have the normal quota of human vanity. Many have the thin skins endemic to writers and intellectuals of any stripe. If one's analysis or prose seems to be ignored, is not used, or is "butchered" (edited), a martyr's role at the hands of "political trimmers" or because of "political pressure" is far more congenial than acknowledgment (private or public) that the prose or analysis in question might have been turgid, poorly written, ill thought-out, irrelevant, or simply unconvincing to equally knowledgeable peers or superiors.

67. Hulnick and Brammer, *Impact of Intelligence,* p. 22.

68. Policy proposals were supposed to include a discussion of all alternative courses of action, as well as an assessment of what would happen if nothing at all were done. Papers written strictly according to these specifications became long-winded, bureaucratic agonies. The State Department under Vance followed a variation of this procedure. Sometimes so many alternatives were advanced in presentations to PRC and SCC meetings that the basic estimate of the situation and proffered course of action itself got lost.

69. Such reexaminations are vital precisely because of usually strong inhibitions on the part of intelligence to reverse its position lest it lose credibility in the eyes of the policy makers.

70. Roger Hilsman, *To Move a Nation* (Garden City, N.Y.: Doubleday, 1967), p. 72.

71. Ibid., p. 79.

72. Ibid., p. 54.

73. Hulnick and Brammer, *Impact of Intelligence,* p. 13.

74. In matters of cover, status, and services in embassies, the Foreign Service still practices discrimination against intelligence officers. This internal tension has not disappeared and perhaps never will; from time to time corrections will have to be administered from above.

Chapter 4: Early Experiences and Later-Day Trials

1. Thomas F. Troy, *Donovan and the CIA* (Frederick, Md.: University Publications of America, Aletheia Books, 1981), p. 355.

2. The very few refugees who were available were apparently not in a position to provide important political information. See Harry Rositzke, *The CIA Secret Operation: Espionage, Counterespionage, Covert Action* (New York: Reader's Digest Press, 1977), chap. 2.

3. Office of Intelligence and Reports (OIR) 13 November 1946, and 1 November 1947.

4. The latter part of the *Review of the World Situation As It Relates to the Security of the United States* was subsequently dropped; henceforth, the publication will be cited in this work as *Review.*

5. *Review,* 26 September 1947.

6. *Review,* 17 December 1947 and 12 January 1948.

7. *Review,* 12 February 1948.

8. *Review,* 10 March 1949.

9. Admiral Roscoe Hillenkoetter, who was then DCI, tried in a memorandum to rebut allegations about five major intelligence failures reported by the *New York Herald Tribune*—lack of information, or mistakes in appraisal, concerning Yugoslavia, the Prague coup, the Arab-Israeli War, the fall of Chiang Kai-shek, and the upheaval in Bogota. His explanations were not convincing. Memorandum ER I-1768, 3 August 1950.

10. The breach between Tito and the Kremlin was considered "the most significant development in international Communism in twenty years." *Review,* 14 July 1948. Having failed to detect Tito's incipient break with the Soviet bloc, the CIA was more or less correct in its evaluations of Yugoslavia's future. The first three-quarters of 1949 were, as Trevor Barnes writes, "largely full of optimism." According to a top-secret review of world communism (Project Jigsaw) there was no masterplan for global domination by Moscow. John Maury, quoted in Trevor Barnes, "The Secret Cold War, Part 2," *Historical Journal* (October 1982): 651. By early 1950 this optimism had faded; nothing remained of it after the invasion of South Korea.

11. Estimate of the *Yugoslav Regime's Ability to Resist Soviet Pressure During 1949.* Office of Research and Evaluation (ORE): 44–49, 20 June 1949.

12. *Review,* 18 January 1950.

13. *Review,* 19 October 1949.

14. *Review,* 14 June 1950.

15. *Review,* 14 July 1948. Trevor Barnes notes that "throughout this [Berlin] crisis the C.I.A. stayed calm." "The Secret Cold War: The C.I.A. and American Foreign Policy in Europe, 1946–56, Part 1," *Historical Journal* (October 1981): 409. Hillenkoetter had warned Truman as early as December 1947 that the Soviets might take steps to oust the West from Berlin. But the CIA did not share General Lucius Clay's assessment in his cable of 5 March 1948, which set off alarm bells all over Washington. The CIA tried to play down the seriousness of the crisis—its March report to the NSC was relaxed in tone, telling the council that reaction to the Czech coup was exaggerated and that nothing violent would happen. But at the end of April 1948 (that is, two months before the event), the ORE announced that Soviet action to force the Western powers out of Berlin was no longer purely speculative.

16. *Review,* 17 May 1949.

17. In an estimate about the probable consequences of U.S. troop withdrawal from Korea, the CIA had stated that American retreat would probably result in the downfall of the South Korean regime, whereas a continued U.S. presence would discourage invasion. ORE: 49, 28 February 1949.

18. *Review,* 16 August 1950.

19. *The New Polish Government,* OIR: 4328, 14 May 1947.

20. On Finland: *Finland's Place in the Soviet Orbit,* OIR: 4819, 3 May 1948; on Greece: *Prospects for the Preservation of the Independence of Greece,* OIR: 4664, 27 April 1948.

21. *The Political Ideas of General de Gaulle,* Rand: A2508, 5 October 1945; CIA, 14 October 1948, DDRA: R21A.

22. OIR: 5024, 31 August 1949.

23. *Britain's Rearmament Policy,* OIR: 4769, 17 November 1948; *The British Commonwealth Approaches a Turning Point,* OIR:4701, 2 August 1948.

24. *The Will of Western European Countries to Resist Aggression,* OIR: 5029, 9 August 1949. The report also credited the Danes and Norwegians with unshakable determination to defend their borders.

25. Hugh de Santis, *The Diplomacy of Silence* (Chicago: University of Chicago Press, 1980), p. 207.

26. There are hardly any references to the CIA in the volumes of *Foreign Relations of the United States for 1949–51.*

27. CIA, (top-secret assessment) NLT: 77-35, 12 October 1950.

28. Allen Dulles, Jackson, and Correa, *The Central Intelligence Agency and National Organization for Intelligence* (Washington, D.C.: GPO, January 1949).

29. ORE: 9, 13 January 1949. The same point was made in the CIA's NIE: 64, 24 December 1952: "Discord within the Politburo's successor and between the Communist Party, the Secret Police and the Soviet army might develop after the first few months [after Stalin's death]."

30. SE: 39, 10 March 1953.

31. The annual NIE of May 1955 made a statement the authors were bound to regret within a year: "Popular resistance of an organized and active kind is unlikely to appear in any of the Satellites during the period of this estimate [namely the years up to 1960]" NIE: 11-3-55, 17 May 1955.

32. NIE: 11-4-57, 12 November 1957.

33. See two preceding NIEs and other contemporary estimates, especially Senate Foreign Relations Committee, *Executive Sessions of the Senate Foreign Relations Committee* (Historical Series), *Briefing on the World Situation,* 85th Cong., 2d sess., 18 January 1960, p. 33. Made public in November 1982. On the other hand, the CIA always conceded that China—unlike the satellites—was not "directly and completely controlled by the Kremlin." (See, for instance, the NIE:64 appendices.)

34. Only in April 1961 did the CIA reach the conclusion that Communist ideology had become a divisive rather than a unifying force, and only in 1963 was it accepted that Soviet and Chinese interests conflicted on almost every issue. CIA, *The Sino-Soviet Dispute and Its Significance,* 1 April 1961. Most outside experts in the field—lacking access to privileged information—had reached these conclusions well before.

35. *The Strength and Capabilities of Soviet Bloc Forces to Conduct Military Operations against NATO,* SE: 16, 12 October 1951.

36. Ibid., p. 3.

37. NIE: 64, part 2.

38. Ibid.

39. SE: 16, p. 18.

40. *Main Trends in Soviet Capabilities and Policies 1957–1962,* NIE: 11-5-57, 12 November 1957. This estimate mentions, perhaps for the first time, the Soviet goal of attaining a position permitting them to control Middle East oil.

41. Quoted here from the summary of the estimate prepared for President Eisenhower: "Important Points in the Estimate of the World Situation," 17 March 1958 (declassified 12 June 1980), pp. 9, 30, 34, 42, 72, 73.

42. *Estimate of the Effects of the Soviet Possession of the Atomic Bomb upon the Security of the United States and upon the Probabilities of Direct Soviet Military Action,* ORE: 91-49, 6 April 1950. The reservations stated by Naval Intelligence concerning this estimate may serve as an illustration for the far-reaching differences of opinion that frequently prevailed in the intelligence community. Naval intelligence argued that there was no sign that the Soviet leaders were about to lose confidence in their system, or lose faith in the collapse of capitalism. They thought the hypothesis that a major war might result from miscalculation quite unrealistic; such a war would result "from a plan, not a blunder." Navy intelligence criticized the lack of integrated analysis: "there is an examination based on several mutually exclusive hypotheses. From these hypotheses one may choose estimates that range from no change in Soviet policy to basic and alarming changes in that policy."

43. NIE: 64, part 1, 12 November 1953; David Holloway, "Research Note," *International Security* 4, no. 3 (Winter 1979–80): 192–199.

44. NSC: 5602, 8 February 1956.

45. NIE: 11-7-54; see also *Probable Warning of Soviet Attack on the U.S. through Mid-1957,* SNIE: 11-8-54, 10 September 1954.

46. The effects of the surprise attack are described in some detail in Stephen Ambrose, *Ike's Spies: Eisenhower and the Espionage Establishment* (Garden City, N.Y.: Doubleday, 1981), p. 256.

47. *The Likelihood of a British-French Resort to Military Action Against Egypt in the Suez Crisis,* SNIE: 30-5-56, 19 September 1956.

48. Donald Neff, *Warriors at Suez* (New York: Simon and Schuster, 1982), frequently refers to the level of CIA knowledge about the Suez expedition preparations. However, his references are based on personal recollections and have to be evaluated with caution. See also Wilbur C. Eveland, *Ropes of Sand: America's Failure in the Middle East* (New York: W.W. Norton, 1980).

49. Senate Foreign Relations Committee, Executive Sessions, (85th Cong., 1st sess., 12 November 1956). These reports were made accessible in Feb., 1980.

50. Senate Foreign Relations Committee, Executive Sessions, *The Situation in the Middle East,* 29 July 1958. These reports were declassified twenty years later.

51. *The Outlook for Iraq,* NIE: 36-2-57, 4 June 1957. Declassified May 1982.

52. *Iraq: The Crisis in Leadership and the Communist Advance,* Intelligence Report 7921, 16 January 1959.

53. When Allen Dulles appeared before the Senate Foreign Relations Committee in April 1959 he painted an even more ominous picture: the Communists had become the strongest single force in Iraq, having taken control of the media and other key positions. Dulles noted that the British were less disturbed; they thought that there was still some hope that Kassem could be saved. The CIA was less sanguine, for if Kassem betrayed any sign of a shift—which seemed unlikely—the Soviets, together with the local Communists, would probably be in a position to see that he was liquidated. Senate Foreign Relations Committee (Historical Series), vol. 11, 86th Cong., 1st sess., March 1982, pp. 320ff.

54. *Approaching Showdown in Jordan,* OIR: 7477, 2 April 1957.

55. *Outlook for the UAR,* OIR: 11 March 1960.

56. *Saudi Arabia: A Disruptive Force in Western-Arab Relations,* OIR: 18 January 1956.

57. OCI: 1758/65, 15 May 1965 and OCI: 1152/66, 3 March 1966.

58. An exceptionally accurate prediction ought to be mentioned in this context. On 24 November 1963, a CIA memorandum predicted a coup in Algeria and named Hawari Boumedienne as its likely leader. The document also outlined the kind of policy he was likely to pursue. Ben Bella was deposed and Boumedienne took over in June 1965, some eighteen months later.

59. For instance, the series *Main Trends in Soviet Capabilities and Policies, Soviet Foreign Development,* INR: 7807.1, 25 September 1958, and *Soviet Foreign Policy,* INR: 8362.1, 31 October 1960.

60. *Moscow Prepares for Showdown,* INR: 8340, 9 September 1960; *Dissidence in the Soviet Union,* INR: 7631, 10 December 1957; *Khrushchev Reaches Top,* INR: 6839, 17 February 1955; and *Interim Evaluation of the Beria Affair,* INR: 6356, 21 July 1953.

61. *Soviet Foreign Developments,* INR: 7807.1, 25 September 1958; and *Soviet Attitudes on Negotiations with the West,* INR: 8427, 27 March 1961.

62. *The Hungarian Explosion: An Analysis,* INR: 7545, 22 July 1957.

63. *Western European Socialist Parties: The United Kingdom,* INR: 7360.1, 17 October 1956; same series: *Italy,* INR: 7360.6, 6 May 1957.

64. *Parties and Power Groups under France's Fifth Republic,* INR: 7936, 3 February 1958. *The Threat from the Extreme Right to French Republican Institutions,* INR: 7823, 27 October 1958.

65. *Senate Foreign Relations Committee,* 83–120.

66. Ibid.

67. Ibid.

68. Dulles, Jackson, Correa Report.

69. *Estimated Soviet Defense Spending in Rubles, 1970–1975.* CIA May 1976, p. 1. There has been considerable literature concerning this controversy. The main arguments are summarized in the following: *CIA Estimates of Soviet Military Expenditure* (1980) and *CIA Estimates of Soviet Defense Spending* (n.d.; declassified 1983); William Lee, *The Estimation of Soviet Defense Expenditures for 1955–1975: An Unconventional Approach* (New York: Praeger, 1977); Franklyn D. Holzman, "Are the Russians Really Outspending the U.S. on Defense?" *International Security* 4, no. 4 (Spring 1980): 86–104; Steven Rosefielde, *False Science: Underestimating the Soviet Arms Build-up* (New Brunswick, N.J.: Transaction Books, 1982). See also various articles by Les Aspin, Abraham

Becker, and Stanley Cohn, to mention only a few of the main figures in the controversy. For a defense of the CIA estimates, see Donald F. Burton, "Estimating Soviet Defense Spending," in *Problems of Communism* 32 (March–April 1983): 85.

70. Rosefielde, *False Science,* p. 252. Some CIA analysts announced in early 1983 that their estimates for Soviet military spending may have been too high during the previous five years.

71. CIA, *The Soviet Decision to Intervene,* memorandum, 21 August 1968. Declassified 2 February 1979.

72. The sequence of events has been discussed in detail in the second volume of Henry Kissinger's *Years of Upheaval* (Boston: Little, Brown, 1982).

73. Senate Select Committee on Intelligence, *Report to the Senate.* 97th Cong., 1st sess., covering the period 1 January 1979–31 December 1980, p. 12.

74. House Select Committtee on Intelligence, Subcommittee on Evaluation *Iran: Evaluation of U.S. Intelligence prior to November 1978,* 96th Cong., 1st sess., January 1979. The report concluded that "The NIE is not worth fighting for . . ."

75. Senate Select Committee on Intelligence, 97th Cong., 2d sess., Subcommittee on Oversight and Evaluation, *U.S. Intelligence Performance on Central America: Achievements and Selected Instances of Concern.* 22 September 1982, p. 1.

Chapter 5: The Missile Gap Controversy and the Cuban Missile Crisis

1. "In mighty enterprises it is enough to have had the determination." Propertius, *Elegies* 10, 5.

2. In this chapter, attention is drawn to the failure of U.S. intelligence to anticipate the Sino-Soviet conflict, yet the possibility was in fact discussed from time to time. See, for instance, Department of State Office of Intelligence, *Sino-Soviet Relations: A Reappraisal,* Research Report 7070, 4 November 1955.

3. The reader will have found more detail on these and other controversies in chapter 4.

4. For the standard discussions, see F. M. Bottome, *The Missile Gap* (Rutherford, N.J.: Fairleigh Dickinson University Press, 1971), chap. 2; L. Freedman, *U.S. Intelligence and the Soviet Strategic Threat* (London: Macmillan, 1977), chap. 4; J. Dick, "The Strategic Arms Race 1957–1962: Who Opened the Missile Gap?" *Journal of Politics* 34 (1972): 1062–1110; C. Gray, "Gap Prediction and America's Defense: Arms Race Behavior in the Eisenhower Years," *Orbis* 16 (1972): 257–74; R. Licklider, "The Missile Gap Controversy," *Political Science Quarterly* 85 (1970): 600–15; L. Aspin, "Debate over U.S. Strategic Forecasts: A Mixed Record," *Strategic Review* 8 (1980): 22–59; and W. Lee, "Debate over U.S. Strategic Forecasts: A Poor Record," *Strategic Review* 8 (1980): 44–59.

5. "Comments: Paul H. Nitze, Joseph Alsop, Morton H. Halperin, and Jeremy T. Stone," *Foreign Policy* 16 (1974): 84.

6. On the vulnerability of U.S. strategic forces in the mid-1950s, see A. Wohlstetter, P. Hoffman, and H. Rowen, *Protecting U.S. Power to Strike Back in the 1950s and 1960s,* Rand Study R-290, (Santa Monica, Calif.: Rand, 1956), especially pp. 30ff, and 41ff. For contemporary projections of this disparity from officially sponsored leakages, Stuart Symington, "Where the Missile Gap Went," *The Reporter,* 15 February 1962, p. 22.

7. W. Lee, *Understanding the Soviet Military Threat: How the CIA Estimates Went Astray,* Agenda Paper 6 (New York: National Strategy Information Center, 1977), p. 26; Freedman, *U.S. Intelligence,* chap. 3, especially pp. 32–36, on the role of the CIA in formulating National Intelligence Estimates.

8. On the bomber gap controversy, Gray, "Gap Prediction," *Orbis* 16 (1972): 258–66.

9. The phrase is Allen Dulles's. Allen Dulles, *The Craft of Intelligence* (New York: Harper and Row, 1965), p. 162. On the overall state of U.S. knowledge regarding the Soviet ICBM development program, see for example, CIA Report, U.S./U.K GM 4–52, 20 July 1953, "Soviet Guided Missile Intelligence. A Summary" (369-page report, including appendices with alphabetical list of known and suspected guided missile activity locations, factories, test centers etc., and directories of Soviet scientists believed to be engaged in missile work). See also CIA, Office of Scientific Intelligence Special Report OSI/ SR-6/49, 10 November 1949, "Flame and Combustion Research and its Relation to Jet Propulsion;" CIA, Directorate of Intelligence Memorandum (no number), 9 October 1958, "Analysis of Soviet ICBM Development Program."

10. Stephen Ambrose, *Ike's Spies: Eisenhower and the Espionage Establishment* (Garden City, N.Y.: Doubleday, 1981), chap. 19.

11. Lieutenant Colonel G. A. Tokaty-Tokaev, *Stalin Means War* (London: Weidenfield and Nicolson, 1951), pp. 103–5, 116–17, and *Comrade X* (London: Harvill Press, 1956). Tokaev's evidence is discussed further in N. Daniloff, *The Kremlin and the Cosmos* (New York: Alfred A. Knopf, 1972), pp. 41ff., with Appendix A an interview with Tokaev.

12. *The Great Soviet Encyclopedia* (Moscow: 1949), p. 562, alluded to the role of the Academy of Artillery Sciences in the development of rockets for military purposes. See also Senate Committee on Aeronautical and Space Sciences, *Soviet Space Program,* 1962, 64–65; Harriet and William Scott, *The Armed Forces of the USSR* (Boulder, Colo.: Westview, 1979), pp. 133ff.; Marshall A. A. Grechko, *The Armed Forces of the Soviet State* in vol. 12 of *Soviet Military Thought,* trans. and pub. by U.S. Air Force, (Washington, D.C.: Supt. of Docs., GPO, 1975), pp. 146–48, for brief accounts of the origin of the rocket forces.

13. V. L. Sokolov, *The Soviet Use of German Science and Technology* (New York: Columbia University, Research Program on the U.S.S.R., 1955), pp. 15ff. See also C. G. Lasby, *Project Paperclip: German Scientists and the Cold War* (New York: Atheneum, 1971).

14. H. Gottrup, "Aus den Arbeiten des Deutschen Raketen Kollektivs in der Sowjet Union," *Raketentechnik und Raumfahrtforschung* 2 (April 1958): 58ff. Dr. Walter Dornberger, former director of the Peenemunde installation, was subsequently employed by the U.S. Air Force at Dayton, Ohio, to collate and evaluate these reports. See E. Schweibert, "USAF Ballistic Missile 1954–1964," *Air Force Digest* (May 1964): chap. 5, for the reaction within the air force to these reports.

15. Some additional gleanings concerning Soviet rocket development may have been obtained through the Gehlen organization, which systematically interrogated all repatriated German POWs from the U.S.S.R. about technical and scientific matters, industrial locations, raw material sites, and so forth. See Heinz Höhne, *The General Was a Spy* (New York: Coward, McCann and Geoghagen, 1972), pp. 77–79; 96–98.

16. Harry Rositzke, *The CIA's Secret Operations* (New York: Reader's Digest Press, 1977), pp. 67–69. William Hood, *Mole* (New York: W.W. Norton, 1982).

17. Freedman, *U.S. Intelligence,* p. 69.

18. Schweibert, "USAF Ballistic Missiles," p. 78. The consensus of leaders from military, industrial, and scientific fields, after briefing by air force intelligence in August 1952, was that there was no immediate cause for alarm. In December 1952, an ad hoc committee (the Millikan committee) examined the evidence collated by Dr. Walter Dornberger under air force auspices; the committee did not recommend a basic acceleration of the U.S. missile program until adequate components had been developed.

19. Ibid., pp. 68–69. The 1952 briefing at Dayton reached the conclusion that the Soviet program was comparable to that of the United States and was proceeding along the lines of the Snark, Navaho, and Atlas programs. Interrogation of some two hundred German rocket and engineering experts established that the Germans had left behind specifications for a 120-metric-ton engine, and that it was possible—but not probable—that the Soviets could develop missiles powered by two, or even four, of these engines. The twin-engine version was estimated to have a maximum range of 4,400 nautical miles.

20. Compare Vannevar Bush, *Modern Arms and Free Men* (New York: Simon and Schuster, 1949), for an example of the skepticism prevailing about German predictions of missiles as practical means of delivering atomic warheads.

21. Unknown to the German scientists and air force intelligence was a massive Soviet hidden missile program. Near the factory at Khimki, where the Germans and Soviets worked side by side, a second Soviet factory had been built that the Germans were not allowed to enter.

22. F. McGuire, "Kaputsin Yar Serves as Russia's Cape Canaveral," *Missiles and Rockets* (February 1958): 61; "How U.S. Taps Soviet Missile Secret," *Aviation Week* (October 21, 1957): 22ff.; see also House Subcommittee of the Committee on Appropriations, *Department of Defense Appropriations for 1960,* pt. 1, 86th Cong., 1st sess., 1959, 831.

23. Until the advent of the U-2, Air Force Intelligence was dependent upon World War II German aerial reconnaissance photographs and target folders for the Soviet Union. On the U-2 program see D. Wise and T. Ross, *The U-2 Affair* (New York: Random House, 1962); Dulles, *The Craft of Intelligence,* pp. 195–96; Ray Cline, *Secrets, Spies, and Scholars* (Washington, D.C.: Acropolis Books, 1976), pp. 155–58; T. Powers, *The Man Who Kept the Secrets* (New York:

Pocket Books, 1981), pp. 119–22. See also G. Powers, *Operation Overflight* (New York: Rinehart and Winston, 1960), pp. 120–22; R. Gaskin, "Flying the U-2," *Air Force Magazine* 60 (April 1977): 66–71; D. Moser, "The Time of the Angel, The U-2, Cuba, and the CIA," *American Heritage*, October 1977, 4–15.

24. On the capabilities of the U-2, see Wise and Ross, *The U-2 Affair*, pp. 10ff.

25. Rositzke, *The CIA's Secret Operations*, chap. 4.

26. Ibid., pp. 59–60.

27. P. Klass, *Secret Sentries in Space* (New York: Random House, 1971); also see Symington, "Where the Missile Gap Went," pp. 21–23, for figures on Soviet bomber forces.

28. Senate Committee on Armed Service, *Military Procurement Authorization, FY 1963*, 87th Cong., 2d sess., 1962, 51.

29. On this document see also M. Halperin, "The Gaither Committee on the Policy Process," *World Politics* 13, no. 3 (April 1961): 360–84, especially 361–64. The complete text of the Gaither Report is only forty-six pages long, including appendices. The correct title is *Deterrence and Survival in the Nuclear Age*.

30. As quoted in Gray, "Gap Prediction," *Orbis* 16 (1972): 268.

31. Ibid. See also, F. McGuire, "Kaputsin Yar," 61ff.

32. C. Murphy, "Khrushchev's Paper Bear," *Fortune*, December 1961, 227.

33. Dick, "Strategic Arms Race," pp. 1069–70.

34. Freedman, *U.S. Intelligence*, p. 69.

35. C. Murphy, "The Embattled Mr. McElroy," *Fortune*, April 1959, 244ff.

36. For a critique of this assumption, see now Lee, *Understanding the Soviet Military Threat*, pp. 24–28.

37. Symington and Bridges quoted in Licklider, "Missile Gap Controversy," p. 604.

38. Murphy, "The Embattled Mr. McElroy," p. 242.

39. Ibid., p. 244.

40. Senate Committee on Armed Services and Committee on Aeronautical and Space Sciences, *Missile and Space Activities*, 86th Cong., 1st sess., 1959.

41. Ibid., pp. 46, 47.

42. Licklider, "Missile Gap Controversy," p. 607, nn. 20, 21.

43. Senate Preparedness Investigating Subcommittee of the Committee on Armed Services and the Committee on Aeronautical and Space Sciences, *Missiles, Space, and Other Defense Matters*, 86th Cong., 2d sess., 1960, 338.

44. Data on failures noted in House Subcommittee on Department of Defense Appropriations of the Committee on Appropriations, *Department of Defense Appropriations for 1960*, pt., 1, 86th Cong., 1st sess., 1959, 831.

45. See Dick, "Strategic Arms Race," p. 1067, for references.

46. See the testimony of General Bernard Schriever, commander, Air Force Ballistic Missile Division, Senate Preparedness Investigating Subcommittee, Committee on Armed Services and Committee on Aeronautical and Space Sciences, *Missile and Space Activities*, 86th Cong., 1st sess., 1959, 93ff. See also Senate Preparedness Investigating Subcommittee, Committee on Armed Services, *Inquiry into Satellite and Missile Programs*, pt. 2, 85th Cong., 1st and 2d sess., 1957–58, 1670, 1774.

47. Dwight Eisenhower, *The White House Years: Waging Peace, 1956–1961* (Garden City, N.Y.: Doubleday, 1965), p. 546.

48. Klass, *Secret Sentries*, pp. 105ff.

49. Ibid., pp. 103–4.

50. Rositzke, *The CIA's Secret Operations*, p. 81. This evidence should refute the contention in Freedman, *U.S. Intelligence*, pp. 73–74, that Penkovsky was not an important source of intelligence. See also D. Martin, *Wilderness of Mirrors* (New York: Harper and Row, 1980), p. 114 and Cline, *Secrets, Spies and Scholars*, p. 198. There is some question as to timing—the first batch of reports handed in by Penkovsky in April may not have been processed in time to be included in the June 1961 NIE.

51. Licklider, "Missile Gap Controvery," p. 609.

52. See note 50 for references.

53. Rositzke, *The CIA's Secret Operations*, p. 59.

54. Eisenhower, *Waging Peace*, p. 220.

55. Figures cited in Freedman, *U.S. Intelligence*, p. 75. In fact, CIA figures were even lower —ten ICBMs for 1960 and 250–350 on launchers in mid-1962. When Freedman wrote his

book, Allen Dulles's evidence before the Senate Foreign Relations Committee in 1960 had not yet been declassified. Senate Foreign Relations Committee, *Executive Sessions, 1960* (Historical Series), 1982, 15.

56. Murphy, "The Embattled Mr. McElroy," p. 244. According to Allen Dulles in 1960, "We are not in agreement as to how they will proceed and I am rather inclined to feel that it is crystal ball gazing to try to fix any very precise goals for future years." Senate Foreign Relations Committee, *Executive Sessions, 1960,* 14.

57. House Committee on Appropriations, *Department of Defense Appropriations for 1961,* part I, 86th Cong., 2d sess., 1960, 5.

58. *New York Times,* 7 February 1961.

59. Dulles, *The Craft of Intelligence,* p. 162.

60. Lee, *Understanding the Soviet Military Threat,* pp. 29ff.

61. Ibid., pp. 34–36. On the importance of this material, see Lee with J. Douglass, *Soviet Military Strategy in Europe* (New York: Pergamon Press, 1980), pp. 1–18.

62. A. Horelick and M. Rush, *Strategic Power and Soviet Foreign Policy* (Chicago: University of Chicago Press, 1966), pp. 5ff.

63. Gates's testimony to House Committee on Science Aeronautics quoted in H. Ransom, *Can American Democracy Survive Cold War?* (Garden City, N.Y.: Doubleday, 1963), p. 164.

64. The best standard accounts are G. Allison, *Essence of Decision: Explaining the Cuban Missile Crisis* (Boston: Little, Brown, 1971); H. Dinerstein, *The Making of a Missile Crisis: October 1962* (Baltimore, Md.: Johns Hopkins University Press, 1976); Roger Hilsman, *To Move a Nation* (Garden City, N.Y.: Doubleday, 1967), pp. 159–229; and J. Prados, *The Soviet Estimate* (New York: Dial Press, 1982), chap. 9. For memoirs of contemporary participants, see also Arthur Schlesinger, *A Thousand Days* (Greenwich, Conn.: Greenwich House, 1983); Theodore Sorensen, *Kennedy* (New York: Harper and Row, 1965); Robert Kennedy, *Thirteen Days* (New York, W. W. Norton, 1969); Walter W. Rostow, *The Diffusion of Power* (New York: Macmillan, 1972).

65. See, for example, President John F. Kennedy, letter to Arthur C. Lundahl, director, National Photo Interpretation Center, 8 November 1962, Kennedy Presidential Library. Jack Anderson, "Getting the Big Picture for the CIA," *Washington Post,* 28 November 1982. See the judgment in Senate Committee on Armed Services, *Interim Report of the Preparedness Investigating Subcommittee with respect to Cuba,* excerpted in *Congressional Record,* 88th Cong., 1st sess., 1963, 109, pt. 6, 8207–12. The dismantlement of the missiles is discussed in House Committee on Appropriations, Subcommittee on Department of Defense Appropriations, 88th Cong., 1st sess., 1962, 12–17.

66. R. Hilsman, State Department, "Talking Paper: Probable Soviet Motives in Deploying Strategic Missiles to Cuba," 14 November 1962; Thomas L. Hughes, director, bureau of Intelligence and Research, intelligence note to secretary of state, 16 April 1963, "Reported Differences between Khrushchev and the Marshalls on Cuban Missile Deployment."

67. Senate Preparedness Subcommittee, Interim Report no. 2, 8211–12; Further, ". . . faulty evaluation and the predisposition of the intelligence community to the philosophical conviction that it would be incompatible with Soviet policy to introduce strategic missiles into Cuba resulted in intelligence judgments and evaluations which later proved to be erroneous." *New York Times,* 10 May 1963.

68. Allison, *Essence of Decision,* chap. 2 (with review in CIA, *Studies in Intelligence,* no. 43); R. Leighton, *The Cuban Missile Crisis of 1962: A Case in National Security Crisis Management,* National Defense University, (Washington, D.C.: GPO, 1978); K. Knorr, "Failures in National Intelligence Estimates. The Case of the Cuban Missiles," *World Politics* 16, no. 3 (1964): 455–67; R. Wohlstetter, "Cuba and Pearl Harbor: Hindsight and Foresight," *Foreign Affairs* 43, no. 4 (1965): 691–707.

69. Prados, *The Soviet Estimate,* chap. 9; Allison, *Essence of Decision,* pp. 113–23; Hilsman, *To Move a Nation,* chap. 14; Cline, *Secrets, Spies and Scholars,* pp. 196–98.

70. The Kennedy Presidential Library's forthcoming declassification of additional intelligence documents on the crisis will expand the boundaries of inquiry, and a new treatment of the Cuban missile crisis may become necessary. The transcript of DCI John McCone's meeting with President Kennedy on 22 August 1962 would make interesting reading, as would the DCI's so-called "honeymoon cables" to his deputy, General Carter, in September of the same year.

71. Hilsman, *To Move a Nation,* chap. 14; "The Military Build-up in Cuba," SNIE: 85-3-62, 19 September 1962; "Soviet Reactions to Certain U.S. Courses of Action on Cuba," SNIE:

11-18-62, 19 October 1962; "Major Consequences of Certain U.S. Courses of Action on Cuba," SNIE. 11-19-62, 20 October 1962; "Recent Soviet Military Aid to Cuba," OCI: 3047/62, 22 August 1962; "Documents on Soviet Military Aircraft in Cuba," OCI: unnumbered, 15 October 1962; "Readiness status of Soviet Missiles in Cuba," OCI: 13927, 23 October 1962; "Readiness, Range, Capabilities, CEP of SS-4 and SS-5 Missiles," OCI: 19 October 1962; CIA, "The Crisis USSR/Cuba," memorandum, 24 October 1962.

72. T. F. Burke, Defense Department, "An Analysis of the Variant Views of the Kremlin," (no provenance), 24 November 1962.

73. Victor Marchetti and John D. Marks, *The CIA and the Cult of Intelligence* (New York: Dell, 1980), p. 271, claim that the military intelligence agencies, including the DIA and NSA, initially viewed the intensified Soviet activity in Cuba during the late spring and summer of 1962 as primarily economic assistance.

74. Senate Committee on Armed Services, Preparedness Investigating Subcommittee, *Interim Report on the Cuban Military Build-up,* 88th Cong., 1st sess., 1963, 11; House, *Defense Appropriations,* 44–46.

75. Thus, for example, Cline, *Secret, Spies and Scholars,* p. 196.

76. House, *Defense Appropriations,* 64, 68, 71.

77. Ibid., 66–70; Senate, *Interim Report on the Cuban Missile Build-up,* 6–8. See Allison, *Essence of Decision,* p. 306, n. 75, on the contradiction in Secretary McNamara's testimony regarding the timetable of U-2 flights in September 1962. According to McNamara, the 5 September flight was the last one made over western Cuba before 14 October; General Carroll, director of the DIA, referred to flights subsequent to 5 September.

78. For an early version, House, *Defense Appropriations,* 24–25, for testimony of Secretary Robert McNamara; Knorr, "Failures in National Intelligence Estimates," pp. 455ff; Hilsman, *To Move a Nation,* pp. 172–73.

79. SNIE: 85-3-62, 19 September 1962, p. 8.

80. House Committee on Armed Services, *Hearings on Sundry Legislation Affecting the Naval and Military Establishments* 88th Cong., 1st sess., 1963, 235–36.

81. Ibid., p. 235.

82. Ibid.; House, *Defense Appropriations,* 64.

83. House, *Defense Appropriations,* 65, 71.

84. Ibid., pp. 8–10.

85. Ibid., p. 25.

86. Allison, *Essence of Decision,* pp. 106–8.

87. To identify deck cargoes, CIA analysts developed the analytical technique of "crateology," which entailed the determination of the contents of large crates. See Marchetti and Marks, *The CIA,* p. 272.

88. Roger Hilsman, "The Cuban Missile Crisis; How Close We Were to War," *Look,* August 1964, p. 18. The *Omsk* and *Poltava* were correctly identified as vessels designed for carrying lumber. However, analysts responsible for shipping intelligence may have assumed that these particular vessels were pressed into service because the Soviets had trouble finding the necessary ships for sending aid to Cuba, and lumber ships could be more readily spared.

89. See Dinerstein, *The Making of a Missile Crisis,* p. 16, arguing that the decision to deploy the missiles was in the beginning of 1962.

90. The role of Penkovsky in the Cuban missile crisis is not altogether clear. The CIA has never revealed the precise information provided by Penkovsky in the spring and summer of 1962, nor has it specified the true date by which Penkovsky had come under KGB control (assuming, of course, that Penkovsky was not a double agent from the start). According to Rositzke, *The CIA's Secret Operations,* p. 71, Penkovsky apparently was under KGB control by mid-September 1962.

91. For example, "The Military Build-up in Cuba," SNIE: 85-3-62, p. 6, par. 22, seems to reflect the "TASS Statement of 11 September 1962," in *Pravda,* 12 September 1962; see also Dinerstein, *The Making of a Missile Crisis,* pp. 195–97.

92. House, *Defense Appropriations,* 70–71. Prados, *Soviet Estimate,* p. 167, presents a figure of six accurate reports of some two hundred Cuban-agent reports bearing on missiles.

93. P. L. Thyraud De Vosjoli, *Lamia* (Boston: Little, Brown, 1970), pp. 295–96. In August, French intelligence apparently provided the CIA with at least one credible eyewitness report of missiles under transport. See Warren Hinckle and W. Turner, *The Fish Is Red* (New York: Harper and Row, 1981), pp. 133–34, on reports from underground sources in Cuba.

94. See, for example, "Recent Soviet Military Aid to Cuba," OCI: 3047/62, 22 August 1962,

p. 2: "Eyewitnesses who saw the material being transported from the port areas report that . . .," and "A refugee from the port of Antilla in Oriente province reported that a Soviet ship unloaded in late July at nearby Nicaro"; p. 3.

95. Ibid. Human sources described the arrival of Soviet personnel; the nature of military construction at two sites near Matanzas (El Bongo and Santa Cruz del Norte); evacuation of Cubans from Mariel and the farming area near Guatana in Pilar de Rio province.

96. There is, admittedly, an element of post facto rationalization here. The agent report received in September initially aroused skepticism. The CIA concluded that the agent had observed a thirty-foot SAM missile on a transporter and not a sixty-foot medium-range ballistic missile. Hilsman, *To Move a Nation,* pp. 186, 189. For indications of the DIA analytical process, see House, *Defense Appropriations,* 64–65. The reasoning of DIA and the military intelligence agencies is indicated in "U.S. Watches for Possible Cuban IRBMs," *Aviation Week* 77 (1 October 1962) pp. 20–21, n. 14. For CIA reasoning see Marchetti and Marks, *The CIA,* pp. 272–73.

97. House, *Defense Appropriations,* 64. In this context information provided from HUMINT sources (Penkovsky) seems to have been important pertaining to the general pattern of Soviet missile sites.

98. Signal intelligence, or SIGINT, is defined here as intelligence information comprising—either individually or in combination—all communications intelligence (COMINT), electronics (ELINT), and foreign instrumentation signals intelligence (SIGINT). The emphasis is upon SIGINT in the form of intercepted radio transmissions (voice and code). For this definition, see House Committee on Foreign Affairs, "The Role of Intelligence in the Foreign Policy Process," 96th Cong., 2d sess., 28 January, 8, 11, and 20 February 1980, p. 236.

99. The exception is Marchetti and Marks, *The CIA,* p. 271, which acknowledges the interception of Cuban communications in the summer of 1962.

100. Ibid. If it were true that the DIA and NSA issued rebuttals to CIA intelligence reports concerning the military build-up in late August, this is prima facie evidence that the NSA had not deciphered Soviet code traffic to Cuba.

101. The intelligence community was far less successful before 17 October 1962 in discovering the actual number and organization of the Soviet army ground units brought to Cuba. These were purportedly first revealed by low-level reconnaissance. See House, *Defense Appropriations,* 24–25.

102. Ibid., p. 65.

103. The San Cristobal MRBM complex was ultimately manned by two Soviet regiments. By 23 October, a probable regimental headquarters location in the San Cristobal area had been identified by photographic surveillance. See "Readiness Status of Soviet Missiles in Cuba," OCI: 13927, 23 October 1962, p. 1. However, ELINT might have been used to locate and identify the SAM radar in the area, while COMINT could have identified the radio communications of this headquarters after it had been located by airborne D/F. It is probable that short-range radio communications within Cuba could be picked up by NSA receivers in southern Florida.

104. House, *Defense Appropriations,* 8–9; Senate, *Cuban Military Build-up,* 236.

105. "As a result of the identification made in the San Cristobal area, it was directed that our high-altitude aircraft survey the island completely in order to determine precisely the nature and extent of Soviet offensive missile base construction in Cuba." House, *Defense Appropriations,* 8. A senior intelligence official told me that the discovery of the San Cristobal site was also accidental—it came from photographs taken by a pilot who took a shortcut back from a mission to a different part of the island.

106. The detailed character of the circumstantial evidence cannot be further analyzed in this context. Agent reports could have been substantiated by the detection of electromagnetic radiation from radio and radar equipment installed to furnish support to the missile sites. It is not known whether the U-2 aircraft that conducted the overflights of Cuban territory were equipped with ferreting gear capable of picking up the characteristic signals of Soviet radar, missile control, and communications equipment in Cuba. It is certain, however, that intercept receivers aboard U.S. Air Force ELINT aircraft and on the ground in southern Florida (under NSA control) were employed in the concerted SIGINT surveillance effort.

107. For background, see Allison, *Essence of Decision,* pp. 190–91.

108. See D. Sullivan, "Evaluating U.S. Intelligence Estimates," in vol. 2 of *Intelligence Require-*

ments for the 1980s, Analysis and Estimates, ed. Roy Godson (Washington, D.C., National Strategy Information Center, 1980), pp. 51–53.

109. SNIE: 85–3–62, p. 4, para. 9; p. 6, para. 22. Compare the rationale offered in "Major Consequences of Certain U.S. Course of Action in Cuba," SNIE: 11–19–62, 20 October 1962, p. 4: "A major Soviet objective in their military build-up in Cuba is to demonstrate that the world balance of forces has shifted so far in their favor that the U.S. can no longer prevent the advance of Soviet offensive power even into its own hemisphere."

110. See "Military Build-up in Cuba" SNIE: 85–3–62, p. 6, para. 22.

111. See A. Krock, *Memoirs: Sixty Years on the Firing Line* (New York: Funk and Wagnalls, 1968), pp. 387ff., on McCone's statement to President Kennedy concerning the arrival of offensive missiles in Cuba. It is averred that Thyraud De Vosjoli, a French intelligence officer who had been sent to Cuba in the summer of 1962, provided McCone with eyewitness evidence of the preparations for the installation of the missiles. The chronology is unclear, and the connection is beyond substantiation pending the publication of the pertinent CIA records. Information on the reasoning of McCone, from Dr. Cline, interview, January 1982.

112. As suggested by Prados, *The Soviet Estimate,* p. 166.

113. President Kennedy and his staff appear to have believed Soviet reassurances as in the TASS statement of 11 September 1962: "The Government of the Soviet Union also authorized TASS to state that there is no need for the Soviet Union to shift its weapons for the repulsion of aggression, for a retaliatory blow, to any other country, for instance Cuba." *Pravda,* 12 September 1962. See also Allison, *Essence of Decision,* pp. 193–94, with Sorensen, *Kennedy,* pp. 668ff., on the reaction of President Kennedy and his inner circle to the photographic evidence of the missiles.

114. SNIE: 85–3–62 nowhere considers the possibility of deliberate Soviet deception. The document presents an acceptance of the Soviet statement and earlier private reassurances conveyed by Ambassador Dobrynin with a minimum of skepticism.

115. "They would almost certainly estimate that this could not be done without provoking a dangerous U.S. reaction." "Military Build-up in Cuba," SNIE: 85–3–62, p. 8, para. 31: Thus, no consideration seems to have been given to the possibility that the Soviet Union did indeed allow for a strong U.S. reaction in its calculations.

116. See Senate Select Committee to Study Governmental Operations with Respect to Intelligence Activities, *Foreign and Military Intelligence,* sect. G, *The Intelligence Culture and Analytical Bias* bk. 1, 94th Cong., 2d sess., no. 94-755 1976, 270–71, noting the opinion of a CIA analyst that in 1962 some analysts judged that the Soviets would not install missiles in Cuba because such a move would have been "aberrational."

117. For an academic explanation, see the summary in Allison, *Essence of Decision,* pp. 44–56, 237–44; Dinerstein, *The Making of a Crisis,* pp. 166ff.; A. Horelick, *The Cuban Missile Crisis: An Analysis of Soviet Calculations and Behavior,* (Santa Monica, Calif.: Rand, 1963); R. Crane, *Soviet Motives and Miscalculations Leading to the Cuban Missile Crisis: A Lesson for the Future,* Hudson Institute Discussion Paper HI–777–DP (Croton-on-Hudson, 1966); J. Kahan, "The Cuban Missile Crisis: A Study of Its Strategic Context," *Political Science Quarterly* 87 (1972): 564–90; B. Bernstein, "The Cuban Missile Crisis: Trading the Jupiters in Turkey?" *Political Science Quarterly* 95 (1980): 97–125; A. Ulam, *Expansion and Coexistence: The History of Soviet Foreign Policy, 1917–1967* (New York: Praeger, 1968), pp. 661–71; L. Kirkpatrick, "Cold War Operations: The Politics of Communist Confrontation, Part V—The Cuban Case History," *Naval War College Review* 20, no. 8 (1968): 40–41.

118. However, note the analysis of T. F. Burke, "Variant Views of the Kremlin," n. 12, and especially pp. 3–8.

119. House, *Defense Appropriations,* 10–11. See also "Readiness Status of Soviet Missiles in Cuba," OCI: 13627, 23 October 1962, p. 1: "While we are unable to confirm the presence of nuclear warheads, photo coverage continues to reveal the construction at several sites of buildings which we suspect are for nuclear storage."

120. A. Katz, *The Soviets and the U-2 Photos—An Heuristic Argument,* Rand Corporation Study RM–3584–PR, (Santa Monica, Calif.: Rand, 1963), p. v; Allison, *Essence of Decision,* pp. 106–7. See House, *Defense Appropriations,* 10, on the inadequate camouflage emplaced to counteract U.S. low-level reconnaissance.

121. It has been argued, for instance, that there is no direct evidence that Khrushchev "miscalculated" by attempting to install offensive missiles in Cuba. But this is stretching imagination well beyond what is plausible.

Chapter 6: Vietnam and the Case of the Missing Missiles

1. Pending publication of the official service histories of the Vietnam War and the declassification of internal post-mortem inquiries by the intelligence agencies, the best general source remains the official Defense Department history, *The Pentagon Papers*. All citations in the text, unless otherwise indicated are from *The Pentagon Papers: The Defense Department History of United States Decisionmaking on Vietnam,* Gravel edition (Boston: Beacon Press, 1971), 4 vols., cited as *PP* 1, 2, and so forth, with page references. The most valuable first-person accounts by CIA officials who served in Vietnam consulted for this work include: Peer de Silva, *Sub Rosa: The CIA and the Uses of Intelligence* (New York: New York Times Publishing Company, 1978); William Colby, *Honorable Men: My Life in the CIA* (New York: Simon and Schuster, 1980); Frank Snepp, *Decent Interval* (New York: Random House, 1977); see also A. Santoli, *Everything We Had: An Oral History of the Vietnam War* (New York: Ballantine Books, 1981), pp. 172–78, 195–96. On military intelligence, two works by former intelligence officials may be noted: Major General Joseph McChristian, *The Role of Military Intelligence 1965–1967,* Vietnam Studies (Washington, D.C.: GPO, 1974), and James Thompson, *Rolling Thunder: Understanding Policy and Program Failure* (Chapel Hill, N.C.: University of North Carolina Press, 1980). Useful accounts by former officials involved with Vietnam are: William Corson, *The Betrayal* (New York: W. W. Norton, 1968); Robert Komer, *Bureaucracy Does Its Thing: Institutional Constraints on US-GVN Performance in Vietnam,* Rand Corporation monograph R–967–ARPA (Santa Monica, Calif.: Rand, 1972); Townsend Hoopes, *The Limits of Intervention* (New York: D. McKay, 1969); Chester Cooper, *The Lost Crusade: America in Vietnam* (New York: Dodd, Mead, 1970); Paul Kattenburg, *The Vietnam Trauma in American Foreign Policy, 1945–75* (New Brunswick: N.J.: Transaction Books, 1982).

2. A notable exception was the CIA-MACV dispute in 1967–1968 about the enemy order of battle. The so-called "Order of Battle Controversy" between MACV and CIA was reopened, though not resolved, by the libel suit against CBS brought by the former commander of MACV, General Westmoreland. The essence of this controversy was the belief of the CIA that the total size of Communist forces in South Vietnam was approximately 500,000 men, not 300,000, as registered in the official MACV order of battle. Despite the mass of intelligence records introduced in evidence, the trial did not settle the issue of whether the Communist forces excluded from the MACV order of battle, namely, the "self-defense forces," played a decisive military role, or establish the true size of these forces in 1967–68. On the other hand, the documents released by the Army and CIA in the trial did establish that the estimates of the enemy order of battle reproduced in SNIE: 14-3-67, "Capabilities of the Vietnamese Communists for Fighting in South Vietnam" (November 1967), were too low. The documents also affirmed that CIA estimates of aggregate Communist troop strength were the most accurate. Intelligence documents relating to the Tet Offensive of February 1968, provided additional evidence to support the CIA argument that MACV estimates of enemy strength were mathematically impossible. MACV estimated that 84,000 enemy soldiers had been committed to the Tet attack, and that enemy losses were 40,000. Using the standard ratio of 1.5 men wounded for each man killed, the number of Communist casualties must have been approximately 100,000, or 16,000 more than the number of troops MACV estimated had been committed. For documentation on the controversy, see House Select Committee on Intelligence, *U.S. Intelligence Agencies and Activities: the Performance of the Intelligence Community,* 94th Cong., 1st sess., September–October 1975, 683–719; ibid., "U.S. Intelligence Agencies and Activities: Risks and Control of Foreign Intelligence," November–December 1975, 1684–1727. For CIA troop estimates, see for example, CIA, Directorate of Intelligence, Memorandum, "The Communist Ability to Recoup their Tet Military Losses," 1 March 1968, especially table 2.

3. F. H. Hinsley, *British Intelligence in the Second World War* (Cambridge: Cambridge University Press, 1981), vol. 2, pp. 3–5; Leslie Gelb, *The Irony of Vietnam: The System Worked* (Washington, D.C.: Brookings Institution, 1979), pp. 268–70, especially pp. 309–10, 319; Frances Fitzgerald, *Fire in the Lake* (Boston: Little, Brown, 1972), pp. 486–94.

4. De Silva, *Sub Rosa,* p. 230. See also David Abshire, "Lessons of Vietnam: Proportion and Credibility," in *The Vietnam Legacy,* ed. Antony Lake (New York: New York University Press, 1976), esp. pp. 397–98: " 'Escalation' became a popular concept, and the theory of 'flexible response' came into popularity among defense planners; thus Vietnam became a testing ground for these two untried strategies; 'gradual escalation,' which might have some validity in nuclear warfare, was misapplied to the ground war in Asia." See also Daniel Ellsberg, "The

Quagmire Myth and the Stalemate Machine," in *Papers on the War* (New York: Simon and Schuster, 1972), pp. 42–131; and Col. Edward King (Ret.) *The Death of the Army* (New York: Saturday Review Press, 1972), pp. 63–65, on the U.S. army version of the "flexible response" doctrine.

5. See McChristian, *Military Intelligence,* pp. 12ff.; Komer, *Bureaucracy,* pp. 59–60.

6. CIA Memorandum, "Intelligence Failure in Vietnam," 24 January 1969, pp. 23–25, 29.

7. See Komer, *Bureaucracy Does Its Thing,* p. 60. The problem was compounded by the fact that the U.S. military and South Vietnamese intelligence organizations were focused in a traditional manner mostly on the enemy order of battle and related information; identifying and locating enemy main force units and movements was the primary task, to the neglect of the local guerrilla militias and the Viet Cong infrastructure. As a result, real enemy strength was often underestimated, a tendency reinforced by the lack of consistent hard intelligence on Viet Cong recruitment in the rural areas. Apart from captured documents, prisoner of war interrogations, and technical systems, much of U.S. military knowledge of the Viet Cong came from combat itself. Hence, U.S. commanders also tended to believe that data about such contacts revealed enemy capabilities, that is, that lessened Viet Cong operations were equivalent to reduced capabilities.

8. See Lucien Bodard, *The Quicksand War: Prelude to Vietnam* (Boston: Little, Brown, 1967), pp. 336ff., on a similar French problem.

9. McChristian, *Military Intelligence,* pp. 94–125. Numerous studies of the Viet Cong organization, and the operational methods and tactics of the Communists were produced. See, for example, V. Pohle, *The Viet Cong in Saigon: Tactics and Objectives during the Tet Offensive,* Rand monograph RM-5799-ISA/ARPA (Santa Monica, Calif: Rand, 1969).

10. See Edward Luttwak, "On the Need to Reform American Strategy," in *Planning U.S. Security,* Philip Kronenberg, ed., (Washington, D.C.: GPO, 1981), p. 19. See especially Komer, "The Military Play out their Institutional Repertories," *Bureaucracy Does Its Thing,* pp. 45–49; and King, *Death of the Army,* pp. 68–69.

11. See for example *PP* 2, pp. 650–51, doc. 102, JCS memorandum to General Maxwell Taylor, 12 October 1962, "Counter-insurgency Operations in South Vietnam." Also *PP* 2, pp. 434–35. For comparison, see Bernard Fall, "The Second Indochina War," in *Street Without Joy* (New York: Schocken Books, 1972), pp. 343–45.

12. On General William Westmoreland's strategy, see *PP* 3, pp. 395–97; Douglas Kinnard, *The War Managers* (Hanover, N.H.: University Press of New England, 1977), chap. 3, especially pp 39–46; Lieutenant Colonel D. R. Palmer, *Readings in Current Military History* (West Point, N.Y.: GPO, 1969), p. 94; Colonel (Ret.) H. G. Summers, *The Strategy of the Vietnam War in Context* (San Francisco: Praesidio Press, 1982); Komer, *Bureaucracy Does Its Thing,* pp. 54–58, especially p. 54. Note, for example, the JCS view on the strategic importance of the Southeast Asian Mainland and the anticipated character of the fighting in *PP* 2, p. 666, doc. 109, memorandum to the Secretary of Defense, 13 January 1962: "Any war in the Southeast Asian Mainland will be a peninsula and island-type of campaign—a mode of warfare in which all elements of the Armed Forces of the United States have gained a wealth of experience and in which we have excelled both in World War Two and Korea." In general, the strategy of "search and destroy" was far more in accord with the doctrinal offensive-mindedness of the U.S. military than the strategy adopted by the British in Malaya. See R. K. Thompson, "The Failure of American Strategy," in *No Exit from Vietnam* (New York: D. McKay, 1970), chap. 9, especially pp 124–31, 134–36. No attempt was made to relate U.S. military effort on the ground to the political aims of the struggle in the South: "The preferred military doctrine dictated the strategy and the strategy determined the policy." Hoopes, *Limits of Intervention,* pp. 62–66.

13. See Fitzgerald, *Fire in the Lake,* chap. 1; Anthony Lewis, "Re-Examining Our Perceptions on Vietnam," in CIA, *Studies in Intelligence* (n.d., internal CIA periodical), pp. 1–7.

14. For background, *PP* 2, pp. 1–125, with Gelb, *Irony of Vietnam,* chap. 3. The National Security Action Memorandum: 52, 11 May 1961, stated the U.S. objective as: "to prevent Communist domination of South Vietnam." See also *PP* 2, pp. 36, 51.

15. On the origins of the insurgency, see *PP* 1, pp. 242ff.; on the war in 1960, *PP* 1, 338ff.; and in general, *PP* 2, pp. 18–21. An NIE (14–3–53–1961) published in August 1961 concluded that Diem faced a "prolonged and difficult struggle" against the insurgency, adding that "the French with their memories of the Indochina that was and the British with their experience in Malaya tend to be pessimistic regarding Government of Vietnam (GVN) prospects for combating the insurgency," *PP* 2, p. 69. "Bloc Support of the Communist Effort against the

Government of Vietnam," SNIE 53-2-61, 5 October 1961, stated that 80 to 90 percent of the estimated 17,000 Viet Cong had been locally recruited, *PP* 2, p. 107. "Probable Communist Reactions to Current U.S. Actions in South Vietnam," concluded that North Vietnam would respond to an increased U.S. commitment with an offsetting increase in infiltrated support for the Viet Cong. "Communist Objectives, Capabilities and Intentions in Southeast Asia," SNIE: 10-62, 21 February 1962, reaffirmed that the primary Communist objective in South Vietnam was reunification with North Vietnam under Communist domination. "The Situation and Short-Term Prospects in South Vietnam," INR memorandum of 3 December 1962, *PP* 2, pp. 690ff., doc. 119, furnished a lucid explication of the nature of the Communist threat, Communist strategy and objectives, Viet Cong organization and capabilities, and the rapid deterioration of the internal situation in South Vietnam. "Prospects in South Vietnam," SNIE: 53-63, 17 April 1963, *PP* 2, pp. 725, doc. 121), provided a rather optimistic judgment of the situation, but concluded that the Communists would continue to wage a war of attrition and that there was "no quick and easy end to the war in sight." See also *PP* 2, pp. 684ff., doc. 117, for an overall analysis of the situation in South Vietnam which emphasizes the strategic hamlet program, 13 July 1962.

16. Memorandum to the President, "A Report on South Vietnam," *PP* 2, pp. 717ff., doc. 120, said "Our overall judgment, in sum, is that we are probably winning. . . . "

17. "Outlook in Mainland Southeast Asia," NIE 50-61, March 1961, *PP* 2, p. 33, concluded that Asian governments tended to regard the Laotian crisis as a symbolic test of strength between the major powers of the West and the Communist bloc. NIE 14-3 53.61, 15 August 1961, *PP* 2, p. 72, reiterated that Vietnam was a critical test of U.S. willingness and ability "to help an anti-Communist Asian Government stand against a Communist 'national liberation' campaign." In June 1964, the Board of National Estimates at the CIA provided a response to President Johnson's query about whether the rest of Southeast Asia would fall if Laos and South Vietnam came under North Vietnamese control:

With the possible exception of Cambodia, it is likely that no nation in the area would quickly succumb to communism as a result of the fall of Laos and South Vietnam. Furthermore, a continuation of the spread of communism in the area would not be inexorable, and any spread which did occur would take time—time in which the total situation might change in any of a number of ways unfavorable to the communist cause. [*PP* 3, p. 178]

18. The NIE: 53-63, of 17 April 1962, *PP* 2, pp. 725ff., concluded that: "We believe that the Communist progress has been blunted and that the situation is improving. Strengthened South Vietnam capabilities and effectiveness, and particularly U.S. involvement, are causing the Viet Cong increased difficulty, although there are as yet no persuasive indications that the Communists have been grievously hurt." "Communist Objectives, Capabilities, and Intentions in Southeast Asia," SNIE: 10-62, 21 February 1962, also offered an optimistic prognosis.

19. See *PP* 1, pp. 265ff.; Colby, *Honorable Men,* pp 159–63. Bernard Fall was the first to establish, on the basis of direct observation, the resurgence of revolutionary war in South Vietnam in 1957. See Bernard Fall, "The Birth of an Insurgency," *Vietnam Witness* (New York: Praeger, 1966), pp. 169–89.

20. See *PP* 3, pp. 32–34. On the shortcomings of U.S. intelligence in this period see Maxwell Taylor, *Swords and Ploughshares* (New York: W. W. Norton, 1972), pp. 236–38, 239. There was, for example, a notable lack of intelligence on the full extent of Viet Cong activities in the countryside from 1958 to 1965. Whereas the Viet Cong concentrated on guerrilla warfare in the rural areas (precisely as stated by Bernard Fall and others), the focus of U.S. intelligence in Saigon seems to have been on the South Vietnamese government in Saigon and on aspects of the conventional military balance.

21. Compare *PP* 3, pp. 20–28, with Bernard Fall, "National Liberation," in his *Two Vietnams,* (New York: Praeger, 1967), especially pp 338ff. It is possible that some of Fall's judgments and prognoses were in fact incorporated into U.S. intelligence estimates. See, for example, Fall, *Street Without Joy,* pp. 349–50: "Hanoi has worked hard for ten years to build up an industrial plant of some dimensions; it does not wish to see it knocked out in a series of even conventional saturation raids." Compare this conclusion with the NSC assessment in November 1964.

22. See *PP* 2, pp. 150–51, 456, 704–716; *PP* 3, pp. 32, 119. But note Colby, *Honorable Men,* pp. 147–50.

23. See *PP* 3, p. 25; David Halberstam, *The Best and the Brightest*, (New York: Crest Books, 1972), pp. 228–29. The official response of General Harkins to the CIA Survey Team report needs to be noted:

> I have no quarrel with most of the statements contained in the CAS Survey Team appraisal. Where the statements are clear-cut, the supporting information was usually provided by my field personnel and reflected in reports already sent to Washington by this headquarters. Where the statements are sweeping, they are based on opinion or an unfortunate penchant for generalizing from the specific. [*PP* 3, pp 34–35.]

This reply exemplified the basic problem of the collaboration between intelligence and decision makers in the war. Harkins's objection to "generalizing from the specific" is tantamount to a disapproval of inductive reasoning—the very basis of the analytical process in intelligence assessment.

24. *PP* 3, pp. 34–35. See also *PP* 3, pp. 41–42, for the special report of the CIA Saigon station chief Peer de Silva. Compare this with the Special Assistant for Counterinsurgency and Special Activities (SACSA) assessment in late 1963, *PP* 3, p. 25.

25. "Short-term Prospects in Southeast Asia," SNIE: 50-64, 11 February 1964, *PP* 3, p. 42, was especially pessimistic, concluding that unless there was marked improvement in the effectiveness of the South Vietnamese government and armed forces "South Vietnam has, at best, an even chance of withstanding an insurgency menace during the next few weeks and months."

26. But see *PP* 2, p. 69, for an allusion to the First Indochina War in an NIE, August 1961. See also Ellsberg, *Papers on the War*, p. 28, n. 16; and Larry Berman, *Planning a Tragedy: The Americanization of the War in Vietnam* (New York: W. W. Norton, 1982), p. 26, on U.S. officials' attitudes to Indochina.

27. On the Taylor mission, *PP* 2, pp. 85–102, 108–9; Gelb, *Irony of Vietnam*, pp. 73–75; and Ellsberg, *Papers on the War*, pp. 52–75.

28. *PP* 2, p. 92, 91: "As an area for the operations of U.S. troops, SVN is not an excessively difficult or unpleasant place to operate."

29. Fall, *Vietnam Witness*, pp. 39, 231–32. Dien Bien Phu was perhaps the exceptional instance. Whereas French military officers and observers agreed that air power on a more massive scale than was then available could not have changed the outcome of the Indochina War, they thought that air power could have saved Dien Bien Phu. See Bernard Fall, *Hell in a Very Small Place: The Siege of Dien Bien Phu* (Philadelphia: Lippincott, 1966), pp. 455ff.

30. See Thompson, *Rolling Thunder*, chap. 4, for a full analysis of intelligence in the bombing program. For background, *PP* 3, pp. 269–388; on the decision, see Kattenburg, *Vietnam Trauma*, pp. 122ff.

31. SNIE: 50-2-64, 25 May 1964, *PP* 3, pp. 124–25, also p. 206; *PP* 3, pp. 406, 408, 427–28. For a discussion, see Berman, *Planning a Tragedy*, pp. 52–57.

32. *PP* 3, pp. 352–53, also pp. 101–4.

33. *PP* 3, pp. 364–65.

34. The CIA estimates of Communist reactions to systematic air attacks in North Vietnam acknowledged a "substantial danger" that the North Vietnamese might send their own regular units on a large scale into the South. SNIE: 10-3-64, 9 October 1964, predicted that China was unlikely to enter the war, even as the result of a systematic U.S. campaign against the North; SNIE: 50-2-64, 25 May 1964, *PP* 3, p. 124, had forecast that air attacks against North Vietnam would not affect enemy capabilities because the major sources of Communist strength in South Vietnam were indigenous. The Sigma II war games (8–11 September 1964), conducted under the JCS, indicated that the bombing of all possible targets in the North would not cripple Hanoi's capacity. See Berman, *Planning a Tragedy*, p. 51.

35. *PP* 3, pp. 210–48; *PP* 3, pp. 651–56 doc. 240, NSC Working Group on Vietnam, November 24, 1964, "Section 1: Intelligence Assessment: The Situation in Vietnam." See also *PP* 3, pp. 656–57 doc. 241 (revised draft).

36. For example, "The Effects of the Bombing of North Vietnam," a June 1965 State Department intelligence note (INR), concluded that U.S. air strikes had no effect on public morale. See Berman, *Planning a Tragedy*, pp. 162–63, n. 45. See also *PP* 4, pp. 12, 168, 180, 188.

37. *PP* 3, pp. 352–53; also pp. 100–1. A pessimistic estimate was submitted to the president by the Board of National Estimates on 27 April 1965. See *PP* 3, p. 364, and pp. 480–81. See also the memorandum to Secretaries Rusk and McNamara by the new CIA director, Admiral

William F. Raborn, *PP* 3, p. 365. Also Thomas Powers, *The Man Who Kept the Secrets,* (New York: Pocket Books, 1979) pp. 210–12.

38. *PP* 4, pp. 345–86, also pp. 26–32.

39. *PP* 4, pp. 71–75; Thompson, *Rolling Thunder,* pp. 50–51; also *PP* 4, p. 76, for a DIA estimate of the effect of the bombing on the petroleum, oil, and lubricants (POL) system.

40. See CIA-DIA joint appraisal of the bombing, "An Appraisal of the Bombing of North Vietnam through 12 September 1966," Lyndon Baines Johnson Library, Austin, Texas (declassified 13 April 1976).

41. *PP* 4, p. 119.

42. *PP* 4, pp. 224–25.

43. *PP* 4, pp. 133–37, 259–76. See William Shawcross, *Sideshow* (New York: Simon and Schuster, 1979), pp. 210–11, on the NSC document.

44. See Berman, *Planning a Tragedy,* pp. 121–29; also *PP* 4, pp. 299–300; Gelb, *Irony of Vietnam,* pp. 124–30.

45. *PP* 3, pp. 424–29, 438–41, 463; *PP* 4, pp. 402–4.

46. *PP* 3, pp. 121, 207, 424–26, 434–35.

47. Kattenburg, *Vietnam Trauma,* pp. 126–30.

48. Berman, *Planning a Tragedy,* pp. 100–5; see p. 168, n. 32, for the final proposal to President Johnson from Secretary McNamara on 20 July 1965.

49. Ray Cline, *Secrets, Spies, and Scholars,* (Washington, D.C.: Acropolis Books, 1976), p. 199: "CIA was the bearer of bad tidings throughout the Vietnam War, and was not very happily received by any of the policymakers who tried to make the Vietnam intervention work." See also Halberstam, *Best and the Brightest,* p. 562. See *PP* 4, p. 505, and the pessimistic analysis of Undersecretary of State Nicholas Katzenbach, *PP* 4, pp. 506–7. For the military view in 1967, see *PP* 4, pp. 516–20; Kinnard, *War Managers,* p. 71, and Gelb, *Irony of Vietnam,* pp. 315–18.

50. *PP* 4, pp. 539, 550–52.

51. See *PP* 4, p. 469, for SNIE on the Soviet attitude. On Chinese Communist intentions, see "Chinese Communist Intentions in the Vietnam Situation," SNIE: 13-66, 4 August 1966 (declassified 12 April 1976).

52. Snepp, *Decent Interval.*

53. For early CIA assessments of North Vietnamese strategy, see for example, Directorate of Intelligence Memorandum SC No. 2226/64, 9 September 1964, "Communist Reactions to Increased U.S. Pressure against North Vietnam;" Directorate of Intelligence Memorandum SC No. 01933/68, 27 February 1968, "Future Communist Military Strategy in South Vietnam"; Office of Current Intelligence Memorandum SC No. 10526/65, 14 December 1965, "Hanoi's View of the War." See also ONE Memorandum, 29 February 1968, "Communist Alternatives in Vietnam." It is noteworthy how few of the declassified CIA and DIA estimates produced before the Tet Offensive deal with North Vietnamese military and political strategy.

54. "The Outlook From Hanoi: Factors Affecting North Vietnam's Policy on the War in Vietnam," 5 February 1970. SNIE: 14-3-70, p. 6.

55. Ibid.

56. Snepp, *Decent Interval,* pp. 21, 23, 27. But there were intelligence failures in this period too. The CIA did not anticipate the North Vietnamese reaction to the South Vietnamese invasion of Laos in 1971; the North Vietnamese show of force predicted for the spring of 1972 in the Central Highlands did not occur; instead, North Vietnam launched an all-out conventional offensive. The CIA also did not appreciate the importance of the Cambodian port of Sihanoukville for the North Vietnamese logistical system.

57. See CIA memorandum, "Stocktaking in Indochina: Longer Term Prospects," 17 April 1970. See also "North Vietnamese Intentions in Indochina," SNIE: 14-3.1-70, 26 June 1970.

58. Snepp, *Decent Interval,* pp. 130ff., on NIE: 53/14-3-74. See also House Select Committee on Intelligence, *U.S. Intelligence Agencies and Activities: The Performance of the Intelligence Community,* pt. 2, 94th Cong., 1st sess., September–October, 1975, 693.

59. House Select Committee on Intelligence, *U.S. Intelligence Agencies and Activities: Risks and Control of Foreign Intelligence,* pt. 5, 94th Cong., 1st sess., 1977 (testimony of DCI William Colby).

60. As quoted in Amron Katz, *Verification and SALT,* (Washington, D.C.: Heritage Foundation, 1979), p. 12. See also D. McLachlan, *Room 39* (New York: Atheneum, 1968), p. 343; Kattenburg, *Vietnam Trauma,* pp. 178–79.

61. Gelb, *Irony of Vietnam,* p. 321; Kattenburg, *Vietnam Trauma,* pp. 138, 174–75; Ellsberg, *Papers on the War,* p. 28, n. 16.

62. William Bundy, assistant secretary of state for Far Eastern affairs under Johnson, was

an exception. He had monitored the pertinent cable traffic and estimates relating to the First Indochina War in the early 1950s while working at the CIA. His predecessor, Roger Hilsman, was another exception, having served with the OSS in Burma. Middle-echelon U.S. military officers read Bernard Fall, but the French experience in Indochina remained unknown to most members of the U.S. high command. General Westmoreland, however, is said to have kept a well-thumbed copy of *Street Without Joy* at his bedside. Westmoreland's memoirs contain nine references to Dien Bien Phu, and mention the destruction of *Groupement Mobile* six times. Both battles seem to have dominated his thinking about the nature of the war and operational behavior of the North Vietnamese. In the siege of Khe Sanh, General Westmoreland had to mind the precedent of Dien Bien Phu. Robert Pisor, *The End of the Line: The Siege of Khe Sanh* (New York: W. W. Norton, 1982), pp. 48–50, 138–39. Other American commanders in Vietnam tended to be overly critical and almost patronizing about the French war in Indochina. See Fall, *Two Vietnams*, p. 349, and *Street Without Joy*, pp. 371–75.

63. For example, the conclusion of "Current Chinese Communist Intentions in the Vietnam Situation," SNIE: 13-66, 22 August 1966,:

The Chinese Communists have responded to recent U.S. air action against North Vietnamese POL facilities and to Ho Chi Minh's July 17 appeal for more aid with massive propaganda demonstrations all over China. These occasions were used to renew pledges of complete support for Hanoi and to reiterate the Chinese view that the war must be continued to final victory.

64. See "Communist Military Capabilities and Near-Term Intentions in Laos and Vietnam," SNIE: 10-65, 1 February 1965, p. 6, Lyndon Baines Johnson Library, declassified 1 June 1976.

65. For example, "Prospects in South Vietnam," NIE: 53-64, *PP* 2, p. 725, doc. 121:

We believe the Communists will continue to wage a war of victory. They evidently hope that a combination of military pressure and political deterioration will in time create favorable circumstances either for delivering a *coup de grace* or for a political settlement which will enable them to continue the struggle on more favorable terms. . . . However, we do not believe that it is possible at this time to project the future course of the war with any confidence. Decisive campaigns have yet to be fought and no quick and easy end to the war is in sight.

A classic of the genre is "Chances for a Stable Government in South Vietnam," SNIE: 52-65, 8 September 1964, Lyndon Baines Johnson Library, declassified June 9, 1976:

At present the odds are against the emergence of a stable government capable of effectively prosecuting the war in South Vietnam. Yet the situation is not hopeless: if a viable regime evolves from the present confusion it may even gain strength from the release of long-pent pressures and the sobering effect of the current crisis.

66. In this connection, Colby comments in *Honorable Men*, pp. 298–99:

I had always felt that the analysts had been slow in appreciating the real changes wrought in the countryside by the pacification program. . . . As I looked at a number of their products now, I had a nagging feeling that they were really academic assertions of what their authors believed to be abstract truth rather than contributions to the difficult decisionmaking process of our national leadership.

67. The exaggeration in military intelligence reports of enemy casualties is only the best known example. See Pisor, *End of the Line*, pp. 262–63. Between 1965 and 1968, the commitment to an attrition strategy encouraged the development of quantitative measurement systems to measure the military "progress" of the war. Because American military commanders were by nature eager for success, any statistical reporting system was bound to be optimistically biased. On the obsession with quantification, see Roger Hilsman, *To Move a Nation*, (Garden City, N.Y.: Doubleday, 1967), pp. 444ff; Colby, *Honorable Men*, pp. 258–59, 299; *PP* 3, p. 385; and Fall, *Vietnam Witness*, pp. 305–7. See *PP* 4, p. 55, for an example of the measurement of bombing results. See Thompson, *Rolling Thunder* pp. 89ff., on sources of

distortion in intelligence collection arising from the manipulation of statistical evidence. See also Kinnard, *The War Managers,* pp. 69–74.

68. House Armed Services Committee, *Statement of Secretary of Defense Melvin B. Laird on Fiscal Year 1971 Defense Program and Budget,* 2 March 1970, 53–54. (Classified Posture Statements henceforth cited as "Classified Posture Statement 1971," and so forth). A. Wohlstetter, "Legends of the Strategic Arms Race, Part 1: The Driving Engine," *Strategic Review* 2, no. 1 (Fall 1974): 71ff., and "Legends of the Strategic Arms Race, Part 2: The Uncontrolled Upward Spiral," *Strategic Review* 3, no. 1 (Winter 1975): 71–86.

69. For additional discussion of the ICBM underestimates, see William Lee, *Underestimating the Soviet Military Threat: How the CIA Estimates Went Astray,* Agenda Paper 6 (New York: Crane and Russak, 1977); D. Sullivan, "Evaluating U.S. Intelligence Estimates," in vol. 2 of *Intelligence Requirements for the 1980s: Analysis and Estimates,* ed. R. Godson (Washington, D.C.: National Strategy Information Center, 1980), pp. 49–73; J. Prados, *The Soviet Estimate,* (New York: Dial Press, 1982), chaps. 12, 13; Freedman, *U.S. Intelligence and the Soviet Strategic Threat,* (London: Macmillan, 1977), chap. 6; L. Aspin, "Debate over U.S. Strategic Forecasts: A Mixed Record," *Strategic Review* 8, no. 3 (Summer 1980): 22–47. See also the testimony of General Daniel Graham, Director of the DIA, Joint Economic Committee, *Allocation of Resources in the Soviet Union and China 1975,* 94th Cong., 1st sess., 1975, 95–98, 120–29. The DIA and the military intelligence services, however, also contributed to the underestimation of ICBM deployments, pp. 95–97. House Permanent Select Committee on Intelligence, *Soviet Strategic Forces,* 96th Cong., 2d sess., February 1980, 5–6, 11–12, 21–22, 25–26. Daniel Graham, "The Intelligence Mythology of Washington," *Strategic Review* 4, no. 3 (Summer 1976): 59–66.

70. "Interview with Robert S. McNamara," *U.S. News and World Report,* 12 April 1965, p. 52: "There is no indication that the Soviets are seeking to develop a strategic nuclear force as large as ours." R. Barnet and M. Raskin, *After Twenty Years: Alternatives to the Cold War in Europe* (New York: Random House, 1965), p. 4: "Where we once believed that the Soviets were bent on surpassing the U.S. in military power, it now appears that . . . they are quite willing to put up with a missile gap: indeed, we have been running much of the arms race with ourselves."

71. Office of Research and Reports, "Soviet Military Policy in 1967: The Challenges and the Issues," 8 June 1967, pp. 7–8 (declassified 10 June 1980); Classified Posture Statement 1967, p. 57.

72. Classified Posture Statement 1968, p. 44. Evidence of major expansion of the Soviet force began to proliferate. As of June 1966, 250 ICBMs had been deployed, with no cessation of silo construction-starts for the SS-9 system. Fifty-four new construction-starts were added to the 1965 SS-9 figures. By October 1966, there were approximately 340 operational ICBMs (an increase of 90 missiles since midyear). There was also a massive increase in new silo construction-starts: 300–400 silos as of November 1966, the largest portion of which were for the SS-11.

73. Classified Posture Statement 1969, p. 58.

74. Classified Posture Statement 1970, p. 77.

75. Freedman, *U.S. Intelligence,* pp. 135, 153; Lee, *Soviet Military Threat,* p. 27. Also see Graham, "Allocation of Resources," p. 97: "Our failure to grasp the magnitude of the Soviet program seems to have been related to the fact that we have been burnt in the early 1960s." William Lee, *The Estimation of Soviet Defense Expenditures, 1955–1975* (New York: Praeger, 1977) and "The Shift in Soviet National Priorities to Military Forces, 1958–1985," *Annals,* AAPSS 457 (September 1981): 54–55, and *Soviet Defense Expenditures in an Era of SALT, USSI: 79-1* (Washington, D.C.: United States Strategic Institute, 1980), pp. 5–7.

76. Testimony of Andrew Marshall and Paul Nitze, Senate Select Committee on Intelligence, *National Intelligence Act of 1980,* 96th Cong., 2d sess., February–March 1980, 356, 359, 363, 368–69.

77. Sullivan, "Evaluating U.S. Intelligence Estimates," p. 54.

78. The short-range predictions of operational ICBM deployments in the annual NIE were duly reproduced in the January or February Posture Statement of the next year's estimate. Therefore, there was not a large basis for error in a one- or two-year aggregate projection. See, for example, the Classified Posture Statement 1964, p. 29, which says "By and large, the latest estimates of Soviet Strategic Forces projected for mid-1967 in the latest National Intelligence Estimate (NIE) are of the same order as those we used last year in developing our five-year Strategic Retaliatory Forces Program."

79. See William Lee, "Debate over U.S. Strategic Forecast: A Poor Record," *Strategic Review* 8 no. 3 (Summer 1980): 44–59; Herbert Goldhammer, *Reality and Belief in Military Affairs:*

A First Draft (June 1977), Rand R-2448-NA (Santa Monica, Calif.: Rand, 1979) esp. pp. 23–25. Also Edward Luttwak, "Nuclear Strategy: The New Debate," in *Strategy and Politics* (New Brunswick, N.J.: Transaction Books, 1980), pp. 32–49.

80. Allen W. Dulles, *Memorandum,* 18 August 1959, pp. 1–4.

81. "Military Build-up in Cuba," SNIE: 85-3-62, "Soviet Policies: The Next Phase," OCI: 1096/63, 18 March 1963, pp. 3–4.

82. CIA, "Trends in the World Situation," 9 June 1964, pp. 3, 6–7. Lyndon Baines Johnson Library (declassified 22 March 1976.)

83. See CIA, "Soviet Military Policy in 1967: The Challenges and the Issues," pp. 1–31.

84. Ibid., pp. 5, 9–11. On the evolution of U.S. strategic doctrine, see L. Freedman, *The Evolution of Nuclear Strategy* (London: St. Martin's, 1981), pp. 173–254. For examples, Luttwak, "Nuclear Strategy," pp. 42–43; F. Y. Kane, "Criteria for Strategic Weapons," *Strategic Review* 2 no. 2 (Spring 1974): 45ff. For more examples of this form of mirror imaging, see note 83, CIA "Soviet Military Policy in 1967," p. 15, referring to the "military lobby" in Soviet political-military relations: Classified Posture Statement 1968, p. 44 (Secretary of Defense McNamara):

> It is this interaction between our strategic force programs and those of the Soviet Union which leads us to believe that there is a mutuality of interests in limiting the deployment of anti-ballistic missile defense systems. If our assumption that the Soviets are also striving to achieve an Assured Destruction capability is correct, and I am convinced it is. . . ."

85. Richard Pipes, *U.S.-Soviet Relations in The Era of Détente* (Boulder, Colo.: Westview, 1981), pp. 135–70; William Scott, "Soviet Military Doctrine and Strategy: Realities and Misunderstanding," pp. 61ff. For an example, see Bernard Brodie, *Strategy in the Missile Age,* 2d ed. (Princeton, N.J.: Princeton University Press, 1965), pp. 171, 215. See William Kaufman, *The McNamara Strategy* (New York: Harper and Row, 1964), p. 97, where McNamara is reported to have been unimpressed by V. D. Sokolovskiy's *Military Strategy* because he could find no sophisticated analysis of nuclear war in the tract. For the earliest public Soviet statement of their objectives, see *Marxism-Leninism on War and the Army,* 2d ed. (Moscow: Ministry of Defense, 1961), p. 57. See also William Lee, "Soviet Perceptions of the Threat and Soviet Military Capabilities," in *Soviet Perceptions of War and Peace,* ed. Graham Vernon (Washington, D.C.: GPO, 1981), pp. 77–79.

86. John Dziak, *Soviet Perceptions of Military Power: The Interaction of Theory and Practice* (New York: Crane and Russak, 1981), pp. 21–29, 39–51. More recently see David Holloway, *The Soviet Union and the Arms Race* (New Haven: Yale University Press, 1983).

87. For analysis and commentary on the text, see V. D. Sokolovskiy, *Soviet Military Strategy,* 3rd ed., ed. Harriet Scott (New York: Crane and Russak, 1975); see also Harriet Scott and William Scott, *The Armed Forces of the USSR* (Boulder, Colo.: Westview, 1979), pp. 75–81.

88. W. Scott, "Soviet Military Doctrine," pp. 61ff. As Soviet military writers explained, Soviet doctrine was concerned with future war, providing a foundation for the formulation of strategy and for weapons systems development. Thus, doctrine may lead military capabilities by several years.

89. Freedman, *Evolution of Nuclear Strategy,* pp. 345–46.

90. Instead of building small, highly accurate ICBMs like the U.S. Minuteman for use in "city-busting," the Soviets began to test and then deploy the enormous SS-9. See Thomas Wolfe, *Worldwide Soviet Military Strategy and Policy, Rand Paper P-5008* (Santa Monica, Calif.: Rand, 1973), pp. 16ff.

91. Edward Epstein and Fredric Feer, "Incorporating Analysis of Foreign Governments' Deception into the U.S. Analytical System," in *Analysis and Estimates,* pp. 123–51. See also R. V. Jones, "Intelligence and Deception," in *Intelligence and National Policy,* ed. Robert Pfaltzgraff, Uri Ra'anan, and W. Milberg, (Hamden, Conn.: Archon Books, 1981), pp. 10–12; R. Heuer, "Cognitive Factors in Deception and Counterdeception," in *Strategic Military Deception,* ed. Donald Daniel and Katherine Herbig, (New York: Pergamon, 1982), pp. 60–63.

92. John Mullen, "Nuclear Exchange Ratios," in AAAS, *Summer Study in Arms Control 1960,* Collected Papers 1, p. 139.

93. See, for example, Classified Posture Statement 1968, p. 46, and Classified Posture Statement 1969, p. 58. The Classified Posture Statement 1969, p. 78, asserted: "The SS-13 in a fixed mode does not appear to offer any particular performance advantages over the SS-11.

It is estimated to have a CEP . . . about the same as the SS-11. . . . Accordingly neither one would have very much value against targets such as our Minuteman silos."

94. A. Legault and G. Lindsey, *The Dynamics of the Nuclear Balance* (Ithaca, N.Y.: Cornell University Press, 1976), pp. 48–69; A. Wohlstetter, "Legends of the Strategic Arms Race," pp. 81–82; Kosta Tsipis, "The Accuracy of Strategic Missiles," *Scientific American,* July 1975: 14–23.

95. The evidence is collected in Harris, *Arms Control,* pp. 73–74. n. 59. See also Senate Select Committee on Intelligence, *The Use of Classified Information in Litigation,* 95th Cong., 2d sess., 1978, 231–32.

96. See Harris, *Arms Control,* pp. 72–76. On the general issue, see also Michael Mihalka, "Soviet Military Deception, 1955–81," *Journal of Strategic Studies* 5 (March 1982): 40–93.

97. See Classified Posture Statement 1968, p. 46; Classified Posture Statement 1969, p. 58.

98. For discussion see Robert Laggett, Kosta Tsipis, and Edward Luttwak, "Missile Accuracy and Strategic Lethality," *Survival,* (March/April 1976): 52–59.

Chapter 7: Secret Services in Open Societies

1. George Washington, for one, was a believer in the virtues of secrecy; he wrote that "upon secrecy success depends in most enterprises of this kind and for want of it, they are generally defeated." General George Washington to Colonel Elias Dayton, his intelligence chief in New Jersey, 26 July 1777. Washington had a good grasp of the essentials of intelligence. Thus in a letter to James Lovell (1 April 1782) thanking him for a specific item of intelligence: "It is by comparing a variety of information, we are frequently enabled to investigate facts, which were so intricate or hidden, that no single clue could have led to the knowledge of them. In this point of view, intelligence becomes interesting which but from its connection and collateral circumstances would not be important."

2. See Francis Dvornik, *Origins of Intelligence Services* (New Brunswick, N.J.: Rutgers University Press, 1974), especially the discussion of espionage as a factor in creating the Egyptian Empire of the New Kingdom during the Eighteenth Dynasty, p. 10.

3. Lassa Francis Lawrence Oppenheim and H. Lauterpacht, eds., *International Law, a treatise,* vol. 2 (London: Longman's Green, 1948), p. 422.

4. His cover was his activity as a lepidopterist. He found spying both patriotic and good for the elan vital: Sir Robert Baden-Powell, *My Adventures as a Spy* (London: C.A. Pearson, 1915).

5. William Joseph Slim, *Defeat into Victory* (London: 1956), p. 39.

6. Geoffrey Till, "Perceptions of Naval Power between the Wars: The British Case," in *Estimating Foreign Military Power* ed. Philip Towle (New York: Holmes and Meier, 1982), p. 172ff.; Patrick Beesly, *Very Special Intelligence* (Garden City, N.Y.: Doubleday, 1977), chap. 1; Wesley K. Wark, "British Intelligence on the German Air Force and Aircraft Industry, 1933–1939," *Historical Journal* 25, no. 3 (September 1982): 627–48.

7. S. W. Roskill, *Hankey, Man of Secrets,* vol. 1 (New York: St. Martin's Press, 1970), p. 81.

8. The high incidence of naval officers among directors of intelligence in the West is probably not a matter of accident. Among them were Hall, Mansfield Cumming, Sinclair, and Cunningham in Great Britain; Souers, Hillenkoetter, Raborn, Inman, and Turner of the United States; Canaris in Germany; and the present head of the French foreign intelligence service, DGSE (Direction Générale à la Sécurité Extérieure).

9. Francis Harry Hinsley, *British Intelligence in the Second World War: Its Influence on Strategy and Operations* (London: H. M. Stationery Office, 1979), p. 25.

10. Ibid., p. 31.

11. Tony Bunyan, *The History and Practice of the Political Police in Britain* (London: J. Friedmann, 1976), p. 186. The directorship seems to rotate among the three services. General Strong, the first director of DIS was an army man; his successor, Sir Alfred Earle, was an air chief marshal; Sir Louis Le Bailly, who succeeded him in 1973, was an admiral.

12. Christopher Andrew, "Government and Secret Services in a Historical Perspective," *International Journal* 34, no. 2 (Spring 1979): 185.

13. U.K. Parliament. *Franks Report.* Vol. 3. Cmnd 5104. 1972. Jones's views were echoed in an interview given by General Y. Hofi, head of the *Mossad* from 1974 to 1982. The general said that he spent many sleepless nights when in office, and that he hoped that it would never be known why. Secrecy was essential in intelligence; publicity, even after the passing of a

considerable time, was usually harmful. It might shed light on the way an intelligence service operated, one revelation might lead to another, and so on. *Ma'ariv,* 20 May 1983. While Allen Dulles, William Colby, Admiral Turner, and other senior officials of U.S. intelligence have written books and articles after retirement, this has been the exception rather then the rule in the other countries under review. One's list would include General Gehlen and Isser Harel, but not many more.

14. The nonrecognition of the existence of the secret services does not stem only from the wish to protect intelligence and to make its operations more efficient. The main reason is probably mid-Victorian prudery—generals and admirals of the Napoleonic era saw nothing objectionable in espionage. Later the view prevailed that it was something to be done but not to be talked about. There were, of course, also other considerations. Intelligence was a function of the Crown, and the Crown, by definition, could do no wrong, even if individual monarchs might be poorly advised by their ministers. The relative neglect into which intelligence fell in the second half of the last century manifested the belief that one's side would prevail over the enemy without using doubtful or unfair means. These, of course, were peacetime attitudes; they began to change toward the end of the century, when European war became a distinct possibility. But they were by no means confined to Great Britain, nor have they entirely disappeared. Bismarck's successor, Caprivi, wanted to have nothing to do with intelligence, and when Ludwig Ehrhardt became West German Chancellor in the 1960s he insisted on removing intelligence officials from his office building. Willy Brandt's attitude was similar. Henry Stimson's views have already been cited. No such reticence has been reported from France or the East European countries, except perhaps in fictional accounts.

15. The true cost is known only to the prime minister, most of the intelligence expenditure is hidden somewhere in the defense estimates. The cost of running the intelligence services, including GCHQ, was estimated at 400 million pounds ($700 million) in 1982.

16. *Lord Denning's Report.* Cmnd. 2152. 1963, p. 80.

17. Ibid., p. 79.

18. David Leigh, *The Frontiers of Secrecy: Closed Government in Britain* (Frederick, Md.: V. Pubns. Amer., Aletheia Books), p. 205.

19. Following the investigation by Lord Trend on Soviet infiltration into MI 5, the directors general of the Secret Service are now appointed by the prime minister, following recommendations made by a Committee of Five which includes the chief of defense staff. Chapman Pincher, *Their Trade is Treachery* (London: Sidgwick & Jackson, 1981), p. 85. The Trend inquiry did not altogether succeed in clearing up what Prime Minister Callaghan (speaking in the Anthony Blunt debate) called a highly complicated case. See also Nigel West, *MI 5, 1945–72* (New York: Stein and Day, 1982), and Chapman Pincher, *Too Secret Too Long* (New York: St. Martin's Press, 1984).

20. At the root of virtually all cases of infiltration after 1960 there were "character defects" (money trouble, drink, unusual sex practices) rather than ideological conviction. The 1982 Security Commission headed by Lord Diplock was more concerned about the abuse of computers in connection with classified information than about the danger of infiltration by foreign intelligence services. Cmnd. 8540. 1982. There are still misgivings with regard to the effectiveness of counterintelligence and internal security; that the British government was surprised by the invasion of the Falkland Islands pointed to certain weaknesses in the operation of the SIS.

21. Anonymous review of four books on the BND, including Gehlen's memoirs, in *Studies in Intelligence* (n.d., internal CIA periodical).

22. Reinhard Gehlen, *Verschlussache* (Mainz: v. Hase & Koehler, 1980), p. 49 and elsewhere.

23. *Der Spiegel,* 31, no. 45, 1977. Gehlen countered by implying that Nollau was a security risk.

24. By way of comparison, in Great Britain the head of foreign intelligence would normally report to the prime minister's adviser on intelligence affairs.

25. The exact size of the BND staff is not known; it was thought to have about 5,500 employees in the 1970s. The official budget was DM 80 million in 1971 and is now much higher. The BfV had about 1,000 full-time employees in the early 1970s; its annual budget was DM 37 million in 1971.

26. Hermann Zolling and Heinz Höhne, *Pullach Intern* (Hamburg: Hoffman u. Campe, 1971), but also an official government handout, undated, probably 1981. According to Zolling and Höhne the CIA learned from the BND about the impending Israeli attack (p. 299), but this

was not what Mr. Helms remembered in 1981. The head of the *Mossad* was in Washington a week before the attack on a special mission.

27. These figures are based on a secret publication, *Foreign Intelligence and Security Services,* published by the CIA Directorate of Operations, Counterintelligence Staff (March 1979). The document was declassified by the young followers of Ayatollah Khomeini who seized the U.S. embassy in Teheran. The figures on the *Mossad* are probably somewhat exaggerated.

28. Several Israeli citizens were arrested on charges of espionage in the early 1950s and 1960s, but not one of them was active in intelligence. There were a few cases of Soviet penetration in the early days of Israeli intelligence, but they affected people on its periphery.

29. A journalistic account published in 1982 is of importance because it used materials inaccessible before. Shlomo Naqdimon, *Sevirut Nemukha* (Tel Aviv: 1982). According to this analysis the *Mossad* took a far more pessimistic view of Egypt's intention than did military intelligence. But the *Mossad*'s director was not even invited to the important consultations during the week preceding the war. It has been generally assumed that Israel would have at least four to five days of warning in the unlikely case that Egypt went to war. As it happened, Israel had just twelve hours of warning, and the decisive evidence came from a human source. Both Israeli and American post mortems showed that there had been literally hundreds of early warning signs, but some were not even processed, and hardly any reached the chief of staff, the minister of defense, or the prime minister.

30. Oded Granot, *Hel Hamodi'in* (Tel Aviv: Ma'ariv, Publishing House, 1981), p. 144.

31. Thus, for example, Ben-Gurion took a less alarmist view than intelligence of the missile designed by German engineers in Egypt under Nasser.

32. According to Colonel Nicolai, head of German intelligence in World War I, the Russians spent almost $7 million (13 million rubles) on intelligence in 1913 and $14 million during the first six months of 1914. Walther Nicolai, *Geheime Maechte* (Leipzig: K. F. Koehler, 1923), p. 34. Intelligence chiefs always tend to exaggerate the manpower and expenditure of the other side, but from other sources it emerged that one of the Russian stations alone—admittedly the most important, Warsaw—spent 5 million rubles.

33. Senator Proxmire introduced his statistics with the following words: "Until such accounting is made, only estimates can be made and by their nature these estimates are entirely variable. Nonetheless, the following information appears to be roughly accurate," *Congressional Record,* 93rd Cong., 1st sess., 10 April 1973, 11504. According to an equally uncertain House Government Operations Committee report (1976, unpublished) the NSA had a budget of $15 billion and employed 120,000 people. But these figures apparently referred to all of intelligence, including military-tactical intelligence.

34. *Electronic Warfare,* November 1978.

35. Victor Marchetti and John D. Marks, *The CIA and the Cult of Intelligence* (New York: Dell, 1980), pp. 57–70.

36. The Russians paid Captain Frank Bossard more, about $40,000 over a period of four years (1961–65); he passed on details about the British guided missile program.

37. Warren Irvin, "The Spy Game," *New York Times Magazine,* 2 July 1939. According to the author, "brilliant minds" were guiding more than 25,000 German spies in Europe and a somewhat lesser number of allied spies. He also noted that the spy must be a good linguist, capable of speaking several languages perfectly. He must have as little concern for honor as for his life. According to Mr. Irvin's exacting standards none of the leading secret agents of World War II would have passed muster. But such was the popular image of intelligence— inaccurate but nonetheless influential.

38. The French intelligence agency which features far more frequently in the media is the Directory for the Surveillance of the Territory (DST). Engaged in domestic counterespionage, it is part of the Ministry of the Interior. The publicity it attracts, like that focusing on the CIA, is usually negative. The SDECE was renamed DGSE (Direction Générale à la Sécurité Extérieure) in 1982.

39. Most major Soviet spies in the West were caught as the result of defection of intelligence officials from the East. Two such defectors, Goleniewski and Golytsin, brought about the arrests of George Blake, Colonel Wennerstrom, Harry Houghton, Heinz Felfe, Israel Beer, and several others.

40. Until the end of World War II, British intelligence agents were not civil servants; their salaries were at the discretion of the director of the service. They paid no income tax, and if they needed money there was always a fund of gold sovereigns over which no accountant general or *Bundesrechnungshof* had any control.

41. This may have happened because, in most countries, intelligence first came into being as a department of the army; whereas counter-intelligence was originally the assignment of the police.

42. Many of the smaller intelligence services, such as Israel's, have no inspector general because the director is supposed to know everything, or at least everything of importance that goes on inside his organization. As General Hofi, head of the *Mossad* from 1974–82, said in an interview: "I knew almost everyone in the organization by name. . . . " *Ma'ariv*, 20 May 1983.

43. In Germany it has been the practice to keep a certain balance as far as the top positions in intelligence are concerned. When Hellenbroich, a Christian Democrat, became head of the BfV in 1983, Stefan Pelny, a Social Democrat was appointed his deputy. Party political appointments were for a long time the exception rather than the rule in the United States; Kennedy at first worked closely with Allen Dulles, and appointed a Republican as his successor.

44. The 1973 British Security Commission was driven to the conclusion that a junior minister was a security risk on the grounds of character defects. Cmnd. 5367. 1973. But it noted, as did the Diplock Commission in 1982, that it was impractical to subject ministers to "positive vetting (PV) clearance" before appointment and "probably politically unacceptable" to invite them to cooperate in PV clearance procedures after appointment. Cmnd 8540. It was suggested that ministers on appointment to a department should be given specific instructions upon security problems and procedures. But this procedure depended on the *bona fides* of the minister. Such an approach became impossible in France once Communist ministers joined the Mitterand government.

45. American intelligence was criticized for not having warned about the impending military coup in Poland in late 1981. Subsequently it emerged that such warning *had* been given but it was so secret that even some of the highest officials did not know about it.

46. Dwight D. Eisenhower, remarks at the cornerstone-laying ceremony for the CIA building, Langley, Virginia, 3 November 1958. The same motive recurred in the messages of virtually every American president in recent times. President Johnson assured the CIA in 1966 that their personal abilities and superior performance "did not go unnoticed and unrecognized," but that they must suffer in silence. Like all in high public positions they were subject to criticism which they must not answer. In a 1969 speech at Langley, President Nixon said "I know that there will be no Purple Hearts, there will be no medals, there will be no recognition. . . . Your successes must never be publicized and your failures will always be publicized."

47. Bilateral exchanges quite apart, there have been general meetings several times yearly, mostly in Bern, in which all major Western intelligence agencies take part. These conferences deal mainly with international terrorism. In addition, there is a European office for the exchange of information on terrorism (TRAVI), which has branches in most European capitals.

48. This refers to the United States, Britain, Canada, Australia, New Zealand, and to some extent to Norway, Belgium, the Netherlands, and Israel. With regard to the other NATO and friendly countries it applies to a lesser degree. There are various patterns of cooperation, but there is probably no NATO country that does not engage in more than liaison activities in respect to others. Such activities have even been reported among the friendliest of neighbors: some time ago an overeager Swiss intelligence official was caught collecting information in Austria.

Chapter 8: The Antagonists: KGB and GRU

1. To emphasize the close cooperation between the armed forces and the KGB (and perhaps to moderate tension), army ranks have been given to most directors of the KGB and their deputies: "Chekist service is military service." With the formal reintroduction of military grades in the military service (1935), an equivalent system for the NKVD was established. Until a uniform ranking system was worked out in 1944–45, security service ranks were two ranks higher than their military equivalent. Thus, in 1935 Yagoda was made "Commissar General;" Yezhov became such in January 1937. Beria became Commissar General in February 1941 and Marshall in July 1945. Since then the order has been Merkulov, Army General;

Kruglov, Colonel General; Abakumov, Colonel General; Serov, Army General; Semichastny, Colonel General; Andropov, Army General; and Fedorchuk, Colonel General. Among the KGB chiefs since Yagoda, only two have not had publicized military grades, Ignatiev (1951–53) and Shelepin (1958–61). On the other hand, in a number of cases (Serov, Abakumov, Fedorchuk, Tsinev) security service generals have been bona fide military men.

2. V. I. Lenin, 8 March 1918, *Report to the VII Congress of R.C.P.* (B) in *Collected Works* 4th ed., trans. by the Institute of Marxism-Leninism, Central Committee of the C.P.S.U., vol. 27 (Moscow: Progress Publishers, 1965), p. 133. At the Stockholm Congress of the Russian Social Democratic party in 1906, Lenin had offered guarantees to Plekhanov and the Menshevik majority that there would be no Asiatic "restoration" following the revolution if there were no socialist revolution in the West. There was to be no standing army, no bureaucracy, and —by implication—no secret police. V. I. Lenin, *Selected Works,* vol. 3 (New York: International Publishers, 1943), pp. 238, 260, 261.

3. George H. Leggett, "Lenin: Terror and the Political Police," *Survey* 4 (Autumn 1975): 171. For more details on the formative period of the secret police, see Leggett's *The Cheka: Lenin's Political Police* (Oxford: Clarendon Press, 1981).

4. Most sources date the formation of Soviet military intelligence to 1921 with the appearance of the Second Directorate of the Red Army General Staff. The origin might be traced, however, to 1918, when the Third Section of Trotsky's Red Army was organized. See Leggett, *The Cheka,* p. 301. The current title, GRU, or Chief Intelligence Directorate *(Glavnoye Razvedyvatelnoye Upravlenye)* of the General Staff, can be traced to early World War II.

5. Leggett, *The Cheka,* p. 355. The secret police heads were apparently more often than not members of successive defense councils (the names for which changed occasionally without affecting their importance). It is certain that Yuri Andropov was a member. See *Krasnaya Zvezda,* 1 November 1977, and J. Dziak, *Soviet Perceptions of Military Power: the Interaction of Theory and Practice* (New York: Crane, Russak, 1981), pp. 43–49.

6. Leonard Schapiro, "The General Department of the CC of the CPSU," *Survey* 3 (Summer 1975): 53.

7. The most comprehensive study of Stalin's personal secretariat is Niels Erik Rosenfeldt's *Knowledge and Power: The Role of Stalin's Secret Chancellery in the Soviet System of Government* (Copenhagen: Rosenkilde and Bagger, 1978). Also see Schapiro, "The General Department of the CC," p. 54; Gordon Brook-Shepherd, *The Storm Petrels* (London: Collins, 1977), pp. 15–84; and Boris Bazhanow (Bajanov), *Ich war Stalins Sekretaer* (Frankfurt, 1977).

8. Poskrebyshev was evidently Stalin's righthand man for supervising incoming reports; Lt. Gen. Golikov, chief of the GRU, tended to play down reports that testified to an upcoming German invasion; as NKVD chief, Beria had seen to the placement of Merkulov as head of the division, which ran the INO (Foreign Department) shared with foreign intelligence. Beria supported Stalin's policy of not provoking the Germans. Ambassador Dekanozov's complacency was not less pronounced. See G. K. Zhukov, *The Memoirs of Marshal Zhukov* (New York: Delacorte Press, 1971); "Discussion of A. M. Nekrich's book 22 June 1941": *Soviet Historians and the German Invasion* (Columbia, S.C.: University of South Carolina Press, 1968); Barton Whaley, *Codeword BARBAROSSA* (Cambridge: MIT Press, 1973); V. A. Anfilov, *Nachalo Velikoy Otechestvennoy Voiny* (Moscow: Voenizdat, 1962).

9. Rosenfeldt, *Knowledge and Power,* pp. 198–202; Schapiro, "The General Department of the CC," pp. 58, 65.

10. There were other reasons besides the desire to have a civilian head of the KGB for Serov's transfer. In late 1958 the Soviets discovered that a GRU officer, Lt. Col. Pyotr Popov, was a CIA agent. As the KGB was responsible for counterintelligence within the military, Serov had to share the blame. See William Hood, *Mole* (New York: W. W. Norton, 1982), pp. 271–74. Moreover, Serov's reputation as a dull-witted thug did not fit in with Khrushchev's more sophisticated plans for the KGB. See Oleg Penkovsky, *The Penkovsky Papers* (New York: Doubleday, 1965), pp. 88–89. In 1963, Serov was replaced at the GRU by another KGB counterintelligence officer, Gen. Pyotr Ivashutin. Ivashutin still ran the GRU in 1982.

11. Andropov was the first chief of intelligence who played an important role in foreign as well as domestic policy. As Podgorny said when awarding Andropov the Order of Lenin: "You play a direct and active part in working out and implementing the home and foreign policies of our Party and of the Soviet state." Under Andropov foreign operations were stepped up; one of the key indicators was the steady growth of "legal" Soviet presence abroad.

12. *Materialy XXV s"ezda KPSS* (Moscow: 1976), p. 82. For more on the legal stature of

security organs, see M. I. Eropkin et al., *Sovetskoe administrativnoe pravo* (Moscow: 1979), section 10; V. V. Korovin, *"Uchastie organov gosudarstvennoy bezopastnosti v osushchestvlenii funkstsii oborony strany,"* in *Sovetskoe Gosudarstvo i Pravo* 5 (May 1975): 53–60.

13. Berzin, the longtime head of the GRU executed in July 1938, was posthumously rehabilitated; by contrast, former NKVD heads Yagoda and Beria have remained "enemies of the people," and Yezhov an "unperson."

14. Cal Carnes, "Soviet Military Intelligence: How Significant," *Military Intelligence* (January–March 1981): 1–5; John J. Dziak, "Soviet Intelligence and Security Services in the 1980's: The Paramilitary Dimension," in vol. 3 of *Intelligence Requirements for the 1980's: Counterintelligence,* ed. Roy Godson (Washington, D.C.: National Strategy Information Center, 1981), pp. 95–121.

15. This results, according to many reports, in a paper flow that surpasses that of U.S. intelligence.

16. Igor S. Glagolev, "The Soviet Decision-Making Process in Arms Control Negotiations," *Orbis* (Winter 1978): 767–76; John Newhouse, *Cold Dawn: The Story of SALT* (New York: Holt, Rinehart and Winston, 1973). The "national means of verification" are controlled in the Soviet Union, as in the West, by the armed forces. But the KGB also has COMINT intercept units of its own. On the Central Committee departments. See Leonard Schapiro, "The International Departments of the CPSU: Key to Soviet Policy," *International Journal,* 32, no. 1 (Winter 1976–77): 41–55; Elisabeth Teague, "The Foreign Department of the Central Committee of the CPSU," *Supplement to the Radio Liberty Research Bulletin,* (27 October 1980): 47.

17. The Cadres Abroad Department was formed in 1959 by Panyushkin, who headed it for many years. The department plays an important part in the selection and evaluation of personnel.

18. There is a certain amount of coming and going between these "think tanks" and the Soviet intelligence community. The heads of IMEMO and ISKAN have access to some classified information as members of the Central Committee, and it may not have been pure accident that Andropov's son has worked for Arbatov at the Institute for the Study of the United States and Canada.

19. See Ladislav Bittmann, *The Deception Game: Czechoslovak Intelligence in Soviet Political Warfare* (Syracuse, N.Y.: Syracuse University Research Corporation, 1972), pp. 214–15, for the part played by both Soviet "active measures" and faulty intelligence in the events leading to the Soviet invasion of Czechoslovakia in 1968. See also Jiri Valenta, "Perspectives on Soviet Intervention," *Survival* (March/April 1982): 54; and J. Valenta, *Soviet Intervention in Czechoslovakia, 1968: Anatomy of a Decision* (Baltimore, Md.: Johns Hopkins University Press, 1981), pp. 123–28.

20. In December 1982 Fedorchuk temporarily became Interior Minister, and Victor Chebrikov, who had been a deputy of Andropov, became head of the KGB.

21. I have no new light to shed on the subject. More than 50 percent of the material transmitted from Switzerland to the "director" in Moscow could have been composed by an intelligent student of military affairs monitoring the German press and radio—and Rudolf Roessler was a near-genius in this respect. But the rest, the more specific items, could not have been obtained in this way nor did it originate with the Western allies (an edited version of Ultra) as some have maintained. Because Roessler, the source of most of the information, had no short wave radio at his disposal, the only plausible explanation is that he received some of the material from the Swiss and the rest by means of the occasional German courier. The Swiss probably reasoned up to 1943 that in the case of a German victory in the East, the occupation of their country would only have been a question of time. They had excellent German sources at their disposal, above all the so-called "Viking line" with Generals Oster, Thomas, and Olbricht as the chief informants. For obvious reasons, they have been reluctant to discuss to this day their sources of information during World War II.

22. But electronic equipment for eavesdropping in the Soviet embassies and other installations abroad is operated by employees of the Eighth Directorate.

23. Western experts surmise that Soviet intelligence has a larger staff for examination of new U.S. patents than the total number of people employed in the U.S. patent office.

24. David A. Phillips, in *The Retired Officer* (January 1982). The East German Ministry for State Security had about 17,000 full-time employees in 1979, not counting the armed units associated with the ministry. The number of employees is now probably nearer 20,000. Most of them, as in the case of the KGB, deal with internal security rather than internal espionage. It is thought that the number of East German agents abroad is now smaller than it was twenty or thirty years ago, but that they are more qualified and better trained.

25. The East German Ministry for State Security, probably the most efficient of the satellite intelligence services, had some 350 defectors to the West between 1950 and 1980. Karl Wilhelm Frick, *Die Staatssicherheit* (Köln: Verlag Wissenschaft und Politik, 1982), p. 224.

Chapter 9: The Causes of Failure

1. Harry H. Turney-High, "Intelligence, Surprise and Countersurprise," in *Primitive War* (Columbia, S.C.: University of South Carolina Press, 1971), chap. 6.

2. Michael Handel wrote in 1977 that the studies of military surprise have reached the point of diminishing returns. The warning came several years too late. M. Handel, "The Yom Kippur War and the Inevitability of Surprise," *International Studies Quarterly* 21, no. 3 (September 1977): 461. The debate began with Roberta Wohlstetter's classic account of Pearl Harbor, *Pearl Harbor: Warning and Decision* (Stanford, Calif: Stanford University Press, 1962). Other noteworthy contributions were Barton Whaley, *Codeword Barbarossa* (Cambridge: MIT Press, 1973) as well as articles by Richard Betts, Abraham Ben-Zvi, Michael Handel, and others between 1975 and 1979. A representative bibliography is in Michael I. Handel, *The Diplomacy of Surprise* (Cambridge: Center for International Affairs, Harvard University, 1981). On the basis of a fair number of case studies Klaus Knorr concluded that the business of minimizing strategic surprise faces very formidable odds. K. Knorr and P. Morgan, ed., *Strategy Military Surprise* (New Brunswick, N.J.: Transaction Books, 1983), p. 264.

3. Carl von Clausewitz, *On War*, ed. and trans. Michael Howard and Peter Paret (Princeton, N.J.: Princeton University Press, 1976), p. 200. Lt. Colonel Jose Sanchez Mendez enlists Clausewitz as a key witness for his thesis that surprise is the most essential factor of victory. "Surprise frequently has ended a war with a single stroke." "Surprise," *Air University Review*, 33, no. 1 November/December 1981): 35. The quotation is correct as far as it goes. But in his following sentence Clausewitz severely restricts the validity of his dictum, for he says that this surprise can be used only if the adversary has committed great, decisive, and rare mistakes. In fact, Clausewitz believed that it was wrong to expect much from surprise in war. See Carl von Clausewitz, *Vom Kriege*, vol. 3, chap 9. Whether Clausewitz's views still apply in nuclear warfare is a different question. Soviet military writers believe that surprise is now of greater importance than in the past because the direct preparation and unleashing of a nuclear war no longer requires several weeks or months. Vasendin and Kuznetsov, *Voyennaya Mysl* (June 1968).

4. Fletcher Pratt argued that the Japanese did not make good aviators because they were near-sighted and because their sense of balance was impaired by certain defects of the inner ear. Fletcher Pratt, *Sea Power and Today's War* (New York: Harrison-Hilton Books, 1939). Captain G. Vivian, the British naval attaché in Tokyo, in his dispatches of 1934–35, repeatedly stressed that the Japanese had "slow brains," were unable to accept new ideas, and were therefore in a poor position to keep abreast of technological innovation. Geoffrey Till, "Perceptions of Naval Power Between the Wars: The British Case," in *Estimating Foreign Military Power*, ed. Philip Towle (London: Croom Helm, 1982), p. 187.

5. Later on, MacArthur ruefully admitted that the real failure was not having pinpointed the exact day and hour of enemy assault, but the strategic failure of not preparing South Korea to meet the attack effectively when it came: "The potential of attack was inherent in the fact that the North Korean forces had tanks, artillery and aircraft with which South Korea was not equipped."

6. There was every reason to believe that war had become highly probable, perhaps inevitable. But there was, as David Kahn has noted, not one intercept, not one shred of intelligence which said anything about an attack on Pearl Harbor. *The New York Review of Books*, 27 May 1982.

7. Richard Betts has rightly pointed out that there have been no totally unexpected attacks in the twentieth century: "All major sudden attacks occurred in situations of prolonged tension during which the victim state's leaders recognized that war might be on the horizon." The author reaches the conclusion that, "in short, the primary problem in major strategic surprises is not intelligence warning but political disbelief." Richard K. Betts, *Surprise Attack* (Washington, D.C.: Brookings Institution, 1982), p. 18.

8. In this respect past experience is not necessarily a guide to the future. In the nuclear age not only the character of war has been changing, there is every reason to reexamine the issue

of strategic surprise. For a recent discussion of this topic see R. L. Pfaltzgraff, U. Ra'anan and W. Milberg, eds., *Intelligence, Policy and National Security* (Hamden, Conn: Archon Books, 1981).

9. *Tactics and Technique of Cavalry,* 6th ed. (Washington, D.C.: 1935), p. 5.

10. This was the classical age of agents and spies in high places and low; of Sir Francis Walsingham it was said that not a mouse could creep out of any ambassador's chamber but "Mr. Secretary" would have one of its whiskers. Counterintelligence was not much less effective in Paris, Vienna, and Madrid; one cannot think of many important events that burst on a truly unsuspecting public.

11. Among them was the Duc de Choiseul, the French Foreign Minister, who predicted in 1765 that a revolution would occur in North America and that as a result the British would get out. (I am grateful to Theodore Draper for having brought this to my attention.)

12. Herbert Albert Laurens Fisher, *Political Prophecies* (Oxford: Clarendon Press, 1919). Ironically, Gibbon wrote in 1788 that the French monarchy stood founded, as it might seem, on the rock of time. The great historian invested part of his fortune in French government loans. See, on the other hand, Roger Boeshe, "Why Could Tocqueville Predict So Well?" *Political Theory* 11, no. 1 (February 1983): 79–104.

13. Richard Cobb, *Second Identity* (New York: Oxford University Press, 1969), p. 16.

14. Ibid., p. 156.

15. The CIA guide *Warnings of Revolution* notes that most warnings are available from open sources and suggests certain techniques to enhance the analyst's ability to record and assess these warnings. The following techniques are recommended: a visual reminder that consists of dropping red or blue poker chips into a clear plastic glass labeled with the name of the country. A red chip records events that adversely affect the stability of the government, blue chips indicate government countermeasures or other events positively affecting stability (p. 7). Thus, an excess of red chips suggests a serious threat. A more dynamic analytical tool is a chart of Comparative Revolutionary Climate, also called "Robert's Rings.":

> The chart shows the degree to which instability is caused by economic problems, social ferment, government repression, or political intrigue. It pinpoints specific events and their impact as revolutionary indicators. When two time periods are plotted, it becomes immediately evident whether the revolution is more or less imminent and which sector is aggravating the public tranquility the most. [p. 8]

A last, and inevitable technique is a computer program that incorporates the warnings of revolution identified in a matrix. This is known as "Status of Political Stability Managements Information System," or SPS:

> It can store, retrieve, and tabulate data as well as display information on tables and graphs. Further, it can explore various hypotheses, thus enhancing the analyst's ability to make political judgments. [p. 8]

The matrix ranges from hurricane and earthquake to crop sabotage and antigovernment coalition. These techniques are clearly meant to be of help to the beginner and it would, therefore, be unfair to submit them to rigorous examination. But it would appear that those who need such techniques should not be expected to assess warnings of revolution in the first place.

16. For a Winston Churchill or a Horace Rumbold (the British ambassador in Berlin in 1933) it was in some respects easier to understand Hitler's aspirations because their political grasp owed more to the eighteenth than to the nineteenth century. They understood instinctively that Hitler was not interested in the expansion of trade but in power, and that his ambitions would sooner or later lead to war. Rumbold's famous *(Mein Kampf)* dispatch to the British Foreign Office on 26 April 1933, predicted that Germany would, on past and present form, look for another European war just as soon as it felt strong enough. It would lull its opponents into security and finish them one by one. Rumbold's prescience has been noted by a few students of international affairs, who regard it as something of a paradox. See Robert Jervis's influential book, *Perception and Misperception in International Politics* (Princeton, N.J.: Princeton University Press, 1976). It is true that Churchill and Rumbold did not open-mindedly view each Nazi action to see if their hypothesis was correct or if perhaps Neville Chamberlain's interpretation was closer to the truth. Mr. Jervis correctly notes that it is difficult to detect differences between their methods and those used by those who were wrong. This shows that

method is not a supreme value, not even the method of open mindedness. It was the political understanding of these men that led them to correct assumptions.

17. Walter Laqueur, "Why the Shah Fell," *Commentary* (March 1979): passim.

18. House Permanent Select Committee on Intelligence, Subcommittee on Evaluation, *Iran: Evaluation of U.S. Intelligence Performance Prior to November 1978,* 96th Cong., 1st sess., 1979, 6–7.

19. Reginald Victor Jones, *Most Secret War* (London: Hamilton, 1978), p. 433.

20. William C. Potter, ed., *Verification and SALT* (Boulder, Colo.: Westview Press, 1980), p. 1.

21. Jones, *Most Secret War,* p. 113.

22. House Permanent Select Committee, Subcommittee on Oversight, *Soviet Strategic Forces Hearings,* 96th Cong., 2d sess., 7 February 1980, 25–28.

23. This, despite the fact that the CIA had received not less than twenty-six intelligence reports already in 1972 that India would soon test a device or was capable of doing so. *Pike Report.* But the DIA report was distributed only to the Joint Chiefs of Staff; furthermore it had the misleading title: *India: A Nuclear Weapons Program Will Not Likely Be Pursued in the Near Term.*

24. The Department of the Army manual on combat intelligence published in 1973 mentions only capabilities. But the army field manual of 1976 says that it is not enough to consider enemy capabilities; intentions have to be taken into account as well.

25. Among the most widely debated contributions to the strategic surprise—intelligence failure debate—have been: B. Wasserman, "The Failure of Intelligence Prediction," *Political Studies* 8 (1964): 156–69; Wohlstetter, *Pearl Harbor;* K. Knorr, "Failures in National Intelligence Estimates," *World Politics* 16 (April 1964): 455; H. A. Weerd, "Strategic Surprise in the Korean War," *Orbis* 6 (1962): 435; R. Jervis, *Perception and Misperception in International Politics* (Princeton, N.J.: Princeton University Press, 1976); A. L. George and R. Smoke, *Deterrence in American Foreign Policy* (New York: Columbia University Press, 1974); Whaley, *Codeword Barbarossa;* G. Allison, *Essence of Decision* (Boston: Little, Brown, 1971); R. Betts, "Analysis, War and Decision," *World Politics* 31, (1978): 61; M. I. Handel, *Perception, Deception and Surprise* (Jerusalem; Hebrew University of Jerusalem, 1976). A summary of these various theories is given by Frank J. Stech in *Political and Military Intention Estimation* (Bethesda, Md.: 1979).

26. Colonel George Furse, an officer in the British army in the late Victorian age, had no special training in cognitive psychology but he did stress when writing his manual *Information in War* that intelligence should not only deal with figures but also with qualitative factors —"elan," as he called it—otherwise one would never understand why the peasants in the Vendee (in the 1790s), the Mahdi in the Sudan, or the Russians in 1812, fought with such tenacity. George Furse, *Information in War* (London: W. Clowes & Sons, 1895). Secretary MacNamara would have done well to take Furse's idea as his motto.

"So in Vietnam we proceed to 'quantify' situations with statistics and graphs and charts that told everything except the only important reality—what the people think." Stanley Karnow, *Washington Post,* 20 July 1970. The CIA, for example, has shown an inclination in this direction. See Anthony Lewis, "Re-examining our Perceptions on Vietnam" in *Studies in Intelligence,* p. 3, (n.d., internal CIA periodical), which treats the theories of the perceptualists with enormous respect.

27. *An Examination of the Intelligence Community Performance before and during the Cyprus Crisis of 1974.*

28. True, there are tens of thousands of Americans with excellent language skills who have lived abroad for years, and who have a good knowledge of many parts of the outside world. But most of these men and women will not find their way into government service; it is also true that knowledge of a foreign language does not of itself provide a key to political grammar, and that more is needed to become an expert on world affairs than exposure to foreign influences.

29. A. L. George and R. Smoke, *Deterrence in American Foreign Policy* (New York: Columbia University Press, 1974); A. L. George, R. Koehane et al., in *App. D to Murphy Report: House Commission on the Organization of the Government for the Conduct of Foreign Policy, Uses of Information,* (Washington, D.C.: GPO, June 1975), 33, 64; Knorr, "Failures in National Intelligence Estimates"; A. L. George, " 'The Operational Code': A Neglected Approach to the Study of Political Leaders and Decision-Making," *International Studies Quarterly* 13, no. 2 (June 1969): 190–222; Captain Robert Bovery, "The Quality of Intelligence Analysis," *American Intelligence Journal,* (Winter 1980).

30. An exception must be made if Mr. Smith is already a knowledgeable student of the

nation in question, in which case the exercise will be unnecessary as knowledge of the opponent's viewpoint will be the starting point of his reasoning.

31. The instances most frequently quoted in this context are the Soviet blockade of Berlin in 1948, and the Soviet decision to deploy missiles in Cuba in 1962, which U.S. analysts regarded as high-risk ventures from the Soviet point of view. The Russians obviously did not share this belief.

32. Alexander L. George, *Propaganda Analysis* (Evanston, Ill. Row, Peterson, 1959). It should be noted, however, that George's example refers to the second half of the war. There is much reason to assume that a comparison between forecast and fulfillment for an earlier period would show less startling results. The FBIS (Foreign Broadcast Information Service) analysis, from what evidence is available, was better in divining and forecasting Nazi intentions after the Allies passed to the offensive.

33. G. M. Trevelyan, "Bias in History," *History*, 32, no. 115 (March 1947): 1–15

34. The parallel with psychoanalysis has been drawn by R. Heuer, "Analyzing the Soviet Invasion of Afghanistan: Hypotheses Causal Attribution Theory," *Studies in Comparative Communism* 13, no. 4 (Winter 1980): 347ff. The author argues that our attribution of causality is biased, that as a rule we do not assign enough weight to external circumstances as far as the behavior of others is concerned, but are too inclined to infer that their behavior was caused by their "nature." Our own behavior, on the other hand, is seen as conditioned almost entirely by the situation in which we find ourselves. Hence the need for increased self-awareness with regard to how people perceive and make analytical judgments concerning foreign events. That there have been such aberrations of judgment goes without saying. But no fetish should be made of increased self-awareness; the CIA record during the 1960s and 1970s shows that there were probably as many mistakes in the opposite direction (attributing too much importance to situational causes—as in the armament action-reaction spiral, the inclination to underrate ideological motives, and so forth).

35. "Prejudice," Edmund Burke wrote, "engages the mind in a steady course of wisdom and virtue." And Hippolyte Adolphe Taine: "Prejudice is a kind of reason which is ignorant of itself."

36. Adam Ulam in *The State of Soviet Studies* ed. Walter Laqueur, (Cambridge: MIT Press, 1965), p. 15.

37. The question of denial is a complex one which has been given relatively little attention by psychologists. The existing psychoanalytical literature is surveyed in *The Mechanism of Denial* ed. Bernard D. Fine et al., by the Kris Study Group of the New York Psychoanalytical Institute, Monograph 3, (New York: International Universities Press, 1969).

38. Catherine Crisholm Cushing, *Pollyanna, the Glad Girl* (New York: Klaw & Erlanger, 1915), p. 36.

39. Keith Clark (CIA), W. Hyland (INR), Lt. Gen. Samuel Wilson (DIA) in their evidence before the Pike Committee. House Select Committee on Intelligence, *U.S. Intelligence Agencies and Activities: The Performance of the Intelligence Community*, 94th Cong., 1st sess., part. 2, 1975, 722, 792. The DIA had even fewer resources on Portugal, as General Graham revealed in a Senate Hearing in 1980:

"When Portugal went bananas, you know, after they had their revolution, everything was going wild in Portugal. I can remember Mr. Clements, then Deputy Secretary of Defense, saying: 'Why are you not giving me more material on Portugal?' I said: Mr. Clements, do you know how many people I have had on Portugal in the whole Defense Intelligence Agency up to now? One sixth of a man, a guy who was handling Spain, Portugal, Angola, Mozambique, and a couple of other places was the analyst for Portugal."

Senate, *National Intelligence Act of 1980*. 1980, 374. The explanation seems persuasive enough but it also shows that the global warning system was not functioning too well: its function is to devote precise attention to potential danger zones.

40. An official British post mortem of the Falkland crisis accepted the explanation of the British Defense attaché in Buenos Aires that this section did not have the capacity to provide critical information, given Argentina's very long coastline, the distance of the southern ports from the capital, and above all, perhaps, the fact that the decision to invade was taken by the junta at a very late stage.

41. This process was known in the State Department as "Wristonization," following the publication of the Wriston report in the 1950s. According to this report, two-thirds of the

INR was staffed by Foreign Service Officers, the remaining third by civil servants exempt from rotation. Observers noted, however, that even after careful screening (many foreign service officers were far more interested in operations than research) the assignment of such officers did not always produce satisfactory results. Robert Ellsworth Elder, *The Policy Machine* (Syracuse, N.Y.: Syracuse University Press, 1960), chap. 3.

42. Fritz Fischer, *Griff nach der Weltmacht* (Dusseldorf: Droste, 1961), p. 394.

43. For an exhaustive treatment of the many misassessments among the powers during World War II, see *Knowing One's Enemies: Intelligence Assessments Before the Two World Wars*, ed. Ernest R. May (Princeton, N.J.: Princeton University Press, 1984), Passim.

44. Walter Nicolai, *Nachrichtendienst, Presse und Volkstimmung im Weltkrieg* (Berlin: E. S. Mittler und Sohn, 1920).

45. Adolf Hitler, *Monologe im Fuehrerhauptquartier* (Hamburg: 1980), p. 61.

46. *Estimates of the Status of Russian Atomic Energy Project,* Papers of Harry S. Truman, President's Secretary's File, Truman Library, 6 July 1948.

47. On Truman and the development of a Soviet nuclear bomb see Robert J. Donovan, *Tumultuous Years* (New York: W. W. Norton, 1982), chap. 9.

48. David Holloway, "Research Note," *International Security,* 4, no. 3 (Winter 1979–80): 192–197.

49. See David Carlton, *Anthony Eden* (London: A. Lane, 1981), p. 416. Ironically, two years earlier Eisenhower had written Churchill that if Indochina passed into the hands of the Communists, the ultimate effect on Western global strategy and position could be disastrous. "We failed to halt Hirohito, Mussolini, and Hitler by not acting in unity and in time. That marked the beginning of many years of stark tragedy and desperate peril. May it not be that our nations have learned something from that lesson?"

50. "Soviet Capabilities and Probable Soviet Course of Action through 1960," NIE, 3 November 1955. Naval intelligence and the Joint Chiefs of Staff took an even more rigid view in a note of dissent on the degree of Chinese independence. This was bad history, for experience had shown that movements of this kind were subject to schisms to the degree to which they expanded. There was also the precedent of Yugoslavia to show that Marxism-Leninism was no panacea against a split.

51. Barton Whaley shows that "covert" German rearmament in the 1920s was largely known at the time to British and French observers. "Covert Rearmament in Germany 1919–1939; Deception and Misperception," *Journal of Strategic Studies,* 5, no. 1 (March 1982): 3–39. No great intelligence effort was needed; the issue was discussed in the German press and even in the *Reichstag.*

52. It could be argued that this intelligence failure had momentous consequences. For if the Western Allies had known that the Soviet Union and Nazi Germany were close to reaching an agreement they might have made even more farreaching concessions to the Russians. But it is still doubtful whether such concessions would have made much difference. The Western Allies were in no position to outbid the Germans. They could not have proposed the dismemberment of Poland. See D. Dilks, "Appeasement and Intelligence," *Retreat from Power,* vol. 1 (London: Macmillan, 1981), p. 158.

53. Charles Cruickshank, *Deception in World War II* (London: Oxford University Press, 1980), pp. 227–228.

54. R. V. Jones, "Intelligence and Deception," *Journal of the Royal Institution* (Spring 1980): 142.

55. Wesley K. Wark, "British Intelligence on the German Air Force and Aircraft Industry, 1933–39," *Historical Journal* 25, no. 3 (1982): 617.

56. British intelligence underrated the number of Soviet divisions by almost 100 and were not aware of the new T-34 tank.

57. The Soviet leadership has faced this problem in one way or another since the end of World War II. The Yugoslav Ambassador to Moscow, Veljko Micunovic, wrote in his diary 16 December 1957, that the Communist party presidium had decided to "correct these mistakes" (the exaggerated propaganda about the strength and technical superiority in the field of armaments following the launching of *Sputnik*) for it is "beginning to have the reverse effect from what they wanted to achieve." Micunovic notes that the Soviet leaders had reached the conclusion that this situation (Soviet superiority) "can be quickly changed by means of vastly increased (American) investments aimed at catching up with the Soviet Union as soon as possible and depriving it of the monopoly it enjoys for the moment." Veljko Micunovic, *Moscow Diary* (New York: Doubleday, 1980), p. 327.

58. R. Heuer, "Strategic Deception and Counter-Deception. A Cognate Process Approach,"

Notes

International Studies Quarterly 25, no. 2 (June 1981): 294–327. See also Barton Whaley "Towards a General Theory of Deception," *Journal of Strategic Studies* 5, no. 1 (March 1982): 178–192, pointing to parallels between deception and the magician's craft.

59. See "Discussions" in ed. Roy Godson *Intelligence Requirements for the 1980s, vol. 2: Analysis and Estimates,* (Washington, D.C.: National Strategy Information Center, 1980), pp. 158–59.

60. Sun-Tzŭ, *Art of War* trans. by Samuel B. Griffith, (New York: Oxford University Press, 1969).

61. Quoted in House Permanent Select Committee on Intelligence, Subcommittee on Oversight, *Soviet Covert Action,* 96th Cong., 2d sess., 1980, 63.

62. If Maclean passed on information on nuclear weapons that the Soviet Union did not already possess, this statement would have to be modified. But it would have been, in any event, a case of espionage rather than deception, and for this reason irrelevant in the present context.

63. *The Listener,* 3 December 1981.

64. Barton Whaley, *Strategem: Deception and Surprise in War* (Cambridge: MIT Press, 1969) deals exclusively with wartime deception. The most recent literature on the subject is discussed in Michael Handel, "Intelligence and Deception," *Journal of Strategic Studies* 5, no. 1 (March 1982): 122–154. See also various contributions on the subject in Klaus Knorr, ed., *Strategic Deception* (New Brunswick, N.J.: Rutgers University Press, 1982).

Chapter 10: Craft or Science?

1. W. O. Aydelotte, A. G. Bogue, R. W. Fogel, eds., *The Dimension of Quantitative Research in History* (Princeton, N.J.: Princeton University Press, 1973), p. 8.

2. Sherman Kent, *Strategic Intelligence for American World Policy,* 2d ed. (Hamden, Conn: Archon Books, 1963), p. 156.

3. Willmore Kendall, *World Politics,* no. 4 "The Function of Intelligence," (July 1949): 551–52.

4. Klaus Knorr, *Foreign Intelligence and the Social Sciences* (Princeton, N.J.: Center of International Studies, Woodrow Wilson School of International and Public Affairs, 1964). Elsewhere Knorr expressed his belief that a theory of intelligence might try to identify and evaluate intelligence practices in terms of efficiency. But he also wrote that one could not say in advance whether systematic attempts at theorizing on intelligence would improve the production and consumption of intelligence. "Failures in National Intelligence Estimates," *World Politics* 16, no. 3 (April 1964): 466.

5. E. Raymond Platig, *International Relations Research: Problems of Evaluation and Advancement* (New York: Carnegie Endowment for International Peace, 1967).

6. Some experts eventually did realize that human emotions and psychological phenomena could not be captured in a computer program, but this discovery came only years later. See J. Weizenbaum, *Computer Power and Human Reason* (San Francisco: W. H. Freeman, 1976), p. 8.

7. Richards J. Heuer, "Adapting Academic Methods and Models to Governmental Needs: The CIA Experience," Paper presented to the 18th Annual Convention of the International Studies Association, St. Louis, Missouri, March 1977.

8. G. J. Graham and G. W. Carey, *The Post Behavioral Era: Perspectives on Political Science* (New York: D. McKay, 1972); Easton's presidential address, 1969.

9. Richards J. Heuer, *Quantitative Approaches To Political Intelligence: The CIA Experience* (Boulder, Colo.: Westview Press, 1978), p. 11; see also Nicholas Schweitzer, "Delphi as a Technique in Intelligence," Paper presented to the 18th Annual Convention of the International Studies Association, St. Louis, Missouri, March 1977; P. Slovic and S. Lichtenstein, "Comparison of Bayesian and Regression Approaches to the Study of Information Processing in Judgement," in *Organizational Behavior and Human Performance* (1971), p. 649; and subsequent writings by P. Slovic, B. Fischoff, and S. Lichtenstein.

10. The quotation is not from one of the Sherlock Holmes stories but from a lesser-known tale, "The Story of the Man with the Watches," *Strand Magazine* 15 (May 1898). Arthur Conan Doyle was a physician, a fact of some relevance with regard to argument on clinical judgment following.

11. A survey of recent literature on the subject is in Wayne W. Daniel, "An Introduction to Computer Assisted Diagnosis," *Journal of the Medical Association of Georgia* (April 1979): 285–89.

12. Heuer, *Quantitative Approaches,* p. 19.

13. Michael K. O'Leary, William D. Coplin, and Howard B. Shapiro, "The Quest for Relevance. Quantitative International Relations Research and Government Foreign Affairs Analysis," *International Studies Quarterly* 18, no. 2 (June 1974): 211.

14. Ibid., p. 228.

15. Heuer, *Quantitative Approaches,* p. 9.

16. Ibid., p. 11.

17. In recent years, new attempts have been made to assist the intelligence analysts in their difficult work. For instance, there has been a proposal to deal mathematically with the problem of surprise attack and, by way of game theory, with the question of deception. R. Axelrod, "The Rational Timing of Surprise," *World Politics* 2 (1979): 228.; A. J. Brams, "Deception on 2 + 2 Games," *Journal of Peace Science* 2 (1977): 171; F. C. Zagare, "The Geneva Conference of 1974: A Case of Tacit Deception," *International Studies Quarterly* 3 (1979): 390.

18. F. Stech, *Estimates of Peacetime Soviet Naval Intentions: An Assessment of Methods,* March 1981, Washington Mathtech. 1981.

19. Stephen J. Andriole, *Indications and Warnings Research and Development* (Marshall, Va.: 1982); Albert Clarkson, Laurence Krasno, and Jerry Kidd, *Indications and Warning Analysis Management System* (Sunnyvale, Calif.: 1978).

20. Jean Fernel, *Pathologiae libri VII,* quoted along with similar observations by later authors in Lester S. King, *Medical Thinking. A Historical Preface* (Princeton, N.J.: Princeton University Press, 1982), p. 79.

21. James Bamford, *The Puzzle Palace* (Boston: Houghton Mifflin, 1982), p. 190.

22. This point seems to have fascinated Émile Littré, one of the first modern medical historians and a translator of Hippocrates (1839).

23. Cabanis, *Du Degré des Certitudes de la Medicine,* Auteurs Modernes, vol. 1 (Paris: 1956), p. 91.

24. R. Koch, *Die Aerztliche Diagnose: Beitrag zur Kenntnis des Aerztlichen Denkens,* 2d ed. (Wiesbaden: Bergmann, 1920), p. 65. This book by my late father-in-law was unknown to me until I began to work on this chapter. Another physician who made the comparison even earlier was the eighteenth-century Swiss physician Zimmermann; his references to politicians were, however, entirely uncomplimentary. Zimmermann, *Erfahrung in der Arzneykunst* (Zurich: 1763), p. 7.

25. Sir James Mackenzie, *The Future of Medicine* (London: H. Frowde, 1919), p. 186.

26. Arthur S. Elstein, *Medical Problem Solving* (Cambridge: Harvard University Press, 1978), p. 302.

27. Lee B. Lusted, *Instruction to Medical Decision Making* (Springfield, Ill: C. C. Thomas, 1968); Henrik R. Wulff, *Rational Diagnosis and Treatment* (Oxford: Blackwell Scientific Publications, 1976), p. 72.

28. Alvin R. Feinstein, *Clinical Judgment,* (Huntington, N.Y.: Krieger, 1967), p. 297; see also C. A. Caceres, *American Journal of Cardiology* 38 (1976): 362; and Bourdilon et al., *European Journal of Cardiology* 8 (1978): 395. Bruce and Yarnell, "Computer-Aided Diagnosis of Cardiovascular Disorders," *Journal of Chronic Disease* (1966): 473. See also D. Vonderschmitt, *Klinische Chemie: Wie hart sind harte Daten?,* Inaugural dissertation, Zürich University, *Neue Zürcher Zeitung,* 12 May 1982.

29. Edmund A. Murphy, *The Logic of Medicine* (Baltimore: Johns Hopkins University Press, 1976), p. 151.

30. Sir Francis Avery Jones, *Richard Asher Talking Sense,* p. 3.

31. Among those active in intelligence there has always been some unhappiness about the belief by outsiders in their predictive powers. They have argued—to little avail—that their success or failure should be measured on the basis of their assessments of current events and developments in foreign parts and not on the basis of predictions.

32. As these lines are written, new editions of Nostradamus prophecies or books about him figure on the best-seller lists in Great Britain, France, West Germany, and other countries.

33. The literature on the subject is enormous. An early attempt to sort the approaches in the social sciences was Daniel Bell, "Twelve Modes of Prediction," *Daedalus* 93, no. 3 (Summer 1964): 845–81; an excellent introduction is E. Cornigh, *The Study of the Future* (Washington, D.C.: 1977), and also Solomon Encel, Mostrand, and Page, *The Art of Anticipation* (New York: Pica Press, 1976); a good collection of relevant essays is Albert Somit, ed., *Political Science and the Study of the Future* (Hinsdale, Ill.: Dryden Press, 1974); J. S. Armstrong, *Long Range Forecasting* (New York: Wiley, 1978) contains one of the most detailed bibliographies.

34. William Ascher, *Forecasting: An Appraisal for Policy-Makers and Planners* (Baltimore, Md.: Johns Hopkins University Press, 1978), p. 58.

35. Robert Nisbet in Albert Somit, ed., *Political Science and the Study of the Future* (Hinsdale, Ill.: Dryden Press, 1974).

Chapter 11: The Future of Intelligence

1. This is not to say that *all* organizational issues are insignificant; it is, for instance, of considerable importance whether the DCI is located in CIA headquarters or in the White House.

2. The 1960 Kirkpatrick report also warned against too much concentration on the military aspects of the power balance, overlooking its political and economic aspects. The warnings went unheard. The report also noted that collection through overt means was "the foundation of all Intelligence" and should not be neglected through overconcentration on less conventional means. Little attention was paid.

3. Philip Agee, ed., *CIA: The Pike Report* (London: 1977), p. 21.

4. The Department of State was a close second for a long time. As F. Mosher wrote: " . . . transition seems to have become a permanent condition in the conduct and the administration of foreign affairs. Transition can breed unsettlement; it often obscures or raises disagreements about goals, directions and values." Frederick C. Mosher, ed. *Foreign Affairs Personnel Studies*, vol. 3 (New York: 1965–66), p. xviii.

5. It is one of the paradoxes of the present system that while it makes for specialization, bureaucratic advancement is "horizontal;" that is, for generalists, not for specialists. As a result, there are few incentives to specialize, and the quality of intelligence suffers. This is one of the fields in which bureaucratic reform could do a great deal of good.

6. One of intelligence managers' most important assignments is to shield creative and innovative people from attempts to force them into bureaucratic molds. In their most creative phases, the OSS during World War II and British intelligence during the same period, were intelligence organizations that often achieved their greatest successes by doing just this. In the CIA, it became increasingly difficult during the 1970s to do it when the preoccupation with "management by objectives," computerization of management, and so on, tended to work everyone into a stereotype and those who did not fit this pattern were judged deficient.

7. The literature is listed in Stephen J. Andriole and Robert A. Young, "Toward the Development of an Integrated Crisis Warning System," *International Studies Quarterly* 21, no. 1 (March 1977): 108.

8. François De Callières, *De la manière de négocier avec les souverains,* was first published in 1716; it is quoted here following A. F. Whyte's translation, *The Practice of Diplomacy* (London: Constable and Co., 1919); Abraham van Wicquefort's book was called *L'ambassadeur et ses fonctions;* Jean Hotman's *L'ambassadeur* was first translated into English in 1603.

9. Quoted in James Westfall Thompson and Saul Padover, *Secret Diplomacy* (New York: F. Ungar, 1963), p. 63.

10. The practice prevails in most fields of intelligence except science and technology.

11. Most of the applicants for intelligence and the foreign service in West Germany are graduates of law schools, in Great Britain they are most likely to have studied arts, history, and/or classics. According to Callieres, the legal mind is not adapted to diplomacy, because the lawyer's training breeds habits of mind not favorable to diplomacy. The German selection boards think differently, but the percentage of lawyers among the recruits is now declining in any case.

12. Senate Select Committee to Study Governmental Operations with Respect to Intelligence Activities, Final Report vol. 1: *Foreign and Military Intelligence,* 94th Cong., 2d sess., no. 94-755 (Washington: GPO, 1976), 270.

13. Ibid.

14. Matters seem no better in Great Britain and France—mainly, it is said, because of insufficient budget allocations. More attention goes into the training of recruits in West Germany, and Soviet bloc intelligence puts more effort into intelligence training than the West would perhaps like to believe.

15. A full list is in Wilfred D. Koplowitz, *Teaching Intelligence,* (Washington, D.C.: National Intelligence Study Center, 1980). Among the literature assigned in some courses one finds

books by Philip Agee, John Le Carré, and Anthony Cave Brown's *Bodyguard of Lies,* (New York: Bantam, 1976), Richard J. Barnet's *The Roots of War* (New York: Atheneum, 1972), David Wise and Thomas Ross's *The Invisible Government,* (New York: Random House, 1969), and so forth.

16. The fact that officers are given a chance of further education in mid-career should be welcomed. But such refresher courses cannot possibly replace early, basic training.

17. Many pertinent examples are found in "Elegant Writing in Intelligence," in *Studies in Intelligence* (n.d., internal CIA periodical).

18. From the beginning, civil service exemptions served the CIA primarily to expedite procedural matters; they have had little impact on the quality of intelligence.

19. The classic discussion is in Max Weber, "Politics as a Vocation," *From Max Weber. Essays in Sociology,* trans. and ed. H. Gerth and C. W. Mills (New York: Oxford University Press, 1958), pp. 120–27.

20. Harold Nicholson, *The Evolution of Diplomatic Method* (London: 1954), pp. 85–86.

21. Nicholas de B. Katzenbach, "Foreign Policy, Public Opinion and Secrecy," *Foreign Affairs* 52, no. 1 (October 1973): 1–19.

22. For practical purposes, there was only one group, which was run by the national security adviser. Under the Reagan administration, the director of Central Intelligence became chairman of this group, SIG-I, which dealt with policy, not operations.

23. Bonner Day, "The Battle over U.S. Intelligence," *Air Force Magazine* (May 1978): 44. There were reportedly some ten operations in 1978–79 that fell into the covert action category, none of them of great importance. The controversy resumed following the decision in November 1981 to support covert operations in Central America.

24. James Michael, *The Politics of Secrecy* (New York: Penguin Books, 1982), pp. 63–64.

25. There is, in fact, a Swedish Secrecy Act. There are such acts in the other Scandinavian countries, in Canada, Australia, New Zealand, and every European country. American attitudes toward secrecy are dominated by the First Amendment's presumption against most forms of censorship. "Prior restraint" can hardly ever be used to stop publication; and legal penalties, if any, can be imposed only after publication.

26. Several DCIs and heads of INR have told me that during their terms of office more leaks came from the White House than from Congress.

27. The government can try to use "prior restraints" against publications if the person in question has signed "secrecy agreements" while in office. This did not help in the case of the Pentagon Papers, though the same approach was later used in the case of Victor Marchetti and John D. Marks, *The CIA and the Cult of Intelligence* (New York: Dell, 1980) with regard to classified information. However, as their attorney rightly noted in his preface to their book: " 'Secrets' are regularly leaked to the press by government officers, sometimes to serve official policy, sometimes only to serve a man's own ambitions. In fact, disclosure of so-called secrets —even CIA secrets—has a long and honorable history in our country, and the practice had proved valuable because it provides the public with important information that it must have in order to pass judgment on its elected officials." Melvin L. Wolf in Marchetti and Marks, *The CIA and the Cult of Intelligence,* p. xxiv.

28. Since the enactment of the 1980 Classified Information Procedures Act it has become possible to give substantial, though not complete, protection to classified information in the course of an espionage prosecution.

29. House Permanent Select Committee on Intelligence, Subcommittee on Legislation, *Espionage Laws and Leaks,* 96th Cong., 1st sess., 24, 25, and 31, January 1979. See in particular evidence given by Robert L. Keuch, Anthony A. Lapham, Harold Edgar, Benno Schmidt, Jr., John H. Maury, and Thomas I. Emerson. See also H. Edgar and B. Schmidt, "The Espionage Statutes and Publication of Defense Information," *Columbia Law Review,* 1973 929,; and the landmark cases of *Gorin v. United States, United States v. Heine, Brady v. Maryland;* the *New York Times-Pentagon Papers* case; and the Jencks Act.

30. There is the danger that effective laws against leaking will be used by the authorities to muzzle inconvenient critics. In the Frank Snepp case, which dealt with this former CIA employee's book on the last stage of the U.S. presence in Vietnam, such steps were taken by the CIA, even though no classified material was involved. The government's case was that it had no wish to muzzle an inconvenient critic, but simply to establish the principle of prepublication review as required under Snepp's CIA employment contract. The case of the Pentagon Papers was more complicated. They contained not just position papers and memoranda, but also some of the most sensitive intelligence material of the day, and the products of operation "Gamma Guppy"—intercepts of conversations between Soviet leaders. This

source, needless to say, dried up after a set of the Pentagon Papers had been passed on to the Russians. James Bamford, *The Puzzle Palace,* (Boston: Houghton Mifflin, 1982), p. 283.

31. The history of the CIA itself began with a leak—the publication in the McCormick-Patterson papers (January 1945) of General William Donovan's and the JCS's plans to create an "all powerful super spy system as disclosed in a secret memo." The leaker, quite likely, was President Roosevelt himself. Thomas F. Troy, *Donovan and the CIA,* (Frederick, Md.: Aletheia Books, 1981), p. vi; Anthony Cave Brown, *Last Hero: Wild Bill Donovan* (New York: Times Books, 1982), p. 627.

32. But it is also true that there has been a strong inclination in the twentieth century to magnify the extent of this tradition. An illustration will show the caution exercised by the Founding Fathers. The Committee of Secret Correspondence of the Continental Congress refused in 1776 to pass on certain information to Congress, since it had found "by fatal experience" that the Congress consisted of too many members to keep secrets. See Daniel N. Hoffman, *Governmental Secrecy and the Founding Fathers* (Westport, Conn.: Greenwood Press, 1981).

33. Peter Szanto and Graham Allison, "Intelligence: Seizing the Opportunity," *Foreign Policy* 22 (Spring 1976): 183–205; the same ideas appear in the Church Report, vol. 1, p. 450; the writings of Ray Cline, and papers presented at the conference on "CIA and Covert Action," September 1974.

34. The Soviet term "active measures" *(aktivnie meropriyatiya)* is more comprehensive and more accurate than "covert action." It includes, according to a CIA study, the manipulation of foreign Communist parties and front organizations; written and oral disinformation (particularly forgeries); manipulation of foreign media; agents of influence; manipulation of mass organizations and demonstrations; covert political, financial and arms support for insurgents, separatist movements and opposition groups and parties; and ad hoc political influence operations—often involving elements of deception, blackmail, or intimidation. This list covers not only clandestine but also overt or semi-overt operations. It is by no means complete; in fact, it should cover all foreign political activity incompatible with normal diplomatic practice. House Permanent Select Committee on Intelligence, *Trends and Developments in Soviet Active Measures,* 13 and 14 July 1982, 97th Cong, 2d sess., 50. The most authoritative discussion of the problems facing covert action organizations in World War II is in Michael R. D. Foot, *SOE in France* (London: H. M. Stationery Off., 1966).

35. George Carver, *Foreign Policy,* (Spring 1976).

36. A point which was made, for instance, by John Bruce Lockhart: "The Relationship between Secret Services and Government in a Modern State," *Journal of the Royal United Service Institute,* (London, June 1974).

37. Roberta Wohlstetter, *Pearl Harbor: Warning and Decision* (Stanford, Calif.: Stanford University Press, 1962), p. 384.

38. The gray zone has always existed; for various reasons Americans have often pretended that it did not, and that there was a sharp line between war and peace. After World War II, there was a better understanding of the concept than in the 1960s, when programs for countering insurgency became fashionable and a large part of the foreign affairs bureaucracy became preoccupied with the problem. In the 1960s the notion of a gray zone was institutionalized, but in a way that distorted the problem and eventually discredited the idea itself; similar attitudes affected the approach to terrorism. There is now a tendency to label the whole gray zone as what it actually is: an area of low-intensity warfare. This concept encompasses everything from insurgency in its various forms to terrorism, propaganda, and more subtle forms of destabilization.

39. According to press reports, a covert action group named "Army Intelligence Support Activity" was set up in 1980–81 in the Pentagon, independent of the CIA and DIA. This unit seems to be similar in function to special anti-terrorist units established in Britain, West Germany, and France. *International Herald Tribune,* 12 May 1983.

40. The idea of a Joint Intelligence Committee was first mooted by Senator Mike Mansfield in 1955; for a variety of reasons, some of them constitutional, the project did not materialize. In retrospect, this seems regrettable, for a Joint Committee—with a small, competent staff—might well be a better vehicle for oversight than two separate committees. There are precedents for such organs, such as the Joint Atomic Energy Committee. But such oversight is likely to work only if there is a consensus between the two political parties. Votes in the House Permanent Select Committee on Intelligence have been all too often along party lines. As the concept of parliamentary democracy is based on the assumption that difference of

view and interest exist and should be fully expressed—except, perhaps, in times of supreme danger—it is unreasonable to expect a consensus on intelligence in "normal" periods.

41. For instance, House Permanent Select Committee on Intelligence, *The Cuban Emigres: Was There a U.S. Intelligence Failure?*, 96th Cong., 2d sess., June 1980.

42. House Permanent Select Committee on Intelligence, Subcommittee on Oversight and Evaluation, 97th Cong., 2d sess., *The U.S. Intelligence Performance on Central America*, 22 September 1982, p. 7.

43. Established according to the recommendation of the Hoover Commission, the PFIAB first became known as the Killian Committee. It was dissolved under Carter, but reestablished by President Reagan. The reason given by the present PFIAB for not increasing its staff is that experience has indicated a danger that an augmented staff would run the committee. While the original PFIAB under Eisenhower was constituted mainly of scientists, James Killian, writing in 1977 (after the PFIAB was abolished by President Carter), noted that none of the new Oversight Board members was a scientist. James R. Killian, Jr., *Sputnik, Scientists and Eisenhower* (Cambridge, Mass.: MIT Press, 1982), p. 93.

44. In the eyes of the Carter administration the great sin of PFIAB was its program of competitive estimates (Team A and Team B). The notion spread that the recommendations made by Team B were intended to limit Carter's latitude in foreign policy. In actual fact the enterprise was started well before Carter became a presidential candidate.

45. The three members of the Intelligence Oversight Board (IOB) established by President Ford also had direct access. But whereas Ford worked fairly closely with both the PFIAB and IOB, it is believed that neither President Carter nor his attorney general ever met with the IOB during their terms of office.

46. Examples are quoted in the Rockefeller Report, *Commission on CIA Activities within the United States, Report to the President* (Washington, D.C.: Supt. of Docs., GPO, 1975), and the Church Report vol. 1, p. 295.

47. The 40 Committee also seldom met; most of its business was transacted over the telephone—a practice at least sometimes preferable to protracted meetings. *Murphy Report*, House Commission on the Organization of the Government for the Conduct of Foreign Policy (Washington, D.C.: GPO, June 1975), p. 74.

48. As one former European intelligence chief put it: "Much of the time we had to explain to them [the academics] what the problem was, and what information we had. Since they had not followed events as closely as we did, their contribution was too vague to be of any use to us."

49. Lawrence Freedman, *U.S. Intelligence and the Soviet Strategic Threat* (Boulder, Colo.: Western Press, 1977).

50. David Dilks, "Appeasement and Intelligence," *Retreat from Power*, vol. 1, (London: Macmillan, 1981) p. 169.

51. In testimony before a Senate committee in September 1982 Admiral Bobby Inman said that while the United States was good at technical intelligence, there have been many times when the country was surprised "because we did not understand events," because there was no real understanding of the motives of other actors on the world scene. Major General William Odom said on the same occasion that "the big intelligence failures of the 1980s and 1990s are likely to be in analysis." *Washington Post*, 23 September 1982.

LIST OF ABBREVIATIONS

ABM—Antiballistic Missile
BND—German External Intelligence Service
CC—Central Committee (USSR)
CFI—Committee on Foreign Intelligence
CIA—Central Intelligence Agency
CIG—Central Intelligence Group
COMINT—Radio Communications Intelligence
COMUSMACV—Commander, U.S. Military Advisory Command, Vietnam
DCI—Director of Central Intelligence
DDI—Directorate of Intelligence (DDI)
DDP—Directorate for Plans (CIA: predecessor of the DDO; renamed in 1973
DGI—Cuban Central Intelligence
DIA—Defense Intelligence Agency
DIC—Defense Intelligence Committee (Great Britain)
DI#5, DI#6—Directorate of Security Services (Great Britain)
DIS—Directorate General of Intelligence (Great Britain)
DOD/ISA—Department of Defense, International Security Affairs
ELINT—Electronic Signal Intelligence
GOSPLAN—State Plan (Soviet Union)
GCHQ—Government Communication Headquarters (Great Britain)
GPO—Government Printing Office
GRU—Soviet Military Intelligence
HUMINT—Human Intelligence
ICA—International Communications Agency
ICBM—Intercontinental Ballistic Missile
ICS—Intelligence Community Staff
IDA—Institute for Defense Analysis
INR—Bureau of Intelligence and Research
IOB—Intelligence Oversight Board
IRBM—Intercontinental Range Ballistic Missile
JCS—Joint Chiefs of Staff
JIB—Joint Intelligence Bureau (Great Britain)
JIC—Joint Intelligence Committee (Great Britain)
JIS—Joint Intelligence Staff (Great Britain)
KGB—Soviet Committee for State Security
KIQ—Key Intelligence Question
MAAG—U.S. Military Assurance Advisory Group
MACV—Military Assistance Command Vietnam
MAD—German Counterintelligence Service
MI#5, MI#6—British Security Service (British Counterintelligence)
MIRV—(Multiple Independent Re-entry Vehicle)
MRBM—Medium Range Ballistic Missile
MVD—Ministry of the Interior (USSR)
NFIP—National Foreign Intelligence Program
NIA—National Intelligence Authority

NIE—National Intelligence Estimate
NIPE—National Intelligence Program Evaluation
NIRB—National Intelligence Resource Board
NIT—National Intelligence Topics List
NKVD—earlier incarnation of KGB
NPIC—National Photographic Interpretation Center
NRC—National Reconaissance Office
NSA—National Security Agency
NSC—National Security Council
NTM—National Technical Means
OAG—Operations Advisory Group
OCI—Office of Coordination of Information
OD—Operational Directive
OEEC—Organization of European Economic Communities
OIR—Office of Intelligence and Reports
ONE—Office of National Estimates
ORE—Office of Research and Evaluation (Intelligence Production Branch of CIG)
OSI—Office of Strategic/Scientific Intelligence
OSS—Office of Special Services
PFIAB—President's Foreign Intelligence Advisory Board
PHOTINT—Photographic Intelligence
PNIO—Priority National Intelligence Objectives
POL—Petroleum, Oil, Lubricants (CIA abbreviation)
PRM—Policy Review Memorandum
PSAC—President's Science Committee
RADINT—Radar Intelligence
RMD—Related Mission Directive
SALT I, II—Strategic Arms Limitation Talks
SAM—Surface-to-Air Missiles
S&T—Science and Technology
SCC—Special Coordinating Committee (of the NSC)
SDECE—French Central Intelligence
SIGINT—Signals Intelligence
SIS—Secret Intelligence Service (MI #6, British Intelligence)
SLAR—Side Looking Airborne Radar
SLBM—Submarine Launched Ballistic Missile
SNIE—Special National Intelligence Estimate
SOE—Special Operations Executive (Great Britain)
STD—Directorate of Science and Technology
STD—Science and Technology Directorate (CIA) (see also TSD—Technical Services Division)
TIARA—Tactical Intelligence and Related Activities
TSD—Technical Services Division
USIB—United States Intelligence Board

INDEX

Index

Data overload: in intelligence, 90, 96–98
Dayan, Moshe, 223
de Callières, François, 319, 320, 322
de Gaulle, Charles, 113–14, 129
Deception: in intelligence, 194–97, 256, 286–91, 367 n114
Decision making, 295, 172, 269, 314, 318, 326, 337, 373 n66; see also Intelligence and policy makers
Defectors: from East Germany, 218; from Eastern Europe, 250, 268, 378 n39; from Soviet Union, 25, 143, 236, 238, 245, 286; from U.S., 196
Defense Council (Soviet Union), 243
Defense Intelligence Agency (DIA), 20, 21, 88, 100; on Arab-Israeli conflict, 134; bureaucracy of, 80; and CIA, 36, 131, 133n, 366 n100; on Cuba, 160, 167; founding of, 18; on India, 268; on Iran, 136, 266; on Poland, 98; on Portugal, 385 n39; on Soviet activities, 52, 374 n69; on Vietnam, 172, 179
Defense Intelligence Committee (DIC), 209, 211
Defense Ministry (West Germany), 217, 218
Department for Liaison with Communist and Workers' Parties of Socialist States (Soviet Union), 241
Department of Defense, 20n, 33, 55, 64–65, 101, 102, 300, 329; on Soviet missiles, 148, 194–96
Department of State, 101, 102, 105, 218, 349 n3, 357 n68, 389 n4; and CIA, 72, 73, 74, 76–79, 80, 100; on Iraq, 124; on Soviet activities, 44, 115, 116; staff, 324; on Vietnam, 184; on Western Europe, 265; see also Bureau of Intelligence and Research; Foreign Service
Détente, 86, 113, 327
Deuxième Bureau (France), 227
Developments Project Division (DPD), 350 n31
Dictatorships, 273
Dilks, David, 339
Diplock Commission, 377 n20, 379 n44
Diplomacy, 294, 320, 326
Diplomats, 101, 111, 127, 218, 246, 272, 320–21, 322, 357 n57
Director of Central Intelligence (DCI), 7, 21, 22, 79, 85–86, 92, 323–24, 337–38; relationship with policy makers, 71, 93, 102, 108; responsibilities, 19, 90, 337, 354 n22, 390 n22; role of, 19–20, 73, 96, 230; see also specific directors, e.g. Helms, Richard
Directorate General of Intelligence (DIS), 208, 209
Directorate of Intelligence (DDI), 32, 88, 226, 335 n
Directorate of Science and Technology, 33, 54–56, 68, 80, 226, 350 n27, 351 n33

Directors of intelligence, 230
Directory for the Surveillance of the Territory (DST), 368 n38
Discoverer Biosatellite Program, 29, 151
Disinformation, 4–5, 27, 64, 231, 247, 288, 291, 350 n23
Disinformation Department (Soviet Union), 238
Dobrynin, Anatoli, 134, 169, 367 n114
Doctrine of intelligence, 292
Donovan, William J., 16, 17, 33, 90
Donovan, William C., 315
Doolittle, James H., 7
Dulles, Allen, 7, 45, 56, 73, 80, 129–31, 155, 191, 289, 311, 324, 338; and congressional committees, x n, 123, 124, 360 n53, 364 n 56; and Eisenhower, Dwight D., 18, 75–79, 80–81, 122, 129, 141, 147; and Kennedy, John F., 79, 379 n43; on role of DCI, 90–91, 355 n34
Dulles-Jackson-Correa Commission (1949), 7, 34, 74, 116, 311
Dulles, John Foster, 18, 76–78, 81
Dzershinsky, Feliks, 234–35, 237, 239, 242

ELINT, see Electronic intelligence
East Germany, 130, 243–44; intelligence services in, 26, 213–14, 215, 249; uprisings in, 117
Eastern Europe, 78, 113, 115, 116, 127, 128, 130, 359 n31; intelligence services in, 216, 226
Economic crises, 295
Economic intelligence, 16, 38–54, 67, 104, 342, 349 n2; American, 44–47, 48, 349 n3; failure of, 267, 280, 307; French, 227–28; German, 38–39; West German, 214, 216
Ecuador, 126
Eden, Anthony, 122, 123, 285
Egypt, 78, 122–23, 124–25; and Soviet Union, 260
Erhard, Ludwig, 377 n14
Eisenhower administration, 76, 78, 88, 143, 146, 147, 151, 153
Eisenhower, Dwight D., 16, 150, 231, 336, 379 n46, 386 n49, 392 n43; see also Dulles, Allen, and Eisenhower, Dwight D.
El Salvador, 137
Electronic intelligence (ELINT), 30, 55, 56, 58, 134, 143–44, 228, 366 nn98, 103, 106
Eshkol, Levi, 223
Espionage, 22, 203, 243–44, 328, 378 n28; see also Spies
Espionage Acts (U.S.), 330–31, 390 n28
Ethiopia, 127
Eurocommunism, 112, 114, 128, 135, 265, 379 n44

Index

Index

INR, *see* Bureau of Intelligence and Research
Ignorance, *see* Knowledge, lack of
Important Points in the Estimate of the World Situation, 120–21
India, 112–13, 135
Indochina War, 76, 113, 174, 176, 177, 183, 184, 372 *n*62, 386 *n*49; *see also* Vietnam War
Information, 91; *see also* Knowledge
Information processing, 31–32, 56–57
Inman, Bobby, 137, 392 *n*51
Institute for Defense Analysis (ISA), 179–80
Institute for the Study of the United States and Canada, 238
Intelligence, 338–44, 387 *n*4; criticism of, 8–9, 327–29, 338; definition of, 12; quality of, 110, 115–20, 144, 174, 328; role of, 89–90, 328; *see also* specific types of intelligence, e.g. Economic intelligence
Intelligence analysis, 4, 8, 55, 75, 138, 240, 269, 294–95, 317–18; methodology in, 5, 185–86, 188–90, 274–76, 295–305, 306–8, 321, 351 *n*37, 383 *n*15; *see also* Worst-case analysis
Intelligence and policy makers, 8, 71, 95, 104, 139–40, 231–32, 269, 343; in U.S., 83, 86, 88–92, 93, 106–8, 110, 174, 183–86, 197, 344, 357 *n*68
Intelligence collection, 4, 8, 18–19, 20, 22–31, 55, 75, 204, 302, 317–18; *see also* specific methods of collection, e.g. Electronic intelligence
Intelligence community, 94, 96, 101–2, 107, 140, 194–95, 317, 376 *n*8
Intelligence Community Staff (ICS), 19, 20*n*, 369 n12
Intelligence cycle, 20–27, 346 *n*3
Intelligence failures, 4*n*, 11, 12, 15, 139, 276–77, 361 *n*2, 372 *n*56; American, 67, 142–43, 147, 155–58, 167, 230, 231, 337, 356 *n*9; British, 202–3; causes of, 8, 221–22, 253–54, 269–72, 289, 319, 339, 352 *n*38; Israeli, 221–23
Intelligence Identities Protection Act (1982), 331
Intelligence Oversight Act (1980), 335*n*
Intelligence perspectives, 90, 98–102
Intelligence priorities, 21, 94, 282
Intelligence successes, 11, 15, 139, 218–19, 220–21, 222, 230, 231, 277
International Department (Soviet Union), 241
International Information Department (Soviet Union), 241
International relations, 294, 295–98, 334
Invisible Government, The (Wise and Ross), 3
Iran, 97, 355 *n*44
Iran-Iraq conflict, 29
Iranian situation, 136–37, 264, 266, 274, 352 *n*38

Iraq, 360 *n*53; coup (1958), 124
Israel, 285; and Egypt, 260; intelligence services in, 201, 220–24, 230, 379 *n*42; *see also* Arab-Israeli conflict
Italy, 114, 128, 250
Ivashutin, Pyotr, 380 *n*10

JCS, *see* Joint Chiefs of Staff
JIC, *see* Joint Intelligence Committee
Jackson, C. D., 77
Japan: foreign opinion of, 382 *n*4
Johnson administration, 103, 172, 180, 182, 183
Johnson, Louis, 73–74
Johnson, Lyndon, 19, 88, 133–34, 178, 336, 370 *n*17, 379 *n*46; *see also* Helms, Richard, and Johnson, Lyndon; McCone, John, and Johnson, Lyndon
Joint Chiefs of Staff (JCS), 178, 179, 181, 182, 337
Joint Intelligence Bureau (JIB), 208
Joint Intelligence Committee (JIC), 206, 207, 209; *see also* Defense Intelligence Committee
Jones, Furnival, 210
Jones, R. V. 268, 277, 288
Jordan, 124
Judgments: about intelligence, 172, 185, 304, 320, 323, 341, 356 *n*48, 385 *n*34
Jung, C. G., 306*n*

KGB, 209, 232, 237–38, 238–40, 249, 287, 379 *n*1; budget, 246, 247; counterintelligence by, 228, 239–40, 246; manpower, 233, 246–47, 248–49, 250, 345 *n*6, 380 *n*10
Kastner, Hermann, 218
Kendall, Willmore, 296
Kennan, George, 74, 100, 114
Kennedy administration, 88, 151, 164, 169, 172, 173, 174–77
Kennedy, John F., 22, 59, 99, 231, 276, 367 *n*113; *see also* McCone, John, and Kennedy, John F.
Kent, Sherman, 34, 35, 89, 90, 296, 348 *n*31, 355 *n*32
Khrushchev, Nikita, 42–43, 127, 129; control of KGB by, 234, 237, 239; and Cuban missile crisis, 141, 367 *n*121; de-Stalinization under, 78, 117, 119–20, 221; and Kennedy, John F., 81; and Mao Zedong, 130; on Soviet capabilities, 45, 46, 57, 59, 158, 191, 193, 197
Killian, James R., 55, 392 *n*43
Kinkel, Klaus, 215
Kirpatrick, Lyman, 312–13